DATE DUE

NOV 1 2 2002	
ttCFU	
due May 26/63	
Fraser Valley Reg	
due Mar 31/0	

BRODART   Cat. No. 23-221

PERSONALITY DISORDERS

AND THE FIVE-FACTOR MODEL OF PERSONALITY

PERSONALITY DISORDERS

AND THE FIVE-FACTOR MODEL OF PERSONALITY

EDITED BY PAUL T. COSTA, JR., AND THOMAS A. WIDIGER

Second Edition

factor

AMERICAN PSYCHOLOGICAL ASSOCIATION ▮ WASHINGTON, DC

Published by
American Psychological Association
750 First Street, NE
Washington, DC 20002
www.apa.org

To order
APA Order Department
P.O. Box 92984
Washington, DC 20090-2984
Tel: (800) 374-2721, Direct: (202) 336-5510
Fax: (202) 336-5502, TDD/TTY: (202) 336-6123
Online: www.apa.org/books/
Email: order@apa.org

In the U.K., Europe, Africa, and the Middle East, copies may be ordered from
American Psychological Association
3 Henrietta Street
Covent Garden, London
WC2E 8LU England

Typeset in Berkeley by EPS Group Inc., Easton, MD
Printer: Sheridan Books, Inc., Ann Arbor, MI
Technical/Production Editor: Amy J. Clarke and Jennifer Powers
Original dust jacket design by Grafik Communications, Ltd., Alexandria, VA;
revision by Naylor Design, Washington, DC.

The opinions and statements published are the responsibility of the authors, and such opinions and statements do not necessarily represent the policies of the American Psychological Association.

Library of Congress Cataloging-in-Publication Data

Personality disorders and the five-factor model of personality, second edition / edited by Paul T. Costa, Jr., and Thomas A. Widiger.—2nd ed.
  p.; cm.
Includes bibliographical references and indexes.
ISBN 1-55798-826-9 (cb : acid-free paper)
1. Personality disorders. 2. NEO Five-Factor Inventory. I. Costa, Paul T., Jr. II. Widiger, Thomas A.
[DNLM: 1. Personality Disorders—classification. 2. Personality Inventiroy. WM 15 P467 2001]
RC554 .P474 2001
616.85'8—dc21

2001033285

British Library Cataloguing-in-Publication Data
A CIP record is available from the British Library.

Printed in the United States of America
First Edition

This book is dedicated to the memory of Jack Digman.
Although not directly involved in the study of personality disorders,
his pioneering work on the five-factor model of personality laid the foundations
not only for this volume but also for this area of research.
His keen intellect, quiet wit, and grace will long be remembered.

Contents

APPENDIXES

Contributors

Samuel A. Ball, *Department of Psychiatry, Yale University School of Medicine, New Haven, CT*

Robert K. Brooner, *Department of Psychiatry and Behavioral Sciences, Johns Hopkins University School of Medicine, Baltimore, MD*

Stephen Bruehl, *Department of Behavioral Science, University of Kentucky College of Medicine, Lexington*

Taisheng Cai, *Clinical Psychological Research Center, 2nd Affiliated Hospital, Hunan Medical University, Changsha, People's Republic of China*

Lee Anna Clark, *Department of Psychology, University of Iowa, Iowa City*

John F. Clarkin, *Department of Psychiatry, Cornell University Medical Center, Ithaca, NY*

Elizabeth M. Corbitt, *Wright State University School of Medicine, Dayton, OH*

Paul T. Costa, Jr., *National Institute of Aging, National Institutes of Health, Baltimore, MD*

Xiaoyang Dai, *Clinical Psychological Research Center, 2nd Affiliated Hospital, Hunan Medical University, Changsha, People's Republic of China*

John M. Digman, *Oregon Research Institute, Eugene, OR*

Jamie A. Dyce, *Department of Psychology, Concordia University of Alberta, Edmonton, Alberta, Canada*

Allen J. Frances, *Department of Psychiatry and Behavioral Sciences, Duke University Medical Center, Durham, NC*

Beiling Gao, *Clinical Psychological Research Center, 2nd Affiliated Hospital, Hunan Medical University, Changsha, People's Republic of China*

Robert D. Hare, *Department of Psychology, University of British Columbia, Vancouver, British Columbia, Canada*

Allan R. Harkness, *Department of Psychology, University of Tulsa, Tulsa, OK*

Timothy J. Harpur, *Department of Psychology, University of Illinois at Urbana–Champaign*

Stephen D. Hart, *Department of Psychology, University of British Columbia, Vancouver, British Columbia, Canada*

Jeffrey H. Herbst, *Gerontology Research Center, National Institute on Aging, Baltimore, MD*

Gregory K. Lehne, *Johns Hopkins University School of Medicine, Baltimore, MD*

W. John Livesley, *Department of Psychiatry, University of British Columbia, Vancouver, British Columbia, Canada*

Donald R. Lynam, *Department of Psychology, University of Kentucky, Lexington*

K. Roy MacKenzie, *Department of Psychiatry, University of British Columbia, Vancouver, British Columbia, Canada*

Robert R. McCrae, *Gerontology Research Center, National Institute on Aging, Baltimore, MD*

Joyce L. McEwen, *Department of Psychology, Southern Methodist University, Dallas, TX*

John L. McNulty, *Department of Psychology, Kent State University, Kent, OH*

Brian P. O'Connor, *Department of Psychology, Lakehead University, Thunder Bay, Ontario, Canada*

Aaron L. Pincus, *Department of Psychology, Pennsylvania State University, University Park*

Cynthia Sanderson, *Department of Psychiatry, Cornell Medical College, Ithaca, NY*

Chester W. Schmidt, Jr., *Department of Psychiatry and Behavioral Sciences, Johns Hopkins University School of Medicine, Baltimore, MD*

Marsha L. Schroeder, *Department of Psychiatry, University of British Columbia, Vancouver, British Columbia, Canada*

Michael H. Stone, *Department of Psychiatry, Columbia University, New York, NY*

Timothy J. Trull, *Department of Psychology, University of Missouri–Columbia*

Lu Vorhies, *Department of Psychology, Southern Methodist University, Dallas, TX*

Thomas A. Widiger, *Department of Psychology, University of Kentucky, Lexington*

Jerry S. Wiggins, *Department of Psychology, University of British Columbia, Vancouver, British Columbia, Canada*

Janice A. Wormworth, *Department of Psychiatry, University of British Columbia, Vancouver, British Columbia, Canada*

Jian Yang, *Gerontology Research Center, National Institute on Aging, Baltimore, MD*

Shuqiao Yao, *Clinical Psychological Research Center, 2nd Affiliated Hospital, Hunan Medical University, Changsha, People's Republic of China*

PERSONALITY DISORDERS

AND THE FIVE-FACTOR MODEL OF PERSONALITY

CHAPTER 1

INTRODUCTION: PERSONALITY DISORDERS AND THE FIVE-FACTOR MODEL OF PERSONALITY

Paul T. Costa, Jr., and Thomas A. Widiger

In the last 20 years, interest in personality disorder research has shown substantial growth. Personality disorders were, no doubt, catapulted into a prominent position by the creation of a special axis, Axis II, in the third edition of the *Diagnostic and Statistical Manual of Mental Disorders* (*DSM-III*; American Psychiatric Association, 1980), a multiaxial classification of mental disorders system. Research interest in personality disorders can be documented by the more than 750 empirical studies that are abstracted in the American Psychological Association's PsycLIT database, covering the 5-year period from January 1987 to June 1992. Since the first edition of this book (Costa & Widiger, 1994), not only has there been a steady flow of empirical research dealing with personality disorders, but there have also been important theoretical and empirical developments, which are pointed out later in this introductory chapter to the second edition of *Personality Disorders and the Five-Factor Model of Personality*.

This large and growing literature on personality disorders should not obscure the fact that there are serious theoretical and methodological problems with the whole *DSM* personality disorder diagnostic enterprise. Officially, the diagnostic criteria sets of the fourth edition of the *Diagnostic and Statistical Manual of Mental Disorders* (*DSM-IV*; American Psychiatric Association, 1994) Axis II are supposed to define or diagnose patients into mutually exclusive, categorical diagnostic entities. But as many reports document, the average number of personality disorder diagnoses is often greater than 4 (Skodol, Rosnick, Kellman, Oldham, & Hyler, 1988; Widiger,

Trull, Hurt, Clarkin, & Frances, 1987). This comorbidity is a serious problem because it suggests redundancy, or a lack of divergent construct validity, for the current set of 10 diagnostic categories of *DSM-IV*-defined personality disorders. Other crucial problems concern the excessive comorbidity of Axis I and Axis II diagnoses (Docherty, Fiester, & Shea, 1986; McGlashan, 1987; Widiger & Hyler, 1987) and the general lack of evidence supporting the construct validity of many of the personality disorder categories.

Problems with the official *DSM*-classification scheme for personality disorders continues to receive the attention of researchers, reviewers, and editors alike. In a Special Feature section of the Spring 2000 issue of the *Journal of Personality Disorders,* editor John Livesley boldly stated that "problems with the *DSM* model are all too obvious" (p. 2). These "obvious problems" concern the limited clinical utility of the categories; the diagnostic constructs that clinicians find useful and the conditions they treat are not included in the system. Personality disorder not otherwise specified is often the most frequent diagnosis, suggesting that the existing diagnostic categories are inadequate in their coverage. Furthermore, Livesley (2000) lamented the limited construct validity of the Axis II system, noting that "almost all empirical investigations fail to support DSM diagnostic concepts" (p. 2).

The fact that personality disorder has its own axis in the multiaxial *DSM* system encourages clinicians to consider the presence of a personality disorder for all patients—a unique position among all other classes of mental disorders. But this prominent place makes the difficulties and problems identified above more acute. Oldham and Skodol (2000) noted that "there is growing debate about the continued appropriateness of maintaining the personality disorders on a separate axis in future editions of the diagnostic manual" (p. 17). But moving the personality disorders back to Axis I (Livesley, 1998) would do more than just reduce their salience. As Millon and Frances (1987) eloquently stated in the initial issue of the *Journal of Personality Disorders,*

> *more relevant to this partitioning decision was the assertion that personality traits and disorders can serve as a dynamic substrate from which clinicians can better grasp the significance and meaning of their patients transient and florid disorders. In the DSM-III then, personality not only attained a nosological status of prominence in its own right but was assigned a contextual role that made it fundamental to the understanding and interpretation of other pathologies. (p. ii)*

How can the difficulties be constructively addressed and solved without seeming to abandon the importance of personality traits and disorders by collapsing the distinction between Axis I and II?

Many of the problems of *DSM-IV* might be resolved by using continuous dimensions instead of discrete categories. Dimensional alternatives have been frequently proposed, but until recently, there was no consensus on which personality dimensional model should be used. The five-factor model (FFM; Digman, 1990; McCrae, 1992) is a taxonomy of personality traits in terms of five broad dimensions (the "Big Five"): Neuroticism (N), Extraversion (E), Openness to Experience (O), Agreeableness (A), and Conscientiousness (C). An emergent and still-growing consensus on the FFM suggests that this is a comprehensive classification of personality dimensions that may be a conceptually useful framework for understanding personality disorders.

By the early 1990s, there had been considerable research confirming the FFM and demonstrating the value of studying individual differences in personality (e.g., Digman, 1990; McCrae, 1992; Wiggins &

Pincus, 1989). But one important question was whether studies using the models and methods of normal personality research could shed light on psychopathological and psychiatric problems, particularly personality disorders.

"Normal" and "abnormal" psychology have traditionally been considered separate fields, but this rigid dichotomy has never made sense to trait psychologists. Trait psychologists know that individual differences in most characteristics are continuously distributed. It therefore seems reasonable to hypothesize that different forms of psychopathology might be related to normal variations in basic personality dispositions.

Considerable evidence in support of this hypothesis is provided by results of analyses relating measures of personality to measures of psychopathology in normal and clinical samples. Several studies (e.g., Costa & McCrae, 1990; Morey, 1986; Trull, 1992) show general parallels between psychopathological and normal personality dimensions. In many of the chapters in this book, authors explore ways in which normal personality dimensions can illuminate clinical constructs. We hoped that the first edition of the book would help promote further research and facilitate integration of research on personality disorders with decades of research on normal personality structure and measurement. As many of the new chapters attest (e.g., chapters 5, 11–14, 20), there has indeed been a substantial amount of new and productive FFM personality disorder research.

From the time this book was first contemplated, interest in and efforts to apply the FFM to a variety of disorders and populations has moved at a rapid pace. We originally limited our focus to diagnostic issues, but the scope has now been enlarged to include treatment implications. A major addition to the second edition is a specific 4-step process for making diagnoses using the FFM (see Widiger, Costa, & McCrae, chapter 25, this volume).

We hope that readers will want to sample directly the fruits of the field, as it were. One aim of this book is to promote greater interest and research between the FFM and personality disorders. The book is intended to give its readers a glimpse of the application of the FFM for the diagnosis and treatment of personality disorders.

BACKGROUND OF THE FIVE-FACTOR MODEL

The FFM is a hierarchical model of the structure of personality traits. *Personality traits* are often defined as enduring "dimensions of individual differences in tendencies to show consistent patterns of thoughts, feelings, and actions" (McCrae & Costa, 1990, p. 23). Traits reflect relatively enduring dispositions and are distinguished from states or moods, which are more transient. The FFM had its origins in analyses of trait-descriptive terms in the natural language. John, Angleitner, and Ostendorf (1988) gave an excellent account of this important line of research, and the contributions of Tupes and Christal (1961), Norman (1963), Goldberg (1982), and Borkenau and Ostendorf (1990) are deservedly recognized by the field of FFM researchers.

But most research and practice of personality assessment has been based on questionnaires. As Wiggins (1968) wrote, the "Big Two" dimensions of N and E have been long associated with Hans Eysenck. Another two-dimensional model that deserves special attention is the interpersonal circle model (i.e., the interpersonal circumplex) associated with Kiesler (1983), Leary (1957), and Wiggins (1982).

With the addition of Psychoticism (P), Eysenck's (Eysenck & Eysenck, 1975) P, E, N model is one of several competing three-factor models. Tellegen (1985) advanced an alternative three-factor model that substitutes Constraint for P. It should be noted that in Tellegen's model both N and E are construed as the dimensions Negative Affectivity (NA) and Positive Affectivity, respectively. Watson, Clark, and Harkness (1994) proffered a four-factor model based on the literature relating personality disorders to the FFM, where the current conceptualizations of the 10 personality disorder categories largely ignore O. Many of the personality disorder diagnostic criteria fail to adequately represent O-related features, such as restricted emotional expression or intolerance of differing views. But even if the personality disorders were completely unrelated to O, which is probably not the case, one would not "downsize" the personality taxonomy to four dimensions because of its currently inadequate representation in the *DSM*. Unlike Eysenck's or Tellegen's models, the Watson,

Clark, and Harkness model is not an alternative to the FFM; it is simply the FFM without the dimension of O. However, Cloninger (1987), a psychiatrist, advanced a neuroadaptive-based personality model with originally three dimensions that is both similar to and different from Eysenck's and Tellegen's three-factor models. In Cloninger's model, N (or NA) is called Harm Avoidance; Novelty Seeking is largely low C; and the third dimension, Reward Dependence, has no simple and direct correspondence to any of the five established dimensions of the FFM because it loads on three or four of the five dimensions (Costa & McCrae, 1993; Herbst, Zonderman, McCrae, & Costa, 2000). Cloninger's original instrument, the Tridimensional Personality Questionnaire, has been revised substantially by splitting off the 8-item subscale, RD2, into a persistence temperament dimension to yield four temperaments and three so-called character dimensions have also been added, leading to a seven-dimensional model (Cloninger, Svrakric, & Przybeck, 1993). An important chapter (14, this volume) by O'Connor and Dyce compares Cloninger's seven-dimensional model with alternative models to identify the optimal structural representation of personality disorders.

Other dimensional models that contain more factors than the familiar five are seen in the 10 factors of Guilford, Zimmerman, and Guilford's (1976) Guilford–Zimmerman Temperament Survey. Of course, Cattell's (Cattell, Eber, & Tatsuoka, 1970) Sixteen Personality Factor Questionnaire represents Cattell's model of 16 primary personality traits.

All of these systems are interesting, and many are valuable in understanding personality disorders, especially the interpersonal circumplex. But mounting evidence suggests that all or nearly all of these models can be either subsumed by the FFM or interpreted in terms of it. Postulated dimensions beyond the Big Five, such as the Guilford–Zimmerman and Cattell models, for example, are generally regarded as tapping trait dimensions at a lower level in the hierarchy.

The consensus currently is that at the second-order level, the five broad dimensions of N, E, O, A, and C are the basic dimensions of personality. For the sake of this text, we adopt the position articulated by McCrae and John (1992) that it is fruitful to assume that the FFM is the correct representation of the structure of traits and move on to its application to important topics and outcomes in psychological and psychiatric practice. This position is well supported by the conclusions of O'Connor and Dyce's (chapter 14, this volume) meta-analysis.

The present collection of chapters, therefore, does not attempt to present a balanced view of alternative dimensional models applied to personality disorders. It specifically adopts the FFM perspective. In fact, this book is organized around the premise that the FFM is the most adequate and comprehensive taxonomy for describing personality and for understanding problems associated with personalities or personality disorders. A special section of the April *Journal of Personality* (2001) entitled "Reconceptualizing Personality Disorder Categories Using Personality Trait Dimensions" and edited by Samuel Ball also acknowledges the promise of the FFM and especially the Revised NEO Personality Inventory (NEO-PI-R). "This special section is admittedly overweighted toward coverage of the NEO-PI-R, in part because this is where the majority of work is occurring at the personality trait-to-disorder interface" (Ball, 2001, p. 147).

DESCRIPTION OF FACTORS

In this section, we briefly describe the broad or higher order dimensions of the FFM. These dimensions are defined by many more specific traits. One specification is provided by the facet scales of the NEO-PI-R (Costa & McCrae, 1992), an instrument designed to measure the FFM. Details on these facets are given in Appendix D.

Neuroticism

N refers to the chronic level of emotional adjustment and instability. High N identifies individuals who are prone to psychological distress. As mentioned earlier, an alternative label is NA, but N also includes having unrealistic ideas, excessive cravings or difficulty in tolerating the frustration caused by not acting on one's urges, and maladaptive coping responses. As shown in Appendix D, N includes the facet scales for anxiety, angry hostility, depression, self-consciousness, impulsivity, and vulnerability.

Extraversion

E refers to the quantity and intensity of preferred interpersonal interactions, activity level, need for stimulation, and capacity for joy. People who are high in E tend to be sociable, active, talkative, person oriented, optimistic, fun loving, and affectionate; whereas people who are low in E tend to be reserved (but not necessarily unfriendly), sober, aloof, independent, and quiet. Introverts are not unhappy or pessimistic people, but they do not experience the exuberant high spirits that characterize extraverts.

Openness to Experience

O is much less well known than either N or E and, in fact, is often construed differently as the alternative label Intellect suggests. But O differs from ability and intelligence and involves the active seeking and appreciation of experiences for their own sake. Open individuals are curious, imaginative, and willing to entertain novel ideas and unconventional values; they experience the whole gamut of emotions more vividly than do closed individuals. By contrast, closed individuals (those who are low in O) tend to be conventional in their beliefs and attitudes, conservative in their tastes, and dogmatic and rigid in their beliefs; they are behaviorally set in their ways and emotionally unresponsive.

Agreeableness

A, like E, is an interpersonal dimension and refers to the kinds of interactions a person prefers along a continuum from compassion to antagonism. People who are high in A tend to be softhearted, good natured, trusting, helpful, forgiving, and altruistic. Eager to help others, they tend to be responsive and empathic and believe that most others want to and will behave in the same manner. Those who are low in A (called antagonistic) tend to be cynical, rude or even abrasive, suspicious, uncooperative, and irritable and can be manipulative, vengeful, and ruthless.

Conscientiousness

C assesses the degree of organization, persistence, control, and motivation in goal-directed behavior. People who are high in C tend to be organized, reliable, hard working, self-directed, punctual, scrupulous, ambitious, and persevering, whereas those who are low in C tend to be aimless, unreliable, lazy, careless, lax, negligent, and hedonistic.

METHODS OF ASSESSMENT

It must be pointed out that there are several instruments to measure the FFM (Briggs, 1992; Widiger & Trull, 1997). These include various adjective-based instruments: Goldberg (1982, 1992) has developed several sets of adjective measures of the FFM, including 50 transparent bipolar adjective sets and 100 unipolar adjective markers. Wiggins and Trapnell (1997) melded the insights from the lexical tradition with the theoretical sophistication of the interpersonal circumplex with the development of the Interpersonal Adjective Scales Revised—Big Five. Q-sort procedures developed by McCrae, Costa, and Busch (1986) and Robbins, John, and Caspi (1994) are also available. In the questionnaire area is the Hogan Personality Inventory (Hogan, 1986), a six-factor variant of the FFM that was designed to reflect Hogan's socioanalytic theory. Many of the authors in this book use the NEO Personality Inventory (NEO-PI; Costa & McCrae, 1985), which was designed to operationalize a hierarchical model of the FFM, and the NEO-PI-R, which became available in 1992 after most of the empirical studies reported in this book were completed.

In addition to self-reports, several procedures can be used to measure the dimensions of the FFM, including observer ratings (Form R) of the NEO-PI-R for spouses and peers and clinician ratings. A semi-structured interview, the Structured Interview for the Five-Factor Model of Personality (Trull & Widiger, 1997), was developed because there was no structured interview to assess the FFM. Many mental health professionals prefer interview-based measures because they allow for an opportunity to pursue follow-up questions and further probe issues that arise in the course of an interview. In sum, the FFM is not just a theoretical model but is operationalized in several different although converging ways. Costa and McCrae (1995) reported convergence among a number of these measures of the FFM.

The *DSM-IV* (American Psychiatric Association, 1994) and the *DSM-IV-Text Revision* (*DSM-IV-TR;*

American Psychiatric Association, 2000) provide criteria to make the diagnosis of each personality disorder, but it does not provide any reliable or valid means of assessing individuals or their personality traits. There are several well-validated measures of the FFM, and if they were to be consistently used in personality disorder research, then they might contribute to advances in the field.

CONTENTS OF THE SECOND EDITION

Aims of the first edition were to

1. examine how personality disorders represent maladaptive variants of the personality traits that are present in all individuals to varying degrees
2. empirically demonstrate the application and utility of the FFM to personality disorders
3. illustrate the power of the FFM to capture the essence of major features of personality disorders through clinical case studies
4. provide possible reconceptualizations of personality disorders.

In any number of ways, these aims were successfully met. For instance, since the appearance of *Personality Disorders and the Five-Factor Model of Personality* at the end of 1994, 81 empirical studies on the topic of personality disorders and the FFM have been published, and the overall volume itself, as well as individual chapters, have been cited over 200 times.

There have been several important changes to this second edition at the same time that there has been significant continuity. This second edition reprints 70% of the original 21 chapters with updated references. For those who are unfamiliar with the first edition, the 15 chapters that have been retained from the first edition are chapters 2–4, 6, 8–11, 13, 17–20, 22, and 23. The second edition retains these chapters and reframes their emphases in terms of the empirical and conceptual advances that have occurred in the last 5 or 6 years.

Part I: Conceptual Background
The first of the four parts that make up this book, Conceptual Background, contains five chapters. In chapter 2, Digman provides an insightful historical

background for the FFM itself. Far from being of recent vintage, the FFM has a hoary pedigree, tracing its roots to McDougall (1932) and Thurstone (1934). But as Digman notes, the model was virtually ignored for years by mainstream personologists and has had a very tardy reception. He ably discusses several reasons and concludes on an optimistic note that there may be a paradigm shift occurring soon in personality studies; the long-ignored FFM may be the new paradigm of personality structure of the future.

In chapter 3, Widiger and Frances comprehensively review the conceptual and empirical support for dimensional and categorical representations of personality disorders. This chapter was retained from the first edition of the book because the findings and arguments provided therein are still applicable today (even with the subsequent revision of the American Psychiatric Association's diagnostic nomenclature). They ably discuss the advantages and disadvantages of the categorical and dimensional models of classification. Particularly useful is their evaluation of the empirical data that are relevant to the respective validity of these two perspectives. They review alternative dimensional models including Cloninger's (1987) neuroadaptive model, the interpersonal circumplex, Siever and Davis's (1991) biogenetic spectrum model, and Gunderson's (Gunderson, Links, & Reich, 1991) hierarchical model. As might be expected, Widiger and Frances pay particular attention to the empirical support for the FFM as the most compelling choice for the representation of personality disorders. Widiger and Frances also raise an issue for future research whether alternative models offer any incremental validity that is not provided in the FFM. O'Connor and Dyce in a new chapter (14) prepared for this second edition speak extensively on this issue raised by Widiger and Frances. They point out important obstacles that the FFM must overcome before clinicians can be expected to use it within their practices.

Because the FFM has only been applied to personality disorders since the 1990s, there are only a handful of studies in the literature. But the few that were found confirm the premise that personality disorders can be understood in terms of the FFM per-

sonality dimensions. In chapter 4, Trull and McCrae review the limited evidence (five studies) that existed before 1994, showing that individuals with different personality disorders differ in predictable ways on the five factors. They suggest that the FFM can aid in understanding each disorder's core symptomatology and the overlap between Axis I and Axis II disorders. They also provide thoughtful analyses of the constructs for the borderline and narcissistic personality disorders and make cogent suggestions for further research.

In chapter 5, Widiger and Costa provide a comprehensive summary of an additional 55 empirical studies that have been published on the relationship of the FFM to personality disorder symptomatology since the research cited in the Trull and McCrae chapter. The studies reviewed by Widiger and Costa do not exhaust the published empirical studies on this topic. Searches in the American Psychological Association's PsycINFO and Institute for Scientific Information's Science and Social Sciences Citation Indices databases from 1994 through March 2000 yielded another 63 studies on this topic, which for space and time are not reviewed here.

Chapter 6, represents a conceptual effort by us and the prominent clinicians Clarkin, Sanderson, and Trull to translate the *DSM-IV* personality disorders into the hierarchical FFM, as operationalized by the scales of the NEO-PI-R. Reprinted from the first edition, Appendix A represents testable hypotheses about the maladaptively extreme facets for each of the 11 *DSM-III-R* personality disorder categories. Appendix B lists the hypothesized facets for the 2 personality disorder categories of negativistic (NEG) and depressive (DPA) originally proposed for *DSM-IV* as well as the self-defeating (SDF) and sadistic (SDS) that were omitted in *DSM-IV*. In this second edition, we present a new Appendix C (see also Table 6.1, this volume), which represents each of the 10 *DSM-IV* categories in terms of the 30 facets of the NEO-PI-R. There is an important difference in Appendix C from Appendix A. Namely, each of the 10 personality disorder categories are defined with respect only to the diagnostic criteria that appear in the *DSM-IV*. Thus, only the uppercase symbols H for high and L for low are used to indicate standing on the relevant facet. Appendix A, reprinted from the first edition, uses other symbols to reflect whether the facet is linked to the disorder through the associated features or the empirical clinical literature.

Part II: Models of Personality Dimensions and Disorders

In chapter 7, Wiggins and Pincus present a forceful account of structural conceptualizations of personality dimensions and personality disorders from the dyadic and FFM interactional perspectives. These authors demonstrate empirically that Millon's influential conceptions of personality disorders, as embodied in the Millon Clinical Multiaxial Inventory (MCMI; Millon, 1982) scales, correspond to the well-established dimensions of normal personality. Wiggins and Pincus also illustrate a unique approach to assessing personality pathology, called *combined model assessment,* which uses the eight interpersonal scales of the interpersonal circumplex along with the domain scores of N, O, and C from the FFM.

Chapters 8 and 9 identify the basic dimensions of personality pathology that underlie the personality disorder categories. Clark, Vorhies, and McEwen (chapter 8) explore the boundaries of normal range personality and abnormal personality. They define the constituent components of maladaptive personality traits through a series of sophisticated conceptual and statistical analyses. They give a clear account of the 22 personality disorder symptom clusters and a self-report inventory, the Schedule for Nonadaptive and Adaptive Personality (SNAP, formerly the Schedule for Normal and Abnormal Personality; Clark, 1993), developed to assess personality disorders. Their results lend strong support for a dimensional approach to the assessment of personality disorders by showing that the FFM is sufficient in scope to account for most of the reliable variance in these personality disorder traits. They also present some interesting analyses that seek to determine whether the O and A dimensions of the FFM add incremental validity to the prediction of maladaptive traits beyond the three dimensional or the N, E, and C dimensions of Tellegen (1985) and Cloninger (1987; cf. Reynolds & Clark, 2001).

In chapter 9, Schroeder, Wormworth, and Livesley provide an important investigation of dimensions

of personality pathology different from those of the *DSM-III-R.* Livesley, Jackson, and Schroeder (1992) developed the Dimensional Assessment of Personality Pathology—Basic Questionnaire (DAPP-BQ) as an alternative to the Axis II categories of *DSM-III-R.* Although all 16 scales of the DAPP-BQ are encompassed by the five personality dimensions, not all disorder scales can be predicted equally or with high levels of precision. Scales with specific behavioral content or focus (e.g., intimacy and conduct problems) are not well predicted by the NEO-PI scales and raise the issue of whether additional dimensions of personality pathology are necessary to give a more comprehensive and precise specification of the personality disorder domain.

In chapter 10, Clark and Livesley collaborate to compare conceptually and empirically the two-trait structures of disordered personality discussed in chapters 8 and 9. SNAP (Clark, 1993) and DAPP-BQ (Livesley et al., 1992) factors were content matched and then correlated with NEO-PI or NEO Five-Factor Inventory (Costa & McCrae, 1989) scores to empirically validate the conceptual matchings across the Clark and Livesley systems. Overall, there were far more convergences or similarities between the SNAP and DAPP-BQ traits in terms of their correlations with the FFM than there were differences. It is rare indeed to observe such high levels of productive collaboration. We express a special note of appreciation for their creative efforts.

In chapter 11, alternative or rival dimensional models of normal personality (i.e., the Zuckerman, Kuhlman, Joireman, Teta, & Kraft, 1993, alternative five and the Cloninger, 1987, seven-factor model) are vigorously compared by Ball with the FFM in a large sample of substance dependent inpatients and outpatients. In several specialized clinical fields, such as substance abuse, field-specific dimensions are important. For example, the impulsive sensation-seeking dimension in the Zuckerman–Kohlman Personality Questionnaire has played a prominent role in the reinvigoration of the substance abuse field. As Ball further notes, the FFM conception of impulsivity is considerably broader and more differentiated, emphasizing distinctions between affective impulsivity (N5: Impulsiveness facet) and cognitive impulsivity (C6: Deliberation facet) that are contrasted with preference for risky and thrilling experiences (E5: Excitement-seeking facet).

Chapter 12 by Pincus shows how the FFM can shed light on different constellations or what he calls *subtypes of dependency*. Rather than restate the problem of heterogeneity of the diagnostic category, Pincus calls attention to the need to recognize the variegation of dependency constructs, and he compellingly argues for distinguishing among love, exploitable, and submissive syndromes. Pincus shows how they can be understood both within the interpersonal circumplex and the 30 facets of the NEO FFM.

Chapter 13 by Yang et al. is a cross-cultural test of the Widiger et al. hypotheses relating the *DSM*-defined personality disorders to the FFM. A large psychiatric sample (1,909 inpatients and outpatients) from the People's Republic of China was administered a Mandarin Chinese version of the NEO-PI-R and the Personality Diagnostic Questionnaire—4+; 525 of whom were also given the Personality Disorder Interview IV. The data provided from this study strongly support hypothesized personality–personality disorder links, even in a different cultural context.

Part II ends with an important contribution by O'Connor and Dyce (chapter 14), which is an adaptation and update of their previously published comparison of general and specific models of personality disorder configuration. In this integrative chapter, they set out to rigorously evaluate conceptually competing models by use of sophisticated statistical techniques. They show that attempts to provide an understanding of the disorders in terms of the latent *DSM* clusters (odd, dramatic, and anxious) or Millon's (1982) polarity distinctions do not provide as optimal a representation as is provided by the FFM.

Part III: Patient Populations and Clinical Cases

In chapter 15, Brooner, Schmidt, and Herbst apply the NEO-PI to a clinical population principally defined by an Axis I disorder, namely, substance abuse. Outpatient opioid abusers with and without comorbid Axis II diagnoses are characterized on the NEO-PI scales. Brooner et al. examine four relatively pure

personality disorder groups: antisocial, avoidant, borderline, and paranoid. The respective personality profiles of these disorders generally support the hypothesized predictions of Widiger et al. in chapter 6. Finally, the authors present several cases that demonstrate how personality characteristics and life history relate to personality disorder diagnoses.

In chapter 16, Lehne (a practicing clinician) explores the usefulness of self-report inventories of clinical and normal personality in the forensic evaluation of sex offenders. Lehne's data and experience present a remarkable counterpoint to the often expressed concern that self-reports are inherently untrustworthy and not relevant to clinical practice. The portrait painted by Lehne's data on the MCMI and the NEO-PI is both reassuring and informative. Data from this clinical sample replicate relations between NEO-PI and MCMI scales and, furthermore, show that sex offenders are high on N (and all six of its facets) and high on excitement seeking. Lehne questions whether traditional reliance on personality disorder diagnoses to transmit information about individuals embroiled in a forensic evaluation is useful and appropriate. He suggests that future research should focus more on personality dispositions to provide information that is useful in understanding forensic clients and their rehabilitation planning.

Single case studies of personality disorder are presented in the next two chapters. Bruehl, in chapter 17, presents the case of Betty, a 45-year-old White divorced woman who is diagnosed with borderline personality disorder. These types of patients are one of the most important variants of personality disordered patients and are discussed in other chapters by Sanderson and Clarkin (chapter 21) and Stone (chapter 24). But Bruehl's case presentation aptly illustrates the theoretical descriptions provided in chapter 6. Bruehl discusses the clinical ratings of Betty on the traits measured by the NEO-PI-R and links both her Axis I symptoms (which include sleep problems, appetite disturbance, and social withdrawal) and borderline symptomatology to high N facets and low E facets of warmth, gregariousness, and positive emotions. Particularly interesting is Bruehl's discussion of Betty's high values, ideas, and openness to fantasy as they relate to her history of childhood sexual abuse and the sexual identity confusion she exhibits.

Corbitt (in chapter 18) deals with narcissism in a sophisticated clinical analysis of the diagnostic construct and suggests that the FFM translation may not be as straightforward as Widiger et al. posit in chapter 6. Corbitt focuses on the ambiguity and complicated evaluation of the narcissistic patient's response to criticism by others and the reasons for seeking treatment. The patient's self-description, as given by her NEO-PI-R profile, illustrates the salient role of low agreeableness facets and low facet scores on self-consciousness and vulnerability as contributing to her narcissistic disorder. Other aspects of the patient's personality profile are used to highlight treatment issues.

The psychopathic personality has long been of gripping interest to personality psychopathologists and those interested in understanding this antisocial personality disorder. The authors of chapter 19, Harpur, Hart, and Hare, are internationally known experts on the topic, and their contribution provides a scholarly comparison of the FFM and the two-factor theory of psychopathy. The Psychopathy Check List (Hare, 1980; Hare & Frazelle, 1980) is compared with Eysenck's (Eysenck & Eysenck, 1975) P, E, N model to illustrate that considerable variance is unaccounted for in Eysenck's model. Harpur et al. help the reader to understand that the key personality characteristics, as opposed to the chronic antisocial behaviors and lifestyle, of the psychopath—the selfishness, callousness, and remorseless use of others—is strongly related to low Agreeableness or antagonism.

Chapter 20 by Lynam is a sophisticated treatment and conceptualization of Revised Psychopathy Checklist defined psychopathy and expert-generated FFM psychopathy prototypes. This chapter is particularly rich in terms of providing common-language Q-sort items that characterize the fledgling psychopathic individual and presents an understanding of the psychopathic deficits in terms of their FFM mappings. In addition, Lynam provides data from the important Levenson Self-Report Psychopathy Scale (Levenson, Kiehl, & Fitzpatrick, 1995; Lynam, Whiteside, & Jones, 1999) and provides a profile of prototypic psychopathy (see Figure 20.1), which we

predict will become increasing important in clinical research and practice.

Part IV: Diagnosis and Treatment Using the Five-Factor Model

Sanderson and Clarkin (chapter 21), with their rich clinical experience, provide a clinically astute examination of how the five personality dimensions of the FFM affect therapy focus, alliance, and outcome. They illustrate with clinical vignettes how patient dimensions assessed by the FFM are related to planning and applying psychological interventions. The authors discuss disorder-specific treatment approaches and the need to individually optimize therapy procedures by taking into account the patient's assets and liabilities, problem complexity, coping style, and reactance level. Sanderson and Clarkin also present an NEO-PI profile for female patients with borderline personality disorder based on 64 carefully diagnosed patients who presented with impulsive acting out (and more direct suicidal behavior) and on a specific 26-year-old female patient in an attempt to show how the personality profile can help in treatment planning.

MacKenzie's chapter 22 provides a practical guide to using structured instruments to assess psychotherapy candidates. MacKenzie attempts to repair what he calls the "diagnostic fragmentation" fostered by the *DSM* by the astute use of formal psychological testing, which he describes. MacKenzie gives helpful information on how to introduce structured assessments to patients so as to ensure compliance and reliable results. He also gives many valuable insights into how to use structured assessments to select intervention strategies that are responsive to different treatment settings or milieus.

In chapter 23, Harkness and McNulty present a broad-sketched perspective of what they call individual differences science (IDS) for clinical work on personality disorders, extending the article by Harkness and Lillienfeld (1997) to incorporate the constructs of the FFM and the constructs of the Minnesota Multiphasic Personality Inventory II. Harkness and McNulty advance the distinction between traits as basic tendencies and their characteristic adaptations or maladaptations and note that it is the maladaptive expressions of the traits and not the basic traits themselves that should be the focus of diagnostic decision making. No matter how extreme one's standing on a trait may be, it might not constitute a disorder unless it is associated with a characteristic maladaptation or problem in living that psychiatrists and clinical psychologists are best qualified to assess and treat clinically. They also indicate how the *DSM* personality disorder criteria mix together traits and symptoms or characteristic maladaptations with confusing results.

The next chapter by Stone, a well-known psychodynamic psychiatrist (chapter 24), is a fascinating presentation of how instruments that operationalize the FFM apply to his patients with borderline personality disorder. He presents nine patients from his extensive clinical practice and single-handedly rediscovers the lexical strengths and roots of the FFM. His wonderful book on *Abnormalities of Personality* (Stone, 1993) was the first illustration by someone outside of traditional FFM research on how the model can provide a vivid and meaningful representation of the essence of patients with a personality disorder. We are delighted that Stone found the time from his busy practice to contribute to this second edition.

Finally, in the concluding chapter (25) of the book, Widiger, Costa, and McCrae present an integration of how the FFM might be used to diagnose personality disorders. They present a 4-step process that should help make the use of the FFM standard in research and clinical practice with personality disorders. Particularly important is their extensive compilation of characteristic maladaptations or problems in living that are associated with each pole of the five broad factors as well as the likely specific maladaptations for the high and low pole of each of the 30 NEO-PI-R facets. With this discussion as a brief guide, we urge readers onward.

References

American Psychiatric Association. (1980). *Diagnostic and statistical manual of mental disorders* (3rd ed.). Washington, DC: Author.

American Psychiatric Association. (1987). *Diagnostic and statistical manual of mental disorders* (3rd ed., rev.). Washington, DC: Author.

American Psychiatric Association. (1994). *Diagnostic and statistical manual of mental disorders* (4th ed.). Washington, DC: Author.

American Psychiatric Association. (2000). *Diagnostic and statistical manual of mental disorders* (4th ed., text rev.). Washington, DC: Author.

Ball, S. A. (2001). Reconceptualizing personality disorder categories using personality trait dimensions: Introduction to special section. *Journal of Personality, 69,* 147–153.

Borkenau, P., & Ostendorf, F. (1990). Comparing exploratory and confirmatory factor analysis: A study on the 5-factor model of personality. *Personality and Individual Differences, 11,* 515–524.

Briggs, S. (1992). Assessing the five-factor model of personality description. *Journal of Personality, 60,* 253–293.

Cattell, R. B., Eber, H. W., & Tatsuoka, M. M. (1970). *The handbook for the Sixteen Personality Factor Questionnaire.* Champaign, IL: Institute for Personality and Ability Testing.

Clark, L. A. (1993). *Manual for the Schedule for Nonadaptive and Adaptive Personality (SNAP).* Minneapolis: University of Minnesota Press.

Cloninger, C. R. (1987). A systematic method for clinical description and classification of personality variants. *Archives of General Psychiatry, 44,* 573–588.

Cloninger, C. R., Svrakic, D. M., & Przybeck, T. R. (1993). A psychobiological model of temperament and character. *Archives of General Psychiatry, 50,* 975–990.

Costa, P. T., Jr., & McCrae, R. R. (1985). *NEO Personality Inventory manual.* Odessa, FL: Psychological Assessment Resources.

Costa, P. T., Jr., & McCrae, R. R. (1989). *The NEO-PI/NEO-FFI manual supplement.* Odessa, FL: Psychological Assessment Resources.

Costa, P. T., Jr., & McCrae, R. R. (1990). Personality disorders and the five-factor model of personality. *Journal of Personality Disorders, 4,* 362–371.

Costa, P. T., Jr., & McCrae, R. R. (1992). *Revised NEO Personality Inventory (NEO-PI-R) and NEO Five-Factor Inventory (NEO-FFI) professional manual.* Odessa, FL: Psychological Assessment Resources.

Costa, P. T., Jr., & McCrae, R. R. (1993). Ego development and trait models of personality. *Psychological Inquiry, 4,* 20–23.

Costa, P. T., Jr., & McCrae, R. R. (1995). Domains and facets: Hierarchical personality assessment using the Revised NEO Personality Inventory. *Journal of Personality Assessment, 64,* 21–50.

Costa, P. T., Jr., & Widiger, T. A. (Eds.). (1994). *Per-

sonality disorders and the five-factor model of personality. Washington, DC: American Psychological Association.

Digman, J. M. (1990). Personality structure: Emergence of the five-factor model. *Annual Review of Psychology, 50,* 116–123.

Docherty, J. P., Fiester, S. J., & Shea, T. (1986). Syndrome diagnosis and personality disorder. In A. Frances & R. Hales (Eds.), *Psychiatry update: The American Psychiatric Association annual review* (Vol. 5, pp. 315–355). Washington, DC: American Psychiatric Press.

Eysenck, H. J., & Eysenck, S. B. G. (1975). *Manual of the Eysenck Personality Questionnaire.* San Diego, CA: EdITS.

Goldberg, L. R. (1982). From ace to zombie: Some explorations in the language of personality. In C. D. Spielberger & J. N. Butcher (Eds.), *Advances in personality assessment* (Vol. 1, pp. 203–234). Hillsdale, NJ: Erlbaum.

Goldberg, L. R. (1992). The development of markers of the Big Five factor structure. *Psychological Assessment, 4,* 26–42.

Guilford, J. S., Zimmerman, W. S., & Guilford, J. P. (1976). *The Guilford–Zimmerman Temperament Survey handbook: Twenty-five years of research and application.* San Diego, CA: EdITS.

Gunderson, J. G., Links, P. S., & Reich, J. H. (1991). Competing models of personality disorders. *Journal of Personality Disorders, 5,* 60–68.

Hare, R. D. (1980). A research scale for the assessment of psychopathy in criminal populations. *Personality and Individual Differences, 1,* 111–117.

Hare, R. D., & Frazelle, J. (1980). *Some preliminary notes on the use of a research scale for the assessment of psychopathy in criminal populations.* Unpublished manuscript, Department of Psychology, University of British Columbia, Vancouver, British Columbia, Canada.

Harkness, A. R., & Lilienfeld, S. O. (1997). Individual differences science for treatment planning: Personality traits. *Psychological Assessment, 9,* 349–360.

Herbst, J. H., Zonderman, A. B., McCrae, R. R., & Costa, P. T., Jr. (2000). Do the dimensions of the Temperament and Character Inventory map a simple genetic architecture? Evidence from molecular genetics and factor analysis. *American Journal of Psychiatry, 157,* 1285–1290.

Hogan, R. (1986). *Hogan Personality Inventory manual.* Minneapolis, MN: National Computer Systems.

John, O. P., Angleitner, A., & Ostendorf, F. (1988). The lexical approach to personality: A historical review of trait taxonomic research. *European Journal of Personality, 2,* 171–205.

Kiesler, D. J. (1983). The 1982 interpersonal circle: A taxonomy for complementarity in human transactions. *Psychological Review, 90,* 185–214.

Leary, T. (1957). *Interpersonal diagnosis of personality.* New York: Ronald Press.

Levenson, M., Kiehl, K., & Fitzpatrick, C. (1995). Assessing psychopathic attributes in a noninstitutional population. *Journal of Personality and Social Psychology, 68,* 151–158.

Livesley, W. J. (1998). Suggestions for a framework for an empirically based classification of personality disorder. *Canadian Journal of Psychiatry, 43,* 137–147.

Livesley, W. J. (2000). Introduction [Special feature: Critical issues in the classification of personality disorders, Part I]. *Journal of Personality Disorders, 14,* 1–2.

Livesley, W. J., Jackson, D. N., & Schroeder, M. L. (1992). A comparison of the factorial structure of personality disorders in a clinical and general population sample. *Journal of Abnormal Psychology, 101,* 432–440.

Lynam, D. R., Whiteside, S., & Jones, S. (1999). Self-reported psychopathy: A validation study. *Journal of Personality Assessment, 73,* 110–132.

McCrae, R. R. (1992). The five-factor model: Issues and applications [Special issue]. *Journal of Personality, 60.*

McCrae, R. R., & Costa, P. T., Jr. (1990). *Personality in adulthood.* New York: Guilford Press.

McCrae, R. R., Costa, P. T., Jr., & Busch, C. M. (1986). Evaluating comprehensiveness in personality systems: The California Q-Set and the five-factor model. *Journal of Personality, 54,* 430–446.

McCrae. R. R., & John, O. P. (1992). An introduction to the five-factor model and its applications. *Journal of Personality, 60,* 175–215.

McDougall, W. (1932). Of the words character and personality. *Character and Personality, 1,* 3–16.

McGlashan, T. (1987). Borderline personality disorder and unipolar affective disorder: Long-term effects of comorbidity. *Journal of Nervous and Mental Disease, 175,* 467–473.

Millon, T. (1982). *Millon Clinical Multiaxial Inventory manual* (3rd ed.). Minneapolis, MN: National Computer Systems.

Millon, T., & Frances, A. (1987). Editorial. *Journal of Personality Disorders, 1,* i–iii.

Morey, L. C. (1986). A comparison of three personality disorder assessment approaches. *Journal of Psychopathology and Behavioral Assessment, 8,* 25–30.

Norman, W. T. (1963). Toward an adequate taxonomy of personality attributes: Replicated factor structure in peer nomination personality ratings. *Journal of Abnormal and Social Psychology, 66,* 574–583.

Oldham, J. M., & Skodol, A. E. (2000). Charting the future of Axis II. *Journal of Personality Disorders, 14,* 17–29.

Reynolds, S. K., & Clark, L. A. (2001). Predicting dimensions of personality disorder from domains and facets of the five-factor model. *Journal of Personality, 69,* 199–222.

Robbins, R. W., John, O. P., & Caspi, A. (1994). Major dimensions of personality in early adolescence: The Big Five and beyond. In C. P. Halverson, G. A. Kohnstamm, & R. P. Martin (Eds.), *The developing structure of temperament and personality from infancy to adulthood* (pp. 261–291). Hillsdale, NJ: Erlbaum.

Siever, L. J., & Davis, K. L. (1991). A psychobiological perspective on the personality disorders. *American Journal of Psychiatry, 148,* 1647–1658.

Skodol, A. E., Rosnick, L., Kellman, H. D., Oldham, J., & Hyler, S. E. (1988). Validating structured *DSM-III-R* personality disorder assessments with longitudinal data. *American Journal of Psychiatry, 145,* 1297–1299.

Stone, M. H. (1993). *Abnormalities of personality: Within and beyond the realm of treatment.* New York: Norton.

Tellegen, A. (1985). Structures of mood and personality and their relevance to assessing anxiety with an emphasis on self-report. In A. H. Tuma & J. D. Maser (Eds.), *Anxiety and the anxiety disorders* (pp. 681–706). Hillsdale, NJ: Erlbaum.

Thurstone, L. L. (1934). The vectors of the mind. *Psychological Review, 41,* 1–32.

Trull, T. J. (1992). *DSM-III-R* personality disorders and the five-factor model of personality: An empirical comparison. *Journal of Abnormal Psychology, 101,* 553–560.

Trull, T. J., & Widiger, T. A. (1997). *Structured interview for the five-factor model of personality (SIFFM).* Odessa, FL: Psychological Assessment Resources.

Tupes, E. R., & Christal, R. (1961). *Recurrent personality factors based on trait ratings* (USAFD Tech. Rep. 67–97). Lackland, TX: Lackland Air Force Base.

Watson, D., Clark, L. A., & Harkness, A. R. (1994). Structures of personality and their relevance to psychopathology. *Journal of Abnormal Psychology, 103,* 18–31.

Widiger, T. A., & Hyler, S. (1987). Axis I/Axis II interactions. In J. Cavenar, R. Michels, & A. Cooper (Eds.), *Psychiatry.* Philadelphia: Lippincott.

Widiger, T. A., & Trull, T. J. (1997). Assessment of the five-factor model of personality. *Journal of Personality Assessment, 68,* 228–250.

Widiger, T. A., Trull, T. J., Hurt, S., Clarkin, J., & Frances, A. (1987). A multidimensional scaling of the *DSM-III* personality disorders. *Archives of General Psychiatry, 44,* 557–563.

Wiggins, J. S. (1968). Personality structure. In P. R. Farnsworth (Ed.), *Annual review of psychology* (Vol. 19, pp. 293–350). Palo Alto, CA: Annual Reviews.

Wiggins, J. S. (1982). Circumplex models of interpersonal behavior in clinical psychology. In P. C. Kendall & J. N. Butcher (Eds.), *Handbook of research methods in clinical psychology* (pp. 183–221). New York: Wiley.

Wiggins, J. S., & Pincus, A. L. (1989). Conceptions of personality disorders and dimensions of personality. *Psychological Assessment: A Journal of Consulting and Clinical Psychology, 1,* 305–316.

Wiggins, J. S., & Trapnell, P. D. (1997). Personality structure: The return of the Big Five. In S. R. Hogan, J. Johnson, & S. Briggs (Eds.), *Handbook of personality psychology* (pp. 737–765). San Diego, CA: Academic Press.

Zuckerman, M., Kuhlman, D. M., Joireman, J., Teta, P., & Kraft, M. (1993). A comparison of three structural models for personality: The big three, big five, and the alternative five. *Journal of Personality and Social Psychology, 65,* 757–768.

PART I

CONCEPTUAL BACKGROUND

CHAPTER 2

HISTORICAL ANTECEDENTS OF THE FIVE-FACTOR MODEL

John M. Digman

The current enthusiasm for the five-factor model (FFM; often referred to as the "Big Five") for organizing the complexities of personality could suggest to those who are unacquainted with its history that it is something quite new, an exciting "new look" at an old field. It comes as a surprise, then, to learn that it was proposed more than a half century ago and that a study demonstrating its essential validity was reported soon thereafter. Now, after many years of lying on the closet shelf of personality theory, the model has been dusted off, "as good as new," and appears to be for many researchers (e.g., Borkenau, 1988; Costa & McCrae, 1985; Digman, 1990; Goldberg, 1983; John, 1990; John, Angleitner, & Ostendorf, 1988; Peabody & Goldberg, 1989) a very meaningful theoretical structure for organizing the myriad specifics implied by the term *personality*.

AN EARLY HYPOTHESIS AND AN EARLY STUDY

It was McDougall (1932), at the time a leading theoretician, who first proposed that "personality may to advantage be broadly analyzed into five distinguishable but separable factors" (p. 5). Soon thereafter, Thurstone (1934) reported a factor analysis of 60 trait adjectives in terms of five factors and expressed his surprise at finding "that the whole list of sixty adjectives can be accounted for by postulating only five independent common factors" (p. 13).

Thus, almost 70 years ago, a model was proposed by a well-known personality theorist, McDougall, and a clear empirical demonstration of it was provided by an eminent psychometrist, Thurstone. Thurstone's article appeared on page 1 (Vol. 41) of *Psychological Review* and had previously been an essential part of his presidential address to the American Psychological Association. This was hardly an obscure introduction by an unknown, yet almost 50 years were to pass before theorists were to take this model seriously as a worthwhile framework for their research.

There are many reasons for the failure of others to follow up on Thurstone's pioneering study. One is that a factor analysis, as carried out before the days of computers, was an incredibly difficult and time-consuming undertaking. Analysis of even a 30-variable problem was a daunting task that could suggest many weeks of clerical work filled with the possibility of errors of calculation at every turn. Thurstone's study, based on a sample of 1,300 subjects and 60 variables, stood alone, Promethean and awe inspiring, for many years. Until Cattell (1947, 1948) undertook his studies in the following decade, no one apparently had the courage to undertake a study of this magnitude.

Second, Thurstone, like so many other early pioneers of the FFM, did not follow up on his finding but turned to other pursuits, notably the field of intelligence. Quite possibly, had he devoted years of work and writing to the implications of his finding,

I express my appreciation to Lewis R. Goldberg for his many thoughtful suggestions over the years.

we would today know the model as the "Thurstone Five."

Later, other investigators would emulate Thurstone both in noting that five factors appeared to explain the variability in trait ratings and in failing to pursue the implications of their findings beyond a published report or two. Thus, Fiske (1949), Tupes and Christal (1961), and Borgatta (1964) published analyses of trait ratings that corroborated and extended Thurstone's findings, yet for one reason or another—other commitments or other interests, perhaps—none of these authors went beyond their initial reports.

A third reason for the model's tardy reception may be traced to the manner in which psychologists, including those interested in the topic, generally viewed the field of personality. As a glance at the textbooks written during the past 50 years will confirm, the field has been long on grand theory and short on systematic research. Generally, research has been undertaken to test some aspect of personality theory, such as Freud's theory of repression or Erikson's theory of personality development.

In addition, as noted by Carver and Scheier (1988), theory and research in personality have been characterized by two quite different approaches. One has been an interest in intrapersonal phenomena, as opposed to individual differences. The former is in the grand tradition, characteristic of continental European tradition, of the search for human identity; the latter, in the tradition of English and American psychometrics. These very different approaches are suggestive of Snow's (1959) distinction between the "two cultures," one with its roots in literature, philosophy, and the arts and the other with its roots in science and technology. One cannot easily imagine an Erikson, a Maslow, or their followers giving close attention to a factor analysis of a set of rating scales.

Finally, the approach to personality study that has been generally known as the "factor approach," dominated by the work of Cattell (e.g., 1943, 1947, 1948, 1957, 1965), Eysenck (e.g., 1947, 1970), and to some degree Guilford (e.g., 1959, 1975), has not been persuasive to personologists or others—and for good reason. Were there 16 or more factors—or only 3? Is Cattell's Extraversion the same as Guilford's? How could the application of a standard statistical technique, factor analysis, produce such different systems? For years, the systems of Cattell, Eysenck, and Guilford have appeared to represent the results of organizing the field of personality descriptors by use of factor analysis: two systems (Cattell's and Guilford's), both rather complex yet different from each other in many respects, and Eysenck's, different from both in its simplicity and in its higher level of abstraction. How could three reputable investigators, using the same technique, arrive at three such different systems? Small wonder that many researchers cast a dubious eye toward factor analysis as a means of bringing order to the field.

FIVE-FACTOR SOLUTIONS FROM 1949 TO 1980

While the textbooks were devoting space to the Cattell and Eysenck systems as representative of factor theories, a series of studies was slowly building a solid, data-based reputation for the FFM. They include the work of Fiske (1949), Tupes and Christal (1961), Norman (1963), Borgatta (1964), and Norman and Goldberg (1966). An interesting aspect of this work is that although most of these studies were conducted independently, generally with no preconception as to outcome, they are in substantial agreement.

Fiske's study was done in conjunction with the Michigan Veterans Administration (VA) Selection Research Project (Kelly & Fiske, 1951). Cattell served as consultant for the project, with the result that 22 of his rating scales were used in the study. Using these scales, VA trainees were rated by peers, by evaluators, and by themselves. Fiske conducted factor analyses of the three sets of correlations and, like Thurstone 15 years before him, could find evidence for no more than five factors. Furthermore, in many respects, his interpretation of these factors was not very different from current interpretations (see Digman & Takemoto-Chock, 1981). The study, impressive for its time, was reported in a journal usually circulated among personality researchers, but it had little impact on the field.

Another consultant to the VA Project, Tupes, subsequently used 30 of Cattell's scales in a study of

U.S. Air Force trainees. Analysis of the data suggested the presence of only five broad factors (Tupes & Christal, 1961). Intrigued by this, these investigators reanalyzed the correlations of Cattell and Fiske and found them to be in good agreement with their own analyses. Not only was agreement impressive with respect to the number of factors, but the factors appeared to be remarkably similar in content across the three different studies. Tupes and Christal interpreted these robust five factors as Surgency (or Extraversion), Agreeableness, Conscientiousness, Emotional Stability, and Culture.

Shortly thereafter, Norman (1963), using 20 of the Tupes–Christal scales, reported a successful replication of their results. Borgatta (1964), familiar with the Tupes–Christal study, devised a set of behavior descriptors that were used by subjects in a study of interactions in small group discussion. Analysis of the scaled descriptors produced five factors very similar in content to the Tupes–Christal factors, except for the Culture factor, which Borgatta felt was better interpreted as Intelligence.

Here, then, by the middle 1960s, were all the ingredients needed for systematic research in personality: five robust trait dimensions that had been originally suggested by an insightful theorist, McDougall, and by a pioneering study by a well-known psychometrist, Thurstone, and clearly demonstrated by four independent studies, all of which were in good agreement. Yet until very recently, few investigators knew of these studies, and the standard textbooks ignored them completely.

Why were these studies almost completely ignored? As I have noted elsewhere (Digman, 1990), the times were not right for the model to catch the attention of personality researchers. For one thing, the 1960s and 1970s witnessed an enthusiasm for behaviorism, with its disdain for anything so subjective as "personality" or ratings. Another factor was the rift between social psychologists and personality psychologists, the former seemingly demonstrating the vastly greater importance of the situation in determining behavior compared with personality traits.

THE 1980S AND THEREAFTER

In the early 1980s, three independent lines of research converged on the FFM as the most appropriate model for ordering the myriad specific constructs of personality. One line was a revival of interest in the model for the field of personality ratings; a second, studies of the structure of the language of personality descriptors; the third, analyses of personality inventories.

My own conversion to the FFM followed unsuccessful attempts to replicate a more complex model of child personality as measured by teacher ratings (Digman, 1963, 1972). A meta-analysis of several studies (Digman & Takemoto-Chock, 1981) demonstrated the robustness of the five-factor solution: "Regardless of whether teachers rate children, officer candidates rate one another, college students rate one another, or clinical staff members rate graduate trainees, the results are pretty much the same" (pp. 164–165). Other studies (Digman & Inouye, 1986; Goldberg, 1980, 1982, 1990; John, 1989; McCrae & Costa, 1985, 1989) amply confirmed this.

The second line of research to converge on the FFM as the appropriate model was the systematic work over the years of Goldberg and his associates on the structure of the everyday language of personality descriptors (Goldberg, 1980, 1981, 1982, 1990; Hampson, 1988; Hampson, John, & Goldberg, 1986). An essential aspect of this work pertaining to the FFM is its investigation of the hierarchical nature of the language of personality, extending from the most specific—and most precise—terms, such as *quiet,* to such broad terms as *Extraversion,* which like other FFM constructs subordinates a broad domain of related, lower level constructs.

Suggestions that the FFM might be noted in the structure of personality inventories as well (Amelang & Borkenau, 1982; Digman, 1979; Goldberg, 1981; Hogan, 1983) led to several studies that confirmed this (Costa & McCrae, 1988a, 1988b; McCrae & Costa, 1987, 1989). Thus, the Sixteen Personality Factor Questionnaire (Cattell, Eber, & Tatsuoka, 1970), the Guilford–Zimmerman Temperament Survey (Guilford & Zimmerman, 1949), the Personality Research Form (Jackson, 1974), the Myers–Briggs Type Indicator (Myers & McCauley, 1985), the Eysenck Personality Inventory (Eysenck & Eysenck, 1964), and the California Q-Set (Block, 1961) represent some or all of the FFM.

The structure of the language of personality, as represented in ratings of self and of others, thus appears to be as well established as any principle coming from empirical research in psychology. Furthermore, when subjects report in inventories what they typically do and what they typically feel, the organization of such behavior and emotion into scales appears to fall into the FFM pattern as well.

LOOKING BACK

Eriksen (1957), reviewing the research efforts of a previous generation, was hopeful that the application of factor analysis to the complexities of personality traits would clarify the field. It appears that it has done just that: Five broad trait dimensions appear to encompass the common features of just about all of the more specific characteristics of personality traits.

But why did it take more than a half century to establish this principle when it was clearly suggested so long ago by McDougall and by Thurstone? The question is disturbing because it suggests that the progress of science is not as straightforward or as rational as it is generally assumed to be. I have proposed some reasons for the slow acceptance of the model. However, only one of these, the difficulty of carrying out a factor analysis in the precomputer era, seems reasonable. The others suggest that such research ran contrary to the paradigms—or fashions—of the day. Perhaps the times and paradigms are different today and a well-grounded theoretical model of personality has at last been accepted.

References

Amelang, A., & Borkenau, P. (1982). Über die faktorielle Struktur und externe Validität einiger Fragebogen-skalen zur Erfassung von Dimensionen der Extraversion und emotionalen Labilität [On the factor structure and external validity of some questionnaire scales measuring dimensions of extraversion and neuroticism]. *Zeitschrift für Differentielle und Diagnostische Psychologie, 3,* 119–146.

Block, J. (1961). *The Q-sort method in personality assessment and psychiatric research.* Springfield, IL: Charles C Thomas.

Borgatta, E. F. (1964). The structure of personality characteristics. *Behavioral Science, 12,* 8–17.

Borkenau, P. (1988). The multiple classification of acts and the Big Five factors of personality. *Journal of Research in Personality, 22,* 337–352.

Carver, C. S., & Scheier, M. F. (1988). *Perspectives on personality.* Boston: Allyn & Bacon.

Cattell, R. B. (1943). The description of personality: Basic traits resolved into clusters. *Journal of Abnormal and Social Psychology, 38,* 476–506.

Cattell, R. B. (1947). Confirmation and clarification of primary personality factors. *Psychometrika, 12,* 197–220.

Cattell, R. B. (1948). The primary personality factors in women compared with those in men. *British Journal of Psychology, 1,* 114–130.

Cattell, R. B. (1957). *Personality and motivation structure and measurement.* New York: World Book.

Cattell, R. B. (1965). *The scientific analysis of personality.* London: Penguin Books.

Cattell, R. B., Eber, H. W., & Tatsuoka, M. M. (1970). *Handbook for the Sixteen Personality Factor Questionnaire.* Champaign, IL: Institute for Personality and Ability Testing.

Costa, P. T., Jr., & McCrae, R. R. (1985). *The NEO Personality Inventory manual.* Odessa, FL: Psychological Assessment Resources.

Costa, P. T., Jr., & McCrae, R. R. (1988a). From catalog to classification: Murray's needs and the five-factor model. *Journal of Personality and Social Psychology, 55,* 258–265.

Costa, P. T., Jr., & McCrae, R. R. (1988b). Personality in adulthood: A six-year longitudinal study of self-reports and spouse ratings on the NEO Personality Inventory. *Journal of Personality and Social Psychology, 54,* 853–863.

Digman, J. M. (1963). Principal dimensions of child personality as seen in teachers' judgments. *Child Development, 34,* 43–60.

Digman, J. M. (1972). The structure of child personality as seen in behavior ratings. In R. M. Dreger (Ed.), *Multivariate personality research* (pp. 587–611). Baton Rouge, LA: Claitor's.

Digman, J. M. (1979, October). *The five major dimensions of personality variables: Analysis of personality questionnaire data in the light of the five robust factors emerging from studies of rated characteristics.* Paper presented at the annual meeting of the Society of Multivariate Experimental Psychology, Los Angeles, CA.

Digman, J. M. (1990). Personality structure: Emergence of the five-factor model. *Annual Review of Psychology, 50,* 116–123.

Digman, J. M., & Inouye, J. (1986). Further specification of the five robust factors of personality.

Journal of Personality and Social Psychology, 50, 116–123.

Digman, J. M., & Takemoto-Chock, N. (1981). Factors in the natural language of personality: Reanalysis, comparison, and interpretation of six major studies. *Multivariate Behavioral Research, 16,* 149–170.

Eriksen, C. W. (1957). Personality. *Annual Review of Personality, 8,* 185–210.

Eysenck, H. J. (1947). *Dimensions of personality.* New York: Praeger.

Eysenck, H. J. (1970). *The structure of human personality* (3rd ed.). London, UK: Methuen.

Eysenck, H. J., & Eysenck, S. B. G. (1964). *Manual of the Eysenck Personality Inventory.* London, UK: University Press.

Fiske, D. W. (1949). Consistency of the factorial structures of personality ratings from different sources. *Journal of Abnormal and Social Psychology, 44,* 329–344.

Goldberg, L. R. (1980, May). *Some ruminations about the structure of individual differences: Developing a common lexicon for the major characteristics of human personality.* Paper presented at the annual convention of the Western Psychological Association, Honolulu, HI.

Goldberg, L. R. (1981). Language and individual differences: The search for universals in personality lexicons. In L. Wheeler (Ed.), *Review of personality and social psychology* (Vol. 2, pp. 141–165). Beverly Hills, CA: Sage.

Goldberg, L. R. (1982). From ace to zombie: Some explorations in the language of personality. In C. D. Spielberger & J. N. Butcher (Eds.), *Advances in personality assessment* (Vol. 1, pp. 203–234). Hillsdale, NJ: Erlbaum.

Goldberg, L. R. (1983, June). *The magical number five, plus or minus two: Some conjectures on the dimensionality of personality descriptors.* Paper presented at a research seminar, Gerontology Research Center, Baltimore, MD.

Goldberg, L. R. (1990). An alternative "description of personality": The Big Five factor structure. *Journal of Personality and Social Psychology, 59,* 1216–1229.

Guilford, J. P. (1959). *Personality.* New York: McGraw-Hill.

Guilford, J. P. (1975). Factors and factors of personality. *Psychological Bulletin, 82,* 802–814.

Guilford, J. P., & Zimmerman, W. S. (1949). *The Guilford–Zimmerman Temperament Survey.* Beverly Hills, CA: Sheridan Supply.

Hampson, S. E. (1988). *The construction of personality: An introduction* (2nd ed.). London: Routledge & Kegan Paul.

Hampson, S. E., John, O. P., & Goldberg, L. R. (1986). Category breadth and hierarchical structure in personality: Studies of asymmetries in judgments of trait implications. *Journal of Personality and Social Psychology, 51,* 37–54.

Hogan, P. (1983). Socioanalytic theory of personality. In M. M. Page (Ed.), *The 1982 Nebraska Symposium on Motivation: Current theory and research* (pp. 59–89). Lincoln: University of Nebraska Press.

Jackson, D. N. (1974). *Personality Research Form manual* (3rd ed.). Port Huron, MI: Research Psychologists Press.

John, O. P. (1989, November). Big Five prototypes for the Adjective Checklist using observer data. In O. P. John (Chair), *The Big Five: Historical perspective and current research.* Symposium conducted at the annual meeting of the Society of Multivariate Experimental Psychology, Honolulu, HI.

John, O. P. (1990). The "Big Five" factor taxonomy: Dimensions of personality in the natural language and in questionnaires. In L. A. Pervin (Ed.), *Handbook of personality* (pp. 66–100). New York: Guilford Press.

John, O. P., Angleitner, A., & Ostendorf, F. (1988). The lexical approach to personality: A historical review of trait taxonomic research. *European Journal of Personality, 2,* 171–205.

Kelly, E. E., & Fiske, D. W. (1951). *The prediction of performance in clinical psychology.* Ann Arbor, MI: University of Michigan Press.

McCrae, R. R., & Costa, P. T., Jr. (1985). Updating Norman's "adequate taxonomy": Intelligence and personality dimensions in natural languages and questionnaires. *Journal of Personality and Social Psychology, 49,* 710–721.

McCrae, R. R., & Costa, P. T., Jr. (1987). Validation of the five-factor model across instruments and observers. *Journal of Personality and Social Psychology, 52,* 81–90.

McCrae, R. R., & Costa, P. T., Jr. (1989). Reinterpreting the Myers–Briggs Type Indicator from the perspective of the five-factor model of personality. *Journal of Personality, 57,* 17–40.

McDougall, W. (1932). Of the words character and personality. *Character and Personality, 1,* 3–16.

Myers, I. B., & McCauley, M. H. (1985). *Manual: A guide to the development and use of the Myers–Briggs Type Indicator.* Palo Alto, CA: Consulting Psychologists Press.

Norman, W. T. (1963). Toward an adequate taxonomy of personality attributes: Replicated factor structure in peer nomination personality ratings. *Journal of Abnormal and Social Psychology, 66,* 574–583.

Norman, W. T., & Goldberg, L. R. (1966). Raters, ratees, and randomness in personality structure. *Journal of Personality and Social Psychology, 4,* 681–691.

Peabody, D., & Goldberg, L. R. (1989). Some determinants of factor structures from personality trait descriptors. *Journal of Personality and Social Psychology, 57,* 552–567.

Snow, C. P. (1959). *The two cultures.* Cambridge, UK: Cambridge University Press.

Thurstone, L. L. (1934). The vectors of mind. *Psychological Review, 41,* 1–32.

Tupes, E. R., & Christal, R. (1961). *Recurrent personality factors based on trait ratings* (USAFD Tech. Rep. 67–97). Lackland, TX: Lackland Air Force Base.

CHAPTER 3

TOWARD A DIMENSIONAL MODEL FOR THE PERSONALITY DISORDERS

Thomas A. Widiger and Allen J. Frances

The purpose of this chapter is to review the conceptual and empirical support for a dimensional classification of personality disorders, focusing in particular on the five-factor model (FFM). The question of whether mental disorders are optimally classified categorically or dimensionally is an ongoing debate (Blashfield, 1984; Kendell, 1975). The issue is particularly pertinent to the topic of personality disorders given the tradition to measure personality with dimensions rather than typologies (Frances, 1982; Gangestad & Snyder, 1985; Livesley, 1985; Widiger & Frances, 1985).

The third edition, revised, of the *Diagnostic and Statistical Manual of Mental Disorders* (*DSM-III-R*; American Psychiatric Association, 1987) personality disorder diagnoses are categorical. It has been suggested that because the *DSM-III-R* diagnoses involve a determination of the number of personality disorder symptoms, the *DSM-III-R* uses a hybrid model that already recognizes and includes a dimensional assessment of each patient (Millon, 1991). However, in practice, the *DSM-III-R* is used and interpreted to make categorical distinctions (Carson, 1991). One does convert the number of symptoms to a categorical distinction on the basis of a cut-off point along a scale (e.g., five of eight for the borderline diagnosis), but the diagnosis that is recorded concerns the presence or absence

of a personality disorder. Clinicians thereafter refer to the presence or absence of a personality disorder, not the degree to which a personality style is maladaptive or the extent to which each personality disorder is present.

The number of symptoms possessed by each patient is assessed to indicate not the extent to which a person is borderline but the likelihood that a person has borderline personality disorder (BDL). The BDL criteria set provides not a scale to indicate the degree to which a person is maladaptively borderline but a set of fallible indicators for determining the category (presence vs. absence of BDL within which the patient falls). An analog would be a set of fallible indicators (e.g., a list of interests, opinions, or attitudes) that could be used either to indicate the likelihood that one is male (a categorical classification) or to indicate the degree to which one is masculine (a dimensional classification). The *DSM-III-R* criteria sets could be used to indicate the extent to which a person is borderline, but they are instead used to indicate whether the personality disorder is either present or absent.

In this chapter, we discuss the advantages and disadvantages of the categorical and dimensional models of classification. We then discuss the empirical data that are relevant to the respective validity of these two perspectives, focusing

This chapter is an extended and updated version of previously published material (Widiger, 1991, 1993).

in particular on the empirical support for the FFM.

ADVANTAGES OF THE CATEGORICAL APPROACH

Three major advantages of the categorical approach have been cited in the literature: (a) ease in conceptualization and communication, (b) familiarity, and (c) consistency with clinical decision making. We discuss each of these advantages in turn.

Ease in Conceptualization and Communication

A categorical model is simpler than a dimensional model in some respects. It is simpler to consider a person as having or not having a disorder than it is to consider various degrees to which a person might have a disorder; similarly, it is simpler to consider the presence of one, two, or three disorders than it is to consider a profile of degrees to which all of the various disorders are present. It is easier to communicate the presence of one or two categorical diagnoses than it is to recall and transmit a profile of scores along five or more dimensions. Also one category (e.g., BDL) can communicate a great deal of vivid information (Frances, 1993).

Diagnosis within a categorical model requires only one decision: whether the person does or does not have a particular personality disorder. Diagnosis within a dimensional model requires more specific and detailed assessment, increasing the complexity of clinical diagnosis. To the extent that a dimensional model retains more information than a categorical model, it requires the obtainment and the communication of more information.

For example, it could be apparent that a patient does not have a histrionic, a dependent, a borderline, an avoidant, a narcissistic, or an antisocial personality disorder. The patient might have a few symptoms of each of these disorders but not have enough to suggest that any of these disorders is present. The clinician could then simply ignore the diagnostic criteria for all of these disorders, focusing instead on the one or two personality disorders most likely to be present. With a dimensional model, a comprehensive assessment would require considera-

tion of all of the dimensions, even if only a few symptoms were present for any one of them.

Familiarity

The second major advantage of the categorical system is that it is more familiar to clinicians. All previous versions of the *DSM* personality disorder diagnoses and all of the other diagnoses within *DSM-III-R* are categorical. It would represent a major shift in clinical practice to convert to a dimensional system (Frances, 1990). The categorical approach is also consistent with the neo-Kraepelinian emphasis on identifying homogeneous, distinct syndromes (Guze & Helzer, 1987; Klerman, 1986). The concept of disorder implies to many clinicians the presence of a distinct syndrome that is in some respects qualitatively different from normality.

The *DSM* has always used a categorical format for clinical diagnoses, and it would be a major disruption to clinical practice to replace the Axis II personality disorders with the FFM dimensions (Frances, 1993). Such a major revision would likely result in considerable opposition by many clinicians and researchers (Zimmerman, 1988). The criteria for revisions to the American Psychiatric Association's nomenclature are much more conservative for the fourth edition of the *DSM* (*DSM-IV*; American Psychiatric Association, 1994) than they were for the third edition (*DSM-III*; American Psychiatric Association, 1980) or *DSM-III-R* (Frances, Widiger, & Pincus, 1989). In the absence of clear guidance as to how the FFM would be used to guide the forensic, disability, insurance, and clinical decisions that are currently guided by the *DSM-III-R* Axis II personality disorders, it might not be practical or realistic to replace Axis II with the FFM.

Consistency With Clinical Decisions

A third argument in favor of the categorical model is that clinical decision making tends to be categorical. A primary function of diagnosis is to suggest treatment, and treatment decisions are not usually in shades of gray. One either hospitalizes or one does not; one either prescribes a medication or one does not. If treatment, insurance, forensic, and other clinically relevant decisions were along a continuum rather than being largely categorical, then the diagnostic system would likely have been more quantitative than qualitative.

Many clinicians convert a dimensional system to categories to facilitate their decision making. The Minnesota Multiphasic Personality Inventory (MMPI; Hathaway & McKinley, 1967), for example, provides the potential for making detailed assessments along a number of dimensions, yet it is often converted to typological code types. One might then question the advantage of potentially increasing the work and complexity of diagnosis by requiring ratings along a continuum that are then ignored in clinical practice.

DISADVANTAGES OF THE CATEGORICAL APPROACH

The only ambiguity that occurs within the categorical model is the decision regarding presence versus absence. If the case is not a literally borderline condition, then the diagnosis is often straightforward. With a dimensional model, there is the potential for a variety of difficult and ambiguous decisions for every patient. For example, even if a personality disorder is clearly present, a dimensional classification still requires an assessment of whether the person is moderately or severely disordered.

In practice, however, the *DSM-III-R* categorical system can be more complex and cumbersome than can a dimensional model. The current system requires the assessment of 104 diagnostic criteria. A systematic and comprehensive assessment of the 11 *DSM-III-R* personality disorders usually requires 2 hr but can take over 4 hr (e.g., Loranger, 1988; Pfohl, Blum, Zimmerman, & Stangl, 1989). Although 2 hr is substantial, even this amount of time allows for an average of only 1 min and 9 sec to assess each personality disorder criterion. A systematic and comprehensive assessment of five dimensions would require much less time and effort. The categorical system is easier to use only if one fails to conduct a comprehensive or systematic assessment (e.g., ignoring most of the categories). Clinicians, in fact, rarely provide a complete assessment of the *DSM-III-R* personality disorders because it is neither feasible nor practical (e.g., Morey & Ochoa, 1989; Pfohl, Coryell, Zimmerman, & Strangl, 1986). As a result, chart diagnoses contain substantially fewer diagnoses

than would be provided by a semistructured interview. This may not be so much a failing of the clinician as perhaps a failing of the nomenclature (Frances, Pincus, Widiger, Davis, & First, 1990).

ADVANTAGES OF THE DIMENSIONAL APPROACH

The major advantages of the dimensional system are (a) resolution of a variety of classificatory dilemmas, (b) retention of information, and (c) flexibility. We discuss each of these advantages in turn.

Classificatory Dilemmas

The ease in conceptualizing and communicating the categorical model is advantageous only if the model provides accurate information. To the extent that it involves the loss of valid information, it is likely to impair decision making and contribute to classificatory dilemmas. One difficulty with a categorical distinction is identifying a nonarbitrary boundary. In *DSM-III* and *DSM-III-R*, only the number of criteria needed to establish a diagnosis or "cut-off points" for the schizotypal disorder and BDL are based on empirical data (Spitzer, Endicott, & Gibbon, 1979), and subsequent research indicates that the cut-off points would have been different if the data had been collected in different settings (Finn, 1982; Widiger, Hurt, Frances, Clarkin, & Gilmore, 1984).

The arbitrary nature of the cut-off points is not problematic for prototypical cases, but it is problematic for cases closer to the boundaries. Cases near the boundaries of a categorical distinction are not adequately characterized by the category on either side (i.e., either presence or absence of the disorder). For example, Widiger, Sanderson, and Warner (1986) indicated that with respect to MMPI profile scores, patients with five BDL symptoms (i.e., patients with the disorder) were more like patients with four symptoms or fewer (i.e., patients without the disorder) than they were like patients with more than five symptoms (i.e., other patients with the disorder).

The cut-off points provided in the *DSM-III-R* are clearly problematic. One does not need any external validator to recognize that there are problems with the prevalence rates and with multiple diagnoses

(Morey, 1988b; Widiger & Rogers, 1989). Some diagnoses occur too often (e.g., BDL), and some too infrequently (e.g., schizoid). Patients may meet the criteria for as many as 5, 6, 7, and even 11 personality disorder diagnoses. The average number of personality disorder diagnoses per patient has been reported to be 2.8 (Zanarini, Frankenburg, Chauncey, & Gunderson, 1987), 3.75 (Widiger, Trull, Hurt, Clarkin, & Frances, 1987), and 4.6 (Skodol, Rosnick, Kellman, Oldham, & Hyler, 1988).

Nurnberg et al. (1991) assessed the comorbidity of *DSM-III-R* BDL with the other Axis II personality disorders in 110 outpatients. Twenty percent (*n* = 22) met the *DSM-III-R* criteria for BDL, with 82% of these having at least one other personality disorder diagnosis. These investigators concluded that the overlap was extensive and not confined to any one of the three broad clusters in which *DSM-III-R* organizes the personality disorders. Nurnberg et al. (1991) suggested that "borderline personality disorder appears to constitute a broad, heterogeneous category with unclear boundaries" (p. 1371) and that "a better understanding of personality disorder awaits a paradigmatic shift away from discrete nosologic categories to alternative models" (p. 1376).

The arbitrariness of the categorical distinctions contributes to diagnostic dilemmas and diagnostic disagreements. To the extent that the presence-versus-absence distinction is arbitrary, clinicians are required to make major distinctions, for which there is no valid or meaningful distinction. If the distinction between the presence versus absence of an avoidant personality disorder is arbitrary, then it is understandable that there has been substantial disagreement and poor reliability (Angus & Marziali, 1988; Mellsop, Varghese, Joshua, & Hicks, 1982). All studies that have compared interrater reliability of the categorical models with that of the dimensional models have found better reliability for the latter (e.g., Heumann & Morey, 1990).

A more dimensional rating (e.g., degrees of severity) also includes arbitrary distinctions—in fact, more of them. But the availability of additional options is less problematic. For example, it is less problematic or controversial to determine whether someone has four versus five symptoms of BDL than it is to determine whether the disorder is either present or absent. Four or five symptoms out of eight (borderline) symptoms is still within a literally borderline range, but presence versus absence suggests qualitatively distinct and substantially different conditions. The distinction of four versus five symptoms is as arbitrary as is presence versus absence, but the impact of the arbitrariness is less severe.

The accepted thresholds for the *DSM-III-R* diagnoses are also somewhat misleading. Even if there is a consensus that a person has BDL when five of the eight criteria are present, there will still be considerable disagreement regarding the threshold for the presence of each criterion. The point at which a person has clinically significant identity disturbance, affective instability, or chronic feelings of emptiness and boredom is undefined in *DSM-III-R* and probably cannot be defined in any manner that would not be arbitrary. Research programs have obtained adequate levels of interrater reliability for the diagnosis of BDL, but this is typically the result of developing local operational criteria for each symptom that are unlikely to agree with the operationalizations used at another research site or with another semistructured interview (Angus & Marziali, 1988; Kavoussi, Coccaro, Klar, Bernstein, & Siever, 1990).

Retention of Information

The second advantage of the dimensional approach is the retention of information. Members and nonmembers of a category tend not to be homogeneous with respect to the criteria used to make the diagnosis. There are 93 different ways to meet the *DSM-III-R* criteria for BDL (Clarkin, Widiger, Frances, Hurt, & Gilmore, 1983) and 848 different ways to meet the *DSM-III-R* criteria for antisocial personality disorder (not even counting the number of different ways to meet the criteria for the conduct disorder and parental irresponsibility items), yet only one diagnostic label (i.e., presence of the disorder) is given to characterize all of these cases. There are 162 different possible combinations of BDL symptomatology in people who do not have BDL, and all of these cases are simply labeled as "not having the disorder."

The handicap to research (and clinical practice) of the failure of the categorical system to adequately characterize personality disorder pathology was discussed by McGlashan (1987). McGlashan was researching the comorbidity of BDL and depression and needed a comparison group of subjects with depression but without BDL. He therefore obtained a group of depressed subjects who did not meet the *DSM-III* criteria for BDL. However, these subjects had on average three of the BDL criteria.

> In short, the "pure" . . . cohort was not pure. . . . The result is that our comparison groups, although defined to be categorically exclusive, may not have been all that different, a fact which, in turn, may account for some of the similarities [between the supposedly pure depressives and the borderlines]. (p. 472)

In other words, the subjects diagnosed as not having BDL did in fact have BDL pathology. McGlashan therefore concluded that the *DSM* "emerges as poorly constructed for the study of comorbidity" (p. 473).

DSM-III-R adopted a polythetic format for the categorical diagnoses (i.e., multiple, optional criteria) in recognition that patients do not fit neatly into distinct categories (Spitzer, 1987). Not all BDL, histrionic, or avoidant patients are alike with respect to the degree or manner in which they are borderline, histrionic, or avoidant (Livesley, 1985; Widiger & Frances, 1985). However, accepting this heterogeneity does not resolve the problems that arise from the heterogeneity, given that the polythetic categories tend to be inadequate for providing sufficiently precise information regarding the individual patient (Widiger & Kelso, 1983). Categories do provide vivid and clear images of each personality disorder, thereby facilitating communication, but to the extent that the patient is not a prototypical case, the communication is misleading and stereotypical (Cantor & Genero, 1986; Schacht, 1985). The categorical format is simpler, but this simplicity can be at the expense of not recognizing the complexity that actually exists.

A dimensional model diminishes stereotyping by providing more precise information. The heterogeneity is retained and informs clinical decisions. It is, in fact, a paradox that for a diagnosis in which reliability and validity are very problematic (e.g., Mellsop et al., 1982), reliable and valid information is excluded from the classification. The ordinal-interval scales that are inherent to the dimensional model have more statistical power, yet *DSM-III-R* currently uses nominal scales. One would expect that one would want to be as accurate as possible when diagnosing BDL pathology; describing personality symptomatology; and determining empirically the familial, treatment, or other correlates of a personality disorder (Widiger, 1993).

Flexibility

A final advantage of the dimensional approach is its flexibility. The categorical format does have advantages. Perhaps its greatest advantage is its compatibility with clinical decision making. This advantage, however, can be retained within a dimensional model by simply providing cut-off points. A conversion from the categorical to the dimensional format, however, is not possible. Once the categorical diagnosis is provided, the ability to return to a more precise classification (e.g., the number of personality disorder symptoms) cannot be recovered. Many clinicians do convert an MMPI dimensional profile to a categorical code type, but most prefer to be provided with a dimensional profile that they can then convert according to their specific clinical needs. Some coding systems are more preferable in some situations than in others. Clinicians often use code types, but the code types that they use vary across situations and clinical decisions. The dimensional model allows the option of different cut-off points for different decisions and different clinical issues (Finn, 1982; Widiger et al., 1984).

A handicap of *DSM-III-R* is that it must respond to a variety of needs (Frances et al., 1990). It provides the nomenclature used for decisions regarding hospitalization, medication, psychotherapy, insurance coverage, scientific research, criminal responsibility, disability, and so forth. It is unlikely that the diagnostic thresholds for each of the categories in *DSM-III-R* will be optimal for all of these needs (Kendler, 1990). The points at which BDL traits likely will result in a depressive mood disorder, will be responsive to medications, will be too problematic for some forms of psychotherapy (e.g., group or gestalt), should receive insurance coverage for their treatment, will need hospitalization for their treatment, will be so disabling as to warrant governmental assistance, or will significantly impair the ability of the person to conform to the requirements of the law are not the same. All of these decisions are currently guided by one diagnostic threshold that is unlikely to be optimal for all of these needs (Widiger & Trull, 1991).

DISADVANTAGES OF THE DIMENSIONAL APPROACH

A major limitation of the dimensional approach, particularly the FFM, may be the lack of apparent clinical utility (Frances, 1993). Clinicians are much more familiar with the treatment implications of the borderline, dependent, schizotypal, and narcissistic personality disorder diagnoses than they are with the treatment implications of excessive agreeableness, conscientiousness, or extraversion. It is also unclear how one would use the FFM within clinical practice. Most clinicians rely on interviews to assess personality disorders, and most researchers currently favor the use of semistructured interviews over self-report inventories. As yet, there is no explicit guidance as to how one would assess the various levels of introversion, conscientiousness, or neuroticism with a clinical interview or the facets within any one of these broader domains.

It has been suggested that a dimensional system could impede the effort to discover and validate discrete syndromes and specific etiologies and treatment (Gunderson, Links, & Reich, 1991). A surface continuum can conceal underlying discontinuities (e.g., different viruses produce similar symptomatology that overlap on a continuum but are in fact qualitatively distinguishable on immunological grounds). The empirical questions are whether there are, in fact, latent-class taxons, and, more simply, whether a categorical or a dimensional model is more consistent with the research on personality disorders.

EMPIRICAL SUPPORT FOR THE DIMENSIONAL MODEL

A variety of data are relevant to the issue of empirical support, including (but not limited to) face va-

lidity, concurrent and predictive validity, factor and cluster analyses, multimodality, and a host of taxometric techniques (e.g., discontinuous regression, admixture analysis, latent-class analysis, and maximum covariation analysis). We discuss in turn each of these methods that have been applied to the personality disorders.

Face Validity

It is evident that theorists and researchers are not in agreement with respect to which model of classification is preferable. The authors of review articles who have argued in favor of the dimensional format for the personality disorders include Adamson (1989), Clarkin and Sanderson (1993), Cloninger (1987, 1989), Costa and McCrae (1992), Eysenck (1986, 1987), Gorton and Akhtar (1990), Grove and Tellegen (1991), Kato (1988), Kiesler (1991), Kroll (1988), Livesley (1991), McLemore and Brokaw (1987), McReynolds (1989), Plutchik and Conte (1985), Schacht (1985), Stone (1992), Tyrer (1988), Vaillant (1984), Widiger and Kelso (1983), and J. Wiggins (1982). Some, however, have argued for retaining the categorical approach (i.e., Frances, 1990, 1993; Gunderson, 1987; Gunderson et al., 1991; Millon, 1981; Spitzer & Williams, 1985; O. P. Wiggins & Schwartz, 1991). Others have been more neutral or at least unclear in their position (e.g., Akiskal, 1989; Blashfield, 1984; Frances, 1982; Kernberg, 1984; Millon, 1990; Oldham, 1987; Robins & Helzer, 1986; Rutter, 1987).

It is also unclear whether practicing clinicians prefer a categorical or a dimensional format. A variety of surveys regarding *DSM-III* and *DSM-III-R* have been conducted, but none has surveyed clinicians with respect to whether they prefer a categorical or a dimensional format for diagnosing personality disorders. Hine and Williams (1975) suggested that there would be little difficulty in obtaining acceptance of a dimensional approach within psychiatry based on their empirical study with medical students. Kass, Skodol, Charles, Spitzer, and Williams (1985) indicated that feedback from staff and trainees during their study indicated that a 4-point severity rating was both feasible and acceptable in routine clinical practice. Maser, Kaelber, and Weise (1991) surveyed 146 psychologists and psychiatrists from

42 countries not including the United States and found that 89% considered *DSM-III-R* to be at least fairly successful in providing diagnostic categories. However, this survey question concerned all of the disorders considered together. Specifically, "the personality disorders led the list of diagnostic categories with which respondents were dissatisfied" (Maser et al., 1991, p. 275). Maser et al. did not ask whether the respondents would prefer a more dimensional classification.

Concurrent and Predictive Validity

Many studies have obtained statistically significant differences on a variety of variables between patients with a personality disorder and patients without the respective disorder (Gunderson & Zanarini, 1987). These findings are consistent with and have been cited as support for the categorical model of classification (Gunderson, 1987). However, although these findings do suggest that a valid construct is measured by the diagnostic algorithm, they are not at all informative with respect to the question of whether the construct is a category or a dimension (Grove & Andreasen, 1989; Kendell, 1975). One can take any continuum, such as height or IQ, define two groups on the basis of scores along the continuum (e.g., IQ scores from 70 to 85 and from 86 to 100), and obtain statistically significant differences between the groups with respect to variables associated with the continuum (e.g., educational achievement, family history, or parental education).

A more compelling datum is whether the strength of the relationship between the diagnostic construct and an external variable is increased or decreased when it is dichotomized. A dimensional variable shows reduced relationships with external variables when it is dichotomized, whereas a truly dichotomous variable shows decreased relationships or at least no change when it is dimensionalized (Cohen & Cohen, 1975). The former occurs as a result of the loss of information; the latter occurs as a result of the inclusion of irrelevant, invalid information (Miller & Thayer, 1989).

Of the personality disorder studies that reported results with the data analyzed both categorically and dimensionally, results in all but one favor the dimensional analyses (e.g., Hart & Hare, 1989; Heu-

mann & Morey, 1990; Hogg, Jackson, Rudd, & Edwards, 1990; Hyler et al., 1989; Kavoussi et al., 1990; Loranger, Susman, Oldham, & Russakoff, 1987; Nazikian, Rudd, Edwards, & Jackson, 1990; O'Boyle & Self, 1990; Reich, Noyes, & Troughton, 1987; Skodol, Oldham, Rosnick, Kellman, & Hyler, 1991; Standage & Ladha, 1988; Walton, 1986; Widiger & Sanderson, 1987; Widiger et al., 1987, 1991; Zimmerman & Coryell, 1990; Zimmerman, Pfohl, Coryell, Stangl, & Corenthal, 1988). The exception was obtained by Zimmerman and Coryell (1989) in a case in which there was a ceiling effect, with both the categorical and dimensional ratings obtaining maximal reliability values. The consistency of this finding is not a statistical artifact. Rather, it indicates that reliable and valid information is lost by converting the data to a nominal scale. If the additional information with respect to the degree to which a person has a personality disorder were not providing reliable or valid information, then including it would have decreased the reliability and validity of the diagnosis.

Factor and Cluster Analyses

Factor analysis (FA) and multidimensional scaling (MDS) have been used to identify the dimensions that might underlie or explain the correlation among variables. A number of such studies have been conducted with the *DSM-III* personality disorders (e.g., Blashfield, Sprock, Pinkston, & Hodgin, 1985; Hyler & Lyons, 1988; Kass et al., 1985; Millon, 1987; Morey, Waugh, & Blashfield, 1985; Widiger et al., 1987) and with other nomenclatures (e.g., Plutchik & Platman, 1977; Presley & Walton, 1973; Tyrer & Alexander, 1979). It has been suggested that factor analytic results provide support for the dimensional approach to classification. Eysenck (1986), for example, suggested that factor analytic studies do not support a categorical model because factor scores are almost always continuous, with individuals often scoring on all of the factors. However, although these analyses can indicate the feasibility of such a model and the dimensions that might underlie a set of variables, the results have not been compelling with respect to whether the variable domain is fundamentally categorical or dimensional. The geometric model on which scaling and factor analytic techniques are based hampers their use for determining whether a categorical or a dimensional model is most appropriate (Kendell, 1975; Morey, 1988a). Factors can be derived from measures of a class variable. One can identify dimensions of masculinity and femininity that are useful and valid in the measurement of personality, but the underlying variable may still be a latent-class taxon.

A complementary limitation occurs with cluster analysis. Cluster analyses are useful in developing types or categories by which to classify subjects. Morey (1988a) demonstrated through a cluster analysis of the *DSM-III-R* personality disorder criteria sets that most of the categorical distinctions in *DSM-III-R* do have empirical support because the clustering recreated the *DSM-III-R* categories (with only a few exceptions). However, clustering methods create subgroups regardless of whether they actually exist (Aldenderger & Blashfield, 1984; Grove & Andreasen, 1989). Cluster analysis may then be more suitable in confirming a particular categorical system than in determining whether the categorical system is more valid than a dimensional one.

An application of FA that is relevant to the appropriateness of a dimensional versus a categorical model is the comparison of factor solutions across groups that are purportedly distinct with respect to a latent-class taxon. Measures that are highly discriminating between such groups should not correlate substantially within the groups; nor should the factor solution of the intercorrelation among such measures replicate across groups (Eysenck, 1987). Tyrer and Alexander (1979), for example, reported that the factor solutions of the intercorrelations among 24 personality variables assessed by a semi-structured interview replicated across 65 patients with a primary clinical diagnosis of personality disorder and 65 patients with other diagnoses. These investigators suggested that the findings support the concept of personality disorders as being extreme variants of a multidimensional continuum. Similar findings were reported by Livesley (1991) using a self-report measure of 79 dimensions of personality disorder pathology, the intercorrelations of which were factor analyzed in a sample of 274 healthy subjects and 158 patients. Livesley (1991) concluded that "a dimensional model is . . . supported

by empirical evidence that the structure of traits describing the features of personality disorder pathology is the same in personality-disordered and non-personality-disordered individuals" (p. 53).

Lack of Empirical Support for Categorical Approaches: Evidence From Taxometric Analyses

Multimodality indicates a discontinuity in the distribution of a variable, thereby suggesting the existence of categories or types (Kendell, 1975; Mendelsohn, Weiss, & Feimer, 1982). Neither multimodality nor a distinct break in the distribution of scores of a personality disorder measure has ever been obtained with data on personality disorder. Frances, Clarkin, Gilmore, Hurt, and Brown (1984) obtained personality disorder ratings on 76 outpatients and concluded that "the DSM-III criteria for personality disorders do not select out mutually exclusive, categorical diagnostic entities. . . . [The] frequency of multiple diagnoses supports the argument for a dimensional rather than a categorical system of personality diagnosis" (p. 1083). Kass et al. (1985) obtained personality disorder ratings from a consecutive sample of 609 outpatients and concluded that "our data do not lend support to the usefulness of a categorical approach" (p. 628). "Since many more patients had some [maladaptive] personality traits or almost met DSM-III criteria than actually met the full criteria[,] . . . the categorical judgments of DSM-III necessarily resulted in the loss of information" (p. 630). Zimmerman and Coryell (1990) obtained personality disorder ratings on 808 first-degree relatives of patients and normal controls and concluded that the "scores are continuously distributed without points of rarity to indicate where to make the distinction between normality and pathology" (p. 690). Nestadt et al. (1990) obtained histrionic ratings from a representative sample of a local community ($N = 810$) and reported that "this personality diagnosis is rather arbitrarily given individuals who extend beyond a cut-off level[;] . . . others less severe but similar in the nature of their dispositional features might have identical symptoms under certain life circumstances" (p. 420). Oldham et al. (1992) administered both the Structured Clinical Interview for *DSM-III-R* Personality Disorders (Spitzer,

Williams, & Gibbon, 1987) and the Personality Disorders Examination (Loranger et al., 1987) to 106 consecutively admitted inpatients. These investigators reported substantial comorbidity among the personality disorders to the point that they questioned the validity of the categorical distinctions (particularly for the narcissistic and avoidant personality disorders and for the distinction between the borderline and the histrionic disorders). However, they did conclude that "there may be merit in maintaining the categorical diagnostic system to allow further research to be done" (Oldham et al., 1992, p. 219). They suggested that in the meantime, clinicians provide the categorical diagnosis when the patient meets the criteria for only one or two disorders: "For patients with more than two disorders, a single diagnosis of 'extensive personality disorder' might be made, with a dimensional description of the predominate characteristics" (p. 219).

The absence of multimodality and distinct breaks, however, is not conclusive, particularly in the absence of any objective technique for interpreting the results (Gangestad & Snyder, 1985; Hicks, 1984). The assessment of multimodality should be conducted with the full range of personality disorder pathology. Such large-scale, epidemiologic research has not yet been conducted, although the studies by Nestadt et al. (1990) and Zimmerman and Coryell (1990) may be close enough.

A compelling approach to the problem of identifying multimodality is admixture analysis, which examines the distribution of canonical coefficient scores derived from a discriminant function analysis for evidence of bimodality. This technique suggests the presence of discrete breaks in the distribution of measures of somatoform and psychotic disorders (Cloninger, Martin, Guze, & Clayton, 1985). Cloninger (1989) indicated that he used admixture analysis with personality disorder data and "found that underlying [the] relatively distinct subgroups appeared to be multiple dimensions of personality that were normally distributed" (p. 140).

> *The real take-home message to me is not that we do not have methods to detect relatively discrete groups but that with psychiatric disorders the groups are not totally*

discrete, and this finding may be consistent with extreme syndromes that develop superimposed on top of underlying dimensional variation. (p. 140)

Lenzenweger and Moldin (1990) applied admixture analysis to items from the Perceptual Aberrations Scale (Chapman, Chapman, & Raulin, 1978) and reported that the results suggested the presence of qualitative discontinuities in the distribution of schizotypal indicators. Others, however, have been somewhat skeptical regarding the power of admixture analysis to detect latent-class taxons (Grayson, 1987a, 1987b; Grove & Andreasen, 1989). It is possible that the lack of sufficiently reliable and valid measurement instruments, sampling biases (e.g., confining the analysis to a limited range along the distribution), and item biases (e.g., items with narrow or skewed levels of difficulty) can distort the findings in either direction.

Additional statistical approaches include latent class analysis, discontinuous regression, and maximum covariation analysis (MAXCOV; Gangestad & Snyder, 1985; Golden & Meehl, 1979; Hicks, 1984; Mendelsohn et al., 1982). Only MAXCOV has been applied to the personality disorders. MAXCOV capitalizes on the fact that the covariation between any two signs of a categorical variable is minimized in groups of subjects who share class membership and is maximized in mixed groups, whereas no such variation in covariation is found across levels of a dimensional variable (Meehl & Golden, 1982). MAXCOV suggests the presence of latent-class taxons for some personality variables (Gangestad & Snyder, 1985; Strube, 1989) and for a "schizoid" taxon that would include the full spectrum of schizophrenic pathology (including the schizotypal, schizoid, and other personality disorders that might share a genetic liability for schizophrenia; Golden & Meehl, 1979). Trull, Widiger, and Guthrie (1990) applied MAXCOV to the *DSM-III-R* criteria for BDL. The charts of 409 psychiatric inpatients were systematically coded for symptoms of dysthymia (a dimensional variable), fallible indicators of biological sex (a categorical variable), and BDL. A clear peak was found for biological sex, the curve was flat for dysthymia, and no middle peak was found for BDL.

Trull et al. concluded that "the results are most consistent with the hypothesis that [BDL] is optimally conceptualized as a dimensional variable" (p. 47). It should also be noted, however, that the Trull et al. findings were not unambiguous. The MAXCOV curve for BDL did not peak in the center of the distribution, although it did peak at the end, which could be inconsistent using both the dimensional and the categorical models. Lenzenweger and Korfine (1992) obtained the same results using indicators of schizotypia from the Perceptual Aberrations Scale and interpreted the peak at the end of the curve to be most consistent with a low-base-rate latent-class taxon.

EMPIRICAL SUPPORT FOR THE FIVE-FACTOR DIMENSIONAL MODEL

Overall, the empirical research does appear to be more consistent with a dimensional than a categorical model of classification. The research indicates that reliable and valid information is lost by the use of the categorical model and that more reliable and valid data are obtained with the dimensional model. Studies using more sophisticated statistical techniques, such as admixture analysis and MAXCOV, also give more support to the dimensional model than to the categorical model, with perhaps the exception of the schizotypal personality disorder (Lenzenweger & Korfine, 1992).

However, this research does not suggest which dimensional model is preferable. A variety of dimensional models have been proposed for personality and personality disorders (Clark, 1990; Cloninger, 1987; Eysenck, 1987; Frances, 1982; Hyler & Lyons, 1988; Kiesler, 1986; Tyrer, 1988; Widiger & Frances, 1985). Many studies have also attempted to identify empirically the dimensions that underlie the personality disorders (Blashfield et al., 1985; Clark, 1989, 1990; Costa & McCrae, 1990; Hyler & Lyons, 1988; Hyler et al., 1990; Kass et al., 1985; Livesley & Jackson, 1986; Livesley, Jackson, & Schroeder, 1989; Lyons, Merla, Ozer, & Hyler, 1990; Millon, 1987; Morey, 1985, 1986; Morey et al., 1985; Plutchik & Platman, 1977; Presley & Walton, 1973; Romney & Bynner, 1989; Schroeder, Wormworth, & Livesley, 1992; Strack & Lorr, 1990; Trull, 1992;

Tyrer & Alexander, 1979; Widiger et al., 1987, 1991; J. Wiggins & Pincus, 1989), but there is no obvious consistency in the findings (Morey, 1986) due in part to the substantial variability in the methodologies and the unreliability of personality disorder assessment. The studies have varied in the analyses used (e.g., MDS vs. FA), the methods of data collection (e.g., clinical interview, self-report inventories, and ratings of analogue case studies), the populations sampled (e.g., inpatients, outpatients, and college students), and the variables analyzed (e.g., trait scales and diagnostic ratings). Even when consistent factor solutions have been obtained across studies, the interpretation of these factors has varied substantially (Widiger et al., 1991).

Romney and Bynner (1989) subjected the factor analytic solutions of Livesley and Jackson (1986), Kass et al. (1985), and Hyler and Lyons (1988) to a confirmatory covariance-structure analysis to assess the extent to which the results were consistent with the interpersonal circumplex (Benjamin, 1993; Kiesler, 1986; Widiger & Kelso, 1983; J. Wiggins, 1982). The results indicated that the narcissistic, paranoid, schizoid, dependent, and histrionic personality disorders could be adequately described with respect to the interpersonal circumplex dimensions but that additional dimensions were needed to account for the other personality disorders. The investigators suggested, for example, that a cognitive dimension was needed to represent the compulsive personality disorder.

Widiger et al. (1987) averaged the correlations among the personality disorders provided in or obtained from nine studies (Dahl, 1986; Kass et al., 1985; Livesley & Jackson, 1986; Millon, 1987; Morey, 1988b; Morey et al., 1985; Pfohl et al., 1986; Widiger et al., 1987; Zanarini et al., 1987). The averaged correlations were then submitted to both MDS and FA. A four-factor solution was optimal for the FA and a three-dimensional solution for the MDS. The three MDS dimensions were identical to the second through fourth dimensions of the FA. Widiger et al. interpreted the first FA dimension as representing the five-factor dimension of Neuroticism. The third MDS and the fourth FA dimensions contrasted the compulsive personality disorder with other diagnoses, replicating the findings of Kass et al. (1985) and Hyler and Lyons (1988). Neither Kass et al. nor Hyler and Lyons, however, offered a substantive interpretation for this dimension, dismissing it simply as a methodological artifact and therefore concluding that the findings supported a three-dimensional model (i.e., the three clusters of odd–eccentric, dramatic–emotional, and anxious–fearful). Widiger et al. indicated that this factor clearly represented the five-factor dimension of Conscientiousness. The remaining two dimensions obtained by Widiger et al. were interpreted as representing the interpersonal dimensions of introversion–extraversion and dominance–submission, which are rotated variants of the five-factor dimensions of Extraversion and Agreeableness (McCrae & Costa, 1989). Widiger et al., however, did not identify an Openness to Experience dimension.

A consistent difficulty with the FA and MDS research, however, is the failure to provide an independent measure of the dimensions that are used to interpret the FA and MDS solutions. The interpretations by the investigators are subjective, inconsistent, and readily debatable in the absence of any independent, objective measure. Only seven studies have assessed empirically the relationship between an independent, objective measure of a dimensional model and the personality disorders. Two concerned the interpersonal circumplex (Dejong, Brink, Jansen, & Schippers, 1989; Morey, 1985), one concerned the interpersonal circumplex and the FFM (J. Wiggins & Pincus, 1989), and four concerned the FFM (Costa & McCrae, 1990; Lyons et al., 1990; Schroeder et al., 1992; Trull, 1992).

Morey (1985) administered the Millon Clinical Multiaxial Inventory (MCMI; Millon, 1977) and the Interpersonal Check List (ICL) to 66 psychiatric inpatients. Canonical correlation analyses indicated that 36% of the variance among the ICL variables was accounted for by the MCMI scales, and 47% of the MCMI was accounted for by the ICL. A plotting of the MCMI scales with respect to the circumplex indicated substantial differentiation among the MCMI scales with respect to the power (or control) axis but very little differentiation with respect to affiliation (extraversion–introversion). This finding is somewhat surprising given the apparent ease with which one can conceptually distinguish the person-

ality disorders with respect to their degree of extraversion–introversion. A limitation of their study is that most of their subjects would have been diagnosed with major Axis I disorders, such as schizophrenia, bipolar disorder, or major depression. The effect of these disorders on the self-report personality scores could be substantial. However, Dejong et al. (1989) obtained quite similar findings using the ICL and the Structured Interview for *DSM-III-R* Personality Disorders (Pfohl et al., 1986). There was again substantial differentiation with respect to the power (control) dimension and little differentiation with respect to affiliation. In fact, all of the personality disorders were placed on the hate half of the love–hate dimension, including the dependent personality disorder.

J. Wiggins and Pincus (1989) administered a variety of personality disorder and five-factor measures to 581 college students. They found that the interpersonal circumplex dimensions were useful in differentiating among and accounting for the variance for some of the personality disorders but that the additional dimensions of Neuroticism, Openness to Experience, and Conscientiousness were necessary to account for all of the personality disorders. For example, Conscientiousness was particularly useful in differentiating compulsive (maladaptively extreme conscientiousness) from passive–aggressive and antisocial disorders. BDL was defined largely by excessive and global neuroticism. The schizotypal personality disorder was the only personality disorder to load on Openness, but additional predictions regarding Openness were confirmed by the bivariate correlations of Openness with the compulsive, schizoid, and avoidant (low openness) and the schizotypal and histrionic (high openness) scales.

Costa and McCrae (1990) obtained self-report, spouse, and peer ratings of the five factors and self-report measures of the personality disorders with the MMPI (Morey et al., 1985), the MCMI, and the MCMI-II (Millon, 1987). The results were largely consistent with the findings of J. Wiggins and Pincus (1989). The FFM accounted for a substantial proportion of the variance in personality disorder pathology, with each of the five dimensions providing substantial contributions. The Conscientiousness dimension, for example, was again useful in characterizing and differentiating the compulsive personality disorder as well as being negatively correlated with the antisocial, passive–aggressive, and histrionic disorders. Narcissism was positively correlated with antagonism and negatively correlated with neuroticism. The avoidant and dependent disorders were both characterized by neuroticism, but the avoidant was also characterized by introversion (on the MCMI). The avoidant and schizoid disorders were both characterized by introversion, but the avoidant was also characterized by neuroticism. The weakest findings occurred for the Openness to Experience dimension.

Schroeder et al. (1992) factor analyzed the Dimensional Assessment of Personality Pathology— Basic Questionnaire (DAPP-BQ; Livesley et al., 1989) along with the NEO Personality Inventory (NEO-PI; Costa & McCrae, 1985) in a sample of 300 normal subjects. The DAPP-BQ contains 18 dimensions of personality pathology, such as affective lability, interpersonal disesteem, narcissism, and stimulus seeking (Livesley et al., 1989). A five-factor solution was obtained, four factors of which corresponded to the FFM domains (Neuroticism, Extraversion, Agreeableness, and Conscientiousness). The third factor was defined jointly by introversion and closedness to experience. Most of the DAPP-BQ scales involve some aspect of neuroticism; compulsivity was associated primarily with conscientiousness; passive oppositionalism was associated with low conscientiousness; lack of interpersonal esteem, suspiciousness, conduct problems, and rejection were associated with antagonism; diffidence was associated with agreeableness; intimacy problems, social avoidance, and restricted expression were associated with introversion; and conduct problems, stimulus seeking, and insecure attachment were associated with extraversion. Schroeder et al. (1992) suggested that the "dimension of Openness to Experience appears to play a relatively minor role in explicating personality disorder" (p. 52). However, although openness was not of primary importance with respect to any of the 18 DAPP-BQ scales, it did provide unique and important contributions with respect to accounting for variance in compulsivity, diffidence, identity problems, restricted expression (low openness), and affective lability (high openness). These latter findings are consistent with those obtained by J. Wiggins and

Pincus (1989). Overall, Schroeder et al. concluded that "the evidence suggests that personality disorders are not characterized by functioning that differs in quality from normal functioning; rather, personality disorders can be described with traits or dimensions that are descriptive of personality, both disordered and normal" (p. 52) and that "the domain of personality pathology can be explained reasonably well within the five-factor model" (p. 51).

In an extensive study, Trull (1992) administered the NEO-PI (Costa & McCrae, 1985), the MMPI personality disorders scales (developed by Morey et al., 1985), the Personality Diagnostic Questionnaire —Revised (PDQ-R; Hyler & Rieder, 1987; Hyler, Rieder, Spitzer, & Williams, 1983), and the Structured Interview for *DSM-III-R* Personality Disorders —Revised (SIDP-R; Pfohl et al., 1989) to 54 outpatients. This was the first published study to assess the relationship of the FFM to the personality disorders in a clinical sample assessed with a multimethod design, including both a semistructured interview and a self-report inventory. Trull found extensive support for the FFM interpretation of the personality disorders. For example, antisocial personality disorder was negatively correlated with agreeableness and conscientiousness, BDL was defined essentially by excessive neuroticism and antagonism, avoidant by introversion and neuroticism (whereas schizoid personality disorder correlated negatively with neuroticism), and histrionic personality disorder was characterized by excessive extraversion. Trull, however, did not replicate the previously reported findings of a correlation of dependency with agreeableness or compulsive personality disorder with conscientiousness.

ALTERNATIVE MODELS

To the extent that the *DSM-III-R* personality disorders involve maladaptive variants of normal personality traits, a model that provides the fundamental dimensions of personality should also provide the fundamental dimensions of abnormal personality (Widiger & Kelso, 1983). The FFM of personality is thus a compelling choice for use with the personality disorders in part because of the substantial empirical support it has received as a model of personality (Digman, 1990). Prior research has also indicated how the five factors subsume the variance and constructs provided in alternative personality disorder dimensional models, including the interpersonal circumplex model (McCrae & Costa, 1989) and the dimensional model (proposed by Eysenck, 1987). Although research concerning the empirical relationship between the five factors and the personality disorders is only a decade old, the findings are encouraging. Even the most vocal critics of the FFM acknowledge that it provides the point of departure for a dimensional formulation of the personality disorders. Grove and Tellegen (1991) asserted that their "view is that the Big Five . . . provides a good starting point for describing normal and disordered personality" (p. 36).

There are other compelling alternatives, including (a) the dimensions of reward dependence, harm avoidance, and novelty seeking proposed by Cloninger (1987); (b) the interpersonal circumplex models proposed by Kiesler (1986) and Benjamin (1993); (c) the seven-factor model proposed by Tellegen and Waller (in press); (d) the three clusters by which the *DSM-III-R* categorical diagnoses are arranged (i.e., odd–eccentric, dramatic–emotional, and anxious–fearful); (d) the four spectra of Axis I-II pathology of anxiety–inhibition, impulsivity–aggression, affective instability, and cognitive–perceptual disorganization proposed by Siever and Davis (1991); and (e) the hierarchical model proposed by Gunderson (1984, 1992). None, however, appears to have compelling empirical support as a model for all of the personality disorders.

We indicated earlier that the interpersonal circumplex is unable to account for all of the personality disorder pathology and is subsumed by the two factors of Extraversion and Agreeableness (Dejong et al., 1989; McCrae & Costa, 1989; J. Wiggins & Pincus, 1989). Kass et al. (1985) and Hyler and Lyons (1988) obtained factor analytic solutions that they suggested provided substantial support for the three clusters presented in the *DSM-III-R*. Both studies obtained three factors that were consistent with the dramatic–emotional, odd–eccentric, and anxious–fearful clusters. However, the results may have been compelled in part by the implicit diagnostic theory of the clinicians who provided the personality disor-

der ratings (Widiger et al., 1987). More important, both studies obtained a fourth factor that the investigators dismissed as a methodological artifact. The fourth factor was in each case consistent with the Conscientiousness dimension, as suggested by J. Wiggins and Pincus (1989).

Fabrega, Ulrich, Pilkonis, and Mezzich (1991) reported a variety of demographic and clinical differences among 2,344 patients who were classified within the three *DSM-III* clusters of odd–eccentric, dramatic–emotional, or anxious–fearful. For example, the odd–eccentric patients were more likely to be male (72%) than were the dramatic–emotional (48%) or the anxious–fearful (43%) patients. Odd–eccentric patients were least likely to have a comorbid Axis I disorder, and dramatic–emotional patients were most likely to have substance abuse disorders. Fabrega et al. suggested that the results supported the validity of the three clusters. It is likely, however, that a variety of other cluster arrangements would have obtained similarly substantial findings. Morey (1988a) provided a more direct test of the three-cluster arrangement. Morey cluster analyzed the *DSM-III-R* personality disorder diagnostic criteria on the basis of data obtained from 291 patients. The cluster analysis did recover most of the personality disorder diagnoses, but Morey acknowledged a "failure to confirm the existence of three superordinate classes of personality disorder . . . [as] suggested both in *DSM-III* and *DSM-III-R*" (p. 320).

Cloninger's (1987) model is appealing from a biogenetic perspective, given that it is derived from theory and research on the neurobiology of motivation and learning (also see Cloninger & Gilligan, 1987). Cloninger related each dimension to a relatively specific but interactive neurotransmitter system. Harm avoidance is thought to reflect variation in the behavioral inhibition system. Its principle monoamine neuromodulator is serotonin, with the locus of activity primarily within the septohippocampal system. Reward dependence is said to involve the behavioral maintenance system, mediated by noradrenergic projections to the neocortex, with norepinephrine being the major neuromodulator. Novelty seeking is thought to reflect variation in the brain's incentive system involving mesolimbic dopaminergic pathways. The model is intriguing, but the neural pathways and neuromodulators that underlie motivation and learning may be only indirectly and often remotely related to the phenotypic variation in personality traits. In addition, there has not yet been any published study that relates empirically Cloninger's dimensions to the personality disorders.

The biogenetic spectrum model proposed by Siever and Davis (1991) is a compelling alternative to the model suggested by Cloninger (1987). There is substantial empirical support for a biogenetic association for many of the personality disorders with near-neighbor Axis I mental disorders (Siever, Klar, & Coccaro, 1985). For example, schizotypal personality disorder may represent a characterologic variant of schizophrenic pathology, avoidant personality disorder a variant of anxiety pathology, BDL a variant of mood and impulsivity pathology, antisocial a variant of impulsivity pathology, compulsive a variant of anxiety pathology, and schizoid a variant of schizophrenic pathology. From this perspective, the personality disorders would represent not extreme variants of normal traits but characterologic variants of Axis I mental disorders. The dimensions that define the personality disorders would not be the same as those that define normal personality but the dimensions that underlie most Axis I psychopathology. However, Widiger and Trull (1992) indicated that the anxiety, impulsivity–hostility, and mood spectra of Siever and Davis are already facets of Neuroticism, a dimension that is involved in almost all of the personality disorders. Widiger and Trull suggested that the cognitive–perceptual spectrum may also represent an additional facet of Neuroticism. It would be of interest in future research to assess whether the phenomenological and biogenetic association of the personality disorders with Axis I disorders is consistent with this extension of the FFM. No study, however, has yet assessed directly the Siever and Davis model, in part because of the absence of a measure of their proposed dimensions. Although it is the case that Neuroticism and its facets are integral to an understanding of personality disorder pathology, it is possible that a complete and comprehensive understanding would also need to consider the dimensions of Introversion, Antagonism, Conscientiousness, and perhaps even Openness.

Tellegen and Waller (in press) suggested that a limitation in the development of the FFM is its exclusion of state and evaluative terms from the original analyses of the English language by Norman (1963) and Goldberg (1981). Evaluative terms may be particularly important when characterizing abnormal personality. Tellegen and Waller suggested that the inclusion of these term results in seven factors rather than five. Five of the factors are equivalent to the FFM, but a few provide a more explicit representation of abnormal variants due to the inclusion of the evaluative terms. For example, the Openness to Experience dimension contrasts being traditional, conventional, conservative, and unimaginative with being unconventional, progressive, radical, unusual, surprising, uncanny, odd, and strange. This formulation of openness (which Tellegen and Waller referred to as *conventionality*) might be better suited than openness for characterizing the peculiar ideation, speech, and behavior of the schizotypal personality disorder. The two additional dimensions are identified as positive evaluation and negative evaluation. Positive evaluation contrasts being excellent, first rate, outstanding, exceptional, special, lofty, and refined with being run-of-the-mill. Negative evaluation contrasts being depraved, evil, immoral, deceitful, detestable, lousy, cruel, destructive, stupid, and mentally imbalanced with being fair and decent. Positive evaluation may be better at characterizing the narcissistic personality disorder and negative evaluation better at characterizing the sadistic (and perhaps the antisocial) disorder than may the FFM.

However, Tellegen and Waller (in press) have not yet published their research concerning the seven-factor model, and it is difficult to evaluate its cogency. It is readily conceivable, for example, that the evaluative terms could be subsumed by the FFM if the respective dimensions were extended to include the more extreme, aberrant manifestations of these dimensions. The original emphasis by Costa and McCrae (1985) on characterizing normal personality with the NEO-PI could have resulted in an inadequate representation of the more extreme and abnormal variants of these traits. The results of Tellegen and Waller do suggest that odd, peculiar, and eccentric behaviors represent extreme variants of Openness to Experience, and the same may be true for the terms contained within the positive and negative evaluation dimensions. The positive evaluation dimension may represent an extreme variant of low Neuroticism (i.e., an excessive absence of insecurity, anxiety, doubts, and vulnerabilities), consistent with the negative correlation of narcissism and psychopathy with Neuroticism (Costa & McCrae, 1990; J. Wiggins & Pincus, 1989). The negative evaluation dimension might represent in large part an extreme variant of antagonism. This dimension already includes socially undesirable traits such as rude, suspicious, vengeful, ruthless, irritable, and manipulative behavior, and it is possible that the traits of evil, depraved, immoral, deceitful, cruel, and detestable are simply more extreme variants of these traits. It will be of interest in future research to explore the relationship between the five factors and the evaluative terms identified by Tellegen and Waller (cf. McCrae & Costa, 1995). McCrae and Costa showed that positive and negative valence are not separate factors of personality, but reflections of the social and personal value of objective features of personality encompassed by the FFM.

Gunderson (1987) has been one of the more outspoken opponents of a dimensional model for classifying personality disorders. However, he has also suggested that only a subset of the personality disorders involve a qualitatively distinct mental disorder (Gunderson, 1984, 1992; Gunderson et al., 1991). Gunderson suggested, for example, that the borderline, schizotypal, paranoid, antisocial, narcissistic, and schizoid personality disorders involve pathologies that are deeper, more severe, earlier, or all of the above in their origins than the pathologies of the compulsive, avoidant, histrionic, and dependent disorders. Their etiologies and pathologies may, then, be more discrete and distinctive.

> The dimensional model deals with the observable surface characteristics and is most applicable to the less severe personality disorders that move imperceptibly into normally occurring traits. The categorical model assumes primary, nonobservable defining characteristics. (Gunderson et al., 1991, p. 65)

As yet, however, there are no data to suggest that the paranoid, schizotypal, borderline, antisocial, narcissistic, and schizoid personality disorders are more consistent with a categorical model than are the compulsive, avoidant, histrionic, and dependent disorders.

Gunderson's (1987) model is similar to that proposed by Meehl (1986). Meehl suggested that a subset of the personality disorders (e.g., antisocial and schizotypal) could be taxonomic in nature (i.e., categorical), although most would be more appropriately classified dimensionally. To the extent that there is a specific etiology and pathology for a particular personality disorder, a categorical model could prove to be optimal for its diagnosis and classification. Underlying the phenotypic distribution of masculine and feminine personality traits is a qualitative genotypic distinction. However, it may still be more accurate and informative to characterize people with respect to their overt personality traits of masculinity and femininity than to lump and stereotype people as being simply men or women. There is likely to be a genetic predisposition for most, if not all, personality traits, but the interaction of these apparently specific etiologies with social, cultural, and other environmental experiences can alter these originally black and white distinctions into more complex and idiosyncratic shades of gray. It is useful to know that schizotypal personality traits are due in part to a genetic predisposition that is associated with schizophrenia (Siever & Davis, 1991), but characterizing the personalities of individuals with the schizotaxic genotype by one diagnostic label can be as stereotyping and misleading as can characterizing the personalities of biogenetically female patients as being simply feminine.

CONCLUSION

Our review of the literature suggests that it is difficult to dismiss the arguments and data favoring a dimensional model of classification for the personality disorders. The few studies to provide data supporting the categorical model have been confined to the schizotypal personality disorder or have concerned simply group (mean or frequency) differences. The latter results are the least informative with respect to determining which model offers the best fit to the data. Data with respect to bimodality, admixture analysis, MAXCOV, and predictive validity have been most consistent with the dimensional model. Research has consistently indicated that reliable and valid information is lost by the failure to use the dimensional approach. A dimensional model resolves the major classificatory dilemmas, provides a more specific and precise description of the traits of the individual patient, and is flexible enough to allow categorical distinctions when they are desirable.

The major limitation of the dimensional model appears to be lack of familiarity, and it is hoped that this book will contribute to an increased appreciation, understanding, and acquaintance with the dimensional perspective. The FFM provides a particularly compelling alternative to the *DSM-III-R* categorical diagnoses. Clinicians who use the FFM will be able to provide a reasonably comprehensive description of their patients' personalities with respect to their adaptive and maladaptive traits. The empirical support for the FFM is substantial with respect to normal personality and encouraging with respect to the personality disorders. It is suggested that future research assess whether the alternative models offer any incremental (concurrent or predictive) validity that is not provided by the FFM or whether the alternative models can in fact be subsumed by one or more of the dimensions and their facets (cf. O'Connor & Dyce, 1998, and chapter 14, this volume). We also suggest further research with clinical populations to assess whether the findings from the relatively normal populations generalize to a personality disordered sample and to consider the issue of how maladaptivity would be defined and assessed by the FFM.

References

Adamson, J. (1989). An appraisal of the *DSM-III* system. *Canadian Journal of Psychiatry, 34,* 300–310.

Akiskal, H. (1989). The classification of mental disorders. In H. Kaplan & B. Sadock (Eds.), *Comprehensive text book of psychiatry* (Vol. 1, 5th ed., pp. 583–598). Baltimore: Williams & Wilkins.

Aldenderger, M., & Blashfield, R. (1984). *Cluster analysis.* Beverly Hills, CA: Sage.

American Psychiatric Association. (1980). *Diagnostic and statistical manual of mental disorders* (3rd ed.). Washington, DC: Author.

American Psychiatric Association. (1987). *Diagnostic and statistical manual of mental disorders* (3rd ed., rev.). Washington, DC: Author.

American Psychiatric Association. (1994). *Diagnostic and statistical manual of mental disorders* (4th ed.). Washington, DC: Author.

Angus, L., & Marziali, E. (1988). A comparison of three measures for the diagnosis of borderline personality disorder. *American Journal of Psychiatry, 145,* 1453–1454.

Benjamin, L. (1993). *Interpersonal diagnosis and treatment of personality disorders: A structural approach.* New York: Guilford Press.

Blashfield, R. (1984). *The classification of psychopathology.* New York: Plenum Press.

Blashfield, R., Sprock, J., Pinkston, K., & Hodgin, J. (1985). Exemplar prototypes of personality disorder diagnoses. *Comprehensive Psychiatry, 26,* 11–21.

Cantor, N., & Genero, N. (1986). Psychiatric diagnosis and natural categorization: A close analogy. In T. Millon & G. Klerman (Eds.), *Contemporary directions in psychopathology* (pp. 233–256). New York: Guilford Press.

Carson, R. C. (1991). Dilemmas in the pathway of *DSM-IV. Journal of Abnormal Psychology, 100,* 302–307.

Chapman, L. J., Chapman, J. P., & Raulin, M. L. (1978). Body-image aberration in schizophrenia. *Journal of Abnormal Psychology, 87,* 399–407.

Clark, L. (1989, August). The basic traits of personality disorder: Primary and higher-order dimensions. In R. R. McCrae (Chair), *Personality disorders from the perspective of the five-factor model.* Symposium conducted at the 97th Annual Convention of the American Psychological Association, New Orleans, LA.

Clark, L. (1990). Towards a consensual set of symptom clusters for assessment of personality disorder. In J. Butcher & C. Spielberger (Eds.), *Advances in personality assessment* (Vol. 8, pp. 243–266). Hillsdale, NJ: Erlbaum.

Clarkin, J. F., & Sanderson, C. (1993). The personality disorders. In A. Bellack & M. Hersen (Eds.), *Psychopathology in adulthood: An advanced text* (pp. 252–274). Boston: Allyn & Bacon.

Clarkin, J. F., Widiger, T. A., Frances, A. J., Hurt, S., & Gilmore, M. (1983). Prototypic typology and the borderline personality disorder. *Journal of Abnormal Psychology, 92,* 263–275.

Cloninger, C. R. (1987). A systematic method for

clinical description and classification of personality variants. *Archives of General Psychiatry, 44,* 573–588.

Cloninger, C. R. (1989). Establishment of diagnostic validity in psychiatric illness: Robins and Guze's method revisited. In L. Robins & J. Barrett (Eds.), *The validity of psychiatric diagnosis* (pp. 9–18). New York: Raven Press.

Cloninger, C. R., & Gilligan, S. (1987). Neurogenic mechanisms of learning: A phylogenetic perspective. *Journal of Psychiatry Research, 21,* 457–472.

Cloninger, C. R., Martin, R., Guze, S., & Clayton, P. (1985). Diagnosis and prognosis in schizophrenia. *Archives of General Psychiatry, 42,* 15–25.

Cohen, J., & Cohen, P. (1975). *Applied multiple regression/correlation analysis for the behavioral sciences.* Hillsdale, NJ: Erlbaum.

Costa, P. T., Jr., & McCrae, R. R. (1985). *The NEO Personality Inventory manual.* Odessa, FL: Psychological Assessment Resources.

Costa, P. T., Jr., & McCrae, R. R. (1990). Personality disorders and the five-factor model of personality. *Journal of Personality Disorders, 4,* 362–371.

Costa, P. T., Jr., & McCrae, R. R. (1992). The five-factor model of personality and its relevance to personality disorders. *Journal of Personality Disorders, 6,* 343–359.

Dahl, A. (1986). Some aspects of the *DSM-III* personality disorders illustrated by a consecutive sample of hospitalized patients. *Acta Psychiatrica Scandinavica, 73,* 61–66.

Dejong, C., Brink, W., Jansen, J., & Schippers, G. (1989). Interpersonal aspects of *DSM-III* Axis II: Theoretical hypotheses and empirical findings. *Journal of Personality Disorders, 3,* 135–146.

Digman, J. (1990). Personality structure: Emergence of the five-factor model. *Annual Review of Psychology, 41,* 417–440.

Eysenck, H. (1986). A critique of contemporary classification and diagnosis. In T. Millon & G. Klerman (Eds.), *Contemporary directions in psychopathology* (pp. 73–98). New York: Guilford Press.

Eysenck, H. (1987). The definition of personality disorders and the criteria appropriate for their description. *Journal of Personality Disorders, 1,* 211–219.

Fabrega, H., Ulrich, R., Pilkonis, P., & Mezzich, J. (1991). On the homogeneity of personality disorder clusters. *Comprehensive Psychiatry, 32,* 373–386.

Finn, S. (1982). Base rates, utilities, and *DSM-III:*

Shortcomings of fixed-rule systems of psychodiagnosis. *Journal of Abnormal Psychology, 91,* 294–302.

Frances, A. J. (1982). Categorical and dimensional systems of personality diagnosis: A comparison. *Comprehensive Psychiatry, 23,* 516–527.

Frances, A. J. (1990, May). *Conceptual problems of psychiatric classification.* Paper presented at the 143rd annual meeting of the American Psychiatric Association, New York.

Frances, A. J. (1993). Dimensional diagnosis of personality—Not whether, but when and which. *Psychological Inquiry, 4,* 110–111.

Frances, A. J., Clarkin, J., Gilmore, M., Hurt, S., & Brown, S. (1984). Reliability of criteria for borderline personality disorder: A comparison of *DSM-III* and the Diagnostic Interview for Borderline Patients. *American Journal of Psychiatry, 141,* 1080–1084.

Frances, A. J., Pincus, H. A., Widiger, T. A., Davis, W. W., & First, M. B. (1990). *DSM-IV:* Work in progress. *American Journal of Psychiatry, 147,* 1439–1448.

Frances, A. J., Widiger, T. A., & Pincus, H. A. (1989). The development of *DSM-IV. Archives of General Psychiatry, 46,* 373–375.

Gangestad, S., & Snyder, M. (1985). "To carve nature at its joints": On the existence of discrete classes in personality. *Psychological Review, 92,* 317–349.

Goldberg, L. (1981). Language and individual differences: The search for universals in personality lexicons. In L. Wheeler (Ed.), *Review of personality and social psychology* (Vol. 2, pp. 141–165). Beverly Hills, CA: Sage.

Golden, R., & Meehl, P. (1979). Detection of the schizoid taxon with MMPI indicators. *Journal of Abnormal Psychology, 88,* 217–233.

Gorton, G., & Akhtar, S. (1990). The literature on personality disorders, 1985–1988: Trends, issues, and controversies. *Hospital and Community Psychiatry, 41,* 39–51.

Grayson, J. (1987a). Can categorical and dimensional views of psychiatric illness be distinguished? *British Journal of Psychiatry, 151,* 355–361.

Grayson, J. (1987b). Discussion. *Psychiatric Developments, 4,* 377–385.

Grove, W. M., & Andreasen, N. (1989). Quantitative and qualitative distinctions between psychiatric disorders. In L. Robins & J. Barett (Eds.), *The validity of psychiatric diagnosis* (pp. 127–141). New York: Raven Press.

Grove, W. M., & Tellegen, A. (1991). Problems in the classification of personality disorders. *Journal of Personality Disorders, 5,* 31–41.

Gunderson, J. G. (1984). *Borderline personality disorder.* Washington, DC: American Psychiatric Press.

Gunderson, J. G. (1987, May). Competing models of personality disorders. In H. Klar (Chair), *Current controversies in personality disorders.* Symposium conducted at the 140th annual meeting of the American Psychiatric Association, Chicago, IL.

Gunderson, J. G. (1992). Diagnostic controversies. In A. Tasman & M. Riba (Eds.), *Review of psychiatry* (Vol. 11, pp. 9–24). Washington, DC: American Psychiatric Press.

Gunderson, J. G., Links, P. S., & Reich, J. H. (1991). Competing models of personality disorders. *Journal of Personality Disorders, 5,* 60–68.

Gunderson, J. G., & Zanarini, M. (1987). Current overview of the borderline diagnosis. *Journal of Clinical Psychiatry, 48,* 5–11.

Guze, R., & Helzer, J. (1987). The medical model and psychiatric disorders. In J. Cavenar, R. Michels, & A. Cooper (Eds.), *Psychiatry* (Vol. 1, pp. 1–12). Philadelphia: Lippincott.

Hart, S., & Hare, R. (1989). Discriminant validity of the Psychopathy Checklist in a forensic psychiatric population. *Psychological Assessment: A Journal of Consulting and Clinical Psychology, 1,* 211–218.

Hathaway, S. R., & McKinley, J. C. (1967). *Minnesota Multiphasic Personality Inventory manual.* New York: Psychological Corporation.

Heumann, K., & Morey, L. (1990). Reliability of categorical and dimensional judgments of personality disorder. *American Journal of Psychiatry, 147,* 498–500.

Hicks, L. (1984). Conceptual and empirical analysis of some assumptions of an explicitly typological theory. *Journal of Personality and Social Psychology, 46,* 1118–1131.

Hine, F., & Williams, R. (1975). Dimensional diagnosis and the medical student's grasp of psychiatry. *Archives of General Psychiatry, 32,* 525–528.

Hogg, B., Jackson, H., Rudd, R., & Edwards, J. (1990). Diagnosing personality disorders in recent-onset schizophrenia. *Journal of Nervous and Mental Disease, 178,* 194–199.

Hyler, S. E., & Lyons, M. (1988). Factor analysis of the *DSM-III* personality disorder clusters: A replication. *Comprehensive Psychiatry, 29,* 304–308.

Hyler, S. E., Lyons, M., Rieder, R. O., Young, L., Williams, J. B. W., & Spitzer, R. L. (1990). The factor structure of self-report *DSM-III* Axis II symptoms and their relationship to clinicians' ratings. *American Journal of Psychiatry, 147,* 751–757.

Hyler, S. E., & Rieder, R. O. (1987). *Personality Diagnostic Questionnaire—Revised.* New York: Author.

Hyler, S. E., Rieder, R. O., Spitzer, R., & Williams, J. (1983). *Personality Diagnostic Questionnaire.* Unpublished manuscript, New York State Psychiatric Institute, New York.

Hyler, S. E., Rieder, R. O., Williams, J., Spitzer, R., Lyons, M., & Hendler, J. (1989). A comparison of clinical and self-report diagnoses of *DSM-III* personality disorders in 552 patients. *Comprehensive Psychiatry, 30,* 170–178.

Kass, F., Skodol, A. E., Charles, E., Spitzer, R. L., & Williams, J. B. W. (1985). Scaled ratings of *DSM-III* personality disorders. *American Journal of Psychiatry, 142,* 627–630.

Kato, M. (1988). Issues on diagnosing and classifying personality disorders. In J. Mezzich & M. von Cranach (Eds.), *International classification in psychiatry* (pp. 166–172). Cambridge, UK: Cambridge University Press.

Kavoussi, R., Coccaro, E., Klar, H., Bernstein, D., & Siever, L. (1990). Structured interviews for borderline personality disorder. *American Journal of Psychiatry, 147,* 1522–1525.

Kendell, R. (1975). *The role of diagnosis in psychiatry.* Oxford, UK: Blackwell Scientific.

Kendler, K. S. (1990). Towards a scientific psychiatric nosology: Strengths and limitations. *Archives of General Psychiatry, 47,* 969–973.

Kernberg, O. F. (1984). *Severe personality disorders.* New Haven, CT: Yale University Press.

Kiesler, D. (1986). The 1982 Interpersonal Circle: An analysis of *DSM-III* personality disorders. In T. Millon & G. Klerman (Eds.), *Contemporary directions in psychopathology* (pp. 571–597). New York: Guilford Press.

Kiesler, D. (1991). Interpersonal methods of assessment and diagnosis. In C. R. Snyder & D. R. Forsyth (Eds.), *Handbook of social and clinical psychology: The health perspective* (pp. 438–468). Elmsford, NY: Pergamon Press.

Klerman, G. (1986). Historical perspectives on contemporary schools of psychopathology. In T. Millon & G. Klerman (Eds.), *Contemporary directions in psychopathology* (pp. 3–28). New York: Guilford Press.

Kroll, J. (1988). *The challenge of the borderline patient.* New York: Norton.

Lenzenweger, M. F., & Korfine, L. (1992). Confirming the latent structure and base rate of schizotypy: A taxometric analysis. *Journal of Abnormal Psychology, 101,* 567–571.

Lenzenweger, M. F., & Moldin, S. O. (1990). Discerning the latent structure of hypothetical psychosis proneness through admixture analysis. *Psychiatry Research, 33,* 243–257.

Livesley, W. J. (1985). The classification of personality disorder: I. The choice of category concept. *Canadian Journal of Psychiatry, 30,* 353–358.

Livesley, W. J. (1991). Classifying personality disorders: Ideal types, prototypes, or dimensions? *Journal of Personality Disorders, 5,* 52–59.

Livesley, W. J., & Jackson, D. (1986). The internal consistency and factorial structure of behaviors judged to be associated with *DSM-III* personality disorders. *American Journal of Psychiatry, 139,* 1360–1361.

Livesley, W. J., Jackson, D., & Schroeder, M. (1989). A study of the factorial structure of personality pathology. *Journal of Personality Disorders, 3,* 292–306.

Loranger, A. (1988). *Personality Disorder Examination (PDE) manual.* New York: DV Communications.

Loranger, A., Susman, V., Oldham, J., & Russakoff, L. (1987). The Personality Disorder Examination: A preliminary report. *Journal of Personality Disorders, 1,* 1–13.

Lyons, M., Merla, M., Ozer, D., & Hyler, S. (1990, August). *Relationship of the "Big Five" Factors to DSM-III personality disorders.* Paper presented at the 98th Annual Convention of the American Psychological Association, Boston, MA.

Maser, J. D., Kaelber, C., & Weise, R. E. (1991). International use and attitudes toward *DSM-III* and *DSM-III-R:* Growing consensus in psychiatric classification. *Journal of Personality Disorders, 100,* 271–279.

McCrae, R. R., & Costa, P. T., Jr. (1989). The structure of interpersonal traits: Wiggins's circumplex and the five-factor model. *Journal of Personality and Social Psychology, 56,* 586–595.

McCrae, R. R., & Costa, P. T., Jr. (1995). Positive and negative valence within the five-factor model. *Journal of Research in Personality, 29,* 443–460.

McGlashan, T. (1987). Borderline personality disorder and unipolar affective disorder: Long-term effects of comorbidity. *Journal of Nervous and Mental Disease, 175,* 467–473.

McLemore, C. W., & Brokaw, D. (1987). Personality disorders as dysfunctional interpersonal behavior. *Journal of Personality Disorders, 1,* 270–285.

McReynolds, P. (1989). Diagnosis and clinical assessment: Current status and major issues. *Annual Review of Psychology, 40,* 83–108.

Meehl, P. E. (1986). Diagnostic taxa as open concepts: Meta-theoretical and statistical questions about reliability and construct validity in the grand strategy of nosological revision. In T. Millon & G. Klerman (Eds.), *Contemporary directions in psychopathology* (pp. 215–231). New York: Guilford Press.

Meehl, P. E., & Golden, R. (1982). Taxometric methods. In P. Kendall & J. Butcher (Eds.), *Handbook of research methods in clinical psychology* (pp. 127–181). New York: Wiley.

Mellsop, G., Varghese, F., Joshua, S., & Hicks, A. (1982). The reliability of Axis II of *DSM-III. American Journal of Psychiatry, 139,* 1360–1361.

Mendelsohn, G., Weiss, D., & Feimer, N. (1982). Conceptual and empirical analysis of the typological implications of patterns of socialization and femininity. *Journal of Personality and Social Psychology, 42,* 1157–1170.

Miller, M., & Thayer, J. (1989). On the existence of discrete classes in personality: Is self-monitoring the correct joint to carve? *Journal of Personality and Social Psychology, 57,* 143–155.

Millon, T. (1977). *Millon Clinical Multiaxial Inventory.* Minneapolis, MN: National Computer Systems.

Millon, T. (1981). *Disorders of personality:* DSM-III, *Axis II.* New York: Wiley.

Millon, T. (1987). *Manual for the MCMI-II.* Minneapolis, MN: National Computer Systems.

Millon, T. (1990). The disorders of personality. In L. A. Pervin (Ed.), *Handbook of personality: Theory and research* (pp. 339–370). New York: Guilford Press.

Millon, T. (1991). Classification in psychopathology: Rationale, alternatives, and standards. *Journal of Abnormal Psychology, 100,* 245–261.

Morey, L. C. (1985). An empirical comparison of interpersonal and *DSM-III* approaches to classification of personality disorders. *Psychiatry, 48,* 358–364.

Morey, L. C. (1986). A comparison of three personality disorder assessment approaches. *Journal of Psychopathology and Behavioral Assessment, 8,* 25–30.

Morey, L. C. (1988a). The categorical representations of personality disorder: A cluster analysis of *DSM-III-R* personality disorders. *Journal of Abnormal Psychology, 97,* 314–321.

Morey, L. C. (1988b). Personality disorders in *DSM-III* and *DSM-III-R:* Convergence, coverage, and internal consistency. *American Journal of Psychiatry, 145,* 573–577.

Morey, L. C., & Ochoa, E. (1989). An investigation of adherence to diagnostic criteria: Clinical diagnosis of the *DSM-III* personality disorders. *Journal of Personality Disorders, 3,* 180–192.

Morey, L. C., Waugh, M., & Blashfield, R. (1985). MMPI scales for *DSM-III* personality disorders: Their derivation and correlates. *Journal of Personality Assessment, 49,* 245–251.

Nazikian, H., Rudd, R., Edwards, J., & Jackson, H. (1990). Personality disorder assessment for psychiatric inpatients. *Australian and New Zealand Journal of Psychiatry, 24,* 37–46.

Nestadt, G., Romanoski, A., Chahal, R., Merchant, A., Folstein, M., Gruenberg, E., & McHugh, P. (1990). An epidemiological study of histrionic personality disorder. *Psychological Medicine, 20,* 413–422.

Norman, W. (1963). Toward an adequate taxonomy of personality attributes: Replicated factor structure in peer nomination personality ratings. *Journal of Abnormal and Social Psychology, 66,* 574–583.

Nurnberg, H. G., Raskin, M., Levine, P. E., Pollack, S., Siegel, O., & Prince, R. (1991). The comorbidity of borderline personality disorder and other *DSM-III-R* Axis II personality disorders. *American Journal of Psychiatry, 148,* 1371–1377.

O'Boyle, M., & Self, D. (1990). A comparison of two interviews for *DSM-III-R* personality disorders. *Psychiatry Research, 32,* 85–92.

O'Connor, B. P., & Dyce, J. A. (1998). A test of models of personality disorder configuration. *Journal of Abnormal Psychology, 107,* 3–16.

Oldham, J. M. (1987). *DSM-III* personality disorders: Assessment problems. *Journal of Personality Disorders, 1,* 241–247.

Oldham, J. M., Skodol, A. E., Kellman, H. D., Hyler, S. E., Rosnick, L., & Davies, M. (1992). Diagnosis of *DSM-III-R* personality disorders by two structured interviews: Patterns of comorbidity. *American Journal of Psychiatry, 149,* 213–220.

Pfohl, B., Blum, N., Zimmerman, M., & Stangl, D. (1989). *Structured Interview for DSM-III-R Personality Disorders—Revised (SIPD-R).* Iowa City: University of Iowa, Department of Psychiatry.

Pfohl, B., Coryell, W., Zimmerman, M., & Stangl, D. (1986). *DSM-III* personality disorders: Diagnostic overlap and internal consistency of individual *DSM-III* criteria. *Comprehensive Psychiatry, 27,* 21–34.

Plutchik, R., & Conte, H. R. (1985). Quantitative assessment of personality disorders. In R. Michels & J. O. Cavenar (Eds.), *Psychiatry* (Vol. 1, pp. 1–13). Philadelphia: Lippincott.

Plutchik, R., & Platman, S. (1977). Personality connotations of psychiatric diagnoses. *Journal of Nervous and Mental Disease, 165,* 418–422.

Presley, A., & Walton, H. (1973). Dimensions of abnormal personality. *British Journal of Psychiatry, 122,* 269–276.

Reich, J., Noyes, R., & Troughton, E. (1987). Lack of agreement between instruments assessing *DSM-III* personality disorders. In C. Green (Ed.), *Conference on the Millon clinical inventories* (pp. 223–234). Minnetonka, MN: National Computer Systems.

Robins, L., & Helzer, J. (1986). Diagnosis and clinical assessment: The current state of psychiatric diagnosis. *Annual Review of Psychology, 37,* 409–432.

Romney, D., & Bynner, J. (1989). Evaluation of a circumplex model of *DSM-III* personality disorders. *Journal of Research in Personality, 23,* 525–538.

Rutter, M. (1987). Temperament, personality and personality disorder. *British Journal of Psychiatry, 150,* 443–458.

Schacht, T. (1985). *DSM-III* and the politics of truth. *American Psychologist, 40,* 513–521.

Schroeder, M. L., Wormworth, J. A., & Livesley, W. J. (1992). Dimensions of personality disorder and their relationships to the Big Five dimensions of personality. *Psychological Assessment, 4,* 47–53.

Siever, L. J., & Davis, K. L. (1991). A psychobiological perspective on the personality disorders. *American Journal of Psychiatry, 148,* 1647–1658.

Siever, L., Klar, H., & Coccaro, E. (1985). Psychobiologic substrates of personality. In H. Klar & L. Siever (Eds.), *Biologic response styles: Clinical implications* (pp. 37–66). Washington, DC: American Psychiatric Press.

Skodol, A. E., Oldham, J. M., Rosnick, L., Kellman, H. D., & Hyler, S. E. (1991). Diagnosis of *DSM-III-R* personality disorders: A comparison of two structured interviews. *International Journal of Methods in Psychiatric Research, 1,* 13–26.

Skodol, A. E., Rosnick, L., Kellman, H. D., Oldham, J., & Hyler, S. E. (1988). Validating structured *DSM-III-R* personality disorder assessments with longitudinal data. *American Journal of Psychiatry, 145,* 1297–1299.

Spitzer, R. L. (1987). Nosology. In A. Skodol & R. Spitzer (Eds.), *An annotated bibliography of DSM-*

III (pp. 3–11). Washington, DC: American Psychiatric Press.

Spitzer, R. L., Endicott, J., & Gibbon, M. (1979). Crossing the border into borderline personality and borderline schizophrenia. *Archives of General Psychiatry, 36,* 17–24.

Spitzer, R. L., & Williams, J. B. W. (1985). Classification of mental disorders. In H. I. Kaplan & B. J. Sadock (Eds.), *Comprehensive textbook of psychiatry* (pp. 591–613). Baltimore: Williams & Wilkins.

Spitzer, R. L., Williams, J. B. W., & Gibbon, M. (1987). *Structured Clinical Interview for* DSM-III-R *Personality Disorders (SCID-II).* New York: New York State Psychiatric Institute, Biometric Research Unit.

Standage, K., & Ladha, N. (1988). An examination of the reliability of the Personality Disorder Examination and a comparison with other methods of identifying personality disorders in a clinical sample. *Journal of Personality Disorders, 2,* 267–271.

Stone, M. (1992). The treatment of severe personality disorders. In A. Tasman & M. Riba (Eds.), *Review of psychiatry* (Vol. 11, pp. 98–115). Washington, DC: American Psychiatric Press.

Strack, S., & Lorr, M. (1990). Item factor structure of the Personality Adjective Check List. *Journal of Personality Assessment, 55,* 86–94.

Strube, M. (1989). Evidence for the type in Type A behavior: A taxometric analysis. *Journal of Personality and Social Psychology, 56,* 972–987.

Tellegen, A., & Waller, N. (in press). Exploring personality through test construction: Development of the Multidimensional Personality Questionnaire. In S. R. Briggs, J. M. Cheek, & E. M. Donohue (Eds.), *Personality measures: Development and evaluation* (Vol. 1, pp. 133–161). New York: Plenum Press.

Trull, T. J. (1992). *DSM-III-R* personality disorders and the five-factor model of personality: An empirical comparison. *Journal of Abnormal Psychology, 101,* 553–560.

Trull, T. J., Widiger, T. A., & Guthrie, P. (1990). The categorical versus dimensional status of borderline personality disorder. *Journal of Abnormal Psychology, 99,* 40–48.

Tyrer, P. (1988). What's wrong with *DSM-III* personality disorders? *Journal of Personality Disorders, 2,* 281–291.

Tyrer, P., & Alexander, J. (1979). Classification of personality disorder. *British Journal of Psychiatry, 135,* 163–167.

Vaillant, G. (1984). The disadvantages of *DSM-III* outweigh its advantages. *American Journal of Psychiatry, 141,* 542–545.

Walton, H. (1986). The relationship between personality disorder and psychiatric illness. In T. Millon & G. Klerman (Eds.), *Contemporary directions in psychopathology* (pp. 553–569). New York: Guilford Press.

Widiger, T. A. (1991). Personality disorder dimensional models proposed for *DSM-IV. Journal of Personality Disorders, 5,* 386–398.

Widiger, T. A. (1993). The *DSM-III-R* categorical personality disorder diagnoses: A critique and an alternative. *Psychological Inquiry, 4,* 75–90.

Widiger, T. A., & Frances, A. J. (1985). The *DSM-III* personality disorders: Perspectives from psychology. *Archives of General Psychiatry, 42,* 615–623.

Widiger, T. A., Frances, A. J., Harris, M., Jacobsberg, L. B., Fyer, M., & Manning, D. (1991). Comorbidity among Axis II disorders. In J. Oldham (Ed.), *Axis II: New perspectives on diagnostic validity* (pp. 163–194). Washington, DC: American Psychiatric Press.

Widiger, T. A., Hurt, S., Frances, A. J., Clarkin, J., & Gilmore, M. (1984). Diagnostic efficiency and *DSM-III. Archives of General Psychiatry, 41,* 1005–1012.

Widiger, T. A., & Kelso, K. (1983). Psychodiagnosis of Axis II. *Clinical Psychology Review, 3,* 491–510.

Widiger, T. A., & Rogers, J. (1989). Prevalence and comorbidity of personality disorders. *Psychiatric Annals, 19,* 132–136.

Widiger, T. A., & Sanderson, C. (1987). The convergent and discriminant validity of the MCMI as a measure of the *DSM-III* personality disorders. *Journal of Personality Assessment, 51,* 228–242.

Widiger, T. A., Sanderson, C., & Warner, L. (1986). The MMPI, prototypal typology, and borderline personality disorder. *Journal of Personality Assessment, 50,* 540–553.

Widiger, T. A., & Trull, T. J. (1991). Diagnosis and clinical assessment. *Annual Review of Psychology, 42,* 109–133.

Widiger, T. A., & Trull, T. J. (1992). Personality and psychopathology: An application of the five-factor model. *Journal of Personality, 60,* 363–395.

Widiger, T. A., Trull, T. J., Hurt, S., Clarkin, J., & Frances, A. (1987). A multidimensional scaling of the *DSM-III* personality disorders. *Archives of General Psychiatry, 44,* 557–563.

Wiggins, J. (1982). Circumplex models of interpersonal behavior in clinical psychology. In P. Kendall & J. Butcher (Eds.), *Handbook of research methods in clinical psychology* (pp. 183–221). New York: Wiley.

Wiggins, J., & Pincus, A. (1989). Conceptions of personality disorders and dimensions of personality. *Psychological Assessment: A Journal of Consulting and Clinical Psychology, 1,* 305–316.

Wiggins, O. P., & Schwartz, M. A. (1991). Research into personality disorders: The alternatives of dimensions and ideal types. *Journal of Personality Disorders, 5,* 69–81.

Zanarini, M., Frankenburg, F., Chauncey, D., & Gunderson, J. (1987). The Diagnostic Interview for Personality Disorders: Interrater and test–retest reliability. *Comprehensive Psychiatry, 28,* 467–480.

Zimmerman, M. (1988). Why are we rushing to publish *DSM-IV*? *Archives of General Psychiatry, 45,* 1135–1138.

Zimmerman, M., & Coryell, W. H. (1989). The reliability of personality disorder diagnoses in a nonpatient sample. *Journal of Personality Disorders, 3,* 53–57.

Zimmerman, M., & Coryell, W. H. (1990). *DSM-III* personality disorder dimensions. *Journal of Nervous and Mental Disease, 178,* 686–692.

Zimmerman, M., Pfohl, B., Coryell, W. H., Stangl, D., & Corenthal, C. (1988). Diagnosing personality disorder in depressed patients. *General Psychiatry, 45,* 733–737.

CHAPTER 4

A FIVE-FACTOR PERSPECTIVE ON PERSONALITY DISORDER RESEARCH

Timothy J. Trull and Robert R. McCrae

The premise of this book is that personality disorders can be understood in terms of the dimensions of personality identified in the five-factor model (FFM). Perhaps the most obvious question, then, is whether there is good empirical evidence that individuals with different personality disorders can in fact be characterized by distinctive and appropriate personality profiles across the five factors, or dimensions, of the FFM. The answer is "not yet." In one respect this is not surprising: It is only within the past decade that the FFM has commanded any attention from psychiatric researchers, and there has simply not been sufficient time to accumulate a body of data on personality disordered patients using measures of this model.

In this chapter, we review research on personality disorders from the perspective of the FFM. We believe this can aid in the understanding of a disorder's core symptomatology, its overlap with other personality disorders, and its overlap with syndromes described in Axis I of the third edition, revised, of the *Diagnostic and Statistical Manual of Mental Disorders* (*DSM-III-R*; American Psychiatric Association, 1987). Many of the controversies that plague personality disorder research can be illuminated from this perspective. In particular, we focus on the overlap between Axis I and Axis II disorders, heterogeneity within the borderline personality disorder (BDL) category, and the nature of the narcissistic personality disorder (NAR) construct.

One might suppose that there would be much literature on the personality traits that characterize various disorders using older instruments like the Eysenck Personality Inventory (Eysenck & Eysenck, 1964), the Sixteen Personality Factor Questionnaire (Cattell, Eber, & Tatsuoka, 1970), or the Guilford–Zimmerman Temperament Survey (Guilford, Zimmerman, & Guilford, 1976). Because the FFM is comprehensive, it is usually possible to interpret scales from other instruments such as these in its terms. Thus, it might be possible to organize a literature review in terms of the five factors even if they were never measured directly.

Somewhat surprisingly, there is relatively little information to organize in this way. A great deal of research (for a review, see Widiger & Frances, 1987) focuses on the reliability and comparability of different instruments designed specifically for assessing the personality disorders, such as the Minnesota Multiphasic Personality Inventory (MMPI; Hathaway & McKinley, 1967), the Personality Disorder Scales (Morey, Waugh, & Blashfield, 1985), and the Millon Clinical Multiaxial Inventory (MCMI; Millon, 1983). Studies link the scales of these instruments to measures of normal personality in normal samples (e.g., Wiggins & Pincus, 1989). But the strategy of administering normal personality measures to characterize individuals diagnosed with specific disorders has only rarely been followed.

Two studies, however, merit special attention as

We thank Thomas A. Widiger for his comments and suggestions regarding earlier versions of this chapter. The research described in this chapter was supported, in part, by a Summer Research Fellowship from the Research Council of the University of Missouri–Columbia.

steps in this direction. Lyons, Merla, Ozer, and Hyler (1990) administered a self-report personality disorder inventory, the Personality Diagnostic Questionnaire (PDQ; Hyler et al., 1989), to a clinical sample for which clinicians' ratings of personality disorders were available; over half of the subjects met diagnostic criteria for at least one personality disorder. Although the initial intent was to examine correspondence between the PDQ scales and clinician ratings, interest in the FFM led to a secondary analysis. By administering the PDQ and Goldberg's (1990) Adjective Scales to a second sample, Lyons et al. were able to select PDQ items that approximated four of the five factors (an Openness to Experience scale could not be created from PDQ items). When these new PDQ scales were compared with clinicians' ratings in the original sample, several significant relations were found. Specifically, Extraversion (E) was positively related to clinicians' ratings of histrionic personality disorder (HST) and negatively related to schizoid personality disorder (SZD), avoidant personality disorder (AVD), and several other personality disorders. Agreeableness (A) was positively related to dependent personality disorder (DEP) and negatively related to paranoid personality disorder (PAR), NAR, and antisocial personality disorder (ATS). Conscientiousness (C) was positively related to obsessive–compulsive personality disorder (OBC) and negatively related to ATS and BDL. All of these findings replicate associations found between personality disorder scales and measures of the five factors in normal samples (Costa & McCrae, 1990). However, Neuroticism (N) was only weakly related to clinicians' ratings, and the pattern of findings did not resemble that found in normal samples.

Trull (1992) provided more direct evidence on this question by administering the NEO Personality Inventory (NEO-PI; Costa & McCrae, 1985)—a standard measure of the FFM—to 54 psychiatric outpatients. The patients were rated for the presence of personality disorder symptoms on the basis of a semistructured interview; in addition, patients completed two self-report personality disorder inventories. Results were generally consistent across the three assessments of personality disorders and replicated most findings previously reported for nonpsychiatric samples. In contrast to the Lyons et al. re-

sults, the NEO-PI's measure of N proved to be a powerful predictor of several personality disorders, especially BDL. Both these studies provide evidence that individuals with diagnosable personality disorders do differ in predictable ways on the five factors.

PERSONALITY, PERSONALITY DISORDERS, AND CLINICAL SYNDROMES

The multiaxial system of the *DSM-III-R* is based on the premise that mental disorders in adults can be categorized as clinical syndromes (Axis I) or personality disorders (Axis II). The latter are inflexible and maladaptive forms of enduring personality traits; the former are typically more florid conditions that may be intermittent or have a late-life onset. How should these two kinds of disorders be related? Certainly they are not mutually exclusive—the whole notion of providing diagnoses on both axes was intended to underscore the possibility that patients might have personality disorders in addition to clinical syndromes. But the degree of comorbidity might be considered surprising.

Docherty, Fiester, and Shea (1986) reviewed studies that presented comorbidity rates for personality disorders and affective disorders as well as for personality disorders and anxiety. Studies varied as to whether they reported on Axis I syndromes in individuals with personality disorders or, conversely, the rate of personality disorder in individuals with Axis I syndromes. Axis I comorbidity rates with BDL diagnosis were reported most frequently; only a few studies reported comorbidity rates in non-BDL personality disordered patients. Across studies, the prevalence rates for a comorbid affective disorder in BDL patients fell in the 25–60% range. In patients with major depression, a comorbid BDL was frequently found as well. In one study that examined other (non-BDL) personality disorder diagnoses in a sample of depressed patients (Pfohl, Stangl, & Zimmerman, 1984), relatively high rates of HST, DEP, and AVD were found. Docherty et al. also reviewed the few studies that examined the comorbidity of personality disorders and anxiety disorders. For example, Akiskal (1981) reported that 10% of the 100 BDL patients in his sample met criteria for agoraphobia, phobic disorders, or both and that 8% met criteria for OBC.

Other investigators have also noted the high comorbidity rates of depressive disorders and personality disorders (Gunderson & Elliot, 1985; Millon & Kotik, 1985; Widiger & Hyler, 1987). For example, Millon and Kotik discussed each third edition of the *Diagnostic and Statistical Manual of Mental Disorders* (*DSM-III*; American Psychiatric Association, 1980) personality disorder with respect to the likelihood that this personality style increased vulnerability to depressive episodes. They reported that those patients with DEP, HST, AVD, BDL, OBC, and passive–aggressive personality disorder (PAG) were particularly prone to depression. In addition, Millon and Kotik reported that acute anxiety states are likely in these patients as well.

If personality disorders are understood as variants of normal personality dimensions, then these comorbidity data suggest that personality traits may themselves be linked to the Axis I syndromes of depression and anxiety—a suggestion that has been made for a number of years (Eysenck, 1970). In particular, the relation between personality and depression has been the subject of a great deal of attention (e.g., Hirschfeld & Klerman, 1979; Hirschfeld, Klerman, Clayton, & Keller, 1983). There are four basic ways in which maladaptive personality traits can interact with depression: (a) Personality can be a predisposition to the development of depression; (b) personality can result from depression; (c) personality and depression can be independent yet affect the manifestation, course, and treatment of each other; or (d) personality and depression can both be manifestations of a common underlying etiology (Hirschfeld et al., 1983; Widiger & Trull, 1992).

Because of these different possibilities, early studies that measured personality in individuals who were clinically depressed or in remission from an episode of depression were difficult to interpret. Some studies suggest that personality traits are indeed a predisposing factor. Hirschfeld et al. (1989) reported a true prospective study of the first onset of major depression that showed elevated N scores in individuals who subsequently developed clinical depression. Zonderman, Herbst, Costa, and McCrae (1993) also showed that a brief measure of N was a significant risk factor for subsequent hospital diagnoses of depression and other psychiatric disorders in a national sample.

These findings are understandable in view of the fact that N (or negative affectivity, as Watson & Clark, 1984, called it) predisposes individuals to experience negative affect. At moderate levels, N is associated with unhappiness and lowered life satisfaction (Costa & McCrae, 1980). At very high levels, it can lead to clinically significant depression or anxiety.

From the perspective of the FFM, comorbidity of these Axis I syndromes and Axis II disorders might therefore be interpreted in terms of shared links to N. This view leads to the hypothesis that personality disorders that are associated with N should also show comorbidity with anxiety and depression. Millon and Kotik (1985) noted links between these Axis I syndromes and DEP, HST, AVD, PAG, BDL, and OBC. With the exception of HST, scales that measured all of these were positively and substantially correlated with the NEO-PI's measure of N (Costa & McCrae, 1985, 1990). By contrast, the scales for NAR, PAR, and ATS show little relation to N, and these personality disorders typically show little comorbidity with depression or anxiety.

DSM-III-R tends to treat personality traits and affects as different phenomena. Research on personality, however, shows that these two are intimately linked and that one of the five major factors of personality—N—is chiefly defined by the tendency to experience a variety of negative affects. Any diagnostic system that attempts to separate personality traits from affective predispositions is liable to be arbitrary and ambiguous. Akiskal (1981), for example, has been a strong proponent of conceptualizing BDL as a subtype of affective disorder—a view that would transfer that diagnosis to Axis I. Conversely, arguments have been made that some of the Axis I disorders—notably dysthymia and social phobia—should be construed as personality disorders and transferred to Axis II (Keller, 1989; Turner & Biedel, 1989).

There is a meaningful distinction between predisposing factors and the phenomena to which they predispose. After all, many individuals who are high in N never suffer from a diagnosable mental disorder. But comorbidity is inevitable when both are present, and much of this can be understood as the operation of underlying personality traits. It would be of substantial interest in research on the comorbidity of depression (or anxiety) with DEP, AVD, OBC, HST, and other personality disorders to assess whether the comorbidity still occurs when variance due to N is controlled or, conversely, whether personality disorder diagnoses have some incremental validity in predicting episodes of depression or anxiety over and above the predictions that can be made from measures of N. It may be that comorbidity with anxiety and depression for most of the personality disorders is simply due to their shared variance with N.

BORDERLINE PERSONALITY DISORDER

BDL is a popular, yet controversial, diagnosis. More literature has been published on BDL than on any other personality disorder. Blashfield and McElroy (1987) estimated that BDL accounted for 40% of all personality disorder articles in 1985, and in their estimation, ATS was a distant second, accounting for 25%. BDL is also by far the most commonly diagnosed personality disorder (Widiger & Trull, 1993). The variety of definitions (American Psychiatric Association, 1987; Gunderson & Zanarini, 1987; Kernberg, 1984) and uses of the term *borderline* has made integration of the research literature difficult, and the label continues to be used to describe a wide variety of patients.

Clinical Heterogeneity

A number of researchers have noted the clinical heterogeneity of patients within the BDL category (e.g., Clarkin, Widiger, Frances, Hurt, & Gilmore, 1983). With *DSM-III-R*'s polythetic format for diagnosing BDL, there are literally 93 ways to be diagnosed as having BDL (eight items taken five or more at a time). Because any five of the eight criteria can satisfy the BDL diagnostic decision rule, BDL patients are heterogeneous with respect to clinical symptomatology. For example, a patient can meet the criteria for BDL by exhibiting symptoms of inappropriate–intense anger, recurrent suicidal threats–behavior, identity disturbance, chronic feelings of emptiness–boredom, and frantic efforts to

avoid real–imagined abandonment, without showing the unstable–intense interpersonal relations, impulsivity, and affective instability that many clinicians would consider to be hallmarks of the BDL diagnosis. However, another BDL patient might manifest the latter three symptoms as well as inappropriate–intense anger and chronic feelings of emptiness–boredom but not suicidal threats–behavior, identity disturbance, or frantic attempts to avoid abandonment. A comparison of these two hypothetical BDL patients reveals markedly different clinical pictures and may suggest different treatment approaches. Clearly, the polythetic system for diagnosing BDL is a breeding ground for clinical heterogeneity.

Several investigators have reported distinct clusters of symptoms within the BDL criteria set. For example, Hurt et al. (1990) examined the interrelations among the eight BDL criteria in a sample of 465 *DSM-III* patients with BDL and 114 patients with other personality disorders. A single linkage-clustering algorithm was used to determine the homogeneity of the entire BDL criteria set. It was found that the BDL criteria varied in their correlation with each other. On the basis of similarity ratings, three subsets of criteria were identified: an identity cluster (chronic feelings of emptiness–boredom, identity disturbance, and intolerance of being alone), an affective cluster (intense–inappropriate anger, instability of affect, and unstable interpersonal relationships), and an impulse cluster (self-damaging acts and impulsive behavior). When BDL patients were sorted according to symptom cluster membership, further evidence for heterogeneity within the BDL category was found. All three clusters were represented by a substantial number of BDL cases, although most cases manifested symptoms from the affective and impulse criteria clusters. These results point to the substantial heterogeneity within the BDL criteria set and among patients diagnosed with BDL.

Nurnberg, Hurt, Feldman, and Shu (1988) also found heterogeneity within the BDL criteria set. In an investigation that compared borderline symptomatology of a narrowly defined BDL group with a nonpatient control group, various combinations of two, three, four, and five BDL symptoms all resulted in high sensitivity and high positive predictive

TABLE 4.1

Mean Minnesota Multiphasic Personality Inventory (MMPI) Scales *T* Scores of Patients Diagnosed With Borderline Personality Disorder

Study	N	L	F	K	1	2	3	4	5	6	7	8	9	0
													MMPI scale	
Evans et al. (1984)	45	48	76	50	67	80	71	84	57	75	77	85	68	64
Gustin et al. (1983)	29	44	85	46	78	89	70	84	68	78	89	98	70	68
Hurt et al. (1985)														
Inpatient	21	46	71	48	68	79	70	77	—	72	77	80	64	63
Outpatient	21	46	83	42	67	81	67	80	—	78	81	91	75	67
Kroll et al. (1981)	21	48	84	47	62	82	70	84	60	78	74	85	65	63
Loyd et al. (1983)	27	48	73	46	70	75	73	81	60	64	78	64	70	65
Patrick (1984)	27	44	77	46	64	78	65	80	55	74	68	87	61	60
Resnick et al. (1988)	37	45	66	47	56	73	63	76	54	70	71	71	61	61
Snyder et al. (1982)	26	46	86	45	75	86	68	85	68	79	88	98	72	65
Trull (1991)	61	48	73	49	64	80	70	80	50	73	72	79	64	63
Widiger et al. (1986)	44	47	78	46	70	81	67	82	60	80	80	91	68	65
Mdn		46	77	46	67	80	70	81	60	75	77	85	68	64

Note. Loyd et al. (1983) used the MMPI-168 short form of the Minnesota Multiphasic Personality Inventory (MMPI); *T* scores from this study were reported in Evans et al. (1984). The borderline group in Kroll et al. (1981) was defined by a score of >7 on the Diagnostic Interview for Borderlines (Kolb & Gunderson, 1980). Evans et al. (1984), Gustin et al. (1983), Loyd et al. (1983), Snyder et al. (1982), Trull (1991), and Widiger et al. (1986) all indicated that MMPI scores were K-corrected. *n* = sample size.

power rates for the BDL diagnosis. Nurnberg et al. concluded that the *DSM-III* BDL criteria set is not homogeneous and that these criteria do not appear to identify a distinct, categorical diagnostic entity. BDL patients exhibited a wide variety of symptom combinations, and no prototypical pattern was found.

MMPI Profiles of BDL Patients

Another example of the heterogeneity within the BDL category comes from the literature reporting MMPI clinical scale scores of *DSM-III* and *DSM-III-R* patients with BDL. We reviewed 10 published studies that reported mean MMPI *T* scores for adult BDL patients or presented figures from which mean *T* scores could be estimated. Most of these studies sampled BDL inpatients, and two of the studies (Hurt, Clarkin, Frances, Abrams, & Hunt, 1985; Resnick et al., 1988) sampled BDL outpatients. Four of the studies (Hurt et al., 1985; Kroll et al., 1981; Resnick et al., 1988; Widiger, Sanderson, & Warner, 1986) established the BDL diagnosis through a

semistructured interview; the remaining studies relied on clinical diagnoses.

Table 4.1 presents the mean MMPI *T* scores reported in each respective study. As indicated, at least one study reported mean MMPI *T* scores at or above 70 on all scales except on the Lie, Defensiveness, Superlative Self-Presentation, and Social Introversion–Extraversion scales. There is clearly no definitive BDL MMPI code type (Morey & Smith, 1988). BDL appears instead to be represented by a nonspecific elevation across most scales, and substantial variability occurs with respect to the MMPI code types obtained by BDL patients.

The lack of specificity for an MMPI code type (and the heterogeneity among individual subjects) can be understood when BDL is reinterpreted from the perspective of the FFM. Elevations on the MMPI Scales 1–4 and 6–9 indicate the presence of anxiety, dysphoria, hostility, feelings of inadequacy, difficulty concentrating, suspiciousness, feelings of alienation, rumination, and the possibility of brief psychotic episodes. This range of symptoms is very similar to the group of traits that covary to define N in normal individuals. For example, in studies of the NEO-PI, N is defined by scales that measure anxiety, hostility, depression, self-consciousness, impulsiveness, and vulnerability. With the possible exception of self-consciousness, a strong case can be made that a patient with BDL would score high on all of these scales. The findings of studies that used the MMPI in clinical samples thus parallel the findings from studies that used normal samples: Measures of BDL are correlated with measures of N (Costa & McCrae, 1990; Wiggins & Pincus, 1989).

We do not suggest that BDL is equivalent to and indistinguishable from extreme N. The diagnostic criteria in *DSM-III-R* include not only some N traits (e.g., constant anger) but also some specific symptoms or behaviors (e.g., suicide attempts) that do not characterize all high-N individuals. A better formulation would be that BDL reflects a set of behaviors and symptoms to which high-N individuals are particularly prone. Interpretation of BDL as a result of extreme N would explain the prevalence of this diagnosis. N is related to a wide variety of psychiatric diagnoses (Costa & McCrae, 1987; Zonderman et al., 1993), and the psychological distress it creates is probably the reason most patients seek psychological or psychiatric help. It is, therefore, not surprising that clinical populations show consistently elevated means on measures of N (e.g., Miller, 1991; Muten, 1991). Within this population of high-N individuals, a large proportion would likely meet the criteria for BDL.

N can be considered a cluster of covarying traits, but individuals differ in the extent to which these specific traits characterize them. Some are characterized primarily by hostility and depression; some by hostility and anxiety; some by depression, vulnerability, and impulsivity; and so forth. In extreme form, any of these patterns might lead to the symptoms of BDL, but they would also lead to differences that could explain in part the heterogeneity of BDL patients.

A high total score on N can be reached in many different ways, just as the diagnosis of BDL can be reached by different patterns of symptoms. Although this heterogeneity is an embarrassment in categorical models that attempt to define a qualitatively distinct entity, it is understandable in terms of factor models of personality for which factors are defined by covarying but distinct traits. As an alternative to the single diagnostic category of BDL, it would be considerably more informative to describe each individual patient on measures of several traits in the domain of N. By including multifaceted measures of N in studies of BDL patients, more detailed information could be obtained, and the comparability of different samples of BDL patients could be ascertained.

The covariation of facets of N is well established; by contrast, the criteria symptoms of BDL do not covary as neatly. This can be seen in factor analyses of personality disorder symptoms, which do not recover a single BDL factor (Clark, 1989), and in research by Hurt et al. (1990), showing that it is possible to identify BDL subtypes. One important question for research is the relation of BDL criteria elements to measures of N and its facets (cf. Clarkin, Hull, Cantor, & Sanderson, 1993). Correlation with N might be used as a basis for selecting a more coherent subset of BDL symptoms.

Comorbidity

It is an implicit assumption of the categorical model of psychiatric diagnoses that disorders refer to distinct conditions (e.g., Trull, Widiger, & Guthrie, 1990). BDL, from this perspective, is a distinct personality disorder that can be distinguished from HST, DEP, AVD, and other mental disorder diagnoses. This assumption was the impetus for revising the criteria for HST and NAR in *DSM-III-R*; an attempt was made to increase or improve the differentiation of these two disorders from BDL (Widiger, Frances, Spitzer, & Williams, 1988). Gunderson (1982, 1987) has explicitly argued that BDL is a discrete mental disorder that can be distinguished from other personality disorders, and he presented empirical data (Gunderson, 1982) to support the validity of this distinction.

In fact, however, BDL shows extensive comorbidity with other diagnoses. We have already reviewed evidence on the co-occurrence of BDL with Axis I affective and anxiety disorders. Swartz, Blazer, George, and Winfield (1990), using a new diagnostic algorithm derived from the Diagnostic Interview Schedule (Robins, Helzer, Croughan, & Ratcliff,

1981) to identify cases of BDL in a community sample, also reported frequent comorbid alcohol abuse–dependence and noted that 98% of BDL subjects met criteria for at least one additional psychiatric disorder in the past year. Viewing BDL as an expression of extreme N can explain these high rates of comorbidity because mood disorders, anxiety disorders, substance use disorders, and somatic disorders are themselves all associated with N.

With regard to other personality disorders, Widiger et al. (1991) examined the comorbidity rates of BDL and other personality disorders averaged across 13 studies that provided relevant data. They noted that at least one comorbid personality diagnosis occurred in 96% of all BDL patients. A factor analysis of averaged covariation showed that BDL, along with PAG, defined "a non-specific factor and/or a general factor of Neuroticism" (Widiger et al., 1991, p. 187).

If one assumes that personality disorders are pathological expressions of the five basic personality factors, then the comorbidity of disorders should be predictable. Disorders that are related to the same dimensions should covary, those that are oppositely related to the same factor (as OBC and ATS are oppositely related to C) should be mutually exclusive, and those that are related to different factors should co-occur in proportion to their mutual base rates.

The data reviewed and reanalyzed by Widiger et al. (1991) are roughly consistent with this premise. In addition to the general or N factor, a second factor contrasts SZD and AVD with HST and NAR; this factor can be interpreted as E. A third factor contrasts PAR, SZD, and NAR with DEP and has some resemblance to (reversed) A. A final factor is defined solely by OBC, with small negative loadings on ATS and BDL; this factor might be interpreted as C.

The disorders that show low levels of comorbidity with BDL ought themselves to be unrelated to N. In the Widiger et al. (1991) review, BDL showed the lowest covariation with SZD and OBC, which appear to be more closely related to low E and C, respectively, than to N (Wiggins & Pincus, 1989). However, it must be noted that the highest levels of comorbidity with BDL are with HST, AST, and PAG. Only one of these—PAG—is chiefly related to N in

studies of normal samples using personality disorder questionnaires (Costa & McCrae, 1990).

There are several possible explanations for this anomaly. Perhaps individuals who are diagnosed as having HST and ATS are, in fact, higher in N than it would appear from studies of instruments like the MMPI and MCMI—recall that Millon and Kotik (1985) found comorbidity of HST with depression and anxiety. Perhaps BDL contains other features besides N that it shares with these two disorders—the dramatic, emotional, or erratic features that led *DSM-III-R* to class them together in Cluster B. Perhaps this clustering itself led to bias in diagnosis: Individuals with BDL were presumed to be more likely to have HST or ATS. Only assessment of the five factors in individuals who are diagnosed as having personality disorders can resolve these questions.

Borderline Personality Organization

The view of BDL as extreme N is consistent with analytic formulations of borderline personality organization (BPO), a level of personality dysfunction that cuts across diagnostic categories (Kernberg, 1975, 1984). According to Kernberg, at a descriptive level patients with BPO exhibit a number of symptoms that are considered to be characteristic of N, including free-floating anxiety, "polysymptomatic neurosis," impulsivity, and proneness to addiction. Kernberg also proposed that those with BPO may exhibit any number of phobic, obsessive–compulsive, dissociative, hypochondriacal, or conversion symptoms. Most important, Kernberg considered the borderline construct as defining a level of personality organization that cuts across other domains or styles of personality functioning. Kernberg did not consider BDL a distinct personality disorder but rather a level of personality functioning that distinguishes among people with, for example, a histrionic, dependent, or compulsive personality style. Thus, Kernberg did not attempt to determine whether a patient who is diagnosed as being BDL is instead actually histrionic (a differential diagnosis that would be important to Gunderson, 1987) but whether a patient who is diagnosed as being HST is functioning at a borderline level of personality organization.

This conception is structurally and substantively consistent with the interpretation of BDL as a manifestation of extreme N. Structurally, the FFM recognizes that individuals must be characterized on all five dimensions and differ only in their level on each of these. For example, an HST patient who is functioning at a borderline level might correspond to an extravert with a high level of N. Substantively, the nonspecific manifestations of ego weakness that Kernberg (1984) listed essentially describe the various facets of N. As a descriptive dimension, the origin and dynamics of N are unspecified; Kernberg provided a psychoanalytically oriented theory of BPO that is based on internal structural factors (e.g., ego weakness, variability in reality testing, use of primitive defenses, quality of object relations). At the phenomenological level, however, BPO shares much with the FFM conceptualization of N.

NARCISSISTIC PERSONALITY DISORDER

The widespread interest in BDL may be attributed to the frequency with which BDL patients are encountered in clinical practice. Interest in NAR must have another basis because NAR is one of the less frequently diagnosed of the personality disorders (Cooper, 1987). Although there are relatively few cases of NAR, there are many theories and descriptions. The narcissistic personality has been of interest to clinicians for almost a century (Millon, 1981), and narcissism has been included in the taxonomies of personality theorists such as Murray (1938) and Leary (1957). Freud's description of this construct has influenced many contemporary psychoanalytic theorists (e.g., Kernberg, Mahler, Kohut).

Interpreting the Narcissistic Personality Inventory

Because of continued clinical interest in narcissism, a number of scales have been developed to assess this construct, including the Narcissistic Personality Inventory (NPI; Raskin & Hall, 1979), the Narcissistic Personality Disorder Scale (Ashby, Lee, & Duke, 1979), and scales from the MMPI and MCMI. Of these, the NPI has received the most empirical attention. The NPI was developed through a rational–empirical strategy of test construction in which items that assessed the *DSM-II* criteria for NAR were generated and subjected to a series of internal con-

sistency and item-total correlational analyses (Raskin & Hall, 1979).

A conceptual analysis of the content of the NPI suggests that it measures chiefly high E and low A. Raskin and Terry (1988) reported a factor analysis of NPI items, which yielded seven factors. The Authority and Exhibition factors include such items as "I am assertive" and "I would do almost anything on a dare," which appear to tap the dominance and excitement-seeking facets of E; the Superiority, Exploitation, and Entitlement factors appear to reflect the opposites of such defining traits of A as modesty, straightforwardness, and compliance.

These interpretations are supported by studies of the correlates of the NPI. Raskin and Terry (1988) reported correlations between NPI scores and both observational and self-report personality scores. Correlations were found with the observational ratings of sensation seeking, dominance, extraversion, energy level, exhibitionism, assertiveness, leadership, extent of participation in a group, and self-confidence—all traits associated with E—and with criticality, aggressiveness, autocracy, and self-centeredness versus submissiveness, patience, modesty, gentleness, peaceableness, and sensitivity—all contrasting definers of A. Positive correlations were found with the California Personality Inventory (CPI; Gough, 1956) scales for dominance, sociability, social presence, and capacity for status, which are related to E; and negative correlations were found with CPI scales for femininity, self-control, and tolerance, which are related to A (McCrae, Costa, & Piedmont, 1993).

Raskin and Novacek (1989) subsequently reported a number of significant correlations between the NPI and MMPI scales. The NPI correlated positively with the MMPI Scale 9 (Mania) and negatively with MMPI Scales 2 (Depression), 7 (Psychasthenia), and 0 (Social Intraversion–Extraversion) as well as the scales for repression, anxiety, and ego control. These correlates suggest that the NPI scores are negatively related to N; that is, NAR individuals are well adjusted. This association is not as easily seen from an examination of NPI items or factors, which do not directly tap chronic negative affect. However, it is well known that N is inversely related to self-esteem (e.g.,

Costa, McCrae, & Dye, 1991); high NPI scorers certainly seem to have high self-esteem.

Problems in Conceptualization and Measurement of NAR

The associations between narcissism and high E, low A, and low N are not unique to the NPI. Both the MMPI NAR scale and the MCMI NAR scale show the same pattern when correlated with NEO-PI factors (Costa & McCrae, 1990). The negative association of NAR with N could account for its relative rarity in clinical samples, just as the positive association of BDL with N accounts for its high prevalence. Thus, there is a good deal of empirical evidence to support the conceptualization of NAR as a combination of high E, low A, and low N.

We might, therefore, suggest that there is no need for a separate narcissistic construct or for separate scales to measure narcissism: Combinations of scores on any measure of the FFM could be used more parsimoniously. Proponents of the construct would probably object to this proposal. Raskin and Shaw (1988), for example, showed that associations between NPI scores and the use of first person pronouns remained significant even after controlling for the Eysenck Personality Questionnaire (Eysenck & Eysenck, 1975) E, P, and N scales and a measure of locus of control. Whether the association (between NPI scores and use of first person pronouns) would have remained after controlling for measures of A remains to be tested. The basic issue—one that recurs for all the personality disorders—is whether measures of NAR have incremental validity over measures of the five factors themselves.

It is also possible to argue that the elements of the NAR—high E, low A, and low N—in combination represent a uniquely important configuration of traits. For example, there may be a specific etiology associated with this constellation of traits, or there may be something about the combination that is pathological, even though the elements themselves are not. In general, it would be of interest to determine whether some constellations of the five-factor dimensions are, in fact, more common than others or are more clearly associated with personal, social, or occupational dysfunction (Widiger & Trull, 1992).

Psychometrically, however, summary scores on multidimensional measures are ambiguous (Briggs & Cheek, 1986). Well-adjusted and highly extraverted individuals might score high on the NPI even if they were somewhat agreeable—a combination we would hardly characterize as narcissistic. Raskin and Terry (1988) also noted this problem and suggested analyses at the level of the more homogeneous NPI factors. The same criticism, of course, applies to the MMPI and MCMI NAR scales. The appropriate way to assess a true configuration of traits is by measuring each component separately and requiring that all be present to meet diagnostic criteria.

Interpreting narcissism as high E, low A, and low N succinctly summarizes the correlates of narcissistic scales and makes conceptual analysis easier. From this formulation, it is easy to see that most narcissistic scales do not square well with *DSM-III-R* criteria for NAR. The diagnostic criteria certainly suggest low A: NAR patients are envious, lack empathy, have a sense of entitlement, and are interpersonally exploitative. But nothing in the *DSM-III-R* definition suggests high E: Sociability, leadership, and excitement seeking are not mentioned at all. Worse yet, *DSM-III-R* suggests that individuals with NAR should score high, not low, on N. They are hypersensitive to criticism, painfully self-conscious, and frequently depressed (Trull, 1992). Concordance between narcissistic scales and NAR diagnoses might well be low.

Of course, it is possible that the *DSM-III-R* definition of NAR is incorrect and should be amended to emphasize high E and low N as well as low A. But such a redefinition does not specify why narcissism should be considered a disorder. Well-adjusted, sociable, albeit somewhat egotistical individuals do not have obvious pathology. Personal vanity may be a vice, but it is also an accepted part of contemporary culture. Those who wish to operationalize narcissism by scales that correlate with extraversion and adjustment must provide a rationale for claiming that high scorers—even extremely high scorers—are suffering from a personality disorder. Analyses of narcissistic scales in terms of the FFM cannot resolve this issue, but they may quickly force clinicians and researchers to face it.

One final issue in the assessment of narcissism

should be noted. Psychoanalytically oriented theorists—and to some extent *DSM-III-R*—emphasize the illusory nature of the narcissist's self-esteem and the disparity between overt grandiosity and covert fragility and insecurity (Cooper, 1987). Self-reports on personality instruments always reflect the self-concept; if there are truly distortions in the self-concept, then the validity of self-reports is questionable. One of the chief merits of the FFM is the fact that its factors can be validly assessed from observer ratings and from self-reports. Research on individuals with NAR should certainly include ratings made by knowledgeable informants and self-reports; indeed, the discrepancies between these two may prove to be the most useful indicators of NAR.

CONCLUSION

We have attempted to show that a consideration of the *DSM-III-R* Axis II disorders from the perspective of the FFM can be useful in understanding previous research on personality disorders. The FFM appears to provide a comprehensive model of normal personality traits; to the extent that personality disorders involve maladaptive or extreme variants of these personality traits, the model should be relevant. We believe that reconceptualizing the personality disorders in these terms helps to resolve many of the controversies in personality disorder research.

The FFM helps to explain the high comorbidity rates of certain personality disorders and mood disorders. Consideration of the FFM reveals why the controversy over BDL as a personality disorder versus a subaffective disorder has developed and suggests that the *DSM-III-R*'s distinction between mood disorder and personality disorder may be artificial.

Heterogeneity within the BDL category can be explained by recognizing that the BDL diagnosis applies to those who are extreme on the traits that define the dimension of N. These traits are ubiquitous within clinical populations, which explains why BDL is so prevalent and diagnostically nonspecific. Conceptualizing BDL as extreme N is also consistent with Kernberg's (1984) formulation of BPO.

From the perspective of the FFM, scales that measure narcissism (especially the NPI) can be seen as measures of high E, low A, and low N. This formulation points out difficulties with multidimensional scales, highlights differences between scales that measure narcissism and diagnostic criteria for NAR, and directs attention to the question of why certain combinations of traits should be considered pathological.

We encourage personality disorder researchers to include measures of the FFM in their studies. The chosen instruments would ideally include measures of specific traits, as well as the global dimensions, to specify in detail the personality characteristics of individuals with Axis II diagnoses. In many cases, it would be wise to supplement self-reports with ratings from knowledgeable informants. The routine inclusion of such measures in studies of personality disorders would help refine the definition of particular disorders, assess the incremental validity of personality disorder scales, examine the role of N and other personality factors in accounting for comorbidity among mental disorders, and develop hypotheses about tailoring treatment to the personality profile of the individual patient.

References

Akiskal, H. S. (1981). Subaffective disorders: Dysthymic, cyclothymic, and bipolar 11 disorders in the "borderline" realm. *Psychiatric Clinics of North America, 4,* 25–46.

American Psychiatric Association. (1980). *Diagnostic and statistical manual of mental disorders* (3rd ed.). Washington, DC: Author.

American Psychiatric Association. (1987). *Diagnostic and statistical manual of mental disorders* (3rd ed., rev.). Washington, DC: Author.

Ashby, H. V., Lee, R. R., & Duke, E. H. (1979, August). *A narcissistic personality disorder MMPI scale.* Paper presented at the 87th Annual Convention of the American Psychological Association, New York.

Blashfield, R., & McElroy, R. (1987). The 1985 journal literature on personality disorders. *Comprehensive Psychiatry, 28,* 536–546.

Briggs, S. R., & Cheek, J. M. (1986). The role of factor analysis in the development and evaluation of personality scales. *Journal of Personality, 54,* 106–148.

Cattell, R. B., Eber, H. W., & Tatsuoka, M. M. (1970). *The handbook for the Sixteen Personality Factor Questionnaire.* Champaign, IL: Institute for Personality and Ability Testing.

Clark, L. A. (1989, August). The basic traits of personality disorder: Primary and higher order dimensions. In R. R. McCrae (Chair), *Personality disorders from the perspective of the five-factor model.* Symposium conducted at the 97th Annual Convention of the American Psychological Association, New Orleans, LA.

Clarkin, J. F., Hull, J. W., Cantor, J., & Sanderson, C. (1993). Borderline personality disorder and personality traits: A comparison of SCID-II BPD and NEO-PI. *Psychological Assessment, 5,* 472–476.

Clarkin, J. F., Widiger, T. A., Frances, A., Hurt, S., & Gilmore, M. (1983). Prototypic typology and the borderline personality disorder. *Journal of Abnormal Psychology, 92,* 263–275.

Cooper, A. M. (1987). Histrionic, narcissistic, and compulsive personality disorders. In G. L. Tischler (Ed.), *Diagnosis and classification in psychiatry: A critical appraisal of DSM-III* (pp. 290–299). New York: Cambridge University Press.

Costa, P. T., Jr., & McCrae, R. R. (1980). Influence of extraversion and neuroticism on subjective well-being: Happy and unhappy people. *Journal of Personality and Social Psychology, 38,* 668–678.

Costa, P. T., Jr., & McCrae, R. R. (1985). *The NEO Personality Inventory manual.* Odessa, FL: Psychological Assessment Resources.

Costa, P. T., Jr., & McCrae, R. R. (1987). Neuroticism, somatic complaints, and disease: Is the bark worse than the bite? *Journal of Personality, 55,* 299–316.

Costa, P. T., Jr., & McCrae, R. R. (1990). Personality disorders and the five-factor model of personality. *Journal of Personality Disorders, 4,* 362–371.

Costa, P. T., Jr., McCrae, R. R., & Dye, D. A. (1991). Facet scales for Agreeableness and Conscientiousness: A revision of the NEO Personality Inventory. *Personality and Individual Differences, 12,* 887–898.

Docherty, J. P., Fiester, S. J., & Shea, T. (1986). Syndrome diagnosis and personality disorder. In A. Frances & R. Hales (Eds.), *Psychiatry update: The American Psychiatric Association annual review* (Vol. 5, pp. 315–355). Washington, DC: American Psychiatric Press.

Evans, R., Ruff, R., Braff, D., & Ainsworth, T. (1984). MMPI characteristics of borderline personality inpatients. *Journal of Nervous and Mental Disease, 172,* 742–748.

Eysenck, H. J. (1970). A dimensional system of psychodiagnosis. In A. R. Mahrer (Ed.), *New approaches to personality classification* (pp. 169–208). New York: Columbia University Press.

Eysenck, H. J., & Eysenck, S. B. G. (1964). *Manual of the Eysenck Personality Inventory.* London, UK: University Press.

Eysenck, H. J., & Eysenck, S. B. G. (1975). *Eysenck Personality Questionnaire manual.* San Diego, CA: EdITS.

Goldberg, L. R. (1990). An alternative "description of personality": The Big-Five factor structure. *Journal of Personality and Social Psychology, 59,* 1216–1229.

Gough, H. G. (1956). *California Psychological Inventory.* Palo Alto, CA: Consulting Psychologists Press.

Guilford, J. S., Zimmerman, W. S., & Guilford, J. P. (1976). *The Guilford–Zimmerman Temperament Survey handbook: Twenty-five years of research and application.* San Diego, CA: EdITS.

Gunderson, J. G. (1982). Empirical studies of the borderline diagnosis. In L. Grinspoon (Ed.), *Psychiatry 1982 annual review* (pp. 415–437). Washington, DC: American Psychiatric Press.

Gunderson, J. G. (1987, May). *Competing models of personality disorders.* Paper presented at the annual meeting of the American Psychiatric Association, Chicago, IL.

Gunderson, J. G., & Elliot, G. R. (1985). The interface between borderline personality disorder and affective disorder. *American Journal of Psychiatry, 142,* 277–288.

Gunderson, J. G., & Zanarini, M. C. (1987). Current overview of the borderline diagnosis. *Journal of Clinical Psychiatry, 48*(Suppl. 8), 5–11.

Gustin, Q., Goodpaster, W., Sajadi, C., Pitts, W., LaBasse, D., & Snyder, S. (1983). MMPI characteristics of the *DSM-III* borderline personality disorder. *Journal of Personality Assessment, 47,* 50–59.

Hathaway, S. R., & McKinley, J. C. (1967). *Minnesota Multiphasic Personality Inventory manual.* New York: Psychological Corporation.

Hirschfeld, R. M., & Klerman, G. (1979). Personality attributes and affective disorders. *American Journal of Psychiatry, 136,* 67–70.

Hirschfeld, R. M., Klerman, G., Clayton, P. J., & Keller, M. B. (1983). Personality and depression: Empirical findings. *Archives of General Psychiatry, 40,* 993–998.

Hirschfeld, R. M., Klerman, G., Lavoni, P., Keller, M. B., Griffith, P., & Coryell, W. (1989). Premorbid personality assessments of first onset of major depression. *Archives of General Psychiatry, 46,* 345–350.

Hurt, S., Clarkin, J., Frances, A., Abrams, R., &

Hunt, H. (1985). Discriminant validity of the MMPI for borderline personality disorder. *Journal of Personality Assessment, 49,* 56–61.

Hurt, S., Clarkin, J., Widiger, T., Fyer, M., Sullivan, T., Stone, M., & Frances, A. (1990). Evaluation of *DSM-III* decision rules for case detection using joint conditional probability structures. *Journal of Personality Disorders, 4,* 121–130.

Hyler, S. E., Rieder, R. O., Williams, J. B. W., Spitzer, R. L., Hendler, J., & Lyons, M. (1989). A comparison of self-report and clinical diagnosis of *DSM-III* personality disorders in 552 patients. *Comprehensive Psychiatry, 30,* 170–178.

Keller, M. (1989). Current concepts in affective disorders. *Journal of Clinical Psychiatry, 50,* 157–162.

Kernberg, O. (1975). *Borderline conditions and pathological narcissism.* Northvale, NJ: Aronson.

Kernberg, O. (1984). *Severe personality disorders.* New Haven, CT: Yale University Press.

Kolb, J. E., & Gunderson, J. G. (1980). Diagnosing borderlines with a semi-structured interview. *Archives of General Psychiatry, 37,* 37–41.

Kroll, J., Sines, L., Martin, K., Lari, L., Pyle, R., & Zander, J. (1981). Borderline personality disorder: Construct validity of the concept. *Archives of General Psychiatry, 38,* 1021–1026.

Leary, T. (1957). *Interpersonal diagnosis of personality.* New York: Ronald Press.

Loyd, C., Overall, J., & Click, M. (1983). Screening for borderline personality disorders with the MMPI-168. *Journal of Clinical Psychology, 39,* 722–726.

Lyons, M. J., Merla, M. E., Ozer, D. J., & Hyler, S. E. (1990, August). *Relationship of the "Big-Five" factors to DSM-III personality disorders.* Paper presented at the 98th Annual Convention of the American Psychological Association, Boston, MA.

McCrae, R. R., Costa, P. T., Jr., & Piedmont, R. L. (1993). Folk concepts, natural language, and psychological constructs: The California Psychological Inventory and the five-factor model. *Journal of Personality, 61,* 1–26.

Miller, T. (1991). The psychotherapeutic utility of the five-factor model of personality. *Journal of Personality Assessment, 57,* 415–433.

Millon, T. (1981). *Disorders of personality: DSM-III, Axis II.* New York: Wiley.

Millon, T. (1983). *Millon Clinical Multiaxial Inventory manual* (3rd ed.). Minneapolis, MN: Interpretive Scoring Systems.

Millon, T., & Kotik, D. (1985). The relationship of depression to disorders of personality. In E. Beckham & W. Leber (Eds.), *Handbook of depression* (pp. 700–744). Homewood, IL: Dorsey Press.

Morey, L. C., & Smith, M. (1988). Personality disorders. In R. Greene (Ed.), *The MMPI: Use with specific populations* (pp. 110–158). Philadelphia: Grune & Stratton.

Morey, L. C., Waugh, M. H., & Blashfield, R. K. (1985). MMPI scales for *DSM-III* personality disorders: Their derivation and correlates. *Journal of Personality Assessment, 49,* 245–251.

Murray, H. A. (1938). *Explorations in personality.* New York: Oxford University Press.

Muten, E. (1991). Self-reports, spouse ratings, and psychophysiological assessment in a behavioral medicine program: An application of the five-factor model. *Journal of Personality Assessment, 57,* 449–464.

Nurnberg, H. G., Hurt, S. W., Feldman, A., & Shu, R. (1988). Evaluation of diagnostic criteria for borderline personality disorder. *American Journal of Psychiatry, 145,* 1280–1284.

Patrick, J. (1984). Characteristics of *DSM-III* borderline MMPI profiles. *Journal of Clinical Psychology, 40,* 655–658.

Pfohl, B., Stangl, D., & Zimmerman, M. (1984). The implications of *DSM-III* personality disorders for patients with major depression. *Journal of Affective Disorders, 7,* 309–318.

Raskin, R., & Hall, C. S. (1979). A narcissistic personality inventory. *Psychological Reports, 45,* 590.

Raskin, R., & Novacek, J. (1989). An MMPI description of the narcissistic personality. *Journal of Personality Assessment, 53,* 66–80.

Raskin, R., & Shaw, R. (1988). Narcissism and the use of personal pronouns. *Journal of Personality, 56,* 393–404.

Raskin, R., & Terry, H. (1988). A principal-components analysis of the Narcissistic Personality Inventory and further evidence of its construct validity. *Journal of Personality and Social Psychology, 54,* 890–902.

Resnick, R. J., Goldberg, S., Schulz, S. C., Schulz, P. M., Hamer, R., & Friedel, R. (1988). Borderline personality disorder: Replication of MMPI profiles. *Journal of Clinical Psychology, 44,* 354–360.

Robins, L. N., Helzer, J. E., Croughan, J., & Ratcliff, K. S. (1981). National Institute of Mental Health Diagnostic Interview Schedule: Its history, characteristics, and validity. *Archives of General Psychiatry, 38,* 381–389.

Snyder, S., Pitts, W., Goodpaster, W., Sajadi, C., & Gustin, Q. (1982). MMPI profile of *DSM-III* borderline personality disorder. *American Journal of Psychiatry, 139,* 1046–1048.

Swartz, M., Blazer, D., George, L., & Winfield, L. (1990). Estimating the prevalence of borderline personality disorder in the community. *Journal of Personality Disorders, 4,* 257–272.

Trull, T. J. (1991). Discriminant validity of the MMPI–Borderline Personality Disorder Scale. *Psychological Assessment: A Journal of Consulting and Clinical Psychology, 3,* 232–238.

Trull, T. J. (1992). *DSM-III-R* personality disorders and the five-factor model of personality: An empirical comparison. *Journal of Abnormal Psychology, 101,* 553–560.

Trull, T. J., Widiger, T. A., & Guthrie, P. (1990). The categorical versus dimensional status of borderline personality disorder. *Journal of Abnormal Psychology, 99,* 40–48.

Turner, S., & Biedel, D. (1989). Social phobia: Clinical syndrome, diagnosis, and comorbidity. *Clinical Psychology Review, 9,* 3–18.

Watson, D., & Clark, L. A. (1984). Negative affectivity: The disposition to experience aversive emotional states. *Psychological Bulletin, 96,* 465–490.

Widiger, T. A., & Frances, A. J. (1987). Interviews and inventories for the measurement of personality disorders. *Clinical Psychology Review, 7,* 49–75.

Widiger, T. A., Frances, A. J., Harris, M., Jacobsberg, L., Fyer, M., & Manning, D. (1991). Comorbidity among Axis II disorders. In J. Oldham (Ed.), *Axis II: New perspectives on validity* (pp. 165–194). Washington, DC: American Psychiatric Press.

Widiger, T. A., Frances, A. J., Spitzer, R., & Williams, J. (1988). The *DSM-III-R* personality disorders: An overview. *American Journal of Psychiatry, 145,* 786–795.

Widiger, T. A., & Hyler, S. (1987). Axis I/Axis II interactions. In J. Cavenar, R. Michels, & A. Cooper (Eds.), *Psychiatry* (pp. 1–10). Philadelphia: Lippincott.

Widiger, T. A., Sanderson, C., & Warner, L. (1986). The MMPI, prototypal typology, and borderline personality disorder. *Journal of Personality Assessment, 50,* 540–553.

Widiger, T. A., & Trull, T. J. (1992). Personality and psychopathology: An application of the five-factor model. *Journal of Personality, 60,* 363–394.

Widiger, T. A., & Trull, T. J. (1993). Borderline and narcissistic personality disorders. In H. Adams & P. Sutker (Eds.), *Comprehensive handbook of psychopathology* (2nd ed., pp. 371–394). New York: Plenum Press.

Wiggins, J. W., & Pincus, A. (1989). Conceptions of personality disorders and dimensions of personality. *Psychological Assessment: A Journal of Consulting and Clinical Psychology, 1,* 305–316.

Zonderman, A. B., Herbst, J. H., Costa, P. T., Jr., & McCrae, R. R. (1993). Depressive symptoms as a nonspecific, graded risk for psychiatric diagnoses. *Journal of Abnormal Psychology, 102,* 544–552.

FIVE-FACTOR MODEL PERSONALITY DISORDER RESEARCH

Thomas A. Widiger and Paul T. Costa, Jr.

Trull and McCrae include within their chapter (4) on personality disorder (PD) research an overview of the limited number of published and unpublished studies that were available to them at the time of the first edition of this text and that were concerned explicitly with the relationship between PD symptomatology and the five-factor model (FFM). One of the major intentions of their chapter was to illustrate the potential value and significance of including measures of the FFM within PD research. Since the original publication of their call for such research, a substantial number of studies on the relationship of the FFM to PD symptomatology have been published. The purpose of this chapter is to provide a reasonably comprehensive summary of this new extensive research.

One difficulty immediately faced by any effort to provide a comprehensive summary of FFM research is to define an appropriate limit to its coverage; otherwise, the review can become overwhelming in its scope. One arbitrary limitation that we used was to require that the authors of the study discuss explicitly the relationship of the FFM to the PD symptomatology. Therefore, excluded were studies that administered a measure of the FFM and PD symptomatology but failed to include any analyses or discussion of the relationship of the FFM and the PD symptomatology (e.g., Wise, Mann, & Randell, 1995, administered both the NEO Five-Factor Inventory [NEO-FFI], Costa & McCrae, 1992a, and a measure of alexythymia but did not provide any analyses of the relationship between them). Not included as well were the many studies in which re-

searchers were concerned with the relationship of the FFM to other (Axis I) mental disorders (e.g., Bagby, Bindseil, et al., 1997; Bagby, Kennedy, Dickens, Minifie, & Schuller, 1997; Bagby, Young, et al., 1996; Duberstein, Seidlitz, Lyness, & Conwell, 1999; Fagan et al., 1991; Quirk & McCormick, 1998; Trull & Sher, 1994), although some of the Axis I measures used in this research could be interpreted as measures of PD symptomatology (e.g., the assessment of delinquency by Heaven, 1996).

FIRST WAVE OF FIVE FACTOR MODEL PERSONALITY DISORDER RESEARCH

An equally difficult decision was demarcating the domains of PD symptomatology to include or to exclude. Costa, McCrae, and their colleagues have conducted a substantial number of studies indicating how the FFM can account for constructs contained within alternative models of personality, including (but not limited to) the constructs of the interpersonal circumplex (McCrae & Costa, 1989a), Henry Murray's 20 need dispositions (Costa & McCrae, 1988), the California Psychological Inventory (McCrae, Costa, & Piedmont, 1993), the Myers–Briggs Type Indicator (McCrae & Costa, 1989a), the Minnesota Multiphasic Personality Inventory (MMPI; Costa, Zonderman, McCrae, & Williams, 1985), and many others.

This research is traditionally classified as studies of normal personality functioning. However, the results of much of this research are relevant to the question of the extent to which the FFM accounts for PD symptomatology because most of the instruments and scales they have investigated over the years have been and continue to be used within clinical populations to assess maladaptive personality traits. Each of the models of personality assessed by these scales includes clinically significant maladaptive personality traits, such as the irritability and verbal hostility from the Buss–Durkee Hostility Inventory (Buss & Durkee, 1957; Costa & McCrae, 1992b), aggression from the Personality Research Form (Costa & McCrae, 1988; Jackson, 1984), aloof–introverted traits from the interpersonal circumplex (McCrae & Costa, 1989b; Wiggins, 1982), and an extrapunitive disposition from the California Q-Sort (CQS; Block, 1961; McCrae, Costa, & Busch, 1986). A brief description of one of these earlier studies is provided here to illustrate the relevance of this research to the relationship of the FFM to PD symptomatology. A more complete summary of this extensive research is provided by Costa and McCrae (1992a, 1995a), Digman (1990), John and Srivastava (1999), McCrae and Costa (1990, 1999), Piedmont (1998), and others.

McCrae et al. (1986) demonstrated in the 1980s how the 100 items within the CQS can be readily understood from the perspective of the FFM. The CQS items were developed by successive panels of psychodynamically oriented clinical psychologists seeking a common language for the description of psychological functioning. McCrae et al. administered the CQS and the NEO Personality Inventory (NEO-PI; Costa & McCrae, 1985) to 110–403 of the participants in the Baltimore Longitudinal Study of Aging (the numbers varied depending on whether the NEO-PI data were self, peer, or spouse ratings). A factor analysis of the complete set of items (N = 403) yielded five factors that corresponded closely to the five domains of the FFM. For example, the Neuroticism (N) factor contrasted such CQS items as "thin skinned," "irritable," "extrapunitive," "self-defeating," and "brittle ego defenses" with "socially poised," "satisfied with self," and "calm, relaxed"; Extraversion contrasted such items as "talkative," "behaves assertively," "initiates humor," and "self-dramatizing" with "submissive, "avoids close relationships," and "emotionally bland"; Openness to Experience contrasted "values intellectual matters,"

"rebellious nonconforming," "unusual thought processes," "introspective," and "engages in fantasy, daydreams" with "moralistic," "uncomfortable with complexities," and "favors conservative values"; Agreeableness (A) contrasted "sympathetic, considerate," "behaves in giving way," and "warm, compassionate" with "basically distrustful," "expresses hostility directly," and "critical, skeptical"; and Conscientiousness contrasted "dependable, responsible," "productive," and "has high aspiration level" with "enjoys sensuous experiences," "self-indulgent," and "unable to delay gratification."

The CQS FFM scores were correlated by McCrae et al. (1986) with the self-report, peer-report, and spouse-report NEO-PI ratings, yielding excellent convergent and discriminant validity. For example, self-report NEO-PI N correlated .73 with CQS neuroticism ($p < .001$) and correlated no higher than .19 with any other scale (N = 233); peer-report NEO-PI N correlated .38 with CQS neuroticism ($p < .001$) and correlated no higher than .14 with any other scale (N = 122); and spouse-report NEO-PI N correlated .48 with CQS neuroticism ($p < .001$) and no higher than $-.16$ with any other scale (N = 110). Comparable results were obtained for each FFM scale. It has been suggested that "the analysis of natural language . . . may be deficient because laypersons do not use concepts derived from psychodynamic perspectives on personality traits" (McCrae et al., 1986, p. 442). However, the results of this study clearly demonstrate a close correspondence of a sophisticated psychodynamic nomenclature with the FFM. The CQS "represents a distillation of clinical insights, and the fact that very similar factors can be found in it provides striking support for the five-factor model" (p. 442).

SECOND WAVE OF FIVE-FACTOR MODEL PERSONALITY DISORDER RESEARCH

The series of studies by Costa and McCrae provide a substantial empirical foundation for a second wave of FFM studies that focus more explicitly and specifically on the application of the FFM to PD symptomatology (Trull & McCrae, 1994; Widiger & Costa, 1994). Table 5.1 provides a list of 56 studies in which researchers were concerned with or have addressed explicitly the description, classification, or understanding of PD symptomatology from the perspective of the FFM (including those studies that were published in the first edition of this text or that chapter authors include within this second edition).

It is evident from Table 5.1 that the research concerning the relevance of the FFM to an understanding of PD symptomatology has been extensive (even if one excludes the few studies cited in Table 5.1 that involve overlapping data sets). FFM PD research has at times been characterized as being confined largely to studies of the naive or ill-informed impressions of college freshman (Westen, 1995). Some of the studies have indeed been confined to college students. Nonetheless, research with college students is not inappropriate or irrelevant to the study of PD symptomatology (Lenzenweger, 1999; Lenzenweger, Loranger, Korfine, & Neff, 1997; Trull, 1995; Trull, Useda, Conforti, & Doan, 1997), and some of the most significant and informative FFM PD research has been conducted within this population (e.g., Shopshire & Craik, 1994; Wiggins & Pincus, 1989; Zuroff, 1994). Nevertheless, it is also evident from Table 5.1 that most of the FFM PD research has in fact involved other populations. Only a third of the 56 studies (*n* = 17) were confined to college students; 9 studies were confined to people sampled from the broader community (some of which involved people at high risk for psychopathology; e.g., John, Caspi, Robins, Moffitt, & Stouthamer-Loeber, 1994; Miller, Lynam, Widiger, & Leukefeld, 2001); and 30 of the 56 studies (54%) sampled from clinical populations, including (but not limited to) patients enrolled in a group therapy for PDs (Soldz, Budman, Demby, & Merry, 1993; Wilberg, Urnes, Friis, Pedersen, & Karterud, 1999), borderline personality disorder (BDL) inpatients at Cornell University Medical Center (Clarkin, Hull, Cantor, & Sanderson, 1993), substance abuse and dependence patients (Ball, Tennen, Poling, Kranzler, & Rounsaville, 1997; Brooner, Herbst, Schmidt, Bigelow, & Costa, 1993), paraphilic forensic patients (Lehne, 1994), chronically depressed patients (Lyoo, Gunderson, & Phillips, 1998), depressed outpatients (Bagby, Gilchrist, Rector, Joffe, & Levitt, in press), inmates (Hart & Hare, 1994), veterans with post-

traumatic stress disorder (PTSD; Hyer et al., 1994), adolescent outpatients (Huey & Weisz, 1997), general outpatients (Trull, 1992), and general inpatients (Pukrop, Herpertz, Sass, & Steinmeyer, 1998).

Most importantly, the vast majority of the authors of these studies have concluded that the PD symptomatology were well accounted for by the FFM. Each of these studies are summarized briefly in turn, with the presentation organized loosely with respect to whether the study involved sets of PD constructs, facets of the FFM, specific PD constructs, other dimensional models, or negative research findings.

SETS OF PERSONALITY DISORDER CONSTRUCTS

Wiggins and Pincus (1989) provided the first published study concerned explicitly with the empirical relationship of the FFM to PD symptomatology. Wiggins and Pincus administered to 581 Canadian college students two measures of PD symptomatology, the Minnesota Multiphasic Personality Inventory (MMPI) PD scales (Morey, Waugh, & Blashfield, 1985) and the Personality Adjective Check List (PACL; Strack, 1987), and two measures of the FFM, the NEO-PI and the Revised Interpersonal Adjective Scales—Big Five version (IAS-R-B5; Trapnell & Wiggins, 1990). They concluded that "conceptions of personality disorders were strongly and clearly related to dimensions of normal personality traits" (Wiggins & Pincus, 1989, p. 305), including (but not limited to) a close relationship of schizotypal symptomatology with Openness; dependent with A; antisocial, paranoid, and narcissistic with antagonism; borderline with N; histrionic and narcissistic with Extraversion; schizoid with introversion, and compulsive with Conscientiousness. They also analyzed their results with respect to the interpersonal circumplex scales embedded within the IAS-R-B5. Although the interpersonal circumplex was able to provide a meaningful and informative understanding of a subset of the PDs, Wiggins and Pincus (1989) reached the conclusion that "the full 5-factor model was required to capture and clarify the entire range of personality disorders" (p. 305). Further details of their study are provided in chapter 7 of this volume.

TABLE 5.1

Empirical Research on the Five-Factor Model of Personality Disorders

Study	FFM instrument	Sample	PD construct
Axelrod et al. (1977)	NEO-PI-R, SIFFM	89 college students	Cluster B DSM-IV PDs
Bagby et al. (1994)	NEO-PI	83 college students	Alexithymia
Bagby et al. (in press)	NEO-PI-R	165 depressed outpatients	Sociotropy, autonomy
Ball et al. (1997)	NEO-FFI	370 substance patients	DSM-III-R PDs
Blais (1997)	ACL	100 personality disorder patients	DSM-IV PDs
Bradlee & Emmons (1992)	NEO-PI	175 college students	Narcissism
Brooner et al. (1993)	NEO-PI	203 opioid outpatients	Antisocial
Cappeliez (1993)	NEO-PI	73 college students	Sociotropy, autonomy
Clark (1993b)	NEO-FFI	82 patients	SNAP, DSM-III-R PDs
Clark & Livesley (1994)	NEO-PI, NEO-FFI	300 community, 225 students, 76 patients	DAPP-BQ and SNAP
Clark et al. (1994)	NEO-PI, ACL	194 college students	SNAP
Clarkin et al. (1993)	NEO-PI	62 female BDL inpatients	Borderline
Coolidge et al. (1994)	NEO-PI	180 college students	DSM-III-R PDs
Costa & McCrae (1990)	NEO-PI	62–274 community adults	DSM-III and DSM-III-R PDs
Duijsens & Diekstra (1996)	23BB5, 5PFT	210–450 community adults	DSM-III-R and ICD-10 PDs
Dyce & O'Connor (1998)	NEO-PI-R	614 college students	DSM-IV PDs
Harpur et al. (1994)	NEO-PI	28 inmates	Psychopathy
Hart & Hare (1994)	IASR-B5	12 inmates	Psychopathy
Huey & Weisz (1997)	California Q-Sort	116 outpatient children	Resiliency, control
Hyer et al. (1994)	NEO-PI	80 male veteran PTSD patients	DSM-III-R PDs
John et al. (1994)	California Q-Sort	350 community adolescents	Antisocial
Lehne (1994)	NEO-PI	99 clinic male patients with paraphilias	DSM-III PDs
Livesley et al. (1998)	None	656 patients, 393 community, 686 twin pairs	DAPP-BQ scales
Luminet et al. (1999)	NEO-PI-R	101 college students	Alexithymia
Lynam et al. (1999)	BFI	739 college students	Psychopathy
Lyoo et al. (1998)	NEO-FFI	46 chronic depressed patients	Depressive PD
McCrae et al. (2001)	NEO-PI-R	1,909 patients	DSM-IV PDs
Miller et al. (2001)	NEO-PI-R	481 community high-risk adults	Psychopathy
Mongrain (1993)	NEO-PI	129 college students	Sociotropy, autonomy
Nestadt et al. (1994)	None	810 community adults	DSM-III PDs
O'Connor & Dyce (1998)	None	Data from 9 studies	DSM-III and DSM-II-R PDs

Study	Instrument	Sample	Construct
Pincus & Gurtman (1995)	NEO-PI, IASR-B5	654 college students	Dependency
Pincus & Ruiz (1997)	NEO-FFI	355 college students	SASB constructs
Pukrop et al. (1998)	SFT	165 inpatients, 100 healthy adults	*DSM-III-R, ICD-10*
Ramanaiah et al. (1994)	NEO-PI-R	188 college students	Narcissistic
Ramanaiah & Sharpe (1998)	NEO-FFI	220 college students	*DSM-III-R* PDs
R. W. Robins et al. (1994)	California Q-Set	350 community adolescents	Resiliency, control
Schroeder et al. (1992)	NEO-PI	300 community adults	DAPP-BQ scales
Schroeder et al. (1994)	NEO-PI	300 community adults	DAPP-BQ scales
Shopshire & Craik (1994)	10 bipolar traits	260 college students	*DSM-III-R* PDs
Soldz et al. (1993)	50-BSRS	102 PD group therapy patients	*DSM-III-R* PDs
Soldz et al. (1995)	50-BSRS	156 group psychotherapy outpatients	Defenses
Svrakic et al. (1993)	NEO-PI	136 psychiatric inpatients	*DSM-III-R* PDs
Trull (1992)	NEO-PI	54 outpatients	*DSM-III-R*, PSY-5
Trull et al. (1995)	NEO-PI-R	170 community; 44–57 outpatients	*DSM-III-R*, PSY-5
Trull et al. (1998)	NEO-PI-R, SIFFM	46 outpatients, 187 students	*DSM-IV* PDs
Trull et al. (2001)	SIFFM	46 outpatients, 187 students	*DSM-IV* PDs
Widiger et al. (1991)	None	Data from 9 studies	*DSM-III* and *DSM-III-R* PDs
Wiggins & Pincus (1989)	NEO-PI, IASR-B5	581 college students	*DSM-III* PDs
Wilberg et al. (1999)	NEO-PI-R	63 group therapy outpatients	Borderline, Avoidant
Wise et al. (1992)	NEO-FFI	114 outpatients, 71 adult volunteers	Alexithymia
Wise & Mann (1994)	NEO-FFI	101 outpatients	Alexithymia
Yang et al. (chapter 13, this volume)	NEO-PI-R	1,909 patients	*DSM-IV* PDs
Yeung et al. (1993)	NEO-FFI (T-F)	224 first degree relatives of patients	*DSM-III* PDs
Zuroff (1994)	NEO-PI	172 college students	Sociotropy, autonomy
Zweig-Frank & Paris (1995)	NEO-PI-R	59 prior patients	Borderline

Note. ACL = Adjective Check List (Blais, 1997; Clark et al., 1994); BFI = Big Five Inventory (John, 1995); California Q-Sort (Block, 1961; J. Block & Block, 1980); Cluster B = borderline, antisocial, histrionic, and narcissistic; DAPP-BQ = Dimensional Assessment of Personality Disorder Pathology—Basic Questionnaire (Livesley et al., 1998); *DSM-III* = third edition of the *Diagnostic and Statistical Manual of Mental Disorders* (American Psychiatric Association [APA], 1980); *DSM-III-R* = third edition, revised, of the *DSM* (APA, 1987); *DSM-IV* = fourth edition of the *DSM* (APA, 1994); FFM = five-factor model; 5PFT = Five Personality Factor Test (Duijsens & Diekstra, 1996); IAS-R-B5 = Interpersonal Adjective Scales Revised—Big Five (Trapnell & Wiggins, 1990); *ICD-10* = *International Classification of Diseases* (World Health Organization, 1992); NEO-FFI = NEO Five-Factor Inventory (Costa & McCrae, 1992a); NEO-PI = NEO Personality Inventory (Costa & McCrae, 1985); NEO-PI-R = Revised NEO Personality Inventory (Costa & McCrae, 1992a); PDs = personality disorders; PSY-5 = Personality Psychopathology Five Scales (Harkness et al., 1995). PTSD = posttraumatic stress disorder; SASB = Structural Analysis of Social Behavior (Benjamin, 1993b); SIFFM = Structured Interview for the Five-Factor Model of Personality (Trull & Widiger, 1997); SFT = *Sechs Faktoren Test* (von Zerssen, 1994); SNAP = Schedule for Nonadaptive and Adaptive Personality Traits (Clark, 1993a); T–F = true–false format; 50-BSRS = 50 Bipolar Self-Rating Scale (Goldberg, 1992); 23BB5 = 23 Bipolar Big Five (Duijsens & Diekstra, 1996).

Wiggins and Pincus (1989) cited a more preliminary factor analytic study by Widiger et al. (1991). Widiger et al. averaged the correlations among the *Diagnostic and Statistical Manual of Mental Disorders* (3rd ed. [*DSM-III*]; American Psychiatric Association [APA], 1980) PDs reported in 9 published studies. The averaged correlations were submitted to both multidimensional scaling and factor analyses, yielding four dimensions of personality functioning that Widiger et al. interpreted as N, Extraversion versus introversion, dominance versus submission, and Conscientiousness. Widiger et al. failed to obtain a factor of Openness but suggested that this domain of personality functioning was necessary to account for the magical thinking and aberrant perceptions of the schizotypal PD.

Costa and McCrae (1990) administered the NEO-PI, the MMPI PD scales, and the first and second editions of the Millon Clinical Multaxial Inventory (MCMI-I and MCMI-II, respectively; Millon, Millon, & Davis, 1994) to samples of community adults participating in the Baltimore Longitudinal Study of Aging. Confirmation of expected relationships were obtained, including (but not limited to) an association of obsessive–compulsive symptomatology with Conscientiousness, A with dependency, avoidant with introversion and N, schizoid with introversion but not N, and borderline with N. Their study was also intriguing in its inclusion of self, peer, and spousal ratings of the FFM (indicating, e.g., a negative relationship between N and narcissism when based on self-ratings) and in its comparison of the two editions of the MCMI (indicating, e.g., the removal of items concerning N from the MCMI-I Antisocial scale and the addition of items to the MCMI-II Antisocial scale concerning low Conscientiousness). Costa and McCrae (1990) concluded that the FFM "appears to account for the major dimensions underlying personality disorder scales developed by a number of different investigators" (p. 370) and that "with shared measures, shared constructs, and a shared vocabulary, the fruitful integration of personality research and psychiatric nosology seems much more likely today" (p. 371).

Trull (1992) provided the first study to include the administration of measures of the FFM and PD symptomatology within a clinical sample. He administered the NEO-PI and three independent measures of the third edition, revised, of the *DSM* (*DSM-III-R*; APA, 1987) PD symptomatology, including the PD scales of the MMPI, the Revised Personality Diagnostic Questionnaire (PDQ-R; Hyler & Rieder, 1987), and the Structured Interview for *DSM-III-R* Personality Disorders—Revised (SIDP-R; Pfohl, Blum, Zimmerman, & Stangl, 1989). He concluded that "all of the *DSM-III-R* personality disorders are related to at least one of the personality dimensions of the FFM, and scores on the five NEO-PI domains together were significantly correlated with individual PD scores in almost every case" (Trull, 1992, p. 559). "In general, the FFM appears to be useful in conceptualizing and differentiating among the *DSM-III-R* personality disorders" (p. 557), with some findings replicating "across all three personality disorder assessment instruments" (p. 557).

Nestadt et al. (1994) factor analyzed 93 of the *DSM-III* PD diagnostic criteria identified in 810 of the people participating in the influential and widely cited National Institute of Mental Health Epidemiology Catchment Area Study (L. N. Robins & Regier, 1991). "The results did not confirm the . . . *DSM-III* definition of disorders or of clusters of disorders; [instead,] the five factors that emerged in our analysis are reminiscent of a long tradition in personality trait theory" (Nestadt et al., 1994, p. 60). Nestadt et al. interpreted the five factors as scrupulousness, timidity, animation, trust, and warmth, and they concluded that these five factors aligned well with the five domains of the FFM: "Our five factors can be positioned . . . as follows: our scrupulousness with their conscientiousness; our timidity with their neurotic; our animation with their extroversion; our trust with their agreeable; and our warmth with their open" (pp. 60–61). The construct of warmth would not normally be placed with a construct of Openness; however, we would note that the schizotypal symptoms of magical thinking, referential ideas, and recurrent illusions loaded substantially on their warmth factor.

John et al. (1994) analyzed California Child Q-Set (CCQS) descriptions of 350 boys by their mothers as part of the Pittsburgh Youth Study, a longitudinal investigation of the antecedents and correlates of delinquency (approximately half of the 350 boys were considered to be at risk for future delinquency and drug use). The CCQS was originally developed by J. Block and Block (1980) for use by professional observers to describe children's personalities. As indicated above, McCrae et al. (1986) demonstrated how the adult version of the CQS was readily understood from the perspective of the FFM and that the underlying or latent dimensions of the CQS yield the canonical Big 5 dimensions. Similar results in an adolescent sample were revealed by a factor analysis of the 100 CCQS items by John et al. that resulted in a seven-factor solution, five of which were again readily interpreted by John et al. as being the five domains of the FFM. The two remaining factors they interpreted as irritability (e.g., cries, whines, or pouts) and positive activity (e.g., energetic, physically active, or fast paced). John et al. noted that research with adults indicates that irritability is a component of N and positive activity a component of Extraversion (Costa & McCrae, 1995b).

John et al. (1994) discouraged researchers from placing much importance on the two additional factors until they were replicated in subsequent studies: "Until this is done, we recommend that researchers use the Big Five scales" (p. 174). It is their expectation that positive activity and irritability "will eventually merge with sociability and anxious distress, respectively, to form the superordinate dimensions of extraversion and neuroticism in adulthood" (R. W. Robins, John, & Caspi, 1994, p. 280). Seventy-eight of the 100 CCQS items were identified as potential markers of the FFM and were subsequently reduced to a more manageable and homogeneous set of 48 items. Scores on the CCQS FFM scales successfully differentiated boys with externalizing and internalizing disorders. "As predicted, boys who had committed severe delinquent behaviors were more than three-fourths of a standard deviation lower on agreeableness and conscientiousness" (John et al., 1994, p. 168).

Hyer et al. (1994) administered the NEO-PI and the MCMI-II to 80 male veterans being treated for PTSD: "On the whole, personality disorder scales [were] reflected by the NEO-PI domains and facets as one would expect" (p. 701), including (but not limited to) a substantial association of the obsessive–compulsive symptomatology with Conscientiousness, dependent with A, borderline with N, histrionic with Extraversion, schizoid with introversion but not N, and avoidant with introversion and N. Hyer et al. (1994) concluded that "it may be said that the NEO-PI is reflective of personality disorder pathology in this clinical group. This applies both to domains and facets, both of which accurately reflect the personality disorders" (p. 704).

Lehne (1994; see also chapter 16, this volume) administered the NEO-PI and the MCMI-I to 99 men who were undergoing evaluation or treatment for a paraphilia at the Sexual Disorders Clinic at Johns Hopkins Hospital (Baltimore, MD). Lehne discussed the results in terms of a potential FFM profile of people with a paraphilia and the association of FFM constructs with the *DSM-III* PDs assessed by the MCMI. Lehne (1994) concluded that "the correlation of the results from the MCMI and NEO-PI provides support for the idea that there are common personality factors that underlie the personality disorders" (p. 182), although Lehne also emphasized that each instrument provides information that is optimally used in a complementary rather than mutually exclusive fashion.

Duijsens and Diekstra (1996) administered two Dutch measures of the FFM, the 23 Bipolar Big Five (23BB5) Self-Report Questionnaire, and the 70-item Five Personality Factor Test (5PFT) to various samples of community adults, some of whom were attending lectures on personality problems advertised in a local newspaper. The participants also completed a self-report questionnaire developed to assess the PD diagnostic criteria for both the *DSM-III-R* and the World Health Organization (WHO; 1992) *International Classifications of Disease 10* (*ICD-10*) taxonomies (i.e., the *Vragenlijst voor Kenmerken van de Persoonlijkheid*). Duijsens and Diekstra concluded that "the correlations between the dimensions of normal personality, such as those used in the Big Five model on the one hand, and personality disorders on the other hand, do indeed have strong and understandable associations with one another" (p. 131). They noted the substantial replication across the *DSM-III-R* and the *ICD-10* taxonomies, indicating "that in terms of underlying personality dimensions[,] the criteria in both systems are more or less the same" (p. 132). They concluded that

> *trying to break personality disorder characteristics down into combinations of certain positions or scores on Big Five dimensions may be a fruitful undertaking [and that] it might be possible to develop a theory of personality disorders that can be seen as an extension of a theory based on normal personality. (p. 131)*

Pukrop et al. (1998) administered the *Sechs Faktoren Test* (*SFT*; von Zerssen, 1994) to 165 adult psychiatric inpatients and 100 psychologically healthy community adults. The *SFT* includes 52 items that assess the five domains of the FFM, along with a sixth dimension for conventional religious attitudes. They also administered self-report measures of PD symptomatology as described within the *DSM-III-R* and the *ICD-10*. They submitted the correlations among these measures to a statistical program yielding a radex structure that they interpreted as supporting "the hypothesis of a universal personality model, and a continuous transition from normal personalities to personality disorders" (Pukrop et al., 1998, p. 226).

Shopshire and Craik (1994) asked 260 college students to provide judgments of the extent to which *DSM-III-R* PD diagnostic criteria exemplified either pole of the five domains of the FFM, thereby exploring the associations with respect to their internal coherence and meaningfulness. The reliability of the ratings was excellent, and the results were consistent with other research.

> *The histrionic and narcissistic personality disorders are associated with the FFM extroversion dimension; the dependent personality disorder is related to the positive pole of the FFM agreeableness; obsessive–compulsive personality disorder is linked to the FFM conscientiousness dimension[,] and passive–aggressive personality disorder bears upon its negative pole. (Shopshire & Craik, 1994, p. 49)*

Shopshire and Craik noted in particular how "this convergence between studies using the methodically different internal and external forms of analysis is impressive" (p. 49).

Blais (1997) provided data obtained from a nationwide survey of 100 clinicians. These clinicians were asked to rate one of their patients who carried a primary diagnosis of a PD and had been in treatment with the clinician for at least 10 sessions (average length of treatment was 3.4 years). The clinicians rated each patient with respect to each of the fourth edition of the *DSM* (*DSM-IV*; APA, 1994) PD diagnostic criteria, and a full range of PD symptomatology was obtained. Blais also requested that each clinician rate each patient with respect to 40 single-term adjectives representing the FFM (Saucier, 1994). As indicated by Blais (1997), "it has been argued that the language of the FFM fails to capture clinically important aspects of personality functioning and that clinicians will have difficulty applying this model to their patients" (p. 388). Despite the assessment of the FFM constructs with a limited number of single-term adjectives, Blais concluded that such "findings [were] highly consistent with the results from previous research that [used] different samples and measurement instruments" (p. 391), including (but not limited to) an association of compulsive PD symptomatology with Conscientiousness and dependent with A. Furthermore, "the use of clinician ratings provides insights into how clinicians view personality disordered patients and increases [the] understanding of the phenomenology of personality disorders" (p. 391). For example, "the antisocial personality disorder was negatively correlated with agreeableness, conscientiousness, and openness, suggesting that clinicians see [their] patients as interpersonally antagonistic, lacking self-discipline, and as having rigid narrowly defined interests" (p. 391). "The avoidant personality disorder was correlated negatively with extraversion and positively with neuroticism, suggesting that it is seen as having both social isolation and emotional instability" (p. 392). Rather than finding that clinicians considered the FFM constructs to be too superficial or irrelevant, Blais concluded that his "data suggest that clinicians can meaningfully apply the FFM to their patients and that the FFM of personality has utility for improving [the] understanding of the DSM personality disorders" (p. 392).

Yang et al. (chapter 13, this volume) report the results of a cross-cultural application of both the FFM and the *DSM-IV* within the People's Republic of China. The self-reported Revised NEO Personality Inventory (NEO-PI-R; Costa & McCrae, 1992a) and the Personality Diagnostic Questionnaire—4 (PDQ-4; Hyler, 1994) were completed by 1,909 patients across 13 hospitals and clinics. The correlations between the NEO-PI-R profile scores for each *DSM-IV* PD (Widiger, Trull, Clarkin, Sanderson, & Costa, 1994) and the PDQ-4 scale scores ranged from .20 (schizoid, $p < .01$) to .59 (borderline). Yang et al. conclude that their findings confirm the hypotheses of Widiger et al. However, McCrae et al. (2001), in an additional report from this data set, emphasized the absence of an association between the categorical PD diagnoses and the NEO-PI-R profile scores (whether provided by the PDQ-4 or by the Personality Disorder Interview—IV; Widiger, Mangine, Corbitt, Ellis, & Thomas, 1995). The weak agreement between NEO-PI-R profile scores and PD diagnoses was comparable with the weak agreement typically obtained between two independent measures of the diagnostic categories (Westen, 1997; Widiger & Sanderson, 1995). McCrae et al. argued that the most likely explanation for their results was the absence of sufficient personality profile homogeneity among the people receiving the same personality disorder diagnoses to justify or warrant the categorical distinctions. They suggested that the search for personality disorder diagnostic categories was largely a "fool's errand."

Facets of the Five-Factor Model

Many of the earliest studies assessing the relationship of the FFM to PD symptomatology were confined largely to the broad domains of N, Extraversion, Openness, Conscientiousness, and A (e.g., Costa & McCrae, 1990; Soldz et al., 1993; Trull, 1992), although a few did provide a limited amount of analyses at a lower order of traits (e.g., Clarkin et al., 1993; Hyer et al., 1994; Wiggins & Pincus, 1989). A substantial amount of information is provided by analyses confined to the five broad domains, but adequate differentiation among the PDs

ultimately requires more specific assessments (Briggs, 1992; Harkness, 1992). That is why Widiger et al. (1994; chapter 6, this volume) translated the PDs into facets, not merely domains.

Three FFM studies emphasize analyses at the facet level. Dyce and O'Connor (1998) administered the NEO-PI-R and the third edition of the MCMI (MCMI-III; Millon et al., 1994) to 614 college students to assess the relationships between the domains and facets of the FFM and the PDs predicted by Widiger et al. (1994). They confirmed most of the specific predictions, including (but not limited to) associations of obsessive–compulsive symptomatology with facets of Conscientiousness (order, dutifulness, self-discipline, and deliberation), and avoidant with facets of N (anxiousness, self-consciousness, and vulnerability) and introversion (low assertiveness, gregariousness, excitement seeking, and activity). Dyce and O'Connor (1998) concluded that "facet-level analyses provided much better discrimination between personality disorders than domain-level analyses" (p. 31). Further details of their research are provided in chapter 14 (this volume).

Axelrod, Widiger, Trull, and Corbitt (1997) reached a similar conclusion with respect to the *DSM-IV* PDs characterized by high levels of antagonism (i.e., antisocial, borderline, narcissistic, paranoid, and passive–aggressive). Axelrod et al. administered the Structured Interview for the Five-Factor Model (SIFFM; Trull & Widiger, 1997), the MMPI PD scales, and the PDQ-R to 89 college students. Axelrod et al. (1997) indicated that

> the antisocial, borderline, narcissistic, paranoid, and passive–aggressive composite scales all correlated significantly with the higher order antagonism domain . . . [but, for example,] narcissism involved the facets of low modesty (or arrogance), low tender-mindedness (or tough-mindedness), and low altruism (or exploitiveness), whereas paranoia involved primarily low trust (or suspiciousness). (p. 309)

"From the perspective of the facets, low tender-mindedness is evident in antisocial and narcissistic traits, but not in borderline, paranoid, or passive–aggressive traits, whereas low modesty (or arrogance) was evident only within narcissism" (p. 309). Their specific facet predictions were confirmed for all but one of the six facets of antagonism.

Trull et al. (1998) administered the SIFFM, NEO-PI-R, and the PDQ-R to 46 outpatients and 187 college students. The results confirmed again the ability of the FFM to account for PD symptomatology, particularly when the SIFFM and the NEO-PI-R were used conjointly. More specific findings were provided in a subsequent report by Trull, Widiger, and Burr (2001). Trull et al. (2001), for example, indicated that both the dependent PD and avoidant personality disorder (AVD) correlated highly with N but with different facets of N. AVD symptomatology was related most highly with the facet of self-consciousness, whereas the dependence was related more highly with the facet of depressiveness. In addition, whereas AVD and schizoid PD were both highly related to introversion, schizoid symptomatology was associated primarily with low positive emotions (along with low gregariousness and low warmth) and AVD was associated primarily with low assertiveness and low excitement seeking, which is consistent with the predictions of Widiger et al. (1994). They indicated that an FFM understanding of these and other PDs helps to explain not only why they co-occurred (i.e., involving the same broad domains of personality) but also how they might be more adequately differentiated with respect to the facets within these domains.

Specific Personality Disorder Constructs

Many authors of the FFM studies have been concerned with only a particular subset of PD symptomatology, such as borderline, sociotropic, depressive, dependent, narcissistic, alexithymic, antisocial, and psychopathic personality traits. For example, Clarkin et al. (1993) explored empirically the conceptualization of BDL by the FFM, the latter assessed by the NEO-PI. Their sample consisted of 62 female inpatients with BDL diagnoses provided by clinicians at Cornell University Medical Center who specialize in the treatment of this PD (the diagnoses were confirmed by the Structured Clinical Interview for *DSM-III-R* Personality Disorders [SCID-II]; Spitzer, Wil-

liams, Gibbon, & First, 1990). Despite the restrictions in range on BDL symptomatology within this sample, Clarkin et al. (1993) confirmed a close correspondence between facets of the FFM and BDL symptomatology: "The borderline personality disorder patient is characterized by extreme and distressing feelings of trait anxiety, hostility, and depression; painful self-consciousness and vulnerability in relating to others; and dyscontrol of impulses" (p. 475). The average NEO-PI profile for their female BDL patients is provided in chapter 21 (Figure 21.1, this volume).

The findings of Clarkin et al. (1993) were subsequently replicated by Wilberg et al. (1999). Wilberg et al. administered the NEO-PI-R to a sample 63 people participating in a day hospital, group psychotherapy program for poorly functioning outpatients with PDs. The NEO-PI-R was administered as a part of the intake assessment. Wilberg et al. obtained assessments of the diagnostic criteria for BDL and AVD after the 18-week treatment ended, based in part on data obtained from an administration of the SCID-II (First, Spitzer, Gibbon, & Williams, 1995) at the time of admission and on the impressions of the clinicians during the course of the treatment. Twenty-nine of the patients met the *DSM-IV* criteria for BDL; 34 met the criteria for avoidant (12 patients who met the criteria for both PDs were excluded).

Wilberg et al. (1999) confirmed all of the facet level predictions of Widiger et al. (1994) for AVD and 8 of the 12 predictions for BDL. The BDL facet predictions for Extraversion were not confirmed, which may reflect in part the fact that the facets of Extraversion are not considered central to this PD, being based instead on only the associated features of the disorder (Widiger et al., 1994; see also chapter 6). Figure 5.1 provides NEO-PI-R profiles for these AVD and BDL patients. There are interesting differences at both the domain and facet level within and across the two disorders. Consider only two of the five dimensions, N and A. Whereas patients with AVD and BDL are very high in overall N and four of the six facets, only the patients with BDL are characterized by very high angry hostility and impulsiveness, which are conceptually linked to the BDL category. Considering A versus antagonism, at

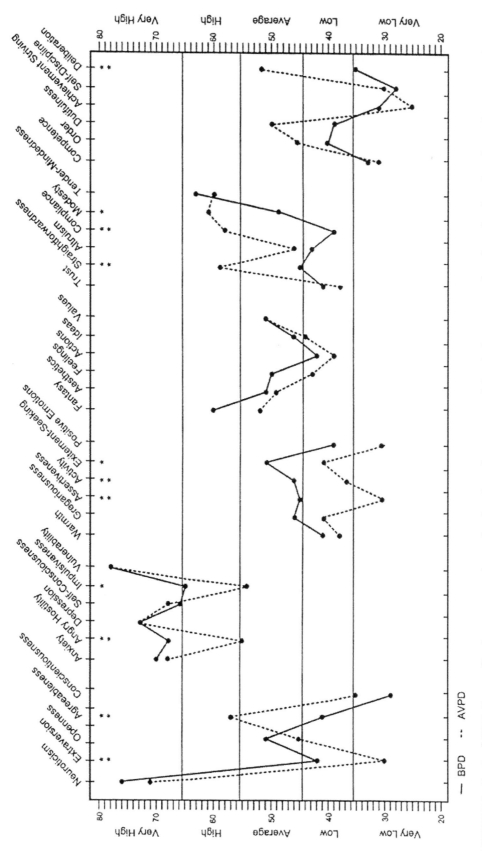

FIGURE 5.1. Revised NEO Personality Inventory scales and subscales of patients with borderline personality disorder (BPD) and avoidant personality disorder (AVPD). *t* test, two tailed (Bonferroni adjustment, .05/.35). **p* = .001. ***p* = .0001. From "Borderline and Avoidant Personality Disorders and the Five-Factor Model of Personality: A Comparison Between DSM-IV Diagnoses and NEO-PI-R," by T. Wilberg, O. Urnes, S. Friis, G. Pedersen, and S. Karterud, 1999, *Journal of Personality Disorders, 13*, p. 232. Copyright 1999 by Guilford Press. Reprinted with permission.

the domain level, patients with AVD are agreeable, whereas patients with BDL show the characteristic antagonistic orientation. Interestingly, the facets within A show considerable scatter: Both patients with AVD and BDL are low on trust (high in suspicion), whereas they are both above average in tender mindedness. Patients with BDL are well differentiated from patients with AVD, displaying characteristically low levels of straightforwardness and significantly lower compliance and modesty.

In a cluster analysis, 53 of the 63 patients (84%) were correctly identified on the basis of the Extraversion and A scales alone. Wilberg et al. (1999) concluded that "the FFM had good discriminating ability regarding a diagnosis of avoidant personality disorder versus borderline personality disorder in a sample of poorly functioning patients" (p. 239). Wilberg et al. did note that "fewer patients with borderline personality disorder than avoidant personality disorder had the hypothesized [FFM] profiles" (p. 237), which is consistent with the findings of Clarkin et al. (1993), who indicated that only 48% of their BDL patients obtained a prototypical FFM profile. However, Wilberg et al. acknowledged that this may reflect the substantial heterogeneity among people who would meet the *DSM-IV* BDL criteria (Clarkin, Widiger, Frances, Hurt, & Gilmore, 1983) and the infrequency of prototypic cases (see chapter 21, this volume). Wilberg et al. also conducted analyses at the level of individual AVD and BDL diagnostic criteria. No significant relationship was found between any NEO-PI-R facet scale and the following BDL diagnostic criteria: frantic efforts to avoid abandonment, identity disturbance, suicidal behavior, and chronic emptiness. Wilberg et al. (1999) suggested that these particular diagnostic criteria "may represent features that are qualitatively different from normal personality dimensions" (p. 237). However, it is also possible that there was inadequate range, reliability, or validity of these individual symptom assessments (no reliability data were provided for the assessments of the individual diagnostic criteria).

Two of the more heavily researched PD constructs hypothesized to contribute to episodes of depression are dependency (sociotropy) and narcissistic autonomy (self-criticism; Beck, 1983; Blatt & Zuroff, 1992). Dependent individuals are predicted to be-

come depressed in response to relationship failures (e.g., separation or loss), whereas narcissistically autonomous people become depressed in response to achievement failures. Three studies explored an understanding of these constructs from the perspective of the FFM (i.e., Cappeliez, 1993; Mongrain, 1993; Zuroff, 1994). This research confirms the predicted association of dependency (sociotropy) with FFM N, Extraversion, and A; and narcissistic autonomy (or self-criticism) with N, introversion, and antagonism (Widiger et al., 1994). These authors have also noted how the FFM was particularly useful in explaining both the overlap among these constructs (e.g., sharing the anxiousness and vulnerability facets of N) and their key distinguishing features (e.g., the Extraversion and A of the dependent person vs. the introversion and arrogance of the narcissistically autonomous). Zuroff (1994) concluded that "research addressing vulnerability to depression may be able to profit from work on the five-factor model of personality" (p. 453). Mongrain (1993) likewise concluded that "the data from the current study may enrich [the] understanding of dependency and self-criticism by considering the abundant findings that have accrued from the research on neuroticism and extraversion" (pp. 460–461).

Lyoo, Gunderson, and Phillips (1998) reported results for the *DSM-IV* diagnosis of depressive PD that were consistent with the studies by Cappeliez (1993), Mongrain (1993), and Zuroff (1994). Lyoo et al. administered the NEO-FFI to a sample of 46 patients with chronic, early-onset dysthymia, 26 of whom were diagnosed with depressive PD by the Diagnostic Interview for Depressive Personality (Gunderson, Phillips, Triebwasser, & Hirschfeld, 1994). Despite the restriction in range, scores on the abbreviated NEO-FFI differentiated the chronic and early-onset dysthymic patients with depressive PD from other chronic and early-onset dysthymic patients with respect to elevations on N and introversion. Lyoo et al. (1998) concluded that "the results of this study begin to add meaning to the depressive personality construct" (p. 53).

Pincus and Gurtman (1995) explored different variants of dependency, which they identified as love dependency, exploitable dependency, and submissive dependency. They administered both the IAS-R-B5 and the NEO-PI, along with a variety of measures of dependency, to a sample of 654 introductory psychology students. Their results indicated strong support for their differentiation of dependency with respect to the interpersonal circumplex. However, they also indicated that the fundamental dimensions of the interpersonal circumplex are rotated variants of the FFM dimensions of Extraversion and A, which is consistent with the research of Wiggins and Pincus (1989), and that "a more comprehensive picture of dependency and its variations emerges when the analysis of the construct is extended beyond the space of the interpersonal circumplex and includes the remaining factors of the FFM: conscientiousness, neuroticism, and openness" (Pincus & Gurtman, 1995, p. 753). All three forms of dependency were related to N, exploitable and submissive dependency were negatively related to Conscientiousness and Openness, and love dependency was positively related to Conscientiousness and Openness. They concluded that "the construct of dependency is a complex individual difference with diverse interpersonal components" (p. 753), which were well captured by the interpersonal circumplex including its assessment from the perspective of the FFM. In addition, the "noninterpersonal components were well captured by FFM dimensions of neuroticism, conscientiousness, and openness" (p. 753). Further details and a discussion of this research is provided in chapter 12 (this volume).

Bagby et al. (in press) explored the relationship of particular facets of the FFM to sociotropy and autonomy. They administered the NEO-PI-R to 165 people participating in an outpatient treatment program for depression. At the domain level, they verified that sociotropy and autonomy could be differentiated with respect to the FFM, with sociotropy "described, in descending degree of importance, as neurotic, agreeable, and extroverted, while the autonomous individual can be best described, also in descending degree of importance, as introverted, neurotic, and disagreeable." Equally intriguing was that the two depressive personality constructs were differentiated further with respect to particular facets of N and Extraversion. "The extraversion facets of warmth and non-assertiveness characterized the sociotropy dimension, while a lack of positive emotions

and warmth characterized autonomy." Both sociotropy and autonomy involved high N, but "sociotropy was the most strongly related to the self-consciousness and anxiety facets, and the angry hostility and depression facets were most strongly related to autonomy."

Bradlee and Emmons (1992) assessed the convergence of the FFM with various components of narcissism assessed by the popularly researched Narcissistic Personality Inventory (NPI; Raskin & Terry, 1988). Bradlee and Emmons confirmed the relationship between antagonism and Extraversion but also obtained a significant negative correlation with N, which is consistent with an earlier study by Costa and McCrae (1990). "The overall portrait that emerges of a narcissistic individual is that of one who is extraverted yet disagreeable and low in anxiety" (Bradlee & Emmons, 1992, p. 828). Their findings were subsequently replicated by Ramanaiah, Detwiler, and Byravan (1994), who administered the NEO-PI-R and the NPI to a sample of 188 college students. An advantage of the NPI as a measure of narcissism is the availability of subscales for different components of this constellation of personality traits. Bradlee and Emmons indicated that the negative correlation with N reflected primarily the subscales assessing feelings of superiority and self-sufficiency. "The lack of significant negative relationship between neuroticism and four of the NPI components, entitlement, exploitiveness, and exhibition, and vanity, suggests that not all aspects of narcissism offer protection from emotional instability" (Bradlee & Emmons, 1992, p. 828).

Alexithymia is a personality construct that includes difficulties in identifying and expressing feelings to others, along with an impoverished imaginal life. A substantial amount of research on alexithymia has been conducted over the past decade, focusing in particular on the clinically significant implications of this PD for both mental and medical functioning (Taylor, Bagby, & Parker, 1997). In four published studies, the authors were concerned with the relationship of alexithymia to the FFM that demonstrates (in part) the importance of the FFM domain of Openness. Openness has failed to provide a significant contribution in some studies of PD symptomatology, which might be due in part to the failure of the official diagnostic nomenclature to provide adequate coverage of this domain (Widiger & Costa, 1994). Two initial studies of FFM and alexithymia were conducted by Wise, Mann, and Shay (1992) and Wise and Mann (1994). They administered the NEO-FFI and the Toronto Alexithymia Scale (TAS; Taylor et al., 1997) to a diverse set of psychiatric outpatients. Partial correlation coefficients that controlled for depressed mood indicated a substantial correlation of $-.40$ with Openness as well as with N ($r = .38$) and introversion ($r = .40$). More detailed research has since been conducted by Bagby, Taylor, and Parker (1994) and Luminet, Bagby, Wagner, Taylor, and Parker (1999). Bagby et al. administered the NEO-PI-R and the TAS to 83 college students, obtaining the most substantial correlation with Openness ($r = -.49$), with a secondary correlation with N ($r = .27$) and insignificant correlations with Extraversion, A, and Conscientiousness (alexithymia correlated $-.55$ with the facet of openness to feelings). Luminet et al. (1999) administered the NEO-PI-R and the TAS to 101 college students and confirmed the primary association with Openness, particularly with the facet of openness to feelings: "These findings indicate that alexithymia is associated strongly with a lack of receptivity to feelings, a limited range of emotional experience, and a negative evaluation of emotion as an important part of life" (p. 354).

Brooner et al. (1993) administered the NEO-PI and the SCID-II to 203 patients in outpatient treatment for opioid abuse and dependence, 23% of whom met the *DSM-III-R* criteria for antisocial personality disorder (ATS). Brooner et al. compared 46 ATS patients with 30 patients having other PDs and 127 having no PD diagnosis. "Several of the hypotheses regarding the relationship of personality disorder to standings on the FFM of personality were confirmed in this study of drug abusers" (Brooner et al., 1993, p. 317). They noted, for example, how the presence of comorbid PD symptomatology in the ATS patients was accounted for by levels of N (see also chapter 15, this volume). "Thus, the present study confirms Alterman and Cacciola's (1991) speculation; axis II comorbidity among antisocial drug abusers was associated with a greater tendency toward emotional distress compared with those with

the antisocial diagnosis alone" (Brooner et al., 1993, p. 317).

Harpur, Hart, and Hare (1994) administered the NEO-PI and the Hare Psychopathy Checklist—Revised (PCL-R; Hare, 1991) to 47 college students and 28 prison inmates, 12 of whom were diagnosed with psychopathy. They confirmed the expected relationships of psychopathy with antagonism and low conscientiousness, but they were limited in their analyses due to the low sample size. Hart and Hare (1994) asked college students to rate videotaped administrations of an abbreviated version of the PCL-R to 12 prison inmates and 12 students with respect to the FFM adjectives on the IAS-R-B5. They obtained the expected negative correlations with N and Conscientiousness but were again sorely limited by the small sample size and abbreviated FFM assessments. Further details of this research are provided in chapter 19 (this volume).

Lynam, Whiteside, and Jones (1999) administered the Big Five Inventory (BFI; John, 1995) and the Levenson Self-Report Psychopathy Scale (LSRP; Levenson, Kiehl, & Fitzpatrick, 1995) to 1,958 undergraduate college students. Total scores on the LSRP correlated as predicated with A ($-.48$, $p < .001$) and Conscientiousness ($-.39$, $p < .001$). Lynam et al. also noted that the two factors of psychopathy (see chapter 13) obtained a different pattern of results that were largely consistent with the predictions of Widiger and Lynam (1998). For example, whereas the second factor was positively correlated with N, the first factor was nonsignificantly negatively correlated; the difference between these correlations was statistically significant ($p < .001$). Further details and discussion of this study are provided in chapter 20.

Miller et al. (2001) developed a prototypic NEO-PI-R profile that represented the mean of the ratings of a prototypic case of psychopathy with respect to the 30 facets of the FFM provided by 15 nationally recognized experts on psychopathy. The experts' FFM profile of psychopathy matched closely the theoretical expectations of Widiger and Lynam (1998), including low anxiousness, depressiveness, self-consciousness, vulnerability, and warmth; high angry–hostility, impulsiveness, excitement seeking, and assertiveness; and low in all facets of A and in the Conscientiousness facets of dutifulness, self-discipline, and deliberation. Miller et al. also obtained NEO-PI-R data from a sample of 481 young adults participating in the Lexington Longitudinal Study, an ongoing, prospective longitudinal study examining antisocial behavior and related outcomes. The degree to which each person's self-reported NEO-PI-R profile matched the expert-based prototype was assessed through the use of an intraclass Q correlation (Westen, Muderrisoglu, Shedler, Fowler, & Koren, 1997). Participants also provided data with respect to their scores on the LSRP, ATS symptomatology, and life history data, including their current and historical substance use disorders, anxiety disorders, and arrest record. The NEO-PI-R Psychopathy index correlated significantly with the presence of ATS to a degree consistent with reported research using the Hare Revised Psychopathy Checklist (Hare, 1991). Miller et al. noted that "this finding is especially interesting, given the lack of explicitly antisocial items in the NEO-PI-R psychopathy index, in contrast to the PCL-R, which explicitly assesses antisocial behavior" (p. 272). The NEO-PI-R Psychopathy index also correlated with the total LSRP score (particularly with the subscale that assesses the core psychopathic traits) and with a variety of external validators for the presence of psychopathy, including arrest history, drug usage, and absence of internalizing disorders, such as anxiety and depression. Miller et al. concluded that "the results support the contention that psychopathy can be understood as an extreme variant of common dimensions of personality" (pp. 253–254). Further details and discussion of this research are provided in chapter 20 (this volume).

Other Dimensional Models

Many of the FFM studies involve a comparison or integration of the FFM with an alternative dimensional model of PD symptomatology (e.g., Wiggins & Pincus, 1989). For example, Pincus and Ruiz (1997) administered to 355 college students the NEO-FFI and the Intrex Short Form Assessment of the Structural Analysis of Social Behavior (SASB). The SASB model of interpersonal behavior is a sophisticated object-relational model of the interpersonal circumplex (Benjamin, 1993b). It has been

suggested that the FFM would not relate well to the more clinically sophisticated SASB (Benjamin, 1993a). Nevertheless, Pincus and Ruiz (1997) reported that "all dimensions of the FFM and SASB exhibited significant intercorrelations" (p. 442) and that "relations found between dimensions of the SASB and FFM provide support for the position that parental representations significantly relate to adult personality" (p. 445). For example,

> *individuals whose parental representations were generally affiliative described themselves as less prone to emotional distress (lower neuroticism); more interpersonally oriented and experiencing of positive emotions (higher extraversion); more peaceable and trustworthy (higher agreeableness); and more dutiful, resourceful, and dependable (higher conscientiousness).* (p. 445).

Pincus and Ruiz (1997) indicated that "this broadens empirical support for a general psychodynamic theory of personality and links descriptive trait models with clinically useful concepts" (p. 445). They concluded that the object-relational, psychodynamic interpersonal circumplex model of personality provided by the SASB is not inconsistent or incompatible with the FFM. These are readily integrated models of personality covering the same ground of personality functioning. "We believe strongly that combining information from both domains provides a richer and more informed basis for clinical personality assessment than either does independently" (p. 451).

Soldz, Budman, Demby, and Merry (1995) administered the 50 Bipolar Self-Rating Scale (50-BSRS; Goldberg, 1992), the Personality Disorder Examination (PDE; Loranger, 1988), and the Defense Style Questionnaire (DSQ; Bond, Gardner, Christian, & Sigal, 1983) to 257 outpatients participating in various group psychotherapy treatment programs. The DSQ assesses various immature defenses (e.g., acting out, splitting, projective identification), withdrawal defenses (e.g., isolation), and mature defenses (e.g., sublimation, supression). Soldz et al. indicated that the DSQ was more highly correlated with some of the PD symptomatology than the FFM, but this could have been due in large part to the limited power provided by the 50-BSRS, at least in comparison to the DSQ. They concluded "overall, these findings suggest substantial empirical overlap between self-rated defensive style and the Big Five trait approach to personality" (Soldz et al., 1995, p. 366). "[Al]though the constructs involved may be conceptualized differently, their operationalization seems to cover much of the same domain" (p. 366).

Trull, Useda, Costa, and McCrae (1995) assessed the convergence of the FFM with the MMPI-2 Personality Psychopathology Five (PSY-5) Scales developed by Harkness, McNulty, and Ben-Porath (1995) in a sample of community and clinical participants. They reported substantial convergence of the PSY-5 and FFM constructs. For example, "PSY-5 positive emotionality and negative emotionality strongly resembled the NEO-PI dimensions of extraversion and neuroticism, respectively" (Trull et al., 1995, p. 514). The other three PSY-5 scales—aggressiveness, constraint, and psychoticism—had more complex relationships but were nevertheless clearly convergent: "Aggressiveness appears to combine some aspects of low agreeableness and high extraversion; constraint may be characterized by high agreeableness and high conscientiousness; and psychoticism was positively related to neuroticism and negatively related to some facets of agreeableness" (p. 514). Trull et al. also compared the two models with respect to their ability to account for PD symptomatology as assessed by a semistructured interview (SIDP-R) and a self-report inventory (PDQ-R). "As hypothesized, these trait measures were systematically related to personality disorder symptom counts, whether based on interviews or on self-reports" (p. 515). When the PD symptomatology was assessed by the PDQ-R, the PSY-5 scales correlated significantly with 7 of the 13 PDQ-R scales after controlling for mood and anxiety; the NEO-PI-R correlated with all 13 PDQ-R scales after controlling for mood and anxiety (the results were 8 and 7 scales, respectively, when the SIDP-R was used).

Soldz et al. (1993) compared the ability of the FFM and the interpersonal circumplex to account for PD symptomatology in a sample of 102 consecutive patients referred for group psychotherapy for PDs at Harvard Community Health Plan, the largest health maintenance organization in New England. PD symptomatology was assessed by both a self-report inventory (MCMI-II) and a semistructured interview (PDE). The FFM was assessed by a set of 50 single-term adjective markers (Goldberg, 1992); the interpersonal circumplex was assessed by the Inventory of Interpersonal Problems (IIP; Alden, Wiggins, & Pincus, 1990). Soldz et al. (1993) concluded that "despite the fact that many of the PDs could be meaningfully mapped into the two-dimensional circumplex space marked by the IIP circumplex scales, this space did not distinguish clearly among the personality disorders" (p. 46). Despite the rather limited power provided a single-term adjective assessment in comparison with the comprehensive set of clinically relevant interpersonal problems assessed by the IIP, "the use of the Big Five model led to even better placement for several disorders" (p. 41), which is consistent with the results of Wiggins and Pincus (1989). Soldz et al. (1993) concluded that "our results lend strong support to the position that the Big Five personality factors can adequately represent the distinctions among the personality disorders" (p. 51).

R. W. Robins et al. (1994) studied the relationship of the FFM as assessed in a sample of Pittsburgh adolescents with the constructs of ego resiliency and ego control emphasized by Block (1995). Ego control refers to the degree to which individuals express their impulses; ego resiliency describes the internal personality structures that function to modulate these impulses adaptively (J. H. Block & Block, 1980). Block's constructs of ego control and ego resiliency have a rich history, both historically and empirically. Ego undercontrolled individuals show a variety of externalizing, delinquent disorders; ego resiliency is linked to secure attachment, delay of gratification, and problem-solving abilities; ego overcontrol and ego brittleness are associated with a variety of internalizing disorders. Robins et al. obtained substantial correlations of ego undercontrol with antagonism and low Conscientiousness and ego resiliency with A, Conscientiousness, and low N. They also demonstrated how an FFM understanding of these constructs helped to explain their relationship with antisocial acts.

Both undercontrolled and antisocial boys were low in conscientiousness, but they differed in their levels of extraversion and agreeableness: undercontrolled boys were more extraverted than antisocial boys, and antisocial boys were less agreeable than undercontrolled boys. Thus, our findings further delineate the meaning and behavioral consequences of these developmental constructs. (R. W. Robins et al., 1994, p. 274)

R. W. Robins et al. (1994) also responded to the concern that dynamic constructs, such as ego control, are not equivalent to a set of personality traits, such as Conscientiousness. They indicated that their findings should not be understood as indicating that ego control is simply Conscientiousness or that Conscientiousness is simply ego control. Rather, the domain of personality functioning mediated by ego control is in large part Conscientiousness (and A).

The relation between conscientiousness and ego overcontrol may indicate that adolescent boys who engage in the types of behaviors that define the conscientiousness factor do so, or are capable of doing so, because they control and contain their emotional and motivational impulses. (p. 274)

Huey and Weisz (1997) further explored the incremental validity of the FFM and the constructs of ego resiliency and ego control to understand the behavioral and emotional problems of 116 clinic-referred children. Huey and Weisz (1997) compared their ability to account for a variety of internalizing and externalizing childhood psychopathology. "Within the FFM, extraversion and agreeableness were independent predictors of externalizing problems, whereas only neuroticism predicted internalizing problems" (p. 404). "All personality variables except openness were significantly associated with measures of child psychopathology and were at least somewhat effective in discriminating between the diagnostic groups of externalizing, internalizing, comorbid, and nonclinical children" (p. 412). With respect to their comparative validity, the FFM was

equally predictive of internalizing problems as the ego-control and ego-resilience model and was even "a stronger predictor of externalizing problems" (p. 412). "Given the fact that the FFM scales were derived from a subset of the CCQ (48 of 100 items), these findings should argue for the theoretical and empirical strength of the FFM" (p. 412).

Two models of PD symptomatology that are comparable with the FFM in the spirit and method of their construction are the 18-factor model of Livesley, as assessed by the Dimensional Assessment of Personality Pathology—Basic Questionnaire (DAPP-BQ; Livesley & Jang, 2000) and the 22-factor model of Clark (1993a), as assessed by the Schedule for Nonadaptive and Adaptive Personality (SNAP). Both of these dimensional models were developed through systematic and reasonably comprehensive searches of the clinical and empirical literature for virtually every PD trait concept, followed by extensive analyses of the correlations among the traits to reduce them to a manageable set of fundamental dimensions of PD symptomatology (Clark, McEwen, Collard, & Hickok, 1993; Livesley, Jackson, & Schroeder, 1989, 1992), including, for example, submissiveness, compulsivity, anxiousness, rejection, narcissism, and social avoidance (Livesley et al., 1989, 1992) and dependency, social isolation, dramatic exhibitionism, impulsivity, and antisocial behavior (Clark, 1993a). Not surprisingly, there is substantial convergence of these two alternative models. In a direct comparison of them, Clark, Livesley, Schroeder, and Irish (1996) indicated considerable convergence and compatibility, with only a few, relatively minor differences (e.g., DAPP-BQ Intimacy Problems may not be well represented within the SNAP, and SNAP Workaholism may not be well represented within the DAPP-BQ). Equally important, Clark et al. (1996) also indicated that the higher order factor structure of the joint set of instruments yielded four factors "which corresponded to the well-established dimensions of neuroticism, introversion, (dis)agreeableness (aggression–hostility), and (low) conscientiousness (impulsive sensation seeking)" (p. 300).

Clark et al. (1994; also see chapter 8, this volume) administered the NEO-PI, an adjective checklist from Goldberg's (1992) markers for the FFM, and the SNAP to 194 college students. Clark et al. (1994) reported that the

> *separate measures of the five factors yielded a clear convergent and discriminant pattern. More important, [SNAP] scales that assess maladaptive personality traits were shown to be related to measures of all five factors, which indicates the general relevance of the FFM for Axis II phenomena. (p. 109)*

Some of the significant findings included substantial correlations of SNAP self-harm and dependency with N, exhibitionism and entitlement with Extraversion, detachment with introversion, aggression and manipulativeness with antagonism, workaholism and propriety with Conscientiousness, and eccentric perceptions with Openness. A joint factor analysis indicated a strong FFM solution.

> *The factor analytic results lend considerable support to related hypotheses. First, the same underlying personality trait structure has been shown to emerge from analyses of normal and maladaptive personality traits. Once again, these data provide evidence of structural continuity across normal and abnormal personality. Second— and more specifically—a comprehensive (although perhaps not exhaustive) set of maladaptive traits has been shown to correlate significantly with all of the dimensions of the FFM, which supports the notion that this particular model of personality has relevance for understanding personality disorder. (p. 110)*

Schroeder, Wormworth, and Livesley (1992; also see chapter 9, this volume) administered the NEO-PI and the DAPP-BQ to 300 adult members of the general community recruited to participate in a study of personality. A joint factor analysis of the 16 DAPP-BQ included in this study and the five NEO-PI scales yielded a stable and meaningful FFM solution. Schroeder et al. (1992) concluded that "the results of the factor analysis suggest that the domain of personality pathology can be explained reasonably well within the five-factor model normal personality"

(p. 51). "The evidence suggests that personality disorders are not characterized by functioning that differs in quality from normal functioning; rather, personality disorder can be described with traits or dimensions that are descriptive of personality, both disordered and normal" (p. 52). More specifically, "the results of this study largely confirm our expectations that these dimensions of personality disorder are closely related to the Big Five factors of normal personality" (p. 52).

Livesley, Jang, and Vernon (1998) factor analyzed the 18 lower order traits included within the DAPP-BQ in samples of 656 patients with a PD, 939 general population subjects, and 686 twin pairs. Principal components analysis yielded four broad domains, which are comparable with those reported earlier by Widiger et al. (1991). "Multivariate genetic analyses also yielded 4 genetic and environmental factors that were remarkably similar to the phenotypic factors" (Livesley et al., 1998, p. 941). Livesley et al. labeled them as emotional dysregulation, dissocial behavior, inhibitedness, and compulsivity and acknowledged a convergence of the four factors with four of the five domains of the FFM: Emotional dysregulation was essentially equivalent to N, dissocial behavior (defined by interpersonal hostility, judgmental attitudes, callousness, and conduct problems) coordinated well with antagonism, inhibition (characterized by intimacy problems and restricted affect) was essentially equivalent to FFM introversion, and compulsivity was equivalent to Conscientiousness. Livesley et al. did emphasize that they did not obtain a factor that would correspond to FFM Openness but, as noted by an accompanying commentary, "four out of five ain't bad" (Widiger, 1998, p. 865). The absence of a factor representing Openness may simply reflect the failure to provide much representation of this domain of personality functioning within the DAPP-BQ; "the breadth and depth of the convergence is far more compelling" (p. 865) than the absence of this particular FFM domain.

Clark and Livesley (1994; also see chapter 10, this volume) explored in more detail the convergence of all three models (DAPP-BQ, SNAP, and FFM) using data sets in which measures of the FFM are included; they concluded that "these data thus provide further support for the notion that the personality trait dimensional structure defined by the FFM is very robust and will emerge reliably as long as a broad range of personality traits are assessed" (p. 275). As mentioned earlier, chapters 8, 9, and 10 (this volume) provide further details concerning this research with the SNAP and the DAPP-BQ.

In perhaps one of the more thorough and extensive comparisons of alternative dimensional models, O'Connor and Dyce (1998) conducted 12 independent principal-axes common factor analyses on the correlation matrices among the PDs using a variety of samples and assessment instruments provided by nine published studies. The PD matrices were rotated to a least squares fit to the target matrices generated by the alternative dimensional models of personality offered by (a) Widiger et al. (1994; FFM), (b) Millon and Davis (1996), (c) Torgersen and Alnaes (1989), (d) APA (1987; the cluster arrangement of the PDs in *DSM-III-R*), (e) Kiesler (1996) and Wiggins (1982; the interpersonal circumplex), and (f) Cloninger (1987b; Cloninger & Svrakic, 1994; the three-factor and seven-factor models). As indicated by O'Connor and Dyce (1998), their analyses were not exploratory searches of data sets, obtaining whatever factor analytic solution might capitalize on the particular measures and samples that were used. Instead, their confirmatory analyses

> were powerful, support-seeking attempts to find the view on a correlational structure that was most consistent with a given model. Failures to find support are thus more likely due to shortcomings with a model than to shortcomings with the method. (O'Connor & Dyce, 1998, p. 14)

Their study was a testing of alternative explanations for the covariations among the PDs obtained empirically in many independent studies. "The highest and most consistent levels of fit were obtained for the five-factor model" (p. 14), along with Cloninger and Svrakic's seven-factor model. A further discussion of their research is provided in chapter 14 (this volume).

Negative Conclusions
There have been a few studies in which the authors have emphasized the failure of the FFM to adequately account for PD symptomatology. Each of these studies are discussed in turn.

Yeung, Lyons, Waternaux, Faraone, and Tsuang (1993) administered a modified version of the NEO-FFI to 224 first degree relatives of patients. The NEO-FFI was altered to a more simplified true-false format to conform to other questionnaires completed by the respondents. The respondents had been given the SIDP 2.27 years earlier. Only a small minority of the sample met the criteria at that time for each PD (e.g., no AVD, three dependent, one paranoid, and four ATS), with the exception of passive–aggressive. "Results . . . suggest that the five personality factors can explain some important features of every personality disorder, since all personality disorders are related to one or more of the five factors" (Yeung et al., 1993, p. 232). However, the correlations were low; Yeung et al. suggested that "the low correlations between personality disorder scales and five-factor scales may imply that these two scales are measuring different aspects of the individuals" (p. 233). "It seems that the five personality factors describe important features of *DSM-III* personality disorders, but are not sufficient to completely explain their characteristics" (p. 227). However, the lower correlations obtained in this study as compared with the prior research are readily attributed to the limited range of SIDP data obtained over 2 years prior to the administration of the NEO-FFI (which is a 60-item shortened version of the 240-item NEO-PI-R that measures all 30 facets). The 2-year test–retest reliability of SIPD diagnoses of people who originally provided only a few marginal elevations on the PD scales would represent a substantial limitation for researchers attempting to identify the actual relationship of the FFM to PD symptomatology.

Zweig-Frank and Paris (1995) conducted a comparable study. They obtained *DSM-III-R* PD diagnoses on 150 female patients, 78 of whom had met the *DSM-III-R* criteria for BDL. Two years after this original study, they were able to find 71 of the original sample, 59 of whom agreed to complete the NEO-PI-R. Twenty-nine of the 59 participants in the follow-up study had been diagnosed with BDL 2 years earlier; the others had been diagnosed with other PDs. Zweig-Frank and Paris (1995) found only a few marginal differences between the 29 patients previously diagnosed with BDL and the 30 patients previously not diagnosed with BDL; they concluded that there were "few overall differences on the five factors between borderline and nonborderline patients" (p. 525). Paris (1998) argued elsewhere that "the best way of understanding [PDs] is as amplifications of normal personality traits" (p. 289). Zweig-Frank and Paris acknowledged that their particular results were inconsistent with the studies by Clarkin et al. (1993), Soldz et al. (1993), and Trull (1992). They suggested that the inconsistent nature of their findings "is accounted for by our methodology, which compared only those patients with a narrowly and categorically defined diagnosis of borderline personality disorder, as opposed to using dimensional scores" (Zweig-Frank & Paris, 1995, p. 525). They indicated that there would probably have been a significant correlation between the extent of BDL symptomatology and NEO-PI-R scores, but they were concerned instead with "the question as to whether or not the FFM could actually discriminate borderline personality disorder cases from cases with [other] personality disorders, and the results here indicate that such a discrimination is not readily made" (p. 525).

Nonetheless, the failure of Zweig-Frank and Paris (1995) to find any differences for their patients with BDL is readily attributed to the low test-retest reliability of their categorical diagnoses (Bronisch & Mombour, 1998; McDavid & Pilkonis, 1996). Paris, Brown, and Nowlis (1987) themselves reported a considerable change in BDL diagnoses across time, with 75 of their patients with BDL no longer meeting the diagnostic criteria for the disorder at their subsequent follow-up. It is possible that there were few meaningful differences remaining between the two categorically distinguished groups of BDL and "nonborderline" PD 2 years after they had been originally diagnosed (and subsequently treated). Regrettably, the authors did not attempt to confirm that the categorical distinctions were still valid 2 years later when they administered the NEO-PI-R.

Clark (1993b) administered the NEO-FFI, SNAP, and SIDP-R to 82 psychiatric patients. Each of the *DSM-III-R* PD scales correlated significantly with a NEO-FFI scale, but the correlations were in some

instances marginal and certainly lower than those reported in other studies. For example, the correlation of NEO-FFI N with SIPD-R BDL was only .09 ($r < .05$). In addition, the SNAP accounted for additional variance in PD symptomatology after the variance accounted for by the NEO-FFI was removed for seven SIDP-R PD scales. Clark (1993b) concluded that

> the five-factor model of personality has much to recommend it as a higher order structural model [, but] it may be inadequate for the clinical assessment of personality disorder because the characterizations it provides are too broad. . . . Moreover, empirical relations between personality pathology and at least one current measure of the five-factor model were low to moderate. (p. 104)

However, Clark's findings are clearly limited by two considerations: (a) criterion contamination and (b) reliance on a measure of the FFM (NEO-FFI) that was substantially less sensitive than the measure she used to assess her alternative dimensional model (SNAP). The methodology was similar to comparing the validity of the 30 facet scales of the NEO-PI-R with the three domain scales of the SNAP to provide specific or differentiated descriptions of the PDs. With respect to the issue of criterion contamination, it would be difficult for any instrument to outperform the SNAP in predicting PD symptomatology, given that the SNAP scales include items intended to represent explicitly the *DSM-III-R* PD diagnostic criteria in a manner comparable with the PDQ-R (Widiger & Costa, 1994). In any case, Clark's subsequent research and conclusions have been more supportive of the FFM (i.e., Clark & Livesley, 1994; Clark et al., 1994, 1996; also see chapter 10, this volume).

Coolidge et al. (1994) administered the NEO-PI and the Coolidge Axis II Inventory (CATI; Coolidge & Merwin, 1992) to 180 college students. Significant and substantial correlations were obtained for the NEO-PI domain scales with each of the CATI PD scales that were consistent with the predictions of Widiger et al. (1994). For example, ATS obtained significant correlations with antagonism ($r = .59$)

and low Conscientiousness ($r = -.38$), histrionic correlated significantly with Extraversion ($r = .46$) and marginally with N ($r = .29$), narcissistic correlated significantly with N ($r = .45$) and antagonism ($r = .34$), AVD correlated with N ($r = .58$) and introversion ($r = .66$), and schizoid correlated with low N ($r = -.41$) and introversion ($r = .32$).

Coolidge et al. (1994), nevertheless, argued that the results indicated at best "a limited usefulness of the five-factor model in the understanding of personality disorders" (p. 11). For example, they argued that the correlations were primarily with N, with less contribution from the other domains, despite the apparent contributions by the other domains as indicated in the summary above of just some of their results. Their rejection of the FFM was based largely on an assumption that FFM N should not be more highly correlated with the CATI PD scales than other domains of the FFM. "The name [Big Five] itself suggests that all five factors are of relatively equal weight in terms of their ability to explain the personality disorders" (p. 18). However, this is not in fact a meaningful assumption or requirement (Widiger & Costa, 1994). There is no compelling reason that the domains of normal personality functioning should have equivalent implications for maladaptivity. PDs can be maladaptive variants of common personality traits without being equally related to all personality traits.

Coolidge et al. (1994) also questioned whether N is a single domain of personality: "If neuroticism must be broken down into these six disparate concepts, then it is not useful to conceive of them as facets of a single factor except in the most figurative sense" (p. 18). They further suggested that two of the facets of N, vulnerability and self-consciousness, are not relevant to the *DSM-III-R* (or *DSM-IV*) PDs because "vulnerability and self-consciousness are not listed as diagnostic entities or symptoms" (p. 18) for any of the *DSM-III-R* PDs. These objections to the FFM understanding of the PDs are well discussed elsewhere (Costa & McCrae, 1995a; Widiger et al., 1994). In the end, the supportive data they obtained should perhaps speak for themselves.

Ramanaiah and Sharpe (1998) subsequently attempted to replicate the findings of Coolidge et al. (1994) in a comparable sample of 220 college stu-dents. Ramanaiah and Sharpe addressed in particular the absence of substantial loadings of the CATI on the final two of the five canonical variates extracted by Coolidge et al. Ramanaiah and Sharpe suggested that their absence was due in large part to the decision of Coolidge et al. not to rotate the structural loadings from the canonical correlation analyses to obtain a simple structure. Ramanaiah and Sharpe replicated the bivariate correlations obtained by Coolidge et al., even though they used the NEO-FFI rather than the NEO-PI-R. More importantly, the rotated canonical structure coefficients supported a more distinct and differentiated association of the CATI with each of the domains of FFM. Ramanaiah and Sharpe (1998) concluded that

> the present study supported the hypothesis that the results of the Coolidge et al. (1994) study might be attributed to the fact that the results of their canonical correlation analysis were not rotated to a simple structure and meaningful canonical variate pairs. (p. 952)

They also concluded more generally that "the results also supported the generality and comprehensiveness of the five-factor model for describing the structure of the Coolidge Axis II Inventory personality disorder scales" (p. 952).

Svrakic, Whitehead, Przybeck, and Cloninger (1993) administered the NEO-PI, the Temperament and Character Inventory (TCI; Cloninger, Svrakic, & Przybeck, 1993), and the SIDP-R to 136 psychiatric inpatients and compared the ability of the TCI and the NEO-PI to account for the total number of PD diagnostic criteria. "The TCI accounted for more of the personality-specific variance in number of PD symptoms than did the NEO (18% vs 11%)" (Svrakic et al., 1993, p. 996). Svrakic et al. concluded that "low self-directedness and cooperativeness are core features of all PDs and are validly measured by the seven-factor TCI but not the five-factor [NEO-PI]" (p. 991).

Ball et al. (1997) attempted to replicate the results of Svrakic et al. (1993) in a sample of 370 substance-dependent patients (188 outpatients, 182 inpatients) diagnosed with PDs using the SCID-II. Ball et al.'s study is particularly intriguing because they were independent researchers who administered the complete TCI but only the abbreviated NEO-FFI. They were anticipating much greater success with the TCI, given its original development for and application within substance-dependence populations (Cloninger, 1987a). Ball et al. (1997), however, reported that the NEO-FFI outperformed the TCI across all of their analyses: "The proportion of variance accounted for in all personality disorders was higher for the NEO than the TCI scales with NEO neuroticism, extraversion, and agreeableness being consistently stronger predictors across several disorders than the TCI dimensions" (p. 549). "The NEO dimensions were related to specific personality disorders as predicted, and most disorders were associated with a unique pattern of scores" (p. 550). TCI scales did correlate with personality disorder symptomatology, but the "results did not support most predictions made for the TCI" (p. 545). They concluded that "our study indicates that the TCI should not be used to screen or diagnose personality disorders in substance abusers" (p. 551). Further details and discussion of their study is provided in chapter 11 (this volume).

CONCLUSION

It is evident from the review above that a substantial amount of research on the relationship of the FFM to PD symptomatology has been published since the original review by Trull and McCrae (1994). In addition, it is also apparent that much of this research indicates strong support for understanding PD symptomatology as maladaptive variants of the personality traits included with the FFM. Further research needs to be conducted. For example, we expect future FFM research to provide a greater emphasis on the facets or even more specific personality traits covered within the broad domains of the FFM. Research confined to the broad domains will continue to be highly informative, indicating, for example, how a particular PD can be understood within the broad context of personality functioning provided by the five domains of the FFM. Nevertheless, the differentiation among and within individual PDs is often most informed by a more differentiated and specific assessment of FFM traits and facets.

We also expect researchers in the future to be concerned with further assessments of the convergent, discriminant, and predictive validity of alternative dimensional and categorical models of personality. The FFM is not the only dimensional model of PDs; this second edition of the text includes discussions of many of the more prominent alternative models. Research concerned with their convergence to the FFM and comparisons of their validity in predicting external criteria or outcomes will have considerable value and importance. In addition, we would encourage not only research on the relative merits of each alternative perspective but also research on the convergence, compatibility, and integration of alternative perspectives. Many of the previous studies focused on which alternative model is more valid or informative than the other. Such research has substantial importance. However, there is often more in common among the alternative dimensional models than there are differences between or distinct advantages among them. An important task for the future is to show how these commonalities can be integrated conceptually and clinically.

Finally, we also expect researchers in the future to be concerned with the clinical applications of the FFM. Stone (chapter 24), Sanderson and Clarkin (chapter 21), MacKenzie (chapter 22), Harkness and McNulty (chapter 23, all this volume), and others illustrate well the utility of the FFM for clinical practice. The clinical application of the FFM has been informed by a substantial body of research (Harkness & Lilienfeld, 1997; Piedmont, 1998) that we expect will expand considerably over the third wave of FFM research, as clinicians and researchers continue to develop their understanding of PDs as maladaptive variants of the personality traits included within the FFM.

References

Alden, L. E., Wiggins, J. S., & Pincus, A. L. (1990). Construction of circumplex scales for the Inventory of Interpersonal Problems. *Journal of Personality Assessment, 55,* 521–536.

Alterman, A. I., & Cacciola, J. S. (1991). The antisocial personality disorder diagnosis in substance abusers: Problems and issues. *Journal of Nervous and Mental Disease, 179,* 401–409.

American Psychiatric Association. (1980). *Diagnostic and statistical manual of mental disorders* (3rd ed.). Washington, DC: Author.

American Psychiatric Association. (1987). *Diagnostic and statistical manual of mental disorders* (3rd ed., rev.). Washington, DC: Author.

American Psychiatric Association. (1994). *Diagnostic and statistical manual of mental disorders* (4th ed.). Washington, DC: Author.

Axelrod, S. R., Widiger, T. A., Trull, T. J., & Corbitt, E. M. (1977). Relationships of five-factor model antagonism facets with personality disorder symptomatology. *Journal of Personality Assessment, 67*, 297–313.

Bagby, R. M., Bindseil, K. D., Schuller, D. R., Rector, N. A., Young, L. T., Cooke, R. G., Seeman, M. V., McCay, E. A., & Joffe, R. T. (1997). Relationship between the five-factor model of personality and unipolar, bipolar, and schizophrenic patients. *Psychiatry Research, 70*, 83–94.

Bagby, R. M., Gilchrist, E. J., Rector, N. A., Joffe, R. T., & Levitt, A. (in press). The stability and validity of the sociotropy and autonomy personality dimensions. *Cognitive Therapy and Research.*

Bagby, R. M., Kennedy, S. H., Dickens, S. E., Minifie, C. E., & Schuller, D. R. (1997). Personality and symptom profiles of the angry hostile depressed patient. *Journal of Affective Disorders, 45*, 155–160.

Bagby, R. M., Taylor, G. J., & Parker, J. D. A. (1994). The twenty-item Toronto Alexithymia Scale—II: Convergent, discriminant, and concurrent validity. *Journal of Psychosomatic Research, 38*, 23–32.

Bagby, R. M., Young, L. T., Schuller, D. R., Bindseil, K. D., Cooke, R. G., Dickens, S. E., Levitt, A. J., & Joffe, R. T. (1996). Bipolar disorder, unipolar depression, and the five-factor model of personality. *Journal of Affective Disorders, 41*, 25–32.

Ball, S. A., Tennen, H., Poling, J. C., Kranzler, H. R., & Rounsaville, B. J. (1997). Personality, temperament, and character dimensions and the *DSM-IV* personality disorders in substance abusers. *Journal of Abnormal Psychology, 106*, 545–553.

Beck, A. T. (1983). Cognitive therapy of depression: New perspectives. In P. J. Clayton & J. E. Barrett (Eds.), *Treatment of depression: Old controversies and new approaches* (pp. 265–290). New York: Raven Press.

Benjamin, L. S. (1993a). Dimensional, categorical, or hybrid analysis of personality: A response to Widiger's proposal. *Psychological Inquiry, 4*, 91–94.

Benjamin, L. S. (1993b). *Interpersonal diagnosis and treatment of personality disorders.* New York: Guilford.

Blais, M. A. (1997). Clinician ratings of the five-factor model of personality and the *DSM-IV* personality disorders. *Journal of Nervous and Mental Disease, 185*, 388–393.

Blatt, S. J., & Zuroff, D. (1992). Interpersonal relatedness and self-definition: Two prototypes for depression. *Clinical Psychology Review, 12*, 527–562.

Block, J. (1961). *The Q-sort method in personality assessment and psychiatric research.* Springfield, IL: Charles C Thomas.

Block, J. (1995). A contrarian view of the five-factor approach to personality description. *Psychological Bulletin, 117*, 187–215.

Block, J., & Block, J. H. (1980). *The California Child Q-Set.* Palo Alto, CA: Consulting Psychologists Press.

Block, J. H., & Block, J. (1980). The role of ego-control and ego-resiliency in the organization of behavior. In W. A. Collins (Ed.), *Minnesota Symposium on Child Psychology* (Vol. 13, pp. 39–101). Hillsdale, NJ: Erlbaum.

Bond, M., Gardner, S., Christian, J., & Sigal, J. J. (1983). Empirical study of self-rated defense styles. *Archives of General Psychiatry, 40*, 333–338.

Bradlee, P. M., & Emmons, R. A. (1992). Locating narcissism within the interpersonal circumplex and the five-factor model. *Personality and Individual Differences, 13*, 821–830.

Briggs, S. R. (1992). Assessing the five-factor model of personality description. *Journal of Personality, 60*, 253–293.

Bronisch, T., & Mombour, W. (1998). The modern assessment of personality disorders: Part 2. Reliability and validity of personality disorders. *Psychopathology, 31*, 293–301.

Brooner, R. K., Herbst, J. H., Schmidt, C. W., Bigelow, G. E., & Costa, P. T., Jr. (1993). Antisocial personality disorder among drug abusers: Relations to other personality diagnoses and the five-factor model of personality. *Journal of Nervous and Mental Disease, 181*, 313–319.

Buss, A. H., & Durkee, A. (1957). An inventory for assessing different kinds of hostility. *Journal of Consulting Psychology, 21*, 343–348.

Cappeliez, P. (1993). The relationship between Beck's concepts of sociotropy and autonomy and the NEO Personality Inventory. *British Journal of Clinical Psychology, 32*, 78–80.

Clark, L. A. (1993a). *Manual for the Schedule for Nonadaptive and Adaptive Personality (SNAP)*. Minneapolis: University of Minnesota Press.

Clark, L. A. (1993b). Personality disorder diagnosis: Limitations of the five-factor model. *Psychological Inquiry, 4*, 100–104.

Clark, L. A., & Livesley, W. J. (1994). Two approaches to identifying the dimensions of personality disorder: Convergence on the five-factor model. In P. T. Costa, Jr., & T. A. Widiger (Eds.), *Personality disorders and the five-factor model of personality* (pp. 261–277). Washington, DC: American Psychological Association.

Clark, L. A., Livesley, W. J., Schroeder, M. L., & Irish, S. L. (1996). Convergence of two systems for assessing personality disorder. *Psychological Assessment, 8*, 294–303.

Clark, L. A., McEwen, J. L., Collard, L., & Hickok, L. G. (1993). Symptoms and traits of personality disorder: Two new methods for their assessment. *Psychological Assessment, 5*, 81–91.

Clark, L. A., Vorhies, L., & McEwen, J. L. (1994). Personality disorder symptomatology from the five-factor model perspective. In P. T. Costa, Jr., & T. A. Widiger (Eds.), *Personality disorders and the five-factor model of personality* (pp. 95–116). Washington, DC: American Psychological Association.

Clarkin, J. F., Hull, J. W., Cantor, J., & Sanderson, C. (1993). Borderline personality disorder and personality traits: A comparison of SCID-II BPD and NEO-PI. *Psychological Assessment, 5*, 472–476.

Clarkin, J. F., Widiger, T. A., Frances, A., Hurt, S., & Gilmore, M. (1983). Prototypic typology and the borderline personality disorder. *Journal of Abnormal Psychology, 92*, 263–275.

Cloninger, C. R. (1987a). Neurogenetic adaptive mechanisms in alcoholism. *Science, 236*, 410–436.

Cloninger, C. R. (1987b). A systematic method for clinical description and classification of personality variants. *Archives of General Psychiatry, 44*, 573–588.

Cloninger, C. R., & Svrakic, D. M. (1994). Differentiating normal and deviant personality by the seven-factor personality model. In S. Strack & M. Lorr (Eds.), *Differentiating normal and abnormal personality* (pp. 40–64). New York: Springer.

Cloninger, C. R., Svrakic, D. M., & Przybeck, T. R. (1993). A psychobiological model of temperament and character. *Archives of General Psychiatry, 50*, 975–990.

Coolidge, F. L., Becker, L. A., Dirito, D. C., Durham, R. L., Kinlaw, M. M., & Philbrick, P. B. (1994). On the relationship of the five-factor personality model to personality disorders: Four reservations. *Psychological Reports, 75*, 11–21.

Coolidge, F. L., & Merwin, M. M. (1992). Reliability and validity of the Coolidge Axis II Inventory: A new inventory for the assessment of personality disorders. *Journal of Personality Assessment, 59*, 223–238.

Costa, P. T., Jr., & McCrae, R. R. (1985). *NEO Personality Inventory (NEO-PI) professional manual*. Odessa, FL: Psychological Assessment Resources.

Costa, P. T., Jr., & McCrae, R. R. (1988). From catalogue to classification: Murray's needs and the five-factor model. *Journal of Personality and Social Psychology, 55*, 258–265.

Costa, P. T., Jr., & McCrae, R. R. (1990). Personality disorders and the five-factor model of personality. *Journal of Personality Disorders, 4*, 362–371.

Costa, P. T., Jr., & McCrae, R. R. (1992a). *Revised NEO Personality Inventory (NEO-PI-R) and NEO Five-Factor Inventory (NEO-FFI) professional manual*. Odessa, FL: Psychological Assessment Resources.

Costa, P. T., Jr., & McCrae, R. R. (1992b). Trait psychology comes of age. In T. B. Sonderegger (Ed.), *Nebraska Symposium on Motivation: Psychology and aging* (pp. 169–204). Lincoln: University of Nebraska Press.

Costa, P. T., Jr., & McCrae, R. R. (1995a). Domains and facets: Hierarchical personality assessment using the Revised NEO Personality Inventory. *Journal of Personality Assessment, 64*, 21–50.

Costa, P. T., Jr., & McCrae, R. R. (1995b). Solid ground in the wetlands of personality: A reply to Block. *Psychological Bulletin, 117*, 216–220.

Costa, P. T., Jr., Zonderman, A. B., McCrae, R. R., & Williams, R. B. (1985). Content and comprehensiveness in the MMPI: An item factor analysis in a normal adult sample. *Journal of Personality and Social Psychology, 48*, 925–933.

Digman, J. M. (1990). Personality structure: Emergence of the five-factor model. *Annual Review of Psychology, 41*, 417–440.

Duberstein, P. R., Seidlitz, L., Lyness, J. M., & Conwell, Y. (1999). Dimensional measures and the five-factor model: Clinical implications and research directions. In E. Rosowsky, R. C. Abrams, & R. A. Zweig (Eds.), *Personality disorders in older adults: Emerging issues in diagnosis and treatment* (pp. 95–117). Hillsdale, NJ: Erlbaum.

Duijsens, I., & Diekstra, R. F. W. (1996). *DSM-III-R* and *ICD-10* personality disorders and their relationship with the Big Five dimensions of personality. *Personality and Individual Differences, 21,* 119–133.

Dyce, J. A., & O'Connor, B. P. (1998). Personality disorders and the five-factor model: A test of facet-level predictions. *Journal of Personality Disorders, 12,* 31–45.

Fagan, P. J., Wise, T. N., Schmidt, C. W., Ponticas, Y., Marshall, R. D., & Costa, P. T., Jr. (1991). A comparison of five-factor personality dimensions in males with sexual dysfunction and males with paraphilia. *Journal of Personality Assessment, 57,* 434–448.

First, M. B., Spitzer, R. L., Gibbon, M., & Williams, J. B. W. (1995). The Structured Clinical Interview for *DSM-III-R* Personality Disorders (SCID-II): Part I. Description. *Journal of Personality Disorders, 9,* 83–91.

Goldberg, L. R. (1992). The development of markers of the Big-Five factor structure. *Psychological Assessment, 4,* 26–42.

Gunderson, J. G., Phillips, K. A., Triebwasser, J., & Hirschfeld, R. M. A. (1994). The Diagnostic Interview for Depressive Personality Disorder. *American Journal of Psychiatry, 151,* 1300–1304.

Hare, R. D. (1991). *The Revised Psychopathy Checklist.* Toronto, Ontario, Canada: Multi-Health Systems.

Harkness, A. R. (1992). Fundamental topics in the personality disorders: Candidate trait dimensions from lower regions of the hierarchy. *Psychological Assessment, 4,* 251–259.

Harkness, A. R., & Lilienfeld, S. O. (1997). Individual differences science for treatment planning: Personality traits. *Psychological Assessment, 9,* 349–360.

Harkness, A. R., McNulty, J. L., & Ben-Porath, Y. S. (1995). The Personality Psychopathology Five (PSY-5): Constructs and MMPI-2 scales. *Psychological Assessment, 7,* 104–114.

Harpur, T. J., Hart, S. D., & Hare, R. D. (1994). Personality of the psychopath. In P. T. Costa, Jr., & T. A. Widiger (Eds.), *Personality disorders and the five-factor model of personality* (pp. 149–173). Washington, DC: American Psychological Association.

Hart, S. D., & Hare, R. D. (1994). Psychopathy and the Big 5: Correlations between observers' ratings of normal and pathological personality. *Journal of Personality Disorders, 8,* 32–40.

Heaven, P. C. L. (1996). Personality and self-reported delinquency: Analysis of the "Big Five"

personality dimensions. *Personality and Individual Differences, 20,* 47–54.

Huey, S. J., & Weisz, J. R. (1997). Ego control, ego resiliency, and the five-factor model as predictors of behavioral and emotional problems in clinic-referred children and adolescents. *Journal of Abnormal Psychology, 106,* 404–415.

Hyer, L., Brawell, L., Albrecht, B., Boyd, S., Boudewyns, P., & Talbert, S. (1994). Relationship of NEO-PI to personality styles and severity of trauma in chronic PTSD victims. *Journal of Clinical Psychology, 50,* 699–707.

Hyler, S. E. (1994). *Personality Diagnostic Questionnaire—4 (PDQ-4).* Unpublished test. New York State Psychiatric Institute, New York.

Hyler, S. E., & Rieder, R. O. (1987). *Personality Diagnostic Questionnaire—Revised (PDQ-R).* New York: New York State Psychiatric Institute.

Jackson, D. N. (1984). *Personality Research Form manual* (3rd ed.). Port Huron, MI: Research Psychologists Press.

John, O. P. (1995). *Big Five Inventory.* Berkeley: University of California, Institute of Personality and Social Research.

John, O. P., Caspi, A., Robins, R. W., Moffitt, T. E., & Stouthamer-Loeber, M. (1994). The "little five": Exploring the nomological network of the five-factor model of personality in adolescent boys. *Child Development, 65,* 160–178.

John, O. P., & Srivastava, S. (1999). The Big Five trait taxonomy: History, measurement, and theoretical perspectives. In L. A. Pervin & O. P. John (Eds.), *Handbook of personality: Theory and research* (2nd ed., pp. 102–138). New York: Guilford.

Kiesler, D. J. (1996). *Contemporary interpersonal theory and research: Personality, psychopathology, and psychotherapy.* New York: Wiley.

Lehne, G. K. (1994). The NEO-PI and the MCMI in the forensic evaluation of sex offenders. In P. T. Costa, Jr., & T. A. Widiger (Eds.), *Personality disorders and the five-factor model of personality* (pp. 175–188). Washington, DC: American Psychological Association.

Lenzenweger, M. F. (1999). Stability and change in personality disorder features: The Longitudinal Study of Personality Disorders. *Archives of General Psychiatry, 56,* 1009–1015.

Lenzenweger, M. F., Loranger, A. W., Korfine, L., & Neff, C. (1997). Detecting personality disorders in a nonclinical population: Application of a 2-stage procedure for case identification. *Archives of General Psychiatry, 54,* 345–351.

Levenson, M., Kiehl, K., & Fitzpatrick, C. (1995). Assessing psychopathic attributes in a noninstitutionalized population. *Journal of Personality and Social Psychology, 68,* 151–158.

Livesley, W. J., Jackson, D. N., & Schroeder, M. L. (1989). A study of the factorial structure of personality pathology. *Journal of Personality Disorders, 3,* 292–306.

Livesley, W. J., Jackson, D. N., & Schroeder, M. L. (1992). Factorial structure of traits delineating personality disorders in clinical and general population samples. *Journal of Abnormal Psychology, 101,* 432–440.

Livesley, W. J., & Jang, K. L. (2000). Toward an empirically based classification of personality disorder. *Journal of Personality Disorders, 14,* 137–151.

Livesley, W. J., Jang, K. L., & Vernon, P. A. (1998). Phenotypic and genetic structure of traits delineating personality disorder. *Archives of General Psychiatry, 55,* 941–948.

Luminet, O., Bagby, R. M., Wagner, H., Taylor, G. J., & Parker, J. D. A. (1999). Relation between alexithymia and the five-factor model of personality: A facet-level analysis. *Journal of Personality Assessment, 73,* 345–358.

Loranger, A. W. (1988). *Personality Disorder Examination (PDE) manual.* Yonkers, NY: DV Communications.

Lynam, D. R., Whiteside, S., & Jones, S. (1999). Self-reported psychopathy: A validation study. *Journal of Personality Assessment, 73,* 110–132.

Lyoo, K., Gunderson, J. G., & Phillips, K. A. (1998). Personality dimensions associated with depressive personality disorder. *Journal of Personality Disorders, 12,* 46–55.

McCrae, R. R., & Costa, P. T., Jr. (1989a). Reinterpreting the Myers–Briggs Type Indicator from the perspective of the five-factor model of personality. *Journal of Personality, 57,* 17–40.

McCrae, R. R., & Costa, P. T., Jr. (1989b). The structure of interpersonal traits: Wiggins' circumplex and the five-factor model. *Journal of Personality and Social Psychology, 56,* 586–595.

McCrae, R. R., & Costa, P. T., Jr. (1990). *Personality in adulthood.* New York: Guilford.

McCrae, R. R., & Costa, P. T., Jr. (1999). A five-factor theory of personality. In L. A. Pervin & O. P. John (Eds.), *Handbook of personality: Theory and research* (2nd ed., pp. 139–153). New York: Guilford.

McCrae, R. R., Costa, P. T., Jr., & Busch, C. M. (1986). Evaluating comprehensiveness in personality systems: The California Q-Set and the five-factor model. *Journal of Personality, 54,* 430–446.

McCrae, R. R., Costa, P. T., Jr., & Piedmont, R. L. (1993). Folk concepts, natural language, and psychological constructs: The California Psychological Inventory and the five-factor model. *Journal of Personality, 61,* 1–26.

McCrae, R. R., Yang, J., Costa, P. T., Jr., Dai, X., Yao, S., Cai, T., & Gao, B. (2001). Personality profiles and the prediction of categorical personality disorders. *Journal of Personality, 69,* 155–174.

McDavid, J. D., & Pilkonis, P. A. (1996). The stability of personality disorder diagnoses. *Journal of Personality Disorders, 10,* 1–15.

Miller, J. D., Lynam, D. R., Widiger, T. A., & Leukefeld, C. (2001). Personality disorders as extreme variants of common personality dimensions: Can the five-factor model adequately represent psychopathy? *Journal of Personality, 69,* 253–276.

Millon, T., & Davis, R. D. (1996). *Disorders of personality: DSM-IV and beyond.* New York: Wiley.

Millon, T., Millon, C., & Davis, R. (1994). *MCMI-III manual.* Minneapolis, MN: National Computer Systems.

Mongrain, M. (1993). Dependency and self-criticism located within the five-factor model of personality. *Personality and Individual Differences, 15,* 455–462.

Morey, L. C., Waugh, M. H., & Blashfield, R. K. (1985). MMPI scales for *DSM-III* personality disorders: Their derivation and correlates. *Journal of Personality Assessment, 49,* 245–251.

Nestadt, G., Eaton, W. W., Romanoski, A. J., Garrison, R., Folstein, M. F., & McHugh, P. R. (1994). Assessment of *DSM-III* personality structure in a general-population survey. *Comprehensive Psychiatry, 35,* 54–63.

O'Connor, B. P., & Dyce, J. A. (1998). A test of models of personality disorder configuration. *Journal of Abnormal Psychology, 107,* 3–16.

Paris, J. (1998). Psychotherapy for the personality disorders: Working with traits. *Bulletin of the Menninger Clinic, 62,* 287–297.

Paris, J., Brown, R., & Nowlis, D. (1987). Long-term follow-up of borderline patients in a general hospital. *Comprehensive Psychiatry, 28,* 530–535.

Pfohl, B., Blum, N., Zimmerman, M., & Stangl, D. (1989). *Structured Interview for DSM-III-R personality (SIDP-R).* Iowa City: University of Iowa Medical Center.

Piedmont, R. L. (1998). *The Revised NEO Personality*

Inventory: Clinical and research applications. New York: Plenum Press.

Pincus, A. L., & Gurtman, M. B. (1995). The three faces of interpersonal dependency: Structural analysis of self-report dependency measures. *Journal of Personality and Social Psychology, 69,* 744–758.

Pincus, A. L., & Ruiz, M. A. (1997). Parental representations and dimensions of personality functioning: Empirical relations and assessment implications. *Journal of Personality Assessment, 68,* 436–454.

Pukrop, R., Herpertz, S., Sass, H., & Steinmeyer, E. M. (1998). Personality and personality disorders: A facet theoretical analysis of the similarity relationships. *Journal of Personality Disorders, 12,* 226–246.

Quirk, S. W., & McCormick, R. A. (1998). Personality subtypes, coping styles, symptom correlates, and substance of choice among a cohort of substance abusers. *Assessment, 5,* 157–170.

Ramanaiah, N. V., Detwiler, F. R. J., & Byravan, A. (1994). Revised NEO Personality Inventory profiles of narcissistic and nonnarcissistic people. *Psychological Reports, 75,* 512–514.

Ramanaiah, N. V., & Sharpe, J. P. (1998). Structure of the Coolidge Axis II Inventory personality disorder scales from the five-factor model perspective. *Psychological Reports, 83,* 947–952.

Raskin, R. N., & Terry, H. (1988). A principal-components analysis of the Narcissistic Personality Inventory and further evidence of its construct validity. *Journal of Personality and Social Psychology, 54,* 890–902.

Robins, L. N., & Regier, D. A. (Eds.). (1991). *Psychiatric disorders in America: The Epidemiologic Catchment Area Study.* New York: Free Press.

Robins, R. W., John, O. P., & Caspi, A. (1994). Major dimensions of personality in early adolescence: The Big Five and beyond. In C. F. Halverson, G. A. Kohnstamm, & R. P. Martin (Eds.), *The developing structure of temperament and personality from infancy to adulthood* (pp. 267–291). Hillsdale, NJ: Erlbaum.

Saucier, G. (1994). Mini-markers: A brief version of Goldberg's unipolar Big-Five markers. *Journal of Personality Assessment, 63,* 506–516.

Schroeder, M. L., Wormworth, J. A., & Livesley, W. J. (1992). Dimensions of personality disorder and their relationship to the Big Five dimensions of personality. *Psychological Assessment, 4,* 47–53.

Schroeder, M. L., Wormworth, J. A., & Livesley, W. J. (1994). Dimensions of personality disorder

and the five-factor model of personality. In P. T. Costa, Jr., & T. A. Widiger (Eds.), *Personality disorders and the five-factor model of personality* (pp. 117–127). Washington, DC: American Psychological Association.

Shopshire, M. S., & Craik, K. H. (1994). The five factor model of personality and the *DSM-III-R* personality disorders: Correspondence and differentiation. *Journal of Personality Disorders, 8,* 41–52.

Soldz, S., Budman, S., Demby, A., & Merry, J. (1993). Representation of personality disorders in circumplex and five-factor space: Explorations with a clinical sample. *Psychological Assessment, 5,* 356–370.

Soldz, S., Budman, S. Demby, A., & Merry, J. (1995). The relation of defensive style to personality pathology and the Big Five personality factors. *Journal of Personality Disorders, 9,* 356–370.

Spitzer, R. L., Williams, J. B. W., Gibbon, M., & First, M. B. (1990). *User's guide for the Structured Clinical Interview for* DSM-III-R *(SCID).* Washington, DC: American Psychiatric Press.

Strack, S. (1987). Development and validation of an adjective checklist to assess the Millon personality types in a normal population. *Journal of Personality Assessment, 51,* 572–587.

Svrakic, D. M., Whitehead, C., Przybeck, T. R., & Cloninger, C. R. (1993). Differential diagnosis of personality disorders by the seven-factor model of temperament and character. *Archives of General Psychiatry, 50,* 991–999.

Taylor, G. J., Bagby, R. M., & Parker, J. D. A. (1997). *Disorders of affect regulation: Alexithymia in medical and psychiatric illness.* Madison, CT: International Universities Press.

Torgersen, S., & Alnaes, R. (1989). Localizing *DSM-III* personality disorders in three-dimensional structural space. *Journal of Personality Disorders, 3,* 274–281.

Trapnell, P. D., & Wiggins, J. S. (1990). Extension of the Interpersonal Adjective Scales to include the Big Five dimensions of personality. *Journal of Personality and Social Psychology, 59,* 781–790.

Trull, T. J. (1992). *DSM-III-R* personality disorders and the five-factor model of personality: An empirical comparison. *Journal of Abnormal Psychology, 101,* 553–560.

Trull, T. J. (1995). Borderline personality disorder features in nonclinical young adults: I. Identification and validation. *Psychological Assessment, 7,* 33–41.

Trull, T. J., & McCrae, R. R. (1994). A five-factor

perspective on personality disorder research. In P. T. Costa, Jr., & T. A. Widiger (Eds.), *Personality disorders and the five-factor model of personality* (pp. 59–71). Washington, DC: American Psychological Association.

Trull, T. J., & Sher, K. J. (1994). Relationship between the five-factor model of personality and Axis I disorders in a nonclinical sample. *Journal of Abnormal Psychology, 103,* 350–360.

Trull, T. J., Useda, D., Conforti, K., & Doan, B.-T. (1997). Borderline personality disorder features in nonclinical young adults: 2. Two-year outcome. *Journal of Abnormal Psychology, 106,* 307–314.

Trull, T. J., Useda, J. D., Costa, P. T., Jr., & McCrae, R. R. (1995). Comparison of the MMPI-2 Personality Psychopathology Five (PSY-5), the NEO-PI, and the NEO-PI-R. *Psychological Assessment, 7,* 508–516.

Trull, T. J., & Widiger, T. A. (1997). *Structured Interview for the Five-Factor Model of Personality.* Odessa, FL: Psychological Assessment Resources.

Trull, T. J., Widiger, T. A., & Burr, R. (2001). A structured interview for the assessment of the five-factor model of personality: 2. Facet-level relations to the Axis II personality disorders. *Journal of Personality, 69,* 175–198.

Trull, T. J., Widiger, T. A., Useda, J. D., Holcomb, J., Doan, D.-T., Axelrod, S. R., Stern, B. L., & Gershuny, B. S. (1998). A structured interview for the assessment of the five-factor model of personality. *Psychological Assessment, 10,* 229–240.

von Zerssen, D. (1994). Personlichkeitzuge als Vulnerabilitatsindikatoren: Probleme ihrer Erfassung [Personality characteristics as indications of vulnerability: Problems with their determination]. *Fortschritte in Neurologie und Psychiatrie, 62,* 1–13.

Westen, D. (1995). A clinical–empirical model of personality: Life after the Mischelian Ice Age and the NEO-Lithic Era. *Journal of Personality, 63,* 495–524.

Westen, D. (1997). Divergences between clinical and research methods for assessing personality disorders: Implications for research and the evolution of Axis II. *American Journal of Psychiatry, 154,* 895–903.

Westen, D., Muderrisoglu, S., Shedler, J., Fowler, C., & Koren, D. (1997). Affect regulation and affective experience: Individual differences, group differences, and measurement using a Q-sort procedure. *Journal of Consulting and Clinical Psychology, 65,* 420–440.

Widiger, T. A. (1998). Four out of five ain't bad. *Archives of General Psychiatry, 55,* 865–866.

Widiger, T. A., & Costa, P. T., Jr. (1994). Personality and personality disorders. *Journal of Abnormal Psychology, 103,* 78–91.

Widiger, T., Frances, A., Harris, M., Jacobsberg, L., Fyer, M., & Manning, D. (1991). Comorbidity among Axis II disorders. In J. Oldham (Ed.), *Axis II: New perspectives on validity* (pp. 163–194). Washington, DC: American Psychiatric Press.

Widiger, T. A., & Lynam, D. R. (1998). Psychopathy from the perspective of the five-factor model of personality. In T. Millon, E. Simonsen, M. Birket-Smith, & R. D. Davis (Eds.), *Psychopathy: Antisocial, criminal, and violent behaviors* (pp. 171–187). New York: Guilford.

Widiger, T. A., Mangine, S., Corbitt, E. M., Ellis, C. G., & Thomas, G. V. (1995). *Personality Disorder Interview—IV: A semistructured interview for the assessment of personality disorders.* Odessa, FL: Psychological Assessment Resources.

Widiger, T. A., & Sanderson, C. J. (1995). Assessing personality disorders. In J. N. Butcher (Ed.), *Clinical personality assessment: Practical approaches* (pp. 380–394). New York: Oxford University Press.

Widiger, T. A., Trull, T. J., Clarkin, J. F., Sanderson, C., & Costa, P. T., Jr. (1994). A description of the *DSM-III-R* and *DSM-IV* personality disorders with the five-factor model of personality. In P. T. Costa, Jr., & T. A. Widiger (Eds.), *Personality disorders and the five-factor model of personality* (pp. 41–56). Washington, DC: American Psychological Association.

Wiggins, J. S. (1982). Circumplex models of interpersonal behavior in clinical psychology. In P. Kendall & J. Butcher (Eds.), *Handbook of research methods in clinical psychology* (pp. 183–221). New York: Wiley.

Wiggins, J. S., & Pincus, H. A. (1989). Conceptions of personality disorder and dimensions of personality. *Psychological Assessment, 1,* 305–316.

Wilberg, T., Urnes, O., Friis, S., Pedersen, G., & Karterud, S. (1999). Borderline and avoidant personality disorders and the five-factor model of personality: A comparison between *DSM-IV* diagnoses and NEO-PI-R. *Journal of Personality Disorders, 13,* 226–240.

Wise, T. N., & Mann, L. S. (1994). The relationship between somatosensory amplification, alexithymia, and neuroticism. *Journal of Psychosomatic Research, 38,* 515–521.

Wise, T. N., Mann, L. S., & Randell, P. (1995). The stability of alexithymia in depressed patients. *Psychopathology, 28,* 173–176.

Wise, T. N., Mann, L. S., & Shay, L. (1992). Alexithymia and the five-factor model of personality. *Comprehensive Psychiatry, 33,* 147–151.

World Health Organization. (1992). *The ICD-10 classification of mental and behavioural disorders: Clinical descriptions and diagnostic guidelines.* Geneva, Switzerland: Author.

Yeung, A. S., Lyons, M. J., Waternaux, C. M., Faraone, S. V., & Tsuang, M. T. (1993). The relationship between *DSM-III* personality disorders and the five-factor model of personality. *Comprehensive Psychiatry, 34,* 227–234.

Zuroff, D. C. (1994). Depressive personality styles and the five-factor model of personality. *Journal of Personality Assessment, 63,* 453–472.

Zweig-Frank, H., & Paris, J. (1995). The five-factor model of personality in borderline and nonborderline personality disorders. *Canadian Journal of Psychiatry, 40,* 523–526.

CHAPTER 6

A DESCRIPTION OF THE *DSM-IV* PERSONALITY DISORDERS WITH THE FIVE-FACTOR MODEL OF PERSONALITY

Thomas A. Widiger, Timothy J. Trull, John F. Clarkin, Cynthia Sanderson, and Paul T. Costa, Jr.

In this chapter, we provide a five-factor translation of the personality disorders within the fourth edition of the American Psychiatric Association's (APA) *Diagnostic and Statistical Manual of Mental Disorders* (*DSM-IV*; APA, 1994). Widiger, Costa, and McCrae in chapter 25 of this book present a four-step process for the diagnosis of a personality disorder solely from the perspective of the five-factor model (FFM) of personality. Many clinicians, however, are more familiar with the personality disorder diagnoses presented in the *DSM-IV*. In this chapter, we specify how each of the *DSM-IV* personality disorders can be translated as maladaptively extreme variants of the 30 facets of personality.

Table 6.1 presents a summary of our translations of each of the 10 *DSM-IV* personality disorders. These translations are based on the diagnostic criteria presented in *DSM-IV* (APA, 1994). In the first edition of this text (Widiger, Trull, Clarkin, Sanderson, & Costa, 1994), we used three sources of information to translate each of the disorders into high or low standing on the personality facets: (a) the diagnostic criteria, (b) associated features provided in the third edition, revised, of the *Diagnostic and Statistical Manual of Mental Disorders* (*DSM-III-R*; APA, 1987), and (c) clinical literature concerning each respective disorder. In this edition of the book, the hypotheses are confined solely to the diagnostic criteria sets for each disorder. The purpose of this change is to elucidate more clearly the source for the hypotheses and thereby remove the ambiguity provided by the inclusion of hypotheses based on associated features and clinical literature. These hypotheses can be tested at the level of the five broad domains; however, more adequate differentiation among prototypic cases of the personality disorders would be achieved by conducting studies at the level of the facets. It is also worth noting that adequate tests of the hypotheses provided in Table 6.1 should involve prototypic cases of each respective personality disorder. A representative sample of people with, for example, paranoid personality disorder (PAR) are high on angry hostility. Prototypic cases are at the very highest levels of this facet of Neuroticism, but any particular sample of people with PAR may in fact fail to include this component of Neuroticism, given the polythetic (optional) nature of the *DSM-IV* diagnostic criteria (i.e., not all of the diagnostic criteria are in fact required).

PARANOID PERSONALITY DISORDER

PAR "is a pattern of pervasive distrust and suspiciousness of others such that their motives are interpreted as malevolent" (APA, 1994, p. 634). Individuals with PAR tend to be suspicious, mistrustful, hypervigilant, and argumentative (Bernstein, Useda, & Siever, 1993). PAR is therefore characterized primarily by excessively low Agreeableness (antagonism), particularly on the facet of suspiciousness (low trust), which provides an explicit representation of the core feature of and first diagnostic criterion for this personality disorder (most of the personality disorder criteria sets are presented within *DSM-IV* in a descending order of diagnostic value; Widiger, Mangine, Corbitt, Ellis, & Thomas, 1995).

TABLE 6.1

DSM-IV Personality Disorders and the Five-Factor Model

NEO-PI-R domains and facets	PAR	SZD	SZT	ATS	BDL	HST	NAR	AVD	DEP	OBC
Neuroticism										
Anxiety			H		H			H	H	
Angry-hostility	H			H	H		H			
Depression					H	H		H		
Self-consciousness			H			H	H	H	H	
Impulsiveness					H					
Vulnerability					H			H	H	
Extraversion										
Warmth		L	L			H			H	
Gregariousness		L	L			H		L		
Assertiveness								L	L	H
Activity										
Excitement seeking				H		H		L		
Positive emotions		L	L			H				
Openness to Experience										
Fantasy			H			H	H			
Aesthetics										
Feelings		L				H				
Actions			H							
Ideas			H							
Values										L
Agreeableness										
Trust	L		L		L	H			H	
Straightforwardness	L			L						
Altruism				L			L		H	
Compliance	L			L	L				H	L
Modesty							L		H	
Tender mindedness				L			L			
Conscientiousness										
Competence					L					H
Order										H
Dutifulness				L						H
Achievement striving							H			H
Self-discipline				L						
Deliberation				L						

Note. NEO-PI-R = Revised NEO Personality Inventory. H, L = high, low, respectively, based on the fourth edition of the *Diagnostic and Statistical Manual of Mental Disorders* (*DSM-IV*; American Psychiatric Association, 1994) diagnostic criteria. Personality disorders: PAR = paranoid; SZD = schizoid; SZT = schizotypal; ATS = antisocial; BDL = borderline; HST = histrionic; NAR = narcissistic; AVD = avoidant; DEP = dependent; OBC = obsessive–compulsive.

PAR also includes the low Agreeableness facets of excessively low straightforwardness (Costa, McCrae, & Dye, 1991), which represents the paranoid tendencies to be secretive, devious, and scheming; excessively low compliance, which represents the paranoid tendency of antagonistic oppositionalism; and the Neuroticism facet of angry hostility (e.g., quick to react with anger). Other *DSM-IV* personality disorders also involve low Agreeableness, particularly the narcissistic (NAR) and antisocial–psychopathic (ATS) personality disorders (see Table 6.1 and our later discussion), which explains the comorbidity of these *DSM-IV* categorical diagnoses. Prototypic cases of these personality disorders, however, can be distinguished in part by the particular facets of antagonism. NAR, for example, is characterized by low Agreeableness but emphasizes primarily the facets of low modesty (arrogance, conceit, and grandiosity), low altruism (entitlement, self-centered stinginess, and exploitation), and low tendermindedness (lack of empathy) rather than low trust or low straightforwardness. ATS also involves the antagonism facets of excessively low straightforwardness (deceptive manipulation) and low compliance (failure to conform to social norms with respect to lawful behaviors), but it can be distinguished from prototypical PAR by its lack of emphasis on low trust (suspiciousness) and the greater emphasis on low altruism (exploitation).

It is evident that the domain and facets of low Agreeableness (or antagonism) are helpful to explain the overlap and the distinctions among PAR, ATS, and NAR. However, it is also evident that the categorical distinction among these personality disorders often is arbitrary. Some patients are more paranoid (low trust) than narcissistic (low modesty), but the diagnosis of many patients involves varying degrees and shades of the respective facets of Agreeableness. Rather than the arbitrary placement of a patient within an overly simplified diagnostic category that ignores the particular constellation of the facets of antagonism (and the other dimensions of personality), it would be more descriptive and precise to indicate the extent to which the patient is characterized by the respective facets of antagonism.

SCHIZOID PERSONALITY DISORDER

The essential features of the schizoid personality disorder (SZD) are "a pervasive pattern of detachment from social relationships and a restricted range of expression of emotions in interpersonal settings" (APA, 1994, p. 638). Individuals with SZD have a profound defect in their ability to form social relationships (Kalus, Bernstein, & Siever, 1993). They are typically loners, isolated and withdrawn from others. They may live as hermits, but more often they are within society but live emotionally and socially detached. They usually have jobs that require little or no social interaction. They prefer to keep to themselves, declining most opportunities to socialize. They rarely marry because the emotional intensity of a romantic or sexual relationship is foreign and has little interest.

In other words, SZD involves excessive introversion, particularly the facets of excessively low warmth (indifference to social relationships and neither desires nor enjoys close relationships; APA, 1994), low gregariousness (almost always chooses solitary activities), and low positive emotions (takes pleasure in few, if any, activities). Our prior description of this disorder (Widiger et al., 1994) included low excitement seeking, as suggested by the associated feature of being overly staid, cautious, and reserved. Low excitement seeking might be evident in some people with this disorder, but it is only suggested rather than required by the diagnostic criteria set (e.g., an absence of any interest in sexual activities). *DSM-IV* provides a greater emphasis on low positive emotions by its inclusion of a variety of indicators of anhedonia (i.e., an inability to experience pleasure from activities that usually produce pleasurable feelings), such as flattened affectivity, detachment, taking pleasure in few activities, and little interest in sexual activities (Kalus et al., 1993).

SZD also includes low openness to feelings. Individuals with SZD are not necessarily closed to all aspects of experience and may even be elevated on the broad domain of low Openness to Experience. They may in fact have substantial interests in areas of life that involve little social involvement (e.g., ideas, theories, aesthetics). However, prototypic cases of SZD include a low awareness or appreciation of emotionality. To the extent that a highly introverted person displays an excessive openness to ideas and fantasy, the person is more likely to be diagnosed with the schizotypal personality disorder (SZT) than with SZD (as discussed later).

SCHIZOTYPAL PERSONALITY DISORDER

The essential features of SZT are said to be "a pervasive pattern of social and interpersonal deficits marked by acute discomfort with, and reduced capacity for, close relationships as well as by cognitive or perceptual distortions and eccentricities of behavior" (APA, 1994, p. 641). SZT and SZD are quite similar (Siever, Bernstein, & Silverman, 1991). Both are largely characterized by excessive introversion (see Table 6.1), but they are differentiated by the relative emphasis on social and physical anhedonia in SZD and by the relative emphasis on cognitive–perceptual aberrations in SZT (Widiger, Frances, Spitzer, & Williams, 1988).

Many of these schizotypal cognitive–perceptual aberrations do not have an obvious representation in the FFM. Some researchers have suggested that SZT does not actually belong within the personality disorders section of *DSM-IV* (Siever et al., 1991). SZT is genetically and phenotypically associated closely with schizophrenia. However, most of the personality disorders have a comparable relationship to one or more Axis I mental disorders. SZT is perhaps best understood as a characterologic (personality) variant of schizophrenic pathology (broadly defined). Widiger and Trull (1992) speculated that the cognitive–perceptual aberrations of SZT may represent additional aspects or manifestations of Neuroticism. Neuroticism is said to involve a disposition to unrealistic and irrational beliefs, in addition to anxiety, depression, impulsivity, hostility, vulnerability, and self-consciousness (Costa & McCrae, 1985; McCrae, Costa, & Busch, 1986).

Prototypical SZD and SZT patients can be differentiated in part by their respective degree of Neuroticism. The prototypical individual with SZT displays excessively high anxiousness and self-consciousness (social anxiety and pervasive discomfort with others; APA, 1994), whereas some SZD patients may display low Neuroticism. However, SZT people are perhaps more clearly differentiated with respect to the domain of Openness, particularly fantasy, actions, and ideas. The cognitive aberrations of the SZT person can reflect, in part, an excessive maladaptive openness to unusual fantasy and ideation. This conceptualization of schizotypic ideation is somewhat controversial (Widiger, 1993). There are a variety of interpretations of this FFM domain, including culture, intellect, and unconventionality. An interpretation of Openness including unconventionality is perhaps best suited to capture the eccentricities, peculiarities, and odd behaviors of the SZT person. In summary, to the extent that an excessively introverted person also displays excessive Neuroticism and openness to fantasy and ideas, the *DSM-IV*

personality disorder diagnosis is more likely to be SZT rather than SZD. It should again be emphasized, however, that this categorical distinction is often arbitrary and misleading. It would be more informative to simply describe the extent to which an introverted person is anxious, self-conscious, and open to aberrant fantasies and ideas than to impose an arbitrary, black-or-white categorical distinction.

ANTISOCIAL PERSONALITY DISORDER

ATS is defined in *DSM-IV* as "a pervasive pattern of disregard for, and violation of, the rights of others" (APA, 1994, p. 645). The diagnostic criteria for ATS essentially provide a set of behavioral examples of excessively low Conscientiousness (e.g., irresponsible and delinquent acts, inability to sustain consistent work behavior, failure to honor obligations, failure to plan ahead) and low Agreeableness (e.g., deceitfulness, failure to conform to the law, fights and assaults, disregard for the safety and welfare of others, and lack of remorse; APA, 1994). People low in Conscientiousness tend to be aimless, unreliable, lax, negligent, and hedonistic (Costa & McCrae, 1985); the most extreme variants of these tendencies describe the indulgent and irresponsible antisocial individual. The ATS person, however, is also manipulative, exploitative, vengeful, criminal, and ruthless, which are aspects of antagonism (particularly the facets of excessively low straightforwardness, altruism, compliance, and tender mindedness). Impulsivity is included within the diagnostic criteria for ATS, but it is described more specifically in *DSM-IV* as a failure to plan ahead. This understanding of impulsivity is best represented within the domain of Conscientiousness (low deliberation) rather than by the FFM Neuroticism facet of impulsivity. The FFM Neuroticism facet of impulsivity refers instead to an inability to control one's urges or desires (Costa & McCrae, 1985, 1992).

The combination of low Conscientiousness and low Agreeableness is also characteristic of the passive–aggressive personality disorder (PAG) included in an appendix to *DSM-IV* (APA, 1994). However, PAG and ATS can be distinguished, in part, by the different facets of Agreeableness and Conscientiousness that are emphasized in each case (see Appendix A). The person with PAG tends to be more sloppy and careless (low in competence), whereas the ATS person is more reckless, unreliable, and hedonistic (low in self-discipline and deliberation). More important, perhaps, is the fact that the ATS person displays more of the facets of low Agreeableness, particularly the tendencies to be tough minded and ruthlessly exploitative. The excitement-seeking facet of Extraversion can also be useful to distinguish ATS from PAG.

BORDERLINE PERSONALITY DISORDER

Borderline personality disorder (BDL) is defined in *DSM-IV* as a "pervasive pattern of instability of interpersonal relationships, self-image, and affects, and marked impulsivity" (APA, 1994, p. 650). As is evident from Table 6.1, BDL is primarily a disorder of extreme Neuroticism. Describing people with this severe personality disorder as being simply high in Neuroticism may not adequately convey the seriousness of their psychopathology, but simultaneously the people who are at the very highest levels of FFM angry hostility, impulsivity, vulnerability, depressiveness, and anxiousness display severe psychopathology and would be diagnosed with BDL.

Affective instability is a central feature of BDL (Gunderson, 1984), and the tendency to experience negative affect is a central component of Neuroticism (Watson & Clark, 1984). The tendency to experience negative affect is represented directly by the Neuroticism facets of anxiety, depression, and angry hostility. The *DSM-IV* diagnostic criteria provide a variety of examples of this emotional instability, including unstable and intense interpersonal relationships; impulsivity; affective instability; inappropriate or intense anger; recurrent self-mutilation or suicidal threats, gestures, or behaviors; identity disturbance (e.g., uncertainty regarding self-image, long-term goals, and preferred values); chronic feelings of emptiness or boredom; and frantic efforts to avoid real or imagined abandonment (APA, 1994). These features correspond closely to the five Neuroticism facets of hostility, impulsivity, vulnerability, depression, and anxiety. A person elevated on Neuroticism tends to be hot tempered, angry, and easily frustrated (hostility); unable to resist impulses and tran-

sient urges (impulsivity); easily rattled, panicked, and unable to deal with stress (vulnerable); tense, fearful, worried, and apprehensive (anxiety); hopeless and blue (depressed); and is strickened by feelings of guilt, shame, inferiority, and embarrassment (self-consciousness; Costa & McCrae, 1992). These traits provide a good description of the BDL patient.

In the FFM, there are two aspects of hostility: the experience of hostility and the expression of hostility. In its former manifestation, it is represented as angry hostility within the domain of Neuroticism; in its latter manifestation, as low compliance of the domain of antagonism (Costa & McCrae, 1992). The hostility of BDL patients is evident in part by their explosive outbursts of anger, temper tantrums, intense rage, and hatred. This hostility of BDL patients may not be for the purpose of inflicting pain and suffering on others but reflects instead their inability to control their affective rage. Antagonism is characteristic of prototypic BDL, particularly the facets of low compliance (i.e., oppositionalism) and low trust (e.g., paranoid ideation). However, it is important to recognize that only two of the six facets of Agreeableness are salient for this personality disorder, and the polythetic nature of the criteria set does not ensure that these components of the disorder are always present. This same point applies to Conscientiousness, where only one of the six facets is involved (i.e., the low sense of self-efficacy evident within an identity disturbance).

Conceptualizing BDL as extreme Neuroticism is consistent with the psychoanalytic construct of borderline personality organization (BPO). BPO refers to a level of personality functioning that cuts across the *DSM-IV* diagnostic categories (Kernberg, 1984). The nonspecific manifestations of BDL functioning identified by Kernberg (e.g., anxiety tolerance, impulse control, and vulnerability to stress) are consistent with the facets of Neuroticism identified by Costa and McCrae (1992). The unstable, intense relations, recurrent suicidal threats, chronic feelings of emptiness, frantic efforts to avoid abandonment, self-mutilation, and transient, stress-related, severe dissociative symptoms are indirect manifestations of the Neuroticism facets of impulsiveness, vulnerability, self-consciousness, anxiety, and depression—what Kernberg (1984) referred to as "nonspecific manifestations of ego weakness." Frantic effort to avoid abandonment is an expression of panicked, helpless, and desperate vulnerability; unstable, intense relationships result from the tendency to be impulsive, vulnerable, hostile, anxious, and depressed. Each of the other *DSM-IV* personality disorders may or may not be at a borderline level of personality organization (or in terms of the FFM, may or may not involve the highest levels of Neuroticism). It would not be meaningful from this perspective to attempt to differentiate BDL from HST, ATS, or SZT because it is likely that inpatients with these personality disorders would also be at a borderline level of personality organization (Kernberg, 1984). Neuroticism, like BPO, is a characteristic level of personality dysfunction that cuts across other important individual differences (e.g., degree of Extraversion and Conscientiousness).

Conceptualizing BDL as extreme Neuroticism is also helpful for addressing the problematic heterogeneity of patients who meet the *DSM-IV* criteria for the BDL diagnosis (Clarkin, Widiger, Frances, Hurt, & Gilmore, 1983). Few cases are prototypical, with some characterized primarily by affective instability, some by impulsivity, and others by intense anger and hostility (Hurt et al., 1990). The dimensional nature of the five-factor formulation of Neuroticism recognizes that not all individuals share the same facets of Neuroticism to the same degree. Clinicians should not lump together all of the diverse presentations of borderline symptomatology within one undifferentiated category but instead should provide a more detailed and specific description of the individual patient with respect to the various facets of Neuroticism. Some patients may be characterized primarily by the facet of hostility, some by impulsivity, and others by anxiety, vulnerability, depression, or self-consciousness.

Conceptualizing BDL as extreme Neuroticism also helps to explain the excessive prevalence and comorbidity of this popular but controversial diagnosis (Widiger & Frances, 1989). Neuroticism, as a characteristic level of personality dysfunction (i.e., vulnerability to stress, impulse dyscontrol, and negative emotionality) is almost ubiquitous within clinical populations (Eysenck & Eysenck, 1985). Personality dysfunction to the point of needing inpatient

hospitalization usually involves excessive Neuroticism. A diagnostic category that consists essentially of excessive Neuroticism should be prevalent and be the most common personality disorder within inpatient settings. To the extent that the other personality disorders involve some degree of Neuroticism (see Table 6.1), one would also expect considerable overlap and comorbidity with BDL, particularly within inpatient settings. The excessive prevalence and comorbidity of BDL, which is so problematic to its validity as a distinct personality disorder (Cloninger, 1989; Gunderson & Zanarini, 1987; Widiger & Frances, 1989), is then readily understandable from the perspective of the FFM.

HISTRIONIC PERSONALITY DISORDER

Histrionic personality disorder (HST) is defined in *DSM-IV* as "excessive emotionality and attention-seeking behavior" (APA, 1994, p. 655). HST individuals express emotions with an inappropriate exaggeration and theatricality (excessively high positive emotions); they are sexually provocative and show attention-seeking behavior (high excitement seeking); they consider relationships to be more intimate than they actually are (high warmth); and they work hard at being the center of attention (high gregariousness). In summary, HST represents to a great extent an extreme variant of Extraversion. Extraversion involves the tendency to be outgoing, talkative, and affectionate (high warmth); to be convivial; to have many friends; to actively seek social contact (high gregariousness); to be assertive and dominant (high assertiveness); to be energetic, fast paced, and vigorous (high activity); to be flashy; to seek strong stimulation; to take risks (high excitement seeking); and to be high spirited, buoyant, optimistic, and joyful (high positive emotions). These facets of Extraversion provide a vivid description of the prototypical HST person. As described in Millon's (1981) alternative model for *DSM-IV*, HST is seen as the "gregarious pattern" (p. 131). Being outgoing, optimistic, and gregarious is not inherently maladaptive, but being extremely extraverted means being at a high risk for HST.

Prototypic cases of HST also involve facets of Openness that are characteristically excessive in the

HST person (e.g., flights into romantic fantasy, creative imagination, novelty craving, and bored with routine; APA, 1994). Thus, HST is contrasted strongly with SZD, which involves low openness to feelings (and introversion), whereas HST involves high openness to feelings and fantasy (as well as Extraversion). Openness to fantasy is only an associated feature of the *DSM-III-R* formulation of HST (APA, 1987; also see Appendix A, this volume). *DSM-IV* elevated this component to a diagnostic criterion. People with this disorder consider relationships to be more intimate than they actually are, and "flights into romantic fantasy are common" (APA, 1994, p. 655).

Another new diagnostic criterion for HST included in *DSM-IV* is "suggestible (i.e., easily influenced by others or circumstances)" (APA, 1994, p. 658). This criterion indicates the presence of the Agreeableness facet of trust (e.g., gullibility). This facet of Agreeableness was included in our previous translation of the *DSM-III-R* personality disorders (Widiger et al., 1994) but was again considered only an associated feature of the disorder (see Appendix A). Excessively high trust, like openness to fantasy, is now among the diagnostic criteria for this personality disorder.

NARCISSISTIC PERSONALITY DISORDER

NAR is "a pervasive pattern of grandiosity, need for admiration, and lack of empathy" (APA, 1994, p. 658). This personality disorder is characterized primarily by particular facets of antagonism, including low modesty (i.e., arrogance, grandiosity, superiority, haughty attitudes), low altruism (i.e., expecting favorable treatment, exploitation of others), and tough mindedness (i.e., lack of empathy). In fact, the first three diagnostic criteria for this disorder concern excessively low modesty.

Low Agreeableness or antagonism is also characteristic of PAR, ATS, BDL, and PAG, but as indicated earlier, prototypical cases of these personality disorders are largely differentiated by the facets of antagonism that are emphasized in each. For example, the excessive suspiciousness (low trust) of PAR is not characteristic of NAR, and the oppositionalism and manipulativeness of ATS, BDL, and PAG (low compliance and low straightforwardness) are not as characteristic of NAR. The narcissistic person also tends to display relatively higher levels of Conscientiousness than do ATS, BDL, HST, and PAG individuals. These other personality disorders are characterized, in part, by low Conscientiousness, whereas NAR involves more normal and often high levels of achievement striving. Achievement striving is not included in the *DSM-III-R* criteria for NAR (see Appendix A), but it is described in the clinical literature (Kernberg, 1984; Ronningstam & Gunderson, 1988) and is now included more explicitly within the *DSM-IV* criteria set as indicated by the reference to an excessive need to associate with high-status institutions (and people).

An ambiguity in the five-factor description of NAR is the characteristic level of Neuroticism. Individuals who are grandiose, overly self-confident, and arrogant and have an inflated self-esteem often describe themselves as being excessively low in Neuroticism, particularly with respect to the facets of self-consciousness, anxiety, and vulnerability. Most people have some degree of self-consciousness and vulnerability, but it is characteristic of the NAR person to deny the presence of any substantial faults, fallibilities, or foibles (Watson & Clark, 1984). Excessively low scores on self-report measures of Neuroticism may then be indicative of NAR, particularly when these scores are not confirmed by ratings provided by a peer or spouse (Costa & McCrae, 1990). Close associates are often more aware of the NAR individual's flaws and insecurities, and a substantial discrepancy between peer and self-ratings of vulnerability can be useful in suggesting an inflated self-esteem.

People with NAR, however, often experience cracks in their armor of grandiosity. They are, in fact, vulnerable to threats to self-esteem (Kernberg, 1984). This vulnerability is particularly evident in people with NAR who seek treatment. *DSM-IV* does not explicitly include a criterion that represents this vulnerability, although some might infer it from the excessive need for admiration and enviousness of others. The *DSM-IV* criteria for NAR place somewhat less emphasis on high Neuroticism (e.g., by deleting the hypersensitivity to criticism item) and more emphasis on arrogant antagonism (by adding the items of arrogance, haughty attitudes, and the belief that others are envious of them).

AVOIDANT PERSONALITY DISORDER

Avoidant personality disorder (AVD) is defined in *DSM-IV* as "a pattern of social inhibition, feelings of inadequacy, and hypersensitivity to negative evaluation" (APA, 1994, p. 662). From the perspective of the FFM, AVD involves (a) introversion, particularly the facets of low assertiveness (restraint within intimate relationships, inhibited in interpersonal situations, and avoids occupational activities that involve significant interpersonal contact), low gregariousness (unwilling to get involved with people), and low excitement seeking (reluctant to take personal risks or engage in any new activities; APA, 1994); and (b) Neuroticism, particularly the facets of self-consciousness, anxiousness, vulnerability, and depressiveness (e.g., fears of criticism, disapproval, or rejection; feelings of inadequacy; views self as inferior to others). In other words, the AVD person is not simply introverted but is withdrawn and inhibited because occupational, interpersonal, and other activities may prove embarrassing. They are willing to get involved with others but only if they are sufficiently reassured that they will be accepted.

Both the comorbidity and the differentiation of AVD and SZD are understandable from the perspective of the FFM. These two personality disorders both involve introversion, but the prototypical SZD and AVD people are readily distinguished with respect to Neuroticism. To the extent that an introverted person is elevated on Neuroticism (particularly the facets of self-consciousness, anxiety, and vulnerability), the more likely diagnosis is AVD rather than SZD. AVD and SZD can also be distinguished to some extent by facets of introversion. AVD introversion tends to emphasize the facets of low assertiveness (submissive and unassuming) and low excitement seeking (cautious and inhibited), whereas SZD introversion involves primarily the facets of low warmth (cold and distant) and low positive emotions (anhedonia). Prototypical avoidant individuals may, in fact, be characterized by high warmth (see Appendix A) because they are fully ca-

pable of expressing strong feelings of affection. Avoidant individuals can at times appear on the surface to be low in warmth, given their tendency to avoid social situations, but they actually strongly desire social contact.

It is useful to emphasize again, however, that the avoidant and schizoid behavior patterns tend to shade into one another. Most patients are not prototypical cases but instead involve shades of gray of avoidant and schizoid traits. Some have low gregariousness and low assertiveness or low warmth and low assertiveness with moderate Neuroticism. It would then be more precise and informative to indicate the respective levels on the relevant facets of introversion and Neuroticism than to characterize the patient as either AVD or SZD (or both).

DEPENDENT PERSONALITY DISORDER

Dependent personality disorder (DEP) is defined in the *DSM-IV* as an "excessive need to be taken care of that leads to submissive and clinging behavior and fears of separation" (APA, 1994, p. 665). From the perspective of the FFM, DEP represents primarily an extreme variant of Agreeableness with high levels of Neuroticism and low assertiveness (see Table 6.1). DEP individuals are characterized by a marked need for social approval and affection and often sacrifice many of their own needs, values, options, pleasures, and goals to live in accordance with the desires of others. They are self-effacing, docile, submissive, and sacrificial. Agreeableness is often adaptive and desirable, involving such traits as being trusting, good natured, helpful, forgiving, and accommodating, but "agreeableness can also assume a pathological form, in which it is usually seen as dependency" (Costa & McCrae, 1985, p. 12).

The *DSM-IV* diagnostic criteria set includes many explicit examples of pathological Agreeableness, such as excessive compliance (difficulty expressing disagreement), altruism (volunteering to do unpleasant things), and modesty (needing advice and reassurance from others to make everyday decisions). Many of the other *DSM-IV* criteria include facets of Neuroticism, particularly vulnerability, anxiety, and self-consciousness (e.g., feels unable to take care of self, feels uncomfortable or helpless when alone, lacks self-confidence in judgment or abilities, fears loss of support or approval).

The diagnoses of AVD and DEP often co-occur, even more so perhaps than the comorbidity of AVD and SZD. This can appear to be somewhat odd, given that the social withdrawal and aloneness that characterize AVD people would appear to be mutually exclusive with the strong attachment needs of DEP people. However, their comorbidity is due primarily to sharing of similar facets of Neuroticism (vulnerability, anxiety, and self-consciousness) and the facet of low assertiveness from Extraversion. Nevertheless, prototypic cases can be distinguished. Prototypical cases of DEP exhibit a pathological high warmth, as manifested in the new *DSM-IV* diagnostic criterion of "urgently seeks another relationship as a source of care and support when a close relationship ends" (APA, 1994, p. 669). This new diagnostic criterion is consistent with the general shift in the definition of DEP from one that emphasizes low self-confidence to a greater emphasis on the attachment component of dependency and emotional reliance on others (Hirschfeld, Shea, & Weise, 1991; Pilkonis, 1988). From the perspective of the FFM, this represents a shift from Neuroticism toward Extraversion and Agreeableness.

Prototypical cases of AVD and DEP are also distinguishable with respect to the domain of Agreeableness. To the extent that a person who is moderately anxious, self-conscious, vulnerable, and depressed is also excessively trustworthy, gullible, compliant, modest, and tenderminded, the person is more likely to be diagnosed as DEP rather than AVD. Once again, however, it is important to emphasize that the categorical distinction between DEP and AVD is arbitrary at its boundaries. Patients with diagnoses of DEP and AVD are characterized by varying degrees of elevations on Agreeableness, Neuroticism, and Extraversion–introversion. Many of these individuals provide a problematic differential diagnosis to the clinician, who is using the categorical *DSM-IV* taxonomy because the patient appears to have both AVD and DEP. From the perspective of the

FFM, these patients would simply be described by their precise elevations on the respective facets of Neuroticism, introversion, and Agreeableness.

OBSESSIVE–COMPULSIVE PERSONALITY DISORDER

Obsessive–compulsive personality disorder (OBC) is defined in *DSM-IV* as "a preoccupation with orderliness, perfectionism, and mental and interpersonal control at the expense of flexibility, openness, and efficiency" (APA, 1994, p. 669). From the perspective of the FFM, OBC is primarily a disorder of excessive Conscientiousness, including such facets as order (preoccupation with details, rules, lists, order), achievement striving (excessive devotion to work and productivity), dutifulness (overconscientious, scrupulousness about matters of ethics and morality), and competence (perfectionism). Conscientiousness involves a person's degree of organization, persistence, and motivation in goal-directed behavior. Conscientious individuals tend to be organized, reliable, hardworking, self-disciplined, businesslike, and punctual (Costa & McCrae, 1992). People who are maladaptively conscientious are excessively devoted to work; perfectionistic, to the point that tasks are not completed (e.g., unable to complete projects because their own strict standards are not met), and preoccupied with organization, rules, and details.

It appears to be a paradox for people who are unable to complete projects effectively or efficiently as being considered high in Conscientiousness. However, the paradox is in fact that people with OBC often make significant achievements yet routinely fail to accomplish even the most mundane and ordinary of tasks due to their personality disorder. People with OBC are essentially their own worst enemy because their hypertrophic sense of competence sets unrealistically high standards that often cannot be met. They may achieve and accomplish a great deal, but they also become stalled and derailed by their severe standards and expectations. Even when a decision is trivial (e.g., which movie to attend, where to have dinner, what apparently worthless objects to throw away), they may ruminate endlessly (excessive deliberation). OBC people are obsessed with making correct decisions, contributing paradoxically to both high achievement and high task failure.

The OBC person is also closed to values (inflexible in matters of morality, ethics, or values; APA, 1994). *DSM-III-R* includes a diagnostic criterion representing closedness to feelings (restricted expression of affection), but this criterion has been removed (Pfohl & Blum, 1991). A new diagnostic criterion for OBC included in the *DSM-IV* is rigidity and stubbornness (APA, 1994), which provides another representation of low openness to values. However, the criterion of stubbornness can also reflect an antagonism (low compliance). The OBC person's reluctance to delegate tasks or to work with others unless they submit to exactly his or her way of doing things reflects a clinically significant form of oppositionalism, perhaps manifestations of the facets of low compliance (antagonism) and high assertiveness (Extraversion).

References

American Psychiatric Association. (1987). *Diagnostic and statistical manual of mental disorders* (3rd ed., rev.). Washington, DC: Author.

American Psychiatric Association. (1994). *Diagnostic and statistical manual of mental disorders* (4th ed.). Washington, DC: Author.

Bernstein, D. P., Useda, D., & Siever, L. J. (1993). Paranoid personality disorder: Review of the literature and recommendations for *DSM-IV*. *Journal of Personality Disorders, 7,* 53–62.

Clarkin, J. F., Widiger, T. A., Frances, A. J., Hurt, S. W., & Gilmore, M. (1983). Prototypic typology and the borderline personality disorder. *Journal of Abnormal Psychology, 92,* 263–275.

Cloninger, C. R. (1989). Establishment of diagnostic validity in psychiatric illness: Robins and Guze's method revisited. In L. Robins & J. Barrett (Eds.), *The validity of psychiatric diagnosis* (pp. 9–18). New York: Raven Press.

Costa, P. T., Jr., & McCrae, R. R. (1985). *The NEO Personality Inventory manual*. Odessa, FL: Psychological Assessment Resources.

Costa, P. T., Jr., & McCrae, R. R. (1990). Personality disorders and the five-factor model of personality. *Journal of Personality Disorders, 4,* 362–371.

Costa, P. T., Jr., & McCrae, R. R. (1992). *Revised NEO Personality Inventory: Professional manual*. Odessa, FL: Psychological Assessment Resources.

Costa, P. T., Jr., McCrae, R. R., & Dye, D. A. (1991). Facet scales for agreeableness and conscientiousness: A revision of the NEO Personality Inventory. *Personality and Individual Differences, 12,* 887–898.

Eysenck, H., & Eysenck, M. (1985). *Personality and individual differences: A natural science approach.* New York: Plenum Press.

Gunderson, J. G. (1984). *Borderline personality disorder.* Washington, DC: American Psychiatric Press.

Gunderson, J. G., & Zanarini, M. (1987). Current overview of the borderline diagnosis. *Journal of Clinical Psychiatry, 48*(Suppl.), 5–11.

Hirschfeld, R. M. A., Shea, M. T., & Weise, R. (1991). Dependent personality disorder: Perspectives for *DSM-IV*. *Journal of Personality Disorders, 5,* 135–149.

Hurt, S. W., Clarkin, J. F., Widiger, T. A., Fyer, M. R., Sullivan, T., Stone, M. H., & Frances, A. J. (1990). Evaluation of *DSM-III* decision rules for case detection using joint conditional probability structures. *Journal of Personality Disorders, 4,* 121–130.

Kalus, O., Bernstein, D. P., & Siever, L. J. (1993). Schizoid personality disorder: A review of its current status. *Journal of Personality Disorders, 7,* 43–52.

Kernberg, O. F. (1984). *Severe personality disorders.* New Haven, CT: Yale University Press.

McCrae, R. R., Costa, P. T., Jr., & Busch, C. M. (1986). Evaluating comprehensiveness in personality systems: The California Q-Set and the five-factor model. *Journal of Personality, 54,* 430–446.

Millon, T. (1981). *Disorders of personality:* DSM-III, *Axis II.* New York: Wiley.

Pfohl, B., & Blum, N. S. (1991). Obsessive–compulsive personality disorder: A review of available data and recommendations for *DSM-IV*. *Journal of Personality Disorders, 5,* 363–375.

Pilkonis, P. A. (1988). Personality prototypes among depressives: Themes of dependency and autonomy. *Journal of Personality Disorders, 2,* 144–152.

Ronningstam, E., & Gunderson, J. (1988). Narcissistic traits in psychiatric patients. *Comprehensive Psychiatry, 29,* 545–549.

Siever, L. J., Bernstein, D. P., & Silverman, J. M. (1991). Schizotypal personality disorder: A review of its current status. *Journal of Personality Disorders, 5,* 178–193.

Watson, D., & Clark, L. (1984). Negative affectivity:

The disposition to experience aversive emotional states. *Psychological Bulletin, 96,* 465–490.

Widiger, T. A. (1993). The *DSM-III-R* categorical personality disorder diagnoses: A critique and an alternative. *Psychological Inquiry, 4,* 75–90.

Widiger, T. A., & Frances, A. J. (1989). Epidemiology, diagnosis, and comorbidity of borderline personality disorder. In A. Tasman, R. E. Hales, & A. J. Frances (Eds.), *Review of psychiatry* (Vol. 8, pp. 8–24). Washington, DC: American Psychiatric Press.

Widiger, T. A., Frances, A. J., Spitzer, R. L., & Williams, J. B. W. (1988). The *DSM-III-R* personality disorders: An overview. *American Journal of Psychiatry, 145,* 786–795.

Widiger, T. A., Mangine, S., Corbitt, E., Ellis, C., & Thomas, G. (1995). *Personality Disorder Interview—IV (PDI-IV) manual.* Odessa, FL: Psychological Assessment Resources.

Widiger, T. A., & Trull, T. J. (1992). Personality and psychopathology: An application of the five-factor model. *Journal of Personality, 60,* 363–394.

Widiger, T. A., Trull, T. J., Clarkin, J. F., Sanderson, C., & Costa, P. T., Jr. (1994). A description of the *DSM-III-R* and *DSM-IV* personality disorders with the five-factor model of personality. In P. T. Costa, Jr., & T. A. Widiger (Eds.), *Personality disorders and the five-factor model of personality* (pp. 41–56). Washington, DC: American Psychological Association.

PART II

MODELS OF PERSONALITY DIMENSIONS AND DISORDERS

CHAPTER 7

PERSONALITY STRUCTURE AND THE STRUCTURE OF PERSONALITY DISORDERS

Jerry S. Wiggins and Aaron L. Pincus

In this chapter, we advocate the use of operationalized structural models of personality in the interpretation of dimensions that underlie the interrelations among conceptions of personality disorders. We begin with an overview of empirical studies of the structure of personality disorders and consider two major perspectives on the nature of these disorders. We then provide an overview of dimensional approaches to personality and consider four theoretical perspectives on the five-factor model (FFM) of personality. Next, we consider in detail the relations between personality structure and the structure of personality disorders. Finally, we illustrate the advantages of a combined FFM and interpersonal circumplex model in the assessment of personality disorders. Throughout the chapter, we present reanalyses of our previously published data that illustrate the specific points of our discussion.

STRUCTURE OF PERSONALITY DISORDERS

Empirical Studies

Current conceptualizations of personality disorders are products of a brief but intensive 15 years of theoretical development and empirical investigation. Only in the latter half of this period has research focused on the "structure" underlying conceptions of personality disorders. In Tables 7.1 and 7.2, we present a summary of these empirical investigations

of personality disorder structure. As Widiger (1989) pointed out, one clear distinction among these studies is the presence or absence of an independently operationalized dimensional model that is used to evaluate empirical findings concerning the structure of personality disorders. Studies conducted in the absence of a dimensional model may nonetheless be important if they reveal a consistent empirical pattern of results. However, such studies are vulnerable to a subjectivity of interpretation of dimensions that may contribute to an apparent lack of consistency of results across studies. Studies that include an operationalized dimensional model have selected models that have emerged from a 50-year history of investigations into personality structure (Wiggins & Trapnell, 1997). From Tables 7.1 and 7.2, it is clear that such studies provide a more coherent pattern of results than studies that do not relate the structure of personality disorders to validated taxonomies of personality traits.

A second distinction that influences the structural study of personality disorders involves the assumption that is made about the relation between normal and disordered personality. If one assumes that disordered personality is qualitatively different from normal personality, then the inclusion of a dimensional model of personality may be insufficient or inappropriate for investigation. If one assumes that disordered personality reflects quantitative differ-

The preparation of this chapter was greatly facilitated by Social Sciences and Humanities Research Council of Canada Grant 410-90-1374 and by a University of British Columbia Killam Predoctoral Fellowship. We thank Anita DeLongis, Dimitri Papageorgis, Paul Trapnell, and Candace Taylor Wiggins for their helpful comments on an earlier version of this chapter.

TABLE 7.1

Methods and Dimensions Identified in Structural Investigations of Personality Disorders (PDs): Studies Lacking Independent Operationalization of Dimensions

Study	Method	Dimension
Blashfield et al. (1985)	MDS of case diagnosis across clinicians	Acting out Interpersonal involvement
Clark (1989)	Factor analysis of *DSM-III* Axis II and some Axis I criteria	Negative emotionality Positive emotionality Impulsivity
Hyler & Lyons (1988)	Factor analysis of PD severity ratings on a nationwide sample	Asocial Unstable Anxious Compulsive
Kass et al. (1985)	Factor analysis of PD severity ratings on a clinical sample	Odd–eccentric Dramatic–erratic Anxious–fearful Compulsive
Livesley & Jackson (1986)	Factor analysis of "prototypical" PD behavioral acts	Interpersonal–cognitive dysfunction Impulsivity Compulsive
Livesley et al. (1989)	Factor analysis of 100 scales that assess PD behavioral dimensions	15 primary dimensions
Livesley & Schroeder (1990)	Factor analysis of *DSM* Cluster A-associated behavioral dimensions	Paranoid behaviors Sensitivity Social avoidance Perceptual–cognitive distortion
Morey (1988)	Cluster analysis of *DSM* PD criteria-rated on diagnosed PD patients	11 clusters corresponding to *DSM* PD categories 2 higher order clusters; acting out and anxious rumination
Morey et al. (1985)	Factor analysis of MMPI PD scales	Odd–eccentric Dramatic–erratic Anxious–fearful
Strack (1987)	Factor analysis of the PACL in normal subjects	Affective neuroticism vs. affective control Assertion vs. submission Extraversion vs. intraversion
Widiger et al. (1987)	MDS of *DSM* criteria rated on inpatient PD sample	Social involvement Dominance Anxious rumination vs. acting out

Note. This table excludes studies that used the full Millon Clinical Multiaxial Inventory. *DSM = Diagnostic and Statistical Manual of Mental Disorders*; DSM-III = *DSM*, third edition; MDS = Multidimensional Scaling; MMPI = Minnesota Multiphasic Personality Inventory; PACL = Personality Adjective Check List.

ences in the manifestation or severity of normal personality traits (i.e., a dimensional approach), then the adoption of a personality taxonomy for use as a structural referent becomes a necessary or even fundamental conceptual task.

The dimensions underlying the personality disorders identified in studies lacking an operationalized model of personality reflect solutions extracted at different levels within the hierarchy of personality constructs (Comrey, 1988). These levels range from first order, narrow-band factors (e.g., 15 primary dimensions identified by Livesley, Jackson, & Schroeder, 1989; Livesley & Schroeder, 1990) to superordinate, broad-band factors (e.g., "acting out" and "interpersonal involvement"; Blashfield, Sprock, Pinkston, & Hodgin, 1985). The varying levels of

TABLE 7.2

Methods and Dimensions Identified in Structural Investigations of Personality Disorders (PDs)

Study	Model	Method	Dimensions
Costa & McCrae (1990)	Five-factor model	Factor analysis of MCMI, MCMI-II, and NEO-PI combined	Neuroticism Extraversion Openness Agreeableness Conscientiousness
DeJong et al. (1989)	Interpersonal circumplex[a]	Correlated SIDP scales with ICL octant scales	Power (control) vs. submission
Morey (1985)	Interpersonal circumplex	Correlated MCMI scales with ICL octant scales	Power (control) vs. submission
Pincus & Wiggins (1990a)	Interpersonal circumplex	Correlated PACL and MMPI PD scales with IIP-C octant scales; projected scales onto IIP-C circumplex	Dominance vs. submission Nurturance vs. coldness
Plutchik & Conte (1986)	Interpersonal circumplex	Factor analysis of clinician's trait ratings for *DSM-III* PDs	Dominance vs. submission Nurturance vs. coldness
Plutchik & Platman (1977)	Interpersonal circumplex	Factor analysis of clinician's trait ratings for *DSM-II* PDs	Dominance vs. submission Nurturance vs. coldness
Romney & Bynner (1989)	Interpersonal circumplex	Confirmatory factor analysis of data sets to test the goodness of fit for circular model	Dominance vs. submission Nurturance vs. coldness
Strack et al. (1990)	Interpersonal circumplex	Evaluated circular ordering of PACL and MCMI-II scales	PACL: Extraversion vs. introversion, resistance vs. conformity MCMI-II: Expressive vs. impassive, compulsive vs. impulsive
Wiggins & Pincus (1989)	Interpersonal circumplex	Projected PACL and MMPI PD scales onto IAS-R circumplex	Dominance vs. submission Nurturance vs. coldness

Note. DSM-II = Diagnostic and Statistical Manual for Mental Disorders, second edition; *DSM-III = DSM*, third edition; IAS-R = Revised Interpersonal Adjective Scales; IASR-B5 = Extended Interpersonal Adjective Scales; ICL = Interpersonal Check List; IIP-C = Inventory of Interpersonal Problems Circumplex Scales; MCMI = Millon Clinical Multiaxial Inventory; MCMI-II = Revised MCMI; MMPI = Minnesota Multiphasic Personality Inventory; NEO-PI = NEO Personality Inventory; PACL = Personality Adjective Check List; SIDP = Structured Interview for *DSM-III* Personality Disorders. [a]Empirical results consistently demonstrate that the interpersonal circumplex is related to a subset of PDs.

extraction in combination with subjective interpretation of factors are likely to be the greatest sources of confusion to interpret results. Another challenge to the investigation of structural relations between personality disorders and personality traits is the operationalization of personality disorder constructs. Attempts to investigate the relations between dimensions of personality and clinically diagnosed personality disorders are embroiled in a "criterion problem" due to the low reliability of clinical diagnoses (Wiggins & Pincus, 1989). Furthermore, the various interview schedules and self-report measures of personality disorders have not been empirically evaluated in a systematic manner (Widiger & Frances, 1987). There are also conceptual divergences among the different methods of assessment. For these reasons, we chose to operationalize the personality disorders by using self-report instruments that reflect the major perspectives on the disorders.

Two Perspectives on Personality Disorders

Millon.   Millon (1981, 1986, 1990) proposed a dimensional model of personality based on three basic polarities from which one can derive the personality disorder categories. The three polarities are (a) the nature of reinforcement (whether the person generally experiences positive reinforcement, negative reinforcement, both, or neither), (b) the source of reinforcement (self, other, or ambivalent), and (c) the instrumental coping style of the individual (actively initiating or passively accommodating). Millon (1990) articulated the personality disorders with reference to how these polarities combine to give rise to individual differences in eight clinical domains: expressive acts, interpersonal conduct, cognitive style, object representations, self-image, regulatory mechanisms, morphologic organization, and mood–temperament.

Two instruments are currently available that assess Millon's conception of personality disorders as syndrome derivations from the three basic polarities: the second edition of the Millon Clinical Multiaxial Inventory (MCMI-II; Millon, 1987) and the Personality Adjective Check List (PACL; Strack, 1987).

The *Diagnostic and Statistical Manual of Mental Disorders.*   The publication of the third edition of

the *Diagnostic and Statistical Manual of Mental Disorders* (*DSM-III*; American Psychiatric Association, 1980), the third edition, revised (*DSM-III-R*; American Psychiatric Association, 1987), and the fourth edition (*DSM-IV*; American Psychiatric Association, 1994) marked major conceptual changes in classification of personality disorders. Along with developmental disorders, personality disorders are placed on a separate axis (Axis II) in this multiaxial diagnostic system. This ensures that in the evaluation of adults, these disorders are not overlooked when attention is directed to the usually more florid Axis I disorders (Widiger, Frances, Spitzer, & Williams, 1988).

For a number of reasons, the construct validity of the *DSM* personality disorders requires continued investigation. Most diagnoses are currently based on limited empirical data. The *DSM* groups personality disorders into three clusters: (a) odd–eccentric (paranoid, schizoid, and schizotypal), (b) dramatic–erratic (histrionic, narcissistic, antisocial, and borderline), and (c) anxious–fearful (avoidant, dependent, compulsive, and passive–aggressive). This clustering is not based on any explicit assumptions or hypotheses regarding the personality disorders (Widiger, 1989). Instead, the placement is based on presumably similar phenomenologies, analogous to the organization of the Axis I syndromes (Frances, 1980; Spitzer, Williams, & Skodal, 1980). It is clear from Tables 7.1 and 7.2 that structural investigations of personality disorders provide only limited support for the *DSM* clusters. A number of self-report measures and interviews have been developed to assess the *DSM* personality disorders (Reich, 1987, 1989; Widiger & Frances, 1987). Two selected examples are considered in the following section.

Assessment Instruments

Personality Adjective Check List.   The PACL was derived under a combined rational–empirical scale construction strategy to yield self-report measures of the 11 personality styles described in Millon's (1981, 1986) theory of psychopathology. Reliable adjective scales were constructed for 8 of Millon's 11 personality styles. It was not possible to construct reliable scales for the 3 "severe" personality styles of borderline, schizotypal, and paranoid. Validity studies of the PACL scales include studies of their convergence with other self-report measures (Strack, 1987; Strack, Lorr, & Campbell, 1990) and their relations to the major dimensions of personality (Pincus & Wiggins, 1990a; Wiggins & Pincus, 1989). In results presented later in the chapter, our analyses are based on a set of nonoverlapping PACL scales constructed by Wiggins and Pincus. Representative items for each PACL scale can be seen in Table 7.3.

TABLE 7.3

Characteristic Items of the PACL and MMPI Personality Disorder Scales

Scale	PACL items	MMPI items
Schizoid	Detached	I like parties and socials. (False)
	Distant	I enjoy social gatherings just to be with people. (False)
	Remote	I am a good mixer. (False)
Avoidant	Ignored	I am easily embarrassed.
	Excluded	I am certainly lacking in self-confidence.
	Insecure	Criticism or scolding hurts me terribly.
Dependent	Sweet	At times I think I am no good at all.
	Warm hearted	I am entirely self-confident. (False)
	Respectful	I have several times given up doing a thing because I thought too little of my ability.
Histrionic	Outgoing	I find it hard to make small talk when I meet new people. (False)
	Lively	While in trains, buses, etc., I often talk to strangers.
	Talkative	I like to go to parties and other affairs where there is lots of loud fun.
Narcissistic	Egoistic	When in a group of people I have trouble thinking of the right things to talk about. (False)
	Conceited	If given the chance, I would make a good leader of people.
	Arrogant	I have no dread of going into a room by myself where other people have already gathered and started talking.
Antisocial	Domineering	In school, I was sometimes sent to the principal for cutting up.
	Forceful	As a youngster, I was suspended from school one or more times for cutting up.
	Aggressive	If I could get into a movie without paying and be sure I would not be seen, I would probably do it.
Compulsive	Organized	I frequently find myself worrying about something.
	Orderly	I must admit that I have at times been worried beyond reason over something that did not matter.
	Neat	I have met problems so full of possibilities that I have been unable to make up my mind about them.
Passive–aggressive	Moody	I find it hard to keep my mind on a task or job.
	Annoyed	I have more trouble concentrating than others seem to have.
	Temperamental	I have difficulty in starting to do things.
(Schizotypal)	(No PACL scale)	I have strange and peculiar thoughts.
		I have had very strange and peculiar experiences.
		I often feel as if things were not real.
(Borderline)	(No PACL scale)	I am not easily angered. (False)
		I get mad easily and then get over it soon.
		I sometimes feel that I am about to go to pieces.
(Paranoid)	(No PACL scale)	There are persons who are trying to steal my thoughts and ideas.
		I have often felt that strangers were looking at me critically.
		I feel that I have often been punished without cause.

Note. MMPI = Minnesota Multiphasic Personality Inventory; PACL = Personality Adjective Check List. From "Conceptions of Personality Disorders and Dimensions of Personality," by J. S. Wiggins and A. L. Pincus, 1989, *Psychological Assessment: A Journal of Consulting and Clinical Psychology, 1,* p. 307. Copyright 1989 by the American Psychological Association. Reprinted with permission.

Minnesota Multiphasic Personality Inventory Personality Disorder Scales. The Minnesota Multiphasic Personality Inventory (MMPI; Hathaway & McKinley, 1967) personality disorder scales (Morey, Waugh, & Blashfield, 1985) were derived under a combined rational–empirical strategy to yield self-report measures of the 11 personality disorders described in *DSM-III*. Both overlapping and nonoverlapping scale sets are available, and the results, presented later, are restricted to the set with non-overlapping items. The results of validity studies suggest that the scales have meaningful relations to major dimensions of personality (Pincus & Wiggins, 1990a; Wiggins & Pincus, 1989) and that they warrant further investigation (Dubro, Wetzler, & Kahn, 1988; Greene, 1987; Trull, 1991). Representative items for each MMPI scale can be seen in Table 7.3.

Principal Components of Personality Disorders

Because the MMPI and PACL personality disorder scales were generated from different conceptual perspectives, it is important to examine their similarities and differences with reference to the structural dimensions that underlie them. With this in mind, we administered the two sets of self-report measures to 581 undergraduate psychology students at the University of British Columbia (Wiggins & Pincus, 1989). We computed the correlations among all 19 scales and with the resultant intercorrelation matrix conducted a principal components analysis. The retention of five components was clearly indicated by both Kaiser–Guttman and Scree test criteria. These five components were analytically rotated to a varimax criterion of simple structure. The resultant component matrix is provided in Table 7.4.

As shown in Table 7.4, conjoint factor analysis of the personality disorder scales from the MMPI and PACL yields a relatively clear simple structure solution of five orthogonal components. It is also apparent that there are a number of clear-cut structural convergences between corresponding scale pairs from the two instruments. In contrast, there are several instances in which corresponding scale pairs

---

TABLE 7.4

Principal Components of Personality Disorder Scales

Scale (test)	Component				
	I	II	III	IV	V
Dependent (MMPI)	.75				
Avoidant (PACL)	.70	.42			
Avoidant (MMPI)	.61	.45			
Narcissistic (PACL)	−.53				
Narcissistic (MMPI)	−.66				
Antisocial (PACL)	−.81				
Schizoid (PACL)		.81			
Schizoid (MMPI)		.80			
Histrionic (MMPI)	−.36	−.74			
Histrionic (PACL)		−.77			
Passive–Aggressive (PACL)			.80		
Passive–Aggressive (MMPI)			.58		
Borderline (MMPI)[a]			.68		
Dependent (PACL)	.57		−.61		
Compulsive (MMPI)				.69	
Compulsive (PACL)			−.47	.63	
Antisocial (MMPI)				−.63	
Schizotypal (MMPI)[a]					.81
Paranoid (MMPI)[a]					.61

Note. N = 581; loadings <.33 omitted. MMPI = Minnesota Multiphasic Personality Inventory; PACL = Personality Adjective Check List. [a]No PACL scales for these disorders.

show clearly divergent structural patterns from one another. Finally, for the first four components at least, it is evident that the factors that underlie the scale intercorrelations are bipolar in nature. Thus, we have established a clear factorial structure that suggests both convergences and divergences among the conceptions of personality disorders reflected in two promising self-report measures. The next and more important question is, how should we interpret this solution?

One approach would be to compare the present factor solution with those obtained in the studies listed in Table 7.1. For example, how does the present five-factor structure compare with the four-factor structure obtained by Kass, Skodal, Charles, Spitzer, and Williams (1985)? As we emphasized, the problem with such a comparison, and with comparisons of our findings with any of the studies listed in Table 7.1, is one of subjectivity. We would, in effect, be comparing our own implicit theory of personality disorders with those of other investigators. Such differences are not easily resolved in the absence of an explicit and operationalized model of personality structure.

The structural convergences and divergences among the corresponding pairs of the personality disorder scales from the MMPI and PACL might be interpreted with respect to judged similarities and differences in item content, as suggested by the examples in Table 7.3. The strong factorial convergence of the two schizoid scales might be interpreted as reflecting the common item theme of detachment in the PACL and MMPI scales. The two antisocial scales are just as clearly different in their factorial composition, and this might be attributed to the domineering content of the PACL items in contrast to the rule infraction theme of the MMPI items.

Content analytic rating procedures can sometimes illuminate the similarity and differences among personality scales. However, in the absence of an explicit and operationalized model, such procedures are inherently subjective and thus do not lend themselves to interpretations of the underlying dimensionality of sets of scales (McCrae, Costa, & Piedmont, 1993). For that reason, we now turn to a consideration of personality structure and an examination of operationalized models that may illuminate the nature of the structure presented in Table 7.4.

PERSONALITY STRUCTURE

Dimensional Approaches

In dimensional approaches to personality, the term *structure* had its origins in the classical distinction between personality structures and personality dynamics (Rapaport, 1960); the present-day meaning however is more delimited (Wiggins, 1968). The literature of personality structure encompasses investigators' efforts over the last half century to provide a structural representation of the interrelations among what they believed to be comprehensive sets of variables reflecting individual differences in human dispositions. Perhaps more than any other area of personality study, personality structure research has been dependent on, inspired by, and even subordinated to the development of mathematical–statistical procedures for data analysis. Computers and their associated software have dramatically transformed this field from one in which conceptualizations exceeded possibilities of data analysis to one in which software capabilities now exceed both the quality of data and the scope of conceptualization.

The interdependence between theory and method in personality structure research is due to the fact that most attempts to provide multivariate representations of personality structure are based on the method of factor analysis. The latter is a set of procedures for reducing a matrix of intercorrelations among observed personality variables to a matrix of smaller rank for the purpose of identifying the latent variables (factors) that give rise to the original matrix of intercorrelations. The logic underlying this procedure is precisely that which led Spearman (1927) and Thurstone (1934) to seek the factor(s) underlying correlations among performances judged to reflect "intelligence."

There are many different computational procedures whereby intercorrelations among personality variables may be reduced to factors; unfortunately, there is substantial disagreement as to which set of procedures is optimal (see Society of Multivariate Experimental Psychology, 1990). As a consequence, theories of personality structure may differ not only in substance but in preferred method, and it is often difficult to determine the extent to which apparent substantive differences are due to differences in computational procedures. To further complicate matters, some theories of personality structure use multivariate models, such as the circumplex, which depart in significant ways from the factor analytic tradition.

The field of personality structure as it is known today began with the comprehensive, cumulative, and systematic research programs of Cattell (1943), Eysenck (1947), and Guilford (1948). The programs of Cattell and Eysenck and their many followers are still pursued actively. By the 1980s, use of well-validated structural models of personality for purposes of integrating the huge variety of operationalized personality constructs became the central task of a number of investigators (e.g., Costa & McCrae, 1988; Wiggins & Broughton, 1985). A "third force," as it were, that promises possible consolidations among these and other schools of thought may be found in the work of those investigators who advocate an FFM personality structure (see Digman, chapter 2, this volume). One of the reasons for the current widespread interest in the FFM is that it has been found to be a highly robust structure that is invariant across many different computational procedures for deriving factors (Goldberg, 1980). Another reason is that the model may be interpreted from a number of different theoretical perspectives (Wiggins & Trapnell, 1997). As discussed later, the FFM has been interpreted from such perspectives as the enduring-dispositional (McCrae & Costa, 1990), dyadic-interactional (Trapnell & Wiggins, 1990), social-competency (Hogan, 1983), and lexical (Goldberg, 1981) perspectives.

Theoretical Perspectives on the FFM

In Table 7.5, we provide examples of some of the ways in which the major theoretical perspectives on the FFM differ from one another. The focus of convenience (Kelly, 1955) of a perspective refers to the research problem or goal the theorists had in mind when they developed their version of the FFM. In general, FFM representations perform best in areas of their original focus of convenience. The theoretical orientation of each perspective influences the overall research strategy adopted, the substantive choices that are made in scale development, and the generalizability claimed for the FFM representation. The universe of content from which items and scales are sampled is largely determined by the focus of convenience and theoretical orientation of the perspective and is itself an important determinant of existing substantive differences among the theoretical perspectives of the FFM.

In addition to substantive differences, the assessment instruments used to implement the various perspectives differ from one another in terms of item format, scale construction strategies, and psychometric characteristics. Any of the instruments listed may be used to investigate the FFM, but their representative applications tend to reflect the focus of convenience and theoretical orientation of the perspective that gave rise to a given measure. Further discussion of the four theoretical perspectives and the differences among them are discussed by Wiggins and Trapnell (1997).

Assessment Instruments

As shown in Table 7.5, each of the four theoretical perspectives on the FFM is associated with a particular assessment instrument that serves as an operational definition of that perspective. In later sections, we present empirical data relevant to three of these instruments: the NEO Personality Inventory (NEO-PI; Costa & McCrae, 1985), the Extended Revised Interpersonal Adjective Scales—Big Five (IASR-B5; Trapnell & Wiggins, 1990), and the Hogan Personality Inventory (HPI; Hogan, 1986).[1] In the following subsections, we briefly describe the manner in which these instruments were constructed.

NEO Personality Inventory. The NEO-PI evolved from a series of studies of the stability of trait dimensions across age groups (e.g., Costa & McCrae, 1976). Three age-invariant factors were identified in instruments such as the Sixteen Personality Factor Questionnaire (Cattell, Eber, & Tatsuoka, 1970), the

[1] Goldberg's (1992) standard markers were not available to us at the time of data collection.

TABLE 7.5

Characteristics of Four Theoretical Perspectives on the Five-Factor Model

Characteristic	Enduring–Dispositional (Costa & McCrae, 1989)	Dyadic–Interactional (Trapnell & Wiggins, 1990)	Social–Competency (Hogan, 1983)	Lexical (Goldberg, 1981)
Focus of convenience	Longitudinal studies of personality and aging	Dyadic interactions in psychotherapeutic settings	Prediction of effective performance in work and social settings	Development of compelling taxonomy of personality-descriptive terms in the natural language
Theoretical orientation	Traditional multivariate trait theory of individual differences is a legitimate alternative to other theories of personality	Agency and communion are propaedutic to the study of characterological, emotional, and cognitive dispositions	Actors have needs for social approval, status, and predictability; observers use trait terms to evaluate social usefulness of actors	Those individual differences that are of the most significance in the daily transactions of people will eventually become encoded in their language
Universe of content	Literature review of earlier scales with a reference to the study of aging	Theoretically based taxonomy of trait terms derived from Goldberg's (1992) earlier taxonomy	Review of earlier five-factor studies from a social–competency perspective	Semantic relations among trait terms selected from dictionary searches
Assessment instruments	NEO-PI: domains of neuroticism, extraversion, openness, agreeableness, and conscientiousness; each measured by six facets	IASR-B5: domains of dominance and nurturance form eight circumplex scales; domain scores for neuroticism, openness, and conscientiousness	HPI: primary scales of ambition, likability, sociability, adjustment, prudence, and intellect; each measured by subsets of homogeneous item clusters	Standard markers: domain scores for surgency, agreeableness, conscientiousness, emotional stability, and intellect; each marked by 20 adjectives
Representative application	Relations between NEO-PI instruments from major research traditions in personality assessment	Relations between IASR-B5 and conceptions of personality disorders	Prediction of organizational and occupational performance	Investigations of generalizability of English taxonomy to Dutch and German languages

Note. HPI = Hogan Personality Inventory; IASR-B5 = extended Interpersonal Adjective Scales; NEO-PI = NEO Personality Inventory.

Eysenck Personality Inventory (Eysenck & Eysenck, 1964), the EASI Temperament Survey (Buss & Plomin, 1975), and the Experience Inventory (Coan, 1974). The five broad domains (or dimensions) of Neuroticism (N), Extraversion (E), Openness to Experience (O), Agreeableness (A), and Conscientiousness (C) are represented in the NEO-PI. The domains of N, E, and O are represented in the NEO-PI by six original facets that reflect previously identified substantive components; facet scales for A and C have subsequently been developed (Costa, McCrae, & Dye, 1991). Representative items for each of the NEO-PI factors may be found in Table 7.6.

Extended Revised Interpersonal Adjective Scales —Big Five. The IAS evolved from a program of research initiated by Goldberg (1977). On the basis of a priori distinctions among different domains of trait categories, Wiggins (1979) provided a conceptually based definition of the universe of content of the interpersonal domain that distinguish that domain from others (e.g., temperamental, characterological, cognitive). This definition of the interpersonal domain was influenced by the earlier conceptual and empirical work of others in the dyadic–interactional tradition (e.g., Carson, 1969; Foa, 1961; Leary, 1957; Lorr & McNair, 1963).

Theoretically guided circumplex methodology was used in the construction of eight adjective scales, which are arrayed in a circular order around the principal axes of dominance and nurturance (Wiggins, 1979). A short form of the IAS was subsequently developed (the IAS-R) that more clearly distinguished the dominance axis from the presumably orthogonal domain of C (Wiggins, Trapnell, & Phillips, 1988). The IAS-R was also found to meet the strong geometric and substantive assumptions involved in the assessment from the dyadic–interactional perspective (Wiggins, Phillips, & Trapnell, 1989). The IAS-R was extended to include adjectival scales that index the remaining three domains of the FFM: C, N, and O (Trapnell & Wiggins, 1990). This extended instrument—the IASR-B5—was used in the empirical work discussed later in this chapter. Representative IASR-B5 items are listed in Table 7.6.

Hogan Personality Inventory. The HPI operationalizes the social–competency perspective with a six-factor variant of the FFM (Hogan, 1986). The first factor of the FFM was originally designated as the Surgency–Extraversion dimension (Norman, 1963; Tupes & Christal, 1961). Subsequent formulations have emphasized the assertive component of this factor (e.g., Trapnell & Wiggins, 1990), the sociability component (e.g., Costa & McCrae, 1985), or both (e.g., Goldberg, 1992). Hogan (1983) felt that assertiveness and sociability were conceptually sufficiently distinct to warrant their representation by the two global domains of Ambition and Sociability, respectively. These two global domains of the HPI and the other four (Likability, Prudence, Adjustment, and Intellectance) clearly reflect Hogan's (1986) intention to measure dimensions that have "broad, general importance for personal and social effectiveness" (p. 5). Items were generated for each of these dimensions by considering what a person might say to convince others that he or she was leaderlike, sociable, likable, self-controlled, well adjusted, or intelligent (p. 9). These items were grouped into homogeneous item clusters (HICs) within the appropriate global domains. Thus, for more fine-grained analyses, the global domains can be decomposed into 5–10 HICs. Representative HPI items are listed in Table 7.6.

Principal Components of the Five-Factor Domain Scales

As should be evident by now, the three instruments above were generated from different theoretical perspectives but were developed with reference to a common FFM structure. To the extent that the instruments can be demonstrated to share a common underlying factor structure, it is possible to interpret variations in patterns of factor loadings among the three instruments as differences in substantive emphasis that arise from differences in theoretical perspectives. To provide a simplified illustration of this point, we return to the data gathered on the 581 undergraduate psychology students, which included complete NEO-PI, IASR-B5, and HPI protocols.

We computed the intercorrelations among the 16 domain scales from the three instruments and subjected the intercorrelation matrix to a principal-components analysis. Both Kaiser–Guttman and Scree test criteria clearly indicate retention of five components, and these were rotated to a varimax

TABLE 7.6

Characteristic Five-Factor Items From Three Tests

NEO Personality Inventory	Hogan Personality Inventory	Extended Interpersonal Adjective Scale
Extraversion	Sociability	Dominance
(+) I like to have a lot of people around me.	(+) I like parties and socials.	(+) Dominant
(+) I am a very active person.	(+) I like to be the center of attention.	(+) Assertive
(−) I usually prefer to do things alone.	(−) I don't care for large, noisy crowds.	(−) Unauthoritative
(−) I don't consider myself especially "high spirited."	(−) In a group, I never attract attention to myself.	(−) Unaggressive
	Ambition	
	(+) In a group, I like to take charge of things.	
	(+) I have a natural talent for influencing people.	
	(−) I am a follower, not a leader.	
	(−) I am not a competitive person.	
Agreeableness	Likability	Love
(+) I would rather cooperative with others than compete with them.	(+) I work well with other people.	(+) Gentlehearted
(+) Most people I know like me.	(+) I'm good at cheering people up.	(+) Kind
(−) If I do not like people, I let them know it.	(−) I would rather work with facts than people.	(−) Coldhearted
(−) I often get into arguments with my family and coworkers.	(−) When people are nice to me, I wonder what they want.	(−) Unsympathetic
Conscientiousness	Prudence	Conscientiousness
(+) When I make a commitment, I can always be counted on to follow through.	(+) It bothers me when my daily routine is interrupted.	(+) Organized
(+) I am a productive person who always gets the job done.	(+) I am a hard and steady worker.	(+) Orderly
(−) Sometimes I'm not as dependable or reliable as I should be.	(−) I am often careless about my appearance.	(−) Disorganized
(−) I never seem to be able to get organized.	(−) Life is no fun when you play it safe.	(−) Disorderly
Neuroticism	Adjustment	Neuroticism
(+) I often feel helpless and want someone else to solve my problems.	(+) I am a happy person.	(+) Worrying
(+) I often feel tense and jittery.	(+) Most of the time I am proud of myself.	(+) Tense
(−) I am seldom sad or depressed.	(−) I get depressed a lot.	(−) Not nervous
(−) I am not a worrier.	(−) I'm uncertain about what to do with my life.	(−) Not worrying
Openness	Intellectance	Openness
(+) I often enjoy playing with theories or abstract ideas.	(+) I enjoy solving riddles.	(+) Philosophical
(+) I am intrigued by the patterns I find in art and nature.	(+) I read at least ten books a year.	(+) Imaginative
(−) I seldom notice the moods or feelings that different environments produce.	(−) In school, I didn't like math.	(−) Unphilosophical
(−) I don't like to waste my time daydreaming.	(−) I hate opera singing.	(−) Uninquisitive

Note. + = a positive response; − = a negative response.

solution. As seen in Table 7.7, the rotated component matrix of the FFM domain scales is highly compatible with the hypothesis that the NEO-PI, IASR-B5, and HPI domain scales share a common underlying factor structure.

The pattern of factor loadings in Table 7.7 suggests that the NEO-PI and IASR-B5 are more similar to one another than they are to the HPI. The former two instruments provide the "defining" loadings on all five factors. The NEO-PI and IASR-B5 have similar conceptions of the nature of N, O, and C; and both were developed in part with reference to Gold-

---

TABLE 7.7

Principal Components of the Five-Factor Domain Scales

Scale (test)	Component				
	I	II	III	IV	V
Extraversion (NEO)	.84				
Dominance (IAS)	.82				
Sociability (HPI)	.81				
Ambition (HPI)	.71		.38		
Neuroticism (NEO)		.92			
Neuroticism (IAS)		.89			
Adjustment (HPI)		−.84			
Openness (IAS)			.85		
Openness (NEO)			.80	.35	
Intellectance (HPI)			.72		
Love (IAS)				.83	
Agreeableness (NEO)				.81	
Likability (HPI)	.45			.68	
Conscientiousness (IAS)					.84
Conscientiousness (NEO)					.83
Prudence (HPI)					.65

Note. N = 581; loadings <.33 omitted. NEO = NEO Personality Inventory; IAS = Interpersonal Adjective Scales; HPI = Hogan Personality Inventory.

berg's (1992) work on trait-descriptive adjectives. Table 7.7 also suggests that dominant and sociable interpretations of the first factor of the model converge on a common E factor, similar to that identified in earlier studies. Similarly, openness and intellect interpretations converge on a common factor, which suggests that the ultimate nature of this presently controversial dimension must be settled on other than psychometric grounds.

Overall, there are only three instances of significant (>.33) scale factor loadings occurring on more than one factor; these may be interpreted in light of substantive emphases that arise from the different theoretical perspectives. The results of a more fine-grained analysis of these data suggest that the loading of HPI Ambition on both the E and O factors was primarily due to the Ambition HIC of "generates ideas" (e.g., "I'm known for coming up with good ideas"). The loading of NEO O on both the O and A factors was primarily due to the O facet of "openness to feelings" (e.g., "I find it easy to empathize—to feel myself what others are doing"); and finally, the loading of HPI Likability on both the E

and A factors was mainly due to the Likability HIC of "likes people" (e.g., "I enjoy meeting new people").

We noted earlier that the present empirical analysis is a simplified illustration, and we would like to re-emphasize that the scientific case for the robustness of the FFM does not stand or fall on this particular example. A more definitive design would be one in which the dimensionality of the five trait domains is assessed by the multiple methods of questionnaires, self-ratings, and ratings by knowledgeable others and evaluated by the confirmatory procedures of structural equation models. This is precisely what Borkenau and Ostendorf (1990) did, and their findings provide rigorous support for the FFM on the global level of domain scores. Other less elaborate but equally convincing studies could just as easily be cited (e.g., Goldberg, 1980; McCrae & Costa, 1987). The point we are perhaps "beating to death" is that despite differences in substantive emphasis that stem from the different theoretical perspectives, the FFM of personality structure provides a meaningful, representative, and robust framework within which it is possible to interpret the structure of personality disorders as represented in Table 7.4. The converse is not, in our opinion, true.

PERSONALITY STRUCTURE AND THE STRUCTURE OF PERSONALITY DISORDERS

Correlations Among Components

What is the relation between the five factors that we found to underlie the two sets of personality disorder scales and the five factors that we found to underlie the three sets of personality domain scales? A preliminary, and again highly limited, answer to this question can be obtained by examining the zero-order correlations among the five component scores for personality disorders and the five component scores for personality dimensions in our university sample. These correlations are presented in Table 7.8. Until recently, the FFM tradition in normal personality assessment and the quest for a satisfactory taxonomy of disordered personalities have developed in relative isolation from each other. Because of this, we would certainly not expect a complete isomorphism between the two factorial solutions as would be indicated by a diagonal matrix of correlations with only five elements.

The considerable number of moderate and substantial correlations in Table 7.8 is compatible with our general hypothesis that conceptions of personality disorders reflect the well-established five dimen-

TABLE 7.8

Correlations Among the Personality Disorder and Five-Factor Components

Five-factor components	Personality disorder components				
	I	II	III	IV	V
Neuroticism	**.57**		.53	−.19	.27
Extraversion	.14	**−.71**	−.40		
Agreeableness	−.33	−.46	**−.47**		−.20
Conscientiousness	−.27			**.63**	
Openness			−.20		.12

Note. Boldface indicates the alignment of the five-factor components with the personality disorder components derived in Table 7.4. *N* = 581; *r* = .10 is significant at *p* < .01.

sions of personality. Different personality disorders would be expected to reflect different numbers and different combinations of these personality dimensions in ways that can only be understood through conjoint factor analysis. The results of a conjoint factor analysis of personality disorder and five-factor inventories can be interpreted as an identification of the salient personality dimensions underlying conceptions of specific personality disorders.

Conjoint Principal Component Analysis

Having established that the personality disorder scales and the personality domain scales share dimensions in common, we now consider the joint factor space shared by the scale sets. From the intercorrelation matrix formed by the 35 scales, we extracted five components that were clearly indicated by both the Scree test and eigenvalues-greater-than-unity criteria. The varimax-rotated FFM solution is presented in Table 7.9. It is clear from that table that the five factors are the familiar ones of N, E, O, A, and C. Within each factor, corresponding MMPI and PACL personality disorder scales have been paired, where possible, followed by the highest loading personality domain scales with labels in italics.

Because of the clarity with which the FFM appears in Table 7.9, it is now possible to interpret the principal components of personality disorder scales alone (Table 7.4) with reference to an operationalized model of personality structure. Earlier, we cautioned against optimistic expectations of an isomorphism between the five components of personality disorder scales and the five components of personality scales. However, in comparing Table 7.4 with Table 7.9, it is evident that almost complete convergence occurs on four of the five components and that only 4 of the 19 personality disorder scales in Table 7.4 do not load most highly on a corresponding component in Table 7.9.

The first component in Table 7.4 provides a bipolar contrast between avoidant (+) and narcissistic (−) personality disorders and is loaded positively by the MMPI dependent scale. As shown in Table 7.9, it is the global dimension of N (Component II) on which avoidant and dependent personality disorders are similar to each other and in contrast to narcissistic personality disorder. The second bipolar compo-

TABLE 7.9

Principal Components for the Combined Analysis of the Five-Factor and Personality Disorder Scales

Scale (test)	Component I	II	III	IV	V
Histrionic (MMPI)	.79				
Histrionic (PACL)	.73				
Schizoid (PACL)	−.77				
Schizoid (MMPI)	−.81				
Extraversion (NEO)	.86				
Sociability (HPI)	.80				
Dominance (IAS)	.73		−.34		
Likability (HPI)	.61		.50		
Ambition (HPI)	.55		−.38		.40
Borderline (MMPI)[a]		.69			
Passive–Aggressive (PACL)		.67			
Avoidant (PACL)	−.51	.65			
Avoidant (MMPI)	−.53	.64			
Dependent (MMPI)		.63			
Narcissistic (PACL)		−.37	−.36		
Narcissistic (MMPI)	.47	−.52	−.34		
Neuroticism (NEO)		.91			
Neuroticism (IAS)		.81			
Adjustment (HPI)		−.81			
Dependent (PACL)			.73		
Antisocial (PACL)	.36	−.37	−.60		
Paranoid (MMPI)[a]			−.41		
Agreeableness (NEO)			.77		
Love (IAS)			.72		
Compulsive (PACL)		−.35		.76	
Compulsive (MMPI)		.36		.47	
Passive–Aggressive (MMPI)		.34		−.35	
Antisocial (MMPI)				−.49	
Conscientiousness (IAS)				.76	
Conscientiousness (NEO)				.74	
Prudence (HPI)				.66	
Schizotypal (MMPI)[a]					.38
Openness (IAS)					.83
Openness (NEO)					.78
Intellectance (HPI)					.38

Note. N = 581; loadings <.33 were omitted. Within each factor, corresponding MMPI and PACL personality disorder scales have been paired, where possible, followed by the highest loading personality domain scales in italics. MMPI = Minnesota Multiphasic Personality Inventory Personality Disorder Scales; PACL = Personality Adjective Check List; NEO = NEO Personality Inventory; IAS = Interpersonal Adjective Scales; HPI = Hogan Personality Inventory. [a]No PACL scales for these dimensions.

nent in Table 7.4 contrasts histrionic and schizoid personality disorders along the dimension of E, which is found in the first component of Table 7.9. The third bipolar component in Table 7.4 contrasts passive–aggressive and borderline personality disor-

ders with the PACL dependent scale. Although only the latter scale loads on Component III of Table 7.9, components in both tables reflect A (and its opposite pole antagonistic hostility). In Table 7.9, the MMPI borderline and PACL passive–aggressive scales load strongly on Component II (N), reflecting the emotional elements of these disorders. The fourth bipolar component of Table 7.4 contrasts the conceptions of compulsive disorders with the MMPI conception of antisocial personality disorder along the dimension of C (Component IV of Table 7.9). Finally, the fifth component of Table 7.4 is positively loaded by schizotypal and paranoid personality disorder scales, with the former related to O on the fifth component of Table 7.9.

The striking, and admittedly somewhat unexpected, convergences between the component solutions in Tables 7.4 and 7.9 serve to forestall the possible criticism that the inclusion of so many markers of the FFM in the conjoint analysis might have "swamped" the variance of personality disorder scales and forced them into a five-component solution. The original structure of the personality disorder scales was only slightly changed in the conjoint analysis; and these changes, in our opinion, are substantively understandable from the perspective of the FFM.

From a clinical perspective, the secondary loadings of the personality disorder scales on the five interpretable factors of Table 7.9 are perhaps of even greater interest than the primary loadings. These secondary loadings serve to characterize the multidimensional nature of some disorders (e.g., people with avoidant personality disorder are both neurotic and introverted), to distinguish one disorder from another (e.g., in contrast to people with avoidant personality disorder, those with schizoid personality disorder are mainly introverted), and to distinguish between alternative conceptions of personality disorders (e.g., the PACL antisocial disorder scale reflects hostility, surgency, and lack of N; whereas the MMPI antisocial personality disorder scale reflects mainly low C).

We previously provided more extended interpretations of the results of this conjoint component analysis, which are buttressed by regression analyses of the NEO-PI facets onto the component-specific personality disorder scales and by an examination of

the item content of the personality disorder scales (Wiggins & Pincus, 1989).[2] Widiger and Trull (1992) also provided interpretations of the same component matrix within the broader context of the personality disorder literature.

DYADIC–INTERACTIONAL PERSPECTIVE

The Interpersonal Domain

Some of the more salient characteristics of the dyadic–interactional perspective are presented in Table 7.3. Our particular operationalization of this perspective is in the eight interpersonal circumplex scales of the IAS-R (Wiggins et al., 1988) that are embedded within the five-factor measures of the IASR-B5 (Trapnell & Wiggins, 1990). The structural model underlying the IAS-R is presented at the top of Figure 7.1, where it can be seen that the underlying dimensions of dominance and nurturance (DOM and LOV, respectively, in the figure) form a circumplex of eight interpersonal octants. The theoretical location of these octants is indicated by two-letter codes that preserve the 40-year tradition of circumplex representations of interpersonal behavior (Freedman, Leary, Ossorio, & Coffey, 1951). The eight octant labels that correspond to the alphabetic designations in Figure 7.1 are assured–dominant (PA), arrogant–calculating (BC), cold hearted (DE), aloof–introverted (FG), unassured–submissive (HI), unassuming–ingenuous (UK), warm–agreeable (LM), and gregarious–extraverted (NO).

Although the interpersonal circumplex and the FFM were developed independently, personality taxonomists have recognized for some time that the dominance and nurturance axes of the circumplex are conceptually similar to the E and A dimensions of the FFM (e.g., Goldberg, 1981). The empirical correspondences between the two models have been examined in detail (e.g., McCrae & Costa, 1989; Trapnell & Wiggins, 1990). At the level of domain scores, the IASR-B5 and NEO-PI are essentially interchangeable, as seen in Table 7.7. However, within the plane defined by the bipolar, orthogonal compo-

[2]The data set analyzed by Wiggins and Pincus did not include the HPI. Their results were highly similar and, if anything, clearer because the NEO-PI and IASR-B5 domain scales provided substantial and univocal markers of each of the five factors.

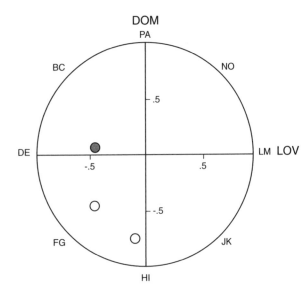

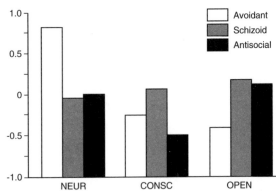

FIGURE 7.1. Combined-model assessment of three personality disorder groups. DOM = dominance; LOV = nurturance; PA = assured–dominant; NO = gregarious–extraverted; LM = warm–agreeable; JK = unassuming–ingenuous; HI = unassured–submissive; FG = aloof–introverted; DE = cold hearted; BC = arrogant–calculating; NEUR = Neuroticism; CONSC = Conscientiousness; OPEN = Openness to Experience. From "Extension of the Interpersonal Adjective Scales to Include the Big Five Dimensions of Personality," by P. D. Trapnell and J. S. Wiggins, 1990, *Journal of Personality and Social Psychology, 59,* p. 789. Copyright 1990 by the American Psychological Association. Reprinted with permission.

tions on the circle (e.g., Gurtman, 1991; Kiesler, 1983; Wiggins et al., 1989). Even small differences in angular displacement between two clinical groups may have clear behavioral implications (e.g., Alden & Capreol, 1993).

The octants of the interpersonal circumplex are, to some extent, analogous to the NEO-PI facets for E and A and to the HPI HICs for Ambition and Likability. The principal difference is that the IAS-R octants are defined structurally, whereas the NEO-PI facets and HPI HICs are not. From the perspective of the FFM, this difference is of no great consequence; from a circumplex perspective, however, it may be important. To demonstrate this point, we projected NEO-PI and HPI domain scores onto the IAS-R circumplex obtained from our university sample. As seen in Figure 7.2, the sets of orthogonal coordinates for the three instruments represent alternative theoretical views on the optimal positioning of the first two axes of the FFM (McCrae & Costa, 1989). These differences span an arc of 135°, which encompasses most of the substantive distinctions among the bipolar variables of the interpersonal cir-

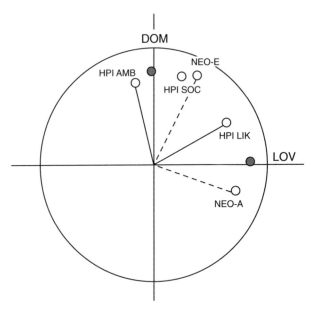

FIGURE 7.2. Projections of NEO Personality Inventory (NEO) and Hogan Personality Inventory (HPI) domain scales onto the circumplex of the Revised Interpersonal Adjective Scales (*N* = 581). HPI AMB = ambition; HPI SOC = sociability; HPI LIK = likability; NEO-E = Extraversion; NEO-A = Agreeableness; DOM = dominance; LOV = nurturance.

nents of dominance and nurturance, there are differences in emphasis between the two models.

The eight octants that constitute the circumplex model are defined with reference to a formal geometric model of personality structure (Wiggins et al., 1989). Consequently, when people (or scales) are projected onto this plane, there are concrete substantive implications associated with different loca-

cumplex. Such differences in emphasis within IAS-R circumplex space have implications for the interpersonal diagnosis of personality. Although there are good arguments for orienting the two NEO-PI domain scales through extraversion and deference (e.g., McCrae & Costa, 1989), interpersonal theory is strongly committed to the proposition that agency (dominance) and communion (nurturance) are more fundamental conceptual coordinates for the measurement and understanding of interpersonal behavior (Wiggins, 1991).

Interpretation of the personality disorders from the structural perspective of the interpersonal circumplex considerably antedates the applications of the FFM perspective. Circumplex interpretations have been made of the personality disorders in the first edition of the *DSM* (American Psychiatric Association, 1952; e.g., Leary, 1957), second edition (American Psychiatric Association, 1968; e.g., Plutchik & Platman, 1977), and third edition (e.g., Kiesler, 1986; Wiggins, 1982). The nine studies listed in Table 7.2 continue this tradition. We conducted a circumplex analysis of the conceptions of personality disorders represented by the MMPI and PACL disorder scales in our university sample. Two principal components were extracted from the intercorrelations among the IAS-R octant scales, and these components were rotated in such a way as to minimize least squared differences between the theoretical angular locations of the octants and their empirical locations. The MMPI and PACL personality disorder scales were then projected onto the rotated circumplex by trigonometric procedures (Wiggins & Pincus, 1989). Six sets of the 11 disorder scales had sufficiently high communality values (distance from the center of the circle) to warrant interpretation of their locations on the circumplex. These scale sets were distributed around the entire circle and were located in the following quadrants: Histrionic in Quadrant I; narcissistic and antisocial in Quadrant II; schizoid and avoidant in Quadrant III; and dependent in Quadrant IV. These locations, as well as the similarities and differences in locations of MMPI and PACL scales with the same labels, were interpreted with reference to other circumplex studies and related conceptions of personality disorders (Wiggins & Pincus, 1989).

Here, we focus on the finding, similar to that reported by others (e.g., Romney & Bynner, 1989), that significant projections on the circumplex were found for 6 of the 11 personality disorders. This finding has been described as indicating the inadequate nature of the circumplex for capturing the full range of personality disorders (e.g., Widiger & Trull, 1992). One could, with equal justification, characterize the FFM as inadequate for capturing the distinctions among 6 personality disorders within the domain of the circumplex model. It is more appropriate to recognize that the two models are complementary and operate at different levels of analysis (McCrae & Costa, 1989, p. 593). For that reason, we advocate a combined five-factor and interpersonal circumplex assessment.

Combined-Model Assessment

We return, for the final time, to the data provided by our 581 university students to illustrate what we mean by combined assessment. In evaluating the discriminant validity of the MMPI personality disorder scales, we determined the location on the interpersonal circumplex of three groups of subjects who had received high scores on the MMPI personality disorder scales of avoidant, schizoid, and antisocial, respectively (Trapnell & Wiggins, 1990). As evident from the top of Figure 7.1, the often difficult differentiation between avoidant and schizoid subjects is achieved by distinguishing the HI tendency of the former from the FG tendency of the latter. The DE tendency of subjects who scored high on the antisocial scale clearly distinguishes them from the other two groups. The bar graphs at the bottom of Figure 7.1 contrast the three groups on the remaining N, C, and O domain scales from the IASR-B5. Here, the critical role of N in further distinguishing avoidant from schizoid groups is quite evident. Avoidant subjects are also relatively closed to experience in relation to the other two groups; as expected, the antisocial group is low on C.

The combined model profile analysis illustrated in Figure 7.1 is a useful method for representing similarities and differences among groups for six of the personality disorders of *DSM-III*. Differences among the remaining five personality disorder groups are expected to occur mainly in the bar graph portion of the profile. This is because the communality values of the interpersonal profiles for these groups were low, and, hence, their location on the circumplex is close to the center of the circle. Does this mean that the circumplex model is inadequate for representing these groups? No, it simply means that these groups did not have significant loadings on the interpersonal factors of the FFM (Factors I and III in Table 7.9).

The lack of significant factor loadings on dominance and nurturance for five of the personality disorder groups may be puzzling on first consideration. Does this mean that these subjects did not have coherent patterns of interpersonal dispositions? This question is best answered with reference to the full interpersonal circumplex profiles in Figure 7.3. The profile at the top of the figure is based on subjects who had elevations on the MMPI schizoid personality disorder scale (which loads on the E factor). Note that the shape of this profile is the characteristic configuration we referred to as the "interpersonal spaceship" (Wiggins et al., 1989). The highest elevation is on the defining octant (FG), which is followed by moderate elevations on adjacent octants (DE and HI) and then diminishes to a highly truncated opposite octant (NO). This group profile suggests that there is a coherent pattern of interpersonal dispositions associated with elevations on the schizoid personality disorder scale, namely, the aloof–introverted personality.

The profile at the bottom of Figure 7.3 is based on a group of subjects who had elevations on the MMPI borderline personality disorder scale (which loads mainly on the N factor). This profile does not have the distinctive shape we would expect from the semantic constraints of the circumplex (Wiggins et al., 1989): It is essentially circular in shape. If this were an individual profile of one of our subjects, then it would be considered unusual. However, it is a group profile, which is based on subjects whose individual profiles tend to have characteristic spaceship configurations but that differ from one another in their defining octants to the extent that they tend to cancel each other out (Pincus & Wiggins, 1990b). The group profile suggests that there is no single pattern of interpersonal dispositions associated with elevations on the borderline personality disor-

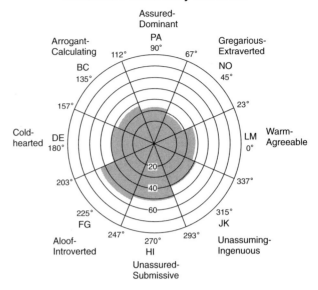

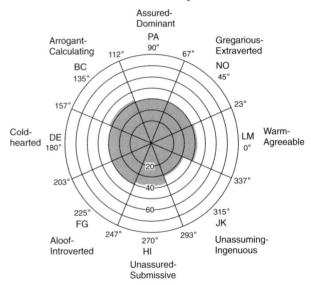

FIGURE 7.3. Interpersonal profiles for schizoid and borderline personality disorder groups.

der scale. A global disposition toward N may be associated with different interpersonal styles in different individuals (Shapiro, 1989). (In the rather special case of the borderline personality, different interpersonal styles might be observed in the same individual over time (American Psychiatric Association, 1987). Thus, within the framework of the combined model, circumplex assessment of individuals who are classified as falling within any taxonomic category of personality disorder may be useful, regardless of whether the first two factors of the FFM are implicated in the definition of that category.

References

Alden, L. E., & Capreol, M. (1993). Interpersonal treatment of avoidant personality disorder. *Behavior Therapy, 24,* 357–376.

American Psychiatric Association. (1952). *Diagnostic and statistical manual of mental disorders* (1st ed.). Washington, DC: Author.

American Psychiatric Association. (1968). *Diagnostic and statistical manual of mental disorders* (2nd ed.) Washington, DC: Author.

American Psychiatric Association. (1980). *Diagnostic and statistical manual of mental disorders* (3rd ed.). Washington, DC: Author.

American Psychiatric Association. (1987). *Diagnostic and statistical manual of mental disorders* (3rd ed., rev.). Washington, DC: Author.

American Psychiatric Association. (1994). *Diagnostic and statistical manual of mental disorders* (4th ed.). Washington, DC: Author.

Blashfield, R. K., Sprock, J., Pinkston, K., & Hodgin, J. (1985). Exemplar prototypes of personality disorder diagnosis. *Comprehensive Psychiatry, 26,* 11–21.

Borkenau, P., & Ostendorf, F. (1990). Comparing exploratory and confirmatory factor analysis: A study on the five-factor model of personality. *Personality and Individual Differences, 11,* 515–524.

Buss, A. H., & Plomin, R. (1975). *A temperament theory of personality development.* New York: Wiley–Interscience.

Carson, R. C. (1969). *Interaction concepts of personality.* Chicago: Aldine.

Cattell, R. B. (1943). The description of personality: II. Basic traits resolved into clusters. *Journal of Abnormal and Social Psychology, 38,* 476–507.

Cattell, R. B., Eber, H. W., & Tatsuoka, M. (1970). *Handbook for the Sixteen Personality Factor Questionnaire.* Champaign, IL: Institute for Personality and Ability Testing.

Clark, L. A. (1989, August). The basic traits of personality disorder: Primary and higher order dimensions. In R. R. McCrae (Chair), *Personality disorders from the perspective of the five-factor model.* Symposium conducted at the 97th Annual Convention of the American Psychological Association, New Orleans, LA.

Coan, R. W. (1974). *The optimal personality.* New York: Columbia University Press.

Comrey, A. L. (1988). Factor-analytic methods of scale development in personality and clinical psychology. *Journal of Consulting and Clinical Psychology, 56,* 754–761.

Costa, P. T., Jr., & McCrae, R. R. (1976). Age differences in personality structure: A cluster analytic approach. *Journal of Gerontology, 31,* 564–570.

Costa, P. T., Jr., & McCrae, R. R. (1985). *The NEO Personality Inventory manual.* Odessa, FL: Psychological Assessment Resources.

Costa, P. T., Jr., & McCrae, R. R. (1988). From catalogue to classification: Murray's needs and the five-factor model. *Journal of Personality and Social Psychology, 55,* 258–265.

Costa, P. T., Jr., & McCrae, R. R. (1989). *The NEO-PI/NEO-FFI manual supplement.* Odessa, FL: Psychological Assessment Resources.

Costa, P. T., Jr., & McCrae, R. R. (1990). Personality disorders and the five-factor model of personality. *Journal of Personality Disorders, 4,* 362–371.

Costa, P. T., Jr., McCrae, R. R., & Dye, D. A. (1991). Facet scales for agreeableness and conscientiousness: A revision of the NEO Personality Inventory. *Personality and Individual Differences, 12,* 887–898.

DeJong, C. A. J., van den Brink, W., Jansen, J. A. M., & Schippers, G. M. (1989). Interpersonal aspects of *DSM-III* Axis II: Theoretical hypotheses and empirical findings. *Journal of Personality Disorders, 3,* 135–146.

Dubro, A. F., Wetzler, S., & Kahn, M. W. (1988). A comparison of three self-report questionnaires for the diagnosis of *DSM-III* personality disorders. *Journal of Personality Disorders, 2,* 256–266.

Eysenck, H. J. (1947). *Dimensions of personality.* London: Routledge & Kegan Paul.

Eysenck, H. J., & Eysenck, S. B. G. (1964). *The manual of the Eysenck Personality Inventory.* London, UK: University of London Press.

Foa, U. G. (1961). Convergences in the analysis of the structure of interpersonal behavior. *Psychological Review, 68,* 341–353.

Frances, A. J. (1980). The *DSM-III* personality disorders section: A commentary. *American Journal of Psychiatry, 137,* 1050–1054.

Freedman, M. B., Leary, T. F., Ossorio, A. G., & Coffey, H. S. (1951). The interpersonal dimension of personality. *Journal of Personality, 20,* 143–161.

Goldberg, L. R. (1977, August). *Developing a taxon-*

omy of trait-descriptive terms. Invited address at the 86th Annual Convention of the American Psychological Association, San Francisco, CA.

Goldberg, L. R. (1980, May). *Some ruminations about the structure of individual differences: Developing a common lexicon for the major characteristics of human personality.* Paper presented at the annual meeting of the Western Psychological Association, Honolulu, HI.

Goldberg, L. R. (1981). Language and individual differences: The search for universals in personality lexicons. In L. Wheeler (Ed.), *Review of personality and social psychology* (Vol. 2, pp. 141–165). Beverly Hills, CA: Sage.

Goldberg, L. R. (1992). The development of markers of the Big-Five factor structure. *Psychological Assessment, 4,* 26–42.

Greene, R. L. (Chair). (1987, September). *Current research on MMPI personality disorder scales.* Symposium conducted at the 95th Annual Convention of the American Psychological Association, New York.

Guilford, J. P. (1948). Factor analysis in a test development program. *Psychological Review, 55,* 79–94.

Gurtman, M. B. (1991). Evaluating the interpersonalness of personality scales. *Personality and Social Psychology Bulletin, 17,* 670–677.

Hathaway, S. R., & McKinley, J. C. (1967). *Minnesota Multiphasic Personality Inventory manual.* New York: Psychological Corporation.

Hogan, R. (1983). A socioanalytic theory of personality. In M. Page (Ed.), 1982 *Nebraska Symposium on Motivation: Personality—Current theory and research* (pp. 55–89). Lincoln: University of Nebraska Press.

Hogan, R. (1986). *Hogan Personality Inventory manual.* Minneapolis, MN: National Computer Systems.

Hyler, S., & Lyons, M. (1988). Factor analysis of the DSM-III personality disorder clusters: A replication. *Comprehensive Psychiatry, 29,* 304–308.

Kass, F., Skodal, A. E., Charles, E., Spitzer, R. L., & Williams, J. B. W. (1985). Scaled ratings of *DSM-III* personality disorders. *American Journal of Psychiatry, 142,* 627–630.

Kelly, G. A. (1955). *The psychology of personal constructs* (Vol. 1). New York: Norton.

Kiesler, D. J. (1983). The 1982 interpersonal circle: A taxonomy for complementarity in human transactions. *Psychological Review, 90,* 185–214.

Kiesler, D. J. (1986). The 1982 interpersonal circle: An analysis of *DSM-III* personality disorders. In

T. Millon & G. L. Klerman (Eds.), *Contemporary directions in psychopathology: Toward the* DSM-IV (pp. 571–597). New York: Ronald Press.

Leary, T. (1957). *Interpersonal diagnosis of personality.* New York: Ronald Press.

Livesley, W. J., & Jackson, D. N. (1986). The internal consistency and factorial structure of behaviors judged to be associated with *DSM-III* personality disorders. *American Journal of Psychiatry, 143,* 1473–1474.

Livesley, W. J., Jackson, D. N., & Schroeder, M. L. (1989). A study of the factorial structure of personality pathology. *Journal of Personality Disorders, 3,* 292–306.

Livesley, W. J., & Schroeder, M. L. (1990). Dimensions of personality disorder: The *DSM-III-R* cluster A diagnosis. *Journal of Nervous and Mental Disease, 178,* 627–635.

Lorr, M., & McNair, D. M. (1963). An interpersonal behavior circle. *Journal of Abnormal and Social Psychology, 67,* 68–75.

McCrae, R. R., & Costa, P. T., Jr. (1987). Validation of the five-factor model of personality across instruments and observers. *Journal of Personality and Social Psychology, 52,* 81–90.

McCrae, R. R., & Costa, P. T., Jr. (1989). The structure of interpersonal traits: Wiggins's circumplex and the five-factor model. *Journal of Personality and Social Psychology, 56,* 586–595.

McCrae, R. R., & Costa, P. T., Jr. (1990). *Personality in adulthood: Emerging lives, enduring dispositions.* New York: Guilford Press.

McCrae, R. R., Costa, P. T., Jr., & Piedmont, R. L. (1993). Folk concepts, natural language, and psychological constructs: The California Psychological Inventory and the five-factor model. *Journal of Personality, 61,* 1–26.

Millon, T. (1981). *Disorders of personality.* New York: Wiley.

Millon, T. (1986). A theoretical derivation of pathological personalities. In T. Millon & G. L. Klerman (Eds.), *Contemporary directions in psychopathology: Towards the* DSM-IV (pp. 639–669). New York: Guilford Press.

Millon, T. (1987). *Millon Clinical Multiaxial Inventory—II: Manual for the MCMI-II.* Minneapolis, MN: National Computer Systems.

Millon, T. (1990). *Toward a new personology: An evolutionary model.* New York: Wiley.

Morey, L. (1985). An empirical comparison of interpersonal and *DSM-III* approaches to the classification of personality disorders. *Psychiatry, 48,* 358–364.

Morey, L. C. (1988). The categorical representation of personality disorder: A cluster analysis of *DSM-III-R* personality features. *Journal of Abnormal Psychology, 97*, 314–321.

Morey, L. C., Waugh, M. H., & Blashfield, R. K. (1985). MMPI scales for *DSM-III* personality disorders: Their derivation and correlates. *Journal of Personality Assessment, 49*, 245–251.

Norman, W. T. (1963). Toward an adequate taxonomy of personality attributes: Replicated factor structure in peer nomination personality ratings. *Journal of Abnormal and Social Psychology, 66*, 574–583.

Pincus, A. L., & Wiggins, J. S. (1990a). Interpersonal problems and conceptions of personality disorders. *Journal of Personality Disorders, 4*, 342–352.

Pincus, A. L., & Wiggins, J. S. (1990b, August). *Interpersonal traits, interpersonal problems, and personality disorders: Dual circumplex analyses.* Paper presented at the 98th Annual Convention of the American Psychological Association, Boston, MA.

Plutchik, R., & Conte, H. R. (1986). Quantitative assessment of personality disorders. In J. O. Cavenar, Jr. (Ed.), *Psychiatry* (Vol. 1, pp. 1–15). Philadelphia: Lippincott.

Plutchik, R., & Platman, S. R. (1977). Personality connotations of psychiatric diagnosis: Implications for a similarity model. *Journal of Nervous and Mental Disease, 165*, 418–422.

Rapaport, D. (1960). The structure of psychoanalytic theory: A systematizing attempt. *Psychological Issues, 2*, Monograph 6.

Reich, J. H. (1987). Instruments measuring *DSM-III* and *DSM-III-R* personality disorders. *Journal of Personality Disorders, 1*, 220–240,

Reich, J. H. (1989). Update on instruments to measure *DSM-III* and *DSM-III-R* personality disorders. *Journal of Nervous and Mental Disease, 177*, 366–370.

Romney, D. M., & Bynner, J. M. (1989). Evaluation of a circumplex model of *DSM-III* personality disorders. *Journal of Research in Personality, 23*, 525–538.

Shapiro, D. (1989). *Psychotherapy of neurotic character.* New York: Basic Books.

Society of Multivariate Experimental Psychology. (Ed.). (1990, January). [Whole issue] *Multivariate Behavioral Research, 25*(1).

Spearman, C. (1927). *The abilities of man.* London, UK: Macmillan.

Spitzer, R., Williams, J. B. W., & Skodal, A. (1980). *DSM-III*: The major achievements and an overview. *American Journal of Psychiatry, 137*, 151–164.

Strack, S. (1987). Development and validation of an adjective check list to assess the Millon personality types in a normal population. *Journal of Personality Assessment, 51*, 572–587.

Strack, S., Lorr, M., & Campbell, L. (1990). An evaluation of Millon's circular model of personality disorders. *Journal of Personality Disorders, 4*, 353–361.

Thurstone, L. L. (1934). The vectors of mind. *Psychological Review, 41*, 1–32.

Trapnell, P. D., & Wiggins, J. S. (1990). Extension of the Interpersonal Adjective Scales to include the Big Five dimensions of personality. *Journal of Personality and Social Psychology, 59*, 781–790.

Trull, T. J. (1991). Discriminant validity of the MMPI Borderline Personality Disorder Scale. *Psychological Assessment: A Journal of Consulting and Clinical Psychology, 3*, 232–238.

Tupes, E. C., & Christal, R. E. (1961). *Recurrent personality factors based on trait ratings* (U.S. Air Force ASD Tech. Rep. No. 61–97). Washington, DC: U.S. Government Printing Office.

Widiger, T. A. (1989). *Personality disorder dimensional models for* DSM-IV (written for the *DSM-IV* Workgroup on Personality Disorders). Unpublished manuscript, University of Kentucky, Lexington.

Widiger, T. A., & Frances, A. J. (1987). Interviews and inventories for the measurement of personality disorders. *Clinical Psychology Review, 7*, 49–75.

Widiger, T. A., Frances, A. J., Spitzer, R. L., & Williams, J. B. W. (1988). The *DSM-III-R* personality disorders: An overview. *American Journal of Psychiatry, 145*, 786–795.

Widiger, T. A., & Trull, T. J. (1992). Personality and psychopathology: An application of the five-factor model. *Journal of Personality, 60*, 363–393.

Widiger, T., Trull, T., Hurt, S., Clarkin, J., & Frances, A. (1987). A multidimensional scaling of the *DSM-III* personality disorders. *Archives of General Psychiatry, 44*, 557–563.

Wiggins, J. S. (1968). Personality structure. *Annual Review of Psychology, 19*, 293–350.

Wiggins, J. S. (1979). A psychological taxonomy of trait-descriptive terms: The interpersonal domain. *Journal of Personality and Social Psychology, 37*, 395–412.

Wiggins, J. S. (1982). Circumplex models of interpersonal behavior in clinical psychology. In P. S.

Kendall & J. N. Butcher (Eds.), *Handbook of research methods in clinical psychology* (pp. 183–221). New York: Wiley.

Wiggins, J. S. (1991). Agency and communion as conceptual coordinates for the understanding and measurement of interpersonal behavior. In W. Grove & D. Cicchetti (Eds.), *Thinking clearly about psychology: Essays in honor of Paul E. Meehl* (Vol. 2, pp. 89–113). Minneapolis: University of Minnesota Press.

Wiggins, J. S., & Broughton, R. (1985). The interpersonal circle: A structural model for the integration of personality research. In R. Hogan & W. H. Jones (Eds.), *Perspectives in personality* (Vol. 1, pp. 1–47). Greenwich, CT: JAI Press.

Wiggins, J. S., Phillips, N., & Trapnell, P. (1989). Circular reasoning about interpersonal behavior: Evidence concerning some untested assumptions underlying diagnostic classification. *Journal of Personality and Social Psychology, 56,* 296–305.

Wiggins, J. S., & Pincus, A. L. (1989). Conceptions of personality disorders and dimensions of personality. *Psychological Assessment: A Journal of Consulting and Clinical Psychology, 1,* 305–316.

Wiggins, J. S., & Trapnell, P. D. (1997). Personality structure: The return of the Big Five. In R. Hogan, J. A. Johnson, & S. R. Briggs (Eds.), *Handbook of personality psychology* (pp. 737–765). San Diego, CA: Academic Press.

Wiggins, J. S., Trapnell, P., & Phillips, N. (1988). Psychometric and geometric characteristics of the Revised Interpersonal Adjective Scales (IAS-R). *Multivariate Behavioral Research, 23,* 517–530.

CHAPTER 8

PERSONALITY DISORDER SYMPTOMATOLOGY FROM THE FIVE-FACTOR MODEL PERSPECTIVE

Lee Anna Clark, Lu Vorhies, and Joyce L. McEwen

As is well known, beginning with its third edition of the *Diagnostic and Statistical Manual of Mental Disorders* (*DSM-III*; American Psychiatric Association [APA], 1980), APA created a multiaxial system for the diagnosis of psychopathology. Although the general impact of the new system has been substantial, the creation of Axis II for personality disorders has had especially broad and far-reaching effects for several reasons. First, the recognition that personality dysfunction represents a domain of psychopathology separate from the clinical syndromes of Axis I has responded particularly to a perceived need on the part of the therapeutic community. Even without a formal nomenclature to support their distinction, clinicians have long made a general differentiation between the chronic affective–cognitive–behavioral patterns that characterize personality and the more episodic manifestations of psychopathology that define clinical syndromes. Thus, the introduction of a separate axis for personality disorders made official a distinction that was already used informally in clinical settings. Nevertheless, it is important to emphasize that the boundary between the two types of psychopathology often is not distinct, and many disagreements remain regarding the appropriate placement of certain disorders on Axis I versus Axis II. We encounter this issue again later in this chapter.

Second, since the inception of Axis II, the number of research reports addressing issues relevant to personality dysfunction has increased dramatically, and many studies confirm the high prevalence of these disorders (see Widiger & Rogers, 1989), although again many disagreements remain regarding the exact number and nature of specific disorders. Third, the profound impact of personality dysfunction on many other areas of psychopathology—from poor psychosocial functioning in community samples (e.g., Drake & Vaillant, 1985) to poor prognosis for those with various Axis I conditions (e.g., Pfohl, Stangl, & Zimmerman, 1984)—has also been well documented.

Apart from its impact on the clinical world, however, the creation of Axis II is important for another reason. *DSM-III* and its revision (*DSM-III-R*; APA, 1987) explicitly define personality disorders in terms of personality traits that "are inflexible and maladaptive and cause either significant functional impairment or subjective distress" and define personality traits as "enduring patterns of perceiving, relating to, and thinking about the environment and oneself, [that] are exhibited in a wide range of important social and personal contexts" (p. 335). Significantly, this definition of traits—and its extension into abnormality—is congruent with both classical and prevailing views of normal-range personality traits (e.g., Allport, 1937; Janis, Mahl, Kagan, & Holt, 1969; Pervin, 1989), thus creating a theoretical bridge between disordered and normal-range personality. Traditionally, personality research has been carried out separately from research in personality-related pathology, but this new *DSM* view of personality disorders as sets of maladaptive traits provides a basis for an integration of the two domains.

AN INTEGRATIVE VIEW OF PERSONALITY AND PERSONALITY DISORDER

A discussion of the many implications that a trait-based definition of personality dysfunction has for personality theory (and vice versa) goes beyond the scope of this chapter, but two points are particularly important in the present context. First, personality theorists generally view traits as continuously distributed and as exhibiting broad individual differences, such that some individuals may exhibit a trait very strongly whereas others may exhibit a trait very weakly, if at all. In other words, traits are dimensional in nature. Putting this view together with a trait-based conceptualization of personality disorders, we propose that there is a common set of personality traits with both normal-range and extreme variants. With the trait dimension of aggression as an example, extremely aggressive behavior and extremely unaggressive (i.e., very passive or unassertive) behaviors are both likely to be considered abnormal, whereas various expressions of moderately aggressive or assertive behavior—or extreme behaviors that appear only in response to highly unusual situations—generally represent normal-range phenomena.

A second important point is that personality theorists view traits not as fixed behavioral responses but as reflecting adaptations to the environment that are consistent within a certain range for each individual (Pervin, 1989). According to the *DSM* definition, a personality disordered person's traits have lost this adaptive aspect and so have become dysfunctional. Thus, normal-range personality may also be differentiated from abnormal personality on the basis of the flexibility and environmental responsivity of the person's traits.

Integrating these two points leads to the notions that (a) there is a single trait structure encompassing both normal and abnormal personality; (b) within the normal range, personality traits exhibit broad individual differences that represent a person's characteristic and adaptive style of thinking, feeling, and behaving; whereas (c) personality dysfunction is characterized by extreme and inflexible expressions of these personality traits that represent dysfunctional ways of thinking, feeling, and behaving. This integrative view suggests that it should be possible to develop a single system for the assessment of normal and abnormal personality and to study personality variation across the full range of trait expression and adaptability. In this chapter, we describe the development of such an integrated system of assessment and explore its implications for a descriptive understanding of personality dysfunction.

Unfortunately, despite its explicit definition of personality disorders as maladaptive traits, the diagnostic formulation of Axis II personality disorders in the *DSM* was not based on personality theory. Rather, it reflected the prevailing psychiatric approach to diagnosis and thus was categorical, rather than dimensional, in nature. Originally, criteria for 11 diagnostic categories were developed. Two provisional diagnoses were then added in *DSM-III-R*, and the criteria for the primary 11 diagnoses were also revised.

This system has had tremendous impact on the study of dysfunctional personality. One direct result is that the vast majority of research has been based on a categorical model of personality dysfunction; more specifically, most research focuses on one or more of the 13 *DSM* categories. For example, in an issue of the *Journal of Personality Disorders* (Widiger & Frances, 1990) only 1 of 10 articles directly assesses the subjects' personality traits (Livesley, Schroeder, & Jackson, 1990), and this assessment focuses only on those traits relevant to the dependent personality disorder.

Recognition is growing that the current categorical system—indeed any categorical system—may not optimally describe the domain (e.g., Eysenck, Wakefield, & Friedman, 1983; Frances & Widiger, 1986; Gunderson, 1983; Widiger & Frances, 1985). One of the most severe problems with the current system is the high degree of comorbidity among the personality disorders. A review of four studies (Widiger & Rogers, 1989) indicates that on average, 85% of patients with a personality disorder received multiple Axis II diagnoses. Furthermore, the average degree of overlap between any two pairs of personality disorders was 10%, ranging from 0% (between obsessive–compulsive personality disorder and antisocial personality disorder) to 46% (between borderline personality disorder and histrionic personality disorder). It is difficult to reconcile these data with the ideal that classification of psychopathology into separate diagnoses requires that the disorders be distinct and that the number of cases that fall into the boundaries between disorder be relatively few (Kendell, 1975). Some have argued that these criteria should be applied only to classical classification systems because they are too stringent for the prototypical model used for the Axis II disorders (e.g., Cantor, Smith, French, & Mezzich, 1980). Yet even prototypical models are supposed to exhibit distinctiveness at the "basic" or most optimal level for categorization (Cantor et al., 1980), and it would be hard to argue that the personality disorders exhibit this feature.

A second problem with the current system stems directly from its use of a prototypical classification model for diagnosis. To receive a personality disorder diagnosis using the *DSM,* patients must exhibit the required number of symptoms (from a longer list) for that diagnosis. For example, they must have five of nine symptoms to meet criteria for borderline personality disorder or four of eight for avoidant personality disorder. Thus, with this system, two patients who share only a single symptom could both receive the borderline personality disorder diagnosis. However, if two patients had four borderline personality disorder symptoms in common but one of them further exhibited a fifth symptom, then only the latter would receive the diagnosis. This system leads to tremendous potential heterogeneity within diagnoses and to unrecognized similarity between subjects who do not share a diagnosis.

THE TRAIT APPROACH TO PERSONALITY DISORDER

As a result of such difficulties, a number of researchers have proposed that a trait-based dimensional system may be more appropriate for the assessment of personality dysfunction (e.g., Eysenck et al., 1983; Tyrer, 1988; Widiger & Kelso, 1983). However, at the time of this writing, there was relatively little research on personality-related pathology from a trait-dimensional point of view (see Clark, 1990). One reason for this has been mentioned: The categorical model of *DSM* is a powerful force in direct-

ing research. Regrettably, the existence of an official categorical system that focuses on defining personality disorders (i.e., specific diagnostic entities) impedes direct investigation of the maladaptive traits that characterize personality disorder (i.e., the domain of personality dysfunction). Another is simply historical: Because personality disorders have been defined categorically, trait theorists have generally not become involved in personality disorder research. A third important reason for the paucity of trait-based research in personality disorders is that adopting a trait point of view cannot be done in a piecemeal fashion. Although it is certainly possible to research specific personality traits—indeed, personality researchers have done so for years—such research is only maximally useful to the extent that it can fit into a larger context and thus contribute to the understanding of the overall structure of personality. Accordingly, before the trait approach can be extended to Axis II, one must first explore the boundaries of the domain and its constituent components. The considerable time and resources required by such research may have inhibited the application of this approach to personality disorders.

However, if—as we hypothesized earlier—normal and abnormal personality represent aspects of an integrated single domain, then it should not be necessary for personality disorder researchers to start de novo in defining the structure of abnormal personality. Theorists such as Cattell and Eysenck have spent years delineating the fundamental parameters that underlie the manifest differences among individuals. They—and many others—have developed sophisticated methodologies that have led to major advances in understanding personality and its structure.

More specifically, during their early development, the fields of personality and personality assessment were characterized by multiple and conflicting views, and personality itself was viewed by many as a hodgepodge of ever-proliferating trait constructs. However, a broad consensus emerged that there are a limited number of basic personality dimensions. Although several competing models remain—and many specifics are being hotly debated and researched—the five-factor model (FFM) of personality gained wide acceptance as a framework for the global classification of personality traits (e.g., Digman & Takemoto-Chock, 1981; McCrae & Costa, 1987; Wiggins & Trapnell, 1997). Moreover, as the existence of this book attests, the relevance of this model for clinical psychology, especially personality disorders, is gaining recognition as well (see also McCrae & Costa, 1986). We hope that this book will help lead to (a) a broader awareness of the importance of trait research to the understanding of Axis II phenomena; (b) a realization that research on personality disorders can and should be informed by the theoretical, methodological, and empirical advances made in normal personality research, (c) an interest in Axis II on the part of normal-range personality researchers; and finally (d) a fruitful integration of these historically separate fields of inquiry.

In our own research applying a trait approach to personality dysfunction, we built on earlier efforts by investigating three basic questions: (a) What are the basic maladaptive traits that comprise the personality disorders as defined by current conceptualizations? (b) How can personality researchers assess these maladaptive traits—both clinically and through self-report—and what is the relation between these two methods of assessment? and (c) What is the relation between these traits and those already identified in normal-range personality? In investigating these questions, we adapted various methods—which were developed by Cattell, Tellegen, and others—for defining trait structure. Moreover, we were strongly guided by their theoretical and empirical research.

In the remainder of this chapter, we address the first of these questions by describing research that led to the identification of 22 personality disorder symptom clusters (Clark, 1990). To answer the second question, we then discuss the development of a self-report inventory that was designed to assess traits relevant to personality dysfunction (Clark, 1993) and present evidence—using this inventory in conjunction with clinical ratings of the personality disorder symptom clusters—that supports a trait-based approach to the assessment of personality-related pathology. Finally, we relate in some detail our investigations into the final question, that is, the relation between normal and abnormal personality. In particular, through a series of

analyses, we demonstrate that the FFM, which has provided a useful framework for understanding the structure of normal personality traits, is also highly relevant to the traits underlying Axis II. Although some five-factor instruments that were designed for normal personality may need to be adapted for optimal assessment of personality dysfunction, we conclude that the model itself is well suited for exploring the entire domain of adaptive and maladaptive personality.

SYMPTOM CLUSTERS IN PERSONALITY DISORDERS

Our initial approach to identifying the basic maladaptive traits that comprise the domain started with the personality disorder criteria by examining whether the criteria could be grouped into meaningful symptom clusters that reflect underlying trait dimensions (Clark, 1990). We began with all of the *DSM* personality disorder criteria and included criteria from non-*DSM* conceptualizations of personality disorder (e.g., Cleckley, 1964; Liebowitz & Klein, 1981; Perry & Klerman, 1978) and from selected Axis I disorders (dysthymia, cyclothymia, and generalized anxiety disorder) that have been noted to resemble personality disorders in important respects (Akiskal, Hirschfeld, & Yerevanian, 1983; Frances, 1980). Twenty-nine clinical psychologists and psychology graduate students sorted these criteria into synonym groups, and a consensual set of 22 symptom clusters were identified through factor analysis (Clark, 1990). Two detailed examples of these clusters are shown in Table 8.1, and a list of all 22 clusters is given in the first column of Table 8.2 (for a complete listing of the criteria, see Clark, 1990).

The clusters show several important characteristics. First, the symptoms for a diagnosis never form a single cluster; that is, every personality disorder is represented by a set of traits. Second, each of the symptom clusters contain criteria from more than one diagnosis. This result, of course, reflects the well-known problem of symptom overlap among personality disorders (e.g., Frances & Widiger, 1986) and simply confirms the fact that the various maladaptive traits comprising the domain are shared across diagnoses rather than being peculiar to one.

TABLE 8.1

Two Examples of Consensually Defined Personality Disorder Symptom Clusters

Diagnosis	Symptoms
	Social isolation
Schizoid	Almost always chooses solitary activities
	Neither desires nor enjoys close relationships
Schizoid/avoidant/schizotypal	Has no close friends or confidants (or only one) other than first-degree relatives
Avoidant	Avoids social activities or occupations that involve significant interpersonal contact
	Reticent in social situations because of a fear of saying something inappropriate or foolish
	Impulsivity
Antisocial	Fails to plan ahead, or is impulsive
	Reckless regarding his or her own or others' personal safety
	Unable to sustain consistent work behavior
	Lacks life plan[a]
	Fails to learn from experience[a]
	Poor judgment[a]
Borderline	Impulsiveness in at least two areas that are potentially self-damaging

Note. Adapted from *Advances in Personality Assessment* (p. 253–254), edited by J. N. Butcher and C. D. Spielberger, 1990, Hillsdale, NJ: Erlbaum. Copyright 1990 by Erlbaum. See Clark (1990) for a complete listing of the symptom clusters.
[a]From Cleekley's (1964) primary symptoms of psychopathy.

Third, many of the Axis I and non-*DSM* personality disorder criteria combined with the *DSM*-based symptoms in the clusters that emerged. This result can be interpreted in several ways. It may reflect simply a methodological artifact; that is, because the symptoms were included in the factor analysis, they had to load on a factor. However, these symptoms could have low loadings on all factors, which would indicate independence from personality dysfunction; but this did not happen. Also, it was possible for these symptoms to form factors of their own, without any interrelation to the Axis II symptoms; and indeed, three factors (anhedonia, high energy, and negativism–pessimism) were composed primarily of symptoms from current Axis I disorders. Another interpretation is that the domain of personality disorders is somewhat broader than is currently defined by the *DSM*; that is, the same maladaptive traits that define the Axis II disorders may also play an important role in some syndromes that are currently defined as belonging on Axis I or that are not recognized currently in the *DSM*. In particular, some

researchers have noted the overlap of certain anxiety disorders (especially generalized anxiety disorder and social phobia, generalized type) with avoidant personality disorder (e.g., Brooks, Baltazar, & Munjack, 1989; Turner & Beidel, 1989). Similarly, the construct of depressive personality disorder and its relation to dysthymia (especially primary early onset dysthymia) is a topic of current debate (e.g., Klein, 1990). Still others have proposed personality disorders for which affective symptomatology is central (e.g., hysteroid dysphoria; Liebowitz & Klein, 1981). As noted earlier, the boundary between Axis I and Axis II pathology remains in need of clarification.

Once these symptom clusters were identified conceptually, it was important to establish that they were also clinically meaningful and could be rated reliably on actual patients. On the basis of their state hospital charts, 56 inpatients were rated on each of the 22 symptom clusters by two independent judges (for a complete description of the sample and methods, see Clark, McEwen, Collard, & Hickok, 1993). Ratings on 18 Axis I symptom clus-

TABLE 8.2

Conceptual Correspondence Between Personality Disorder Symptoms and Personality Traits

Symptom cluster	Personality trait scale
Suspiciousness	Mistrust
Hypersensitivity	
Self-centered exploitation	Manipulativeness
Passive–aggression	
Anger–aggression	Aggression
Eccentric thought	Eccentric perceptions
Antisocial behavior	Disinhibition
Suicide proneness	Self-harm
Self-derogation	
Negative affect	Negative temperament
Negativism–pessimism	
Dramatic exhibition	Exhibitionism
Grandiose egocentrism	Entitlement
Emotional coldness	Detachment
Social isolation	
Dependency	Dependency
Anhedonia (−)	Positive temperament
High energy	
Impulsivity	Impulsivity
Conventionality	Propriety
	Workaholism

Note. − = inverse correspondence. From the *Manual for the Schedule for Nonadaptive and Adaptive Personality (SNAP)* (p. 16), by L. A. Clark, 1993, Minneapolis: University of Minnesota Press. Copyright 1993 by the University of Minnesota Press. Adapted with permission.

ters were also made to provide a basis for comparing the results. For both sets of symptoms, ratings were made on a 3-point scale: 1 = *not present or of minor clinical significance*; 2 = *present but of moderate significance*; 3 = *a prominent clinical symptom*.

The personality disorder symptom clusters proved to be quite prevalent in the sample: The median base rate for at least subclinical expression of the clusters (a rating of 2) was 44.7%, and several traits were highly prevalent. For example, impulsivity and dependency were judged to be present, at least subclinically, in over 85.0% of the sample. Only two symptom clusters—rigidity and high energy—had a very low prevalence (<10.0%). In contrast, the base rate for the Axis I symptoms

was considerably lower (*Mdn* = 14.3%; range = from 1.8% for phobias to 76.8% for drug abuse or dependence). Thus, there was ample evidence of the existence of personality-related pathology in the hospital charts.

Moreover, the ratings of the symptom clusters proved to be reliable. When the two clusters with very low base rates were omitted, the average interrater reliability for the personality disorder symptom clusters was .73 (range = from .57 for passive–aggression and exploitation to .96 for eccentric thoughts). (Intraclass coefficients, rather than Pearson correlations, were used to compute these reliabilities because the two raters were not always the same people.) This value indicates adequate reliability and is broadly comparable with the value of .88 obtained for the Axis I symptoms (range = from .40 for obsessive–compulsive to .98 for eating disturbance, omitting low base-rate symptoms), which are usually thought to be considerably more reliable. Although the rated clusters represent conceptual categories of broadly synonymous symptoms, they also appear to have certain traitlike properties.

Recall that the judges rated each symptom on a 1–3 scale. All three rating levels were used with some frequency: On average, approximately half (46%) of the patients were rated as showing symptoms of a given cluster either fully (21%) or at a subclinical level (25%). These data suggest that the clusters were seen as having varying degrees of expression and were not simply present or absent. These data contrast sharply with the Axis I symptoms, which were rated, on the average, as subclinically present only 11% of the time, with a mean of 18% of the patients per cluster clearly showing the symptoms and 71% of the patients per cluster rated as symptom free. Thus, subclinical manifestations were more rare for the Axis I symptoms compared with the Axis II symptoms, which suggests that the latter were viewed somewhat more dimensionally by the raters. These findings should be replicated with a longer rating scale to establish more conclusively whether personality disorder symptom clusters are indeed distributed more continuously (i.e., dimensionally) than bimodally (i.e., categorically).

A second traitlike property of the symptom clusters is their apparent stability. The judges rated each set of symptoms twice: first for current manifestations of each cluster and then to reflect the patients' lifetime status. It is noteworthy that with one exception (suicide proneness; $r = .48$), these two sets of ratings were highly correlated: The median r was .95, with a range of .75 (hypersexuality) to 1.00 (rigidity; Clark et al., 1993). This may have resulted because the chart information was not sufficiently detailed to permit differentiation of the two types of ratings; however, an alternative explanation is that the patients' standing on the various clusters was, in fact, stable. That is, it is likely that those who showed evidence of aggressiveness, for example, in their lifetime histories also exhibited aggressive tendencies during their current hospital stay. In support of this interpretation, the corresponding correlations for the Axis I symptoms were somewhat lower, ranging from .33 (hallucinations) to 1.00 (phobias and obsessive–compulsive), with a median r of .84. Although this figure still suggests considerable stability, it nevertheless is consistent with the notion that many Axis I symptoms are episodic in nature.

These results demonstrate that conceptually identified personality disorder symptom clusters also have an empirical basis: The clusters were rated as moderately to highly prevalent in a patient sample, they have acceptable interrater reliability coefficients, and they exhibit certain traitlike properties such as dimensionality and stability. Although these results are encouraging, it may be premature to identify these personality disorder symptom clusters as traits. Before they can be called traits, for example, personality researchers need to establish more firmly that they exhibit certain psychometric properties, that they are identifiable in nonpatient samples, that they can also be assessed through other methods (e.g., self-report), and that they are systematically (and appropriately) related to other personality-relevant variables. We address these issues in the following sections. Also the relations between these clusters and another set of traits designed to assess personality dysfunction are discussed by Clark and Livesley (see chapter 10, this volume).

MALADAPTIVE TRAITS OF PERSONALITY DISORDER

Scale Development

Although the identified symptom clusters appear to have certain traitlike properties, the extent to which they represent personality trait dimensions is not yet clear. For example, the stabilities (i.e., retest reliabilities) of the clusters are unknown. Examining these reliabilities would require rating the individual personality disorder symptoms on multiple occasions, which is clearly a major undertaking, especially because relatively large samples would be needed. Nevertheless, such research would help to illuminate the structure and psychometric properties of personality disorder symptoms. At the same time, however, it is important to investigate the trait structure of personality disorders using more than one method or approach to assess the convergent–discriminant validity of the emergent structure.

Clark (1993) pursued one such alternative method. Specifically, using the symptom clusters as the basis for potential trait dimensions, Clark developed a self-report inventory (the Schedule for Nonadaptive and Adaptive Personality [SNAP]) that assesses 12 primary traits and 3 broad temperament dimensions. Because this instrument plays a central role in the results we present later, we briefly describe its development here. A broad range of items were written to assess 16 of the 22 identified symptom clusters, which were then administered to a large sample of university students. The content of the remaining 6 clusters appeared to be tapped by three broad temperament scales developed by Clark and Watson (1990), so independent scale development was not undertaken (a description of these scales follows shortly). With a broadly followed method described by Tellegen (1982; Tellegen & Waller, in press), factor analytic techniques were used to evaluate both items and constructs. That is, factor analyses indicated (a) the ways in which scales measuring a target construct could be improved (e.g., by eliminating poor items and adding relevant items to enhance internal consistency) and (b) the ways in which constructs could be developed (e.g., through the addition of items that would expand their scope or alter their focus). The independence of the scales from each other was also a consideration. This process was repeated through several rounds of data gathering and scale revision—cross-validation using university, outpatient clinic, and inpatient samples.

The primary scales just described encompass 16 of the 22 symptom clusters; the remaining clusters were assessed with three broad temperament scales developed by Clark and Watson (1990): negative temperament, positive temperament, and disinhibition (vs. constraint). These scales have been incorporated into the SNAP, but they are also available separately as the General Temperament Survey (Clark & Watson, 1990). These scales correspond broadly to three factors of the FFM: negative temperament with Neuroticism, positive temperament with Extraversion, and disinhibition with (low) Conscientiousness.[1] However, it should be noted that two of the temperament scales were specifically designed to assess the affective cores of their respective dimensions rather than to sample their entire content domains (Watson & Clark, 1992, 1997). The relevance of this point is noted in a subsequent analysis.

It is also important to note that the symptom clusters themselves were only twice considered: first, when they guided the initial compilation of the item pool and, second, with the publication of *DSM-III-R*, when the symptom clusters were expanded—and new items were written—to incorporate the revisions. Otherwise, scale construction was driven by the data in terms of both developing the constructs that emerged from the analyses and making the psychometric refinements that these required. As a result, in several cases, clusters that were distinguishable conceptually did not yield independent self-report scales (e.g., the suspiciousness and hypersensitivity clusters combined to form a single self-report scale, mistrust). In other cases, two self-report scales were required to assess the content of a single conceptual cluster (e.g., the conventionality cluster contained content related to both conservative values and willingness to work hard, which split into separate self-report scales). Thus, although having their conceptual basis in the symptoms of personality disorder, the scales were ultimately not constrained by them.

To summarize, on the basis of the initial results, additional items were written to either solidify and refine the assessed constructs or expand them in directions suggested by the factor analyses. This process resulted in 12 primary trait scales that are each homogeneous in item content and maximally distinctive within the broad constraints imposed by the trait domain of personality disorders.[2] The scales are listed in the second column of Table 8.2 in such a way as to indicate their conceptual correspondences with the symptom clusters (shown in the first column). (Hypersexuality and instability have been omitted because of their lack of convergence with any SNAP scale; Clark, 1993.)

Clark (1993) reported extensive data regarding the psychometric properties of the scales. Briefly, the scales are internally consistent in both college and patient samples. Median alpha coefficients for the scales were .81, .83, and .76 in college, mixed-patient, and Veterans Affairs hospital samples, respectively. The scales were also stable (r = .81) over a short (1-week) interval in a patient sample and over moderate (1- and 2-month) time periods (median retest r = .81 and .79, respectively) in a college sample. Moreover, only one scale intercorrelation exceeded .50 in either the college or mixed-patient sample. This is especially noteworthy given the high degree of overlap typically found for self-reported psychopathology (e.g., Gotlib, 1984). Thus, the scales exhibit the psychometric properties that are appropriate to measures of trait dimensions.

---

[1] Various labels have been used for the five factors: (a) *Extraversion,* surgency, positive affectivity; (b) *Agreeableness;* (c) *Conscientiousness,* will to achieve, constraint versus disinhibition; (d) *Neuroticism,* negative affectivity versus emotional stability; and (e) *Openness (to Experience),* culture, intellectance. In this chapter, we primarily use the (italicized) labels of Costa and McCrae (1985) when referring to the FFM model but use our own terminology when referring to the three-factor models.

[2] Diagnostic and validity scales have also been developed but are not relevant in this context and so are not discussed here (for details, see Clark, 1993; see also Clark & Watson, 1990, for more information regarding the General Temperament Survey scales and their development).

Factor Structure

Although the primary SNAP scales are largely independent, an examination of the scale intercorrelation matrix nonetheless revealed notable clusters of interrelated scales (Clark, 1993). Moreover, all but 3 of 12 primary scales (eccentric perceptions, exhibitionism, and entitlement) are substantially correlated with one of the temperament scales. These data suggest a hierarchical arrangement, in which the 12 primary scales represent a lower order level of analyses and in which the temperament scales (each reflecting a group of primaries) comprise the higher order level.

Separate principal factor analyses of all 15 SNAP scales were performed on each of the three samples mentioned earlier to investigate this issue: normal college students ($n = 476$), a mixed-inpatient sample ($n = 55$), and a sample of Veterans Affairs hospital substance abuse patients ($n = 135$). As is typical in analyses of normal-range personality scales, a few higher order dimensions exhausted the common scale variance, regardless of sample type. Specifically, the first three factors accounted for 94%, 89%, and 93% of the common variance (46%, 55%, and 51% of the total variance) in the three samples, respectively. Therefore, the three-factor solution was subjected to varimax rotation in all samples.

The structure proved to be quite robust, with highly similar factors emerging in the three samples, although some sample variation was noted with regard to secondary loadings. In only two cases, however, did these differences also suggest a possible divergence between the normal and patient samples. Thus, it is most likely that they simply represent random sample variation rather than evidence of different structures for normal and abnormal personality. Furthermore, the observed structure clearly replicated that found in analyses of many normal-range personality inventories, such as the Eysenck Personality Questionnaire (Eysenck & Eysenck, 1975), the California Psychological Inventory (Gough, 1987), and the Multidimensional Personality Questionnaire (Tellegen, 1982; Tellegen & Waller, in press). Specifically, the factors were clearly identifiable as Neuroticism or negative affectivity, Extraversion or positive affectivity, and disinhibition versus Conscientiousness.

Neuroticism (negative affectivity) was defined by mistrust, aggression, eccentric perceptions, self-harm, negative temperament, and detachment; manipulativeness also marked this factor in the college sample. Extraversion (positive affectivity) was marked by exhibitionism and entitlement on the high end, with detachment and dependency loading on the low end. Finally, disinhibition. versus Conscientiousness was associated with impulsivity and manipulativeness on the high (disinhibited) end and with propriety and workaholism on the low (conscientious) end. Aggression also marked this factor in the patient samples.

In one sense, given the inclusion of temperament scales that were specifically designed to represent these three higher order factors, the emergence of this structure is not surprising. However, the origin and conceptual basis for the primary SNAP scales is rather different from that of most personality assessment instruments; that is, the items were based on clusters of symptoms of personality disorder, not on trait adjectives or concepts per se. From this point of view, the high degree of similarity between the observed factors and those that have emerged in other instruments is striking, and it adds to the growing body of evidence indicating that the basic structure of personality is quite robust. Furthermore, it supports our hypothesis that there is a common trait structure that encompasses both the adaptive and maladaptive variants of personality.

There remains the question of why the remaining two factors of the FFM (Agreeableness and Openness to Experience) did not emerge in these analyses. One possibility is that their content is not sufficiently represented in personality disorder symptomatology to emerge as higher order factors. The chapters in this book, however, attest to the improbability of this hypothesis (see also Wiggins & Pincus, 1989). Another explanation is more methodological: Three of the higher order factors were directly represented by scales in these analyses, which would facilitate their emergence. In contrast, higher order scales that were specifically designed to assess Agreeableness and Openness were not included, which would likely hinder the expression of these factors. To test this hypothesis, one would need to factor analyze the SNAP together with one or more measures of all of the five factors. We present such analyses later in this chapter.

RELATIONS BETWEEN SELF-REPORT AND CLINICAL ASSESSMENTS

Symptom Clusters

We demonstrated earlier that the personality disorder symptom clusters have both a conceptual and an empirical basis. We also showed that psychometrically sound self-report scales can be derived from these clusters and that they yield a factor structure similar to that found when using other instruments with diverse conceptual histories. It is now important to investigate whether the symptom clusters are related systematically to the trait measures that were developed from them. That is, what is the relation between the patients' self-views of their (maladaptive) personality traits and the clinical ratings of criteria intended to represent behavioral expressions of these traits?

Clark et al. (1993) examined this issue and presented correlations between SNAP scale scores and the chart-based symptom ratings described earlier. Their results demonstrate that there are broad-based relations between the two types of measures: 17 of 22 symptom clusters were significantly correlated with one or more SNAP scales. Moreover, the ob-

served relations were systematic. For example, clinically rated social isolation was related to self-reported detachment, whereas rated dependency correlated with both self-reported dependence and (negatively) aggression. Axis I symptomatology was also related to the SNAP scales, but the correlations tended to be weaker and, therefore, less easily interpreted. Thus, these results suggest that self-reported personality traits are more specifically related to personality disorder symptoms than to other types of psychopathology.

However, Clark et al. (1993) only examined these relations at the lower order level of individual scales. It is also illuminating to examine how the higher order factors are related to personality disorder symptom ratings. Therefore, we computed factor scores based on the three-factor solution described earlier and correlated these factor scores with the symptom cluster ratings, including symptoms from both Axis I and Axis II. All significant correlations ($p < .05$) are presented in Table 8.3.

Several aspects of the table are noteworthy. First, as shown with the lower order scales, the observed correlations are, for the most part, straightforward and easily interpretable. For example, subjects low in self-reported Extraversion (positive affectivity) are likely to be rated as self-derogatory and chronically depressed, whereas disinhibited subjects (i.e., low

TABLE 8.3

Correlations of Three Factor Scales From the Schedule for Nonadaptive and Adaptive Personality (SNAP) With Ratings of Axis I and Axis II Symptom Clusters in a State Hospital Sample

Scale	Axis II		Axis I	
	Symptom	*r*	Symptom	*r*
Negative affectivity (Neuroticism)	Suicide proneness	0.33*	Eating disturbance	−0.27*
	Aggression	0.28*		
	High energy	0.27*		
Positive affectivity (Extraversion)	Hypersensitivity	−0.27*	Chronic depression	−0.44***
	Self-derogation	−0.37**	Cognitive impairment	0.32*
			Inappropriate affect	0.31*
Disinhibition (vs. Conscientiousness)	Antisocial behavior	0.34*	Somatic complaints	−0.35**
	Anhedonia	−0.29*	Alcohol dependence	0.32*
			Vegetative signs	−0.31*
			Acute depression	−0.27*

Note. N = 56; all significant correlations are shown.
*$p < .05$; **$p < .01$; ***$p < .001$.

Conscientiousness) are rated as having prominent antisocial behavior and being prone to alcohol abuse or dependence. Second—in contrast to the lower order scale level, at which the SNAP scales were somewhat more strongly correlated with the Axis II symptoms—the higher order factors are as broadly and as strongly correlated with Axis I symptoms as with personality disorder symptoms. The reason for this is unclear, but it may be that the higher order factors tap very broad-based dimensions of psychopathology that are equally reflected in Axis I and Axis II symptomatology. In contrast, at the lower order level, specific relations between the SNAP scales and rated personality disorder symptomatology can emerge more strongly. This hypothesis is supported by the fact that fewer personality disorder symptom clusters were correlated with the higher order factors than with the lower order scales.

To summarize, the observed relations between higher order factors of self-report and clinically rated symptomatology were systematic and easily interpretable. At the same time, however, it appears that personality-related pathology may be understood more precisely by examining relations at the lower order level. Thus, with regard to the FFM, it may prove important to investigate the lower order or "facet" level rather than simply examining the five higher order factors (cf. Dyce & O'Connor, 1998).

Correlations With Diagnoses

Although our focus in this chapter is on personality disorder symptomatology, it is also interesting to examine relations at the diagnostic level. In addition to symptom ratings, hospital chart diagnoses were recorded for all 56 subjects in the inpatient sample (for details, see Clark et al., 1993). An overall frequency count of the patients' most recent hospital diagnoses was made, and 13 diagnostic groups (8 for Axis I and 7 for Axis II) were created so that no group was either overly broad or too specific. For example, a large number of subjects received substance abuse diagnoses; these were subdivided into three groups: alcohol, single drug, and polydrug

abuse–dependence. In contrast, patients with adjustment disorder and those with depressed mood were grouped together with those having major depression because there were too few with only adjustment disorder to form a separate category.

Each diagnosis was scored dichotomously as either *absent* (0) or *present* (1); Clark et al. (1993) reported correlations between these scores and the SNAP scales. As shown with the symptom ratings, the self-reports and diagnoses were broadly and systematically related. For example, a diagnosis of borderline personality disorder correlated significantly with self-reported dependency, self-harm, negative temperament, and entitlement (negatively). Correlations with Axis I diagnoses were equally strong and systematic. For example, subjects who received a diagnosis of polydrug abuse–dependence obtained higher scores on manipulativeness, disinhibition, impulsivity, and exhibitionism and lower scores on propriety and workaholism.

As with symptomatology, however, correlations with the higher order factors were not previously reported, so we report on those relations here. Table 8.4 presents all significant correlations, together with the sample prevalence for each diagnosis. In each case, scale means and standard deviations are also given for the subgroups of patients with and without each disorder, respectively.[3]

The higher order personality traits proved to be systematically related to both Axis I and Axis II disorders (although some of the data must be interpreted cautiously because of the low prevalence of certain diagnoses in this relatively small sample). One noteworthy finding is that correlates of the disinhibition (vs. the conscientiousness) factor were stronger than at the symptom level. The rather different self-characterizations of subjects who abused or were dependent on a single drug versus multiple drugs is particularly interesting. Those with a single-drug diagnosis portrayed themselves as higher in Neuroticism and Conscientiousness, whereas polydrug users were (not surprisingly) low in Conscientiousness. This difference may have arisen because

---

[3]Because the *p* value of the correlation between a dichotomous and continuous variable is the same as that for the *t* statistic comparing the means of the two groups, all mean differences are also statistically significant.

Correlations of Three Factor Scales From the Schedule for Nonadaptive and Adaptive Personality With Chart Diagnoses in a State Hospital Sample

Factor	Diagnostic group (*n*)	*r*	Present (*M ± SD*)	Absent (*M ± SD*)
Negative affectivity (Neuroticism)	Bipolar disorder (2)	0.28*	1.26 ± 0.17	−0.05 ± 0.87
	Single-drug abuse (7)	0.27*	0.62 ± 0.94	−0.09 ± 0.85
	Eating disorder (4)	−0.38**	−1.18 ± 0.32	0.09 ± 0.85
Positive affectivity (Extraversion)	Borderline PD (22)	−0.40**	0.45 ± 1.01	−0.30 ± 0.75
	Unipolar depression (14)	−0.36**	0.57 ± 0.96	−0.19 ± 0.85
Disinhibition (vs. Conscientiousness)	Antisocial PD (2)	0.42**	2.07 ± 0.64	0.08 ± 0.89
	Polydrug abuse (28)	0.59***	0.55 ± 0.93	−0.57 ± 0.63
	Single-drug abuse (7)	−0.41**	−1.04 ± 0.74	0.15 ± 0.91

Note. Total $N = 56$; PD = personality disorder; *n* = number of subjects receiving each diagnosis. Means and standard deviations are standard scores. All significant correlations are shown. *p* values apply to both correlations and comparisons of mean differences (*t* tests).
*$p < .05$; **$p < .01$; ***$p < .001$.

those who were single-drug abusers included a number of dysphoric subjects who had become addicted to prescription drugs, which they (over)used to cope with stress, whereas those who were polydrug abusers were more likely to be addicted to street drugs, come from dysfunctional families, have a poor employment record, and have a history of antisocial behavior.

It should be noted that—due to substantial comorbidity—the reported correlations are not independent of one another. For example, both of the subjects who were diagnosed with antisocial personality disorder were also polydrug users, and slightly over half (55%) of those with borderline personality disorder received a depressive diagnosis. It may be that the presence of a personality disorder diagnosis is a predisposing factor (either for genetic or psychosocial reasons) for the development of the Axis I syndrome in these cases. (Of course, the reverse could also be true; but because the manifestations of personality disorders are often seen as early as adolescence and are long-standing features of the person's functioning, this seems less compelling.) However, another plausible interpretation of these data is that personality trait factors reflect common substrates that underlie the overlapping diagnoses and that contribute directly to their comorbidity. For example, being extremely low in Conscientiousness

may itself represent a feature of antisocial personality disorder that also predisposes one to drug abuse. These are important questions for future research.

Finally, it is important to emphasize that these correlations represent diagnostic covariations with personality factors within a patient sample. That is, they provide important information regarding differential diagnosis. For example, the data in Table 8.4 indicate that patients with borderline personality disorder score lower on the Extraversion factor than do other patients in the sample; this is a fairly strong diagnostic statement. This fact may also explain the paucity of correlations with the Neuroticism factor. Inpatient samples tend to have a restricted range on this factor because the majority yield highly elevated scores (Clark et al., 1993). Further research is needed to examine this issue.

Summary

Beginning with analyses of personality disorder symptomatology, we examined the broad domain of maladaptive personality traits and presented data that explicated the internal structure of this domain. First, we showed that clusters of personality disorder symptoms have several traitlike properties, such as dimensionality and temporal stability. We then described the development of self-report scales that were derived from these clusters of personality disorder symptoms. The trait structure that emerged from factor analyses of these scales closely resembled that identified in analyses of many normal-range personality inventories. Moreover, these higher order personality factors were shown to be systematically related to both the clinical ratings of symptomatology and diagnoses. Interestingly, these relations were not limited to the personality disorders but included strong Axis I correlates as well, which suggests that these higher order personality factors have broad implications for pathology.

In summary, we have shown that trait-based measures of personality disorder are related to aspects of both normal and abnormal personality, which thereby supports the hypothesis that a single personality trait structure underlies both domains. However, because our analyses examined only personality disorder symptoms and their associated traits and diagnoses, they leave several questions unanswered. First, we have not yet explored directly the relation between abnormal and normal personality traits; nor have we determined whether all factors of the FFM have maladaptive variants that are related to Axis II symptomatology. We now examine these issues.

RELATIONS BETWEEN NORMAL AND ABNORMAL PERSONALITY TRAITS

In this section, we report on a study in which subjects completed two measures of the FFM, which was designed to assess normal personality, and the SNAP, which (as noted earlier) was developed to assess maladaptive traits. Through a series of correlational, factor analytic, and multiple regression analyses, we explored (a) the basic correlations between normal-range and maladaptive traits, (b) the structure of personality traits when both normal and pathological traits are considered together, (c) the ability of the FFM to predict traits of personality disorder, and (d) the relative effectiveness of the three- and five-factor models for predicting these maladaptive traits. Given that Neuroticism, Extraversion, and Conscientiousness have been shown to be related to personality-relevant pathology, we are particularly interested here in the extent to which the dimensions of Agreeableness and Openness are related to this domain.

Method

Subjects and Procedures. Students enrolled in an introductory psychology course at Southern Methodist University (a private southwestern college) completed a packet of self-report questionnaires at the beginning of the 1989 fall semester. Two months later, 225 subjects from these same classes completed a second round of testing. The data we present here are on 194 subjects (68 men and 126 women) who completed both sets of measures. The mean age of the sample was 18.7 years (SD = .99; range = 17–23); 94% were White.

Measures

Goldberg Scales. The Goldberg scales (Goldberg, 1983) originally consisted of 40 bipolar pairs of adjectives, with each of the five factors represented by 8 adjectival pairs. However, McCrae and Costa (1985, 1987) expanded this instrument by adding 8 additional pairs that were intended to assess each factor. They were concerned with increasing the reliability of the factors and broadening the content of the Openness factor. Subjects completed this 80-item version during the first round of testing. They rated which adjective best characterized their personality on a 1–5 scale: 1 = *very much like trait A*; 3 = *about average on this dimension*; 5 = *very much like trait B*. A principal factor analysis of the items was performed for the entire initial sample (N = 603) following McCrae and Costa's (1987) study, and five varimax-rotated factors were extracted. Factor scores were computed for each of these factors and were used in the analyses that follow.

NEO Personality Inventory. The NEO Personality Inventory (NEO-PI; Costa & McCrae, 1985) is a 181-item measure designed to assess the FFM. Items are rated on a 0–4 scale on the basis of whether (and how strongly) the subject agrees or disagrees with each statement. The domains of Neuroticism, Extraversion, and Openness are each composed of six 8-item facets, whereas Agreeableness and Conscientiousness are assessed simply with 18-item scales. Facets have been developed for these factors also but were not available for this study. Costa and McCrae presented extensive psychometric and validational data for the NEO-PI, and the psychometric analyses of our data (e.g., descriptive statistics, internal consistency reliabilities) yielded comparable results (Vorhies, 1990). Subjects completed the NEO-PI during the second round of testing.

SNAP. Subjects completed the SNAP (Clark, 1993) in the second round of testing. The development, content, and psychometric properties of this inventory have already been described. It should be noted that much of the normative data presented earlier (e.g., regarding internal consistency, reliability, and factor structure) included these subjects' data.

Results

Correlational Analyses

Correlations Between Two Sets of FFM Scales. The two measures of the FFM (i.e., the NEO-PI and the Goldberg scales) were first intercorrelated to determine whether corresponding scales were actually tapping the same dimensions. Convergent correlations ranged from .42 for Openness to .62 for Conscientiousness, which confirms the general correspondence of the two sets of scales, especially considering that these coefficients also reflect a 2-month retest interval. Discriminant correlations were all quite low, ranging from .23 (NEO-PI Extraversion with Goldberg's Agreeableness) to −.17 (NEO-PI Neuroticism with Goldberg's Conscientiousness), with a median absolute value of .13.

Correlations between these five-factor measures and the three SNAP temperament scales were also computed, and they again confirmed the convergence of these measures: Convergence coefficients of the SNAP temperament scales with the NEO-PI and Goldberg scales, respectively, were .74 and .55 for Neuroticism–negative temperament, .61 and .46 for Extraversion–positive temperament, and −.59 and −.50 for Conscientiousness versus disinhibition. Once again, it should be noted that the SNAP and NEO-PI were assessed at the same time, whereas the Goldberg scales were completed 2 months earlier. This explains, in part, why the SNAP temperament scales converged better with the NEO-PI than with the Goldberg scales. In addition, because the SNAP and NEO-PI are both questionnaires—whereas the Goldberg scores are based on bipolar adjective ratings scales—it is likely that methodological factors also contributed to this pattern.

Discriminant correlations were again notably lower, ranging from −.28 (negative temperament with NEO-PI Agreeableness) to .35 (positive temperament and NEO-PI Agreeableness), with a median absolute value of .15. These results suggest that the scales possess substantial convergent and discriminant validity. That is, although these measures are not entirely interchangeable, the bulk of their systematic variance appears to reflect the same respective underlying constructs; therefore, they should yield highly similar results in most analyses.

Correlations of the FFM Scales With Personality Disorder Trait Scales. Next, the two sets of five-factor scales were correlated with the primary SNAP scales (a) to replicate the relations observed earlier between the primary trait and higher order temperament scales of the SNAP, using the corresponding NEO-PI and Goldberg measures of Neuroticism, Extraversion, and Conscientiousness; and (b) to examine whether any of the SNAP scales show significant correlations with the other two higher order scales, Agreeableness and Openness. Every SNAP scale proved to be significantly correlated with at least one of the five-factor marker pairs, which thereby supports the hypothesis that there is substantial overlap between measures of normal and abnormal personality. SNAP scales that were significantly correlated ($p < .01$) with a particular five-factor scale in each of the two instruments are given in Table 8.5; a stringent p value was used in this case because of the large number of correlations (12 SNAP scales × 10 Five-Factor scales) that were computed.

With Neuroticism, Extraversion, and Conscientiousness, the five-factor scales yielded correlations similar to those found with the corresponding SNAP temperament scales, with few exceptions. For example, three of the four scales significantly related to Neuroticism in this analysis (self-harm, mistrust, and aggression) also marked the Neuroticism–negative affectivity factor in the previously described analyses. Similarly, three of the four scales that correlated in this sample with Extraversion and four of the five that were related to Conscientiousness marked their respective factors in the earlier analyses. The most notable discrepancy involved dependency, which correlated with Neuroticism and Conscientiousness (negatively) in these analyses but which previously

TABLE 8.5

Replicated Correlations Between the Schedule for Nonadaptive and Adaptive Personality (SNAP) Primary Scales and Two Sets of Scales Measuring the Five-Factor Model

Factor	SNAP scale	NEO-PI	Goldberg
Neuroticism	Self-Harm	0.57	0.32
	Dependency	0.48	0.25
	Mistrust	0.47	0.28
	Aggression	0.35	0.25
Extraversion	Exhibitionism	0.64	0.52
	Detachment	−0.66	−0.54
	Entitlement	0.28	0.20
	Impulsivity	0.19	0.31
Openness	Eccentric Perceptions	0.26	0.30
	Propriety	−0.23	−0.30
	Impulsivity	0.22	0.23
Agreeableness	Aggression	−0.58	−0.48
	Manipulativeness	−0.49	−0.32
	Detachment	−0.38	−0.35
Conscientiousness	Workaholism	0.54	0.49
	Impulsivity	−0.51	−0.52
	Manipulativeness	−0.44	−0.30
	Dependency	−0.41	−0.34
	Propriety	0.26	0.24

Note. N = 194 university students. NEO-PI = NEO Personality Inventory; Goldberg = Goldberg scales.

marked the low end of the Extraversion factor. Nevertheless, it must be said that overall the NEO-PI, Goldberg, and SNAP temperament scales yielded very comparable results, which further demonstrates the convergent validity of these instruments.

As seen in Table 8.5, several SNAP scales were strongly and significantly correlated with Agreeableness and—to a lesser extent—Openness, which indicates that these factors do indeed play a role in personality-related pathology. It is interesting to note that each of the scales that correlated significantly with Agreeableness was also related to another of the five factors. Specifically, aggression was also related to Neuroticism, manipulativeness (negatively) was related to Conscientiousness, and detachment was (negatively) related to Extraversion. This may suggest that (dis)agreeableness is an important modifying element of personality, such that certain traits

become maladaptive only to the extent that they have an additional, disagreeable quality. For example, it may be that "pure" introversion can be adaptive, whereas disagreeable introversion is maladaptive and expresses itself as detachment. Similarly, pure low Conscientiousness may simply reflect adaptively carefree, nondirected behavior; whereas disagreeable, unconscientious behavior may emerge as manipulativeness. This is an interesting hypothesis for further research.

It is important to note that Openness was significantly correlated with several SNAP scales. Although these correlations were not as strong as those with the other factors, they were nevertheless systematic. Eccentric perceptions appear to represent a cognitive pattern that is too open, that is, so open that it begins to lose its reality base. Similarly, being too open to experience may lead to impulsive and disinhibited behavior. Proprietous people, however, are characteristically rigid and closed to new ideas and experiences.

To summarize, separate measures of the five factors yielded a clear convergent and discriminant pattern. More important, scales that assess maladaptive personality traits were shown to be related to measures of all five factors, which indicates the general relevance of the FFM for Axis II phenomena. However, several SNAP scales were correlated with more than one of the five factors, so it should be illuminating to examine the overall structure of these maladaptive traits in relation to the FFM. Therefore, in the next section, we describe a factor analysis of these measures.

Factor Analyses. To investigate the combined structure of normal and abnormal personality traits, we first performed a principal factor analysis of the Goldberg, NEO-PI, and SNAP scales. The SNAP temperament scales were omitted from these analyses to avoid overrepresenting three of the five factors. Examination of the eigenvalues revealed that the first five factors (all with eigenvalues >1) accounted for all of the common variance (55% of the total variance) and that successive factors each contributed an additional 5% or less. Therefore, we extracted five varimax-rotated factors; these results are presented in Table 8.6. For clarity of presentation, the FFM scales are given in boldface, and all load-

TABLE 8.6

Principal Factor Analysis With Varimax Rotation of the Schedule for Nonadaptive and Adaptive Personality Primary Scales and Two Sets of Scales Measuring the Five-Factor Model

Scale	N	E	O	A	C
NEO-PI Neuroticism	**0.79**				
Self-Harm	**0.66**				
Mistrust	**0.62**			−0.36	
Goldberg Neuroticism	**0.57**				
Dependency	**0.50**				−0.39
NEO-PI Extraversion		**0.84**			
Exhibitionism		**0.79**			
Goldberg Extraversion		**0.69**			
Entitlement		**0.44**			
Detachment		**−0.68**		−0.34	
Goldberg Openness			**0.69**		
NEO-PI Openness			**0.60**		
Eccentric Perceptions	0.41		**0.43**		
Propriety			**−0.43**		0.38
NEO-PI Agreeableness				**0.75**	
Goldberg Agreeableness				**0.68**	
Manipulativeness				**−0.62**	−0.33
Aggression				**−0.68**	
NEO-PI Conscientiousness					**0.77**
Goldberg Conscientiousness					**0.74**
Workaholism					**0.69**
Impulsivity			0.31		**−0.66**

Note. N = 194 university students. NEO-PI = NEO Personality Inventory. Goldberg = Goldberg scales. N = Neuroticism; E = Extraversion; O = Openness; A = Agreeableness; C = Conscientiousness. Highest loading for each scale is in boldface. Names of NEO-PI and Goldberg marker scales are also in boldface. Loadings below 0.30 are omitted.

ings below .30 are omitted (for the complete matrix, see Vorhies, 1990).

Several things are evident in the table. First, the five factors of the model emerge cleanly in these data: The corresponding Goldberg and NEO-PI scales each mark one—and only one—of the extracted five factors. Second, each of the factors is also clearly marked by one or more SNAP scales, and conversely, every SNAP scale loads strongly on at least one of the five factors (SNAP marker scale loadings range = .43–.79). These results clearly indicate that the SNAP scales contain content relevant to all five factors and, furthermore, that the dimensions of the FFM account for much of the variance in traits of personality disorder. Third, seven of the SNAP scales have substantial loadings on more than one factor, which indicates—as also suggested by the correlational analyses—that certain (lower order) traits in the domain of personality disorder are factorially complex. For example, as noted earlier, detachment loads negatively on both Extraversion and Agreeableness. Reynolds and Clark (2001) recently replicated these findings in a heterogeneous clinical sample (N = 94). Again, 12 of the 15 SNAP scales displayed factorial complexity. However, the detachment scale was predicted only by Extraversion facets (low E1: Warmth; E2: Gregariousness; and E3: Assertiveness) in their clinical sample (cf. Table 8.2; Reynolds & Clark, 2001).

To summarize, the factor analytic results lend

considerable support to two related hypotheses. First, the same underlying personality trait structure has been shown to emerge from analyses of normal and maladaptive personality traits. Once again, these data provide evidence of structural continuity across normal and abnormal personality. Second—and more specifically—a comprehensive (although perhaps not exhaustive) set of maladaptive traits has been shown to correlate significantly with all of the dimensions of the FFM, which supports the notion that this particular model of personality has relevance for understanding personality disorder and has been replicated in a clinical sample (Reynolds & Clark, 2001).

Several interesting issues remain unresolved by these analyses. Needless to say, the FFM is not without its critics and rivals; most notably, three-factor models also currently have a number of prominent proponents (e.g., Eysenck, Gough, Tellegen, Cloninger). Although we have seen evidence of substantial overlap between the five-factor dimensions of Neuroticism, Extraversion, and Conscientiousness and the three higher order dimensions proposed by these theorists, each personality researcher has his or her own view of the basic composition and nature of these constructs; moreover, the scope of corresponding dimensions varies from researcher to researcher. For example, Eysenck's third dimension (labeled "psychoticism")—although strongly related to (low) Conscientiousness—also clearly encompasses some of the variance accounted for by (dis)Agreeableness in the FFM. However, it is currently unclear whether one model or the other is generally more comprehensive and essentially incorporates the other, or whether each model assesses some portion of the personality trait domain that the other misses.

Therefore, it is interesting to investigate (a) the extent to which the additional dimensions of Agreeableness and Openness contribute to the prediction of maladaptive traits beyond that accounted for by Neuroticism, Extraversion, and Conscientiousness; (b) how well the FFM, as a whole, can predict scores on maladaptive traits; and (c) whether scales developed within the three-factor tradition can contribute information to the prediction of these traits beyond that attributable to the FFM as a whole. To

answer these questions, we turn to multiple regression analyses.

Multiple Regression Analyses

Predicting Maladaptive Personality Traits From the FFM. To focus on the contribution of the FFM per se rather than on a particular set of marker scales, we first created a single composite measure for each five-factor dimension by combining the two corresponding scores from the NEO-PI and Goldberg scales. To adjust for scaling differences in the measures, we standardized the scores for each scale before they were added. We then performed a series of hierarchical multiple regression analyses in which each of the primary SNAP scales was predicted from the five-factor dimensions using the following procedure. First, the dimensions of Neuroticism, Extraversion, and Conscientiousness were entered into the equation (Step 1). For each SNAP scale, the percentage of variance that was accounted for (R^2) at this step is presented in the first column of Table 8.7; the second column of Table 8.7 lists the specific dimensions that made a significant contribution at this step ($p < .05$), with the stronger predictor listed first. Openness and Agreeableness were then entered in Steps 2 and 3, with the stronger predictor entered first at Step 2. These R^2 changes are also shown in Columns 3 (for Openness) and 4 (for Agreeableness). Finally, the overall R^2 is shown in the last column; these values include the contributions of all five dimensions, regardless of significance of contribution.

Several aspects of the results deserve comment. First, as seen in the table, the three dimensions of Neuroticism, Extraversion, and Conscientiousness account for a substantial portion of the variance in some—but not all—of the SNAP scales. Specifically, the multiple correlations (Rs) for impulsivity, exhibitionism, and detachment were all greater than .60, whereas those for several other scales (mistrust, self-harm, dependency, and workaholism) fell between .35 and .60. However, the multiple Rs for the remaining SNAP scales (eccentric perceptions, entitlement, propriety, and aggression) ranged from .26 to .35.

Second, for the most part, these findings parallel the results of the factor analysis (see Table 8.6); for example, manipulativeness split across the

TABLE 8.7

Multiple Regression Analyses Predicting Schedule for Nonadaptive and Adaptive Personality (SNAP) Primary Scales From Three and Five Higher Order Dimensions

SNAP scale[a]	Step 1 R^2	Significant dimensions[b]	Step 2 R^2 change due to: O	A	Final R^2
Detachment	0.46***	E	0.01	0.05***	0.51
Exhibitionism	0.42***	E	0.01	0.04***	0.47
Impulsivity	0.40***	C, E	0.03**	0.06***	0.48
Aggression	0.12***	N	0.00	0.33***	0.45
Dependency	0.29***	N, C	0.04**	0.06***	0.39
Manipulativeness	0.17***	C	0.00	0.23***	0.39
Workaholism	0.35***	C	0.01	0.02*	0.37
Self-Harm	0.28***	N, E	0.00	0.02*	0.31
Mistrust	0.21***	N, E	0.00	0.05***	0.26
Propriety	0.10***	C	0.10***	0.02	0.21
Entitlement	0.09***	E, C	0.03**	0.05**	0.17
Eccentric Perceptions	0.07***	N	0.09***	0.00	0.17
M	0.25		0.03	0.08	0.35

Note. N = 194 university students. N = Neuroticism; E = Extraversion; O = Openness; A = Agreeableness; C = Conscientiousness. N, E, and C were entered as a block, followed by O and A in a stepwise hierarchical regression.
[a]Scales are listed in order of decreasing final squared multiple correlations (R^2). [b]$p < .05$; predictors are listed in order of strength.
*$p < .05$; **$p < .01$; ***$p < .001$.

Agreeableness and Conscientiousness factors in the factor analysis and was significantly predicted by both Agreeableness and Conscientiousness in the regression analysis. However, results for a few scales yielded discrepant results. For example, impulsivity was strongly related to Conscientiousness in both analyses but had a secondary loading on Openness in the factor analysis. In contrast, Extraversion and Agreeableness were better predictors than Openness in the regression analysis. The fact that Neuroticism, Extraversion, and Conscientiousness were entered first into the regression equation may account for some of the observed discrepancies, but it is also possible that some of the SNAP scales are more sensitive to different analytic ap-

proaches, perhaps because they are more factorially complex.

Third, even when controlling for Neuroticism, Extraversion, and Conscientiousness, the dimensions of Agreeableness and Openness account for a significant portion of the variance in every scale, and their contribution is quite substantial in several cases. Specifically, Openness contributed most strongly to eccentric perceptions and propriety, whereas Agreeableness proved to be the strongest predictor for aggression and manipulativeness. It is noteworthy that these findings all support the factor analytic results. Finally, when all five dimensions are taken together, they produce multiple Rs that are quite impressive, ranging from .40

to .70 across the 12 SNAP scales (mean multiple R = .59). Thus, in most cases, the majority of the reliable variance in these traits of personality disorder is explained by the FFM.

Entitlement, eccentric perceptions, and propriety, however, appear to fall somewhat outside the domain assessed by the FFM. These scales may assess traits that are rare in normal-range personality. Alternatively, they may represent pathologically extreme forms of normal traits, so they are not well captured by scales that assess the FFM, which were designed for use with normal subjects. We subsequently investigated this latter possibility.

To summarize, the dimensions of the FFM, as a whole, account for a large portion of the variance in most maladaptive personality traits. Moreover, the higher order factors of Neuroticism, Extraversion, and Conscientiousness do not exhaust the predictable variance; rather, the dimensions of Agreeableness and Openness are also important in understanding this domain. Finally, several traits appear to contain specific variance that is not well represented within the FFM. These may represent types of pathology that are rarely seen in normal populations or that are not well assessed by measures developed for normal personality.

Additional Contributions of the Three-Factor Model in Predicting Maladaptive Personality Traits. We now turn to an investigation of the third issue raised earlier; that is, to what extent do scales that have been developed within the three-factor tradition contribute variance to the prediction of maladaptive traits beyond the variance captured by the FFM as a whole? Similar to the FFM, three-factor models have largely focused on normal-range personality variation. Nevertheless, abnormal behavior has played a more prominent role in the conceptualization of these three-factor models from their inception. Thus, one might expect that scales developed within this tradition would assess some trait variance relevant to psychopathology (and particularly personality disorders) that is not well represented in measures of the FFM. To investigate this issue, we again performed a

series of hierarchical regression analyses to predict the primary SNAP scales. In these analyses, we first entered all of the five-factor scores as a block in Step 1. These results (given in the first column of Table 8.8) correspond to the last column in Table 8.7; Column 2 in Table 8.8 lists the specific dimensions that made significant contributions at this step (results differ slightly in some cases from those presented in Table 8.7 because of the differences in the order of entry). We then entered the three SNAP temperament scales, with the predictors entered in order of strength at each step.[4] These changes in the squared multiple correlation (R^2) are also shown in Table 8.8 in Column 3 for negative temperament, in Column 4 for positive temperament, and in Column 5 for disinhibition. Finally, the overall R^2 change across Steps 2–4 is given in the last column; these figures again include all three temperament dimensions, regardless of the significance of contribution.

First, it is noteworthy that each of the temperament scales contributes significantly to the prediction of five of the seven SNAP scales; in several cases, this contribution is substantial. For example, negative temperament adds an additional 9% to the prediction of eccentric perceptions, whereas positive temperament contributes an additional 9% to both entitlement and workaholism. Because these scales were specifically designed to assess the affective cores of Neuroticism and Extraversion, respectively, these data suggest that some of the emotion-related variance in these maladaptive traits may not be accounted for by the FFM. Disinhibition, however, was designed to assess a broad higher order factor, similar to that described by Tellegen and Waller (in press).

In five-factor terms, we have shown that disinhibition is largely strongly related to (low) Conscientiousness, but it is also correlated significantly (−.32) with Agreeableness. In this regard, it is interesting to note that two of the scales to which disinhibition contributed substantially—aggression and manipulativeness—were strong markers of the Agreeableness factor (see Table 8.6). It may be that

---

[4]The disinhibition scale shares items with several primary SNAP scales; for the regressions involving these scales, the respective overlapping items were removed from the disinhibition scale.

TABLE 8.8

Multiple Regression Analyses Assessing the Additional Contribution of the Three-Factor Model Over the Five-Factor Model in Predicting Schedule for Nonadaptive and Adaptive Personality (SNAP) Primary Scales

SNAP scale[a]	Step 1 R^2	Significant dimensions[b]	R^2 Change, Steps 2–4			Total
			NT	PT	D	
Detachment	0.51***	E, A	0.01*	0.02**	0.00	0.03
Impulsivity	0.48***	C, E, A, O	0.00	0.00	0.08***	0.08
Exhibitionism	0.47***	E. A	0.02**	0.02**	0.00	0.04
Aggression	0.45***	A, N, E	0.02**	0.00	0.08***	0.10
Dependency	0.39***	N, C, O, A	0.00	0.02*	0.00	0.02
Manipulativeness	0.39***	A, C, E	0.02*	0.00	0.06***	0.08
Workaholism	0.37***	C, A	0.03***	0.09***	0.02**	0.14
Self-Harm	0.31***	N, A, E	0.01	0.01	0.02*	0.04
Mistrust	0.26***	N, A	0.04**	0.00	0.01	0.05
Propriety	0.21***	O, C, N	0.01	0.03*	0.01	0.04
Entitlement	0.17***	E, A, O, C	0.00	0.09***	0.00	0.09
Eccentric perceptions	0.17***	O, N	0.09***	0.02*	0.01	0.12
M	0.35		0.02	0.03	0.02	0.07

Note. N = 194 university students. N = Neuroticism; E = Extraversion; O = Openness; A = Agreeableness; C = Conscientiousness; NT = negative temperament; PT = positive temperament; D = disinhibition. N, E, O, A, and C were entered as a block, followed by NT, PT, and D in a stepwise hierarchical regression.
[a]Scales are listed in order of decreasing Step 1 squared multiple correlation (R^2). [b]$p < .05$; predictors are listed in order of strength.
*$p < .05$; **$p < .01$; ***$p < .001$.

these SNAP scales represent such extreme forms of disagreeableness that the FFM scales, which were designed to assess traits within normal range, fail to capture some of this (dis)agreeableness variance. If so, then disinhibition, which was developed with somewhat more concern for the assessment of psychopathology, may tap some of this remaining variance. As mentioned earlier, the role of (dis)agreeableness in personality disorder is an important area for further research.

A second noteworthy point is that the two SNAP scales that were least well predicted by the FFM—entitlement and eccentric perceptions—showed the greatest R^2 change with the addition of the temperament scales, so that a multiple R of .50 or greater is now obtained for all of the primary SNAP scales. This leads us to our final point: By combining the predictive power of the five-factor scales and the SNAP temperament scales, the average percentage of variance accounted for reaches a remarkable .42 (range = .25 for propriety to .56 for impulsivity). In several cases, the R^2 values approach the scale reliabilities (i.e., alpha coefficients), which suggests that —taken together—these models nearly exhaust the reliable variance of certain maladaptive traits. Thus, these results strongly support the claim that basic models of personality are broadly relevant to personality disorder and that these models are valuable in understanding the structure of maladaptive and normal-range personality traits.

TOWARD A DIMENSIONAL APPROACH TO THE ASSESSMENT OF PERSONALITY DISORDER

We have presented evidence to demonstrate that a dimensional approach has a great deal to offer to the assessment of personality disorder. For example, we have shown that self-report measures of maladaptive traits are systematically related to clinical ratings of personality disorder symptom clusters. These data suggest that self-ratings can play as important a role in screening for personality disorder as they do currently in the assessment of Axis I symptomatology, such as depression, anxiety, somatic complaints, hallucinations, and delusions. Moreover, we have shown that the concepts and structures of normal-range personality are highly relevant to personality-related pathology. Specifically, we have presented evidence that the domains of normal and abnormal personality share a common trait structure, and we have hypothesized that what differentiates the ordered from the disordered personality is not its component traits per se but whether the trait expression is moderate or extreme, flexible or rigid, and adaptive or maladaptive.

Although these results may technically represent new information, they come as no surprise to many readers. Indeed, the theoretical merits of a dimensional system for understanding personality disorder have been touted for some time now. Nevertheless, empirical research in this area has not proceeded very far, in part, because of the lack of assessment instruments for investigating personality disorder dimensionally. However, our results suggest that it may not be necessary to develop entirely new instruments to assess the traits underlying personality disorder. Rather, if normal and abnormal personality share a common trait structure, then the development of instruments for assessing maladaptive traits can build on the extensive knowledge base of personality psychology that has been accumulating since the 1930s. Moreover, many existing personality tests (e.g., those we have considered here) may prove useful with personality-disordered populations, although some adaptation may be needed to maximize their util-

ity in clinical settings. In addition, we have shown that the SNAP (the scales of which were based conceptually on personality disorder symptom clusters) provides reliable and reasonably independent measures of maladaptive personality traits. Its scales have been shown to be systematically related both to personality disorder symptoms and to measures of normal-range personality, this is a useful tool in exploring the interface between normal and abnormal personality.

In conclusion, the findings reported here have significant implications for both normal personality and personality disorder. Demonstration of the relevance of normal personality structure for personality disorder gives Axis II researchers access to sophisticated research methodologies, a rich knowledge base, and well-developed theoretical structures. For the traditional field of personality, awareness of its importance to personality disorders opens up a new arena in which to expand its knowledge, apply its methods, and test its theories. We hope that recognition of the structural unity of personality will foster research and promote integration of the fields of normal and abnormal personality. Clearly, the understanding of personality and its pathology will be greatly enhanced as researchers in both domains recognize and develop their common interest.

References

Akiskal, H. S., Hirschfeld, R. M., & Yerevanian, B. I. (1983). The relationship of personality to affective disorder. *Archives of General Psychiatry, 40,* 801–810.

Allport, G. W. (1937). *Personality: A psychological interpretation.* New York: Holt, Rinehart & Winston.

American Psychiatric Association. (1980). *Diagnostic and statistical manual of mental disorders* (3rd ed.). Washington, DC: Author.

American Psychiatric Association. (1987). *Diagnostic and statistical manual of mental disorders* (3rd ed., rev.). Washington, DC: Author.

Brooks, R. B., Baltazar, P. L., & Munjack, D. J. (1989). Co-occurrence of personality disorders with panic disorder, social phobia, and generalized anxiety disorder: A review of the literature. *Journal of Anxiety Disorders, 29,* 259–285.

Butcher, J. N., & Spielberger, C. D. (Eds.). (1990). *Advances in personality assessment* (Vol. 8). Hillsdale, NJ: Erlbaum.

Cantor, N., Smith, E. E., French, R. de S., & Mezzich, J. (1980). Psychiatric diagnosis as prototype categorization. *Journal of Abnormal Psychology, 89,* 181–193.

Clark, L. A. (1990). Toward a consensual set of symptom clusters for assessment of personality disorder. In J. N. Butcher & C. D. Spielberger (Eds.), *Advances in personality assessment* (Vol. 8, pp. 243–266). Hillsdale, NJ: Erlbaum.

Clark, L. A. (1993). *Manual for the Schedule for Nonadaptive and Adaptive Personality (SNAP).* Minneapolis: University of Minnesota Press.

Clark, L. A., McEwen, J., Collard, L. M., & Hickok, L. G. (1993). Symptoms and traits of personality disorder: Two new methods for their assessment. *Psychological Assessment, 5,* 81–91.

Clark, L. A., & Watson, D. W. (1990). *General Temperament Survey (GTS).* Unpublished manuscript, Southern Methodist University, Dallas, TX.

Cleckley, H. (1964). *The mask of sanity* (4th ed.). St. Louis, MO: Mosby.

Costa, P. T., Jr., & McCrae, R. R. (1985). *The NEO Personality Inventory manual.* Odessa, FL: Psychological Assessment Resources.

Digman, J., & Takemoto-Chock, N. K. (1981). Factors in the natural language of personality: Re-analysis and comparison of six major studies. *Multivariate Behavioral Research, 16,* 149–170.

Drake, R. E., & Vaillant, G. E. (1985). A validity study of Axis II of *DSM-III. American Journal of Psychiatry, 142,* 553–558.

Dyce, J. A., & O'Connor, B. P. (1998). Personality disorders and the five-factor model: A test of facet-level predictions. *Journal of Personality Disorders, 12,* 31–45.

Eysenck, H. J., & Eysenck, S. B. G. (1975). *Eysenck Personality Questionnaire manual.* San Diego, CA: EdITS.

Eysenck, H. J., Wakefield, J. A., & Friedman, A. F. (1983). Diagnosis and clinical assessment: The *DSM-III. Annual Review of Psychology, 34,* 167–193.

Frances, A. J. (1980). The *DSM-III* personality disorders section: A commentary. *American Journal of Psychiatry, 137,* 1050–1054.

Frances, A. J., & Widiger, T. (1986). The classification of personality disorders: An overview of problems and solutions. In A. J. Frances & R. E. Hales (Eds.), *Psychiatry update: The American Psychiatric Association annual review* (Vol. 5, pp. 240–257). Washington, DC: American Psychiatric Press.

Goldberg, L. R. (1983, June). *The magical number five, plus or minus two: Some conjectures on the dimensionality of personality.* Paper presented at the Gerontology Research Center Research Seminar, Baltimore, MD.

Gotlib, I. H. (1984). Depression and general psychopathology in university students. *Journal of Abnormal Psychology, 93,* 19–30.

Gough, H. G. (1987). *California Psychological Inventory administrator's guide.* Palo Alto, CA: Consulting Psychologist Press.

Gunderson, J. G. (1983). *DSM-III* diagnoses of personality disorders. In J. P. Frosch (Ed.), *Current perspectives on personality disorders* (pp. 20–39). Washington DC: American Psychiatric Press.

Janis, I. L., Mahl, G. F., Kagan, J., & Holt, R. R. (1969). *Personality: Dynamics, development, and assessment.* New York: Harcourt, Brace & World.

Kendell, R. (1975). *The role of diagnosis in psychiatry.* Oxford, UK: Blackwell Scientific.

Klein, D. N. (1990). The depressive personality: Reliability, validity, and relationship to dysthymia. *Journal of Abnormal Psychology, 99,* 412–421.

Liebowitz, M. R., & Klein, D. F. (1981). Interrelationship of hysteroid dysphoria and borderline personality disorder. *Psychiatric Clinics of North America, 4,* 67–87.

Livesley, W. J., Schroeder, M. L., & Jackson, D. N. (1990). Dependent personality disorder and attachment problems. *Journal of Personality Disorders, 4,* 131–140.

McCrae, R. R., & Costa, P. T., Jr. (1985). Updating Norman's "Adequate taxonomy": Intelligence and personality dimensions in natural language and in questionnaires. *Journal of Personality and Social Psychology, 49,* 710–721.

McCrae, R. R., & Costa, P. T., Jr. (1986). Clinical assessment can benefit from recent advances in personality psychology. *American Psychologist, 41,* 1001–1002.

McCrae, R. R., & Costa, P. T., Jr. (1987). Validation of a five-factor model of personality across instruments and observers. *Journal of Personality and Social Psychology, 52,* 81–90.

Perry, J. C., & Klerman, G. L. (1978). The borderline patient: A comparative analysis of four sets of diagnostic criteria. *Archives of General Psychiatry, 35,* 141–150.

Pervin, L. A. (1989). *Personality: Theory and research.* New York: Wiley.

Pfohl, B., Stangl, D., & Zimmerman, M. (1984). The implications of *DSM-III* personality disorders for patients with major depression. *Journal of Affective Disorders, 7,* 309–318.

Reynolds, S. K., & Clark, L. A. (2001). Predicting dimensions of personality disorder from domains and facets of the five-factor model. *Journal of Personality, 69,* 199–222.

Tellegen, A. (1982). *A brief manual for the Differential Personality Questionnaire.* Unpublished manuscript, University of Minnesota, Minneapolis.

Tellegen, A., & Waller, N. (in press). Exploring personality through test construction: Development of the Multidimensional Personality Questionnaire. In S. R. Briggs, J. M. Cheek, & E. M. Donahue (Eds.), *Handbook of adult personality inventories.* New York: Plenum Press.

Turner, S. M., & Beidel, D. C. (1989). Social phobia: Clinical syndrome, diagnosis, and comorbidity. *Clinical Psychology Review, 9,* 3–18.

Tyrer, P. (1988). What's wrong with *DSM-III* personality disorders? *Journal of Personality Disorders, 2,* 281–291.

Vorhies, L. (1990). *The factor structure of personality dimensions: Three factors or five?* Unpublished master's thesis, Southern Methodist University, Dallas, TX.

Watson, D., & Clark, L. A. (1992). On traits and temperament: General and specific factors of emotional experience and their relations to the five-factor model. *Journal of Personality, 60,* 443–476.

Watson, D., & Clark, L. A. (1997). Extraversion and its positive emotional core. In R. T. Hogan, J. Johnson, & S. R. Briggs (Eds.), *Handbook of personality psychology* (pp. 767–793). San Diego, CA: Academic Press.

Widiger, T. A., & Frances, A. (1985). The *DSM-III* personality disorders: Perspectives from psychology. *Archives of General Psychiatry, 42,* 615–623.

Widiger, T. A., & Kelso, K. (1983). Psychodiagnosis of Axis II. *Clinical Psychology Review, 2,* 115–135.

Widiger, T. A., & Rogers, J. H. (1989). Prevalence and comorbidity of personality disorders. *Psychiatric Annals, 19,* 132–136.

Wiggins, J. S., & Pincus, A. L. (1989). Conceptions of personality disorders and dimensions of personality. *Psychological Assessment, 1,* 305–316.

Wiggins, J. S., & Trapnell, P. D. (1997). Personality structure: The return of the Big Five. In R. T. Hogan, J. Johnson, & S. R. Briggs (Eds.), *Handbook of personality psychology* (pp. 737–765). San Diego, CA: Academic Press.

CHAPTER 9

DIMENSIONS OF PERSONALITY DISORDER AND THE FIVE-FACTOR MODEL OF PERSONALITY

Marsha L. Schroeder, Janice A. Wormworth, and W. John Livesley

The relation between the contemporary classification of personality disorder and the structure of normal personality has only recently received attention (Costa & McCrae, 1990; Wiggins & Pincus, 1989). In many ways, the classification of personality disorders and the study of personality structure have proceeded along independent paths, using different approaches and methods. Conceptions of normal personality structure have emerged from extensive empirical studies, whereas conceptions of personality disorders are largely the consensus of experts who base their decisions on traditional clinical concepts and accumulated clinical experience. Consequently, classifications of personality disorders consist of relatively unstructured lists of diagnoses that reflect multiple theoretical perspectives within the clinical tradition. They do not incorporate, to any significant degree, accumulated empirical knowledge of normal personality structure. The consequence of these developments is that current classifications tend to lack explicit structure and clear conceptual underpinnings.

Several proposals have been advanced to anchor diagnostic concepts to more satisfactory theoretical bases. Millon (1981), for example, suggested that diagnoses and diagnostic criteria could be derived from three basic dimensions based on social cognitive theory: the nature of reinforcement, the source of reinforcement, and the instrumental coping style.

Cloninger (1987) proposed anchoring diagnoses in neurotransmitter systems. The merit of these approaches is that they provide an explicit rationale for determining the number of personality disorder diagnoses to include in the classification and for selecting diagnostic criteria. A problem is the lack of an extensive theoretical rationale for basing the classification on a given set of dimensions. An alternative would be to relate diagnostic concepts to a general model of personality structure. This approach is particularly appealing given the emerging body of evidence in support of the five-factor model (FFM) of personality (Digman, 1990). With this approach, personality disorders would be conceptualized as extremes of normal personality variants rather than as discrete classes of behaviors, as is the case with the classification of the third edition, revised, of the *Diagnostic and Statistical Manual of Mental Disorders* (*DSM-III-R*; American Psychiatric Association, 1987).

Initially, empirical investigations of the relation between personality disorders and personality examined the relation between personality disorder diagnoses and the interpersonal circumplex (Kiesler, 1986; Wiggins, 1968, 1982). Although many diagnostic concepts could be adequately accounted for by a two-factor model—an observation noted by Plutchik and Platman (1977)—the circumplex does not represent all aspects of personality disorder.

The research reported in this chapter was supported by Medical Research Council of Canada Grant MA-99424 and by a National Health and Welfare Canada Research Scholar Award.

Cognitive traits, in particular, do not fit within this model.

More recently, researchers have investigated the relations between personality disorders and the FFM. Wiggins and Pincus (1989; see also Wiggins & Pincus, chapter 7, this volume) reported that personality disorders, assessed using the Minnesota Multiphasic Personality Inventory (MMPI; Hathaway & McKinley, 1967) personality disorder scales (Morey, Waugh, & Blashfield, 1985), could be adequately accommodated by the FFM when assessed using the NEO Personality Inventory (NEO-PI; Costa & McCrae, 1985). Costa and McCrae (1990) also presented evidence that the FFM could adequately account for personality diagnoses. When the five factors were measured by self-report, peer ratings, and spouse ratings, they were found to correlate with personality disorder diagnoses measured by the MMPI scales. Significant correlations were also found with the Millon Clinical Multiaxial Inventory (Millon, 1982). These studies provide convincing preliminary evidence that *DSM-III-R* diagnostic concepts, as measured by the MMPI and Millon scales, can be adequately accounted for by the FFM.

In the study discussed here, we investigated the extent to which these observations generalize when personality disorders are conceptualized using an approach different from that of the *DSM-III-R*. In earlier studies, Livesley (1986, 1987) attempted to identify the basic dimensions underlying the overall domain of personality disorders by investigating the structure of the traits defining each diagnosis. The resulting dimensions provide a representative description of the domain at a primary or ungeneralized level. Investigation of the relation between these dimensions and the five major factors provides alternative ways to test the generality of the relation between personality structure and personality disorders. In the following section, we describe the steps taken to identify the underlying dimensions of personality disorder. We then report on their relation to the NEO-PI dimensions.

DIMENSIONS OF PERSONALITY DISORDER

Those attempting to identify the underlying dimensions of the domain of personality disorders have adopted two research approaches. Hyler et al. (1990) factor analyzed responses to the Personality Diagnostic Questionnaire, a self-report instrument that assesses each *DSM-III* diagnostic criterion with a single item. The authors reported an 11-factor solution that they believed to underlie the diagnostic criteria. The value of this approach is that it suggests a structure underlying the domain defined by the *DSM-III-R* diagnostic concepts and criterion sets. The method relies, however, on the use of single items to assess criteria that differ considerably in generality, tapping content ranging from specific behaviors to general traits. It also assumes that the *DSM-III-R* diagnoses provide a representative sample of the overall domain. Several *DSM-III-R* diagnoses have, however, been criticized for poor content validity. For example, antisocial personality disorder does not include many of the features that clinicians consider important aspects of the diagnosis, particularly, the interpersonal features associated with the traditional concept of psychopathy (Frances, 1980; Hare, 1983; Millon, 1981). Similarly, histrionic personality disorder omits many of the traditional analytic concepts of hysterical personality (Kernberg, 1984).

A second research approach attempts to specify the domain of personality disorders more comprehensively than does the *DSM-III-R* before attempting to identify the underlying structure. Clark (1990), for example, used clinicians' judgments to identify the structural relations among descriptors selected to provide an overall representation of the domain. We used a similar starting point for our investigations.

From an extensive literature review, Livesley (1986) compiled a list of descriptors for each *DSM-III-R* diagnosis. Consensual judgments of panels of clinicians were used to identify the most prototypical features of each diagnosis (Livesley, 1987). He was able to order the features of each *DSM-III-R* diagnosis on the basis of its prototypicality ratings. The list of highly prototypical features for a given diagnosis invariably contained several items that referred to the same characteristic. For example, features highly prototypical of paranoid personality disorder included "mistrustful," "feels persecuted," and "expects trickery or harm." All refer to behaviors that are indicative of "suspiciousness." Therefore, the list of features describing each diagnosis was reduced to fewer traits by grouping together those referring to the same behavior. Livesley then used the most highly rated feature for a given diagnosis to define a trait category. The next most highly rated feature was placed in this category if appropriate. If not, an additional trait category was used. This process was repeated until all features were categorized. Each trait category was then defined on the basis of features from which it was derived; the greatest weight was placed on the most prototypical feature. This procedure was repeated for all categories. Trait categories were then examined across all disorders; definitions were revised until a relatively mutually exclusive set of trait categories was established. Thus, each disorder was defined by a cluster of traits. For example, schizoid personality disorder consisted of low affiliation, avoidant attachment, defective social skills, generalized hypersensitivity, lack of empathy, restricted affective expression, self-absorption, and social apprehensiveness. Initially, 79 traits were required to define all 11 diagnoses in the *DSM-III-R*. These traits provided a representative depiction of the domain of personality disorder.

The next step was to develop self-report scales to assess each trait. This was accomplished using the structured approach to scale development described by Jackson (1971). The scales were administered to two general population samples. During the course of scale development, some proposed scales were found to have low internal consistency; consequently, these scales were subdivided into homogeneous item sets. We developed new scales to assess additional criteria proposed in the *DSM-III-R*. As a result of this process, the number of scales increased to 100. The final scales were administered to two independent samples: a general population sample of 274 subjects and a clinical sample of 158 patients with a primary diagnosis of a personality disorder. The structure of the two data sets was analyzed independently using exploratory factor analysis. Fifteen-factor obliquely rotated solutions provided the closest approximation to a simple structure for data from both the general population sample (Livesley, Jackson, & Schroeder, 1989) and the clinical sample (Livesley & Schroeder, 1990, 1991). Like other investigators (e.g., Clark, 1990; Hyler et al.,

1990), we identified factors with only superficial resemblance to the *DSM-III-R* diagnostic concepts. The factor structures were similar across the general population and clinical samples (Livesley & Schroeder, 1990)—an observation lending substantial support to a dimensional model for representing personality disorders (Eysenck, 1987).

INSTRUMENT DEVELOPMENT

We developed the Dimensional Assessment of Personality Pathology—Basic Questionnaire (DAPP-BQ) because the 100-scale questionnaire is too long for practical research application. Furthermore, 100 scales provide too much information to be easily interpreted and synthesized. Even though efforts were made during scale development to construct relatively distinct measures, substantial intercorrelations were observed among some scales. Thus, it seemed likely that a more parsimonious set of descriptors could be derived from the 100 scales without great loss of descriptive detail. In this section, the term *components* refers to the 100 scales; the term *scales* refers to the 18 DAPP-BQ scales; the term *factor* refers to the previously described factor analytic results. On the basis of the factor analytic studies described earlier, we formed clusters of components that loaded together in both analyses. These clusters provided construct definitions. Thus, the scale content generally was narrower in scope than was the factor content in either analysis. This strategy was used to form the pool of potential items for 14 of the 18 DAPP-BQ scales. A strong factor that we labeled *Identity Disturbance*, which emerged in both factor analyses, was divided into two separate but correlated clusters because of its breadth of content. The scales Identity Problems and Anxiousness were developed from this factor. Two additional clusters of components were formed that resulted in the scales Suspiciousness and Self-Harming Behaviors. These did not emerge clearly as factors in both analyses, but we believe that they have sufficient importance to be included as scales in the DAPP-BQ.

Scale items were chosen from the components in the cluster formed on the basis of the factor analytic results. Each scale has content from multiple components. For example, the Identity Problems scale comprises anhedonia, chronic feelings of emptiness and boredom, labile self-concept, and pessimism. We attempted to ensure satisfactory domain sampling by selecting items in approximately equal numbers from each component. DAPP-BQ scale content was also guided by item analysis. Items with highly skewed distributions were eliminated, as were those that had a low correlation with their total scale score. The scales have 16 items each, except Suspiciousness, which has 14, and Self-Harming Behaviors, which has 12. The scales demonstrated good levels of internal consistency in the general population and clinical samples. Scales and their constituent components are listed in Table 9.1, along with reliability estimates from the two samples on which the DAPP-BQ was developed.

METHOD

Instruments

Dimensions of personality disorder were assessed with the DAPP-BQ. Two DAPP-BQ scales, Self-Harming Behaviors and Perceptual Cognitive Distortion, were not included in the questionnaire used in the present study because of low item endorsement rates in the general population subjects. The second measure used was the NEO-PI, a 181-item inventory that yields measures of the Big Five factors of normal personality.

Subjects and Procedures

The subjects were 300 general population members recruited with posters and newspaper advertisements to participate in a study of personality. The sample included students and staff of the University of British Columbia as well as community members. The mean age of participants was 34.4 years (SD = 11.8). Half of the participants were male. A general population rather than a clinical sample was used to permit the collection of sufficient data for multivariate analyses. Consistent with other studies (Jackson & Messick, 1962; Tyrer & Alexander, 1977), our past research shows similar patterns of responses from the two groups (Livesley & Schroeder, 1990; Livesley, Schroeder, & Jackson, 1990). Subjects completed the test materials in small groups supervised by a research assistant. A subgroup of 59 partici-

pants completed the questionnaire a second time approximately 6 weeks after the initial testing to permit the evaluation of the stability of responses over time.

RESULTS

We examined the psychometric properties of the 16 DAPP-BQ scales. Coefficient alpha values were acceptable for all scales. These ranged from .80 (Conduct Problems) to .93 (Anxiousness). We also calculated coefficients of generalizability (CGs; Cronbach, Gleser, Nanda, & Rajaratnam, 1972) for the 59 cases with retest data. A Design VII CG was calculated for each DAPP-BQ scale. This design corresponds to a three-way fully crossed random effects Persons × Items × Occasions analysis of variance design; it yields seven independent variance components. Estimates of the variance components are calculated from the observed mean square values. For the calculation of the CG, the variance component estimate corresponding to the persons main effect is wanted variance. The variance component estimates corresponding to the Persons × Items, the Persons × Occasions, and the Persons × Items × Occasions interactions represent error variance in this application. We were interested in the extent to which we could differentiate among individuals (i.e., reliably rank order them), generalizing over the item and occasion facets of the design (see Schroeder, Schroeder, & Hare, 1983, for a detailed example of the technique). CGs ranged from .86 (Rejection) to .95 (Anxiousness). Because respondents usually completed the questionnaire only once, we also estimated the CG values for a single occasion. These were only slightly lower, ranging from .82 (Rejection and Social Avoidance) to .93 (Anxiousness). These CG values attest to the stability of the responses.

Principal Component Analyses

To determine the extent to which five personality factors would emerge when the NEO-PI and DAPP-BQ scales are intercorrelated, we performed a principal component analysis on the 21 × 21 matrix of scale intercorrelations. Decomposition of the correlation matrix yielded five eigenvalues greater than unity. The five-factor solution accounted for 70.6%

TABLE 9.1

Dimensional Assessment of Personality Pathology—Basic Questionnaire Dimension Reliabilities and Constituent Scales

	Coefficient alpha	
Dimension	General population sample	Clinical sample
Compulsivity	.88	.86
Orderliness, precision, conscientiousness		
Conduct problems	.87	.84
Interpersonal violence, juvenile antisocial behavior, addictive behaviors, failure to report social norms		
Diffidence	.89	.85
Submissiveness, suggestibility, need for advice		
Identity problems	.94	.92
Anhedonia, chronic feelings of emptiness and boredom, labile self-concept, pessimism		
Insecure attachment	.93	.90
Separation protest, secure base, proximity seeking, feared loss, intolerance of aloneness		
Intimacy problems	.88	.85
Desire for improved attachment relationships, inhibited sexuality, avoidant attachment		
Narcissism	.91	.87
Need for adulation, attention seeking, grandiosity, need for approval		
Suspiciousness	.89	.89
Hypervigilance, suspiciousness		
Affective lability	.91	.86
Affective lability, affective overreactivity, generalized hypersensitivity, labile anger, irritability		
Passive oppositionality	.90	.90
Passivity, oppositional, lack of organization		
Perceptual cognitive distortion	.89	.89
Depersonalization, schizotypal cognition, brief stress psychosis		
Rejection	.87	.85
Rigid cognitive style, judgmental, interpersonal hostility, dominance		
Self-harming behaviors	.92	.94
Ideas of self-harm, self-damaging acts		
Restricted expression	.90	.91
Reluctant self-disclosure, restricted expression of anger, restricted expression of positive sentiments, self-reliance		
Social avoidance	.93	.88
Low affiliation, defective social skills, social apprehensiveness, fearfulness of interpersonal hurt, desire for improved affiliative relationships		
Stimulus seeking	.89	.89
Sensation seeking, recklessness, impulsivity		
Interpersonal disesteem	.87	.80
Contemptuousness, egocentrism, exploitation, interpersonal irresponsibility, lack of empathy, remorselessness, sadism		
Anxiousness	.94	.93
Guilt proneness, indecisiveness, rumination, trait anxiety		

Note. Suspiciousness scale has 14 items; Self-Harming Behaviors scale has 12. $N = 274$ for the general population sample; $N = 158$ for the clinical sample.

of the total variance. The Harris–Kaiser obliquely rotated factor pattern matrix is presented in Table 9.2. The rotated factors were nearly orthogonal; the largest factor intercorrelation was .12.

The first factor, which was marked by the NEO-PI Neuroticism dimension, captured aspects of the DAPP-BQ reflecting distress and dissatisfaction with self; notable were the high loadings by the DAPP-BQ Anxiousness and Affective Lability dimensions. This strong first factor appears to represent core features of personality disorder. The second factor, marked by the NEO-PI Extraversion dimension, had one other salient loading, the DAPP-BQ Stimulus Seeking scale. This dimension is similar to Zuckerman's (1971) sensation seeking construct, which measures the need for high levels of excitement, stimulation, and novelty. On the third factor, the scale with the highest loading was DAPP-BQ Restricted Expression, which measures difficulties with self-disclosure and the overt expression of emotion. The NEO-PI Openness to Experience and Extraversion scales had negative loadings. The other DAPP-BQ scales loading on this factor (Intimacy Problems, Identity Problems, and Social Avoidance) tap dissatisfaction with self and difficulties with interpersonal relationships. The scale with the largest loading on the fourth factor was the NEO-PI Agreeableness dimension. The remaining salient loadings (Interpersonal Disesteem, Rejection, Suspiciousness, and Conduct Problems) were all negative. These scales reflect aspects of interpersonal behavior emphasizing distrust and lack of regard and concern for others. The scale with the largest loading on the fifth factor was the NEO-PI Conscientiousness dimension. Not surprisingly, the

---

TABLE 9.2

Obliquely Rotated Factor Pattern for Combined Analysis of the NEO Personality Inventory (NEO-PI) Factors and Dimensional Assessment of Personality Pathology—Basic Questionnaire (DAPP-BQ) Dimensions

Test and factor-dimension	Factors				
	I	II	III	IV	V
NEO-PI					
Neuroticism	**.84**	−.21	.02	−.16	−.13
Extraversion	−.18	**.72**	**−.42**	−.05	.08
Openness to Experience	−.05	.06	**−.41**	.09	−.16
Agreeableness	−.06	.11	−.09	**.86**	.01
Conscientiousness	−.14	.04	−.05	.08	**.94**
DAPP-BQ					
Anxiousness	**.83**	−.19	.09	−.11	.06
Affective Lability	**.68**	−.01	−.17	−.35	.00
Diffidence	**.64**	.08	.32	.25	−.07
Insecure Attachment	**.61**	.22	−.02	−.10	.04
Social Avoidance	**.59**	−.15	**.42**	−.07	−.09
Identity Problems	**.58**	−.04	**.53**	−.14	−.11
Narcissism	**.58**	.32	.00	−.29	−.06
Stimulus Seeking	−.01	**.64**	−.03	−.27	.00
Restricted Expression	.15	.01	**.81**	.03	−.03
Intimacy Problems	−.11	−.16	**.58**	−.12	−.08
Interpersonal Disesteem	.11	.09	.19	**−.76**	.01
Rejection	.11	.32	−.03	**−.62**	.05
Suspiciousness	.30	.10	.32	**−.58**	.13
Conduct problems	.12	.16	−.08	**−.48**	−.18
Compulsivity	.12	.06	.13	−.05	**.72**
Passive–Oppositionality	**.51**	.09	.22	−.06	**−.55**

Note. N = 300; loadings greater than .40 are in boldface.

DAPP-BQ Compulsivity dimension loaded highly on this factor along with Passive Oppositionality (negatively). The latter scale measures difficulties planning, organizing, and completing tasks.

We also performed a principal component analysis on the intercorrelations among the 16 DAPP-BQ scales by themselves to evaluate the extent to which factors resembling those of the FFM would emerge on their own. Decomposition of the correlation matrix yielded four eigenvalues greater than unity; the scree plot also strongly indicated a four-factor solution. The four factors accounted for 67.3% of the total variance. The obliquely rotated pattern matrix is presented in Table 9.3.

The large first factor contained content suggesting the label *Neuroticism*. The high salient loadings by insecure attachment, anxiousness, diffidence, and affective lability are consistent with this label. The content of the factor is highly similar to the DAPP-BQ content of the first factor in the combined DAPP-BQ–NEO-PI analysis. The second factor in the DAPP-BQ analysis is similar to the fifth factor from the combined analysis. We propose the label *Disagreeableness*. Interestingly, the Stimulus-Seeking

scale also loaded highly on this factor; whereas in the combined analysis, it loaded on a separate factor marked by NEO-PI Extraversion. The DAPP-BQ likely does not contain sufficient content tapping Extraversion for this factor to emerge clearly by itself. The third DAPP-BQ factor had salient loadings by the DAPP-BQ dimensions that loaded on the third factor in the combined analysis. The factor in the combined analysis also had negative salient loadings by NEO-PI Extraversion and Openness to Experience. The third DAPP-BQ factor appears largely to tap introversion. The fourth factor clearly represents compulsivity.

This analysis also suggests that four of the FFM factors are important in describing personality pathology. Factors corresponding to Neuroticism, Conscientiousness, (low) Extraversion, and (low) Agreeableness are apparent in this analysis. Again, a factor resembling Openness to Experience did not emerge.

Canonical Correlation Analysis

We also examined the relations among the NEO-PI and DAPP-BQ scales using canonical correlation analysis. This technique describes dependencies be-

TABLE 9.3

Obliquely Rotated Factor Pattern for the Dimensional Assessment of Personality Pathology—Basic Questionnaire (DAPP-BQ) Dimensions

Dimension	Factor			
	I	II	III	IV
Insecure Attachment	**.82**	.08	−.28	.05
Anxiousness	**.81**	−.08	.16	.09
Diffidence	**.71**	−.32	.21	.09
Affective Lability	**.65**	.30	−.10	−.08
Narcissism	**.60**	.38	−.08	−.01
Social Avoidance	**.57**	−.09	**.44**	−.06
Passive–Oppositionality	**.54**	.00	.16	**−.47**
Rejection	.06	**.80**	−.06	.09
Interpersonal Disesteem	.02	**.74**	.26	.00
Conduct Problems	−.02	**.67**	−.04	−.38
Stimulus Seeking	−.07	**.66**	−.18	−.04
Suspiciousness	.24	**.57**	.35	.21
Intimacy Problems	−.38	.09	**.91**	−.04
Restricted Expression	.05	−.06	**.84**	.05
Identity Problems	**.52**	.04	**.54**	−.07
Compulsivity	.19	.09	.04	**.92**

Note. N = 300; loadings greater than .40 are in boldface.

tween two sets of variables by forming successive pairs of linear combinations, called *canonical variates,* that correlate maximally. The second pair of canonical variates correlates maximally, subject to the constraint that they are orthogonal to the first pair, and so forth, until all possible pairs of variates have been formed. The maximum number of pairs of canonical variates is equal to the number of variables in the smaller set. In the present application, the 5 NEO-PI scales can be thought of as predictor or independent variables and the 16 DAPP-BQ scales as criterion or dependent variables. The canonical correlation analysis demonstrated considerable linkage between the two sets of variables. All five canonical correlations attained statistical significance. Table 9.4 shows the canonical correlations and structure coefficients. The latter are the correlations between the original varia-

bles and the derived canonical variables; these indicate which variables had the greatest weight in forming the linear composite and thus were useful for interpreting the meaning of the canonical variate.

The large first canonical correlation indicates a strong linkage between the two sets of variables. A high score on the first predictor canonical variate resulted from a combination of high Neuroticism, low Extraversion, and low Conscientiousness. The corresponding criterion variate correlated highly with a number of scales, suggesting a pattern that is pervasive in personality pathology. A high scorer on this variate would tend to be passive, anxious, and lacking in self-confidence and to have a diffuse self-concept. The content is similar to that of the first factor from both principal component analyses, except that Narcissism and Insecure Attachment did

TABLE 9.4

Canonical Correlation Analysis of the Dimensional Assessment of Personality Pathology—Basic Questionnaire (DAPP-BQ) and NEO Personality Inventory (NEO-PI) Scales

Variable	Canonical variates				
	I	II	III	IV	V
R	.91	.86	.84	.74	.48
DAPP-BQ					
Anxiousness	.75	.39	.38	.12	−.02
Passive–Oppositionality	.74	−.39	.18	−.18	−.22
Identity Problems	.71	.26	.18	−.16	−.39
Social Avoidance	.71	.35	.02	−.21	.03
Diffidence	.61	.20	.06	.27	−.46
Restricted Expression	.38	.24	−.21	−.26	−.30
Compulsivity	−.30	.74	.09	.06	−.14
Narcissism	.33	.04	.67	.12	−.10
Affective Lability	.51	.21	.66	.11	.23
Interpersonal Disesteem	.06	.16	.66	−.63	−.17
Rejection	−.13	−.00	.66	−.31	−.12
Stimulus Seeking	−.33	−.24	.57	.10	−.15
Conduct Problems	.10	−.11	.54	−.24	.14
Insecure Attachment	.32	.16	.43	.12	−.33
Suspiciousness	.19	.29	.49	−.51	−.16
Intimacy Problems	.23	.14	−.18	−.34	−.25
NEO-PI					
Neuroticism	.84	.27	.45	.11	−.04
Extraversion	−.62	−.36	.53	.43	−.15
Openness to Experience	−.08	−.25	.10	.27	.89
Conscientiousness	−.62	.74	−.05	.23	.12
Agreeableness	−.07	−.16	−.64	.75	.03

Note. N = 30.

not correlate substantially with the first criterion canonical variate.

The second canonical correlation essentially represents the linkage between NEO-PI Conscientiousness and DAPP-BQ Compulsivity. For the third correlation, a high score on the predictor variate indicates a low level of Agreeableness coupled with high Extraversion and Neuroticism. The criterion variate correlates with several DAPP-BQ dimensions, including Affective Lability, Conduct Problems, Stimulus Seeking, and measures indicating low regard for others. This pattern suggests a proactive personal style, in contrast with the more passive style seen in conjunction with the first canonical correlation. The predictor variate for the fourth canonical correlation had a high correlation with Agreeableness and a moderate correlation with Extraversion. The criterion variate had high negative correlations with Interpersonal Disesteem and Suspiciousness, suggesting that a high scorer would be mistrustful of others. The fifth canonical correlation was considerably lower than the other four. The predictor variate correlated highly with Openness to Experience, whereas the criterion variate did not correlate highly with any DAPP-BQ scale. The largest correlation was with Diffidence (negative). This finding again suggests that Openness to Experience is not strongly related to personality pathology. Wiggins and Pincus's (1989) canonical correlation analysis similarly indicated only modest relations between Openness to Experience and self-report measures of the *DSM-III-R* diagnoses.

Multiple Regression Analyses

To examine further the relation between the NEO-PI scales and the DAPP-BQ dimensions, we performed a series of multiple regression analyses. The multiple correlations and standard regression coefficients (beta weights) greater than .15 are presented in Table 9.5. We note again the prominent role that Neuroticism plays in the prediction of several DAPP-BQ scales. As was seen from the combined principal component analysis of the two sets of scales, however, the other NEO-PI scales also play a role in the description of personality pathology.

Agreeableness was negatively related to several scales that measure problematic interpersonal behav-

ior; Agreeableness was positively related to Diffidence, a scale measuring the willingness to acquiesce to others' wishes. The NEO-PI Extraversion dimension showed a strong relation to Stimulus Seeking and played a lesser role in the prediction of nine other DAPP-BQ scales. Conscientiousness was related to the DAPP-BQ Compulsivity and Passive Oppositionality (negatively). Openness to Experience did not play a major role in predicting any DAPP-BQ scales. Nevertheless, Openness to Experience did appear to play a lesser role in a number of DAPP-BQ dimensions; the regression coefficients in Table 9.5 suggest an inverse relation between Openness to Experience and personality disorders.

The values of the multiple correlations indicate that a number of DAPP-BQ scales share a substantial proportion of variance with the NEO-PI factors. The lowest multiple correlation was found with Intimacy Problems. This DAPP-BQ scale measures difficulties with the formation and maintenance of close personal relationships and difficulties with the expression of sexuality. Three other DAPP-BQ scales (Conduct Problems, Restricted Expression, and Insecure Attachment) showed only modest relations with the NEO-PI dimensions; each demonstrated less than 30% shared variance. Thus, not all aspects of personality disorders can be predicted by the NEO-PI dimensions with a high level of precision. The Intimacy Problems and Conduct Problems scales have largely behavioral content, which may help to explain their relatively low multiple correlations; the NEO-PI scales do not tap this content. The Restricted Expression and Insecure Attachment scales describe problems with interpersonal relationships; again, this content is not strongly represented in the NEO-PI. The former scale measures difficulties with the expression of both positive and negative emotions. The Insecure Attachment scale taps content similar to Bowlby's (1969, 1977) concept of *anxious attachment*. Those with a high score on the scale would be expected to have difficulties functioning independently of an attachment figure and to be preoccupied with fears of losing those closest to them.

DISCUSSION

We developed the DAPP-BQ self-report scales as reliable measures of important features of personality

---

TABLE 9.5

Multiple Regression Analyses Predicting Dimensional Assessment of Personality Pathology—Basic Questionnaire (DAPP-BQ) Dimensions With the NEO Personality Inventory (NEO-PI) Scales

DAPP-BQ dimension	R	Standardized regression coefficients
Affective lability	0.75	0.74 N − 0.19 A + 0.18 O + 0.17 E
Anxiousness	0.83	0.84 N
Compulsivity	0.70	0.69 C − 0.16 O + 0.15 N
Conduct problems	0.51	0.21 E − 0.39 A
Diffidence	0.66	0.60 N + 0.29 A − 0.23 O
Identity problems	0.73	0.54 N − 0.20 O − 0.18 E
Insecure attachment	0.52	0.52 N + 0.22 E
Interpersonal disesteem	0.74	−0.70 A
Intimacy problems	0.40	−0.31 E − 0.17 O
Narcissism	0.65	0.59 N + 0.35 E − 0.18 A
Passive–oppositionality	0.78	−0.60 C + 0.32 N
Rejection	0.61	−0.52 A + 0.34 E
Restricted expression	0.50	−0.36 E − 0.21 O
Social avoidance	0.73	0.47 N − 0.41 E
Stimulus seeking	0.61	0.59 E − 0.24 A
Suspiciousness	0.64	−0.52 A + 0.22 N

Note. N = 300. NEO-PI scales, N = Neuroticism, E = Extraversion, O = Openness to Experience, A = Agreeableness, and C = Conscientiousness. Coefficients less than 0.15 are omitted.

pathology. The results of the present study indicate that many of these measures are strongly related to the five factors of normal personality. These results are consistent with those obtained by Costa and Mc-Crae (1990) and Wiggins and Pincus (1989). The fact that we used a different conceptualization of personality pathology provides evidence of the robustness of the relation between the domains of normal personality and personality disorders. Because little information is available about the structure of the domain of personality disorder, it is desirable to relate the DAPP-BQ scales to well-established personality factors like the NEO-PI dimensions.

The 18 DAPP-BQ scales provide an alternative to the *DSM-III-R* Axis II categories for describing personality disorders. The latter system was developed largely on the basis of clinical impressions in the ab-

sence of sound theoretical underpinnings. In developing the DAPP-BQ, we attempted to examine the domain of personality pathology in a comprehensive and systematic manner, using both rational and empirical considerations. We believe that the DAPP-BQ can prove useful in research because it provides more detailed and precise information than can be obtained from the knowledge of category membership.

From the relations between the two tests, it is clear that the NEO-PI Neuroticism factor plays a prominent role in the explication of several aspects of personality disorder. In contrast, the Openness to Experience factor appears have lesser importance. To a great extent, our research and that of others suggests that personality pathology can be described with the same traits that underlie normal personality functioning. The relation between the two domains is not, however, uniformly high. Some DAPP-BQ scales with behavioral content demonstrated only modest relation with the NEO-PI factors. Although not included in the present study, the Self-Harming Behaviors and Perceptual Cognitive Distortion scales from the DAPP-BQ also would not, we believe, be highly related to the NEO-PI. These latter features of personality disorders also may not represent continua.

Future research is needed to investigate the generalizability of the results presented here. It would be desirable to replicate the study with a sample of personality disordered individuals. It also seems important to generalize the findings beyond self-reports. Some aspects of personality disorders may be more readily apparent to a skilled observer or a knowledgeable informant than to an individual making a self-rating. Further research is needed to develop a more precise specification of the domain of personality pathology. Personality disorders are described with terms that vary in specificity. It would be desirable to develop a comprehensive set of trait-level descriptors that map out the domain of personality pathology similar to the way the NEO-PI factors describe normal personality.

References

American Psychiatric Association. (1987). *Diagnostic and statistical manual of mental disorders* (3rd ed., rev.). Washington, DC: Author.

Bowlby, J. (1969). *Attachment and loss* (Vol. 1). London: Hogarth Press.

Bowlby, J. (1977). The making and breaking of affectional bonds. *British Journal of Psychiatry, 130,* 201–210, 421–431.

Clark, L. A. (1990). Toward a consensual set of symptom clusters for assessment of personality disorder. In J. N. Butcher & C. D. Spielberger (Eds.), *Advances in personality assessment* (Vol. 9, pp. 243–266). Hillsdale, NJ: Erlbaum.

Cloninger, C. R. (1987). A systematic method for clinical description and classification of personality variants. *Archives of General Psychiatry, 44,* 573–588.

Costa, P. T., Jr., & McCrae, R. R. (1985). *The NEO Personality Inventory manual.* Odessa, FL: Psychological Assessment Resources.

Costa, P. T., Jr., & McCrae, R. R. (1990). Personality disorders and the five-factor model of personality. *Journal of Personality Disorders, 4,* 362–371.

Cronbach, L. J., Gleser, G. C., Nanda, H., & Rajaratnam, N. (1972). *The dependability of behavioral measurements.* New York: Wiley.

Digman, J. M. (1990). Personality structure: Emergence of the five-factor model. *Annual Review of Psychology, 41,* 417–440.

Eysenck, H. J. (1987). The definition of personality disorders and the criteria appropriate to their description. *Journal of Personality Disorders, 1,* 211–219.

Frances, A. J. (1980). The *DSM-III* personality disorders section: A commentary. *American Journal of Psychiatry, 137,* 1050–1054.

Hare, R. D. (1983). Diagnosis of antisocial personality disorder in two prison populations. *American Journal of Psychiatry, 140,* 887–890.

Hathaway, S. R., & McKinley, J. C. (1967). *Minnesota Multiphasic Personality Inventory manual.* New York: Psychological Corporation.

Hyler, S. E., Lyons, M., Rieder, R. O., Young, L., Williams, J. B., & Spitzer, R. L. (1990). The factor structure of self-report *DSM-III* Axis II symptoms and their relationship to clinicians' ratings. *American Journal of Psychiatry, 147,* 751–757.

Jackson, D. N. (1971). The dynamics of structured personality tests. *Psychological Review, 78,* 229–248.

Jackson, D. N., & Messick, S. (1962). Response styles of the MMPI: Comparison of clinical and normal samples. *Journal of Abnormal Psychology, 65,* 285–299.

Kernberg, O. (1984). *Severe personality disorders.* New Haven, CT: Yale University Press.

Kiesler, D. J. (1986). The 1982 interpersonal circle: An analysis of *DSM-III* personality disorders. In T. Millon & G. L. Klerman (Eds.), *Contemporary directions in psychopathology: Towards* DSM-IV (pp. 571–597). New York: Guilford Press.

Livesley, W. J. (1986). Trait and behavioral prototypes of personality disorder. *American Journal of Psychiatry, 143,* 728–732.

Livesley, W. J. (1987). A systematic approach to the delineation of personality disorders. *American Journal of Psychiatry, 144,* 772–777.

Livesley, W. J., Jackson, D. N., & Schroeder, M. L. (1989). A study of the factorial structure of personality pathology. *Journal of Personality Disorders, 3,* 292–306.

Livesley, W. J., & Schroeder, M. L. (1990). Dimensions of personality disorder: The *DSM-III-R* cluster A diagnoses. *Journal of Nervous and Mental Disease, 178,* 627–635.

Livesley, W. J., & Schroeder, M. L. (1991). Dimensions of personality disorder: The *DSM-III-R* cluster B diagnoses. *Journal of Nervous and Mental Disease, 179,* 320–328.

Livesley, W. J., Schroeder, M. L., & Jackson, D. N. (1990). Dependent personality disorder. *Journal of Personality Disorders, 4,* 131–140.

Millon, T. (1981). *Disorders of personality:* DSM-III, *Axis II.* New York: Wiley.

Millon, T. (1982). *Millon Clinical Multiaxial Inventory manual* (3rd ed.). Minneapolis, MN: National Computer Systems.

Morey, L. C., Waugh, M. H., & Blashfield, R. K. (1985). MMPI scales for *DSM-III* personality disorders: Their derivation and correlates. *Journal of Personality Assessment, 49,* 245–251.

Plutchik, R., & Platman, S. R. (1977). Personality connotations of psychiatric diagnosis. *Journal of Nervous and Mental Disease, 165,* 418–422.

Schroeder, M. L., Schroeder, K., &, & Hare, R. D. (1983). Generalizability of a checklist for assessment of psychopathy. *Journal of Consulting and Clinical Psychology, 51,* 511–516.

Tyrer, P., & Alexander, M. S. (1977). Classification of personality disorders. *British Journal of Psychiatry, 135,* 163–167.

Wiggins, J. S. (1968). Personality structure. *Annual Review of Psychology, 19,* 293–350.

Wiggins, J. S. (1982). Circumplex model of interpersonal behavior in clinical psychology. In P. C. Kendall & J. N. Butcher (Eds.), *Offprints from the handbook of research methods in clinical psychology* (pp. 183–221). New York: Wiley.

Wiggins, J. S., & Pincus, A. L. (1989). Conceptions of personality disorders and dimensions of personality. *Psychological Assessment: A Journal of Consulting and Clinical Psychology, 1,* 305–316.

Zuckerman, M. (1971). Dimensions of sensation seeking. *Journal of Consulting and Clinical Psychology, 36,* 45–52.

CHAPTER 10

TWO APPROACHES TO IDENTIFYING THE DIMENSIONS OF PERSONALITY DISORDER: CONVERGENCE ON THE FIVE-FACTOR MODEL

Lee Anna Clark and W. John Livesley

Since the introduction of a separate axis for personality disorders in the third edition of the *Diagnostic and Statistical Manual of Mental Disorders* (*DSM-III*; American Psychiatric Association, 1980), debate has continued regarding the most valid approach to their description and diagnosis. From the beginning, these disorders have been conceptualized as personality traits that are inflexible and maladaptive and that cause either significant functional impairment or subjective distress (American Psychiatric Association, 1980, 1987). Delineation of the specific traits constituting the personality disorders, however, has been unsystematic and imprecise. Moreover, the *DSM* Axis II criteria, which are intended as manifestations of the component traits, were developed informally on the basis of expert consensus. This approach was necessitated in part by the lack of empirical research into the structure of maladaptive personality traits. Prior to 1980, research in normal-range personality was abundant, and although thousands of studies used the Minnesota Multiphasic Personality Inventory (Hathaway & McKinley, 1967) to examine personality pathology in various settings and diagnostic groups, research specifically investigating the traits of personality-disordered individuals was limited (notable exceptions include Presley & Walton, 1973; and Tyrer & Alexander, 1979). Over the past decade, however, interest in the trait dimensions of personality disorder has increased markedly, with a corresponding increase in relevant research activity.

Investigators have approached the study of maladaptive personality traits in a variety of ways, as is typical of relatively new areas of research. For exam-ple, personality disorder has been studied in relation to the interpersonal circumplex (Kiesler, 1986; Trapnell & Wiggins, 1990; Wiggins, 1982; Wiggins & Pincus, 1989) and, as the chapters in this volume attest, the five-factor model (FFM) of personality. Moreover, Cloninger (1987) developed a three-factor model of personality disorder (which he later expanded to include four "temperament" and three "character" dimensions; Cloninger, Svrakic, & Przybeck, 1993). In each of these cases, an existing theoretical or empirical model of personality was used, either directly or with adaptation, to conceptualize personality disorder. These are termed *top-down* approaches.

In contrast, we (Clark, 1990, 1993; Livesley, 1986, 1987; Livesley, Jackson, & Schroeder, 1989) independently adopted *bottom-up* strategies, in which the research begins with an examination of lower order components and builds gradually toward a final structure. For the Axis II disorders, this meant beginning with the symptomatic traits and behaviors of personality disorder. Then, by combining traits and behaviors that were conceptually related, empirically correlated, or both, we each developed dimensional structures to represent the domain. We are not the only investigators to have used a bottom-up strategy. For example, Morey (1988) used cluster analysis to examine the covariance of clinician-rated personality features, whereas Hyler et al. (1990) reported an item-level factor analysis of a self-report questionnaire that assesses each of the *DSM-III* Axis II criteria. In neither case, however, was the research goal per se to develop a structure that characterized the domain of personality disorders, whereas that was a primary goal of each of our research programs. Therefore, this chapter's focus is a comparison of the structures that emerged from our respective research efforts.

To the extent that a phenomenon is robust, different methods lead to similar conclusions about its nature. For example, although they have gone by many different names, the traits of neuroticism and extraversion have emerged repeatedly in diverse analyses of personality (e.g., Cloninger, 1987; Tellegen, 1985; Zuckerman, Kuhlman, & Camac, 1988). Similarly, we were motivated to write this chapter because we were impressed with the high degree of convergence between our dimensional structures, despite the fact that they had been developed using rather different methods. Given the many difficulties one encounters in attempting to conceptualize and assess personality pathology, it was gratifying to find that the core dimensions of this domain are sufficiently robust to emerge under diverse conditions. Detailed descriptions of the developmental processes followed by each of us are available elsewhere (Clark, 1990, 1993; Livesley, 1986; Livesley et al., 1989), so we only summarize them briefly in this chapter. Because specific comparisons of each dimensional structure to the FFM also can be found elsewhere in this book (Clark, Vorhies, & McEwen, chapter 8, this volume; Schroeder, Wormworth, & Livesley, chapter 9, this volume), we focus here more broadly on how the two trait systems converge on a higher order structure.

LIVESLEY'S STRUCTURE AND ITS DEVELOPMENT

Livesley began his investigation by compiling a comprehensive list of trait descriptors and behavioral acts that were considered to be characteristic of each of the *DSM-III* Axis II categories by a content analysis of the personality disorder literature (Livesley, 1986). These characteristics, which included all *DSM-III* and *DSM-III-R* criteria, were sent to a large number of clinicians who rated the prototypicality of the items for the relevant diagnosis. The results, and those of a follow-up study (Livesley, 1987), indicated good agreement regard-

ing the prototypical characteristics of each diagnosis. Highly prototypical items for each disorder often referred to the same dimension, so that it was possible to characterize each diagnosis using a relatively small number of dimensions, each consisting of conceptually related items (Livesley, 1987; Livesley et al., 1989). For example, "mistrustful," "searches for hidden meanings," and "sees the world as hostile and opposed to him/her" were all prototypical of paranoid personality disorder, and all represented the dimension of suspiciousness. Altogether, 79 dimensions were identified, and self-report items were written to assess each dimension. This initial questionnaire was completed by two samples of normal subjects, and psychometric analyses led to refinement of the scales, including the splitting of some dimensions into subcomponents.

The result was an instrument with 100 dimensions represented by 16 items per dimension, which was administered to a sample of normal subjects and a sample of patients with a primary diagnosis of personality disorder. The data were submitted independently to principal components analysis and, initially, 15 factors were identified from each data set (Livesley et al., 1989). These factors provided the basic structure, and subsequent modification led to the development of 18 dimensions that are the focus of comparison in this chapter (Livesley, 1991; Schroeder, Wormworth, & Livesley, 1992; also see chapter 9, this volume). Specifically, rational considerations led to 1 of the 15 factors being divided into two dimensions. In addition, traits related to suspiciousness did not form a separate factor but nevertheless were used to construct a scale because of the clinical importance of these behaviors. Similar considerations led to the decision to establish a scale for self-harm. Finally, items were chosen to represent these 18 factors. When selecting items from the original pool, steps were taken to ensure that adequate sampling of the domain was retained. The result was a 290-item questionnaire, the Dimensional Assessment of Personality Pathology—Basic Questionnaire (DAPP-BQ; Livesley, 1990). More information about the DAPP-BQ, including its relation to the FFM, is available in chapter 9 of this book.

CLARK'S STRUCTURE AND ITS DEVELOPMENT

Rather than using characteristic traits and behaviors as Livesley did, Clark (1990) began her investigation with the criterial symptoms of personality disorder. All of the *DSM* personality disorder criteria were included, plus criteria from various non-*DSM* conceptualizations of personality disorder (e.g., Cleckley, 1964; Liebowitz & Klein, 1981; Perry & Klerman, 1978) and from selected Axis I disorders (dysthymia, cyclothymia, and generalized anxiety disorder) that resemble personality disorders in important respects; that is, they have relatively chronic, traitlike manifestations (Akiskal, Hirschfeld, & Yerevanian, 1983; Frances, 1980). Complex criteria were divided into subcomponents (e.g., "unduly conventional," "serious and formal," and "stingy" were considered as separate criteria). Clinicians sorted these criteria into synonym groups, and a consensual set of 22 symptom clusters was identified through a factor analysis of the resulting co-occurrence matrix (Clark, 1990).

Because this initial research was completed before the *DSM-III-R* appeared, each Axis II symptom in the *DSM-III-R* was examined to determine whether it represented a new criterion that had not appeared in the *DSM-III*. All new criteria were given to a set of clinicians, who were asked to judge whether each could be placed into one of the 22 previously identified symptom clusters. Only criteria from the two provisional diagnoses (the sadistic and self-defeating personality disorders) were viewed as not categorizable into the 22 clusters. Therefore, it appeared that the basic structures of the primary criterion sets of the *DSM-III* and *DSM-III-R* were essentially the same.

This 22-factor structure is the focus of comparison in this chapter. Examples and a list of these clusters are shown elsewhere in this book (see Clark et al., chapter 8, this volume, Tables 8.1 and 8.2). Ratings on a sample of hospitalized psychiatric patients indicated that the clusters have good interrater reliability (Clark, McEwen, Collard, & Hickok, 1993). Moreover, preliminary analyses of their internal consistency using clinical ratings from a structured interview suggest that they represent homogeneous symptom clusters (Clark, Pfohl, & Blashfield, 1991). Self-report data based on the clusters is reported later.

COMPARISONS OF THE TWO STRUCTURES

Conceptual Considerations

Before a direct examination of the structures, it is interesting to consider the methodological and theoretical implications of these two research strategies and whether there are reasons for why they might be expected to produce convergent or divergent results. The first and most obvious constraint is that both investigators were attempting to identify traits relevant to personality disorder, so that each was broadly addressing the same content domain. However, their methods for defining this domain were quite different. First, neither limited his or her investigation to the *DSM* but used a broader literature to help define the domain of personality disorder. Although the literature reviews most likely overlapped somewhat, many writings were surely unique to one or the other researcher. For example, Clark (1990) included chronic affective trait symptoms from selected Axis I disorders, whereas Livesley did not.

Second, if one considers that various manifestations or characterizations of personality disorder fall along a continuum ranging from the highly abstract and general to the very concrete and specific, it appears that the two investigators sampled from different parts of this continuum. Livesley (1986) selected many terms from the extremes of the continuum, including both general trait terms (e.g., introverted, manipulative, perfectionistic) and specific behavioral items (e.g., "wore eye-catching, revealing clothing," "rechecked timetable several times"). In contrast, Clark's (1990) investigation began with symptom criteria, which tend to vary around the middle of the generality–specificity continuum (e.g., "easily hurt by criticism or disapproval," "overly concerned with hidden motives"). Thus, these criteria tend to be more specific than general trait terms but less narrow than specific behavioral items. Clearly, if the trait structure of personality disorder is robust, one would expect congruence across the range of items from highly general to very specific, but such a result is not determined in advance. Thus, in terms of the items with which the investigations began, there was ample opportunity for the structures to diverge, despite the fact that they broadly addressed the same content domain.

A third major difference in the methodologies of the two investigators was in how they pursued identification of the trait dimensions. Clark used a conceptual free-sort task, in which raters grouped semantically similar symptoms regardless of their diagnostic origin; the question of which symptoms combined to form dimensions was then determined by factor analysis. In contrast, Livesley's initial research was tied conceptually to the Axis II diagnoses, with raters judging the prototypicality of the traits or behaviors for a given disorder. Furthermore, whereas Livesley used both judgments of semantic similarity and factor analysis as data reduction techniques, the basis for evaluating these procedures was self-ratings of the most highly prototypical items, rather than clinical judgments as used by Clark. Therefore, we again see ample opportunity for the emergence of rather diverse trait structures in these different procedures.

Content Comparisons

The first step in comparing the two trait structures was to match each of the factors in one structure with one (or more) factors in the other on the basis of similar content. The factor labels used by the investigators provided an initial indication of corresponding factors (e.g., Livesley's Social Avoidance was expected to correspond to Clark's Social Isolation), but the greatest weight was placed on the specific component dimensions (Livesley) or criteria (Clark) composing the factors. Table 10.1 shows the results of this content-based matching.

As seen in Table 10.1, a clear correspondence emerged across the two structures, with about one third of the factors showing a one-to-one match. Inevitably, differences in degree of differentiation occurred, such that one structure or the other elaborated or simplified certain content areas. Nevertheless, in the remaining cases, two factors from one structure (or three, in one instance only) corresponded to a single factor in the other, and in no case did the content of a factor in one struc-

ture split so much as to map onto more than two factors in the other. Because Clark's 22-cluster structure is slightly more differentiated than Livesley's 18-factor structure, it was more often the case that multiple-symptom clusters represented content tapped by a single Livesley factor, but both types of asymmetry were seen. For example, Livesley's Anxiousness factor overlapped with content in Clark's pessimism and negative affect clusters. Conversely, Clark's self-centered exploitation matched Livesley's rejection and interpersonal disesteem factors. Moreover, one symptom cluster —hypersexuality—failed to emerge in Livesley's analyses.

It is noteworthy that the two-dimensional systems were similar not just at the factor level but at the level of more detailed structures as well. For example, between Livesley's compulsivity and Clark's conventionality–rigidity, three components of the former—orderliness, precision, and conscientiousness—could be matched directly with the latter's symptoms of preoccupation with detail, perfectionism, and overconscientiousness, respectively. Although such exact matching was not seen uniformly, overall the structures were surprisingly congruent at this lower level, given their rather different origins.

A few discrepancies should also be noted. One divergence occurred between the social avoidance and social isolation factors, the former involving a desire for improved affiliative relationships and the latter including the symptom "neither desires nor enjoys close relationships." An examination of the other components of these factors suggests that the former factor leans conceptually toward the avoidant personality disorder, which is said to include desire but fear of interpersonal relationships, whereas the latter represents the more classical schizoid temperament that rejects interpersonal involvement more completely. It is noteworthy that empirical differentiation of these two types has been difficult; perhaps an investigation of the relation between these two factors will shed some light on this problem.

Another point of discrepancy occurred with the trait of pessimism. In Clark's structure, pessimism emerged as a dimension, characterized by such

---

TABLE 10.1

Content-Based Comparison of Structures of the Traits of Personality Disorder

Livesley's (1990) 18-factor scales	Clark's (1993) 22-symptom clusters
Self-harm	Suicide proneness
Ideas of self-harm	Recurrently thinks of death or suicide
Self-damaging acts	Self-mutilating behavior
	Recurrent suicidal threats, gestures, or behavior
Identity problems	Self-derogation
Labile self-concept	Identity disturbance
	Low self-esteem
Anhedonia	Anhedonia
Chronic feelings of emptiness	Low energy
Pessimism	Emptiness; boredom
	Little interest in enjoyment or pleasurable activities
Affective lability	Instability
Affective instability	Shifting, shallow emotional expression
Affective overreactivity	Reacts to criticism with feelings of rage or shame
	Unstable interpersonal relationships
Generalized hypersensitivity	Hypersensitivity
	Easily hurt by criticism or disapproval
	Reacts to criticism with feelings of rage or shame
	Bears grudges or is unforgiving of slights and insults
	Anger–aggression
Labile anger	Inappropriate intense anger, lack of anger control
Irritability	Irritability
Anxiousness	Pessimism
Guilt proneness	Feels guilty concerning past activities
Indecisiveness	Exaggeration of difficulties
Rumination	Broods over past events
	Negative Affect
Trait anxiety	Anxious, worried, on edge
	Excessive social anxiety
	Restlessness, unable to relax
Suspiciousness	Suspiciousness
Hypervigilance	Expects to be exploited or harmed
	Overly concerned with hidden motives
Suspiciousness	Suspiciousness, paranoid ideation
	Reluctant to confide in others
	Questions the loyalty or trustworthiness of friends
Rejection	Self-centered exploitation
Judgmental	Inconsiderate of others
Rigid cognitive style	Lack of generosity when no personal gain will result
Interpersonal hostility	Disregards the personal integrity and rights of others
Dominance	Treats those under his/her control unusually harshly
Interpersonal disesteem	Self-centered exploitation
Interpersonal irresponsibility	Takes advantage of others for his/her own ends
Exploitation	Interpersonally exploitative
Contemptuousness	Humiliates or demeans people in front of others
Remorseless	Treats those under his/her control unusually harshly
Lack of empathy	Lacks empathy
Egocentrism	Indifferent to the feelings of others
	Anger–aggression
Sadism	Aggressive
	Uses cruelty or violence to establish dominance
Passive oppositionality	Passive–aggressiveness
Passivity	Inefficient, ineffective, unproductive
	Fails to accomplish tasks crucial to personal objectives

Continued on next page

TABLE 10.1 *(continued)*	
Livesley's (1990) 18-factor scales	**Clark's (1993) 22-symptom clusters**

Livesley's (1990) 18-factor scales	Clark's (1993) 22-symptom clusters
Oppositional	Obstructs efforts of others by failing to do his/her work
	Resents useful suggestions from others
Lack of organization	Indecisive
	Has difficulty initiating projects
Narcissism	Dramatic exhibitionism
Need for adulation	Requires constant admiration
Attention seeking	Uncomfortable when not the center of attention
	Grandiose egocentrism
Grandiosity	Grandiose sense of self-importance
	Sense of entitlement
Need for approval	Egocentric, vain, demanding
	Insists that others submit to his/her way of doing things
Social avoidance	Social isolation
Defective social skills	Engages in peripheral social and vocational roles
Low affiliation	Has no close friends or confidants
Social apprehension	Chooses solitary activities
Fearful of interpersonal hurt	Distances oneself from close personal attachments
Desire for improved affiliative relations	Neither desires nor enjoys close relationships
Intimacy problems	Emotional coldness
Inhibited sexuality	Restricted ability to express warm and tender feelings
Avoidant attachment	Unresponsive in interpersonal relationships
Desire for improved attachment	
Restricted expression	Emotional coldness
Restricted affective expression	Displays constricted affect
Restricted express of anger and of positive sentiments	Rarely experiences strong emotions such as anger or joy
Reluctant self-disclosure	Rarely makes reciprocal gestures or facial expressions
Self-reliance	
Insecure attachment	Dependency
Separation protest	Preoccupied with fears of being abandoned
Feared loss	Agrees with people for fear of rejection
Intolerant of aloneness	Feels uncomfortable or helpless when alone
Proximity seeking	Goes to great lengths to avoid being alone
Secure base	Feels devastated when close relationships end
Diffidence	Dependency
Submissiveness	Subordinates own needs to those of others
Suggestibility	Allows others to make decisions for him/her
Need for advice	Constantly seeks reassurance
Compulsivity	Conventionality–rigidity
Orderliness	Preoccupation with details, order, organization
Precision	Perfectionism that interferes with task completion
Conscientiousness	Overconscientiousness, scrupulousness
Stimulus seeking	Impulsivity
Impulsivity	Impulsive, fails to plan ahead
Recklessness	Recklessness
	High energy
Sensation seeking	Craves activity and excitement
	Excessive involvement in pleasurable activities
	Elevated or expansive mood, overoptimistic
Conduct problems	Antisocial behavior
Interpersonal violence	Lies for the purpose of harming others
Fails to adopt social norms	Fails to conform to social norms
Addictive behaviors	Fails to honor financial obligations
Juvenile antisocial	
Cognitive distortion	Schizotypal thought
Depersonalization	Depersonalization–derealization
Schizotypal cognition	Magical thinking, ideas of reference, illusions
Brief stress psychosis	

symptoms as guilt, brooding, and exaggeration of difficulties. Together with negative affect, this dimension corresponded to Livesley's anxiousness factor. However, in Livesley's structure, pessimism emerged as a (lower level) aspect of identity problems, along with anhedonia, chronic feelings of emptiness, and labile self-concept, which were represented by the symptom clusters of self-derogation and anhedonia in Clark's structure. It is possible that these discrepancies result from differences in the way that the specific terms were used in the different research protocols. A related possibility is that all of these dimensions actually are facets of a broader higher order trait such as neuroticism and that the noted discrepancies represent methodological artifacts. We hope that further investigation into these structures will clarify the various points of divergence.

Although a few discrepancies were noted, when taken as a whole, the two independently derived structures represent a striking congruence in the identified traits of personality disorder. Given their rather diverse theoretical and methodological origins, this remarkable structural convergence suggests that there are a number of robust traits in the domain of personality disorder. Moreover, given that neither investigator limited his or her research to the traits, symptoms, or behaviors defined by the *DSM,* it is likely that these structures have a high degree of generality. That is, although it is possible that additional traits may be identified if new personality disorders were defined, the likelihood is small that these traits would fall totally outside these structures. Rather, they would probably represent variations on one of the basic themes already identified.

A final noteworthy point is that a comparable number of factors emerged in each of these structures. However, examination of the content of either set of factors suggests that there will be significant intercorrelations among some of the dimensions. Thus, further questions remain regarding (a) whether a consistent higher order level of structure will emerge based on these two sets of dimensions and (b) whether a lower order structure (e.g., those of Livesley or Clark) or a higher order one (e.g., the FFM) is more optimal for characterizing the domain of personality disordered traits. Although a complete answer to these questions awaits more research, it is possible to begin to answer the former on the basis of existing data. We turn now to this question.

Conceptual Convergence With the FFM

In our attempt to match the factors across the two solutions, it was helpful initially to group the dimensions into several very broad categories. Because a number of the dimensions (e.g., affective lability and anxiousness, which corresponded to instability–hypersensitivity–anger–aggression and pessimism–negative affect, respectively) had various negative affective states as one of their main components, they were seen as forming a large general category. Similarly, because several factors (e.g., self-centered exploitation, which corresponded to rejection and interpersonal disesteem and passive oppositionality–passive–aggressiveness) suggested antagonistic interpersonal relationships, they were placed together in a larger group.

Next, as described earlier, we used the descriptive facets of each factor to match specific dimensions across the two structures. When this was completed, we reconsidered the issue of broad higher order dimensions. Somewhat to our surprise, the dimensions of the FFM appeared to emerge in broad outline. For example, the factors having negative affective component states seemed to represent the broad dimension of Neuroticism. Similarly, the factors tapping hostile and exploitative interpersonal relationships were characteristic of the higher order dimension of (dis)agreeableness. Extraversion appeared to be negatively represented by factors such as social avoidance (social isolation) and emotional coldness (intimacy problems, restricted expression), whereas compulsivity (conventionality–rigidity) undoubtedly tapped conscientiousness. Finally, cognitive distortion (schizotypal. thought) was thought to represent extreme openness.

Although the basic dimensions of the FFM generally appeared to be represented by these traits of personality disorder, several dimensions seemed to be related to more than one of the five factors. For example, suspiciousness was thought perhaps to represent aspects of both neuroticism and (dis)agreeableness, and dependency (insecure attachment, diffidence) was thought to represent a facet of neuroticism, introversion, or both. Furthermore, it was not clear whether conduct problems (antisocial behavior) was better characterized as low conscientiousness (conventionality–rigidity) or (dis)agreeableness.

Fortunately, however, it was not necessary to depend only on content considerations to determine the most optimal categorization of the disordered personality dimensions into the five factors. That is, each of us had collected data investigating his or her structures in relation to the FFM. Therefore, we turn now to an examination of these empirical data.

Empirical Evidence

We can use the common metric of the FFM to compare the two trait structures of personality disorder to examine three interrelated questions. First, how accurate are our conceptual matches of specific dimensions? If two factors for which we had hypothesized a correspondence were both related to the same FFM domain(s), this would provide evidence regarding the validity of the match. Conversely, if corresponding factors were related to different FFM domains, our hypothesis about their conceptual identity would be called into question. At the very least, the operational measurement of the factors would be shown to be discrepant.

Second, we can use these same data to examine our hypotheses regarding the higher order arrangement of the personality disorder factors. It is conceivable that a pair of factors were accurately matched but that their placement in the FFM was incorrectly hypothesized. Thus, we can ask if the matched dimensions are in fact correlated with the hypothesized FFM domain. Finally, the empirical relations between the five factors and the dimensions of personality disorder will provide evidence regarding those dimensions that were not clearly or easily classified conceptually in terms of the FFM. For example, is the characterization of certain matched factors unclear because they are correlated with more than one FFM domain?

In this section, we describe the results of comparative analyses using three samples. For Sample 1 —from which the data on Livesley's 18-factor struc-

ture were obtained—the subjects, measures, and procedures are described in chapter 9 of this volume. Briefly, 300 general population subjects (150 men, 150 women) completed the DAPP-BQ and the NEO Personality Inventory (NEO-PI; Costa & McCrae, 1985, 1989).

For Sample 2, the subjects and procedures are described in chapter 8 of this volume. In brief, 225 university students (140 women, 85 men) completed the Schedule for Nonadaptive and Adaptive Personality (SNAP; Clark, 1993) and the NEO-PI. Sample 3 consisted of 76 psychiatric patients who participated in an ongoing project comparing interview-based and self-report assessment of personality disorders. These patients completed the SNAP and the Five-Factor Inventory (FFI; Costa & McCrae, 1989), a short form of the NEO-PI. The FFI scales can be scored from the full NEO-PI completed by the students in Sample 2; therefore, to equate the data derived from Samples 2 and 3, we used FFI scale scores for both samples.

Demographics of Sample 3

The patients (38 women, 38 men) ranged from 18 to 53 years of age ($M = 32.1$, $SD = 8.6$). Most (80%) were White, and 70% of the remainder were Black. The average patient had a high school education (43%), with education levels ranging from 7th grade to postgraduate study. Approximately half (49%) were single, 21% were married, 14% were divorced, and 16% were separated. The majority (59%) was inpatients on one of three units at a state hospital (32% from a substance abuse unit, 14% from a personality disorders unit, and 13% from an acute care unit). The remainder were outpatients from a variety of private and community agencies.

Measures

Symptom Clusters. The SNAP is a 375-item self-report inventory in a true–false format that was designed primarily to provide 15 personality trait scale scores. However, the item pool is constituted so that it also can provide an assessment of the various personality disorder symptoms that constitute the 22 identified clusters. In most cases, two items are provided for each symptom criterion, although in some cases only one or as many as six items represent the criterion. For example, a person with schizoid personality disorder criterion rarely, if ever, claims or appears to experience strong emotions, such as anger or joy, as represented by the two items: "It often seems that I simply have no feelings," and "I rarely feel strong emotions such as anger or joy."

Preliminary scales were constructed for each of the 22 symptom clusters by compiling the SNAP items that represented each of the component symptoms.[1] Scores were derived for each symptom cluster by summing the total number of items endorsed. Internal consistency analyses were then conducted using both Samples 2 and 3. Items with low item-total correlations in both samples were eliminated. Because of limitations in the item pool, one cluster (hypersexuality) was represented by only 4 items, too few to permit the development of a reliable scale. For the other 21 scales, the number of items ranged from 6 (suicide proneness and self-derogation) to 25 (grandiose egocentrism), with an average of 13 items per cluster. Internal consistency reliabilities averaged .71 (range = .50 for suicide proneness to .79 for negative affect and social isolation) in Sample 2 (students) and .75 (range = .55 for emotional coldness to .86 for suspiciousness) in Sample 3 (patients).

Five-Factor Inventory. The FFI is a 60-item questionnaire developed from the item pool of the NEO-PI using factor analytic methods. Each scale consists of 12 items that most strongly and consistently represent one of the five domains assessed by the NEO-PI. Internal consistency reliabilities in Sample 2 were .85 (Neuroticism), .80 (Extraversion), .67 (Openness), .77 (Agreeableness), and .82 (Conscientiousness). In Sample 3, the corresponding values were .82 (Neuroticism), .80 (Extraversion), .65 (Openness), .81 (Agreeableness), and .83 (Conscientiousness).

Empirical Comparison of Two Sets of Personality Disordered Traits

In each of the three samples, correlations were computed between a measure of the FFM (the NEO-PI in Sample 1 and the FFI in Samples 2 and 3) and

either the 18 DAPP-BQ factor scales (Sample 1) or the 21 SNAP-based symptom clusters (Samples 2 and 3). Even in the smallest group, Sample 3 (N = 76), correlations of .22 or greater were significant at the p = .05 level, so it was decided to use a higher cutoff point to represent a conceptually significant correlation, rather than to use statistical significance as an index. Therefore, any DAPP-BQ factor or SNAP cluster that correlated |.35| or stronger with any FFM scale was identified, as were scales whose highest correlation with any FFM scale was less than |.35|. The correlations of conceptually matched traits (shown in Table 10.1) were then examined for the comparability of their correlational patterns with the FFM scales.

The results are shown in Table 10.2. A scale—and its counterpart(s) in the other structure—was included if it met the conditions just described. Openness was not included because no scales correlated consistently with this domain. To highlight the most salient correlations with the FFM scales, we show factor or cluster scale names and correlations in bold if they represent the strongest correlation with a given FFM scale. For example, Identity Problems correlated +.67 with Neuroticism and −.43 with Extraversion. Therefore, it is shown in bold under Neuroticism and in regular under Extraversion because its correlation with Neuroticism was its strongest. For the SNAP symptom clusters, scale names are shown in bold only if the correlation with a particular FFM scale was the highest in both Samples 2 and 3. Thus, negative affect and pessimism (and their correlations) are shown in bold under Neuroticism because those were their highest correlations in both the student and patient samples. However, for suspiciousness, the strongest correlation in Sample 3 (patients) was with Agreeableness, whereas it was highest with Neuroticism in Sample 2 (students). Therefore, only the individual correlations (and not the cluster name) are shown in bold.

As seen in the table, the empirical correspondence of the matched scales was generally quite good. Of the 16 DAPP-BQ scales assessed (self-harm and cognitive distortion were not included in Sam-

---

[1] An earlier version of the SNAP diagnostic criterion scales was used in these samples.

TABLE 10.2

Correlations Between the NEO Personality Inventory and the NEO Five-Factor Inventory Scales and Personality Disordered Traits

DAPP-BQ factor scales	*r*[a]	SNAP symptom clusters	*r*[b]	*r*[c]
		Neuroticism		
Anxiousness	.82	**Negative affect**	.73	.64
		Pessimism	.72	.67
Affective lability	.68	**Instability**	.50	.63
		Hypersensitivity	.53	.50
		Anger–aggression	.17	.31
Identity problems	.67	**Self-derogation**	.32	.38
		Anhedonia	.34	.21
Social avoidance	.62	Social isolation	.47	.27
Diffidence	.57	**Dependency**	.47	.56
Insecure attachment	.46			
Passive oppositionality	.54	Passive–aggressiveness	.32	.26
Narcissism	.52	Dramatic exhibitionism	.00	.03
		Grandiose egocentrism	.34	.25
Self-harm	—[d]	**Suicide proneness**	.46	.36
Suspiciousness	.36	Suspiciousness	.41	.51
		Extraversion		
Social avoidance	−.57	**Social isolation**	−.60	−.69
Stimulus seeking	.56	**High energy**	.57	.56
		Impulsivity	.10	.07
Restricted expression	−.45	**Emotional coldness**	−.52	−.60
Intimacy problems	−.35			
Identity problems	−.43	**Anhedonia**	−.54	−.51
		Self-derogation	−.26	−.22
Narcissism	.14	**Dramatic exhibitionism**	.38	.59
		Agreeableness		
Interpersonal disesteem	−.73	**Self-centered exploitation**	−.65	−.69
Rejection	−.52	**Anger–aggression**	−.56	−.55
Suspiciousness	−.59	Suspiciousness	−.60	−.50
Conduct problems	−.41	**Antisocial behavior**	−.50	−.51
Narcissism	−.32	**Grandiose egocentrism**	−.47	−.30
Affective lability	−.35	Hypersensitivity	−.55	−.38
		Instability	−.42	−.40
		Conscientiousness		
Passive oppositionality	−.71	**Passive–aggressiveness**	−.60	−.61
Compulsivity	.63	**Conventionality–rigidity**	.32	.39
Stimulus seeking	.02	Impulsivity	−.38	−.45
Conduct problems	−.18	Antisocial behavior	−.44	−.44

Note. DAPP-BQ = Dimensional Assessment of Personality Pathology—Basic Questionnaire; SNAP = Schedule for Nonadaptive and Adaptive Personality. A correlation shown in **boldface** indicates the strongest correlation between a factor or cluster and a five-factor measure in a given sample.   [a]Correlation with NEO-PI domain scales; *N* = 300 normal adults.   [b]Correlation with FFI scales; *N* = 76 patients.   [c]Correlation with FFI scales; *N* = 225 university students.   [d]DAPP-BQ self-harm and cognitive distortion factors were unavailable in this sample.

ple 1), 14 shared their highest correlation with at least one of their SNAP-based counterparts, and 8 showed exactly the same correlational pattern across the two structures in all three samples. Of the six conceptual sets that showed some correlational differences, there were two notable patterns. In three cases, a single Livesley scale had two or more counterparts in Clark's structure; not all of the counterparts had the same correlational pattern with the five factors as did Livesley's scale. For example, DAPP-BQ stimulus seeking matched with SNAP high energy and impulsivity; and stimulus seeking and high energy were both strongly correlated with Extraversion, whereas impulsivity was not. Impulsivity's highest correlation was with (low) Conscientiousness, which was uncorrelated with stimulus seeking. In other cases, the matched scales showed the same correlation with one FFM scale but not another. For example, DAPP-BQ passive oppositionality and SNAP passive aggressiveness were both strongly (negatively) correlated with Conscientiousness; however, only passive oppositionality showed a strong secondary correlation with Neuroticism.

Of the two sets of matched scales that showed somewhat different patterns, one pair differed only in emphasis. Specifically, DAPP-BQ social avoidance and SNAP social isolation each correlated both with Neuroticism and (negatively) with Extraversion; however, social avoidance correlated more highly with Neuroticism, whereas social isolation correlated more strongly with Extraversion. Thus, of 16 conceptual matches, only one set—narcissism and its counterparts dramatic exhibitionism and grandiose egocentrism—showed markedly different patterns. This and other differences are discussed further subsequently, but first we examine the similarities between the structures in more detail.

Similarities Between the Two Structures in Relation to the Five-Factor Model

Table 10.3 summarizes the empirically validated correspondences between conceptually matched scales in Clark's and Livesley's structures. Congruent with previous formulations of this higher order dimension, Neuroticism was characterized by scales assessing negative affects and affective instability; by problems with identity and self-esteem; and by

insecurity, dependency, and mistrust in interpersonal relationships. Similarly, the correlates of the domain of Extraversion were consistent with current conceptions of this dimension. Specifically, the low end was characterized by social avoidance and isolation, difficulties in forming close interpersonal relationships, and restricted expression of emotions including anhedonia. In contrast, the high end of the dimension reflected the active and energetic seeking out of arousing stimuli.

Agreeableness was entirely represented by scales tapping the low end of the dimension. Specifically, disagreeableness was characterized by a variety of interpersonal difficulties, including angry, rejecting, unstable, and exploitative relationships; suspiciousness and hypersensitivity toward others; and overt antisocial behaviors or conduct problems. Finally, the domain of Conscientiousness was readily recognizable in its correlates of passive opposition to cooperation or conformity versus rigid compulsivity and conventionality.

In summary, the factor scales of the DAPP-BQ and the SNAP-based personality disorder symptom clusters are themselves highly convergent and yield an elaborated picture of the FFM that is quite consistent with previous descriptions of these domains. It must be noted, however, that the Openness domain was not represented in these structures of personality disordered traits and symptoms. It is possible that cognitive distortion, which was not assessed in Sample 1, would be related to Openness, but its SNAP-based conceptual counterpart, eccentric thought, was not consistently related to this domain. Therefore, the importance of Openness in the structure of the traits of personality disorder remains unknown.

Differences Between the Two Structures in Relation to the Five-Factor Model

An examination of points of divergence between the two structures in relation to the FFM can shed light on the different ways that what is nominally the same trait can be assessed. Conceptual matches between Clark's and Livesley's structures that were not completely confirmed empirically are summarized in Table 10.4. As mentioned earlier, many of the differences were only partial or reflect complementary dif-

Similarities Between the Personality Disordered Traits in Terms of the Five-Factor Model (FFM)

FFM scale	DAPP-BQ factor scales	SNAP symptom clusters
Neuroticism	Anxiousness	Negative affect
		Pessimism
	Affective lability	Instability
		Hypersensitivity
	Identity problems	Self-derogation
	Insecure attachment	Dependency
	Diffidence	
	Suspiciousness	Suspiciousness
Extraversion (introversion)	Social avoidance	Social isolation
	Stimulus seeking	Emotional coldness
	Intimacy problems	
	Restricted expression	
	Identity problems	Anhedonia
(Dis)Agreeableness	Rejection	Self-centered exploitation
	Interpersonal disesteem	Self-centered exploitation
		Anger–aggression
	Suspiciousness	Suspiciousness
	Conduct problems	Antisocial behavior
	Affective lability	Instability
		Hypersensitivity
(Low) Conscientiousness	Passive oppositionality	Passive–aggressiveness
	Compulsivity	Conventionality–rigidity

Note. DAPP-BQ = Dimensional Assessment of Personality Pathology—Basic Questionnaire; SNAP = Schedule for Nonadaptive and Adaptive Personality. Traits are included if they correlated |.35| or stronger with the same FFM domain scale in all three samples examined, or if $r < |.35|$, the correlation was the strongest for that factor or cluster. All scales meeting these conditions were matched conceptually.

ferences in the way the scales divided across two higher order dimensions. It is noteworthy that no simple pattern of divergence emerged. That is, of the seven matches that showed some empirical differences in their correlational patterns with the FFM measures, no pattern appeared exactly the same way twice. Therefore, each one is discussed briefly.

Differences in the relations of DAPP-BQ stimulus seeking to its conceptual matches, SNAP-based high energy and impulsivity, have already been mentioned. Specifically, stimulus seeking and high energy both correlated with Extraversion (and impulsivity did not), whereas impulsivity correlated (negatively) with Conscientiousness (and stimulus seeking did not). This suggests that although stimulus seeking includes items tapping impulsivity and recklessness, they are phrased so that they carry an active, positive emotional tone, whereas SNAP-based

impulsivity items more strongly reflect the nonconscientious, irresponsible aspect of recklessness. For example, contrast the stimulus seeking scale item "I like to flirt with danger" with the impulsivity cluster item "I've gotten a lot of speeding tickets." It is noteworthy that the proper placement of impulsivity in the higher order structure of personality traits has been the subject of some debate (Watson & Clark, 1997), with some writers viewing it as a facet of Extraversion (e.g., Eysenck & Eysenck, 1969), some as a facet of Neuroticism (Costa & McCrae, 1985), and still others as a facet of Conscientiousness (Tellegen, 1985). Thus, this discrepancy is not at all unique to personality disorder and may reflect the fact that impulsivity is not a homogeneous dimension but has several different facets.

In a related vein, both DAPP-BQ conduct problems and SNAP antisocial behavior were related to

TABLE 10.4

Differences Between the Personality Disordered Traits in Terms of the Five-Factor Model (FFM)

DAPP-BQ factor	FFM scale	SNAP symptom cluster	FFM scale
Stimulus seeking	Extraversion	Impulsivity	(−) Conscientiousness
Conduct problems	(−) Agreeableness only	Antisocial behavior	(−) Agreeableness and (−) Conscientiousness
Social avoidance	(−) Extraversion and Neuroticism	Social isolation	(−) Extraversion only
Passive oppositionality	(−) Conscientiousness and Neuroticism	Passive–aggressiveness	(−) Conscientiousness only
Affective lability	(−) Agreeableness and Neuroticism	Anger–aggression	(−) Agreeableness only
Identity problems	Neuroticism and (−) Extraversion	Self-derogation Anhedonia	Neuroticism only (−) Extraversion only
Narcissism	Neuroticism	Dramatic exhibitionism Grandiose egocentrism	Extraversion (−) Agreeableness

Note. DAPP-BQ = Dimensional Assessment of Personality Pathology—Basic Questionnaire; SNAP = Schedule for Nonadaptive and Adaptive Personality. Traits are included if (a) they were matched conceptually and (b) the factor or cluster from one structure correlated |.35| or stronger with a particular FFM domain scale, or if $r < |.35|$, the scale was the strongest correlate of the factor or cluster, and the corresponding scale from the other structure did not meet either of these empirical conditions.

(low) Agreeableness. Only antisocial behavior, however, was correlated also with (low) Conscientiousness. Both scales contain items reflecting irresponsible behavior, so this commonality apparently reflects (low) Agreeableness rather than (low) Conscientiousness. The different correlational patterns suggest that the SNAP antisocial behavior items also imply the rejection of a well-ordered and organized life, whereas the DAPP-BQ conduct problems items do not, although this conclusion is not immediately obvious from an inspection of the item content. Thus, more research is needed to clarify the meaning of the discrepant patterns.

Although it was stated earlier that no two correlational patterns of divergence were exactly the same, there did appear to be one systematic difference between the two structures. That is, in several cases, a DAPP-BQ scale was correlated with both Neuroticism and another of the five-factor dimensions, whereas the corresponding SNAP scale was correlated only with the second dimension and not also with Neuroticism. We mentioned two of these cases earlier. DAPP-BQ social avoidance correlated

most strongly with Neuroticism but had a strong secondary (negative) correlation with Extraversion. Its SNAP-based counterpart, social isolation, correlated most highly with Extraversion and correlated strongly with Neuroticism only in Sample 2. This difference appears to correspond to the *DSM*-based distinction between the interpersonal relations of people with avoidant personality disorder and those with schizoid personality disorder. That is, the former are said to both desire and fear social contact, suggesting a negative emotional component to their social avoidance that would link it with the domain of neuroticism. The latter, however, are more affectively disengaged from other people, which suggests introversion more than neuroticism. It is interesting to note that the names provided by Livesley and Clark for their respective dimensions appear to capture the distinction that is represented in their empirical correlations.

DAPP-BQ passive oppositionality and SNAP-based passive aggressiveness represent the second pair of scales in which the DAPP-BQ scale was correlated with Neuroticism. and the SNAP-based scale was not. The strongest correlation of both scales was (negatively) with Conscientiousness; however, only passive oppositionality was correlated also with Neuroticism. The reason for this phenomenon may lie partly in the history of the development of the SNAP. Because of the overabundance of scales measuring neuroticism (see Watson & Clark, 1984), Clark (1993) was concerned with minimizing the role of this dimension in the SNAP item pool, except for a few scales explicitly designed to tap this domain. Therefore, in developing the SNAP scales, items that correlated |.35| or higher with a measure of neuroticism were systematically eliminated. Although a number of SNAP scales, nevertheless, still had substantial neuroticism-related variance, this process had the effect of reducing the influence of this highly pervasive dimension. Most likely, the differential pattern of DAPP-BQ and SNAP correlations with five-factor Neuroticism reflects this fact.

The two other cases of differential correlations with Neuroticism both involved one DAPP-BQ scale being matched to more than one SNAP-based cluster. First, affective lability matched SNAP-based instability, hypersensitivity, and anger–aggression. All of these scales correlated (negatively) with Agreeableness; moreover, all but anger–aggression were also correlated with Neuroticism. (Indeed, this was the stronger correlation in most cases). Thus, the lack of convergence simply reflects the fact that anger–aggression reflects only Agreeableness. This suggests that this cluster emphasizes the overt behavioral aspects of anger–aggression rather than the more subjective affective experience that underlies them, which is consistent with the explanation of the SNAP item pool offered previously.

Second, DAPP-BQ identity problems, which correlated strongly with both Neuroticism and (low) Extraversion, was matched with SNAP-based self-derogation and anhedonia. These scales, rather than both correlating with the two FFM domains, showed relatively independent correlational patterns. That is, self-derogation was related to Neuroticism but not to Extraversion, whereas anhedonia was related to (low) Extraversion but not to Neuroticism. Thus, in this case, two aspects of DAPP-BQ identity problems were tapped separately by the two SNAP-based cluster scales.

Finally, the only match to show a clear and complete divergence in its empirical relations was that between DAPP-BQ narcissism and SNAP-based dramatic exhibitionism and grandiose egocentrism. Interestingly, narcissism was again correlated with Neuroticism, whereas dramatic exhibitionism and grandiose egocentrism were correlated with Extraversion and (low) Agreeableness, respectively. Inspection of the items of each scale suggests reasons for this divergence. Many of the narcissism items concerning attention seeking have a quality of overt neediness and dissatisfaction when these needs are not met. Items include "I need people to reassure me that they think well of me" and "I am only really satisfied when people acknowledge how good I am." Thus, the items have a negative affective tone that appears to tap the domain of Neuroticism. In contrast, dramatic exhibitionism assesses this need through items that reflect attention-seeking behaviors (e.g., "I wear clothes that draw attention") and that express positive emotions in connection with receiving attention (e.g., "I like being the topic of conversation"), which may serve to link the scale with Extraversion. In contrast, the grandiose egocentrism items express a haughty sense of being entitled to others' attention (e.g., "I deserve special recognition") and a sense of indignation when admiration is not forthcoming (e.g., "People don't give me enough credit for my work"), which seem to tap the interpersonal antagonism of (dis)agreeableness.

It should be noted, however, that the narcissism scale is not devoid of positive or grandiose content (e.g., "I like to dramatize things," "I am destined for greatness"); similarly, both of the SNAP-based scales contain items expressing neediness, negative affect (e.g., "I feel a strong need to have others approve of me," "It irritates me greatly when I am asked to do something I don't want to do"), or both. Thus, the marked lack of convergence in the scales' correlational patterns with the FFM measures remains a bit puzzling. We hope to shed light on this issue using data currently being collected that will permit a direct examination of the intercorrelations of the SNAP and DAPP-BQ scales as well as provide additional evidence regarding their correlations with measures of the FFM.

CONCLUSION

We described two rather different approaches to identifying and assessing the basic traits of personality disorder: One focused on prototypical traits and behaviors for the various personality disorders; the other was based more directly on the criterion symptoms of personality disorder. In addition, we have shown that these diverse strategies nevertheless yielded personality trait structures that were highly comparable in terms of their overt content. Finally, we have demonstrated that measures developed independently to assess these two sets of identified trait dimensions show strongly convergent correlational patterns with measures of the FFM. Moreover, the traits that correlated with each FFM domain clearly represented content consistent with previous interpretation of these higher order dimensions. (It should be noted, however, that Openness was not represented strongly or consistently in the structures.)

Differences in emphasis or focus did emerge for some scales, but most of these were minor, and it is noteworthy that only one pair of scales that were conceptually matched showed no empirical convergence. In general, the DAPP-BQ scales seemed to be more saturated with Neuroticism, and this likely reflects the systematic removal of this variance in the development of the SNAP.

These data thus provide further support for the notion that the personality trait dimensional structure defined by the FFM is very robust and will emerge reliably as long as a broad range of personality traits are assessed. Further research into the observed differences will shed light on the alternative ways that nominally similar constructs of personality disorder can be construed, which will serve to increase the understanding of this domain. Finally, more research is needed to determine the role of Openness in personality disorder.

References

Akiskal, H. S., Hirschfeld, R. M., & Yerevanian, B. I. (1983). The relationship of personality to affective disorder. *Archives of General Psychiatry, 40,* 801–810.

American Psychiatric Association. (1980). *Diagnostic and statistical manual of mental disorders* (3rd ed.). Washington, DC: Author.

American Psychiatric Association. (1987). *Diagnostic and statistical manual of mental disorders* (3rd ed., rev.). Washington, DC: Author.

Clark, L. A. (1990). Toward a consensual set of symptom clusters for assessment of personality disorder. In J. N. Butcher & C. D. Spielberger (Eds.), *Advances in personality assessment* (Vol. 8, pp. 243–266). Hillsdale, NJ: Erlbaum.

Clark, L. A. (1993). *Manual for the Schedule for Nonadaptive and Adaptive Personality (SNAP).* Minneapolis: University of Minnesota Press.

Clark, L. A., McEwen, J. L., Collard, L., & Hickok, L. G. (1993). Symptoms and traits of personality disorder: Two new methods for their assessment. *Psychological Assessment, 5,* 81–91.

Clark, L. A., Pfohl, B., & Blashfield, R. (1991). *Internal consistency analyses of conceptually derived clusters of personality disorder symptoms.* Unpublished raw data, Southern Methodist University, Dallas, TX.

Cleckley, H. (1964). *The mask of sanity* (4th ed.). St. Louis, MO: Mosby.

Cloninger, C. R. (1987). Neurogenetic adaptive mechanism in alcoholism. *Science, 236,* 410–416.

Cloninger, C. R., Svrakic, D. M., & Przybeck, T. R. (1993). A psychobiological model of temperament and character. *Archives of General Psychiatry, 50,* 975–990

Costa, P. T., Jr., & McCrae, R. R. (1985). *The NEO Personality Inventory manual.* Odessa, FL: Psychological Assessment Resources.

Costa, P. T., Jr., & McCrae, R. R. (1989). *The NEO Personality Inventory/NEO Five-Factor Inventory manual supplement.* Odessa, FL: Psychological Assessment Resources.

Eysenck, H. J., & Eysenck, S. B. G. (1969). *Eysenck Personality Inventory manual.* San Diego, CA: EdITS.

Frances, A. J. (1980). The *DSM-III* personality disorders section: A commentary. *American Journal of Psychiatry, 137,* 1050–1054.

Hathaway, S. R., & McKinley, J. C. (1967). *Minnesota Multiphasic Personality Inventory manual.* New York: Psychological Corporation.

Hyler, S. E., Lyons, M., Rieder, R. O., Young, L., Williams, J. B. W., & Spitzer, R. L. (1990). The factor structure of self-report *DSM-III* Axis I symptoms and their relationship to clinicians' ratings. *American Journal of Psychiatry, 147,* 751–757.

Kiesler, D. J. (1986). The 1982 interpersonal circle: An analysis of *DSM-III* personality disorders. In T. Millon & G. L. Klerman (Eds.), *Contemporary directions in psychopathology: Toward the* DSM-IV (pp. 571–597). New York: Guilford Press.

Liebowitz, M. R., & Klein, D. F. (1981). Interrelationship of hysteroid dysphoria and borderline personality disorder. *Psychiatric Clinics of North America, 4,* 67–87.

Livesley, W. J. (1986). Traits and behavioral prototypes of personality disorder. *American Journal of Psychiatry, 143,* 728–732.

Livesley, W. J. (1987). A systematic approach to the delineation of personality disorders. *American Journal of Psychiatry, 144,* 772–777.

Livesley, W. J. (1990). *Dimensional Assessment of Personality Pathology—Basic Questionnaire.* Unpublished manuscript, University of British Columbia, Vancouver, British Columbia, Canada.

Livesley, W. J. (1991). Classifying personality disorders: Ideal types, prototypes, or dimensions? *Journal of Personality Disorders, 5,* 52–59.

Livesley, W. J., Jackson, D., & Schroeder, M. L. (1989). A study of the factorial structure of personality pathology. *Journal of Personality Disorders, 3,* 292–306.

Morey, L. C. (1988). The categorical representation of personality disorders: A cluster analysis of *DSM-III-R* personality features. *Journal of Abnormal Psychology, 97,* 314–321.

Perry, J. C., & Klerman, G. L. (1978). The borderline patient: A comparative analysis of four sets of diagnostic criteria. *Archives of General Psychiatry, 35,* 141–150.

Presley, A. S., & Walton, H. J. (1973). Dimensions of abnormal personality. *British Journal of Psychiatry, 122,* 269–276.

Schroeder, M. L., Wormworth, J. A., & Livesley, W. J. (1992). Dimensions of personality disorder and their relationship to the Big Five dimensions of personality. *Psychological Assessment, 4,* 47–53.

Tellegen, A. (1985). Structures of mood and personality and their relevance to assessing anxiety, with an emphasis on self-report. In A. H. Tuma & J. D. Maser (Eds.), *Anxiety and anxiety disorders* (pp. 681–706). Hillsdale, NJ: Erlbaum.

Trapnell, P. D., & Wiggins, J. S. (1990). Extension of the Interpersonal Adjective Scales to include the Big Five dimensions of personality. *Journal of Personality and Social Psychology, 59,* 781–790.

Tyrer, P., & Alexander, J. (1979). Classification of personality disorder. *British Journal of Psychiatry, 135,* 163–167.

Watson, D., & Clark, L. A. (1984). Negative affectivity: The disposition to experience unpleasant emotional states. *Psychological Bulletin, 95,* 465–490.

Watson, D., & Clark, L. A. (1997). The positive emotional core of extraversion. In R. Hogan, J. Johnson, & S. Briggs (Eds.), *Handbook of personality psychology* (pp. 767–793). San Diego, CA: Academic Press.

Wiggins, J. S. (1982). Circumplex models of interpersonal behavior in clinical psychology. In P. Kendall & J. N. Butcher (Eds.), *Handbook of research methods in clinical psychology* (pp. 183–221). New York: Wiley.

Wiggins, J. S., & Pincus, A. L. (1989). Conceptions of personality disorders and dimensions of personality. *Psychological Assessment: A Journal of Consulting and Clinical Psychology, 1,* 305–316.

Zuckerman, M., Kuhlman, D. M., & Camac, C. (1988). What lies beyond E and N? Factor analyses of scales believed to measure basic dimensions of personality. *Journal of Personality and Social Psychology, 54,* 96–107.

CHAPTER 11

BIG FIVE, ALTERNATIVE FIVE, AND SEVEN PERSONALITY DIMENSIONS: VALIDITY IN SUBSTANCE-DEPENDENT PATIENTS

Samuel A. Ball

For much of this century, theoreticians and researchers have struggled to understand the complex association among personality, personality disorder, and substance abuse.[1] Early psychoanalytic theories of addiction (e.g., Fenichel, 1945; Knight, 1936; Rado, 1933) implicated an oral fixation due to unresolved, unconscious early childhood conflicts. Oral traits of dependency, hostility, and low frustration tolerance were thought to increase one's susceptibility to a substance's ability to induce an immediate state of comfort, pseudo-independence, and soothing for affective distress. Early psychoanalytic conceptions of addiction never gained credibility, in part, because they never fully acknowledged alcoholism as a primary disorder and never adequately focused therapeutic attention directly on addictive behaviors. More recently, researchers of psychodynamic conceptualizations based on object relations or self psychology theory have modified their approach to focus on addictive behaviors while attending particularly to issues related to narcissistic injury (see the review by Morganstern & Leeds, 1993). Nonetheless, these models have generated limited empirical research and continue to overlook the significant heterogeneity among those who abuse substances.

The 1930s witnessed the repeal of prohibition; the founding of Alcoholics Anonymous; and a revitalized view of alcoholism and addiction as a medical, psychological, and spiritual disease in which a person's character defects or maladaptive personality traits were important. Abstinence combined with lifestyle and personality change was considered necessary for effective recovery. With the rapid growth of psychological testing around World War II, the 1940s and 1950s were a period of extensive research to define an alcoholic or addictive personality type (see the summary by Cox, 1987). Nearly every objective and projective test has been used with drug and alcohol dependent individuals, especially the Minnesota Multiphasic Personality Inventory (MMPI; see reviews by Anglin, Weisman, & Fisher, 1989; and Graham & Strenger, 1988).

The first edition of the American Psychiatric Association's (APA) *Diagnostic and Statistical Manual for Mental Disorders* (DSM; 1952) classified alcoholism and drug addiction as types of "sociopathic personality disturbances," and the second edition (*DSM-II*; APA, 1967) included these disorders under the broader category of "personality disorders." Even though these nosological systems embedded addiction within a personality construct, the search for an addictive personality was mostly abandoned from the 1960s into the 1980s—a time during

I would like to express appreciation for the mentoring I have received from collaborators in my work in the areas of personality (Marvin Zuckerman and Howard Tennen) and substance abuse (Bruce Rounsaville and Kathleen Carroll). The series of studies reviewed in this chapter were funded through National Institute on Drug Abuse Grants R01 DA 04029, R01 DA05592, R18 DA06915, P50 DA09241, and R01 DA10012.

[1]This chapter uses the terms substance use, abuse, and dependence. *Use* refers broadly to the ingestion of any alcohol or street drug. *Abuse* implies use despite harmful consequences. *Dependence* involves evidence of a loss of control and addiction to the substance.

which the concept of personality was attacked by behaviorists and researchers of multiple studies failed to converge on a single addictive personality type (see the review by Sutker & Allain, 1988).

Interestingly, as the search for a common group of addictive personality traits lost momentum, more complex, statistically derived models based on the MMPI clinical scales, Cattell's 16 Personality Factors, Jackson's Personality Research Form (PRF), or other omnibus measures yielded between 2 and 10 subtypes, many of which paralleled and were labeled with *DSM-II's* diagnostic labels (e.g., MMPI psychopathic, neurotic, and psychotic subtypes). In relevance to this chapter, Nerviano (1976; Nerviano & Gross, 1983) evaluated (male) alcoholic subtypes using five broad personality dimensions from the PRF, which were labeled (a) impulse control (high PRF impulsivity, play; low order, cognitive structure), (b) extraversion (high PRF exhibition, affiliation, dominance), (c) defendency, that is, threat sensitivity (low abasement, high PRF aggression, and defendence, which consists of disagreeableness and hostility), (d) intellectual–aesthetic interests (high PRF understanding, sentience, achievement, nurturance, and change), and (e) dependency (high PRF succor, low autonomy, dependency, defendence). From the 12 best PRF marker scales for the factors, Nerviano found seven profile types that paralleled several *DSM-II* personality disorders: (a) obsessive–compulsive, (b) impulsive, (c) aggressive–paranoid (explosive), (d) passive–dependent (inadequate), (e) avoidant–schizoid, (f) asocial–schizoid (asthenic), and (g) passive–independent (narcissistic). Nerviano's attempt 20 years ago to map the terrain among normal personality dimensions, personality disorders, and multidimensional addiction subtypes provides the conceptual framework for the series of studies reviewed in this chapter, which were conducted over the past 5 years with my colleagues from Yale University's Division of Substance Abuse.

The third edition of the *DSM* (*DSM-III*; APA, 1980), third edition, revised, of the *DSM* (*DSM-III-R*; APA, 1987), and fourth edition of the *DSM* (*DSM-IV*; APA, 1994) clearly differentiate substance use disorders from antisocial personality disorder (ATS) and the other personality disorders. When addiction and personality disorders were recognized as distinct disorders on separate axes, researchers began a series of studies to evaluate the comorbidity and prognostic significance of personality disorders in people treated for substance abuse (see reviews by Verheul, Ball, & van den Brink, 1998; and DeJong, van den Brink, Harteveld, & van der Wielen, 1993). In fact, personality dimensions and personality disorders have been evaluated more often in those who abuse substances than in any other *DSM* Axis I disorder. On the basis of a review of available comordibity studies, Verheul et al. found that the median rates of personality disorders in various substance abuse samples ranged from 40% to 90%. Although ATS, borderline personality disorder (BDL), and avoidant personality disorder (AVD) were usually the most common, a significant minority of those who abuse substances met the criteria for the full range of Axis II disorders.

In addition to these comorbidity studies, the addiction and personality field began to regain its lost credibility in the 1980s through longitudinal studies of biologically influenced temperament traits (e.g., heightened activity, impulsivity, aggression, negative affect), which appear to precede the development of early behavior problems (e.g., attention, conduct, risk taking, substance use, other deviant behaviors) and predict the later development of ATS and substance use disorders (see reviews by Sher & Trull, 1994; Sutker & Allain, 1988; and Tarter, 1988). These developmental psychopathology models articulate a more complex role for personality in the etiology of addiction than do previous, more unidirectional, causal notions that drugs are used to relieve psychodynamic drives, conflicts, or deprivation; fulfill needs for risk, thrill, or excitement; or maintain an optimal level of arousal (Zuckerman, 1994). Instead, heritable variations in temperaments (e.g., behavioral disinhibition) appear to increase one's risk for problematic interactions with parents, teachers, and peers, which increases one's risk for deficient socialization and early identification with a deviance-prone peer group (with similar experiences of rejection of and by normative social influences), in which use of substances and antisocial behaviors are common (Tarter, 1988).

In addition, theoretical and empirical work by Cloninger (1987a, 1987b) and colleagues on the genetics of alcoholism helped to reposition personality to a central role. In the original biosocial personality model, deviations in Novelty Seeking, Harm Avoidance, and Reward Dependence are tied to specific neurotransmitter and behavioral systems and provide an underlying susceptibility for substance abuse and a range of personality disorders. Cloninger also advocated the concept that different personality dimensions and disorders are associated with different subtypes of alcoholism. Type 1 alcoholism is defined as a later onset, environmentally influenced, less severe disorder characterized by higher Harm Avoidance; Type 2 is defined as an earlier onset, genetically influenced, more chronic disorder characterized by higher Novelty Seeking. Another source of renewed credibility for personality factors comes from researchers evaluating individual differences in sensitivity to the stress-reinforcing or stress-reducing effects of alcohol (Levenson, Oyaama, & Meek, 1987; Sher, 1987) and personality subtypes of those arrested for driving while intoxicated (see the review by Donovan, Marlatt, & Salzberg, 1983). In all of these areas, the traits of Impulsivity, Novelty–Sensation Seeking, or behavioral disinhibition have central roles.

As such, over the past 2 decades, there has been a significant shift away from identifying a single addictive personality type to a greater appreciation of the variability of personality functioning among individuals who use drugs and alcohol (Sutker & Allain, 1988). Although there appears to be no consistent evidence for an addictive personality construct per se, there is substantial evidence that certain personality traits play a critical role in the initiation of substance use, the development of substance abuse, and the maintenance of substance dependence. Summaries of cross-sectional and longitudinal research (Barnes, 1979, 1983; Cox, 1987) indicate that individuals later diagnosed with alcoholism premorbidly exhibited higher impulsivity, hostility, and hyperactivity and lower self-esteem and social conformity. Individuals already diagnosed with alcoholism exhibited many of these traits as well as higher neuroticism–anxiety, introversion, depression, and antisocial behavior.

CURRENT TRAIT MODELS AND SUBSTANCE ABUSE

In the past 15–20 years, there has been a renewed appreciation for the heterogeneity of individuals who abuse substances and the usefulness of normal personality dimensions for subtyping these individuals and understanding the etiology, symptom severity, and treatment response. Certain personality dimensions appear to act as risk factors, mediators, moderators, or consequences of the development, progression, and outcome of both substance abuse and personality disorders (see Barnes, 1983; Cox, 1985; Sher & Trull, 1994; and Sutker & Allain, 1988). In this chapter, I summarize studies using three trait models to understand the relation among substance abuse, personality dimensions and disorders, and multidimensional typologies.

Costa and McCrae's (1992b) Revised NEO Personality Inventory (NEO-PI-R) measures five broad domains (Neuroticism, Extraversion, Openness to Experience, Agreeableness, Conscientiousness), each of which is composed of six narrower facets. The NEO-PI is one of the most extensively researched of the five-factor measures (see Appendix D, this volume, for descriptions of domains and facets). This model has been applied to clinical populations (Costa & Widiger, 1994) to evaluate its validity for different diagnostic groups, for subtyping based on common personality profiles, and adding meaningful information for predicting response to treatment. The Big Five appear to account for significant variation in personality disorder dimensions in both normal (Clark, Vorhies, & McEwen, 1994; Costa & McCrae, 1990; Costa & Widiger, 1994; Schroeder, Wormsworth, & Livesley, 1992; Watson, Clark, & Harkness, 1994; Wiggins & Pincus, 1989) and nonsubstance abusing clinical samples (Soldz, Budman, Demby, & Merry, 1993; Trull, 1992).

The Zuckerman–Kuhlman Personality Questionnaire (3rd ed. [ZKPQ-III]; Zuckerman, Kuhlman, Joireman, Teta, & Kraft, 1993) is an alternative five-factor measure of biologically informed personality traits, derived from the five-factor solution using factor analyses and simultaneous component analyses of 33 personality scales (Zuckerman, Kuhlman, Thornquist, & Kiers, 1991). Impulsive–Sensation

Seeking is characterized by the tendency to act without thinking or planning and take risks but does not include drug or alcohol abuse items; Sociability involves being outgoing, having many friends and spending time with them, and preferring this to being alone; Neuroticism–Anxiety describes experiences of fearfulness, worry, emotional upset, tension, indecisiveness, poor confidence, and sensitivity to criticism; Aggression–Hostility involves a tendency to express verbal aggression, antisocial behavior, impatience, and vengefulness; Activity involves the need for activity, busy life, challenging work, high energy level, and inability to relax. ZKPQ-III Neuroticism–Anxiety is strongly related to what the NEO-PI-R calls Neuroticism or what other models (e.g., Tellegen, 1985; Watson, Clark, & Harkness, 1994) call Negative Emotionality or Affect, and ZKPQ-III Sociability is similar to what the NEO-PI-R and other models call Extraversion. There is a disagreement between the NEO-PI-R and ZKPQ-III about the remaining personality dimensions that centers mostly on whether a particular dimension is a broader primary trait or a narrower component. Zuckerman et al. (1993) viewed Impulsive–Sensation Seeking and Aggression–Hostility as primary traits that are negatively related to Conscientiousness and Agreeableness, respectively, in the NEO-PI-R. However, Costa and McCrae (1992a) viewed impulsiveness and angry hostility as narrower facets of their Neuroticism domain and sensation seeking as a facet within the broader domains of Extraversion (excitement-seeking facet) and Openness to Experience (particularly openness to actions, ideas, and aesthetics facets). They viewed activity as a facet of Extraversion.

Cloninger's (1987b) original biosocial model of personality, as measured by the Tridimensional Personality Questionnaire (TPQ), provides a useful theoretical framework for research on personality disorders and alcoholism. Novelty Seeking is characterized by exploration, impulsiveness, disorderliness, and extravagance. Harm Avoidance is defined by pessimism, fear of uncertainty, shyness, and fatiguability. The original conceptualization of Reward Dependence included dimensions of sentimentality, attachment, dependence, and persistence, but Persistence is now conceptualized as a fourth temperament within the TPQ (Stallings, Hewitt, Cloninger, Heath, & Eaves, 1996).

Cloninger (1987b) first proposed that deviations in Novelty Seeking, Harm Avoidance, and Reward Dependence form higher order personality traits, which in their extreme form become personality disorders. For example, high Novelty Seeking and low Harm Avoidance dimensions define a broader Impulsive trait that when combined with other traits characterizes ATS. Novelty Seeking, Harm Avoidance, Impulsiveness, and ATS are all strongly associated with substance use and abuse (Cloninger, Sigvardsson, & Przybeck, 1995; Howard, Kivlahan, & Walker, 1997; Sher, Wood, Crews, & Vandiver, 1995). TPQ dimensions are also important dimensions defining Cloninger's (1987a; Cloninger et al., 1988) Type 1–Type 2 alcoholism subtypes (Cannon, Clark, Leeka, & Keefe, 1993).

In 1993, Cloninger, Svrakic, and Przybeck made significant revisions to the model and developed the Temperament and Character Inventory (TCI) to measure their new seven-factor psychobiological model of personality. In addition to the four TPQ temperaments, three broader character dimensions (Self-Directedness, Cooperativeness, Self-Transcendence) are included. Self-Directedness combines dimensions of responsibility, resourcefulness, purposefulness, self-acceptance, and congruence. Cooperativeness is defined as social acceptance, helpfulness, compassion, empathy, and pure heartedness. Self-Transcendence encompasses spiritual acceptance, identification with the transpersonal, and self-forgetfulness. In Cloninger et al.'s (1993) revised model, low Self-Directedness and Cooperativeness are conceptualized as critical dimensions for all personality disorders and the temperaments provide a specific risk for each Axis II cluster: A (Reward Dependence), B (Novelty Seeking), and C (Harm Avoidance; Svrakic, Whitehead, Przybeck, & Cloninger, 1993).

Some of the limitations in studies of personality and addiction over the past century include underemphasizing the heterogeneity of people with addictions and evaluating personality constructs in isolation from other variables that mediate or moderate risk for addiction. A theoretical framework for understanding the relationship among personality, substance abuse, and personality disorders may be found through a typological system (Babor, Dolinsky, Rounsaville, & Jaffe, 1998; Cloninger, 1987b; Morey & Skinner, 1986) that organizes diverse dimensional variables into broader categorical constructs, which are associated with different etiologies, patterns, and courses of the disorder. A broad range of empirical research supports the construct, discriminative, and predictive validity of two subtypes that differ on premorbid risk factors (including personality), severity of symptoms and consequences, and psychopathology (Babor et al., 1992; Ball, 1996; Ball, Carroll, Babor, & Rounsaville, 1995; Ball, Tennen, Poling, Kranzler, & Rounsaville, 1997; Schuckit et al., 1995). Both Babor et al.'s Type A and Cloninger's (1987a) Type 1 alcoholism represent a less severe subtype characterized by a later age of onset, lower heritability, fewer childhood risk factors, and less severe substance dependence and psychosocial impairment. Type B or 2 is more severe with an earlier onset, higher heritability, childhood behavior problems, novelty–sensation seeking, and impulsive–antisocial behavior. This Type A–B distinction has been validated across race, gender, substances of abuse, and treatment settings (Ball, 1996).

In this chapter, I review work examining the relation between personality dimensional (Big Five, big seven, alternative five) and categorical (personality disorders, addiction subtypes) models in several inpatient and outpatient substance abuse samples. I also review in detail comparisons between Costa and McCrae's (1992b) NEO Five-Factor Inventory (NEO-FFI) and Cloninger et al.'s (1993) TCI and the superiority of the Big Five in predicting the severity of personality disorder symptoms (Ball et al., 1997).

THE FIVE-FACTOR MODEL

Substance Abuse

Relatively few researchers have examined the five-factor model (FFM) in substance dependent individuals. Brooner and colleagues (Brooner, Herbst, Schmidt, Bigelow, & Costa, 1993; Brooner, Schmidt, & Herbst, 1994) analyzed the association between different personality disorder subgroups and the NEO-PI dimensions in 203 methadone-maintained opiate abusing outpatients. Patients who were diagnosed with a personality disorder with or without comorbid ATS scored higher on Neuroticism than nonpersonality disordered and ATS-only drug abusing patients. Those diagnosed with comorbid ATS and another personality disorder scored lower on Agreeableness than did personality disordered individuals without ATS or nonpersonality disordered opiate abusing patients. Those who met the criteria for at least one personality disorder scored lower on Conscientiousness than did nonpersonality disordered patients.

Trull and Sher (1994) evaluated the relation of the NEO-FFI and lifetime diagnoses of substance abuse, anxiety, and affective disorders in 468 college students, half of whom were children of fathers who abused alcohol. A lifetime diagnosis of substance abuse or dependence (which included nicotine) was associated with higher Neuroticism and Openness and lower Extraversion, Agreeableness, and Conscientiousness. However, a similar pattern was found for both anxiety and affective disorders. When gender and a measure of psychiatric symptom severity were entered into regression equations and captured much of the variation, only high Openness and lower Agreeableness and Conscientiousness remained significant predictors for lifetime substance use disorders. Interestingly, a canonical correlation analysis suggested two variables: (a) An indicator of general psychopathology (equal weighting of depression, anxiety, and substance abuse) was characterized by higher Neuroticism and Openness and lower Conscientiousness, and (b) a psychopathic personality indicator (positive weighting of substance abuse and negative weighting of depression) was characterized by lower Neuroticism, Agreeableness, and Conscientiousness and higher Extraversion.

Quirk and McCormick (1998) cluster analyzed the NEO-FFI in a sample of 3,256 male substance abusing veterans and related these subtypes to symptom correlates, substance of choice, and coping styles. The three subtypes appeared to vary along a continuum of severity defined by Neuroticism (increasing) and Agreeableness and Conscientiousness (both decreasing). The more extreme scoring subtype on these dimensions reported higher levels of depressive symptoms, hostile cognitions, impulsiveness, and polysubstance use. Individuals with the highest level of Neuroticism and lowest levels of Agreeableness and Conscientiousness (most likely personality disordered) exhibited the highest level of escape–avoidance coping and the lowest level of planful problem solving or positive reappraisal. Piedmont and Ciarrocchi (1999) evaluated 132 outpatients who abused cocaine, alcohol, or heroin with somewhat different measures and similarly found that the NEO-PI-R domains and facets of high Neuroticism and low Agreeableness and Conscientiousness were related to greater psychiatric and personal problem severity and worse coping resources.

In a study conducted by Ball et al. (1997), 370 patients were evaluated after they had completed a clinical evaluation and detoxification and had entered into an active phase of treatment (3–10 days inpatient; 3–6 weeks outpatient) at one of three medical school affiliated drug and alcohol abuse treatment programs: (a) a short term (14-day) inpatient program treating all substance use disorders with or without additional psychiatric disorders in Farmington, CT; (b) an outpatient program treating primary cocaine abuse in New Haven, CT; or (c) an outpatient program treating primary alcohol and opiate abuse in New Haven. Participants were evaluated using the (a) Structured Clinical Interview for *DSM-III-R* (Spitzer, Williams, & First, 1990), a semistructured interview used to assess Axis I (SCID) and II (SCID-II) disorders; (b) NEO-FFI; (c) TCI (Cloninger, Przybeck, Svrakic, & Wetzel, 1994); (d) Addiction Severity Index (ASI; McLellan et al., 1992); and (e) Brief Symptom Inventory (BSI; Derogatis, 1992). All SCID-II interview items were double coded to allow interviewers to exclude positive criterion that could be attributed solely to substance effects. Participants who met the SCID criteria for any depressive disorder (i.e., major depressive, bipolar, or dysthymic disorders) or any anxiety disorder (i.e., generalized anxiety, phobic, agoraphobic, panic, posttraumatic stress, or obsessive–compulsive disorders) were compared with those without these psychiatric diagnoses on the NEO-FFI and TCI scales using *t* tests. For a complete description of this study's sample, method, and results, see Ball et al. (1997) and Rounsaville et al. (1998).

In analyses not previously reported for the NEO-FFI, Neuroticism was related to many substance use and Axis I psychiatric indicators, specifically SCID substance dependence severity; polydrug use; past 30-days drinking frequency; and greater ASI alcohol, drug, family, and psychiatric severity. It also was associated with a higher percentage of family members with alcohol problems and a parental history of substance abuse. Neuroticism was strongly associated with the BSI Global Severity Index (GSI) and current and lifetime SCID diagnoses of anxiety and depressive disorders. Lower Extraversion was associated with a longer duration (years) of heavy substance use, more frequent alcohol use in the past 30 days, and higher ASI alcohol and psychiatric severity. Lower Extraversion also was associated with higher BSI GSI ratings and current and lifetime SCID anxiety and depressive diagnoses. Higher Openness was associated with past 30 days and lifetime use of cannabis and greater ASI family and psychiatric severity. It also was associated with depressive but not anxiety disorder diagnoses. Lower Agreeableness was related to an earlier age of onset for alcohol and drug abuse, polydrug use, SCID substance dependence severity, duration of lifetime opiate use, and higher BSI GSI. Lower Conscientiousness was associated with SCID substance dependence severity, polydrug use, ASI psychiatric severity, higher BSI GSI, and a current SCID diagnosis of depression (see Table 11.1).

Personality Disorders

Costa and McCrae's (1992b) FFM appears to account for significant variation in personality disorder dimensions in both normal and clinical samples (Clark et al., 1994; Costa & McCrae, 1990; Schroeder et al., 1992; Soldz et al., 1993; Trull, 1992; Watson et al., 1994; Wiggins & Pincus, 1989). As reported in Ball et al. (1997), *t* tests for those meeting versus those not meeting categorical *DSM-IV* personality disorder diagnoses indicated that individuals diagnosed with at least one personality disorder scored higher on NEO-FFI Neuroticism and lower on Agreeableness and Conscientiousness. Individuals meeting the diagnostic criteria for any Cluster A disorder scored higher on Neuroticism and lower on Agreeableness. Individuals diagnosed with any Cluster B diagnosis scored higher on Neuroticism and lower on Agreeableness and Conscientiousness. Indi-

TABLE 11.1

Summary of Significant Findings for the NEO Five-Factor Inventory

Domain	Substance abuse	Other Axis I	Axis II disorders
Neuroticism	Dependence severity, ASI alcohol and drug, polydrug, drinking frequency, family history	ASI psychiatric, BSI GSI, current and lifetime anxiety and depressive diagnoses	Paranoid, schizotypal, borderline, histrionic, narcissistic, avoidant, dependent, obsessive–compulsive
Extraversion	− Years of use, − drinking frequency, − ASI alcohol	− ASI psychiatric, − BSI GSI, − Current and lifetime anxiety and depressive diagnoses	− Schizoid, − avoidant
Openness to Experience	Cannabis frequency and duration, ASI family	ASI psychiatric, current and lifetime anxiety and depressive diagnoses	ns
Agreeableness	− Dependence severity, age of onset, − polydrug, − opioid use duration	− BSI GSI	− Paranoid, − schizotypal, − antisocial, − borderline, − narcissistic, − dependent, obsessive–compulsive
Conscientiousness	− Dependence severity, − polydrug	− ASI psychiatric, − BSI GSI, − current and lifetime anxiety and depressive diagnoses	− Antisocial, − borderline, − avoidant, − dependent

Note. Results are from Ball et al. (1997) and unpublished data. − = a significant negative relation; ASI = Addiction Severity Index (McLellan et al., 1992); BSI = Brief Symptom Inventory; GSI = Global Symptom Index (Derogatis, 1992); ns = no significant effect.

viduals with any Cluster C diagnosis scored higher on Neuroticism and lower on Extraversion. Pearson correlations for the association of the NEO-FFI domains with SCID-II personality disorder symptom counts were highly consistent with those found by Trull in a non-substance-abuse sample. Regarding Cluster A, higher Neuroticism and lower Agreeableness were associated with higher paranoid personality disorder (PAR) and schizotypal personality disorder (SZT) severity. Schizoid personality disorder (SZD) was associated with lower Extraversion. Regarding Cluster B, ATS severity was correlated with lower Agreeableness and Conscientiousness. BDL also was associated with lower Agreeableness and Conscientiousness as well as higher Neuroticism. Histrionic personality disorder (HST) severity was associated with higher Neuroticism and Extraversion, and narcissistic personality disorder (NAR) was associated with higher Neuroticism and lower Agree-

ableness. Regarding Cluster C, AVD severity was correlated with higher Neuroticism and lower Extraversion and Conscientiousness. Dependent personality disorder (DEP) was associated with higher Neuroticism and lower Agreeableness and Conscientiousness. OBC was associated with higher Neuroticism (see Table 11.1).

Summary

Consistent with the results of Trull and Sher (1994), substance abuse was associated with a pattern of higher Neuroticism, lower Extraversion, higher Openness, lower Agreeableness, and lower Conscientiousness. Also replicated were the strong associations between Neuroticism and anxiety disorders, depressive disorders, and general psychopathology and findings that higher Openness and lower Conscientiousness were related to depressive but not anxiety disorders. These findings that greater psychiatric and problem severity were associated with higher Neuroticism and lower Agreeableness and Conscientiousness have now been replicated by Quirk and McCormick (1998) and Piedmont and Ciarrocchi (1999).

As a first study of the relation between *DSM-IV* personality disorders and the major dimensions of personality in substance abusers, Ball et al. (1997) found support for the prediction that a diagnosis of personality disorder would be associated with higher NEO Neuroticism and lower Agreeableness and Conscientiousness (see also Brooner et al., 1993, 1994). With relatively few exceptions, the NEO-FFI dimensions were related to specific personality disorders as predicted from Widiger, Trull, Clarkin, Sanderson, and Costa (1994), and most disorders were associated with a unique pattern of scores. Neuroticism was positively associated with all disorders except SZD and ATS. Like Trull (1992), Ball et al. found that PAR and SZT had higher Neuroticism and lower Agreeableness (but not Extraversion). ATS and BDL were both lower in Agreeableness and Conscientiousness and were differentiated by higher Neuroticism in BDL. HST and NAR both had higher Neuroticism and were differentiated by higher Extraversion for HST and lower Agreeableness for NAR (see also Trull, 1992). As predicted, both SZD and AVD were lower in Extraversion, whereas only AVD was associated with higher Neuroticism (and low Conscientiousness as well). Ball et al. did not replicate Trull's findings of lower Openness and Agreeableness in patients with SZD. DEP was associated with higher Neuroticism but also low Agreeableness and Conscientiousness in the Ball et al. study. OBC was associated with high Neuroticism but not lower Extraversion or Agreeableness.

Also building off the work of Trull and Sher (1994), Ball et al. (1997) predicted personality disorders from personality dimensions, taking into account Axis I symptoms. Consistent with predictions, the NEO-FFI dimensions contributed significantly to the prediction of personality disorder severity beyond substance abuse and depression symptoms. Because both depression and Neuroticism reflect the level of subjective distress, negative affect, and mood, entering one in a regression statement seems to capture more of the variation, leaving little for

the other dimension. In contrast, entering a substance dependence severity measure into the regressions had little effect on the contribution of the NEO-FFI to personality disorders. With this approach, the NEO-FFI remained a stronger predictor of personality disorder severity than did the TCI (see the next section). In summary, Ball et al.'s findings were mostly consistent with other studies, despite variability in the use of different substance abuse measures and personality disorder interviews for three versions of the *DSM,* different versions of the NEO measure, and sample differences in demographics and Axis I and II disorders. Their study supports the NEO-FFI's role in predicting personality psychopathology (Clark et al., 1994; Schroeder et al., 1992; Trull, 1992), particularly in comparison with the TCI scales (see the next section).

SEVEN-FACTOR PSYCHOBIOLOGICAL MODEL

Substance Abuse

In 1993, Cloninger et al. made significant revisions to the earlier three-dimensional TPQ model and developed the TCI to measure their new seven-factor psychobiological model of personality (Novelty Seeking, Harm Avoidance, Reward Dependence, Persistence, Self-Directedness, Cooperativeness, Self-Transcendence). In analyses not reported for the TCI, the number of *DSM-III-R* substance dependence criteria met for a participant's substance of choice and the number of drugs used regularly (lifetime) were associated with higher Novelty Seeking and Harm Avoidance and lower Persistence, Self-Directedness, and Cooperativeness. An analysis of the frequency of recent (past 30 days) drinking indicated a positive association with Harm Avoidance and a negative association with Reward Dependence and Self-Directedness. Higher Novelty Seeking and Harm Avoidance and lower Self-Directedness and Cooperativeness were associated with more polydrug use. Higher Harm Avoidance and lower Reward Dependence and Self-Directedness were associated with greater ASI severity of alcohol-related problems, and lower Self-Directedness and Cooperativeness were associated with greater severity of ASI drug abuse problems. Higher Novelty Seeking also was associated with an earlier age of onset of drug use problems but was not associated with family history of substance abuse. Lower Cooperativeness was associated with an earlier age of onset for both drug and alcohol problems. A parental history of drug or alcohol abuse was associated with higher Harm Avoidance and lower Reward Dependence, Self-Directedness, and Cooperativeness (see Table 11.2).

Higher Novelty Seeking, Harm Avoidance, Self-Transcendence and lower Self-Directedness and Cooperativeness were associated with higher global psychiatric severity on the BSI. Harm Avoidance and Self-Directedness also were associated with addiction-related psychiatric impairment on the ASI. Higher Novelty Seeking and lower Reward Dependence, Self-Directedness, and Cooperativeness also were associated with more childhood behavior symptoms. Higher Harm Avoidance was related to having at least one current and lifetime depressive

diagnosis as well as a current and lifetime anxiety diagnosis. Similarly, lower Self-Directedness was found in participants meeting the criteria for current and lifetime depressive disorders and current and lifetime anxiety disorders (see Table 11.2).

Personality Disorders

Svrakic et al. (1993) found that low Self-Directedness and Cooperativeness predicted the presence of any personality disorder and the number of personality symptoms in 136 inpatients. In addition, the temperaments differentiated the following *DSM* clusters: A (low Reward Dependence), B (high Novelty Seeking), and C (high Harm Avoidance). These dimensions explained more variation in personality disorders than did the NEO-FFI, particularly when Self-Directedness, age, and depression were entered into the regression analyses. As previously reported, Ball et al. (1997) found limited support for the pre-

---

TABLE 11.2

Summary of Significant Findings for TCI Dimensions

Scale	Substance abuse	Other Axis I	Axis II disorders
Novelty Seeking	Dependence severity, − age of onset, polydrug, drinking frequency	BSI GSI, childhood symptom severity	Antisocial
Harm Avoidance	Dependence severity, ASI alcohol, polydrug, drinking frequency, family history	ASI psychiatric, BSI, GSI, current and lifetime anxiety and depressive diagnoses	Paranoid, borderline, avoidant
Reward Dependence	− ASI alcohol, − drinking frequency, − family history	− Childhood symptom severity	− Schizoid
Persistence	− Dependence severity	ns	Obsessive–compulsive, − borderline
Self-Directedness	− Dependence severity, − ASI, − ASI alcohol and drug, − drinking frequency, − family history, − polydrug	− ASI psychiatric, − BSI GSI, − current and lifetime anxiety and depressive diagnoses, − childhood symptom severity	− Antisocial, − borderline, − narcissistic
Cooperativeness	− Dependence severity, − ASI drug, − polydrug, − family history, age of onset	− BSI GSI, − childhood symptom severity	− Borderline, − narcissistic
Self-Transcendence	ns	BSI GSI	ns

Note. Results are from Ball et al. (1997). − = a significant negative relation; ASI = Addiction Severity Index (McLellan et al., 1992). BSI = Brief Symptom Inventory, GSI = Global Symptom Index (Derogatis, 1992); ns = no significant effect.

dicted relations between the TCI temperaments and the *DSM* clusters. Among the Cluster A disorders, lower Reward Dependence was associated only with SZD severity. Among the Cluster B disorders, higher Novelty Seeking was associated only with ATS severity. Higher Harm Avoidance was not only associated with AVD (Cluster C) but also PAR (Cluster A) and BDL (Cluster B) and the presence of any personality disorder. Ball et al. also did not find strong support for predictions and preliminary findings that the TCI character dimensions were critical for understanding or predicting all personality disorders. They found that few (three of nine) of the predicted associations among Self-Directedness and personality disorders were significant. Only two of the seven correlations predicted from Svrakic et al. for Cooperativeness were significant. These significant associations were restricted to the Cluster B disorders.

Ball et al. (1997) found that higher Harm Avoidance was associated with higher PAR severity, and lower Reward Dependence was associated with higher SZD severity. ATS severity was correlated with higher Novelty Seeking and lower Self-Directedness. BDL was associated with higher Harm Avoidance and lower Persistence, Self-Directedness, and Cooperativeness. NAR personality severity was associated with lower Cooperativeness and Self-Directedness. AVD severity was correlated with higher Harm Avoidance, and OBC was associated with higher Persistence (see Table 11.2). The number of personality disorder diagnoses received also showed a significant association with higher Harm Avoidance and lower Self-Directedness. Although Self-Directedness did not appear to be critical for predicting all personality disorders, it was consistently associated with general psychopathology indicators, including mood, anxiety, and psychiatric symptoms (Ball et al., 1997).

TCI Versus NEO-FFI

Cloninger et al. (1993) and Svrakic et al. (1993) suggested that the new TCI provides a more complete characterization of personality and better differential diagnosis of personality disorders than do the FFM or *DSM* system. Ball et al. (1997) compared the strength of associations among the NEO-FFI, the TCI, and personality disorder severity. Us-

ing *t* tests for dependent sample (*r* to *z*) correlations for the NEO-FFI versus the TCI, they found that the NEO-FFI domains were more strongly associated than the TCI dimensions with personality disorder severity. NEO-FFI Neuroticism was more strongly correlated than TCI Self-Directedness with PAR, BDL, AVD, DEP, and OBC and more strongly than TCI Cooperativeness with the severity of all personality disorders except SZD, HST, and NAR. Neuroticism was more associated than Novelty Seeking with higher PAR, BDL, AVD, and DEP and more associated than Reward Dependence for PAR and SZT. NEO-FFI Extraversion was more highly negatively correlated than TCI Reward Dependence with SZD severity. NEO-FFI Agreeableness was more negatively correlated than TCI Self-Directedness with ATS severity, and low Agreeableness was more associated than low Cooperativeness with ATS. NEO-FFI Agreeableness also showed a stronger association than the TCI temperaments Novelty Seeking and Harm Avoidance with ATS and NAR severity and than Reward Dependence with PAR and SZT.

In another comparison of the NEO-FFI and TCI dimensions, multiple regression analyses were conducted to predict symptom severity of each personality disorder through three separate analyses: (a) 5 NEO-FFI domains entered, (b) 7 TCI scales entered, and (c) 12 NEO-FFI and TCI scales entered simultaneously. The proportion of variance accounted for in all personality disorders was higher for the NEO-FFI than the TCI scales. NEO-FFI Neuroticism, Extraversion, and Agreeableness were consistently stronger predictors across all disorders than were the TCI dimensions, which were significant predictors only for BDL and AVD severity (see Table 11.3).

Ben-Porath and Waller (1992) suggested that an important test of clinical utility for personality measures is whether they provide incremental knowledge beyond other measures of psychopathology. As reviewed above, Ball et al. (1997) addressed this issue by conducting hierarchical multiple regression analyses to provide a relatively stringent test of the NEO-FFI and TCI scales' contribution beyond the dimensions that are significantly related to personality disorders (see related analyses by Svrakic et al., 1993; and Trull & Sher, 1994). First, they forced a measure of substance dependence severity into the

TABLE 11.3

Multiple Regression Analyses

Disorder severity	Overall R^2			Final model significant dimensions
	NEO-FFI	**TCI**	**NEO-FFI + TCI**	
Paranoid	.09**	.02	.11	NEO-FFI N+, A−, TCI HA+
Schizoid	.09**	.03	.10	NEO-FFI E−
Schizotypal	.10**	.02	.12	NEO-FFI N+, A−, C−
Antisocial	.14**	.03	.15	NEO-FFI A−, E+, C−, N+
Borderline	.20**	.09**	.25	NEO-FFI N+, E+, TCI HA+
Histrionic	.11**	.03	.13	NEO-FFI E+, N+
Narcissistic	.09**	.03	.11	NEO-FFI A−, N+, E+
Avoidant	.26**	.06*	.28	NEO-FFI N+, E−, TCI HA+
Dependent	.11**	.02	.12	NEO-FFI N+, A−
Obsessive–compulsive	.08**	.03	.10	NEO-FFI N+, TCI P+

Note. Predicting *DSM-IV* personality disorder severity from the separate and joint contribution of the NEO Five-Factor Inventory (NEO-FFI) and the Temperament and Character Inventory (TCI). Significant dimensions are listed in order of descending proportion of variance accounted for in the final model ($p < .0001$) with $+/−$ indicating direction of association. N = Neuroticism; E = Extraversion; A = Agreeableness; C = Conscientiousness; HA = Harm Avoidance; P = Persistence; *DSM-IV* = *Diagnostic and Statistical Manual of Mental Disorders* (4th ed.). *$p < .01$. **$p < .0001$. From "Personality, Temperament, and Character Dimension and *DSM-IV* Personality Disorders in Substance Abusers," by S. A. Ball, H. Tennen, J. C. Poling, H. R. Kranzler, and B. J. Rounsaville, 1997, *Journal of Abnormal Psychology, 106,* p. 550. Copyright 1997 by the American Psychological Association. Adapted with permission.

equation (Step 1) and then added a measure of depression symptom severity (Step 2). They next compared the additional contribution of those personality scales that they had found in their analyses to be correlated with more than one personality disorder severity. Four NEO-FFI domains (Neuroticism, Extraversion, Agreeableness, Conscientiousness) were entered as a block, followed by four TCI scales (Harm Avoidance, Persistence, Self-Directedness, Cooperativeness), and then the order of entry of the NEO-FFI and TCI was reversed (Step 3). Substance dependence was a significant predictor for all personality disorders except SZD at Step 1. At Step 2, depression was a significant predictor for the severity of all personality disorders except ATS. At Step 3, the amount of variance accounted for by the NEO-FFI was greater than for the TCI for all disorders, even though the effects of Neuroticism were suppressed by the early entry of depressive symptoms in the model. In summary, the results did not support most of Svrakic et al.'s (1993) predictions made for the TCI. Several TCI dimensions were associated with different personality disorders, al-though not as strongly as the NEO-FFI domains. Overall, NEO-FFI Neuroticism, Extraversion, and Agreeableness were stronger predictors for all personality disorders than were Self-Directedness and Cooperativeness (or the temperaments) in the substance abusing sample (see Table 11.4).

Limited TCI Replicability

Because the TCI did not differentiate personality disorders as predicted by other researchers, Ball, Tennen, and Kranzler (1999) undertook a more comprehensive analysis of the replicability and validity of the TCI dimensions. They evaluated the difference between Cloninger et al.'s (1993) TCI factor matrix and their substance abuse sample matrix using a Procrustes rotation of principal components. They found that the factor, variable, and overall congruence coefficients indicated a poor replication of Cloninger et al.'s seven-factor matrix. The variable congruence coefficients of only 7 out of the 25 TCI subscales exceeded a .90 rule-of-thumb, indicating a good correspondence. In a similar analysis for the NEO-PI-R, Piedmont and Ciarrocchi (1999) used a

TABLE 11.4

Hierarchical Multiple Regression Analyses

Personality disorder severity	Step 1 R^2 substance severity	R^2 change, Steps 2–3			Final R^2
		Step 2 depression symptoms	Step 3A NEO-FFI 1st (NEO-FFI 2nd)	Step 3B TCI 1st (TCI 2nd)	
Paranoid	.02**	.08****	.04** (.04)**	.01 (.01)	.15
Schizoid	.00	.02	.08**** (.07)****	.01 (.01)	.10
Schizotypal	.01*	.04****	.06*** (.06)***	.01 (.01)	.12
Antisocial	.08****	.01	.12**** (.11)****	.02* (.01)	.22
Borderline	.09****	.13****	.06*** (.06)**	.03** (.03)**	.31
Histrionic	.01*	.04***	.09**** (.09)****	.01 (.01)	.15
Narcissistic	.04****	.03***	.08*** (.07)***	.01 (.00)	.15
Avoidant	.03**	.16****	.10**** (.09)***	.02** (.02)**	.31
Dependent	.02**	.07****	.04** (.04)*	.00 (.00)	.14
Obsessive–compulsive	.02*	.03***	.03* (.03)*	.02* (.02)*	.10

Note. A comparison of the contribution of the NEO Five-Factor Inventory (NEO-FFI) and the Temperament and Character Inventory (TCI) scales over substance dependence and depression severity in predicting *DSM-IV* personality disorders. R^2 = additional variance accounted for at each step.   *p < .05.   **p < .01.   ***p < .001.   ****p < .0001. From "Personality, Temperament, and Character Dimension and *DSM-IV* Personality Disorders in Substance Abusers," by S. A. Ball, H. Tennen, J. C. Poling, H. R. Kranzler, and B. J. Rounsaville, 1997, *Journal of Abnormal Psychology, 106,* p. 550. Copyright 1997 by the American Psychological Association. Reprinted with permission.

Procrustes rotation of their substance abuse sample matrix on Costa and McCrae's (1992b) normative target matrix and found that the variable congruence coefficients of 25 out of 30 facets exceeded the .90 rule-of-thumb.

An examination of the scree plots for Ball et al.'s (1999) substance dependent sample and a community sample indicated four clear factors that were replicated using Procrustes rotations. In the clinical sample, Factor 1 consisted of high negative loadings from Harm Avoidance and positive loadings from Novelty Seeking 1 (exploratory excitability) and secondary loadings from four out of five Self-Directedness subscales (responsibility, purposefulness, resourcefulness, congruence). This factor appeared to be Harm Avoidance or perhaps low Vigor,

given some of the additional loadings and its association with other personality dimensions. Factor 2 consisted of most of the Reward Dependence and Cooperativeness subscales and could be labeled "Agreeableness" but is called "Sociability" here to avoid confusion with the NEO-FFI scale. Factor 3 consisted of primary negative loadings from three Novelty Seeking subscales (reflective, reserve, regimentation) and secondary positive loadings from Self-Directedness (purposeful, resourceful, self-acceptance, congruence). This appears to represent Novelty Seeking, perhaps impulsivity–disinhibtion, or low constraint, given some of the additional loadings and its association with other personality dimensions. Factor 4 appears to be Cloninger's Self-Transcendence factor. More importantly, TCI Reward

Dependence, Persistence, Self-Directedness, and Co-operativeness did not emerge as distinct factors and appear in need of further refinement. The four-factor structure was validated on other measures of personality, psychopathology, and substance abuse severity and replicated with few exceptions in a nonclinical, nonsubstance abusing community sample (see Ball et al., 1999). These results raise substantive questions about the replicability of the TCI's seven-factor model as a whole.

ALTERNATIVE FIVE-FACTOR MODEL

In comparison with the Big Five dimensions, sensation seeking, novelty seeking, impulsivity, aggression–hostility, and anxious affect have been assessed extensively in people who abuse substances. For example, sensation seeking appears to be a more powerful and robust predictors of initial drug use and abuse across drug categories than other measures of personality and psychopathology and is highly related to substance abuse and dependence in adults (Zuckerman, 1994). Disinhibition (which includes narrower traits of impulsivity, sensation seeking, activity, and aggression) is associated with adolescent substance use and abuse and general deviance (Block, Block, & Keyes, 1988; Brook, Whiteman, Gorden, & Cohen, 1986; Labouvie & McGee, 1986; Newcomb & McGee, 1991). We completed two studies validating these somewhat different (from the NEO-FFI) personality traits using the ZKPQ in cocaine-abusing outpatients.

ZKPQ Study 1

In the first study (Ball, 1995), 450 patients seeking outpatient treatment for cocaine abuse were evaluated with the (a) ZKPQ, (b) ASI, and (c) clinical chart reviews, which yielded information about treatment response and outcome, including urine results, days in treatment, appointments kept, completion status, and discharge referrals. Pearson correlations indicated that Impulsive–Sensation Seeking, Neuroticism–Anxiety, and Aggression–Hostility were significantly correlated with ASI impairment in the areas of substance abuse and psychiatric functioning. Outpatients reporting more recent use of cocaine scored higher on Impulsive–Sensation Seeking and Neuroticism–Anxiety. Patients scoring higher on Impulsive–Sensation Seeking, Aggression–Hostility, and Activity reported earlier first use of cocaine. Patients scoring higher on Neuroticism–Anxiety reported more past treatment episodes and a stronger family history for alcohol and drug abuse (see Table 11.5).

Impulsive–Sensation Seeking and Neuroticism–Anxiety were also the two scales more strongly related to psychiatric variables. Patients who scored higher on these two scales reported more childhood abuse, attention–concentration problems, lifetime depression and suicide attempts or serious ideation, and history of psychiatric treatment. Patients scoring lower on Sociability more often reported a history of attention–concentration problems and psychiatric treatment. Those who abused cocaine with a history of violence and suicidality scored higher on Aggression–Hostility.

Impulsive–Sensation Seeking, Neuroticism–Anxiety, and Aggression–Hostility were related to abstinence and treatment response at discharge. Analyses of variance indicated that those who abused cocaine and who continued using throughout treatment scored higher on Impulsive–Sensation Seeking and Neuroticism–Anxiety than those who abstained or used cocaine infrequently. Those who scored higher on Impulsive–Sensation Seeking kept fewer treatment appointments, were less successful at remaining in treatment for at least 1 month or completing treatment, and were more often in need of immediate referral for inpatient treatment. Those who were immediately referred for inpatient treatment also scored higher on Neuroticism–Anxiety and Aggression–Hostility than those patients who completed treatment. Early dropouts (<1 month) also scored higher on Aggression–Hostility than those who completed treatment (see Table 11.5).

The five personality scales were then cluster analyzed using a k-means approach to identify a smaller number of personality subtypes. Patients who abused cocaine and who were in Subtype 2 ($n = 210$) scored higher than those in Subtype 1 ($n = 240$) on Neuroticism–Anxiety, Impulsive–Sensation Seeking, and Aggression–Hostility but lower on Sociability. There was no difference between the subtypes on the Activity trait. As expected from the

TABLE 11.5

Summary of Significant Findings for the ZKPQ Alternative Five

Scale	Substance abuse	Other Axis I	Axis II
Impulsive–Sensation Seeking	Dependence severity, ASI alcohol and drug, polydrug, − age of onset, HIV risk, kept fewer appointments, continued abuse during treatment	ASI psychiatric, BDI severity lifetime antisocial, conduct, attention deficit and mood disorders, suicidality, violence, criminal arrests, history of psychiatric treatment, childhood abuse, antisocial family history	NA
Sociability	− ASI drug and medical	− History of psychiatric treatment	
Neuroticism–Anxiety	ASI drug and family, history of treatment, HIV risk, family history, continued abuse during treatment	ASI psychiatric, BDI severity History of psychiatric treatment, suicidality, childhood abuse	NA
Aggression–Hostility	ASI drug, − age of onset, HIV risk, early treatment dropout	ASI psychiatric, BDI severity, suicidality, violence, criminal arrests	NA
Activity	− Age of onset	ns	NA

Note. Results are from Ball (1995), Ball et al. (1994), and Ball et al. (1997). NA = the study of relation between Zuckerman–Kuhlman Personality Questionnaire (ZKPQ) and personality disorders has not been done; − = a significant negative relation; ASI = Addiction Severity Index (McLellan et al., 1992); BDI = Beck Depression Inventory (Beck & Steer, 1972); ns = no significant effects.

findings above, those in Subtype 2 began using cocaine earlier and scored higher than those in Subtype 1 on ASI drug abuse, family, and psychiatric severity. At discharge, patients who were able to abstain or substantially reduce their cocaine use and successfully complete treatment were more often in Subtype 1 than Subtype 2. The less severe patients in Subtype 1 were more commonly men, stipulated by criminal justice, not abused as children, and relatively free of psychiatric symptoms. Patients in Subtype 2 were more commonly women, abused as children, nonstipulated, and recent users of cocaine who reported several lifetime psychiatric symptoms. In contrast to controls (Zuckerman et al., 1993), the female patients scored significantly higher than the male patients on Impulsive–Sensation Seeking with nonsignificant effects for higher Aggression–Hostility and lower Sociability.

ZKPQ Study 2

To follow-up on some of these counterintuitive gender effects, Ball and Schottenfeld (1997) completed a separate study of the relation among addiction severity, psychiatric symptoms, AIDS risk behaviors, and the ZKPQ-III in 92 pregnant and postpartum cocaine-abusing women in a comprehensive day treatment program. These women were initially nontreatment seeking and recruited following self-report of or urine detection of cocaine use at a prenatal appointment or at delivery. Participants were evaluated based on their (a) ZKPQ-III, (b) ASI (c) Beck Depression Inventory (BDI; Beck & Steer, 1972), (d) Risk Assessment for AIDS (Metzger et al., 1991) (e) intake screening, and (f) discharge chart reviews.

Pearson correlations indicated that Neuroticism–Anxiety was positively associated with ASI drug, legal, family, and psychiatric severity. The correlations between Aggression–Hostility and drug, legal and psychiatric severity and Impulsive–Sensation Seeking and drug severity were marginally significant. Women reporting a history of addiction treatment scored higher on Neuroticism–Anxiety than those with no treatment. Impulsive–Sensation Seeking, Neuroticism–Anxiety, and Aggression–Hostility were all correlated with scores on the BDI. Participants reporting a history of depression, anxiety, suicidality, and attention difficulties scored higher on Neuroticism–Anxiety. A history of suicidality, violence, criminal arrests, and attention difficulties also was associated with higher Aggression–Hostility.

Impulsive–Sensation Seeking was related to a history of anxiety, depression, and violence, including arrests. Women reporting a history of psychiatric treatment scored higher on Impulsive–Sensation Seeking and Neuroticism–Anxiety. Women who reported having sex with multiple partners scored higher on Impulsive–Sensation Seeking, Neuroticism–Anxiety, and Aggression–Hostility did than those reporting having sex with few men or none. Women who reported engaging in sex to obtain drugs and money also scored higher on these traits than those who reported never having engaged in these high-risk behaviors. Women who reported being tested multiple times for HIV scored higher on Neuroticism–Anxiety and Aggression–Hostility. None of the personality factors were correlated with the percent of urines positive for cocaine, the total number of clinical contacts, or the number of weeks in which at least some services were used (see Table 11.5).

Because the three personality traits (Impulsive–Sensation Seeking, Neuroticism–Anxiety, and Aggression–Hostility) that were consistently related to the variables under study were strongly correlated with each other (and clustered in Study 1), Ball and Schottenfeld (1997) reanalyzed the individual associations among Impulsive–Sensation Seeking, Neuroticism–Anxiety, Aggression–Hostility, and the severity measures, controlling for the effects of the other two traits through partial correlation or logistic regression analyses. Neuroticism–Anxiety was the only personality dimension for which most of the effects reported previously remained significant when controlling for the effects of the other two traits. None of the effects for Impulsive–Sensation Seeking remained significant when controlling for the effects of Neuroticism–Anxiety and Aggression–Hostility except number of drugs used. None of the effects for Aggression–Hostility remained significant when controlling for the effects of Impulsive–Sensation Seeking and Neuroticism–Anxiety except lifetime violence and suicidality.

In summary, both studies support the construct and criterion validity of the ZKPQ alternative five-factor measure in two samples of cocaine-abusing outpatients. Three of the personality traits (Neuroticism–Anxiety, Impulsive–Sensation Seeking, Aggression–Hostility) were significantly related to measures of addiction severity, various psychiatric symptoms, and high HIV risk behavior. Of these traits, Neuroticism–Anxiety seemed to be the most powerful predictor of symptom severity in women. Impulsive–Sensation Seeking, Neuroticism–Anxiety, and Aggression–Hostility were strongly correlated and clustered together to define two cocaine abuse subtypes in this sample. These traits combined with hyperactivity, psychopathy, and substance abuse have been found to characterize a disinhibitory psychopathology syndrome (see Sher & Trull, 1994). In contrast to the findings from controls (Zuckerman et al., 1991, 1993), women scored higher than men on Impulsive–Sensation Seeking and Aggression–Hostility, traits which are related to psychopathy (Harpur, Hart, & Hare, 1994). In other studies, ATS substance abusing subtypes were not exclusively male (see Ball, 1996; Ball et al., 1998; and Cecero, Ball, Tennen, Kranzler, & Rounsaville, 1999).

A MULTIDIMENSIONAL MODEL

The role of personality dimensions and disorders in substance-abuse patients may be best conceptualized within broader multidimensional addiction subtypes, such as Type A and Type B. Although it is conceptually more parsimonious and practically easier to categorize subtypes by one dimension (e.g., personality traits, age of onset, family history), most of these dimensions are highly related to each other and no single dimension does as well as all of the dimensions considered together in predicting the course or outcome of substance abuse (Babor et al., 1988, 1992). A substantial alcoholism typology literature and a broad range of empirical research (Babor et al., 1988, 1992; Cloninger, 1987a) support the construct and predictive validity of a two-subtype model. One type (variously called Type 1 or A) is characterized by later age of onset, lower heritability, fewer childhood risk factors, and less severe dependence. The second type (Type 2 or B) is characterized by earlier onset, higher heritability, more childhood risk factors, more severe dependence, and psychiatric comorbidity. Babor's and Cloninger's typologies emphasize the role of personality traits and antisocial behavior. Although these models are similar, they differ in the subtypes to which they assign negative affect-related dimensions and disorders. Babor viewed Type B alcoholism as having more global psychiatric distress than Type A, including more prominent antisocial, affective, and anxiety symptoms, disorders, and personality traits. Cloninger also viewed Type 2 alcoholism as associated with an ATS or disinhibited personality profile (impulsivity, novelty–sensation seeking, boredom susceptibility) and perhaps other Cluster B (ATS, BDL, HST, NAR) disorders (see Gurrera, 1990). In contrast, Cloninger hypothesized that Type 1 alcoholism is more associated with an "anxious" or inhibited personality profile (introversion, guilt, fear, dependence, rigidity, perfectionism, Harm Avoidance) and possibly greater susceptibility to Cluster C disorders (AVD, DEP, OBC; Gurrera, 1990).

In a series of studies (Ball, 1996; Ball, Carroll, & Rounsaville, 1994; Ball et al., 1995; Ball et al., 1998; Ball, Jaffe, Crouse-Artus, Rounsaville, & O'Malley, 2000; Feingold, Ball, Kranzler, & Rounsaville, 1996; Kosten, Ball, & Rounsaville, 1993), colleagues and I have extended these alcoholism typologies to other substances of abuse and conducted a detailed mapping of the relation of the personality dimensions and disorders to these broader addiction subtypes. Of most relevance to this chapter, Ball et al. (1998) evaluated substance abuse subtype differences in *DSM-IV* personality disorders and normal personality dimensions in 370 inpatients and outpatients who abused alcohol, cocaine, or opiates. Participants completed the following assessments: (a) SCID, (b) ASI, (c) Research Dignostic Criteria for Family History (Andreason, Rice, Endicott, Reich, & Coryell, 1986), (d) BSI, (e) California Psychological Inventory—Socialization Scale (Gough, 1987), (f) typology survey (Babor, personal communication, October 1994), (g) NEO-FFI, and (h) TCI. Because both Babor's (Type A–B) and Cloninger's (Type 1–2) subtypes are defined in part by antisocial, impulsive, and sensation-seeking behavior and general psychiatric distress, Ball et al. were concerned that finding that one subtype has more ATS, BDL, and other correlated personality disorders and dimensions could be tautological (see Sher & Trull, 1994). They conducted separate cluster analyses that controlled for ATS and psychiatric severity.

K means suggested that a two-cluster solution was optimal for defining clearly separated subtypes of those who abuse substances. Fifty-nine percent of the substance abusing sample were grouped into one cluster (Type A), and 41% were grouped into another cluster (Type B). Proportionately more of these patients in Type B were diagnosed with a personality disorder (70% yes; 30% no) than patients in Type A (47% yes; 53% no). Higher rates of personality disorder diagnoses among those in Type B were found across the three *DSM-IV* clusters, although this difference was more pronounced for the *DSM-IV* Cluster B personality disorders. In addition, Type B patients were diagnosed with more Axis II disorders than were Type A patients. Those in Type B scored higher than those in Type A on symptom counts for all of the *DSM-IV* personality disorders except SZD.

Regarding normal personality dimensions, patients in Type B scored higher on NEO-FFI Neuroticism and lower on Agreeableness and Conscientiousness than those in Type A. With regard to the TCI, those in Type B scored higher on Novelty Seeking and Harm Avoidance and lower on Cooperativeness and Self-Directedness than those in Type A. Schuckit et al. (1995) and Yoshino, Kato, Takeuchi, Ono, and Kitamura (1994) also found that Type B patients had higher scores on Harm Avoidance, which is in contrast to Cloninger's predictions. Type A patients did not score higher than Type B patients on Extraversion or Openness, and SZD was the only personality disorder that was not different between the subtypes.

In summary, the typology studies above suggest that the traits of Impulsivity, Novelty Seeking, Sensation Seeking, Neuroticism, or Harm Avoidance and ATS (aggressiveness, disagreeableness, low Conscientiousness, and low socialization) appear to be core dimensions of the more severe Type B. Schuckit and Irwin (1989) speculated that Type 2 alcoholism and ATS are redundant constructs. Ball et al. (1998) findings suggest that personality disorder and dimension differences are not solely due to the greater prevalence of ATS among Type B patients. The Type A–B distinction and personality dimension and disorder differences that emerged were retained even when a measure of sociopathy and ATS individuals were removed from the clustering procedure. In addition, a significant minority of ATS individuals were classified as Type A, and more Type B patients were not diagnosed with this personality disorder. Perhaps it is more accurate to call Type B patients a psychiatric subtype than specifically those with ATS or any personality disorder. Babor's Type B substance abuse appears to have some similarity to a construct of secondary psychopathy in which Neuroticism, anxiety, and depression may develop as potential consequences of a coexisting substance abuse disorder (see Sher & Trull, 1994; and Verheul et al., 1998). Ball et al.'s findings suggest that most Type B patients are not primarily psychopathic but rather experience significant emotional distress related to their addiction and psychiatric conditions.

DISCUSSION

Through the efforts of many researchers over the past 20 years, personality dimension and disorder constructs have reclaimed their lost niche in the addictions field. Empirical studies have evolved from those searching for an addictive personality type to more complex approaches for understanding the relation between personality and substance use problems. Unidirectional cause–effect concepts have been replaced with developmentally complex models in which temperament–personality, parental behavior, peer and cultural influences, and deviant behavior interact to create greater susceptibility to substance abuse and personality disorders (Sutker & Allain, 1988; Tarter, 1988). Through these and other research efforts, a greater appreciation has developed for the variability of personality functioning among individuals who abuse drugs and alcohol. Although there appears to be no consistent evidence for one addictive personality type, there is substantial evidence that certain personality traits play a critical role in the initiation of substance use, the development of substance abuse, and the maintenance of substance dependence. In this chapter, I reviewed a series of studies from both a dimensional and typological framework that add to this redeveloping field by focusing on the relation between five- and seven-factor personality models, a multidimensional typology, substance abuse, and personality disorders.

As this second edition of Costa and Widiger's (1994) volume indicates, there is substantial empiri-

cal support for the validity of Costa and McCrae's (1992a) FFM in normal and clinical samples. Our analysis indicated that substance abuse most strongly related to higher Neuroticism and Openness and lower Extraversion, Agreeableness, and Conscientiousness (see also Quirk & McCormick, 1998; and Trull & Sher, 1994). Neuroticism, Agreeableness, and Conscientiousness also were related to many personality disorders (see also Brooner et al., 1993, 1994), and specific disorders were differentiated by different patterns of scores, which is consistent with the findings by Trull (1992). These findings were mostly consistent with the results from other studies using the NEO-PI (Brooner et al., 1993, 1994; Soldz et al., 1993; Trull, 1992; Yeung, Lyons, Waternaux, Faraone, & Tsuang, 1992), despite variability in the use of different personality disorder interviews for three versions of the *DSM*, different versions of the NEO instrument, and sample differences in demographics and Axis I and II disorders. Ball et al.'s (1997) study strongly supports the NEO-FFI's role in predicting personality psychopathology (Clark et al., 1994; Schroeder et al., 1992; Trull, 1992).

In regards to the ZKPQ-III alternative five, Ball (1995) and Ball and Schottenfeld (1997) have found that Impulsive–Sensation Seeking, Neuroticism–Anxiety, and Aggression–Hostility were consistently associated with a range of substance abuse and psychiatric indicators. These three dimensions also clustered together to form two subtypes that differed on many severity measures and, in many ways, resembled the NEO-FFI subtypes found by Quirk and McCormick (1998). Regarding the TCI, higher Novelty Seeking and Harm Avoidance and lower Self-Directedness and Cooperativeness were associated with many measures of substance abuse and psychiatric and personality disorder severity (Ball et al., 1997). Although both the NEO-FFI and TCI contributed significantly to the prediction of personality disorder severity beyond substance abuse and depression symptoms, NEO-FFI Neuroticism, Extraversion, and Agreeableness were stronger predictors for all personality disorders than were TCI Self-Directedness and Cooperativeness (or the temperaments) in the sample of substance abusers (Ball et al., 1997).

Cloninger et al. (1993) and Svrakic et al. (1993) emphasized the usefulness of the TCI for defining core features and unique profiles for all personality disorders and for a screening or diagnostic instrument. Ball et al. (1997) did not find convincing support for their predictions and preliminary findings that the TCI character dimensions were critical for understanding or predicting all personality disorders or for the predicted relations among the TCI temperaments and the *DSM* clusters. In addition, Ball et al. (1999) failed to replicate the seven-factor structure of the TCI using a Procrustes rotation. These findings indicate that it is premature to consider the TCI as a screening or diagnostic measure for personality disorders. Further refinement of several of its scales and an extensive series of validating studies is suggested, as was been done with the NEO-PI-R, before it can be considered for general clinical use.

As a greater appreciation for the heterogeneity of people with addictions has developed, personality factors may now be viewed as etiologically or prognostically linked to some, but not necessarily all, subtypes of those who abuse substances. Although a dimensional approach to personality pathology appears superior to a categorical system, a useful theoretical framework for understanding the relation between personality, substance abuse, and personality disorders may be found, nonetheless, through a typological (i.e., categorical) system that organizes these diverse dimensions into broader subtyping constructs, which are associated with different etiologies, patterns, and courses of the disorder. Ball et al. (1998) found that proportionately more Type B substance abusing patients were diagnosed with a personality disorder than were Type A patients. Type B substance abusing patients scored higher than Type A patients on symptom counts for all of the *DSM-IV* personality disorders except SZD. Regarding normal personality dimensions, Type B patients scored higher on NEO-FFI Neuroticism and TCI Novelty Seeking and Harm Avoidance and lower on NEO-FFI Agreeableness and Conscientiousness and TCI Self-Directedness and Cooperativeness than did Type A patients. These subtype differences remained after controlling for the effects of ATS and psychiatric symptoms (Ball et al., 1998).

The NEO-FFI, ZKPQ-III, and TCI all measure constructs that are related to substance abuse and psychiatric indicators. NEO-FFI Neuroticism, ZKPQ-III Neuroticism–Anxiety, and TCI Harm Avoidance are related constructs that appear to be important measures for a range of substance abusing individuals (see the review by Wills & Hirky, 1996) and for psychiatric disorders in general. Higher NEO-FFI Neuroticism was a defining feature of Trull and Sher's (1994) first canonical variable, which appears to be an indicator of general psychopathology (equal weighting of depression, anxiety, and substance abuse). Alternatively, it is possible that Neuroticism is not an overall risk factor for substance abusing individuals but has critical importance only for certain subtypes of addicted individuals (i.e., nonpsychopathic) or develops through the prolonged psychosocial consequences of drug and alcohol dependence. NEO-FFI Extraversion, ZKPQ-III Sociability, and TCI Reward Dependence have conceptual overlap but have fewer relations to substance abuse and psychopathology. Inconsistencies in the literature seem in part related to when individuals are assessed in the development of their substance abuse problems. Lower NEO-FFI Agreeableness and TCI Cooperativeness and higher ZKPQ-III Aggression–Hostility also overlap and have more consistent associations with both personality disorder and substance dependence severity.

However, the three trait inventories reviewed in this chapter differ markedly in their conceptualization of a personality dimension, which appears to be most relevant in cross-sectional, longitudinal studies of substance abuse, that is, impulsivity. Although there is no single addictive personality trait or type, there is little dispute in the field regarding the importance of impulsivity, sensation seeking, or disinhibition in personality studies of those who abuse substances. Research suggests that impulsivity–disinhibition predates the development of both substance abuse disorder and ATS, whereas Neuroticism–emotionality develops more as a consequence of both disorders (see Sher & Trull, 1994). Zuckerman et al. (1991, 1993) viewed Impulsive–Sensation Seeking as a primary trait, and Cloninger (1987b) viewed impulsivity as an interaction of Novelty Seeking (where one subscale is labeled "impulsiveness" vs. "reflection") and Harm Avoidance. On the surface, it appears that impulsivity is measured directly by the impulsiveness facet of Neuroticism. However, Costa and McCrae (1992b) defined this facet more narrowly as an inability to control or resist craving and urges (e.g., for food, items, substances). This definition of impulsiveness is controversial and disputed in the personality field (see Eysenck, 1992) and, more specific to this discussion, may contribute little information for understanding individual differences in clinical samples of addicted individuals.

In fact, Costa and McCrae's (1992b) conceptualization of impulsivity is considerably broader and more complex and includes not only the Neuroticism impulsiveness facet but also facets in the domains of Extraversion (excitement seeking) and Conscientiousness (self-discipline, deliberation). Although this multidimensional conceptualization of impulsivity may be more valid than other models, the inclusion of the NEO-PI-R in addictions research and clinical batteries may be impeded by its failure to provide an unambiguous, efficient assessment of a personality construct of high interest to this field.

My experience as an addiction clinician and researcher has been that the field, much like the clients it treats and studies, is predisposed to search for easy, rapid solutions for complex issues and gets stuck with its habits, despite the availability of better methods. The same self-report screening instruments have remained lodged in clinical and research assessment batteries for the past 20 years, even though their reliability and validity is nowhere near that found for the NEO-PI-R. The only way for the personality field's most promising measure to gain general acceptance into established test batteries is by educating clinicians and researchers about its utility for the assessment of personality dimensions, disorders, and subtypes of those who abuse substances and for treatment planning. In this regard, the 240-item NEO-PI-R is preferred both for its facet-level differentiation of personality disorders and negative affect and impulsivity traits. If researchers are only specifically interested in a measure of impulsivity, the value of using select facets (e.g., N5, C5, C6, E5) could be explored or the Conscientiousness domain (which includes concepts of self-control, deliberation, planning, carelessness, self-discipline, and morality) of the 60-item NEO-FFI possibly could be used as a substitute.

Although Cloninger conceptualized impulsivity as a combination of high Novelty Seeking and low Harm Avoidance, Ball et al.'s (1999) research suggests that impulsivity (i.e., lower constraint) may be better characterized by high Novelty Seeking and low Self-Directedness. In addition, research has not always supported the earlier TPQ's factor structure, and the TCI's use for clinical assessment purposes seems premature. In contrast, the ZKPQ-III provides more straightforward coverage of impulsivity, sensation seeking, aggression and hostility traits, and all five of its biologically influenced traits have been implicated in longitudinal and cross-sectional research on the development, progression, and consequence of substance abuse. However, this alternative FFM is at a much earlier stage of reliability and validity testing than either the TPQ–TCI or the NEO-PI-R and does not have narrower subscales for a more detailed description of the complexity of personality. Its validity for personality disorders and other psychopathological conditions is untested, and it is not ready to be used for clinical assessment purposes. The advantages of the TCI and the NEO-PI-R over the ZKPQ-III include the breadth of these models and their inclusion of narrower facets or subscales that may be useful for subtyping or treatment planning purposes. The NEO-PI-R's advantage over the TCI is its replicability and validity across cross-cultural clinical and community samples and its consistent association with personality disorders.

The FFM as assessed by the NEO-PI-R has become the dominant personality model over the past 2 decades. This popularity seems justified given its substantial empirical support in diverse national and cross-cultural community and clinical samples. Although the TCI, ZKPQ-III, and Types A and B may be useful descriptive models that clinicians can use to educate their patients about temperament and its relation to substance-abuse subtypes and personality problems, the translation of these dimensions into specific treatment recommendations is less advanced than that of the NEO-PI-R, which has a developed system for patient feedback and for which preliminary patient–treatment matching hypotheses have been made (see Miller, 1991). For example, treatment for those scoring higher on Neuroticism might include behavioral techniques to improve coping with stress and emotions. More Extraverted patients may respond better to interpersonally oriented therapy. Openness may predict the ability to benefit from more experiential techniques. Agreeableness may predict the capacity to form a good working alliance, and more Conscientious patients may be better able and motivated to work in therapies that involve homework (e.g., practicing coping skills). Similar predictions could be made for the ZKPQ-III and TCI. For example, addicted patients who are impulsive, novelty, or sensation seekers may need an approach that provides immediate, tangible, and pleasurable contingent reinforcement for abstinence; better coping skills; and more adaptive outlets for satisfying motivational needs for novelty, risk, excitement, and avoiding boredom (Sutker & Allain, 1988). It also would be interesting to evaluate whether addicted patients scoring higher on TCI Self-Transcendence can make better use of a therapy that facilitates involvement in 12-step meetings emphasizing spirituality and the power of the larger community relative to an individual's power to change.

An assessment of personality dimensions, such as those measured by the NEO-PI-R, also may be useful for identifying specific patterns of behavior and coping problems (see the review by Hewitt & Flett, 1996) toward which interventions can be targeted. Substance abuse may be conceptualized, in part, as a form of maladaptive coping with trait anxiety or impulsiveness (avoidance or reduction of negative affect or discharge of built-up tension–frustration; see also reviews by Costa, Somerfield, & McCrae, 1996; and Wills & Hirky, 1996). Consistent with this hypothesis, the more severe NEO-FFI cluster (high Neuroticism and low Agreeableness and Conscientiousness) reported higher levels of depressive symptoms, hostile cognitions, and impulsiveness and exhibited the highest level of escape–avoidance coping and the lowest level of planful problem solving or positive reappraisal (Quirk & McCormick, 1998).

With colleagues, I have been developing a personality trait-based treatment for personality disordered substance abusing patients that targets self-defeating patterns (Ball, 1998; Ball & Cecero, 2001; Ball & Young, 2000). Dual focus schema therapy integrates relapse prevention with attention to person-

ality traits and targeted work on early maladaptive schemas (unconditional, negative views of self, others, and the world) and coping styles. Cognitive, experiential, relational, and behavioral interventions are based on a detailed conceptualization that includes the assessment of and feedback on personality traits, schemas, coping styles, interpersonal conflict, substance abuse, and psychiatric symptoms. In this approach, temperament or personality traits are regarded as heritable dispositions that influence the actions of early caregivers. Repetitive, dysfunctional behaviors on the part of early caregivers contribute to the development of early maladaptive schema, which in turn contribute to the development of maladaptive coping styles.

The NEO-FFI, Young Schema Questionnaire, SCID-II, Inventory of Interpersonal Problems, and measures of trait and state affect are used to guide a discussion with the patient regarding what aspects of their personality (e.g., temperament traits) may not be changeable but can be recognized and coped with better versus what aspects can be changed (e.g., experience of schema-related affects, beliefs, and relationships; coping styles; substance-related personality problems) through this manual-guided individual therapy. Personality disordered patients report that they find this open discussion of personality assessment results to be a helpful part of their treatment planning process (see also Finn & Tonsager, 1997; and Harkness & Lilienfeld, 1997).

CONCLUSION

Normal personality dimensions have an important role in facilitating an understanding of the complex etiology and interrelated course of psychiatric disorders, such as substance abuse and personality disorders (Sher & Trull, 1994). In several longitudinal and retrospective studies, researchers have found that certain temperament and personality dimensions in combination with family and social factors place children at developmental risk for a range of behavioral and personality adjustment problems (see Tarter, 1988). Personality dimensions, such as those assessed in this series of studies, may be direct risk factors for substance use (e.g., Impulsivity, Novelty, Sensation Seeking), risk factors for personality disorders (e.g., low Agreeableness, high Aggression–Hostility) that have substance abuse as an important behavioral expression, or mediators or consequences of the severity of both disorders (e.g., Neuroticism, Harm Avoidance). The measurement of normal temperament or personality dimensions may also facilitate the identification of types of individuals at increased risk for substance abuse and personality disorders toward whom prevention efforts can be targeted and the understanding of relapse vulnerabilities of already addicted individuals. Finally, an understanding of individual differences in personality traits and coping styles appears critical for effective treatment of individuals with substance abuse and personality disorder.

References

American Psychiatric Association (1952). *Diagnostic and statistical manual of mental disorders.* Washington, DC: Author.

American Psychiatric Association (1967). *Diagnostic and statistical manual of mental disorders* (2nd ed.). Washington, DC: Author.

American Psychiatric Association (1980). *Diagnostic and statistical manual of mental disorders* (3rd ed.). Washington, DC: Author.

American Psychiatric Association (1987). *Diagnostic and statistical manual of mental disorders* (3rd ed., rev.). Washington, DC: Author.

American Psychiatric Association (1994). *Diagnostic and statistical manual of mental disorders* (4th ed.). Washington, DC: Author.

Andreason, N. C., Rice, J., Endicott, J., Reich, T., & Coryell, W. (1986). The family history approach to diagnosis: How useful is it? *Archives of General Psychiatry, 43,* 421–429.

Anglin, M. D., Weisman, C. P., & Fisher, D. G. (1989). The MMPI profiles of narcotic addicts. I: A review of the literature. *International Journal of the Addictions, 24,* 867–880.

Babor, T. F., Dolinsky, Z., Rounsaville, B. J., & Jaffe, J. (1988). Unitary versus multidimensional models of alcoholism treatment outcome: An empirical study. *Journal of Studies on Alcohol, 49,* 167–177.

Babor, T. F., Hofmann, M., DelBoca, F. K., Hesselbrock, V., Meyer, R. E., Dolinsky, Z. S., & Rounsaville, B. (1992). Types of alcoholics: I. Evidence for an empirically derived typology based on indicators of vulnerability and severity. *Archives of General Psychiatry, 49,* 599–608.

Ball, S. A. (1995). The validity of an alternative five-factor measure of personality in cocaine abusers. *Psychological Assessment, 7,* 148–154.

Ball, S. A. (1996). Type A and B alcoholism: Applicability across subpopulations and treatment settings. *Alcohol Health and Research World, 20,* 30–35.

Ball, S. A. (1998). Manualized treatment for substance abusers with personality disorders: Dual focus schema therapy. *Addictive Behaviors, 23,* 883–891.

Ball, S. A., Carroll, K. M., Babor, T. F., & Rounsaville, B. J. (1995). Subtypes of cocaine abusers: Support for a type A–type B distinction. *Journal of Consulting and Clinical Psychology, 63,* 115–124.

Ball, S. A., Carroll, K. M., & Rounsaville, B. J. (1994). Sensation seeking, substance abuse, and psychopathology in treatment seeking and community cocaine abusers. *Journal of Consulting and Clinical Psychology, 62,* 1053–1057.

Ball, S. A., & Cecero, J. J. (2001). Addicted patients with personality disorders: Traits, schemas, and presenting problems. *Journal of Personality Disorders, 15,* 72–83.

Ball, S. A., Jaffe, A. J., Crouse-Artus, M. S., Rounsaville, B. J., & O'Malley, S. S. (2000). Multidimensional subtypes and treatment outcome in first-time DWI offenders. *Addictive Behaviors, 25,* 167–181.

Ball, S. A., Kranzler, H. R., Tennen, H., Poling, J. C., & Rounsaville, B. J. (1998). Personality disorder and dimension differences between type A and type B substance abusers. *Journal of Personality Disorders, 12,* 1–12.

Ball, S. A., & Schottenfeld, R. S. (1997). A five-factor model of personality and addiction, psychiatric, and AIDS risk severity in pregnant and postpartum cocaine misusers. *Substance Use and Misuse, 32,* 25–41.

Ball, S. A., Tennen, H., & Kranzler, H. R. (1999). Factor replicability and validity of the Temperament and Character Inventory in substance-dependent patients. *Psychological Assessment, 11,* 514–524.

Ball, S. A., Tennen, H., Poling, J. C., Kranzler, H. R., & Rounsaville, B. J. (1997). Personality, temperament, and character dimension and the *DSM-IV* personality disorders in substance abusers. *Journal of Abnormal Psychology, 106,* 545–553.

Ball, S. A., & Young, J. E. (2000). Dual focus schema therapy for personality disorders and substance dependence: Case study results. *Cognitive and Behavioral Practice, 7,* 270–281.

Barnes, G. E. (1979). The alcoholic personality: A reanalysis of the literature. *Journal of Studies on Alcohol, 40,* 571–634.

Barnes, G. E. (1983). Clinical and prealcoholic personality characteristics. In B. Kissin & H. Begleiter (Eds.), *The pathogenesis of alcoholism: Psychosocial factors* (Vol. 6, pp. 113–196). New York: Plenum Press.

Beck, A. T., & Steer, R. W. (1972). Screening depressed patients in family practice: A rapid technique. *Postgraduate Medicine, 52,* 81–85.

Ben-Porath, Y. S., & Waller, N. (1992). "Normal" personality inventories in clinical assessment: General requirements and the potential for using the NEO Personality Inventory. *Psychological Assessment, 4,* 14–19.

Block, J., Block, J. H., & Keyes, S. (1988). Longitudinally foretelling drug usage in adolescence: Early childhood personality and environmental precursors. *Child Development, 59,* 336–355.

Brook, J. S., Whiteman, M., Gordon, A. S., & Cohen, P. (1986). Dynamics of childhood and adolescent personality traits and adolescent drug use. *Developmental Psychology, 25,* 394–402.

Brooner, R. K., Herbst, J. H., Schmidt, C. W., Bigelow, G. E., & Costa, P. T., Jr. (1993). Antisocial personality disorder among drug abusers: Relations to other personality diagnoses and the five-factor model of personality. *Journal of Nervous and Mental Disease, 181,* 313–319.

Brooner, R. K., Schmidt, C. W., & Herbst, J. H. (1994). Personality trait characteristics of opioid abusers with and without comorbid personality disorders. In P. T. Costa, Jr., & T. A. Widiger (Eds.), *Personality disorders and the five-factor model of personality* (pp. 131–148). Washington, DC: American Psychological Association.

Cannon, D. S., Clark, L. E., Leeka, J. K., & Keefe, C. K. (1993). A reanalysis of the Tridimensional Personality Questionnaire (TPQ) and its relation to Cloninger's type 2 alcoholism. *Psychological Assessment, 5,* 62–66.

Cecero, J. J., Ball, S. A., Tennen, H., Kranzler, H. R., & Rounsaville, B. J. (1999). Concurrent and predictive validity of antisocial personality disorder subtyping among substance abusers. *Journal of Nervous and Mental Disease, 187,* 478–486.

Clark, L. A., Vorhies, L., & McEwen, J. L. (1994). Personality disorder symptomatology from the five-factor model perspective. In P. T. Costa, Jr., & T. A. Widiger (Eds.), *Personality disorders and the five-factor model of personality* (pp. 95–116). Washington, DC: American Psychological Association.

Cloninger, C. R. (1987a). Neurogenetic adaptive mechanisms in alcoholism. *Science, 236,* 410–416.

Cloninger, C. R. (1987b). A systematic method for clinical description and classification of personality variants. *Archives of General Psychiatry, 44,* 573–585.

Cloninger, C. R., Przybeck, T., Svrakic, D. M., & Wetzel, R. (1994). *The Temperament and Character Inventory (TCI): A guide to its development and use.* St. Louis, MO: Center for Psychobiology of Personality.

Cloninger, C. R., Sigvardsson, S., Przybeck, T., & Svrakic, D. M. (1995). Personality antecedents of alcoholism in a national area probability sample. *European Archives of Psychiatry and Clinical Neuroscience, 245,* 239–244.

Cloninger, C. R., Svrakic, D. M., & Przybeck, T. R. (1993). A psychobiological model of temperament and character. *Archives of General Psychiatry, 50,* 975–990.

Costa, P. T., Jr., & McCrae, R. R. (1990). Personality disorders and the five-factor model of personality. *Journal of Personality Disorders, 4,* 362–371.

Costa, P. T., Jr., & McCrae, R. R. (1992a). Normal personality assessment in clinical practice: The NEO Personality Inventory. *Psychological Assessment, 4,* 5–13.

Costa, P. T., Jr., & McCrae, R. R. (1992b). *Revised NEO Personality Inventory and NEO Five-Factor Inventory.* Odessa, FL: Psychological Assessment Resources.

Costa, P. T., Jr., Somerfield, M. R., & McCrae, R. R. (1996). Personality and coping: A reconceptualization. In M. Ziedner & N. S. Endler (Eds.), *Handbook of coping: Theory, research, applications* (pp. 44–61). New York: Wiley.

Costa, P. T., Jr., & Widiger, T. A. (Eds.). (1994). *Personality disorders and the five-factor model of personality.* Washington, DC: American Psychological Association.

Cox, W. M. (1985). Personality correlates of substance abuse. In M. Galizio & S. A. Maisto (Eds.), *Determinants of substance abuse* (pp. 209–246). New York: Plenum Press.

Cox, W. M. (1987). Personality theory and research. In H. T. Blane & K. E. Leonard (Eds.), *Psychological theories of drinking and alcoholism* (pp. 55–89). New York: Guilford Press.

DeJong, C. A. J., van den Brink, W., Harteveld, F. M., & van der Wielen, G. M. (1993). Personality disorders in alcoholics and drug addicts. *Comprehensive Psychiatry, 34,* 87–94.

Derogatis, L. R. I. (1992). *The Brief Symptom Inventory.* Baltimore, MD: Clinical Psychometric Research.

Donovan, D. M., Marlatt, G. A., & Salzberg, P. M. (1983). Drinking behavior, personality factors and high risk driving: A review and theoretical formulation. *Journal of Studies on Alcohol, 44,* 395–428.

Eysenck, H. J. (1992). Four ways five factors are not basic. *Personality and Individual Differences, 13,* 757–785.

Feingold, A., Ball, S. A., Kranzler, H. R., & Rounsaville, B. J. (1996). Generalizability of the type A/type B distinction across different psychoactive substances. *American Journal of Drug and Alcohol Abuse, 22,* 449–462.

Fenichel, O. (1945). *The psychoanalytic theory of neurosis.* New York: Norton.

Finn, S. E., & Tonsager, M. E. (1997). Information-gathering and therapeutic models of assessment: Complementary paradigms. *Psychological Assessment, 9,* 374–385.

Gough, H. G. (1987). *California Psychological Inventory.* Palo Alto, CA: Consulting Psychologists Press.

Graham, J. R., & Strenger, V. E. (1988). MMPI characteristics of alcoholics: A review. *Journal of Consulting and Clinical Psychology, 56,* 197–205.

Gurrera, R. J. (1990). Some biological and behavioral features associated with clinical personality types. *Journal of Nervous and Mental Disease, 178,* 556–566.

Harkness, A. R., & Lilienfeld, S. O. (1997). Individual differences science for treatment planning: Personality traits. *Psychological Assessment, 9,* 349–360.

Harpur, T. J., Hart, S. D., & Hare, R. D. (1994). Personality of the psychopath. In P. T. Costa, Jr., & T. A. Widiger (Eds.), *Personality disorders and the five-factor model of personality* (pp. 149–173). Washington, DC: American Psychological Association.

Hewitt, P. L., & Flett, G. L. (1996). Personality traits and the coping process. In M. Ziedner & N. S. Endler (Eds.), *Handbook of coping: Theory, research, applications* (pp. 410–433). New York: Wiley.

Howard, M. O., Kivlahan, D., & Walker, R. D. (1997). Cloninger's tridimensional theory of personality and psychopathology: Applications to substance use disorders. *Journal of Studies on Alcohol, 58,* 48–66.

Knight, R. (1936). The psychodynamics of chronic alcoholism. *Journal of Nervous and Mental Disorders, 86,* 36–41.

Kosten, T. A., Ball, S. A., & Rounsaville, B. J. (1993). A sibling study of sensation-seeking and opiate addiction. *Journal of Nervous and Mental Disease, 182,* 284–289.

Labouvie, E. W., & McGee, C. R. (1986). Relation of personality to alcohol and drug use in adolescence. *Journal of Consulting and Clinical Psychology, 54,* 289–293.

Levenson, R. W., Oyaama, O. N., & Meek, P. S. (1987). Greater reinforcement from alcohol for those at risk: Parental risk, personality risk, and sex. *Journal of Abnormal Psychology, 96,* 242–253.

McLellan, A. T., Kushner, H., Metzger, D., Peters, R., Smith, L., Grissom, G., Pettinati, H., & Angeriou, M. (1992). The fifth edition of the Addiction Severity Index. *Journal of Substance Abuse Treatment, 9,* 199–213.

Metzger, D. S., DePhilippis, D., Druley, P., O'Brien, C. P., et al. (1991). *The impact of HIV testing on risk for AIDS behavior* (NIDA Research Monographs 119, pp. 297–298). Rockville, MD: U.S. Department of Health and Human Services.

Miller, T. (1991). The psychotherapeutic utility of the five-factor model of personality: A clinician's experience. *Journal of Personality Assessment, 57,* 415–433.

Morey, L. C., & Skinner, H. A. (1986). Empirically derived classifications of alcohol-related problems. In M. Galanter (Ed.), *Recent developments in alcoholism* (Vol. 4, pp. 144–168). New York: Plenum Press.

Morganstern, J., & Leeds, J. (1993). Contemporary psychoanalytic theories of substance abuse: A disorder in search of a paradigm. *Psychotherapy, 2,* 194–206.

Nerviano, V. J. (1976). Common personality patterns among alcoholic males: A multivariate study. *Journal of Consulting and Clinical Psychology, 44,* 104–110.

Nerviano, V. J., & Gross, W. (1983). Personality types of alcoholics on objective personality inventories. *Journal of Studies on Alcohol, 44,* 837–851.

Newcomb, M. D., & McGee, L. (1991). Influence of sensation seeking on general deviance and specific problem behaviors from adolescence to young adulthood. *Journal of Personality and Social Psychology, 61,* 614–628.

Piedmont, R. L., & Ciarrocchi, J. W. (1999). The utility of the Revised NEO Personality Inventory in an outpatient, drug rehabilitation context. *Psychology of Addictive Behaviors, 13,* 213–226.

Quirk, S. W., & McCormick, R. A. (1998). Personality subtypes, coping styles, symptom correlates, and substances of choice among a cohort of substance abusers. *Assessment, 5,* 157–170.

Rado, S. (1933). Psychoanalysis of pharmacothymia (drug addiction). *Psychoanalytic Quarterly, 2,* 1–23.

Rounsaville, B. J., Kranzler, H. R., Ball, S., Tennen, H., Poling, J., & Triffleman, E. (1998). Personality disorders in substance abusers: Relation to substance use. *Journal of Nervous and Mental Disease, 186,* 87–95.

Schroeder, M. L., Wormsworth, J. A., & Livesley, W. J. (1992). Dimensions of personality disorder and their relationships to the Big Five dimensions of personality. *Psychological Assessment, 4,* 47–53.

Schuckit, M. A., & Irwin, M. (1989). An analysis of the clinical relevance of type 1 and type 2 alcoholics. *British Journal of Addictions, 84,* 869–876.

Schuckit, M. A., Tipp, J., Smith, T. L., Shapiro, E., Hesselbrock, V. M., Bucholz, K. K., Reich, T., & Nurnberger, J. I. (1995). An evaluation of type A and B alcoholics. *Addiction, 90,* 1189–1203.

Sher, K. J. (1987). Stress response dampening. In H. T. Blane & K. E. Leonard (Eds.), *Psychological theories of drinking and alcoholism* (pp. 227–271). New York: Guilford.

Sher, K. J., & Trull, T. J. (1994). Personality and disinhibitory psychopathology: Alcoholism and antisocial personality disorder. *Journal of Abnormal Psychology, 103,* 92–102.

Sher, K. J., Wood, M. D., Crews, T. M., & Vandiver, P. A. (1995). The Tridimensional Personality Questionnaire: Reliability and validity studies and derivation of a short form. *Psychological Assessment, 7,* 195–208.

Soldz, S., Budman, S., Demby, A., & Merry, J. (1993). Representation of personality disorders in circumplex and five-factor space: Explorations with a clinical sample. *Psychological Assessment, 5,* 41–52.

Spitzer, R. L., Endicott, J., & Robins, E. (1978). Research diagnostic criteria: Rationale and reliability. *Archives of General Psychiatry, 36,* 733–782.

Spitzer, R. L., Williams, J. B. W., & First, M. (1990). *Structured Clinical Interview for DSM-III-R, Patient Version.* Washington, DC: American Psychiatric Press.

Stallings, M. C., Hewitt, J. K., Cloninger, C. R., Heath, A. C., & Eaves, L. J. (1996). Genetic and environmental structure of the Tridimensional Personality Questionnaire: Three or four temperament dimensions? *Journal of Personality and Social Psychology, 70,* 127–140.

Sutker, P. B., & Allain, A. N. (1988). Issues in personality conceptualizations of addictive behaviors. *Journal of Consulting and Clinical Psychology, 56,* 172–182.

Svrakic, D. M., Whitehead, C., Przybeck, T. R., & Cloninger, C. R. (1993). Differential diagnosis of personality disorders by the seven factor model of temperament and character. *Archives of General Psychiatry, 50,* 991–999.

Tarter, R. E. (1988). Are there inherited behavioral traits that predispose to substance abuse? *Journal of Consulting and Clinical Psychology, 56,* 189–196.

Tellegen, A. (1985). Structures of mood and personality and their relevance to assessing anxiety, with an emphasis on self-report. In A. H. Tuma & J. D. Maser (Eds.), *Anxiety and anxiety disorders* (pp. 681–706). Hillsdale, NJ: Erlbaum.

Trull, T. J. (1992). *DSM-III-R* personality disorders and the five-factor model of personality: An empirical comparison. *Journal of Abnormal Psychology, 101,* 553–560.

Trull, T. J., & Sher, K. J. (1994). Relationship between the five-factor model of personality and Axis I disorders in a nonclinical sample. *Journal of Abnormal Psychology, 103,* 350–360.

Verheul, R., Ball, S., & van den Brink, W. (1998). Substance abuse and personality disorders. In H. R. Kranzler & B. J. Rounsaville (Eds.), *Dual diagnosis and treatment: Substance abuse and comorbid medical and psychiatric disorders* (pp. 317–363). New York: Marcel Dekker.

Watson, D., Clark, L. A., & Harkness, A. R. (1994). Structures of personality and their relevance to psychopathology. *Journal of Abnormal Psychology, 103,* 18–31.

Widiger, T. A., Trull, T. J., Clarkin, J. F., Sanderson, C., & Costa, P. T., Jr. (1994). A description of the *DSM-III-R* and *DSM-IV* personality disorders with the five-factor model of personality. In P. T. Costa, Jr., & T. A. Widiger (Eds.), *Personality disorders and the five-factor model of personality* (pp. 41–56). Washington, DC: American Psychological Association.

Wiggins, J. S., & Pincus, A. C. (1989). Conceptions of personality disorders and dimensions of personality. *Psychological Assessment, 1,* 305–316.

Wills, T. A., & Hirky, E. (1996). Coping and substance abuse: A theoretical model and review of the evidence. In M. Ziedner & N. S. Endler

(Eds.), *Handbook of coping: Theory, research, applications* (pp. 279–302). New York: Wiley.

Yeung, A. S., Lyons, M. J., Waternaux, C. M., Faraone, S. V., & Tsuang, M. T. (1993). The relationship between *DSM-III* personality disorders and the five-factor model of personality. *Comprehensive Psychiatry, 34,* 227–234.

Yoshino, A., Kato, M., Takeuchi, M., Ono, Y., & Kitamura, T. (1994). Examination of the Tridimensional Personality Questionnaire hypothesis of alcoholism using empirically multivariate typology. *Alcoholism: Clinical and Experimental Research, 18,* 1121–1124.

Zuckerman, M. (1994). *Behavioral expressions and biosocial bases of sensation seeking.* New York: Cambridge University Press.

Zuckerman, M., Kuhlman, D. M., Joireman, J., Teta, P., & Kraft, M. (1993). A comparison of three structural models for personality: The big three, the Big Five, and the alternative five. *Journal of Personality and Social Psychology, 65,* 757–768.

Zuckerman, M., Kuhlman, D. M., Thornquist, M., & Kiers, H. (1991). Five (or three) robust questionnaire scale factors of personality without culture. *Personality and Individual Differences, 23,* 929–941.

CHAPTER 12

CONSTELLATIONS OF DEPENDENCY WITHIN THE FIVE-FACTOR MODEL OF PERSONALITY

Aaron L. Pincus

This chapter addresses the description of dependent personality disorder (DEP) and its pathology from the perspective of the five-factor model (FFM) of personality. Costa and Widiger (1994) provided strong evidence that personality disorders could be understood from the FFM perspective. This has stimulated significant theoretical and empirical efforts to derive and validate FFM profiles correspondent to specific *Diagnostic and Statistical Manual of Mental Disorders* (fourth edition [*DSM-IV*]; American Psychiatric Association, 1994) categories of personality disorder (e.g., Widiger, Trull, Clarkin, Sanderson, & Costa, 1994).[1] One potential concern for such efforts is the assumption that the *DSM* personality disorder categories (and their diagnostic criteria) combine descriptive elements appropriately in both scope and substance. Specific to DEP, Bornstein (1997) criticized the *DSM-IV* diagnostic criteria as too narrow in scope, that is, overemphasizing passivity and helplessness. He also noted that certain diagnostic criteria were inconsistent with empirical research on dependency. Bornstein suggested that reconceptualization of DEP should be broadened with reference to the empirical literature on dependency as an individual difference related to both normality and psychopathology.

Consistent with this suggestion, this chapter applies the FFM to dependent personality and its pathology, without limiting the FFM description to a single proposed profile based exclusively on the *DSM* category of DEP. It is suggested that dependency is a multifaceted personality construct that takes three different forms (Pincus & Gurtman, 1995; Pincus & Wilson, 2001) and that stronger and clearer associations with FFM traits are articulated if these different forms of dependency are recognized. I conclude by providing three potential approaches for incorporating the FFM description of these forms of dependency into a reconceptualization of DEP. This effort emphasizes the continuity between normal personality and personality pathology (Widiger, Verhuel, & van den Brink, 1999) and provides a common dimensional framework in which to integrate the research on dependency and its pathology.

DEPENDENCY, DEPENDENT PERSONALITY DISORDER, AND THE FIVE-FACTOR MODEL

In their translation of *DSM* personality disorders into FFM profiles, Widiger et al. (1994) proposed that DEP mainly reflects high Neuroticism (N) and high Agreeableness (A). In a recent meta-analysis of dependency-FFM links, Bornstein and Cecero (2000) summarized the theoretical and empirical literature and hypothesized that dependency should exhibit strong positive correlations with N and A and small negative correlations with Extraversion (E), Openness to Experience (O), and Conscientiousness (C). Across 18 studies using self-report measures of de-

---

[1] McCrae (1994a, 1994b) suggested an alternative approach involving the identification of personality-related problems associated with high and low scores on the FFM dimensions.

pendency, self-report measures of DEP, and diagnostic interviews for DEP, correlations between dependency and the FFM exhibited considerable variation that was not moderated by the method of assessment. The meta-analytic effect sizes were invariably small to moderate, with N accounting for approximately 14% of the variance in dependency and A accounting for less than 1% of the variance. Correlations between dependency and A ranged approximately from −.2 to .4, suggesting that all forms of dependency are not well represented solely by a combination of high N and high A. A broader consideration of theory and research on dependency may provide a more comprehensive picture on which to build FFM descriptions.

VARIEGATION IN DEPENDENT PERSONALITY DISORDER

I do not focus on dependent personality and DEP because of the latter's existence on Axis II of the *DSM*. Instead, I see the concept of dependency as a ubiquitous construct in developmental, personality, social, and clinical psychology that appears to be a fundamental but complex aspect of personality, reflecting a core motivation to obtain and maintain nurturant and supportive relationships (Birtchnell, 1988; Bornstein, 1992, 1993). Dependency is a good candidate for inclusion in a reconceptualized personality disorder nosology because it is consistent with the dimensional assumption that normal and abnormal personality are on a continuum. Dependency is associated with both maladaptive (Bornstein, 1995b; Greenberg & Bornstein, 1988) and adaptive functioning (Bornstein, 1998a). Additionally, a variety of developmental perspectives on dependency have been articulated (Ainsworth, 1969; Blatt, Zohar, Quinlan, Zuroff, & Mongrain, 1995; Bornstein, 1996), and its importance across the lifespan has been acknowledged (Baltes, 1996; Baumeister & Leary, 1995).

However, a complication arises from deriving a single FFM profile to reconceptualize DEP because both theory and research suggest that dependency is a broad-band individual difference that exhibits significant variegation both in behavioral expression and in the needed psychological resources dependent people rely on others to provide (Bornstein, 1998b; Heathers, 1955). At the lowest levels of the construct hierarchy, dependent individuals exhibit significant variability in phenotypic behavioral expression (e.g., active and passive strategies for obtaining needed psychological and instrumental resources from others; Bornstein, 1995a, 1998c). In a therapeutic situation, one DEP patient may indirectly seek help by displaying passive, helpless behavior during a session, whereas another may directly seek help by assertively demanding that the therapist give him or her advice, schedule additional sessions, or reassure him or her. Such behavioral variability suggests that it may not be possible to characterize DEP with only a single FFM profile because dependency reflects a consistency of motivation to initiate and maintain ties to potential care and support providers, which may be reflected in different preferred behavioral strategies (e.g., Bornstein, 1998b).

In addition to proposing variegated behavioral expression, many theorists have proposed that dependency can take several characteristic forms, reflecting differences in the needed psychological resources others are depended on to provide. Heathers (1955) offered that individuals may develop *instrumental dependence,* which focuses on seeking help to reach goals and complete tasks, or *emotional dependence,* which focuses on receiving affection, acceptance, and approval. Blatt et al. (1995) and Rude and Burnham (1995) suggested that dependence may be expressed in immature and mature forms. Both investigations concluded that measures of dependency reflect two facets. The first facet typified immature dependency and was labeled "neediness," reflecting "a generalized, undifferentiated dependence on others and feelings of helplessness and fears of desertion and abandonment" (Blatt et al., 1995, p. 334). Neediness appears to reflect the motivation to obtain and maintain instrumental support and guidance from powerful others to negotiate the daily demands of life. The second facet typified mature dependency and was labeled "connectedness" or "relatedness," reflecting "feelings of loss and loneliness in reaction to disruption of a relationship with a *particular* person" (p. 319, emphasis added). Relatedness appears to reflect the motivation to obtain and maintain positive reciprocal affective bonds with specific attachment figures.

Pincus and Gurtman (1995) investigated the structure of dependency by relating the universe of content defined by the combined item pool of several widely used self-report measures of dependency to the interpersonal circumplex (IPC; Wiggins, 1979). Because the core motivation of dependent people is inherently interpersonal, the IPC was selected as a structural referent to identify the range of interpersonal traits associated with dependency. Their results suggest that dependency spanned three octants of the IPC in a continuous arc from submissive–nonassertive through trusting–exploitable to affiliative–overly nurturing (see Figure 12.1). This arc is typically referred to as the friendly–submissive quadrant of the IPC, reflecting a range of trait expression from low to average dominance and average to high nurturance in terms of the latent IPC traits. Component traits of friendly submissiveness can be based on a choice to segmen-

talize the IPC into octants, generating three interpersonal vectors of dependency that reflect meaningful variegation in the expression of dependency and are labeled "submissive dependence," "exploitable dependence," and "love dependence" (Pincus & Gurtman, 1995).

Recently, Pincus, and Wilson (2001) replicated this structure and developed a reliable self-report instrument, the 3-Vector Dependency Inventory (3VDI). They also presented evidence that individuals characterized most strongly by submissive dependence, exploitable dependence, or love dependence exhibited differential levels of pathological attachment behavior and experiences of loneliness, differences in the quality of parental representations, and differing adult attachment styles, respectively.

As an application of trait dimensional models to the reconceptualization of personality disorders preserves the continuity between normal personality and its pathology (Clark & Watson, 1999), DEP may be equally variegated and difficult to describe

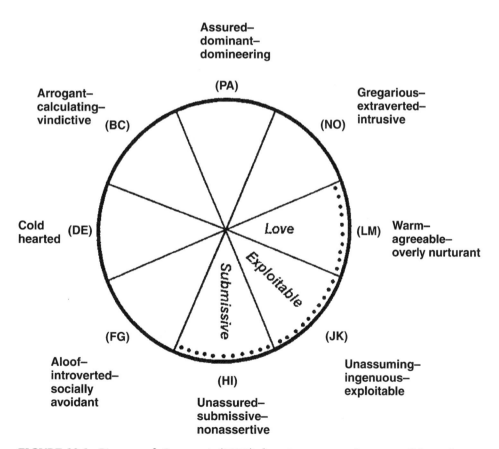

FIGURE 12.1. Pincus and Gurtman's (1995) three interpersonal vectors of dependency.

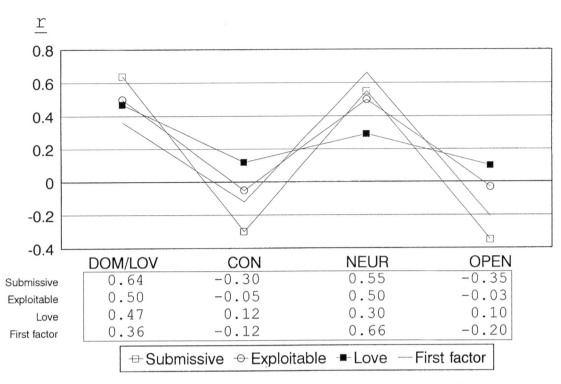

FIGURE 12.2. Correlational patterns for the three interpersonal vectors of dependency and Neuroticism, Openness to Experience, and Conscientiousness. From "The Three Faces of Interpersonal Dependency: Structural Analyses of Self-Report Dependency Measures," by A. L. Pincus and M. B. Gurtman, 1995, *Journal of Personality and Social Psychology, 69*, p. 754. Copyright © 1995 by the American Psychological Association. Reprinted with permission.

with a single FFM profile. At minimum, efforts to represent DEP using the FFM should take into consideration the variegation noted in the theoretical and empirical literature, as summarized in Figures 12.1 and 12.2.

CONSTELLATIONS OF DEPENDENCY WITHIN THE FIVE-FACTOR MODEL

Interpersonal Traits of Dependency

Using the three vectors of interpersonal dependency (Pincus & Gurtman, 1995; Pincus & Wilson, 2001) as the core model for variegation in DEP, one can consider whether this variability sheds light on the inconsistent results of studies examining the relationship between dependency and the FFM. The arc of dependency on the IPC, spanning from affiliative–overly nurturing to submissive–nonassertive, runs from 22.5° counterclockwise to 247.5°. The relationship between the FFM dimensions of A and E and the IPC model are well documented (McCrae &

Costa, 1989; Wiggins & Pincus, 1994). A and E are rotational variants of IPC dominance and love, with A typically falling around 330° and E typically falling around 60°. Thus, one would expect that the facet structure underlying these two dimensions would be dispersed appropriately around the IPC. This was evaluated in a sample of 281 young adults who completed the Revised NEO Personality Inventory (NEO-PI-R; Costa & McCrae, 1992) and the Interpersonal Adjective Scales (Wiggins, 1995). Facet and domain scales for A and E were projected onto the circumplex using standard trigonometric procedures (Wiggins & Broughton, 1985, 1991). These results are summarized in Table 12.1.

Facets of A spanned an arc of 82.2°, ranging from A1 trust (17.8°) counterclockwise to A5 modesty (295.7°). Facets of E spanned an arc of 51.0°, ranging from E3 assertiveness (83.2°) counterclockwise to E1 warmth (32.2°). As predicted, the domain scale of A was located at 340.7° and the domain scale of E was located at 54.8°, suggesting that

TABLE 12.1

Interpersonal Circumplex Projections of NEO-PI-R Extraversion and Agreeableness

NEO-PI-R scale	DOM	LOV	θ	VL	Core dependency traits		
					Love	Exploitable	Submissive
A1 Trust	.159	.494	17.8°	.52	(+)		
A2 Straightforwardness	−.298	.538	331.0°	.62		(+)	
A3 Altruism	.032	.660	2.3°	.66	(+)		
A4 Compliance	−.292	.487	329.0°	.57		(+)	
A5 Modesty	−.458	.220	295.7°	.51		(+)	
A6 Tender mindedness	−.038	.343	353.7°	.35	(+)		
Agreeableness	−.245	.686	340.7°	.73	(+)	(+)	
E1 Warmth	.413	.655	32.2°	.77			
E2 Gregariousness	.428	.389	47.7°	.58			
E3 Assertiveness	.708	.085	83.2°	.71			(−)
E4 Activity	.527	.147	74.4°	.55			(−)
E5 Excitement seeking	.407	.153	69.4°	.43			(−)
E6 Positive emotions	.416	.535	37.9°	.68			
Extraversion	.692	.489	54.8°	.85			(−)

Note. Interpersonal circumplex projections of the Revised NEO Personality Inventory (NEO-PI-R) of Extraversion and Agreeableness domains and facets and their relations with the core traits of dependency. Empty blocks indicate no relationship between these FFM facets and the core traits of dependency. N = 281. DOM = dominance; LOV = nurturance; VL = vector length.

these two FFM dimensions are orthogonal rotational variants of the IPC axes.

Given the dispersion of the E and A facets, it is also possible to link the facets to the respective elements of love, exploitable, and submissive dependence (summarized in the last three columns of Table 12.1). Here, one can see that one reason for the inconsistent relationship between A and dependency in the literature is that the three elements of dependency are differentially related to the A facets. On the basis of their locations on the IPC, love dependence is associated with A1 Trust, A3 Altruism, and A6 tender mindedness and exploitable dependence is associated with A2 Straightforward, A4 Compliance, and A5 Modesty, whereas submissive dependence is unrelated to the facets of A. In fact, submissive dependence is best described by its negative relationship to the facets of E.[2] Specifically, submissive dependence is associated with low E3 Assertiveness, low E4 Activity, and low E5 Excitement seeking.

Pincus and Gurtman (1995) demonstrated that the widely used self-report measures of dependency typically assess only one of the three elements of the 3VDI. Furthermore, self-report measures of the *DSM* conception of DEP tend to consistently reflect the submissive element of dependency (Pincus, 1996; Pincus & Gurtman, 1995). Thus, it appears that the lack of consistent support for an association among dependency, DEP, and A is due to the variegation in dependency and an emphasis on submissiveness in conceptions of dependent personality pathology (see also Bornstein, 1997). In this analysis, submissive elements of dependence were unrelated to A.

Beyond Extraversion and Agreeableness

In addition to the interpersonal traits of E and A, it is useful to evaluate dependency in relation to the remaining dimensions of the FFM. Meta-analytic effect sizes for these relations were .38 for N, −.20 for O, and −.13 for C (Bornstein & Cecero, 2000). Whereas the effect size for N was moderate, the re-

[2] In the circumplex system, one can locate "low" scores on facets by adding 180° to their projected angle.

maining effect sizes were small. Pincus and Gurtman (1995) correlated their three vectors of dependence with N, C, and O and found that all three elements of dependency correlated positively with N but exhibited differential relations with C and O (see Figure 12.2).

In Figure 12.2, DOM–LOV represents the interpersonal dimensions and uniform positive correlations reflecting dependence vectors' communality within interpersonal space. All vectors of dependence are positively related to N, although magnitude increases from love dependence to submissive dependence. Love dependence exhibits positive correlations with C and O, exploitable dependence exhibits no relationship with C and O, and submissive dependence exhibits negative correlations with C and O. These differential relations also support the notion that dependence is a complex construct that cannot be summarized by a single FFM profile.

PERSONALITY DISORDER AND THE FIVE-FACTOR MODEL

Definition Versus Diagnosis, Pathology Versus Phenomenology

The translation of *DSM* personality disorder categories into prototypic FFM profiles has not yet demonstrated substantial validity and diagnostic efficiency. However, shortcomings of specific *DSM* criteria sets (Bornstein, 1997) and a lack of validity of the *DSM* categorical system itself (Clark, Livesley, & Morey, 1997; McCrae et al., 2001; Westen & Shedler, 1999a) limits the success of efforts to translate the *DSM* personality disorder categories into prototypic FFM profiles. If personality pathology is not categorical in nature, the current trend of attempting to translate *DSM* categories found on Axis II into FFM profiles rests on slippery ground. However, this does not rule out the use of the FFM as part of a comprehensive reconceptualization of personality pathology.

Several possible alternatives have been suggested. One view suggests that personality pathology reflects extreme variants of the FFM traits (e.g., Trull & Widiger, 1997). It is currently unclear how to best measure the extreme ends of the dimensional trait continuum to reflect maladaptive content. One might write items that reflect rigidity (e.g., "I always" or "I never") or reflect negative consequences. Alternatively, new maladaptive facets might be generated, or a more quantitative approach could be applied using empirically derived cut-off scores. An alternative approach suggested by McCrae (1994a, 1994b; McCrae et al., 2001) avoids the sticky issue of defining pathology altogether by simply cataloguing a range of life problems associated with high or low standings of FFM traits.

Widiger (1991) and Widiger and Trull (1991) differentiated the definition of a disorder from the diagnosis of a disorder. The former reflects a conceptualization of what is meant by the disorder, whereas the latter reflects a fallible set of indicators for determining if the disorder is present or absent. Widiger also discussed a related distinction between pathology, that is, pathogenic causality, and phenomenology, that is, the manifestation of the pathology. I suggest that continuing efforts to integrate personality and personality disorder using the FFM must first clarify whether the goal is definition or diagnosis and whether personality traits relate to the pathology or the phenomenology of personality disorder. Those who suggest personality pathology reflects extreme levels of particular traits appear to be discussing definition and pathology, whereas McCrae (1994a, 1994b) appears to be discussing a phenomenological approach.

My view is that it is unlikely that one can comprehensively define personality pathology strictly in terms of FFM traits. Rather, the FFM may have greater utility in providing a consensual set of fundamental traits that can be used to describe the phenomenology of personality pathology and aid in its diagnosis. This view is compatible with recent developments in FFM theory that suggest the traits be conceived of as basic tendencies, which are a part of a much more comprehensive conceptualization of personality, including characteristic adaptations, self-concept, objective biography, external influences, and dynamic processes (McCrae & Costa, 1996). Perhaps the definition of personality pathology would require explication of all the elements of personality theory posited in the theoretical framework.

Such an effort, using FFM theory, could be the basis of a comprehensive reconceptualization of personality disorder. A broader framework appears necessary in light of Westen and Shedler's (1999b) conclusion that the *DSM* categories of personality disorder "do not encompass the domains of functioning relevant to personality" (p. 274).

Dependent Phenomenology and the Five-Factor Model

In the case of DEP, it appears much more likely that what is consistent or stable is the core motivation to obtain and maintain supportive and nurturant relationships rather than specific behavioral manifestations of this motive. How the individual accomplishes this varies, as noted throughout this chapter. The FFM traits can be used to describe the variegation in phenomenology of dependency rather than be the sole basis for a definition of DEP. When such a goal is made explicit, it is not necessary that a single, prototypal FFM profile be assigned to a conception of a particular class of personality pathology. This is exemplified in the profiles in Table 12.2, which propose a facet structure describing the variegated phenomenology of love, exploitable, and submissive dependence (as a referent, the profile of Widiger et al., 1994, is also presented). The facet structures proposed can be viewed as a set of rational hypotheses derived from a synthesis of the dependency literature and the FFM domain-level correlations presented by Pincus and Gurtman (1995; see Figure 12.2).

The phenomenological profiles in Table 12.2 provide a distinct advantage because they allow for all dimensions of the FFM to be used. Love dependency manifests itself in phenomena associated with N+, O+, A+, and C+ (Pincus & Gurtman, 1995). Love dependency reflects the desire to obtain and maintain proximal relations with nurturing attachment figures (i.e., emotional dependence; Heathers, 1955). It is associated with the development of a secure attachment style, lower levels of pathological attachment, lower levels of loneliness, and more loving and less controlling parental representations than exploitable and submissive dependence (Pincus & Wilson, 2001). At the facet level, it is proposed that

the valuing of attachment bonds may lead to anxiety over current attachments and vulnerability under stress if needed others are not available to help provide emotional as opposed to instrumental support. A notable absence involves the facet of depression, which has often been considered strongly related to dependency. Love dependence is not consistently related to depressive experiences (Strauss & Pincus, 2001). In valuing relationships with others, love dependence is associated with the openness to feelings, ideas, and values because it seems essential in the formation and maintenance of needed relationships. If one were closed with respect to differences, attachment figures would be hard to find. Love dependence is also proposed to be associated with trust, altruism, and tendermindedness, all of which further serve to deepen reciprocal attachment bonds. C in love dependence is proposed to reflect a sense of competence derived from secure attachments and emotionally rewarding relationships. Dutifulness is proposed to reflect a sense of loyalty to important others.

Exploitable dependence is associated with N+ and A+ (Pincus & Gurtman, 1995) and may be the closest to the prototype reflected in Widiger et al.'s (1994) profile. Exploitable dependence reflects a motivation to obtain and maintain acknowledgement and appreciation from others, often by putting others needs in front of one's own and avoiding conflict (Pincus & Wilson, 2001). For example, individuals high in exploitable dependence were less able to refuse unwanted sexual petting and intercourse than individuals high in love dependence or submissive dependence (Newes et al., 1998) and engaged in more compulsive care-seeking behaviors (Pincus & Wilson, 2001). At the facet level, exploitable dependence is associated with anxiety, depression, self-consciousness, and vulnerability. However, the facet of Neuroticism–hostility is proposed to be low, reflecting a conflict-avoidant style. Additionally, the phenomenology of exploitable dependence is reflected in compliance, modesty, and straightforwardness.

Submissive dependence is associated with N+, E−, O−, and C− (Pincus & Gurtman, 1995). Submissive dependence reflects a motivation to obtain and maintain relationships with powerful others

TABLE 12.2

Descriptions of Variegation in Dependent Phenomenology and Dependent Personality Disorder

NEO-PI-R domains and facets	Love	Exploitable	Submissive	DPD
Neuroticism				
Anxiety	H	H	H	H
Hostility		L	H	
Depression		H	H	H
Self-consciousness		H	H	H
Impulsiveness				
Vulnerability	H	H	H	H
Extraversion				H
Warmth				
Gregariousness			L	L
Assertiveness			L	
Activity			L	
Excitement seeking			L	
Positive emotions				
Openness to Experience				
Fantasy				
Aesthetics				
Feelings	H			
Actions			L	
Ideas	H		L	
Values	H		L	
Agreeableness				
Trust	H			
Straightforwardness		H		H
Altruism	H			H
Compliance		H		H
Modesty		H		H
Tender mindedness	H			
Conscientiousness				
Competence	H		L	
Order				
Dutifulness	H		L	
Achievement striving			L	L
Self-discipline			L	
Deliberation				

Note. Empty blocks indicate no relationship is proposed for these facets and the core traits of dependency or DPD. NEO-PI-R = Revised NEO Personality Inventory; DPD = dependent personality disorder, based on hypotheses of Widiger et al. (1994).

who provide instrumental support (i.e., Heathers, 1955). Individuals high in submissive dependence were more likely to endorse a fearful adult attachment style; to have greater loneliness, greater anger at perceived unavailability of needed others, and less loving and more controlling parental representations; and to receive higher scores on self-report measures of the *DSM* DEP than individuals scoring higher in exploitable or love dependence (Pincus, 1996, Pin-cus & Wilson, 2001). At the facet level, submissive dependence reflects significant anxiety, depression, self-consciousness, hostility, and vulnerability. Interpersonally, submissive dependence is not strongly related to A but reflects several facets indicative of low E. Their view of the self as helpless and ineffective leads to low levels of assertiveness, activity, and excitement seeking. The phenomenology of submissive dependence is proposed to be related to being closed—particularly regarding actions, ideas, and values—and lacking in dutifulness, achievement striving, and self discipline.

RECONCEPTUALIZING DEPENDENT PERSONALITY DISORDER

If the FFM is used to describe phenomenology of DEP, a definition of the pathology must be cast in a broader theoretical and personological context. Below, I review three possible extensions of the FFM phenomenology of dependency that could be used as a basis for a definition of DEP to generate testable hypotheses in future research.

An Interpersonal Perspective

The interpersonal tradition in clinical psychology bases conceptions of psychopathology on the intensity of specific interpersonal behaviors and the rigidity of people's interpersonal behavioral repertoire over time (Pincus, 1994).

> *Abnormality consists of the rigid reliance on a limited class of interpersonal behaviors regardless of the situational influences or norms, that are often enacted at an inappropriate level of intensity. Normality, then, is simply the flexible and adaptive deployment, within moderate levels of intensity, of behaviors encompassing the entire interpersonal circle, as varied situations dictate (Carson, 1991, p. 190).*

From this perspective, three aspects of dependent phenomenology can be adaptive or maladaptive. DEP may then be conceptualized as the rigid reliance on behaviors expressing any or all aspects of dependency in situations that are not congruent with such expression. For example, extremely intense expressions of love dependence (e.g., a clinging need to absolutely maintain physical proximity to a nurturant figure) might be just as maladaptive as extreme expressions of exploitable and submissive dependence. In this case, extreme love dependence may reflect a failure in the development of the capacity to be alone (Winnicott, 1965). Such a view is compatible with conceptions of personality disorder suggesting pathology involves extreme variants of FFM traits (e.g., Trull & Widiger, 1997; Widiger, 1993).

A Configurational Perspective

N was consistently correlated with all elements of dependent phenomenology, that is, submissive dependence, exploitable dependence, and love dependence (Pincus & Gurtman, 1995). One might conclude that the variegated phenomenology of dependence, reflected in differing constellations of A, E, O, and C could be defined as "disordered" in terms of N. Whereas normal dependency may include mild levels of affective reactivity, vulnerability to distress, or both, perhaps DEP is associated with higher levels of N. That is, individuals with a core motive to obtain and maintain nurturant and supportive relationships who are also highly reactive and distress prone might experience greater impairment when those on whom they depend for needed psychological and instrumental resources are unavailable or unresponsive.

A Comprehensive Five-Factor Model Reconceptualization

Westen and Shedler (1999b) asserted that the *DSM* categories of personality disorder fail to encompass the necessary domains of personality functioning. McCrae and Costa (1996) presented a framework for incorporating the FFM traits into a comprehensive theory of personality. This theoretical framework could be used to reconceptualize personality pathology by specifying the appropriate and necessary domains of personality that should be reflected in a definition of personality pathology. The FFM traits are among an individual's *basic tendencies* (which also include genetics, physical characteristics, cognitive capacities, physiological drives, and focal vulnerabilities). Additional elements of their FFM theory include an individual's *characteristic adaptations* (i.e., learned behaviors, interpersonal roles, acquired competencies, attitudes, beliefs, and goals), *self-concept* (i.e., self-representations, self-esteem, identity, and life narrative), *objective biography* (i.e., historical accidents and career path), and *external influences* across the lifespan (e.g., early family environment, trauma, peer relations, cultural influences). All identified domains of personality are linked through *dynamic processes,* such as information processing, coping and defense, volition, affect regulation, interpersonal processes such as attachment, and identity formation.

McCrae and Costa's (1996) theory provides a promising framework for a reconceptualization of personality pathology that places FFM at the phenomenological core while also expanding well beyond the traits in the definition of personality and its pathology. Both personality and personality pathology can be understood in reference to basic tendencies, characteristic adaptations, self-concept, objective biography, external influences, and dynamic processes. Hypotheses regarding the nature of these aspects of personality in the personality disorders can be generated and tested. As an example, DEP may be reflected in the FFM phenomenology of love, exploitable, or submissive dependencies. The core traits can be associated with characteristic adaptations reflecting perceptual schemas of others as more powerful and competent (Bornstein, 1993) and habitual interpersonal patterns reflecting a range of friendly–submissive role behaviors (Pincus & Gurtman, 1995). In addition, the self-concept reflects a range of views from helpless and incompetent to connected and lovable (Bornstein, 1993). Objective biography and external influences can include traumatic losses, authoritarian parenting, peer rejection (Bornstein, 1996), or a family history of punishing autonomy and rewarding dependence (e.g., Thompson & Zuroff, 1998). Hypotheses regarding the dynamic processes linking these elements could also be posited.

CONCLUSION

The three approaches incorporating the FFM into phenomenological description and ultimately the definition of DEP are clearly not mutually exclusive. It appears McCrae and Costa's (1996) framework for personality theory is a promising context in which to integrate the other two views for both dependency and other personologically defined disorders of personality. I believe the future of the FFM as an integrative model for personality and personality dis-

order rests in disengaging from the current *DSM* nosology and expanding to generate a comprehensive account of both the phenomenology and definition of personality pathology from the ground up. In this chapter, I suggested that DEP is a good candidate for membership in an FFM-based reconceptualization of personality disorders. A complete elaboration of DEP and the identification of other characteristic forms of personality pathology from this perspective are tasks for the next revisions of both *Personality Disorders and the Five-Factor Model of Personality* and Axis II of the *DSM.*

References

Ainsworth, M. D. (1969). Object relations, dependency, and attachment: A theoretical review of the mother–infant relationship. *Child Development, 40,* 969–1025.

American Psychiatric Association. (1994). *Diagnostic and statistical manual of mental disorders* (4th ed.). Washington, DC: Author.

Baltes, M. M. (1996). *The many faces of dependency in old age.* New York: Cambridge University Press.

Baumeister, R. F., & Leary, M. R. (1995). The need to belong: Desire for interpersonal attachments as a fundamental human motive. *Psychological Bulletin, 117,* 497–529.

Birtchnell, J. (1988). Defining dependency. *British Journal of Medical Psychology, 61,* 111–123.

Blatt, S. J., Zohar, A. H., Quinlan, D. M., Zuroff, D. C., & Mongrain, M. (1995). Subscales within the dependency factor of the Depressive Experiences Questionnaire. *Journal of Personality Assessment, 64,* 319–339.

Bornstein, R. F. (1992). The dependent personality: Developmental, social, and clinical perspectives. *Psychological Bulletin, 112,* 3–23.

Bornstein, R. F. (1993). *The dependent personality.* New York: Guilford.

Bornstein, R. F. (1995a). Active dependency. *Journal of Nervous and Mental Disease, 183,* 64–77.

Bornstein, R. F. (1995b). Comorbidity of dependent personality disorder and other psychological disorders: An integrative review. *Journal of Personality Disorders, 9,* 286–303.

Bornstein, R. F. (1996). Beyond orality: Toward an object relations/interactionist reconceptualization of the etiology and dynamics of dependency. *Psychoanalytic Psychology, 13,* 177–203.

Bornstein, R. F. (1997). Dependent personality disorder in the *DSM-IV* and beyond. *Clinical Psychology: Science and Practice, 4,* 175–187.

Bornstein, R. F. (1998a). Depathologizing dependency. *Journal of Nervous and Mental Disease, 186,* 67–73.

Bornstein, R. F. (1998b). Dependency in the personality disorders: Intensity, insight, expression, and defense. *Journal of Clinical Psychology, 54,* 175–189.

Bornstein, R. F. (1998c). Implicit and self-attributed dependency strivings: Differential relationships to laboratory and field measures of help seeking. *Journal of Personality and Social Psychology, 75,* 778–787.

Bornstein, R. F., & Cecero, J. J. (2000). Deconstructing dependency in a five-factor world: A meta-analytic review. *Journal of Personality Assessment, 74,* 324–343.

Carson, R. C. (1991). The social-interactionist viewpoint. In M. Hersen, A. Kazdin, & A. Bellack (Eds.), *The clinical psychology handbook* (pp. 185–199). New York: Pergamon Press.

Clark, L. A., Livesley, W. J., & Morey, L. (1997). Personality disorder assessment: The challenge of construct validity. *Journal of Personality Disorders, 11,* 205–231.

Clark, L. A., & Watson, D. (1999). Personality, disorder, and personality disorder: Towards a more rational reconceptualization. *Journal of Personality Disorders, 13,* 142–151.

Costa, P. T., Jr., & McCrae, R. R. (1992). *The NEO-PI-R and NEO-FFI professional manual.* Odessa, FL: Psychological Assessment Resources.

Costa, P. T., Jr., & Widiger, T. A. (Eds.). (1994). *Personality disorders and the five-factor model of personality.* Washington, DC: American Psychological Association.

Greenberg, R. P., & Bornstein, R. F. (1988). The dependent personality: II. Risk for psychological disorders. *Journal of Personality Disorders, 2,* 136–143.

Heathers, G. (1955). Acquiring dependence and independence: A theoretical orientation. *Journal of Genetic Psychology, 87,* 277–291.

McCrae, R. R. (1994a). Psychopathology from the perspective of the five-factor model. In S. Strack & M. Lorr (Eds.), *Differentiating normal and abnormal personality* (pp. 26–39). New York: Springer.

McCrae, R. R. (1994b). A reformulation of Axis II: Personality and personality-related problems. In P. T. Costa, Jr., & T. A. Widiger (Eds.), *Personal-ity disorders and the five-factor model of personality* (pp. 303–309). Washington, DC: American Psychological Association.

McCrae, R. R., & Costa, P. T., Jr. (1989). The structure of interpersonal traits: Wiggins's circumplex and the five-factor model of personality. *Journal of Personality and Social Psychology, 56,* 586–595.

McCrae, R. R., & Costa, P. T., Jr. (1996). Toward a new generation of personality theories: Theoretical contexts for the five-factor model. In J. S. Wiggins (Ed.), *The five-factor model of personality: Theoretical perspectives* (pp. 51–87). New York: Guilford.

McCrae, R. R., Yang, J., Costa, P. T., Jr., Dai, X., Yao, S., Cai, T., & Gao, B. (2001). Personality profiles and the prediction of categorical personality disorders. *Journal of Personality, 69,* 155–174.

Newes, S. L., Pincus, A. L., Claudius, M., Jones, K., Skinner, S., & Wilson, K. R. (1998, August). *Dependent subtypes: Abilities to refuse dating, kissing, petting, and intercourse.* Paper presented at the 106th Annual Convention of the American Psychological Association, San Francisco, CA.

Pincus, A. L. (1994). The interpersonal circumplex and the interpersonal theory: Perspectives on personality and its pathology. In S. Strack & M. Lorr (Eds.), *Differentiating normal and abnormal personality* (pp. 114–136). New York: Springer.

Pincus, A. L. (1996, August). The three faces of interpersonal dependency: Attachment, parental representations, and personality disorder. In A. L. Pincus (Chair), *Interpersonal dependency and dependent personality disorder: Theory, research, and treatment.* Symposium conducted at the 104th Annual Convention of the American Psychological Association, Toronto, Ontario, Canada.

Pincus, A. L., & Gurtman, M. B. (1995). The three faces of interpersonal dependency: Structural analyses of self-report dependency measures. *Journal of Personality and Social Psychology, 69,* 744–758.

Pincus, A. L., & Wilson, K. R. (2001). Interpersonal variegation in dependent personality. *Journal of Personality, 69,* 223–251.

Rude, S. S., & Burnham, B. L. (1995). Connectedness and neediness: Factors of the DEQ and SAS dependency scales. *Cognitive Therapy and Research, 19,* 323–340.

Strauss, K., & Pincus, A. L. (2001, May). *Interpersonal dependency, depression, and the moderating role of socially desirable responding.* Paper presented at the annual meeting of the Society for Interpersonal Theory and Research, Montreal, Quebec, Canada.

Thompson, R., & Zuroff, D. C. (1998). Dependent and self-critical mothers' responses to adolescent autonomy and competence. *Personality and Individual Differences, 24,* 311–324.

Trull, T. J., & Widiger, T. A. (1997). *Structured Interview for the Five-Factor Model of Personality: Professional manual.* Odessa, FL: Psychological Assessment Resources.

Westen, D., & Shedler, J. (1999a). Revising and assessing Axis II: Part I. Developing a clinically and empirically valid assessment method. *American Journal of Psychiatry, 156,* 258–272.

Westen, D., & Shedler, J. (1999b). Revising and assessing Axis II: Part II. Toward an empirically based and clinically useful classification of personality disorders. *American Journal of Psychiatry, 156,* 273–285.

Widiger, T. A. (1991). Definition, diagnosis, and differentiation. *Journal of Personality Disorders, 5,* 42–51.

Widiger, T. A. (1993). The *DSM-III-R* categorical personality disorder diagnoses: A critique and an alternative. *Psychological Inquiry, 4,* 75–90.

Widiger, T. A., & Trull, T. J. (1991). Diagnosis and clinical assessment. *Annual Review of Psychology, 42,* 109–133.

Widiger, T. A., Trull, T. J., Clarkin, J. F., Sanderson, C., & Costa, P. T., Jr. (1994). A description of the *DSM-III-R* and *DSM-IV* personality disorders with the five-factor model of personality. In P. T. Costa, Jr., & T. A. Widiger (Eds.), *Personality disorders and the five-factor model of personality* (pp. 41–56). Washington, DC: American Psychological Association.

Widiger, T. A., Verhuel, R., & van den Brink, W. (1999). Personality and psychopathology. In L. Pervin & O. John (Eds.), *Handbook of personality* (2nd ed., pp. 347–366). New York: Guilford.

Wiggins, J. S. (1979). A psychological taxonomy of trait descriptive terms: The interpersonal domain. *Journal of Personality and Social Psychology, 37,* 395–412.

Wiggins, J. S. (1995). *Interpersonal Adjective Scales professional manual.* Odessa, FL: Psychological Assessment Resources.

Wiggins, J. S., & Broughton, R. (1985). The interpersonal circle: A structural model for the integration of personality research. In R. Hogan & W. H. Jones (Eds.), *Perspectives in personality* (Vol. 1, pp. 1–47). Greenwich, CT: JAI Press.

Wiggins, J. S., & Broughton, R. (1991). A geometric taxonomy of personality scales. *European Journal of Personality, 5,* 343–365.

Wiggins, J. S., & Pincus, A. L. (1994). Personality structure and the structure of personality disorders. In P. T. Costa, Jr., & T. A. Widiger (Eds.), *Personality disorders and the five-factor model of personality* (pp. 73–93). Washington, DC: American Psychological Association.

Winnicott, D. W. (1965). The capacity to be alone. In D. W. Winnicott (Ed.), *The maturational processes and the facilitating environment: Studies in the theory of emotional development* (pp. 124–139). New York: International Universities Press.

PERSONALITY DISORDERS AND THE FIVE-FACTOR MODEL OF PERSONALITY IN CHINESE PSYCHIATRIC PATIENTS

Jian Yang, Xiaoyang Dai, Shuqiao Yao, Taisheng Cai, Beiling Gao, Robert R. McCrae, and Paul T. Costa, Jr.

The personality disorders (PDs) described in the *Diagnostic and Statistical Manual of Mental Disorders* (4th ed. [*DSM-IV*]; American Psychiatric Association [APA], 1994) are a set of discreet psychiatric categories (Loranger, 1999; Oldham, 1994), but similarities between features characterizing PDs and normal personality trait dimensions have repeatedly been pointed out (Eysenck, Wakefield, & Friedman, 1983; Wiggins & Pincus, 1989). Both PDs and traits are construed as enduring dispositions that affect behavior and experience in a variety of contexts, and both are likely to have a substantial genetic basis (Livesley, Jang, & Vernon, 1998; Loehlin, 1992).

Until recently, however, there was little agreement on which personality traits were relevant to PDs. A substantial literature points to overlaps between PDs and normal traits in the interpersonal circumplex (Kiesler, 1986), but Wiggins and Pincus (1989) noted that several PDs could not be adequately characterized in terms of interpersonal traits alone. They argued that a more comprehensive personality model was needed and suggested the five-factor model (FFM; Digman, 1990). In 1994, Costa and Widiger edited a volume hypothesizing associa-

tions among PDs and the broad dimensions of the FFM, and considerable empirical evidence supports these hypotheses (Ball, Tennen, Poling, Kranzler, & Rounsaville, 1997; Trull, Useda, Costa, & McCrae, 1995).

However, the five personality factors are broad constructs that combine many more specific traits, and many distinctions among PDs cannot clearly be made at the factor level. For example, both paranoid PD and narcissistic PD are associated with traits defining the low pole of Agreeableness such as suspiciousness and arrogance, but suspiciousness is more characteristic of paranoid PD and arrogance of narcissistic PD. Widiger, Trull, Clarkin, Sanderson, and Costa (1994) therefore made more detailed predictions, linking the third edition, revised, of the *DSM* (*DSM-III-R*; APA, 1987) PDs and the proposed PDs to the 30 specific traits (or facets) measured by the Revised NEO Personality Inventory (NEO-PI-R; Costa & McCrae, 1992). To date, in only one study have researchers examined all these hypotheses. Dyce and O'Connor (1998) administered the NEO-PI-R and the self-report of the third edition of the Millon Clinical Multiaxial Inventory (Millon, 1994) to a sample of 614 Canadian undergraduates; they

For their assistance in conducting interviews and gathering data, we thank Chengge Gao, Department of Psychiatry, 1st Affilated Hospital, Xian Medical University; Donghua Xiu and Hongge Zhand, Hunan Provincial Mental Hospital; Huikai Zhang, Mental Health Center, Huaxi Medical University; Ren Xiaopeng, Clinical Psychological Research Center, 2nd Affiliated Hospital, Hunan Medical University; Runde Pan and Tianwei Pan, Guangxi Longquanshan Hospital; Shumao Ji and Zanli Wang, Xian Mental Health Center; Xiaochun Sheng and Xiaolin Liu, Wuhan Mental Health Center; Xiaonian Luo, Department of Psychiatry, 1st Affilated Hospital, Hubei Medical University; Yiping Yu and Xiaoling Shen, Shanghai Mental Health Center; Yunping Yang, Zhenkang Jiang, and Tao Xi, Beijing Andi Hospital; Yuping Ning, Guangzhou Mental Hospital; Zhenzhu Song and Jing Li, Qiqihar, 1st Neuropsychiatric Hospital; and Zhian Jiao, Shangdong Provincial Mental Health Center. We thank Jeffrey Herbst for assistance with data analyses. Portions of this article were presented at the 107th Annual Convention of the American Psychological Association in Boston, MA, August, 1999.

confirmed 63% of the hypotheses proposed by Widiger et al.

Encouraging as that study is, it falls short of a definitive test. More clinically relevant tests require the use of a patient population and assessments of PDs based on clinical interviews and self-reports. In another study, a large sample of psychiatric inpatients and outpatients completed self-report measures of both personality (NEO-PI-R) and PDs (Personality Diagnostic Questionnaire [PDQ-4+]; Hyler, 1994). A subset of the patients were interviewed by a psychiatrist or clinical psychologist using the Personality Disorder Interview (4th ed. [PDI-IV]; Widiger, Mangine, Corbitt, Ellis, & Thomas, 1995). Both PD instruments provide scores for the 10 PDs recognized in *DSM-IV* and the proposed depressive and passive–aggressive PDs.

Correlations of personality traits with PD symptom scores may be distorted or inflated by method bias because patients serve as the ultimate source of information for both self-report questionnaires and clinical interviews. However, spouse ratings of patient personality were also available for some patients, and correlations of these ratings with patients' self-reports or clinicians' ratings of PDs are unlikely to be due to measurement artifacts. Data from this study provide the basis for both mono- and heteromethod evaluations of personality trait–PD associations.

Cross-cultural research supports the view that the structure of normal personality is a human universal (McCrae & Costa, 1997), and psychiatric disorders are often presumed to be found in every culture (Fossati et al., 1998). However, little research documents the presence or nature of PDs outside Western cultures, and no researchers have examined the links between the FFM and PDs in non-Western samples. This study was conducted in the People's Republic of China, a culture that differs dramatically from the West in terms of history, language, and social structure. Personality trait–PD correlations in this sample provide a rigorous test of the cross-cultural validity of Widiger et al.'s (1994) hypotheses.

METHOD

Subjects

Patients (*N* = 1,926; 54.5% male) were recruited from 13 psychiatric hospitals and clinics in 10 cities in the People's Republic of China. Inclusion criteria included age (18 years and older), education (8th grade or above), definite or probable psychiatric diagnosis, and willingness to participate voluntarily. Exclusion criteria included acute psychosis, organic brain syndrome, and recent illicit drug use. Primary diagnoses, using the *Chinese Classification and Diagnostic Criteria for Mental Disorders* (Chinese Medical Association, Psychiatric Division, 1992), were neuroses (37.5%), major depression (19.0%), schizophrenia (17.4%), bipolar mood disorder (11.8%), and substance abuse (9.0%; Yang et al., 1999). After the study was explained to patients, written informed consent was obtained.

Measures

The PDQ-4+ is a 99-item, self-administered true–false questionnaire designed to yield diagnoses consistent with the *DSM-IV* (Hyler, 1994). The PDI-IV is a semistructured interview administered by psychiatrists or clinical psychologists (Widiger et al., 1995). Both instruments yield dimensional scores that correspond to the number of *DSM-IV* criteria present for each PD. Both instruments were translated into Mandarin Chinese, with minor modifications to adapt them to Chinese culture. Studies of retest, interrater reliability, and cross-instrument validity suggest that the two instruments preserve their psychometric properties in translation (Yang et al., 2000).

The NEO-PI-R is a 240-item questionnaire that measures personality traits. Thirty facet scales measure traits that define the five basic personality factors. Evidence on the reliability and validity of the original instrument is summarized in the manual (Costa & McCrae, 1992). A Hong Kong Chinese translation of the NEO-PI-R (McCrae, Costa, & Yik, 1996) was modified for use in Mainland China. Studies in this sample of internal consistency, retest reliability, factor structure, cross-observer agreement, and construct validity suggest that the Mandarin version of the NEO-PI-R is a valid measure of traits in the FFM (Yang et al., 1999).

An observer rating form of the NEO-PI-R was created by rephrasing items in the third person. The English version of this form has been used in psychiatric populations (Bagby et al., 1998); in this study, spouse ratings on the Chinese version showed significant correlations with self-reports for all five factors (Yang et al., 1999).

Procedure

The PDQ-4+ and NEO-PI-R were administered to patients individually or in groups of 2–10 patients. The PDI-IV was given to 525 patients. Interviewers —experienced clinicians who had received 10 days of intensive training in the background and methods of this study—were unaware of the patients' scores on the NEO-PI-R and the PDQ-4+. The full interview was given to 234 patients; because of time constraints, other patients were randomly assigned to one of three groups and completed only a portion of the interview, corresponding to one of the three PD clusters. Preliminary analyses of means and correlations suggested that PD scores from the partial interviews did not differ systematically from those obtained in the full interview; all data were therefore pooled. Spouse ratings of personality were obtained for 160 patients, of whom 154 had complete PDQ-4+ data.

Analyses

Pearson correlations were calculated between dimensional scores on the two PD instruments and the 30 self-report NEO-PI-R facet scales. The PDQ-4+ scores were used for the primary analysis, based on the full sample; because of the large sample size, only correlations at $p < .001$ were considered significant. Data from the subsample of patients interviewed on the PDI-IV were used to replicate self-report findings; correlations were considered replications if they were significant at $p < .05$, one tailed. A final analysis examined correlations between spouse ratings of personality and PD scores.

RESULTS

Table 13.1 reports the correlations between the PDQ-4+ scales and the facet scales of the NEO-PI-R. Most of the associations are meaningful. For example, the largest correlations of paranoid PD were with Angry–Hostility, low Trust, and low Compliance scale scores; the chief correlates of antisocial PD were low Straight-Forwardness, high Excitement Seeking, and low Deliberation scale scores; and the

chief correlates of (proposed) depressive PD were Depression, Self-Consciousness, and Anxiety scale scores. Formally hypothesized associations, derived by Widiger et al. (1994) from a conceptual analysis of *DSM-III-R* descriptions of the PDs, are shown in boldface in Table 13.1.

Of the 119 hypotheses, 87 (73%) were supported. All hypothesized associations for borderline and passive–aggressive PDs were significant, and at least half the hypotheses were supported for each of the other PDs. Furthermore, 63 of the 87 confirmed hypotheses were replicated when clinical judgments on the PDI-IV were correlated with NEO-PI-R facet scales (Ns = 325–358). By contrast, only 11 correlations in Table 13.1 were significant in the direction opposite to the hypothesis, all of these were small in magnitude ($r < .20$), and only 3 were replicated in PDI-IV analyses. There is, however, consistent, cross-instrument evidence in this sample that schizotypal PD was associated with high rather than low Openness to Feelings scale score; that histrionic PD was associated with low Trust scale score; and that dependent PD was associated with low Altruism scale score. Because Dyce and O'Connor (1998) found none of these associations in their Canadian sample, these results may be specific to Chinese.

Although most of the associations predicted by Widiger et al. (1994) were observed, many other correlations were also found. Table 13.1 includes 188 significant correlations not predicted by other hypotheses, of which 111 were replicated in PDI-IV analyses. For example, avoidant and depressive PDs were negatively related to all six facets of Conscientiousness, and passive–aggressive PD was associated with all facets of Neuroticism, not merely angry–hostility.

Correlations of the spouse ratings on the NEO-PI-R with patient self-reports of PD symptoms on the PDQ-4+ reached significance for 48 of the 119 hypotheses (rs = .16 to .35, N = 154, $p < .05$); none of the correlations was significant in the direction opposite to the hypotheses. Twelve more hypothesized correlations were marginally significant ($p < .10$). Only a few patients (Ns = 22 to 27) had both spouse ratings and PDI-IV scores, but of the 23 significant correlations between spouse-rated NEO-PI-R facets and clinician-rated PDI-IV scale scores, none

TABLE 13.1

Correlations Among the NEO-PI-R Facet Scales and the PDQ-4+ Dimensional Scores

NEO-PI-R scale	Personality disorder											
	PAR	SZD	SZT	ATS	BDL	HST	NAR	AVD	DEP	OBC	DPS	PAG
Neuroticism												
N1 Anxiety	**.27**[a]	.17	**.34**[a]	.07	**.47**[a]	.18[a]	.23[a]	**.48**[a]	**.39**[a]	.25[a]	**.55**[a]	.30[a]
N2 Angry–Hostility	**.39**[a]	**.19**[b]	.34[a]	**.32**[a]	**.51**[a]	**.30**[a]	**.36**[a]	.36[a]	.28[a]	**.22**[a]	.40[a]	**.41**[a]
N3 Depression	.27[a]	.24	**.35**[a]	.15	**.50**[a]	.19	**.23**[a]	**.52**[a]	**.46**[a]	**.29**[a]	**.59**[a]	.33[a]
N4 Self-Consciousness	.28[a]	**.19**[b]	**.33**	.12	**.45**[a]	.17	.23	**.55**[a]	**.41**[a]	.26[a]	.48[a]	.31[a]
N5 Impulsiveness	.25[a]	.07	.26	**.31**[a]	**.46**[a]	.31[a]	.30[a]	.31[a]	.28[a]	.17[a]	.34[a]	.33[a]
N6 Vulnerability	.15[a]	.14[a]	**.20**	.08	**.44**[a]	**.12**	.10	**.41**[a]	**.38**[a]	.11[a]	.46[a]	.24[a]
Extraversion												
E1 Warmth	−**.09**[a]	−**.31**[a]	−**.18**[a]	−**.06**	−.23	**.12**	−.03	−**.28**[a]	−**.15**[a]	−**.01**	−.27[a]	−**.10**[a]
E2 Gregariousness	−**.19**[a]	−**.42**[a]	−**.30**[a]	−.10	−.29	**.03**	−.14	−**.36**[a]	−**.19**[a]	−**.18**[a]	−.34[a]	−**.22**[a]
E3 Assertiveness	.00	−.14	−.05	.06	−.13	.12	.11[a]	−**.28**[a]	−**.21**[a]	−**.02**	−.22[a]	−.06
E4 Activity	−.03	−.16[a]	−.11	.11[a]	−.18	**.13**	.09	−**.29**[a]	−**.22**[a]	−.06	−.27[a]	−.03
E5 Excitement Seeking	.18	−.11[a]	.15	**.39**[a]	.17[a]	**.34**[a]	.28[a]	**.01**	.06	.07	.02	.15[a]
E6 Positive Emotions	−.04	−**.25**[a]	−.13	.07	−.18	**.16**	.05	−**.29**[a]	−**.20**[a]	−**.07**	−.32[a]	−**.08**[a]
Openness to Experience												
O1 Fantasy	.18	−.01	**.17**	.20	.28[a]	**.23**[a]	**.24**[a]	.17[a]	.14[a]	.06	.19[a]	.16[a]
O2 Aesthetics	**.06**	−.14[a]	.06	.01	−.01	.16	.11	−.02	−.05	.11	−.02	.00
O3 Feelings	**.13**[b]	−.11	**.16**[a,b]	.11	.14[a]	**.23**[a]	.20[a]	.08	.02	**.12**[b]	.11	.10
O4 Actions	.00	−.14[a]	−.00	.13	.00	**.07**	.06	−**.10**	−.11	−.09	−.03	−.01
O5 Ideas	.05	−.11	**.09**	.07	−.07	**.10**[b]	.13	−**.09**[a]	−**.13**[a]	.09	−.07	.00
O6 Values	−.16[a]	−.24	−**.16**[b]	−.15[a]	−.18[a]	−.13	−.16	−.17	−**.25**[a]	−**.20**	−.14	−.20
Agreeableness												
A1 Trust	−**.37**[a]	−**.17**[a]	−**.27**[a]	−.22[a]	−**.32**[a]	−**.10**[a,b]	−**.25**[a]	−.22[a]	−.17[a]	−**.10**[a]	−.25[a]	−.24[a]
A2 Straightforwardness	−**.30**[a]	−.06	−.25	−**.39**[a]	−.27[a]	−**.30**[a]	−**.32**[a]	−.10	−.13	−.11	−**.09**[a]	−**.24**[a]
A3 Altruism	−.17[a]	−.17[a]	−.19[a]	−**.16**	−.26[a]	−**.05**	−**.11**	−.20[a]	−**.14**[a,b]	−**.02**	−.20[a]	−**.16**[a]
A4 Compliance	−**.30**	−.02	−.14	−**.28**[a]	−**.24**[a]	−.21	−**.28**[a]	−**.33**[a]	.03	−.02	−.07	−**.23**[a]
A5 Modesty	−**.20**	.08	−.12	−.23[a]	−.11[a]	−.28	−**.33**[a]	.03	.06	−.02	.04	−.13
A6 Tender Mindedness	**.03**	.04	.06	−**.01**	.03	.10	**.10**[b]	.08	.09	.19[a]	.04	.09
Conscientiousness												
C1 Competence	−**.09**[b]	−.20[a]	−.14	−.11	−.32	−**.03**	.01	−.30[a]	−.32[a]	−.04	−.33[a]	−**.18**[a]
C2 Order	−.10	−.13	−.15	−.16	−.24	−.07	−.07	−.18[a]	−.22[a]	.08	−.17[a]	−**.19**[a]
C3 Dutifulness	−.15[a]	−.08	−.14	−**.31**[a]	−.30[a]	−.16	−.15	−.16[a]	−.16[a]	**.10**[a]	−.19[a]	−.10
C4 Achievement Striving	−.04	−**.09**	−.07	−.09	−.23	−.02	.01	−.20[a]	−**.21**[a]	**.10**[a]	−.19[a]	−.14
C5 Self-Discipline	−.21[a]	−.17	−.25	−**.27**[a]	−**.41**[a]	−**.18**	−.18	−.32[a]	−.34[a]	−.08	−.33[a]	−**.26**[a]
C6 Deliberation	−.15[a]	−.09	−.16	−**.32**[a]	−**.38**[a]	−.21	−.16	−.20[a]	−.20[a]	**.01**	−.25[a]	−.22[a]

Note. N = 1,909. Hypothesized correlations are in boldface. For |r| > .07, p <.001, two tailed. NEO-PI-R = Revised NEO Personality Inventory; PDQ-4+ = Personality Disorder Questionnaire—4+. Personality disorders: PAR = paranoid; SZD = schizoid; SZT = schizotypal; ATS = antisocial; BDL = borderline; HST = histrionic; NAR = narcissistic; AVD = avoidant; DEP = dependent; OBC = obsessive–compulsive; DPS = depressive; PAG = passive–aggressive. [a]Significant, p < .05, one tailed, as a replication in correlations among NEO-PI-R facet scales and PDI-IV symptom ratings. [b]The direction of significant correlation opposite to the hypothesis.

contradicted the Widiger et al. (1994) hypotheses, and 14 supported them. For example, clinician-rated schizoid PD was related to spouse-rated low Gregariousness scale score; borderline PD to Angry–Hostility scale score; and passive–aggressive PD to low Compliance scale score.

CONCLUSION

Overall, these data provide strong support for Widiger et al.'s (1994) hypotheses. Three-quarters of the specified links were confirmed using a self-report measure of PDs; more than half were replicated us-

TABLE 13.2

Clinician-Rated *DSM-IV* Criteria Associated With Self-Reported Revised NEO Personality Inventory Factors

Personality disorder	Criterion
Neuroticism	
Avoidant	Is preoccupied with being criticized or rejected
Borderline	Makes frantic efforts to avoid abandonment
Dependent	Is preoccupied with the fear of being left alone
Histrionic	Has rapidly shifting emotions
Narcissistic	Is preoccupied with fantasies of success
Obsessive–compulsive	Shows perfectionism that interferes with task completion
Paranoid	Suspects others of harm and exploitation
Schizotypal	Has ideas of reference (*DSM-IV* diagnostic criteria)
Depressive	Is derogatory toward self
Passive–aggressive	Is sullen and argumentative
High Extraversion	
Antisocial	Fails to plan ahead
Borderline	Shows potentially self-damaging impulsivity
Histrionic	Considers relationships more intimate than they really are
Narcissistic	Is interpersonally exploitative
Low Extraversion	
Avoidant	Is reluctant to take personal risks that may prove embarrassing
Dependent	Lacks confidence to initiate a project
Schizoid	Always chooses solitary activities
Schizotypal	Lacks close friends or confidants
Depressive	Broods
High Openness to Experi-ence	
Borderline	Has identity disturbance and an unstable sense of self
Histrionic	Is uncomfortable when not the center of attention
Narcissistic	Has grandiose sense of self-importance
Schizotypal	Shows odd beliefs or magical thinking
Low Openness to Experience	
Avoidant	Views self as inferior to others
Dependent	Needs others to assume responsibility
Paranoid	Has doubts trustworthiness of friends
Schizoid	Takes pleasure in few activities
High Agreeableness	
Dependent	Has difficulty expressing disagreements with others
Obsessive–compulsive	Is overconscientious and scrupulous
Low Agreeableness	
Antisocial	Shows reckless disregard for the safety of others
Borderline	Has difficulty controlling anger
Histrionic	Shows inappropriate sexually seductive behavior
Narcissistic	Requires excessive admiration
Obsessive–compulsive	Shows rigidity and stubbornness
Paranoid	Reads hidden meanings into benign remarks
Schizotypal	Has paranoid ideation
Depressive	Is negativistic, critical, and judgmental
Passive–aggressive	Resists performing tasks
High Conscientiousness	
Narcissistic	Has a sense of entitlement
Obsessive–compulsive	Is excessively devoted to work
Low Conscientiousness	
Antisocial	Is irresponsible in work or finances
Avoidant	Is unwilling to get involved with people
Borderline	Shows chronic feelings of emptiness and a lack of purpose
Dependent	Has difficulty making decisions
Depressive	Has low self-esteem

Note. N = 319–357. *DSM-IV* = *Diagnostic and Statistical Manual of Mental Disorders* (4th ed.; American Psychiatric Association, 1994). All associations are significant, *p* < .05.

ing clinician ratings. About half the hypotheses were also supported by analyses using spouse ratings of personality in place of self-reports, substantially ruling out the possibility that results were attributable solely to method of measurement.

Yet many more correlations were found than were predicted. Some—such as the associations of vulnerability with depressive PD, impulsiveness with histrionic PD, and low self-discipline with borderline PD—contribute to a clearer conceptualization of the disorders. But all the PDs were related to facets of Neuroticism, and there were pervasive links to both low Agreeableness and low Conscientiousness facets. In these respects, PDs apparently do not have as distinctive a personality profile as other hypotheses suggest. That lack of specificity is probably related to the well-known problem of comorbidity among PDs (Widiger et al., 1991). One explanation for comorbidity is that many PDs are influenced by the same underlying personality traits. Neuroticism is manifested in dysphoric affect, low Agreeableness in poor interpersonal relations, and low Conscientiousness in problems with achievement and self-control. It is therefore perhaps not surprising that these trait factors are associated with a variety of PDs (Trull & McCrae, 1994).

One way to illustrate the overlap of personality traits across PDs is by examining correlations with individual criteria. Table 13.2 provides examples of *DSM-IV* PD criteria associated with the five NEO-PI-R factors. All but six of the 93 criteria were associated with one or more personality factors, and those six were rarely diagnosed. As Table 13.2 shows, personality trait correlations cut across PDs. Impairments related to Neuroticism can be found among the criteria for almost all disorders, and criteria from diverse PDs are associated with the high or low ends of the other factors.

The data in Table 13.2 also illustrate the utility of an entirely different approach to the assessment of personality pathology (Costa, & McCrae, chapter 25, this volume). By measuring personality traits, we can anticipate significant life problems. For example, someone who is high in Openness to Experience may be judged by clinicians to have an unstable sense of self, a grandiose sense of self-importance (cf. McCrae, 1994), or odd and magical beliefs.

These problems do not define any single PD, but they surely merit clinical concern.

Data for the study discussed above were collected in a psychiatric sample in the People's Republic of China, yet results closely resemble those reported by Dyce and O'Connor (1998) in a Canadian undergraduate sample. Studies from many cultures support the hypothesis that personality traits themselves are universal aspects of human psychology (McCrae & Costa, 1997). The data above also suggest the parallel hypothesis that personality-related pathology may also transcend culture. Both PDs and personality traits may reflect biologically based individual differences common to the human species as a whole.

References

American Psychiatric Association. (1987). *Diagnostic and Statistical Manual of Mental Disorders* (3rd ed., rev.). Washington, DC: Author.

American Psychiatric Association. (1994). *Diagnostic and Statistical Manual of Mental Disorders* (4th ed.). Washington, DC: Author.

Bagby, R. M., Rector, N. A., Bindseil, K., Dickens, S. E., Levitan, R. D., & Kennedy, S. H. (1998). Self-report ratings and informant ratings of personalities of depressed outpatients. *American Journal of Psychiatry, 155,* 437–438.

Ball, S. A., Tennen, H., Poling, J. C., Kranzler, H. R., & Rounsaville, B. J. (1997). Personality, temperament, and character dimensions and the *DSM-IV* personality disorders in substance abusers. *Journal of Abnormal Psychology, 4,* 545–553.

Chinese Medical Association, Psychiatric Division. (1992). *Chinese classification and diagnostic criteria for mental disorders* (2nd ed., rev.). Changsha, Hunan, People's Republic of China: Author.

Costa, P. T., Jr., & McCrae, R. R. (1992). *Revised NEO Personality Inventory (NEO-PI-R) and NEO Five-Factor Inventory (NEO-FFI) professional manual.* Odessa, FL: Psychological Assessment Resources.

Costa, P. T., Jr., & Widiger, T. A. (Eds.). (1994). *Personality disorders and the five-factor model of personality.* Washington, DC: American Psychological Association.

Digman, J. M. (1990). Personality structure: Emergence of the five-factor model. *Annual Review of Psychology, 41,* 417–440.

Dyce, J. A., & O'Connor, B. P. (1998). Personality

disorders and the five-factor model: A test of facet-level predictions. *Journal of Personality Disorders, 12,* 31–45.

Eysenck, H. J., Wakefield, J. A., Jr., & Friedman, A. F. (1983). Diagnosis and clinical assessment: The *DSM-III. Annual Review of Psychology, 34,* 167–193.

Fossati, A., Maffei, C., Bagnato, M., Donati, D., Donini, M., Fiorilli, M., Novella, L., & Ansoldi, M. (1998). Criterion validity of the Personality Diagnostic Questionnaire—4+ (PDQ-4+) in a mixed psychiatric sample. *Journal of Personality Disorders, 12,* 172–178.

Hyler, S. E. (1994). *PDQ-4+ Personality Questionnaire.* New York: Author.

Kiesler, D. J. (1986). The 1982 interpersonal circle: An analysis of *DSM-III* personality disorders. In T. Millon & G. L. Klerman (Eds.), *Contemporary directions in psychopathology: Toward the* DSM-IV (pp. 571–597). New York: Guilford.

Livesley, W. J., Jang, K. L., & Vernon, P. A. (1998). Phenotypic and genetic structure of traits delineating personality disorder. *Archives of General Psychiatry, 55,* 941–948.

Loehlin, J. C. (1992). *Genes and environment in personality development.* Newbury Park, CA: Sage.

Loranger, A. W. (1999). Categorical approaches to assessment and diagnosis of personality disorders. In C. R. Cloninger (Ed.), *Personality and psychopathology* (pp. 201–217). Washington, DC: American Psychiatric Press.

McCrae, R. R. (1994). Openness to Experience: Expanding the boundaries of Factor V. *European Journal of Personality, 8,* 251–272.

McCrae, R. R., & Costa, P. T., Jr. (1997). Personality trait structure as a human universal. *American Psychologist, 52,* 509–516.

McCrae, R. R., Costa, P. T., Jr., & Yik, M. S. M. (1996). Universal aspects of Chinese personality structure. In M. H. Bond (Ed.), *The handbook of Chinese psychology* (pp. 189–207). Hong Kong, People's Republic of China: Oxford University Press.

Millon, T. (1994). *Manual for the MCMI-III.* Minneapolis, MN: National Computer Systems.

Oldham, J. M. (1994). Personality disorders: Current perspectives. *Journal of the American Medical Association, 272,* 1770–1776.

Trull, T. J., & McCrae, R. R. (1994). A five-factor perspective on personality disorder research. In P. T. Costa, Jr., & T. A. Widiger (Eds.), *Personality disorders and the five-factor model of personality* (pp. 59–71). Washington, DC: American Psychological Association.

Trull, T. J., Useda, J. D., Costa, P. T., Jr., & McCrae, R. R. (1995). Comparison of the MMPI-2 Personality Psychopathology Five (PSY-5), the NEO-PI, and the NEO-PI-R. *Psychological Assessment, 7,* 508–516.

Widiger, T. A., Frances, A. J., Harris, M., Jacobsberg, L. B., Fyer, M., & Manning, D. (1991). Comorbidity among Axis II disorders. In J. Oldham (Ed.), *Axis II: New perspectives on validity* (pp. 165–194). Washington, DC: American Psychiatric Press.

Widiger, T. A., Mangine, S., Corbitt, E. M., Ellis, C. G., & Thomas, G. V. (1995). *Personality Disorder Interview—IV: A semi-structured interview for the assessment of personality disorders.* Odessa, FL: Psychological Assessment Resources.

Widiger, T. A., Trull, T. J., Clarkin, J. F., Sanderson, C., & Costa, P. T., Jr. (1994). A description of the *DSM-III-R* and *DSM-IV* personality disorders with the five-factor model of personality. In P. T. Costa, Jr., & T. A. Widiger (Eds.), *Personality disorders and the five-factor model of personality* (pp. 41–56). Washington, DC: American Psychological Association.

Wiggins, J. S., & Pincus, A. L. (1989). Conceptions of personality disorders and dimensions of personality. *Psychological Assessment: A Journal of Consulting and Clinical Psychology, 1,* 305–316.

Yang, J., McCrae, R. R., Costa, P. T., Jr., Dai, X., Yao, S., Cai, T., & Gao, B. (1999). Cross-cultural personality assessment in psychiatric populations: The NEO-PI-R in the People's Republic of China. *Psychological Assessment, 11,* 359–368.

Yang, J., McCrae, R. R., Costa, P. T., Jr., Yao, S., Dai, X., Cai, T., & Gao, B. (2000). The cross-cultural generalizability of Axis-II constructs: Evaluation of two personality disorder assessment instruments in the People's Republic of China. *Journal of Personality Disorders, 14,* 249–263.

CHAPTER 14

TESTS OF GENERAL AND SPECIFIC MODELS OF PERSONALITY DISORDER CONFIGURATION

Brian P. O'Connor and Jamie A. Dyce

Models of personality disorder (PD) configuration help researchers understand and simplify the complex world of these disorders. They simultaneously place PDs in the same multivariate space, thereby revealing the fundamental dimensions of PDs and their similarities and differences on these dimensions. The five-factor model (FFM) serves as one such configurational model. This chapter focuses on two issues on the topic that have pre-occupied us since the publication of the first edition of this book. The first issue concerns the validities of the competing models of PD configuration that have been proposed to date. Does the FFM provide a representation of PD dimensions and interrelationships that is more accurate than the representations provided by other models discussed in the literature? The second issue is more specific and focuses on the predictions made by Widiger (1993) and Widiger, Trull, Clarkin, Sanderson, and Costa (1994) regarding associations between PDs and the facets of the Big-Five dimensions. What are the benefits of facet-level analyses, and how much support is there for Widiger et al.'s predictions?

COMPETING MODELS OF PERSONALITY DISORDER CONFIGURATION

Although only a few models of PD configuration can be found in the literature, the existing models have rarely been tested and their relative degrees of fit with the same data sets have never been assessed nor compared. We (O'Connor & Dyce, 1998) therefore designed a competition between the models to assess their degrees of fit with the primary PD data sets from clinical and community samples reported in the more recent literature. Their methods and findings are the focus of this section of our chapter.

Personality Disorder Data Sets

In our model-testing review (O'Connor & Dyce, 1998), we used the PD correlation matrices reported by Hyler and Lyons (1988); Kass, Skodol, Charles, Spitzer, and Williams (1985); Klein et al. (1993); Livesley and Jackson (1986); Millon (1987); Moldin, Rice, Erlenmeyer-Kimling, and Squires-Wheeler (1994); Morey, Waugh, and Blashfield (1985); Widiger, Trull, Hurt, Clarkin, and Frances (1987); and Zimmerman and Coryell (1989). The PD correlation matrices (see Table 14.1 for descriptions) were generally derived from large samples. Some of the matrices were based on data from clinical populations, whereas others were from general community populations.

A variety of assessment techniques were used by these researchers to collect their PD data, including structured and semistructured interviews, ratings by clinicians, and self-report tests (e.g., the Minnesota

This chapter is an adapted and updated presentation of two articles: (a) "A Test of Models of Personality Disorder Configuration," by B. P. O'Connor and J. A. Dyce, 1998, *Journal of Abnormal Psychology, 107*, 3–16. Copyright 1998 by the American Psychological Association. Adapted with permission. (b) "Personality Disorders and the Five-Factor Model: A Test of Facet-Level Predictions," by J. A. Dyce and B. P. O'Connor, 1998, *Journal of Personality Disorders, 12*, 31–45. Copyright 1998 by the Guilford Press. Adapted with permission.

<table>
<thead>
<tr><th colspan="4" style="text-align:center">TABLE 14.1</th></tr>
</thead>
</table>

Sources of the Correlation Matrices

Study	Sample type	Sample size	Personality disorder assessment technique
Hyler & Lyons (1988)	Clinical	358	Ratings by clinicians based on *DSM-III* criteria
Kass et al. (1985)	Clinical	609	Ratings by clinicians based on *DSM-III* criteria
Klein et al. (1993)	Clinical and community	1,230	Wisconsin Personality Disorder Inventory
Livesley & Jackson (1986)	University students	115	*DSM-III* behavior prototypicality ratings
Millon (1987)	Clinical	769	Millon Clinical Multiaxial Inventory (2nd ed.)
Moldin et al. (1994)			
Women	Community	143	Personality Disorder Examination (semistructured interviews), based on *DSM-III-R* criteria
Men	Community	159	Personality Disorder Examination (semistructured interviews), based on *DSM-III-R* criteria
Morey et al. (1985)	Clinical	475	Minnesota Multiphasic Personality Inventory personality disorder scales
Widiger et al. (1987)	Clinical	87	Semistructured interviews, based on *DSM-III* criteria
Zimmerman & Coryell (1989)	Community	797	Structured Interview for *DSM-III* Personality Disorders (SIDP)

Note. DSM-III = third edition of the *Diagnostic and Statistical Manual of Mental Disease; DSM-III-R* = third edition, revised, of the *DSM.*

Multiphasic Personality Inventory PD scales and the Million Clinical Multiaxial Inventory (2nd ed. [MCMI-II]). In other words, the data were from the primary, recent studies on PDs and encompassed a range of populations and assessment techniques. For each data set, we used only correlations between the 11 primary PDs (i.e., schizoid, avoidant, dependent, histrionic, narcissistic, antisocial, compulsive, passive–aggressive, schizotypal, borderline, and paranoid) and excluded correlations that were sometimes reported for proposed PDs (e.g., depressive, self-defeating, sadistic) but were not assessed in all of the studies. Our focus was also on the relationships among continuous dimensions of PD scores (Widiger & Costa, 1994; Widiger & Sanderson, 1995), not on the configuration of highly questionable, categorical PD "entities" (Clark, Watson, & Reynolds, 1995).

Factor Analytic Techniques

Factor analyses are typically performed to discover or confirm simple structures. Users are confronted with a number of subjective and controversial decisions, such as choosing between factor extraction and rotation techniques and conflicting rules regarding the number of factors to extract. Although differing paths through the decision tree sometimes produce differing end results, the structure that exists in a correlation matrix never changes. It is merely viewed from different vantage points (Watson, Clark, & Harkness, 1994, p. 20). In the case of PD configurations, structures have been proposed, but their existence has rarely been tested; the vantage points offered by routine factor analytic techniques may not reveal the structures that could in fact exist. The purpose of targeted extractions and rotations is to determine whether the relationships between variables can be aligned to conform with a specified configuration. Procrustes targeted rotations are considered the most appropriate for testing complex models (see McCrae, Zonderman, Costa, Bond, & Paunonen, 1996) and are necessary for testing models that are not consistent with simple structure (e.g., convergence is impossible in perfect circumplex configurations). We (O'Connor & Dyce, 1998) therefore examined the degrees to which relationships between PDs could be rotated to conform with particular configurational models. In other words, when the structure in a correlation matrix is examined from the vantage point that maximizes congruence with a particular model, is the picture that emerges consistent with the model?

The power of this support-seeking statistical technique can be illustrated by an analogy to the familiar Rubic's cube. In this context, a PD configuration model would be a specific target pattern (e.g., the picture on a jigsaw puzzle box) for the rotation of the cube segments (PDs). A Procrustes rotation would be equivalent to a device that could rapidly rotate the cube segments to the coordinates that provide the closest possible approximation to the target without destroying the cube (PD) structure. Although such a device would take the fun out of a Rubic's cube and would provide unfair advantage to whoever used it, a Procrustes statistical equivalent is a much-needed blessing for PD researchers who must deal with 11 PDs on each surface of a structure that may have more than three dimensions.

The first step in testing a particular model was to generate a target factor loading matrix consisting of coefficients representing the relative positionings of PDs predicted by the model. In the second step, principal-axes common factor analyses (CFAs), with squared multiple correlations on the diagonal, were conducted on the correlation matrices from other research (see Table 14.1), extracting as many factors as specified by the target model (essentially the same findings emerged when principal components analysis [PCA] was used instead). In the third step, the PD loading matrices were rotated to least square fits to the target matrices using the orthogonal Procrustes technique, as described by Schonemann (1966) and McCrae et al. (1996). Oblique targeted rotations were also conducted, using the procedure described by Hurley and Cattell (1962), to determine whether substantially stronger degrees of support for the models could be obtained for nonorthogonal rotations.

We then assessed the degrees to which the rotated matrices conformed to the model-based target matrices by computing the Tucker–Burt–Wrigley–Neuhaus congruence coefficient (see Guadagnoli & Velicer, 1991), which is an index of proportional similarity between two sets of factor loadings. Congruence coefficients can be (and were) computed for each factor from each comparison. But reporting all of these coefficients for every data set and model

test would require an inordinate amount of space and would quickly become overwhelming. We therefore computed the Tucker et al. congruence coefficient for all corresponding elements in the matrix comparisons (this procedure was recommended and used by McCrae et al., 1996). The result is an overall fit coefficient based on all factor loadings instead of multiple congruence coefficients based on the loadings for single factors. The overall coefficients are roughly equivalent to the mean of the factor congruence coefficients and are efficient summaries of the total degree of fit between the target and rotated loading matrices. They provide broad overviews of which models best fit the data. Little additional information was provided by the individual factor congruences when the overall congruences were very low or very high.

One drawback with targeted rotations is that they capitalize on chance (Horn, 1967), although the problem is less severe for the orthogonal targeted rotations. Researchers must therefore demonstrate that a given targeted rotation displays a degree of fit that is superior to the fit achieved by chance rotations. In our review, the degree of fit was statistically assessed using the procedure described by Paunonen (1997) and McCrae et al. (1996). The technique is a random data permutation test of statistical significance (Edgington, 1995). Specifically, a Monte Carlo investigation of the distribution of congruence coefficients was conducted for each targeted rotation (i.e., for each target matrix vs. CFA loading matrix comparison). In these investigations, the elements in a given target matrix were randomly rearranged, the CFA loading matrix was rotated to maximum fit with the rearranged target, and the congruence coefficient was computed. (Randomly rearranging elements in a matrix provides a more conservative test than using random numbers.) This was repeated 1,000 times. The upper 95th and 99th percentiles of each distribution of coefficients were identified and used to determine whether the fit indices for nonrandomly rearranged coefficients exceeded the fit achieved by randomly rearranged coefficients. Coefficients higher than the 95th percentiles were considered significant at the .05 level; coefficients higher than the 99th percentiles were considered significant at the .01 level; and coefficients higher than all

1,000 values observed for rotations to randomly re-arranged target matrices were considered significant at the .001 level.

Diagnostic and Statistical Manual of Mental Disorders Clusters

In the fourth edition of the *Diagnostic and Statistical Manual of Mental Disorders* (*DSM-IV*; American Psychiatric Association, 1994), PDs are organized into three clusters based on common underlying themes. Cluster A involves odd or eccentric behavior; Cluster B involves dramatic, emotional, or erratic behavior; and Cluster C involves anxiety and fearfulness. The specific PDs associated with these clusters and the target loading matrix constructed to represent them are shown in Table 14.2. Values of 1.00 and .00 were chosen to represent high and low loadings in the target matrix. Substituting alternative "high" values in place of 1.00 (e.g., 0.45, 0.75) does not change the congruence coefficients. Alternative values only make a difference when there are varying degrees of high loadings, low loadings, or both across elements in a matrix. The fit coefficients from the targeted rotations and their significance levels derived from the Monte Carlo simulations are re-ported in Table 14.3. The coefficients were significant for 10 of the data sets, and the coefficients for oblique rotations were only marginally higher than the coefficients for orthogonal rotations. Support for the *DSM* as a model of the correlational structure of PDs can be considered statistically significant and substantial but somewhat variable and less than perfect. At this point, we were curious to see if alternative PD configurations could surpass the fit levels achieved by the *DSM* model.

Millon's Biosocial Learning Theory

Theodore Millon has been an influential figure in the development of the *DSM* section on PDs and a creative contributor to the literature on PD configuration. His models of PD dimensions and interrelationships have been evolving, and we tested both his often-described, earlier model (Millon, 1987, 1990, 1994) and a recently revised version, both of which are called "biosocial learning" theories (Millon, 1996). We began by deriving a target matrix that represents the earlier model from a table that Millon (e.g., 1987, p. 19; 1990, p. 128) repeatedly published depicting the various PDs in relation to the dimensions of his theory. There are at least three

---

TABLE 14.2

Personality Disorder Configurations for the *DSM* Clusters, Millon, and Torgersen and Alnaes Studies

Personality disorder	DSM clusters A	B	C	Millon (1990) Pleas–pain	Self–other	Passive–active	Millon (1996) Pleas–pain	Self–other	Passive–active	Torgersen & Alnaes (1989) Reality–weak	Oral	Extra version	Obsessive
Schizoid	1	0	0	0.707	0.000	0.707	0.00	0.50	1.00	no	no	no	no
Avoidant	0	0	1	0.707	0.000	−0.707	−1.00	0.00	−1.00	no	yes	no	no
Dependent	0	0	1	0.000	0.707	0.707	0.00	−1.00	1.00	no	yes	no	no
Histrionic	0	1	0	0.000	0.707	−0.707	0.00	−1.00	−1.00	no	yes	yes	no
Narcissistic	0	1	0	0.000	−0.707	0.707	0.00	1.00	1.00	no	no	yes	no
Antisocial	0	1	0	0.000	−0.707	−0.707	0.50	1.00	−1.00	no	no	yes	no
Compulsive	0	0	1	0.000	0.000	1.000	−0.50	−1.00	1.00	no	yes	no	yes
Passive–aggressive	0	0	1	0.000	0.000	−1.000	−0.50	−0.50	−0.25	no	yes	no	no
Schizotypal	1	0	0	1.000	0.000	0.000	0.00	0.00	0.00	yes	yes	no	no
Borderline	0	1	0	0.000	0.707	0.000	0.00	0.00	0.00	yes	yes	yes	no
Paranoid	1	0	0	0.000	−0.707	0.000	0.00	0.00	0.00	yes	yes	no	yes

Note. DSM = Diagnostic and Statistical Manual of Mental Disorders; Pleas–pain = pleasure–pain; *DSM* clusters: A = odd or eccentric; B = dramatic, emotional, or erratic; C = anxious and fearfulness.

TABLE 14.3

Congruences With Target Loading Matrices for the *DSM*, Millon, and Torgersen and Alnaes Configurations

Study	DSM clusters		Millon (1990)				Millon (1996)				Torgersen & Alnaes (1989)	
			Three factors		Seven factors		Three factors		Six factors			
	orth	obl	orth	obl	orth	obl	orth	obl	orth	obl	orth	obl
Hyler & Lyons (1988)	89***	91***	34	38	83**	87	33	34	57	73	84***	84**
Kass et al. (1985)	90***	91***	45	47	79*	85	34	37	62	77	85***	85**
Klein et al. (1993)	75**	79**	33	46	74	85	31	48	52	69	82**	81*
Livesley & Jackson (1986)	73*	73	41	49	75	81	43	60	60	77	81**	81*
Millon (1987)[a]	71	70	54	63	80*	88*	39	39	63	74	80**	76
Millon (1987)[b]	65	70	64	67	79*	84	47	51	63	78	77**	78
Moldin et al. (1994): women	77**	79**	41	56	77	82	38	50	59	74	79**	77
Moldin et al. (1994): men	81***	86***	39	50	78	83	36	50	57	80	82**	78
Morey et al. (1985)[a]	79**	80**	43	46	78	84	33	40	56	72	79**	82*
Morey et al. (1985)[b]	81***	83***	42	49	77*	86	34	42	59	78	79**	84**
Widiger et al. (1987)	78**	80**	49	53	72	80	42	46	65	76	79**	83**
Zimmerman & Coryell (1989)	81***	85***	46	63	81**	85	38	55	61	76	83**	82*

Note. Decimals omitted. *DSM* = *Diagnostic and Statistical Manual of Mental Disorders*; orth = orthogonal rotation; obl = oblique rotation.   [a]nonoverlapping item scales.   [b]overlapping item scales.   *$p < .05$.   **$p < .01$.   ***$p < .001$.

dimensions inherent in this earlier view: pleasure–pain (frequency of reinforcement), self–other (source of reinforcement), and passive–active (coping style). The translation of Millon's early model into a target loading matrix is less than straightforward (see O'Connor & Dyce, 1998, p. 6, for details), and the three-factor matrix reported in Table 14.2 is the best target representation that could be derived.

The fit indices for this three-factor target pattern were low and not significant (see Table 14.3), so numerous other *n*-factor target patterns were tested in an attempt to find a pattern that was consistent with both the model and the data. The target pattern that produced the best fit coefficients and was at least roughly consistent with the model is a seven-factor matrix consisting of a column of loadings for each column in Millon's table and one column of loadings for each of the active, passive, and dysfunctional coping styles. The fit coefficients from the targeted rotations and their significance levels are reported in

Table 14.3. Coefficients for seven of the data sets were significant, and the fit levels were comparable with those achieved by the *DSM* model. However, the seven-factor model stretches the logic underlying Millon's theory. Active and passive coping styles seem like opposites, as do the rewards-from-self and rewards-from-others reinforcement patterns, but they are coded as unrelated in the seven-factor target matrix. In summary, a variety of patterns were tested and overall support for Millon's early model can best be described as modest. The fit levels for the seven-factor pattern indicate at least some support for the model, but the data also indicate that revisions to the theory are required.

Millon's (1996) revised model involves the same three dimensions as the earlier model, but the positioning of some PDs on the dimensions have been altered and relative weights ("weak," "average," or "strong") have been given to each PD. Furthermore, Millon provided two weights for each PD on each dimension (e.g., a weight for the active pole and a weight for the passive pole of the active–passive dimension); in a number of cases, the two weights for a PD on a dimension are the same for each pole (e.g., both weak or both average). The three-factor matrix of target weights (not loadings) that was constructed to represent this revised model is shown in Table 14.2. In constructing the target weight matrix, weights of 0 were assigned when Millon's weights for the two poles were the same; weights of .5 or −.5 were used when there was one weak and one average weight; and weights of 1 or −1 were used when there was one strong and one weak weight. Other weight-assignment rules were either not logical or were inconsistent with Millon's model. The analyses were run twice, once using the target weights in Table 14.2 and again using a target loading matrix computed from the weights. The loadings were computed by dividing each weight by the sum of its row weights, computing the square roots of the results, and assigning the proper signs. This procedure results in 100% of the variance accounted for by the loadings in a row. Only the target weights are reported in Table 14.2 because the loadings might have been confusing if one attempted to match the magnitudes of the loadings to the polarity weights provided by Millon (1996).

The fit coefficients for the targeted rotations were essentially identical, regardless of whether target weights or target loadings were used. The fit coefficients were low, and none were significant (the coefficients from the target loading matrix rotations are reported in Table 14.3). A six-factor target weight matrix was then constructed, with the two polarities of each dimension represented as separate factors. The weights of 1, 0, and −1 were simply substituted for strong, average, and weak weights provided by Millon (1996). Once again, a target loading matrix was computed from the weights, using the procedures described above. The fit coefficients for the targeted rotations were again essentially the same, regardless of whether target weights or loadings were used (the fit coefficients from rotations to the target loading matrix are reported in Table 14.3). These fit coefficients were stronger than those for the three-factor model, but none were significant.

Circumplex Configurations

A number of theorists have proposed circular, or circumplex, configurations of PDs. These models all specify that PDs are dispersed around the wheel-like structure that can be formed from scores on two orthogonal dimensions. The models differ from one another in the nature of the two dimensions involved and in the relative positionings of the PDs around the circles in question. Circumplex models are also geometrically precise because the translation of a circumplex structure into a target factor loading matrix is direct and unambiguous. The position of any variable (or PD) on a circle is indexed by the angular displacement of the variable from 0 (3:00 in clock terms). To compute loadings on the north–south dimension of a circle, one merely computes the sines of the angular locations of the variables. Loadings on the east–west dimension are the cosines of the angular locations (Wiggins & Broughton, 1991).

Millon (1987, p. 20) published a circumplex configuration of PDs that he believed represented his theory, although no description of the leap from his theory or table to the circumplex was provided. The angular locations for the 11 *DSM* PDs in Millon's circumplex are reported in Table 14.4. The fit coefficients from attempts to rotate the two-factor CFA structures from the data sets to the two-factor target matrix of sines and cosines are reported in Table 14.5; none were significant.

The most widely discussed circumplex is the interpersonal circle, which is an orthogonal two-dimensional structural representation of the universe of interpersonal traits that has been confirmed in numerous lexical and factor analytic investigations of trait adjectives describing interpersonal behavior (Wiggins, 1982). The circle is bisected by two orthogonal axes, love–warmth–affiliation (horizontal) and dominance–status–control (vertical), which together yield a circular array of categories or segments in Euclidian space. The heuristic value of the circumplex is that it permits any given interpersonal trait or behavior to be interpreted as a particular blend of the two primary dimensions, with a corresponding angular location on the circle. Wiggins noted that seven of the PDs from the *DSM* appear to have substantial interpersonal components; his hy-

TABLE 14.4

Angular Locations (in Degrees) of Personality Disorders in Circumplex Configurations

Personality disorder	Millon (1987)	Wiggins (1982)	Romney & Bynner (1989)	Kiesler (1996)	Widiger & Kelso (1983)	Blashfield et al. (1985)	Plutchik & Conte (1985)
Schizoid	180	225	225	205	225	135	205
Avoidant	235			225	225	225	213
Dependent	275	315	315	255	315	270	324
Histrionic	10	0	0	35	0	315	65
Narcissistic	40	135	135	55	135	315	127
Antisocial	90			180	180	45	140
Compulsive	150	90		215	45	195	240
Passive–aggressive	345	270		195	270	350	210
Schizotypal	205				225	90	207
Borderline	325				337	15	115
Paranoid	67	180	180	155	157	165	180

Note. In clock terms, $0° = 3:00$, and $180° = 9:00$. Empty cells indicate no predictions.

pothesized angular locations of the seven PDs are reported in Table 14.4. A two-factor target loading matrix representing Wiggins's predictions was derived by computing the sines and cosines of the angular locations, as described above. The fit coefficients from the targeted rotations are reported in Table 14.5, and none were significant.

Wiggins's (1982) circumplex ordering of PDs was

also evaluated by Romney and Bynner (1989, 1997), who analyzed three of the same correlation matrices we did (Hyler & Lyons, 1988; Kass et al., 1985; Livesley & Jackson, 1986; O'Connor & Dyce, 1998). Their statistical technique was somewhat different, but they also concluded that the fit to Wiggins's model was poor. However, Romney and Bynner conducted supplementary analyses and found more evi-

TABLE 14.5

Congruences With Target Loading Matrices for the Circumplex Configurations

Study	Millon (1987)	Wiggins (1982)	Romney & Bynner (1989)	Widiger & Kelso (1983)	Kiesler (1996)	Blashfield et al. (1985)	Plutchik & Conte (1985)
Hyler & Lyons (1988)	42	43	49	36	66	34	45
Kass et al. (1985)	36	41	54	53	54	48	38
Klein et al. (1993)	26	18	28	26	58	29	36
Livesley & Jackson (1986)	31	41	38	41	57	26	44
Millon (1987)[a]	46	45	69	49	76*	31	37
Millon (1987)[b]	57	37	64	50	74*	44	40
Moldin et al. (1994): women	33	25	38	31	50	36	32
Moldin et al. (1994): men	33	22	38	29	61	27	33
Morey et al. (1985)[a]	42	46	47	34	75*	29	44
Morey et al. (1985)[b]	45	37	54	40	82**	36	46
Widiger et al. (1987)	57	56	72	41	44	42	34
Zimmerman & Coryell (1989)	29	28	41	23	53	27	36

Note. Decimals omitted. [a] = nonoverlapping item scales. [b] overlapping item scales. $*p < .05$. $**p < .01$.

dence of circularity in a subset of five PDs (but only for two of the three correlation matrices they examined). Their revised circumplex model of PDs is identical to Wiggins's model but excludes obsessive–compulsive and passive–aggressive. We therefore conducted targeted rotations to their model using CFA loading matrices derived from the intercorrelations between the five PDs. The fit coefficients are reported in Table 14.5, and none were significant.

The discrepancies between our findings and those of Romney and Bynner (1989, 1997) were due to different tests for circular pattern. Their factor analytic tests were less stringent: They merely examined whether correlations displayed the incremental pattern ($r1 > r2 > r3 > r4$, etc.) required for circular structure, whereas our target matrices specified the precise angular locations of PDs on the circle, as indicated by the models. When we plotted the unrotated loadings from factor analyses of the data used by Romney and Bynner, we found rough circular patterns in isolated regions of the factor spaces (see O'Connor & Dyce, 1998, p. 10). These rough patterns were apparently responsible for Romney and Bynner's significant results. However, genuine circumplexes did not exist because the data points for the circles did not fully encompass the two dimensions on which the data points were based. In other words, two dimensions may have existed in the correlations between the five PDs in Romney and Bynner's model, but the PDs were not dispersed in circular form around the two dimensions.

Kiesler (1986, 1996) offered another arrangement of the DSM PDs on the interpersonal circle. Lexical analyses of the terms describing PDs and interpersonal traits resulted in the circle placements listed in Table 14.4. (Kiesler's predictions for the schizotypal and borderline PDs were not tested because they span nonadjacent segments of the circle, thus preventing their translation into factor loadings.) The targeted rotations produced congruence coefficients that were significant for four data sets, but the congruences were generally modest in size (e.g., below .80; see Table 14.5). Targeted rotations for the subsets of PDs specified by Kiesler (e.g., for PDs from his "octant prototypes") yielded congruence coefficients that were lower than those in Table 14.5. However, it should also be noted that Kielser did

not actually propose a circular configuration of PDs. Instead, he merely made predictions regarding the positioning of PDs on the interpersonal circle. His positionings resulted in many PDs being clustered together in the same regions of the circle instead of being dispersed around the circle (see the angular locations in Table 14.4). The slightly greater support for Kiesler's hypotheses should therefore not be misconstrued as evidence for mild degrees of circularity. Kiesler also claimed that PDs vary in their interpersonal intensity or distance from the origin of the interpersonal circle. However, his distance from the origin hypotheses was incomplete and sometimes varied within PDs, thus preventing tests of this additional feature of his model.

Other circumplex configurations of PDs have been proposed by Widiger and Kelso (1983); Blashfield, Sprock, Pinkston, and Hodgin (1985); and Plutchik and Conte (1985). These models were derived from reviews of the literature, ratings by clinicians, or both. The angular locations of PDs specified in these models are reported in Table 14.4, and none of the fit coefficients for the targeted rotations were significant (see Table 14.5). Finally, a three-dimensional interpersonal approach to PDs was proposed by Benjamin (1993), but her model could not be tested in this study because each PD has more than one high point on each dimension and the high points are often not adjacent (p. 394), thus preventing the computation of dimension loadings for a target matrix.

In summary, there is little support for the various circumplex configurations of PDs proposed to date. This does not mean that the primary dimensions of interpersonal behavior are not relevant to PDs. Some PDs do have notable projections in interpersonal space, but these projections do not form a meaningful or complete circular configuration, and other dimensions are required to capture, clarify, and discriminate between the PDs (Kiesler, 1996, p. 194; Soldz, Budman, Demby, & Merry, 1993; Widiger & Hagemoser, 1997; Wiggins & Pincus, 1989).

Torgersen and Alnaes's Decision Tree

Torgersen and Alnaes (1989) examined scores on PDs in relation to scores on four dimensions of personality traits, which they labeled "reality–weak," "extroversion," "oral," and "obsessive." Their findings led them to propose a decision tree for PD diagnosis: One merely determines the presence or absence of traits on the four dimensions to arrive at a PD diagnosis (although some PDs are not yet differentiated in their decision tree and have the same yes–no scores on all four dimensions). Their predictions are reported in Table 14.2 and were translated into a target loading matrix by (a) assigning 1s to represent "yes" codes and 0s to represent "no" codes (by no Torgersen & Alnaes meant that a trait was absent, not that the opposite of a trait was present), (b) dividing each code by the sum of the row codes, and (c) computing the square roots of the results. This procedure results in 100% of the variance accounted for by the row loadings for each PD. The fit coefficients for the targeted rotations are reported in Table 14.3. All coefficients were significant and in the .75–.85 range, indicating substantial, consistent, but less-than-perfect congruence.

Cloninger's Three-Dimensional Model

Cloninger's (1987) three-dimensional model is one of the few configurations that roots PDs in underlying biological and psychological processes. He claimed that three fundamental dimensions of personality (novelty seeking, harm avoidance, and reward dependence) are associated with activity in three brain systems (behavioral activation, behavioral inhibition, and behavioral maintenance) and three neurotransmitters (dopamine, serotonin, and norepinephrine). Cloninger predicted the relative positionings of nine PDs from the *DSM* on his three key dimensions (see Cloninger, 1987, Table 8 and p. 583). To construct a target matrix to represent his hypothesized configuration, one needs to (a) substitute the values of 1.00 and −1.00 first for the "high" and "low" terms used by Cloninger and use 0.00 in the two cases where no predictions were made; (b) divide the elements in a row by the total number of nonzero elements in a row; and (c) use the square roots of the results (with appropriate signs) as the target loadings (see Table 14.6). This procedure ensures that the percentages of variance accounted for by the loadings in a row add up to 100%. (Essentially identical findings emerged when target loadings of 1.00 and −1.00 were tested instead.)

Cloninger (1987) claimed that the adaptive optimum for each dimension is in the intermediate or average range. It is clear from his theory that highs and lows on his dimensions are considered opposites, which means lows should be given negative weights and should not be coded as .00. In testing this model, we conducted CFAs on the correlations among the nine PDs specified in the model (correlations for the other two PDs were excluded). The fit coefficients from the targeted rotations and their significance levels are reported in Table 14.7. For orthogonal rotations the coefficient for only one of the data sets was significant, whereas for oblique rotations the coefficients for five of the data sets were significant. However, the congruence levels remained slightly lower than those for the *DSM* cluster dimensions.

Cloninger and Svrakic's Seven-Factor Model

Cloninger and Svrakic (1994) proposed an empirically derived seven-factor model for all of the *DSM* PDs. The model consists of the three original Cloninger factors (Novelty Seeking, Harm Avoidance, and Reward Dependence) and four new ones (Persistence, Self-Directedness, Cooperativeness, and Self-Transcendence). The first four factors are believed to be temperamental traits based on genetics, whereas the latter three factors are believed to be character dimensions based on aspects of self-concept as described by humanistic and developmental psychologists.

Cloninger and Svrakic (1994) developed measures of the seven factors, which were then administered to 136 psychiatric inpatients who had also taken from both the original and the second editions of the Structured Interview for *DSM-III-R* Personality Disorder. The researchers reported correlations among the seven factors and the numbers of symptoms of individual PDs (see Cloninger & Svrakic, 1994, p. 52, and Svrakic, Whitehead, Przybeck, & Cloninger, 1993, p. 995). These Pearson correlations were used as the target matrix in the model tests because Cloninger and Svrakic did not make specific hypotheses regarding the positionings of PDs on the seven factors and did not report a factor loading matrix. The seven factors are not orthogonal, so

TABLE 14.6

Target Loading Matrices

Personality disorder or dimension	Widiger et al. (1994) five-factor model					Loadings from Dyce & O'Connor (1998)									Cloninger (1987)		
						Five-factor model					Four-factor model				Novelty seeking	Harm avoidance	Reward dependence
	N	E	O	A	C	N	E	O	A	C	N	E	A	C			
Schizoid	-47	-67	-33	33	-33	24	-66	09	-35	15	28	-61	-36	16	-58	-58	-58
Avoidant	67	-67	-33	00	00	66	-54	05	-08	-02	68	-51	-07	-01	[a]	71	71
Dependent	67	00	00	67	-33	83	00	-04	14	09	83	01	16	09	-58	58	58
Histrionic	48	62	39	-28	-39	-11	84	07	-20	06	-12	84	-19	04	58	[a]	58
Narcissistic	52	30	30	-60	43	04	11	27	-73	15	08	19	-73	15	71	-58	71
Antisocial	45	00	00	-71	-55	12	10	00	-67	-37	13	09	-66	-37	58	-58	-58
Compulsive	48	-39	-39	-39	55	02	-04	-12	09	87	01	-06	09	87	-58	58	-58
Passive-aggressive	41	00	00	-58	-71	66	-08	-16	-46	-09	65	-11	-44	-10	58	58	58
Schizotypal	67	-47	47	-33	00	55	-30	32	-40	-10	59	-22	-40	-10	[a]	[a]	[a]
Borderline	71	50	00	-41	-29	71	-17	07	-35	-23	72	-15	-34	-23	58	-58	58
Paranoid	38	-46	-46	-60	27	49	-23	-07	-61	08	50	-22	-60	08	[a]	[a]	[a]
Neuroticism						80	-22	-08	01	-24	80	-23	01	-24			
Extraversion						-15	82	25	04	09	-16	85	04	08			
Openness						-07	17	90	03	-11							
Agreeableness						03	12	27	77	24	04	17	77	24			
Conscientiousness						-25	19	02	09	84	-25	10	08	84			

Note. Decimals omitted; N = Neuroticism; E = Extraversion; O = Openness to Experience; A = Agreeableness; C = Conscientiousness. [a] no predictions were made by Cloninger.

TABLE 14.7

Congruences With Target Loading Matrices

Study	Five-factor model (Widiger et al., 1994)		Five-factor model (Dyce & O'Connor, 1998)		Four-factor model (Dyce & O'Connor, 1998)		Three-factor model (Cloninger, 1987)		Cloninger & Svrakic (1994)			
	orth.	obl.	orth.	obl.	orth.	obl.	orth.	obl.	Three factors obl.	Four factors obl.	Five factors obl.	Seven factors obl.
Hyler & Lyons (1988)	81***	86***	88***	89***	88***	90***	62	74*	82***	92***	95***	95***
Kass et al. (1985)	79***	85***	86***	89***	88***	92***	69*	81**	87***	91***	94***	94***
Klein et al. (1993)	81***	91***	85***	85**	87***	91***	49	71	93***	95***	96***	95***
Livesley & Jackson (1986)	82***	87***	92***	95***	94***	96***	52	63	85***	95***	96***	96***
Millon (1987)[a]	79***	88***	94***	95***	96***	97***	56	68	85***	93***	95***	95***
Millon (1987)[b]	84***	87***	92***	94***	93***	94***	64	71	85***	93***	95***	94***
Moldin et al. (1994): women	81***	84***	84***	87***	81***	83***	56	74*	93***	96***	96***	95***
Moldin et al. (1994): men	78***	81**	88***	91***	88***	91***	59	79**	90***	94***	95***	95***
Morey et al. (1985)[a]	83***	86***	86***	87***	84***	88***	48	62	85***	90***	95***	94***
Morey et al. (1985)[b]	83***	85***	88***	89***	87***	89***	53	65	86***	91***	92***	93***
Widiger et al. (1987)	82***	89***	80***	83**	75**	76*	64	70	87***	90***	93***	92***
Zimmerman & Coryell (1989)	79***	85***	79**	80*	79**	79**	60	77*	86***	92***	92***	94***

Note. Decimals omitted. orth. = orthogonal rotation; obl. = oblique rotation. [a]nonoverlapping item scales. [b]overlapping item scales. *p < .05.
**p < .01. ***p < .001.

only oblique targeted rotations could be conducted. The congruence coefficients were all very high and significant (see Table 14.7). Subsets of the factors were then used as targets in further tests because (a) the extraction of seven factors from the PD correlation matrices is probably excessive, and (b) perusal of the correlations revealed that two of the factors (Persistence and Self-Transcendence) are almost unrelated to PD symptoms, and two other factors (Self-Directedness and Cooperativeness) provide little differentiation among the PDs. A five-factor target consisting of the PD correlations for the first three factors plus Self-Directedness and Cooperativeness yielded congruence coefficients that were essentially identical to the coefficients for the seven-factor target (see Table 14.7). The congruence coefficients from rotations to four-factor targets, consisting of the first three factors plus either Self-Directedness or Cooperativeness, were slightly lower but still very high and consistently significant (almost identical findings emerged, regardless of whether Self-Directedness or Cooperativeness was used as the fourth factor; the four-factor coefficients in Table 14.7 are based on Self-Directedness). Congruence coefficients from rotations to a target consisting of the first three factors produced slightly lower but still high and significant congruences that were comparable with those obtained for the FFM (see Table 14.7). It is also worth noting that the PD correlations with the first three factors do not greatly resemble the theory-based predictions of Cloninger (1987). The factor congruence coefficients computed for comparisons of the theory-based target matrix with the Pearson correlations were .77, .46, and .47.

The Five-Factor Model

The dimensions of the FFM—Neuroticism, Extraversion, Openness to Experience, Agreeableness, and Conscientiousness—are assumed to underlie both normal and abnormal personality characteristics. Abnormal personalities are viewed as "maladaptively extreme variants of the five basic factors of personality" (Widiger et al., 1994, p. 41; see also Widiger & Costa, 1994). It has therefore been argued that PDs can be understood in terms of their relative positionings on the five primary dimensions. In our model-testing review (O'Connor & Dyce, 1998), we

devised two target matrices to assess the degree of support for the FFM. One target matrix was derived from the review of the literature conducted by Widiger et al., and the other target matrix was derived from data we collected on the FFM and PDs.

Widiger et al. (1994) conducted an extensive review of the DSM PD diagnostic criteria and of the clinical literature on PDs and outlined the predicted relationships with the FFM in tabular form (p. 42). However, their predictions were for facets of the each of the five factors, not for the broader domains or dimensions. Target loadings for domains were computed from their facet predictions as follows: We first counted the number of PD facet predictions for each domain (six facets in each domain); the PD counts for the domains–factors were then divided by the sum of the row counts; the square roots of the results were computed and given positive or negative signs to reflect high or low predicted loadings. This procedure results in 100% of the variance accounted for by the loadings in a row. The resulting target loading matrix is reported in Table 14.6, and the fit coefficients for the targeted rotations are reported in Table 14.7. The coefficients were consistent, and all were significant, although the levels of fit were less than perfect. The lowest individual factor congruences (in the .21–.57 range) were for the Openness dimension, a finding that was consistent across PD data sets. The FFM target matrix derived from Widiger et al.'s review of the literature thus provided relatively impressive degrees of fit with extensive PD data gathered from independent sources, although there is still room for improvement.

We also assessed the degrees of fit for a target matrix derived from empirical data. We used data that we collected (Dyce & O'Connor, 1998) because, surprisingly, a FFM loading matrix for the DSM PDs had not yet been published. These data was based on scores from the Revised NEO Personality Inventory (NEO-PI-R; Costa & McCrae, 1992) and the third edition of the MCMI (MCMI-III; (Millon, 1994) obtained from 614 college students. We computed five-factor domain scores for the NEO-PI-R and PD scores from the nonoverlapping item scales of the MCMI-III and conducted a PCA with varimax rotation on the scale intercorrelations. CFA was also conducted, but the loadings for the FFM variables were more dispersed across factors than was the case for the PCA loadings; PCA has been the more frequently used analytic technique in other FFM research. The target loadings for the model tests were the PD loadings on the five components (see Table 14.6). The fit coefficients for the targeted rotations are reported in Table 14.7, and all were significant (the coefficients were essentially identical for target matrices based on PCA and CFA). As a group, the coefficients indicated better overall fit than was obtained in any of the other model tests, although there is still room for improvement. The lowest factor congruences were once again for the Openness dimension, with the other factor congruences being consistently high. The FFM thus generally appears consistent with existing, independently assessed PD data sets.

A Four-Factor Model

Even though the findings above for the FFM are encouraging, the extraction of five factors or more from the correlation matrices for just 11 PDs may be excessive. Smaller PD factor solutions are the norm in the PD literature, although these solutions are typically based on questionable procedures for determining the number of factors (e.g., the eigenvalues-greater-than-one rule). Two more highly recommended tests for determining the number of factors, parallel analyses (using 1,000 random data sets) and Velicer's Minimum Average Partial Test (Zwick & Velicer, 1986), were therefore conducted on the correlation matrices listed in Table 14.1. The results indicated the existence of between one and four factors, depending on the test and data set, with a norm of two to three factors. Extractions of five components or more would be excessive in every case.

In a review of personality structure and psychopathology, Watson et al. (1994) concluded that four factors from the FFM were most relevant. There were no high-loading PDs on the excluded factor, Openness to Experience in our (Dyce & O'Connor, 1998) data (see Table 14.6); this factor also had lower factor congruences in the model tests. This dimension may be important to understand nonclinical personality characteristics, but the degree of differentiation that it provides among the 11 PDs in

the *DSM* is arguably minimal, although it may be important to as-yet-undiscovered PDs. We also found that the eigenvalues for the fourth factor and its components were low for some of the PD correlation matrices, but the fourth dimension should probably be retained. It typically has only one high-loading PD, compulsiveness, which does not load strongly on any other factor-component (a finding replicated in our data; Dyce & O'Connor, 1998; also see Table 14.6). A PCA with varimax rotation was therefore conducted again on the NEO-PI-R and MCMI-III data from Dyce and O'Connor, excluding Openness, and the results are reported in Table 14.6. Four-factor PCAs were then conducted on the PD correlation matrices, and targeted rotations to the PD loadings in Table 14.6 produced fit coefficients highly similar to those for the FFM (see Table 14.7).

Cloninger and Svrakic's (1994) model and the FFM are both based on the assumption that a relatively small number of basic personality dimensions exist and can be found in both normal and clinical populations, which are presumed to differ quantitatively, not qualitatively. Substantial degrees of similarity between the two models should therefore be expected and have in fact been observed. Cloninger and Svrakic also administered the NEO-PI in their data collection and reported high degrees of overlap between their seven factors and the FFM domain scores. The multiple correlations predicting the FFM variables from the seven factors were .84 for Neuroticism, .79 for Extraversion, .46 for Openness, .69 for Agreeableness, and .57 for Conscientiousness. The two measurement devices are not identical, but to a large extent, they seem to be merely giving differing views on the same structure. A targeted rotation of the FFM matrix from our other work (Dyce & O'Connor, 1998, p. 35, Table 14.7) to the five-factor Cloninger and Svrakic matrix described above yielded an overall congruence coefficient of .95 ($p < .0001$).

Discussion

The tests above were powerful, support-seeking attempts to find the views on the PD correlational structures that were most consistent with the PD configuration models. The level of fit with other data sets achieved by the three-dimensional *DSM* configuration proved to be a challenging standard. The fit levels for all circumplex models and for Millon's biosocial learning theory fell below this standard and were rarely statistically significant. For Millon's (1987, 1990, 1994) original model, an alternative, better fitting representational matrix was found, but it requires important adjustments to the original theory. The fit levels for Cloninger's (1987) tridimensional theory were moderate, and the fit levels for Torgersen and Alnaes's (1989) four-dimensional model were generally similar to those for the *DSM* configuration. The highest and most consistent levels of fit were obtained for the FFM and for Cloninger and Svrakic's (1994) seven-factor model. The levels of fit for these models surpassed the fit levels for the *DSM* cluster dimensions. However, extraction of five factors or more from existing PD correlation matrices is probably excessive, and four factors provide comparable degrees of differentiation among the PDs and similar levels of fit to the data.

In one sense, our (Dyce & O'Connor's, 1998) FFM and Cloninger and Svrakic's (1994) model had an unfair advantage in the competition. The target matrices for these models were based on actual PD data, whereas the targets for the other models were based largely on clinical observations and theoretical speculation. There seems to be less risk in claiming that PDs should display alignments with normal personality traits and then use the observed alignments to specify the details of the target that represents the model. This simple strategy was nevertheless effective and could be used by supporters of other models.

The FFM and Cloninger and Svrakic's (1994) model both provide high levels of fit to the PD data, so it is not surprising that the two models are highly similar. In fact, one configuration can be rotated to align with the other quite closely. The evidence for Cloninger and Svrakic's configuration was nevertheless slightly stronger than the evidence for the FFM dimensions. Further research is obviously required to identify similarities and differences among the two models. Some of the differences between the two targets may account for the slightly different findings. The target for Cloninger and Svrakic's

model was based on clinical respondents who had been through the third edition, revised, of the *DSM* (*DSM-III-R*; American Psychiatric Association, 1987) PD interviews, whereas the FFM target was based on student respondents who completed a self-report measure of PDs. There may also be important breadth-of-measurement differences between Cloninger and Svrakic's measure of basic personality dimensions and the NEO-PI-R measure of the FFM. The NEO-PI-R analyses were based on the five broad domains of the FFM. PDs may be more specific phenomenon that are only roughly tapped by domain scores (Dyce & O'Connor, 1998). Cloninger's measure has been less extensively researched; it could yield slightly stronger findings if it assesses traits at the same level as PDs in the general-versus-specific hierarchy.

One disadvantage with Cloninger and Svrakic's (1994) model is that it provides less differentiation among PDs than does the target based on the FFM. The lack of differentiation has been a long-standing problem in the assessment and diagnosis of PDs. For example, between 67% and 85% of patients who meet the criteria for one PD, using modern assessment instruments, also meet the criteria for at least one other PD (Clark, Livesley, & Morey, 1997; Stuart et al., 1998). In fact, people who meet the criteria for at least one PD typically meet the criteria for three or four PDs (Widiger & Sanderson, 1995, p. 381). There may be genuine comorbidities between PDs, but the observed comorbidity levels are almost certainly excessive and are due, at least in part, to problems in PD conceptualization and assessment. Models of PD configuration that provide more differentiation would therefore be more useful than models that provide less differentiation.

We therefore quantified the degrees of differentiation provided by the FFM and by Cloninger and Svrakic's (1994) model, instead of merely making eyeball judgments of the coefficients in the two target matrices. The quantification procedure involved comparing the target matrix coefficients for each PD with the target matrix coefficients for every other PD. Specifically, the sums of the absolute values of the differences among the target matrix coefficients for pairs of PDs were computed. These sums for the PD-to-PD comparisons represent the degrees of dispersion between the PDs across the multivariate space defined by a given target matrix. There are 10 PDs, which means that a sum for each of 55 PD-to-PD comparisons should be computed. We then calculated the total of the 55 sums to arrive at a total dispersion index for each configuration model. The total degree of dispersion for the FFM configuration was 24% higher than the total dispersion for Cloninger and Svrakic's seven-factor model (the actual values were 79.7 and 64.2). In other words, the additional dispersion provided by the two extra dimensions in Cloninger and Svrakic's matrix still resulted in notably less overall differentiation than that for the FFM. The total degree of dispersion for the four-factor configuration derived from the FFM (as described above) was 57% higher than the total dispersion index for the four-factor model derived from Cloninger and Svrakic's data (the actual values were 71.6 and 45.7). These findings confirm that the FFM provides greater differentiation among PDs than does Cloninger and Svrakic's model.

Unfortunately, the greater differentiation provided by the FFM almost certainly reduced the magnitude of the fit coefficients from the targeted rotations for this model. Least squares deviations from targeted rotations are greater when there are greater discrepancies between elements in a target matrix. One must therefore weigh the slight difference in degrees of support for the two configurations in relation to the more substantial difference in degrees of differentiation that the models provide.

The PD configurations most strongly supported in this review were the two based on attempts to identify basic dimensions of personality existing in both clinical and nonclinical populations. Some clinician psychologists (e.g., Ben-Porath & Waller, 1992; Butcher & Rouse, 1996) have expressed doubts that models of normal personality characteristics are sufficiently comprehensive to incorporate clinical phenomena such as PDs. However, the results of our model testing review indicate that the structures in PD data for both clinical and nonclinical samples are well captured by the FFM and by Cloninger and Svrakic's (1994) model of normal personality characteristics. In fact, models of PD configuration based on clinical speculation (Millon's, 1987, 1990, 1994, 1996, models and the *DSM* clus-

ters) provided lower levels of fit to the PD data than did the models of normal personality characteristics. Furthermore, the PD structures in data from clinical and nonclinical samples are essentially identical. Normal and abnormal personalities (and normal and abnormal personality characteristics) exist in the same universe of basic psychological dimensions. The differences between clinical and nonclinical populations are matters of extremity and degree, at least in the case of PDs.

A TEST OF FIVE-FACTOR MODEL FACET-LEVEL PREDICTIONS

The research above clearly indicates that the representation of the PD dimensions and interrelationships provided by the FFM provides a reasonably accurate representation of the PDs. The focus of our work therefore shifted from broad comparisons of PD configuration models to the more specialized predictions that have been made regarding the FFM and PDs.

There have been numerous reports of associations among PDs and measures of the FFM (Ball, Tennen, Poling, Kranzler, & Rounsaville, 1997; Coolidge et al., 1994; Costa & McCrae, 1990; Duijsens & Diekstra, 1996; Hyer et al., 1994; Lehne, 1994; Soldz et al., 1993; Trull, 1992; Wiggins & Pincus, 1989; Yeung, Lyons, Waternaux, Faraone, & Tsuang, 1993). The findings are surprisingly consistent, especially given the variety of samples (e.g., clinical, community) and methods (interviews, self-reports, expert ratings) used. However, some researchers have claimed that the magnitudes of the overall relationships seem noticeably weaker than the strong claims made by supporters of the FFM and that reducing the various forms of personality pathology to five factors is an oversimplification (Clark, 1993; Coolidge et al., 1994; Schmidt, Wagner, & Kiesler, 1993; Yeung et al., 1993).

The primary retort to these objections is that a distinction should be made between domains and facets of the FFM (Costa & McCrae, 1992, 1995; Widiger & Costa, 1994; Widiger & Trull, 1992). Researchers have thus far measured only the broad, higher order, domain-level aspects of the five dimensions and have not examined PDs in relation to the more numerous lower order facets of each dimension. A focus on facets should increase specificity and discrimination between PDs and provide the richer descriptions preferred by clinicians. For example, on the Neuroticism dimension, paranoid PD individuals may be higher on the hostility facet, whereas schizotypal individuals may be higher on the depression, self-consciousness, and vulnerability facets. Furthermore, analyses at the facet level might reveal stronger relationships because the contribution of any single, important facet is submerged and diluted in broader domain scores (Ashton, Jackson, Paunonen, Helmes, & Rothstein, 1995; Costa & Mc-Crae, 1995).

Specific predictions regarding PDs and facets of the FFM were made by Widiger (1993) and Widiger et al. (1994). They assembled descriptions of *DSM-III-R* PD diagnostic criteria and associated features as well as descriptions of PDs in the clinical literature. They then compared these descriptions with the facets of the FFM assessed by the NEO-PI-R (Costa & McCrae, 1992). We tested the predictions that resulted from these efforts and sought to determine whether facet-level analyses increase the discrimination between PD scores and produce stronger effect sizes. Our methods and results are described below (a more detailed presentation can be found in Dyce & O'Connor, 1998).

Sample and Procedure

The participants (N = 614) were 427 female and 187 male undergraduates solicited from two universities in different regions of Canada. They were predominantly Caucasian, and the average age was 22 years (range = 18–45 years). Participants completed the NEO-PI-R, which provides scores on six facets for each of the Big Five dimensions. Domain scores were computed by summing scores on the relevant facets. Participants also completed the MCMI-III, which provides scores for the 10 official PDs in the *DSM* and four additional PDs (depressive, passive–aggressive, self-defeating, and sadistic). We computed raw PD scale scores derived from the prototypal, nonoverlapping items, which were designed to directly reflect the content of *DSM* criteria (Millon, 1994, p. 1). Participants completed the MCMI-III

and NEO-PI-R individually or in small groups outside of class times.

Results

Preliminary analyses revealed high degrees of similarity between the scale intercorrelations from our sample and those reported in the NEO-PI-R and MCMI-III test manuals. For example, for the NEO-PI-R, the factor loadings for five varimax-rotated principal components derived from correlations between the 30 facet scales were highly congruent with the factor loadings reported by Costa and Mc-Crae (1992, p. 44). The lowest factor congruence coefficient was .95. Similarly, although a factor loading matrix was not published in the manual for the MCMI-III, a comparison of the MCMI scale intercorrelation matrix from our data with the scale intercorrelation matrix from the manual revealed that the two matrices were almost identical. The correlation between the two sets of z-transformed correlations was .98, and the root mean square residual, which is an index of the average difference in size of the coefficients, was very low (.12). In other words, the correlational structure of the measure of PDs was well replicated in our nonclinical sample, which should increase confidence in the generalizability of our facet-level findings to clinical samples.

A joint PCA with varimax rotation was then conducted on the NEO-PI-R facet and MCMI-III PD scale scores. The loadings (see Dyce & O'Connor, 1998, p. 35) indicated that the facets from the same domain of the FFM loaded most strongly on their proper dimensions. The loadings also confirmed that to a considerable degree, the various PDs are different blends of the five dimensions. However, there was minimal differentiation between the depressive and self-defeating PD scores, and there were no high PD loadings for the Openness dimension. There was only one high loading on Conscientiousness, but the dimension is nevertheless important because the high-loading PD scale, obsessive–compulsiveness, did not load strongly on any other dimension.

Pearson correlation coefficients were then computed between the facets and PD scales (see Table 14.8). (There were a small number of missing minus signs in our Table 2 correlations; O'Connor & Dyce, 1998; however, the errors have been corrected in this chapter's Table 14.8.) Widiger et al.'s facet-level predictions are also listed in Table 14.8 for comparison with the obtained correlations. One difficulty in evaluating support for Widiger et al.'s high and low predictions (low implies a negative relationship, not the absence of a relationship) is that they did specify effect sizes. Using statistical significance as the criteria for evaluating support for the predictions required an application of the Bonferonni adjustment of the significance level due to the large number of tests. The adjusted significance level was .0001 (.05/490), which required that correlations be greater than .15 to be significant. Overall support for the predictions was high: 94 of 150 predicted relationships (63%) were significant. At the bottom of each column of correlations in Table 14.8, we report the numbers of significant predictions for each PD. The strongest support emerged for the schizoid, antisocial, borderline, avoidant, passive–aggressive, and sadistic PD predictions, whereas only modest support (in the 50% range) emerged for the narcissistic, dependent, and obsessive–compulsive PD predictions. Also noteworthy is the number of significant but nonpredicted relationships that emerged: The correlations for 123 of the 275 cases (45%) reached significance where no predictions were made.

Another important pattern that can be discerned from the correlations in Table 14.8 is the tendency for domain-level correlations to be roughly similar to the correlations for the strongest facets in each domain. However, this tendency is not completely consistent. When most of the facets in a domain had low correlations for a given PD (e.g., the correlations for Openness) or when the facet correlations had different signs (e.g., the correlations between histrionic PD and facets of Conscientiousness), then the domain-level correlations tended to be weaker and less similar to the strongest facet-level correlations.

Stepwise regressions were also conducted to further evaluate the relative importance of domains and facets to PD scores. Two regression equations were computed for each PD scale: one for the five domains and one for the 30 facets. The predictor-entry significance level was set at .0001 for all equations. The facet equations provided better discrimination between PDs than the domain equations (see Table

14.9). In many cases, at least two facets from a domain were significant predictors, and the important facets from a domain for one PD were generally not the same important facets from that domain for other PDs. For example, Neuroticism was an important domain for most PDs, but the facets of Neuroticism and their relative weights varied across PDs.

This apparent increase in differentiation among PDs provided by facet-level analyses was confirmed by the total dispersion indices (described above) for domains and facets. The dispersion computations in this case were conducted on the Fisher's z-transformed correlation coefficients for the FFM domains and facets. The dispersion index for the facet-level analyses was 360% higher than the dispersion index for the domain-level analyses (the actual values were 584 and 128). Of course, the greater dispersion is based on a sixfold increase in the number of predictors (5 domains vs. 30 facets), but the increase is nevertheless important.

In our original report, we noted that the stepwise regression multiple Rs for the facet equations were only slightly higher than the multiple Rs for the domain equations (Dyce & O'Connor, 1998, p. 41). We therefore concluded that facet-level analyses do not noticeably increase the amount of variance accounted for in PD scores relative to domain-level analyses. However, the analyses on which this finding is based were stepwise regressions with stringent predictor-entry criterion. The variance accounted for issue is more properly addressed by comparing the domain and facet R^2 values derived from regular multiple regressions using all of the predictors. These analyses revealed that the mean R^2 value from regressions predicting PD scores from the five domain scores was .37. The corresponding value for the facet-level analyses was .46, which is 24% higher. Facet-level analyses thus do provide notable, although not large, increases in PD variance accounted for relative to domain-level analyses.

Discussion

Widiger (1993) and Widiger et al. (1994) provided the first and so far only predictions for how PDs might be related to facets of the FFM. Our findings indicated that 63% of their 150 predicted relationships were statistically significant. Widiger et al. did

TABLE 14.8

Pearson Correlations Between Personality Disorder Scores and NEO-PI-R Domain and Facet Scores

Domain and facet	Paranoid Prediction	Paranoid r	Schizoid Prediction	Schizoid r	Schizotypal Prediction	Schizotypal r	Antisocial Prediction	Antisocial r	Borderline Prediction	Borderline r	Histrionic Prediction	Histrionic r	Narcissistic Prediction	Narcissistic r
Neuroticism		40		28		47		12		64		−29		−02
N1: Anxiety	h	29		21	h	34	h/L	−05	H	44		−29		−07
N2: Hostility	H	43	L	22		35	H	26	H	53	H	−11	H	13
N3: Depression		37	L	31	h	47	h	10	H	63	H	−32	h/L	−03
N4: Self-consciousness		32	L	30	H	38	L	−01	H	46		−36	H	−08
N5: Impulsiveness		17		01		26	H	28	H	38		04		09
N6: Vulnerability		23		19	h	34		00	H	48	h	−23	H	−10
Extraversion		−27		−47		−26		−01		−27		61		09
E1: Warmth	l	−35	L	−44	L	−30	—	−19		−30	H	48		−07
E2: Gregariousness	l	−26	L	−46	L	−25		−04	h	−17	h	42		−08
E3: Assertiveness		−08		−23		−10		07	h	−15		43	H	27
E4: Activity		−08		−25		−14		04		−14	h	39		14
E5: Excitement seeking	L	−03	L	−17		−01	H	23		−03	h	36		13
E6: Positive emotions	l	−31	L	−40		−26		−15	h	−34	H	42		−01
Openness to Experience		−13		−12		10		05		01		19		13
O1: Fantasy		−04		−10	H	16		09		07	h	12	H	09
O2: Aesthetics	l	−08		−06		12		−03		−01		11		05
O3: Feelings	l	−05	L	−16	L	07		04		08	H	21		12
O4: Actions	L	−20		−09		−10		00		−14	h	19		03
O5: Ideas		−06		−05	H	05		01		−05	L	12		15
O6: Values		−05		00	h	00		08		08		−01		03
Agreeableness		−44		−21		−27		−46		−31		00		−40
A1: Trust	L	−48		−34	L	−37		−28		−37	h	18		−17
A2: Straightforwardness	L	−34		−11		−25	L	−48		−27	L	−11	L	−36
A3: Altruism		−27		−22		−23	L	−28		−24	L	16	L	−22
A4: Compliance	L	−39	h	−11		−22	L	−39	L	−34		−05		−27
A5: Modesty	l	−13		03		02	L	−25		07		−23	L	−49
A6: Tendermindedness	l	−19		−12		−05	L	−20		−11		06	L	−12
Conscientiousness		−16		−10		−28		−36		−35		08		00
C1: Competence	h	−18		−16		−30		−21		−37	—	21	h	12
C2: Order		00		02		−11		−19		−11		−04		−03
C3: Dutifulness		−04	l	−05		−11	L	−25		−17		02		01
C4: Achievement striving		−11		−12		−20		−20		−25		17	h	07
C5: Self-discipline	l	−24		−13		−30	L	−30	L	−37	L	14		−07
C6: Deliberation		−10		−02		−18	L	−44		−26		−14		−05
Significant predictions	10 of 14		5 of 9		8 of 11		12 of 15		9 of 12		8 of 17		4 of 12	
Significant nonpredictions	7 of 16		10 of 21		11 of 22		4 of 16		9 of 18		9 of 13		2 of 19	

Domain and facet	Avoidant Prediction	Avoidant r	Dependent Prediction	Dependent r	Obsessive–Compulsive Prediction	Obsessive–Compulsive r	Passive–Aggressive Prediction	Passive–Aggressive r	Self-Defeating Prediction	Self-Defeating r	Depressive Prediction	Depressive r	Sadistic Prediction	Sadistic r
Neuroticism		63		55		−14		55		59		72		35
N1: Anxiety	H	49	H	47		00		37		42		61		23
N2: Hostility		40		25		−14	H	57		42	H	48	h	50
N3: Depression	h	63	H	53	h	−13		51	H	62	H	75		28
N4: Self-consciousness	H	62	h	51	h	01		36		48	H	56	l	22
N5: Impulsiveness		22		20	h	−30		30		26		28		25
N6: Vulnerability	H	46	H	53		−15		41	H	48		56		15
Extraversion		−48		−16		−03		−23		−30		−36		−11
E1: Warmth	L/H	−36	h	−01		04		−27		−25		−25		−26
E2: Gregariousness	L	−37		−03	L	−10		−14		−22		−20		−12
E3: Assertiveness	L	−36	L	−31		00		−11		−19		−21		13
E4: Activity	L	−29		−13	H	06		−08		−14		−24	H	00
E5: Excitement seeking	L	−24		−09		−13		−05		−12		−22		09
E6: Positive emotions		−37		−10	l	02		−31	L	−31		−37		−26
Openness to Experience		−12		−12		−15		−13		−04		−05		−10
O1: Fantasy		−06		−05	l	−28		−01		−05		−04		−05
O2: Aesthetics		−03		02		01		−08		06		00		−08
O3: Feelings		−03		03	l	−04		−03		04		09		−01
O4: Actions	L	−26		−22	l	−12		−18		−14		−20		−18
O5: Ideas		−09		−19		−01		−13		−10		−09		−01
O6: Values		01		−04	L	−14		−05		01		05		−04
Agreeableness		−11		12		22		−36		−18		−12		−52
A1: Trust		−33		−12		12	L	−39		−37		−34		−38
A2: Straightforwardness		−05		06		18		−29	L	−15		−05		−45
A3: Altruism		−13	H	11		23		−24	H	−18		−11	L	−35
A4: Compliance		−10	H	14		19	L	−39	L	−15		−19	L	−49
A5: Modesty		20	H	19		09		−04		16		20		−24
A6: Tendermindedness		−02	h	16		11		−14		−04	L	03	L	−22
Conscientiousness		−22		−16		62		−26		−21		−22		−14
C1: Competence		−33		−32		38		−30		−31		−35		−09
C2: Order		−01		00	H	48	L	−05		−01		−04		01
C3: Dutifulness		−10		−02	H	45		−13		−06		−07		−09
C4: Achievement striving		−24	L	−13	H	43	L	−19	L	−15		−17		−10
C5: Self-discipline		−31		−26	H	51	L	−29	L	−27		−30		−21
C6: Deliberation		00		00	H	43		−20		−14		−02		−14
Significant predictions		10 of 10		6 of 11		6 of 15		5 of 6		4 of 8		3 of 4		4 of 6
Significant nonpredictions		8 of 20		7 of 19		5 of 15		12 of 24		11 of 22		17 of 26		11 of 24

Note. Decimals omitted. Correlations >.15 are significant according to the Bonferonni adjustment. NEO-PI-R = Revised NEO Personality Inventory; H, L = high, low, respectively, based on the third edition, revised, of the *Diagnostic and Statistical Manual of Mental Disorders (DSM-III-R)* diagnostic criteria; h, l = high, low, respectively, based on associated features in *DSM-III-R*; **H/h, L/l** = high, low, respectively, based on clinical literature. All predictions are from Widiger et al. (1994).

TABLE 14.9

Stepwise Regression Coefficients for NEO-PI-R Domains and Facets Predicting Personality Disorder Scores

Personality disorder	NEO-PI-R domains (standardized betas)			NEO-PI-R facets (standardized betas)				
Paranoid	.33 N	−.38 A		.28 N2	−.15 E2	−.32 A1		
Schizoid	−.47 E			.20 N3	−.21 E1	−.31 E2		
Schizotypal	.45 N	.18 O	−.22 A	.43 N3	−.17 E2	.18 O2	−.25 A2	
Antisocial	−.40 A	−.28 C		−.40 A2	−.35 C6			
Borderline	.61 N	−.21 A		.59 N3	−.23 A4	−.16 C6		
Histrionic	.61 E			.37 E1	.23 E3	.16 E5	−.14 A5	
Narcissistic	.20 O	−.43 A		−.19 A2	−.41 A5			
Avoidant	.52 N	−.30 E		.39 N3	.31 N4	−.24 E2		
Dependent	.59 N	.22 A		.23 N3	.21 N4	.26 N6	.19 A4	
Obsessive–compulsive	−.17 E	.65 C		−.14 O1	.24 C2	.16 C3	.24 C5	.17 C6
Passive–aggressive (neg.)	.50 N	−.28 A		.36 N2	.32 N3	−.16 A2		
Self-defeating	.59 N			.55 N3	−.16 A1			
Depressive	.68 N	−.13 E		.13 N2	.69 N3			
Sadistic	.27 N	−.47 A		.40 N2	−.32 A2			

Note. NEO-PI-R = Revised NEO Personality Inventory; N = Neuroticism, E = Extraversion, O = Openness to Experience, A = Agreeableness, C = Conscientiousness; neg. = negative. See Table 14.8 to decode the other abbreviations. $p < .0001$ for all coefficients.

not make predictions regarding the magnitudes of their expected effects, and many of the relationships we observed were modest in size. But the many small effects do combine to produce substantial overall effect sizes, which is consistent with the assumption that PDs are different blends of the FFM and its facets. The more impressive combined effects are also due to a large number (123) of significant relationships not predicted by Widiger et al. In our reading, their predictions were not carved in stone. Rather, their apparent intentions were to stimulate research on PDs and facets of the FFM and to provide guidelines and best guesses based on existing knowledge. Some of their hypotheses may have to be revised, and many other relationships may have to be added to the picture, but overall support for the general endeavor is strong.

We expected stronger effect sizes for facet-level analyses on the basis of the assumption that stronger relationships may have remained hidden in the studies in which researchers examined PD–FFM relationships only at the domain level. The findings indicate a notable but modest 24% overall increase in effect size for facet-level relationships over domain-level relationships. Domain-level effects are diluted and fail to represent the importance of some facets in the domain only when a small number of facets from a domain are related to a PD or when the facets from a domain differ in the nature of their relationship with a PD. In other words, only occasionally is it true that domain-level relationships misrepresent and underestimate the importance of a personality dimension to PDs.

A more important finding is that facet-level analyses provide greater discrimination among PDs than domain-level analyses. Two PDs may have roughly the same domain-level relationship with a FFM dimension; but in most cases, either different facets of the dimension were responsible for the similar overall relationship or the relative weights of the facets varied across PDs. More generally, when any two PDs are compared across the five dimensions, facets can be found to distinguish among them. The primary exceptions to this rule are the highly similar facet correlations for two proposed PDs that do not appear in the *DSM-IV* but are measured by the MCMI-III (depressive and self-defeating). However, the stepwise regression analyses revealed at least some discrimination between these two similar PD scales. Facet-level analyses thus substantially increase specificity and discrimination between PDs and provide a basis for the richer descriptions of PDs that are preferred by the FFM critics and clinicians who claim the model is excessively simple.

There is one sense in which the FFM may actually be too complex. When correlations among just PD scores were factor analyzed in other work (see Widiger & Costa, 1994, for a brief review and a list of references), only three or four dimensions are typically found. Furthermore, the number-of-components analyses on the PD correlation matrices described in Table 14.1 revealed even fewer components (typically two or three, as reported above). Five orthogonal PD factors have never been reported in other work, and the fourth factor that has been reported seems to be tentative and weak. Our findings indicate that the FFM dimension Openness to Experience is not strongly represented in PD scores. None of the PD scales loaded strongly on the Openness dimension in our data (see Table 14.6, and Dyce & O'Connor, 1998, p. 35). The same phenomenon can be discerned in reports of domain-level correlations among the FFM and PDs (Ball et al., 1997; Coolidge et al., 1994; Costa & McCrae, 1990; Duijsens & Diekstra, 1996; Hyer et al., 1994; Lehne, 1994; Soldz et al., 1993; Trull, 1992; Wiggins & Pincus, 1989; Yeung et al., 1993).

Watson et al. (1994) also concluded that on the basis of domain-level research, only four factors from the FFM were relevant and that Openness seemed unimportant. However, our findings again indicate the importance of distinguishing among facet- and domain-level findings. The facet-level relationships reported in Table 14.8 indicate that paranoid and avoidant PD scores were associated with lower scores on the actions facet of Openness; schizoid PD scores were associated with lower scores on openness to feelings; and histrionic scores were associated with higher scores on openness to feelings. Thus, whereas broad domain-level analyses indicate a small role for Openness, facet-level relationships on the Openness dimension are useful in providing richer descriptions and finer discriminations among PDs. The relatively few such associations apparently prevent the Openness dimension from appearing important in domain-level analyses.

CONCLUSION

It is our belief that the success of the FFM as a general dimensional model of personality characteristics has generated unrealistically high expectations for the model. These high expectations have, in turn, resulted in misunderstandings and fuel for critics. For example, the findings above strongly suggest that the FFM is a "comprehensive" model. In fact, it seems overly comprehensive, given that fewer than five dimensions exist in PD intercorrelation matrices. However, the danger of the comprehensiveness argument is that it creates the expectation that all or most of the variance in PDs should be accounted for by the five factors, which is clearly far from true. As well, clinicians often seem to think (yet are reluctant to believe themselves) that scores on just five dimensions are supposed to provide comprehensive descriptions of the complex disordered personalities they encounter in their work (Ben-Porath & Waller, 1992; Butcher & Rouse, 1996). This expectation is also not realistic or consistent with the nature of the FFM. Dimensional models, whether of *DSM* clusters or the five factors, were designed to simplify complex worlds. They do so by focusing attention on the small numbers of primary, underlying continuums. There is almost always a loss of richness and detail in these endeavors. The variations in PD scores not captured by dimensional models such as the FFM are scale-specific (and error) variances. These scale-specific variances may provide richness and detail in describing individual PDs, but they are not sufficiently important to constitute "dimensions" that can be identified by modern statistical procedures. It is therefore inappropriate to expect dimensional models to provide richness and detail, when their original purpose was to simplify the complex world created by all the richness and detail in the first place.

The adequacy of the FFM as a configurational model of PDs cannot be evaluated by a reference to percentages of variance accounted for and perhaps not even by a reference to the degrees of differentiation provided among PDs. The adequacy of the FFM can be evaluated by comparisons with other dimensional models and by an assessment of the degrees of fit with real PD data. Our model comparison tests indicated that the FFM was highly successful on both counts. In this context, it was probably even unreasonable to expect facet-level analyses to increase substantially the variance accounted for in PDs or for there to be high levels of differentiation among PDs in these analyses. The ceilings for degrees of differentiation and percentages of accounted for variance are low for dimensional models. The emerging FFM PD findings are thus remarkable.

References

American Psychiatric Association. (1987). *Diagnostic and statistical manual of mental disorders* (3rd ed., rev.). Washington, DC: Author.

American Psychiatric Association. (1994). *Diagnostic and statistical manual of mental disorders* (4th ed.). Washington, DC: Author.

Ashton, M. C., Jackson, D. N., Paunonen, S. V., Helmes, E., & Rothstein, M. G. (1995). The criterion validity of broad factor scales versus specific facet scales. *Journal of Research in Personality, 29*, 432–442.

Ball, S. A., Tennen, H., Poling, J. C., Kranzler, H. R., & Rounsaville, B. J. (1997). Personality, temperament, and character dimensions and the *DSM-IV* personality disorders in substance abusers. *Journal of Abnormal Psychology, 106*, 545–553.

Benjamin, L. S. (1993). *Interpersonal diagnosis and treatment of personality disorders.* New York: Guilford Press.

Ben-Porath, Y. S., & Waller, N. G. (1992). "Normal" personality inventories in clinical assessment: General requirements and the potential for using the NEO Personality Inventory. *Psychological Assessment, 4*, 14–19.

Blashfield, R., Sprock, J., Pinkston, K., & Hodgin, J. (1985). Exemplar prototypes of personality disorder diagnoses. *Comprehensive Psychiatry, 26*, 11–21.

Butcher, J. N., & Rouse, S. V. (1996). Personality: Individual differences and clinical assessment. *Annual Review of Psychology, 47*, 87–111.

Clark, L. A. (1993). Personality disorders: Limitations of the five-factor model. *Psychological Inquiry, 4*, 100–104.

Clark, L. A., Livesley, W. J., & Morey, L. (1997).

Personality disorder assessment: The challenge of construct validity. *Journal of Personality Disorders, 11*, 205–231.

Clark, L. A., Watson, D., & Reynolds, S. (1995). Diagnosis and classification of psychopathology: Challenges to the current system and future directions. *Annual Review of Psychology, 46*, 121–153.

Cloninger, C. R. (1987). A systematic method for clinical description and classification of personality variants. *Archives of General Psychiatry, 44*, 573–588.

Cloninger, C. R., & Svrakic, D. M. (1994). Differentiating normal and deviant personality by the seven-factor personality model. In S. Strack & M. Lorr (Eds.), *Differentiating normal and abnormal personality* (pp. 40–64). New York: Springer.

Coolidge, F. L., Becker, L. A., Dirito, D. C., Durham, R. L., Kinlaw, M. M., & Philbrick, P. B. (1994). On the relationship of the five-factor personality model to personality disorders: Four reservations. *Psychological Reports, 75*, 11–21.

Costa, P. T., Jr., & McCrae, R. R. (1990). Personality disorders and the five-factor model of personality. *Journal of Personality Disorders, 4*, 362–371.

Costa, P. T., Jr., & McCrae, R. R. (1992). *Revised NEO Personality Inventory (NEO-PI-R) and NEO Five-Factor Inventory (NEO-FFI) professional manual.* Odessa, FL: Psychological Assessment Resources.

Costa, P. T., Jr., & McCrae, R. R. (1995). Domains and facets: Hierarchical personality assessment using the Revised NEO Personality Inventory. *Journal of Personality Assessment, 64*, 21–50.

Duijsens, I. J., & Diekstra, R. F. W. (1996). *DSM-III-R* and *ICD-10* personality disorders and their relationship with the Big Five dimensions of personality. *Personality and Individual Differences, 21*, 119–133.

Dyce, J. A., & O'Connor, B. P. (1998). Personality disorders and the five-factor model: A test of facet-level predictions. *Journal of Personality Disorders, 12*, 31–45.

Edgington, E. S. (1995). *Randomization tests.* New York: Marcel Dekker.

Guadagnoli, E., & Velicer, W. (1991). A comparison of pattern matching indices. *Multivariate Behavioral Research, 26*, 323–343.

Horn, J. L. (1967). On subjectivity in factor analysis. *Educational and Psychological Measurement, 27*, 811–820.

Hurley, J. R., & Cattell, R. B. (1962). The Procrustes

program: Producing direct rotation to test a hypothesized factor structure. *Behavioral Science, 7,* 258–262.

Hyer, L., Brawell, L., Albrecht, B., Boyd, S., Boudewyns, P., & Talbert, S. (1994). Relationship of NEO-PI to personality styles and severity of trauma in chronic PTSD victims. *Journal of Clinical Psychology, 50,* 699–707.

Hyler, S. E., & Lyons, M. (1988). Factor analysis of the *DSM-III* personality disorder clusters: A replication. *Comprehensive Psychiatry, 29,* 304–308.

Kass, F., Skodol, A. E., Charles, E., Spitzer, R. L., & Williams, J. B. W. (1985). Scaled ratings of *DSM-III* personality disorders. *American Journal of Psychiatry, 142,* 627–630.

Kiesler, D. J. (1986). The 1982 interpersonal circle: An analysis of *DSM-III* personality disorders. In T. Millon & G. Klerman (Eds.), *Contemporary directions in psychopathology: Toward DSM-IV* (pp. 571–597). New York: Guilford Press.

Kiesler, D. J. (1996). *Contemporary interpersonal theory and research: Personality, psychopathology, and psychotherapy.* New York: Wiley.

Klein, M. H., Benjamin, L. S., Rosenfeld, R., Treece, C., Husted, J., & Greist, J. H. (1993). The Wisconsin Personality Disorders Inventory: Development, reliability, and validity. *Journal of Personality Disorders, 7,* 285–303.

Lehne, G. K. (1994). The NEO-PI and MCMI in the forensic evaluation of sex offenders. In P. T. Costa, Jr., & T. A. Widiger (Eds.), *Personality disorders and the five-factor model of personality* (pp. 175–188). Washington, DC: American Psychological Association.

Livesley, W. J., & Jackson, D. N. (1986). The internal consistency and factorial structure of behaviors judged to be associated with *DSM-III* personality disorders. *American Journal of Psychiatry, 143,* 1473–1474.

McCrae, R. R., Zonderman, A. B., Costa, P. T., Jr., Bond, M. H., & Paunonen, S. V. (1996). Evaluating replicability of factors in the Revised NEO Personality Inventory: Confirmatory factor analysis versus Procrustes rotation. *Journal of Personality and Social Psychology, 70,* 552–566.

Millon, T. (1987). *Manual for the MCMI-II.* Minneapolis, MN: National Computer Systems.

Millon, T. (1990). *Toward a new personology: An evolutionary model.* New York: Wiley.

Millon, T. (1994). *Manual for the MCMI-III.* Minneapolis, MN: National Computer Systems.

Millon, T. (1996). *Disorders of personality:* DSM-IV *and beyond.* New York: Wiley.

Moldin, S. O., Rice, J. P., Erlenmeyer-Kimling, L., & Squires-Wheeler, E. (1994). Latent structure of *DSM-III-R* Axis II psychopathology in a normal sample. *Journal of Abnormal Psychology, 103,* 259–266.

Morey, L. C., Waugh, M. H., & Blashfield, R. K. (1985). MMPI scales for *DSM-III* personality disorders: Their derivation and correlates. *Journal of Personality Assessment, 49,* 245–251.

O'Connor, B. P., & Dyce, J. A. (1998). A test of models of personality disorder configuration. *Journal of Abnormal Psychology, 107,* 3–16.

Paunonen, S. V. (1997). On chance and factor congruence following orthogonal Procrustes rotation. *Educational and Psychological Measurement, 57,* 33–59.

Plutchik, R., & Conte, H. R. (1985). Quantitative assessment of personality disorders. In R. Nickols, J. O. Cavenar, & H. K. H. Brodie (Eds.), *Psychiatry* (Vol. 7, pp. 1–13). Philadelphia: Lippincott.

Romney, D. M., & Bynner, J. M. (1989). Evaluation of a circumplex model of *DSM-III* personality disorders. *Journal of Research in Personality, 23,* 525–538.

Romney, D. M., & Bynner, J. M. (1997). Evaluating a circumplex model of personality disorders with structural equation modeling. In R. Plutchik & H. R. Conte (Eds.), *Circumplex models of personality and emotions* (pp. 327–346). Washington, DC: American Psychological Association.

Schmidt, J. A., Wagner, C. C., & Kiesler, D. J. (1993). *DSM-IV* Axis II: Dimensionality ratings? "Yes"; Big Five? "Perhaps later." *Psychological Inquiry, 4,* 119–121.

Schonemann, P. H. (1966). A generalized solution of the orthogonal Procrustes problem. *Psychometrika, 31,* 1–10.

Soldz, S., Budman, S., Demby, A., & Merry, J. (1993). Representation of personality disorders in circumplex and five-factor model space: Explorations with a clinical sample. *Psychological Assessment, 5,* 41–52.

Stuart, S., Pfohl, B., Battaglia, M., Bellodi, L., Grove, W., & Cadoret, R. (1998). The co-occurrence of *DSM-III-R* personality disorders. *Journal of Personality Disorders, 12,* 302–315.

Svrakic, D. M., Whitehead, C., Przybeck, T. R., & Cloninger, C. R. (1993). Differential diagnosis of personality disorders by the seven-factor model of temperament and character. *Archives of General Psychiatry, 50,* 991–999.

Torgersen, S., & Alnaes, R. (1989). Localizing *DSM-*

III personality disorders in three-dimensional structural space. *Journal of Personality Disorders, 3,* 274–281.

Trull, T. J. (1992). *DSM-III-R* personality disorders and the five-factor model of personality: An empirical comparison. *Journal of Abnormal Psychology, 3,* 553–560.

Watson, D., Clark, L. A., & Harkness, A. R. (1994). Structures of personality and their relevance to psychopathology. *Journal of Abnormal Psychology, 103,* 18–31.

Widiger, T. A. (1993). The *DSM-III-R* categorical personality disorder diagnoses: A critique and an alternative. *Psychological Inquiry, 4,* 75–90.

Widiger, T. A., & Costa, P. T., Jr. (1994). Personality and personality disorders. *Journal of Abnormal Psychology, 103,* 78–91.

Widiger, T. A., & Hagemoser, S. (1997). Personality disorders and the interpersonal circumplex. In R. Plutchik & H. R. Conte (Eds.), *Circumplex models of personality and emotions* (pp. 299–325). Washington, DC: American Psychological Association.

Widiger, T. A., & Kelso, K. (1983). Psychodiagnosis of Axis II. *Clinical Psychology Review, 3,* 491–510.

Widiger, T. A., & Sanderson, C. J. (1995). Assessing personality disorders. In J. N. Butcher (Ed.), *Clinical personality assessment* (pp. 380–394). New York: Oxford University Press.

Widiger, T. A., & Trull, T. J. (1992). Personality and psychopathology: An application of the five-factor model. *Journal of Personality, 60,* 363–393.

Widiger, T. A., Trull, T. J., Clarkin, J. F., Sanderson, C., & Costa, P. T., Jr. (1994). A description of the *DSM-III-R* and *DSM-IV* personality disorders with the five-factor model of personality. In P. T. Costa, Jr., & T. A. Widiger (Eds.), *Personality disorders and the five-factor model of personality* (pp. 41–56). Washington, DC: American Psychological Association.

Widiger, T. A., Trull, T. J., Hurt, S. W., Clarkin, J., & Frances, A. (1987). A multidimensional scaling of the *DSM-III* personality disorders. *Archives of General Psychiatry, 44,* 557–563.

Wiggins, J. S. (1982). Circumplex models of interpersonal behavior in clinical psychology. In P. C. Kendall & J. N. Butcher (Eds.), *Handbook of research methods in clinical psychology* (pp. 183–221). New York: Wiley.

Wiggins, J. S., & Broughton, R. (1991). A geometric taxonomy of personality scales. *European Journal of Personality, 5,* 343–365.

Wiggins, J. S., & Pincus, A. L. (1989). Conceptions of personality disorders and dimensions of personality. *Psychological Assessment: A Journal of Consulting and Clinical Psychology, 1,* 305–316.

Yeung, A. S., Lyons, M. J., Waternaux, C. M., & Faraone, S. V., & Tsuang, M. T. (1993). The relationship between *DSM-III* personality disorders and the five-factor model of personality. *Comprehensive Psychiatry, 34,* 227–234.

Zimmerman, M., & Coryell, W. (1989). *DSM-III* personality disorder diagnoses in a nonpatient sample. *Archives of General Psychiatry, 46,* 682–689.

Zwick, W. R., & Velicer, W. F. (1986). Comparison of five rules for determining the number of components to retain. *Psychological Bulletin, 99,* 432–442.

PART III

PATIENT POPULATIONS AND CLINICAL CASES

PERSONALITY TRAIT CHARACTERISTICS OF OPIOID ABUSERS WITH AND WITHOUT COMORBID PERSONALITY DISORDERS

Robert K. Brooner, Chester W. Schmidt, Jr., and Jeffrey H. Herbst

This chapter examines the relation between normal personality traits and specific Axis II personality disorder diagnoses obtained in a sample of opioid abusers. We describe several personality diagnostic categories of the third edition, revised, of the *Diagnostic and Statistical Manual of Mental Disorders* (*DSM-III-R*; American Psychiatric Association, 1987) from the perspective of the five-factor model (FFM) of personality. First, we compare the personality traits of drug abusers with and without comorbid personality disorder. Second, we examine the personality traits of drug abusers with specific Axis II diagnoses in relation to empirically derived hypotheses regarding the personality traits of these conditions (see Widiger et al., chapter 6, this volume).

Drug abusers typically have higher rates of personality disorder compared with the normal population (Blume, 1989). The prevalence of personality disorder among drug abusers has ranged from 65% to 90%, with antisocial personality disorder (ATS) representing the most frequent diagnosis (Khantzian & Treece, 1985; Kosten, Kosten, & Rounsaville, 1989; Kosten, Rounsaville, & Kleber, 1982; Rounsaville, Weissman, Kleber, & Wilber, 1982). In addition, many drug abusers satisfy the criteria for multiple personality diagnoses. For instance, Kosten et al. (1982) found that 68% of 384 opiate abusers met the *DSM-III-R* criteria for an Axis II disorder, with 24% meeting criteria for two disorders or more. Khantzian and Treece reported similar findings in their study of 133 narcotic abusers. Of these patients, 65% (*n* = 86) satisfied *DSM-III-R*

criteria for at least one personality disorder diagnosis.

Other studies have assessed the personality traits of drug abusers from a dimensional perspective. For example, three studies used the Adjective Check List (ACL) to describe the personality trait characteristics of drug abusers (Craig, 1988; Kilmann, 1974; Sutker, Patsiokas, & Allain, 1981). These studies characterized drug abusers as headstrong, impulsive, competitive, aggressive, and markedly indifferent to the concerns of others. Reith, Crockett, and Craig (1975) used the Edwards Personal Preference Schedule to compare the personality traits of drug-abusing criminal offenders with those of non-drug-abusing offenders. The drug-abusing offenders were significantly more impulsive and aggressive and less persistent in tasks compared with the non-drug-abusing offenders. These studies identified several personality trait dimensions common among drug abusers (e.g., impulsiveness, aggressiveness). However, they provide no information on the relation of drug abuse and Axis II comorbidity to a comprehensive taxonomic framework of normal personality traits.

Brooner, Herbst, Schmidt, Bigelow, and Costa (1993) used the NEO Personality Inventory (NEO-PI; Costa & McCrae, 1985, 1989) to examine comprehensively the normal personality traits of 203 opioid abusers. Patients were diagnostically categorized according to the *DSM-III-R* Axis II conditions into four groups: (a) pure antisocial group (ATS with no additional Axis II diagnosis), (b) mixed antisocial group (ATS plus another Axis II diagnosis),

(c) other Axis II group (Axis II diagnosis other than ATS), and (d) non-Axis II group (no personality disorder). The mixed ATS group had a significantly higher level of Neuroticism compared with the pure ATS group. As suggested in a review article by Alterman and Cacciola (1991), ATS drug abusers with other personality diagnoses were significantly more prone to emotional distress and instability compared with drug abusers with ATS only. Not surprisingly, the mixed ATS group and the other Axis II group both scored higher in Neuroticism than did the non-Axis II group. The mixed ATS group also reported lower levels of Agreeableness (i.e., more interpersonal antagonism) than did the non-Axis II and the other Axis II groups. Finally, no significant group differences were found on the Conscientiousness, Extraversion, or Openness to Experience personality domains.

In this chapter, we further examine the NEO-PI profiles of opioid drug abusers to determine the personality characteristics of several diagnostic subgroups not described in the earlier report (Brooner et al., 1993). First, the mean NEO-PI personality profile of the 203 drug abusers is compared with the NEO-PI normative sample. Second, the personality profiles of drug abusers with no personality disorder diagnosis (non-Axis II group) are compared with those of drug abusers with any Axis II disorder (Axis II group) and with those of the NEO-PI normative sample. Third, the NEO-PI personality profiles of pure ATS, pure avoidant (AVD), pure borderline (BDL), and pure paranoid (PAR) drug abusers are examined in relation to empirically derived hypotheses regarding the personality traits of these conditions (see Widiger et al., chapter 6). Finally, the case history and treatment performance of three drug abusers with ATS, AVD, or BDL are discussed with respect to their standing on normal personality trait dimensions.

As noted earlier, Widiger et al. (chapter 6) characterize the *DSM-IV* personality disorders from the perspective of the FFM. They describe the defining (i.e., core) features and associated features of the Axis II diagnoses in terms of domains and facet scales of the five basic dimensions of normal personality as operationalized by the NEO-PI. Table 15.1 presents an adaptation of this translation of NEO-PI facet scales for Neuroticism, Extraversion, and Openness to Experience and domain scales for Agreeableness and Conscientiousness for specific personality diagnoses that are individually examined in this chapter (i.e., pure ATS, pure AVD, pure BDL, and pure PAR).

The following hypotheses were examined. First, ATS drug abusers would have elevated levels on Hostility, Impulsiveness, and Excitement Seeking of the NEO facet scales and low levels of Agreeableness and Conscientiousness. Associated features of ATS would include high levels of Anxiety and Depression and low levels of Warmth. Second, AVD drug abusers would have high levels of Anxiety, Self-Consciousness, and Vulnerability and low levels of Warmth, Gregariousness, Activity, Excitement Seeking, and Openness to Actions. An associated feature of this disorder would include a high level of depression. Third, BDL drug abusers would have high levels of Anxiety, Hostility, Depression, Impulsiveness, and Vulnerability. Finally, PAR drug abusers would have high levels of Hostility and low levels of Agreeableness (i.e., high interpersonal antagonism). Associated features of PAR would include high levels of Anxiety and low levels of Warmth, Gregariousness, Positive Emotions, Aesthetics, and Feelings.

The data presented are from 203 drug abusers who participated in a longitudinal study of the relation between personality and psychopathology to drug abuse treatment outcome. A detailed description of the study method was presented in an earlier report (Brooner et al., 1993). Briefly, all patients were opioid abusers admitted to an outpatient drug treatment program that incorporated methadone hydrochloride as one component of care. Their mean age was 33.75 years, 46% were male, 67% were White, 26% were employed, and 15% were married and living with their spouse. Information for making *DSM-III-R* Axis II personality diagnoses was derived from the Structured Clinical Interview for *DSM-III-R* (Spitzer, Williams, Gibbon, & First, 1988); personality traits were assessed by the NEO-PI. Both instruments were administered between 22 and 28 days after admission to minimize the possible effects of drug intoxication and withdrawal on patient symptom reports.

TABLE 15.1

Conceptual Relationships Among the *DSM-III-R* Diagnostic Criteria for Antisocial (ATS), Avoidant (AVD), Borderline (BDL), and Paranoid (PAR) Personality Disorders and the Five-Factor Model

NEO-PI scales	ATS	AVD	BDL	PAR
Neuroticism facets				
Anxiety	h	H[a]	H	h
Hostility	H[a]		H[a]	H[a]
Depression	h[a]	h[a]	H[a]	
Self-Consciousness		H[a]		
Impulsiveness	H[a]		H[a]	
Vulnerability		H[a]	H[a]	
Extraversion facets				
Warmth	l[a]	L[a]		l[a]
Gregariousness		L[a]		l
Assertiveness				
Activity		L		
Excitement Seeking	H[a]	L		
Positive Emotions				l
Openness to Experience Facets				
Fantasy				
Aesthetics				
Feelings				l
Actions		l		l
Ideas				
Values				
Agreeableness domain	L[a]			L[a]
Conscientiousness domain	L[a]			

Note. Uppercase letters relate to the defining features of the disorder in the third edition, revised, of the *Diagnostic and Statistical Manual of Mental Disorders* (*DSM-III-R*; American Psychiatric Association, 1987), and lowercase letters relate to associated features in the *DSM-III-R*. H or h indicate high on the trait, and L or l indicate low on the trait. From "A Description of the *DSM-III-R* and *DSM-IV* Personality Disorders With the Five-Factor Model of Personality" (p. 42, Table 1), by T. A. Widiger, T. J. Trull, J. F. Clarkin, C. Sanderson, and P. T. Costa, Jr., in P. T. Costa, Jr., and T. A. Widiger (Eds.), *Personality Disorders and the Five-Factor Model of Personality*, Washington, DC: American Psychological Association, 1994. Copyright 1994 by the American Psychological Association. Adapted with permission. [a]Empirical support for the relationship.

PERSONALITY CHARACTERISTICS OF THE 203 OPIOID ABUSERS

The total sample of 203 opioid abusers differed from the NEO-PI normative sample (Costa & McCrae, 1989) on three of the five personality domains. Drug abusers reported high levels (*T* score range = 55–65) of Neuroticism and low levels (*T* score range = 35–45) of Agreeableness and Conscientiousness compared with the normative sample. They also scored within the high range on three of the six Neuroticism facets (Hostility, Depression, and Vulnerability). Although no group differences were found for the Extraversion domain, drug abusers did

score within the low range of the Warmth facet and within the high range of the Excitement-Seeking facet scale. Finally, drug abusers scored within the low range on Openness to Actions. All other NEO-PI domain and facet scales for drug abusers were comparable with those of the NEO-PI normative sample.

Viewed from this perspective, the FFM of personality characterizes opioid drug abusers as prone to high levels of emotional distress, interpersonal antagonism, and excitement seeking and low levels of conscientiousness. It is important to note that the personality profile obtained in this study is consistent with data reported from other studies of drug abusers, despite the use of different self-report personality instruments.

OVERALL AND SPECIFIC PREVALENCE RATES OF PERSONALITY DISORDER

A personality disorder was present in 37% (76 of 203) of the patients included in this report. This overall rate of personality disorder is obviously lower than reported in other studies (e.g., Khantzian & Treece, 1985). The reason for the relatively low rate of personality disorder obtained in this study is unclear but may be related to methodological differences, patient differences, or both. First, other studies have typically examined patients at the time of admission to treatment, a period when the acute effects of intoxication and withdrawal from brain depressants and brain stimulants may result in greater symptom reporting (including symptoms required for many of the Axis II conditions). Methods for determining Axis II comorbidity among drug abusers have also varied across studies. For example, Khantzian and Treece relied on a standard, non-structured clinical interview to detect personality disorder. In contrast, the data presented here were obtained following the patient's initial stabilization in the treatment program (i.e., 3–4 weeks after admission), and all Axis II diagnoses were based on information derived from a structured clinical interview.

Among the 76 drug abusers who met the criteria for a personality disorder, 32% (24 of 76) met the criteria for two diagnoses or more. Among those with only one Axis II disorder, 28 received a sole diagnosis of (pure) ATS, 8 received a sole diagnosis of (pure) AVD, 5 received a sole diagnosis of (pure) BDL, and 5 received a sole diagnosis of (pure) PAR.

PERSONALITY CHARACTERISTICS OF DRUG ABUSERS WITHOUT AN AXIS II DISORDER COMPARED WITH THOSE IN THE NEO-PI NORMATIVE SAMPLE

The profile of the 127 nonpersonality disordered opioid abusers was compared with those of subjects in the NEO-PI normative sample (Costa & McCrae, 1989). As shown in Figure 15.1, drug abusers without an Axis II diagnosis (solid line) differed from subjects in the normative sample on both the Agreeableness and Conscientiousness domains. With respect to the NEO-PI facet scales, the only prominent elevation occurred on the Excitement-Seeking facet scale of Extraversion. In terms of experiential style, drug abusers appeared somewhat set in their ways (low Openness to Actions scale). Interestingly, drug abusers without a personality disorder obtained Neuroticism domain and facet scores that were quite similar to those found in the NEO-PI normative sample. Thus, drug abusers without a personality diagnosis were not highly prone to emotional distress or instability.

PERSONALITY CHARACTERISTICS OF DRUG ABUSERS WITH VERSUS WITHOUT AN AXIS II DIAGNOSIS

Table 15.2 compares the mean NEO-PI domain and facet T scores of the drug abusers without an Axis II disorder (i.e., non-Axis II group; $n = 127$) with those of the drug abusers with at least one Axis II disorder (i.e., Axis II group; $n = 76$). The personality profiles of the two groups are shown in Figure 15.1. A two-group multivariate analysis of variance (MANOVA) including the five NEO-PI domains indicated significant group differences, $T^2 = 0.213$, $F(5, 197) = 8.38$, $p < .001$. Examination of the univariate effects indicated that the Axis II group scored significantly higher on Neuroticism, $F(1, 201) = 25.47$, $p < .001$, and lower on Agreeableness, $F(1, 201) = 21.93$, $p < .001$, and Conscientiousness, $F(1, 201) = 9.72$, $p < .01$, than did the non-Axis II group. In fact, the Axis II group scored within the very low range of the Agreeableness domain ($T = 32.4$). Thus, Axis II comorbidity in drug abusers was generally related to having a strong disposition toward emotional distress and instability, high interpersonal antagonism and mistrust, and low motivation and cooperativeness.

A two-group MANOVA including the six facet scales of Neuroticism also revealed significant group differences, $T^2 = 0.17$, $F(6, 196) = 5.58$, $p < .001$. Univariate analyses showed that the Axis II group scored significantly higher than did the non-Axis II group on all six facet scales of Neuroticism: Anxiety, $F(1, 201) = 8.08$, $p < .01$; Hostility, $F(1, 201) =$

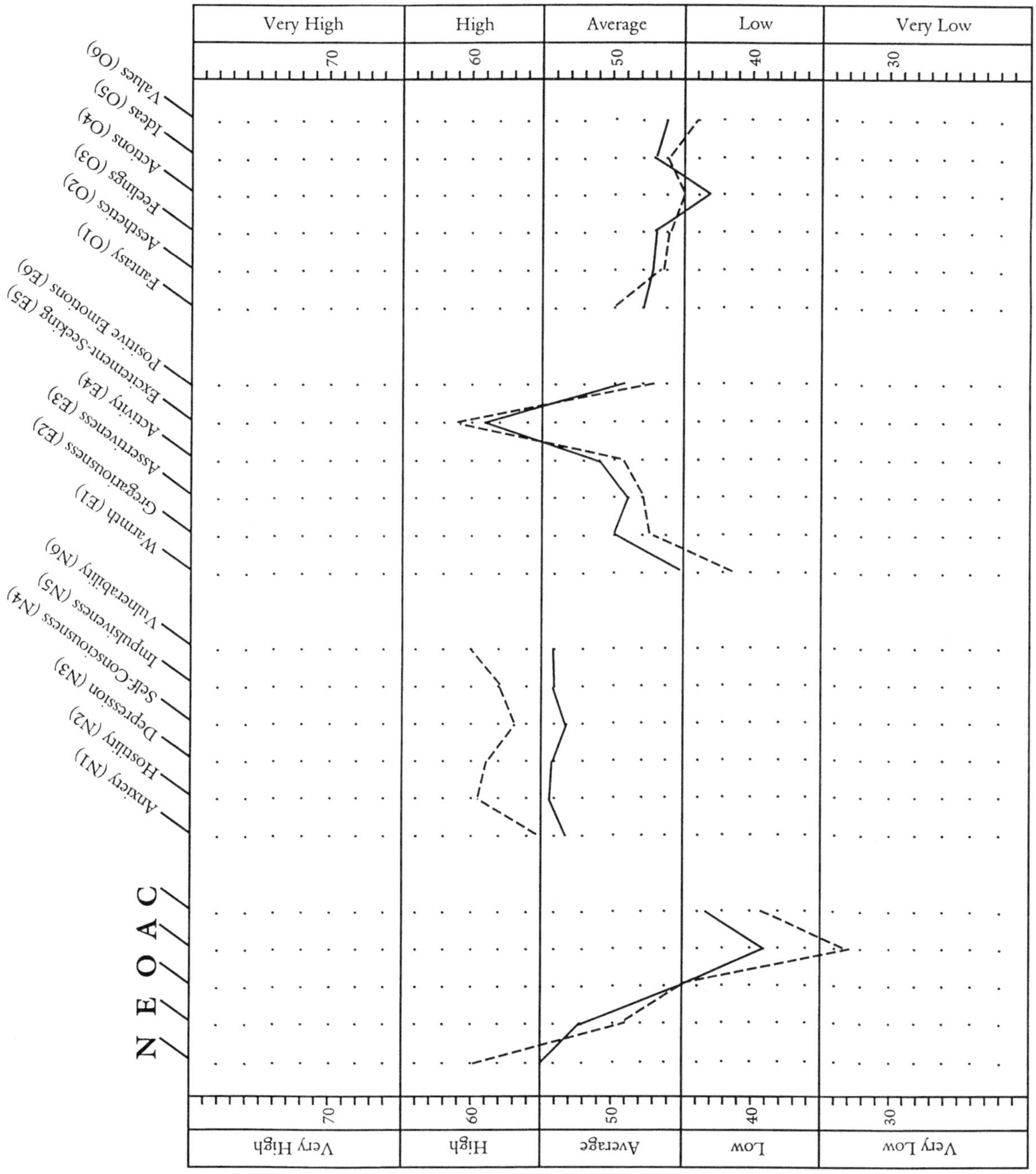

FIGURE 15.1. NEO Personality Inventory (NEO-PI) profile of 127 opioid abusers with no Axis II disorder (solid line) and 76 opioid abusers with an Axis II disorder (broken line). N = Neuroticism; E = Extraversion; O = Openness to Experience; A = Agreeableness; C = Conscientiousness. From the *NEO Personality Inventory*, by P. T. Costa, Jr., and R. R. McCrae, Copyright 1978, 1985, 1989, 1992 by PAR, Inc. Further reproduction is prohibited without permission of PAR, Inc. Reproduced by special permission of the publisher, Psychological Assessment Resources, Inc., 16204 North Florida Avenue, Lutz, FL 33549.

TABLE 15.2

NEO Personality Inventory (NEO-PI) Domain and Facet *T* Scores (*M* ± *SD*) for Opioid Abusers With and Without Personality Disorder Diagnoses

Domain and facet	No Axis II disorder (*N* = 127)		Any Axis II disorder (*N* = 76)	
	M	**SD**	**M**	**SD**
NEO-PI domains				
Neuroticism	54.6	7.8	60.3	7.5
Extraversion	50.7	6.9	48.6	8.8
Openness to Experience	44.9	8.1	45.0	7.7
Agreeableness	39.2	9.7	32.4	10.2
Conscientiousness	42.8	8.3	38.9	8.8
Neuroticism facets				
Anxiety	52.1	7.3	55.2	7.6
Hostility	54.4	8.2	59.6	8.7
Depression	54.2	9.1	58.4	8.4
Self-consciousness	52.6	7.4	56.6	7.7
Impulsiveness	54.0	8.2	57.1	7.4
Vulnerability	54.1	8.9	60.3	11.0
Extraversion facets				
Warmth	45.4	8.6	40.9	10.9
Gregariousness	49.7	8.8	47.4	9.5
Assertiveness	48.6	7.6	47.7	8.3
Activity	50.3	6.7	48.9	8.0
Excitement seeking	58.6	8.7	61.1	7.9
Positive emotions	49.3	7.5	47.0	8.4
Openness facets				
Fantasy	48.2	6.7	50.3	7.3
Aesthetics	47.5	9.1	47.2	9.4
Feelings	47.3	9.2	46.5	8.3
Actions	43.2	7.5	45.0	8.3
Ideas	47.0	7.6	46.6	8.7
Values	46.0	8.2	43.9	7.0

18.3, $p < .01$; Depression, $F(1, 201) = 10.74$, $p < .01$; Self-Consciousness, $F(1, 201) = 13.80$, $p < .01$; Impulsiveness, $F(1, 201) = 7.24$, $p < .01$; and Vulnerability, $F(1, 201) = 19.48$, $p < .01$.

A two-group MANOVA including the six facet scales of Extraversion also indicated significant group differences, $T^2 = 0.12$, $F(6, 196) = 3.81$, $p < .01$. The Axis II group scored higher on Excitement Seeking, $F(1, 201) = 4.29$, $p < .05$, and lower on Warmth, $F(1, 201) = 10.63$, $p < .01$, and Positive Emotions, $F(1, 201) = 3.90$, $p < .05$, than did the non-Axis II group. Finally, a two-group MANOVA, $T^2 = 0.07$, $F(6, 196) = 2.27$, $p < .05$, including the six facet scales of Openness to Experience also

showed significant group differences. The Axis II group scored higher on Openness to Fantasy, $F(1, 201) = 4.04$, $p < .05$, than did the non-Axis II group.

In short, these data provide further information concerning the impact of Axis II comorbidity on normal personality traits in drug abusers. The pattern of group differences on the NEO-PI facet scales of Neuroticism, Extraversion, and Openness to Experience show clearly that having both a drug abuse and a personality disorder diagnosis is associated with a pervasive tendency toward marked emotional distress and instability, very low interpersonal warmth, and low positive emotions compared with drug abusers in the non-Axis II group. High distress among drug abusers in this study was characteristic only of those who received a personality disorder diagnosis. Both the non-Axis II and the Axis II groups were prone to high excitement seeking, high interpersonal antagonism and mistrust (i.e., low Agreeableness), and high disregard for established social rules and conventions (i.e., low Conscientiousness). In general, this finding indicates that high excitement seeking, low Agreeableness, and low Conscientiousness are FFM personality traits characteristic of opioid drug abusers.

PERSONALITY CHARACTERISTICS OF DRUG ABUSERS WITH PERSONALITY DISORDER DIAGNOSES

We subsequently examined the hypotheses generated from Widiger et al.'s (chapter 6) translation of the *DSM-IV* criteria using the FFM (see Table 15.1). Specifically, the mean *T* scores for the NEO-PI domains and facets were determined for the 28 pure ATS drug abusers, 8 pure AVD drug abusers, 5 pure BDL drug abusers, and 5 pure PAR drug abusers drawn from the original sample of 203 patients (see Figure 15.2); statistical comparisons were not made given the small sample size in each of the groups.

The personality profiles presented in Figure 15.2 illustrate some of the similarities and differences in the personality characteristics among the four Axis II groups. For example, the ATS, AVD, and BDL groups scored in the high range on the Neuroticism domain, whereas PAR patients scored within the average range of the domain. On the Extraversion domain, the BDL group scored higher than did the ATS and PAR groups, and each of these groups scored higher than did the AVD group. There were no apparent group differences on the Openness to Experience domain; each scored in the low–average to low range. Finally, all four groups scored within the low to very low range of Agreeableness and within the low range of Conscientiousness. These findings indicate that the interpersonal style of the drug abusers with an Axis II disorder, regardless of the specific diagnosis, was highly antagonistic with a tendency to be suspicious, uncooperative, and

manipulative. They also had strong patterns of unconscientiousness, irresponsibility, and disorganized behavior. The personality traits of each group are discussed in the following sections in relation to the expected findings generated by the FFM translation of these Axis II diagnoses (see Table 15.1).

Pure ATS Drug Abusers

As noted earlier, the defining personality features of the ATS diagnosis were predicted to include high scores on Hostility, Impulsiveness, and Excitement-Seeking facets and low scores on Agreeableness and Conscientiousness domains. Associated features of the diagnosis were expected to include high scores on Anxiety and Depression and low scores on Warmth. In contrast to these expected associated features, the clinical literature indicates that ATS patients would score low on both the Anxiety and Depression facet scales (Brooner et al., 1993; and Widiger et al., 1994).

Consistent with these predictions, the ATS group obtained high scores on the Hostility and Impulsiveness facets of Neuroticism, high scores on the Excitement-Seeking facet of Extraversion, very low scores on the Agreeableness domain, and low scores on the Conscientiousness domain. Each of the defining features of this disorder was present among the group. They also showed slight elevations on the Depression and Vulnerability facets of Neuroticism, a pattern of scores that was somewhat consistent with the associated features of ATS. In fact, Widiger et al. (chapter 6) reported that the profile obtained by this group was especially evident among ATS patients seeking treatment.

In contrast to the expected personality profile, the ATS group reported levels of Anxiety, which were consistent with the clinical literature. Also their high scores on Vulnerability were unexpected. Nonetheless, the basic profile of this group was remarkably similar to the hypothesized findings, despite the fact that all ATS patients also had a chronic drug abuse disorder that had a clear impact on personality. In fact, the ATS group obtained the lowest Agreeableness score of any group. This finding is likely to reflect the combined contribution of the personality disorder and the drug dependence on this aspect of normal personality.

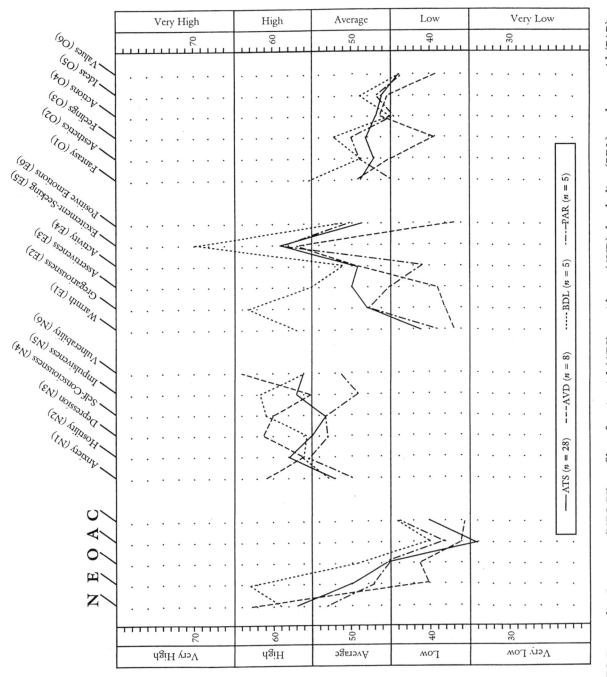

FIGURE 15.2. NEO Personality Inventory (NEO-PI) profiles of antisocial (ATS), avoidance (AVD), borderline (BDL), and paranoid (PAR) personality disordered opioid abusers. N = Neuroticism; E = Extraversion; O = Openness to Experience; A = Agreeableness; C = Conscientiousness. From the *NEO Personality Inventory*, by P. T. Costa, Jr., and R. R. McCrae, Copyright 1978, 1985, 1989, 1992 by PAR, Inc. Further reproduction is prohibited without permission of PAR, Inc. Reproduced by special permission of the publisher, Psychological Assessment Resources, Inc., 16204 North Florida Avenue, Lutz, FL 33549.

Pure AVD Drug Abusers

Briefly, the defining features of AVD are expected to include high Anxiety, Self-Consciousness, and Vulnerability and low Warmth, Gregariousness, Activity, Excitement Seeking, and Openness to Actions. In addition, AVD patients were expected to score high on Depression as an associated feature of the disorder.

This group also produced a NEO-PI profile that was consistent with both the predicted defining and associated features of the disorder. With respect to the defining features, they obtained high scores on the Neuroticism facets of Anxiety, Self-Consciousness, and Vulnerability and low scores on the Extraversion facets of Warmth and Gregariousness. In addition, they had the associated characteristic of high Depression in their personality profiles and low Assertiveness consistent with clinical impression.

The high Hostility and Excitement Seeking and low Agreeableness and Conscientiousness scores were not predicted for the AVD diagnosis. As noted earlier, the high scores on these traits may reflect the independent contribution of chronic drug abuse on personality style.

Pure BDL Drug Abusers

The defining features of this group were expected to include high scores on each of the Neuroticism facets except Self-Consciousness. Associated features of the disorder were expected to include high scores on Gregariousness, Assertiveness, and Excitement Seeking. In fact, the BDL group scored within the high range on each of the six facets of Neuroticism, except Anxiety. They also had high scores on the associated features of Gregariousness and Excitement Seeking.

Although a high level of Self-Consciousness among BDL patients was not predicted, clinical impression indicates that these patients are prone to experience strong feelings of inferiority and embarrassment (Widiger et al., 1994). Finally, low Agreeableness and Conscientiousness scores of these patients were consistent with having a chronic drug use disorder.

Pure PAR Drug Abusers

The PAR group was predicted to score high on Hostility and low on Agreeableness. Associated features

of the diagnosis were expected to include high scores on Anxiety and low scores on Warmth, Gregariousness, Positive Emotions, and Openness to Aesthetics and Feelings.

This group also produced a personality profile consistent with the defining features of the PAR diagnosis. Specifically, they scored high on Hostility and low on Agreeableness. They also scored low on Warmth and Activity and high on Excitement Seeking. Based on this profile, PAR drug abusers are easily frustrated and prone to react with anger. They do not have close emotional ties and are typically mistrusting of others. They are slow and deliberate in their actions and crave excitement, stimulation, and thrills. Although high Excitement Seeking and low Conscientiousness were not predicted for those with a PAR diagnosis, both are characteristic of this drug abusing population.

TREATMENT IMPLICATIONS

All of the drug abusers in the study, including those with an Axis II diagnosis, obtained low scores on the Agreeableness and Conscientiousness personality domains. According to Miller (1991), patients who are disagreeable and unconscientious pose a major challenge for the therapist. Disagreeable or antagonistic patients tend to be skeptical of the therapist and have problems forging an effective therapeutic alliance. Thus, patients who are extremely disagreeable may be at the greatest risk of treatment dropout or premature discharge. Similarly, unconscientious patients are likely to resist treatment plans that are highly structured, particularly if intensive in nature. Recognition of these personality dynamics is important in predicting the patient's general reaction to treatment and in improving the therapist's understanding of the problem and response to the patient's disruptive behaviors. Clinical impression has led many to argue that clear and consistent limit setting is an essential aspect to treating drug abusers. The data reviewed here clearly support that impression. Furthermore, some drug abusers are more antagonistic and disorganized than others. Identification of the highly antagonistic and disorganized patient can assist treatment providers in quickly establishing reasonable therapeutic goals and an appropriate level of limit setting within the treatment plan. The failure to recognize these aspects of personality in the treatment of drug abusers may reduce treatment effectiveness and may increase the likelihood of premature discharge.

Drug abusers with a personality disorder clearly pose a special challenge for both research and clinical practice. Not only do these patients experience the severe and pervasive problems associated with a drug use disorder, but many of these problems are exacerbated by the presence of a personality disorder (Kosten et al., 1989). Recognition of the special problems associated with the care of the dually diagnosed drug abuser is important. It is especially critical to establish reasonable therapeutic goals and target dates for their achievement that will support treatment retention and enhance clinical outcomes. For example, cessation of drug use is a primary and early goal of drug abuse treatment. In fact, the success of this goal is generally seen as essential to addressing the employment, relationship, emotional, and legal problems common among drug abusing patients. Cessation of drug use early in the course of treatment may be an appropriate clinical expectation for many drug abusers who are not challenged further by a personality disorder. However, applying the same expectation to patients with a personality disorder may result in multiple failures early in treatment that may negatively affect the therapeutic process and contribute to lower rates of retention.

It has also been shown that patients with high levels of emotional distress are more motivated to enter and remain in treatment compared with those with little or no distress (Miller, 1991; Woody, McLellan, Luborsky, & O'Brien, 1985). This may be particularly critical in the care of personality disordered drug abusers. In our study, the AVD, BDL, and ATS groups scored within the high range of Neuroticism.

Although high Neuroticism may improve motivation for treatment, Miller (1991) labeled the combination of high Neuroticism, low Extraversion, and low Conscientiousness the "misery triad," often associated with a poor treatment prognosis in nondrug abusing clinical populations. The combination of these traits is especially evident in the personality profile of the AVD group. The AVD abusers were

characterized by high Neuroticism and low Extraversion, Openness, Agreeableness, and Conscientiousness scores. Their low level of Extraversion may be especially detrimental to treatment outcome. Many therapies require active involvement in the therapeutic process and the patients' hope that the therapist can help them. Introversion may negatively affect both of these dimensions in therapy. In addition, the low Openness characteristic of the AVD drug abusers suggests a rigid experiential style associated with low levels of curiosity.

Although standard drug abuse counseling provides some benefits to personality disordered drug abusers, specialized interventions may improve their treatment outcomes. In fact, knowledge about the personality dynamics of drug abusers with AVD or other personality disorder diagnoses may be useful in selecting specialized forms of treatment. For example, Miller (1991) suggested that behavioral interventions or cognitive–behavioral therapy may be particularly useful for patients with the misery triad. Other research with drug abusers provides some support for this therapeutic approach. Woody et al. (1985) showed that drug abusers with high levels of psychiatric distress had better clinical outcomes when they received both standard counseling and cognitive–behavioral therapy compared with a group that received standard counseling only. They also found significant differences in the treatment outcomes of ATS drug abusers with or without a diagnosis (lifetime or current) of major depression. The depressed ATS drug abusers had better outcomes than did the nondepressed group when cognitive therapy was added to standard counseling. Similarly, Kadden, Cooney, Getter, and Litt (1989) reported that "sociopathic" alcoholics who received behavioral coping skills training had lower rates of relapse to alcohol use over a 26-week period than did those who received interactional therapy.

In summary, each of the personality disordered groups considered in this chapter experienced low levels of Agreeableness and Conscientiousness. As noted earlier, patients with these traits may have better clinical outcomes when the treatment plan is clear and consistent and incorporates firm behavioral controls. The recognition of the special problems of these patients should also be reflected in the development of treatment goals that enhance rather than reduce retention in therapy. Finally, existing data suggest that enhancing the standard care of these patients by adding specialized forms of behavioral treatment may also improve both retention and clinical outcomes.

CLINICAL CASE REPORTS

In concluding this chapter, we present three case histories to illustrate the usefulness of the FFM in delineating the personality trait characteristics of drug abusers with specific personality diagnoses. One case was selected from each of the ATS, BDL, and AVD groups after reviewing the personality profiles of all patients in each group. The selected cases were chosen because they represented strong examples of the personality profile predicted for the diagnosis.

Each clinical report reviews the relevant case history, the NEO-PI personality profile, and two measures of 3-month treatment performance. The first treatment outcome measure is the Addiction Severity Index (ASI; McLellan, Luborsky, Woody, & O'Brien, 1980). The ASI is a semistructured interview designed to assess problem severity in seven areas commonly associated with alcohol and drug dependence: medical, legal, drug, alcohol, employment, family, and psychiatric. Scores can range from 0.00 to 1.00, with higher scores reflecting greater problem severity. A comparison of scores obtained at Month 1 and Month 3 of treatment is made to assess changes in problem severity across each of the ASI domains. The second measure involves urinalysis drug test records. All urine specimens were collected on a random basis using direct observation techniques to minimize falsified urine samples. The percentage of urine samples positive for drug and alcohol is shown.

Case Report 1: ATS Opioid Abuser

Rick was a 41-year-old married White man who was admitted for treatment of opioid dependence. Rick's family history was remarkable for alcohol and drug problems in his father and two of four brothers. He described his childhood as being "very" traumatic. Rick's father reportedly murdered his mother when he was "very young" and physically abused him. He was separated from his brothers and placed in foster care following his mother's death. Over the years, he was moved to several foster care homes because of severe behavior problems. He was frequently truant from school, was suspended on several occasions for truancy and fighting, and finally quit school after completing the eighth grade. He began working at age 14 as a bricklayer and had numerous jobs lasting for less than 1 year. Although employed as a bricklayer for the past 5 months, he reported missing "lots" of work because of his drug use.

Rick was married twice, first at age 17. His first marriage ended in divorce after 2 years. He had had multiple extramarital relationships and stated that the marriage had failed because both he and his wife were "too young." At age 26, he married a nurse, who provided the majority of the family's financial support. Although he reported repeated extramarital relationships over the past 15 years, he described his marriage as stable and sexually satisfying.

His legal history included four arrests and numerous illegal behaviors that escaped detection (i.e., robbery and sale of drugs). He was first arrested at age 17 for robbing a bar. Each of his subsequent arrests involved possession of illegal substances. He served a 1-year prison sentence for possession of speed and marijuana and an 18-month prison sentence for possession of heroin. At the time of his admission to the outpatient drug treatment program, Rick was on a 1-year unsupervised probation for possession of marijuana.

Rick denied any significant medical history and chose not to be HIV-1 tested, despite frequent sharing of needles and a history of unprotected sex with multiple partners. His admission history and physical was unremarkable. His social life was relatively barren; he denied having any close friends, hobbies, or recreational interests. In fact, he described himself as "selfish" in his interpersonal relationships and "unmotivated" to set any goals except to "try and stay alive." He began using alcohol on a daily basis at age 16, marijuana at age 18, and stimulants and sedatives at age 20. At age 21, he began intravenous heroin use and by age 30 cocaine use. His first treatment for drug abuse occurred at age 20. Since then, he reported having more than 10 episodes of treatment, usually at different programs, and viewed all of them as unsuccessful. He denied other psychiatric problems or treatment. On a mental state examination, he was fully oriented, and his talk was both logical and directed. His mood was euthymic, and he was negative for delusions, hallucinations, true obsessions or compulsions, and phobias.

Rick's personality profile is presented in Figure 15.3. Compared with the NEO-PI normative sample, Rick scored in the average ranges of Neuroticism, Extraversion, and Openness. He scored in the low range of Agreeableness and in the very low range of Conscientiousness.

Rick's low level of Agreeableness indicated marked interpersonal antagonism and an egocentric, critical, and mistrusting view of others. His extremely low standing on the Conscientiousness domain indicated very little concern about day-to-day responsibilities and little self-discipline. Both the low Agreeableness and very low Conscientiousness are consistent with a diagnosis of ATS and of a drug abuse disorder. These traits were also consistent with many aspects of his early history (e.g., frequent truancy and fighting, school suspensions, and multiple foster care placements) and his adult behaviors (frequent marital infidelity, unstable work history, criminal activities, lack of friends, and no life goals). He reported using any means possible to obtain drugs (e.g., "dealing" and forging prescriptions). His poor drug abuse treatment history may also have been associated with his low Agreeableness and extremely low Conscientiousness.

More detailed information on Rick's personality characteristics was provided by an examination of his NEO-PI facet scores. Specifically, he scored in the high range on the Self-Consciousness and Impulsiveness facet scales of Neuroticism and in the low range on the Anxiety facet scale. We can speculate that his elevated concern over how others perceive him was associated with an effort to present himself well. This is somewhat consistent with his demonstrated ability to attract numerous female sexual partners despite his infidelity and antagonism, obtain multiple jobs despite a very poor work history, and receive unsupervised probation despite an extensive arrest history. His high impulsiveness al-

most certainly contributed to his continued drug use and poor responses to treatment and many life problems (e.g., employment problems). Regardless of the nature or severity of his life problems, his average score on the Anxiety facet scale indicated very little concern or worry.

Rick's scores on the Extraversion facets also provide details that help in understanding the relation of personality disorder diagnosis to personality characteristics and life history. His low interpersonal warmth clearly contributed to his lack of close friends and may have been associated with his poor treatment history. It is interesting that although he clearly preferred to remain formal and distant in his emotional relationships with others, he had maintained a 15-year relationship with his wife. However, he acknowledged chronic problems in the relationship and multiple episodes of extramarital affairs. In light of this, one could speculate that his wife provided the stability and support (including financial) to sustain the marriage. His high level of Excitement Seeking was consistent with both his ATS and drug-dependence diagnoses and with his criminal behaviors and extramarital relationships. Finally, on the facets of Openness to Experience, he scored low on Fantasy and high on Feelings. This pattern of scores indicated a very limited imagination and a strong belief in the value of his emotional experience.

Given Rick's personality profile, we expected a poor treatment prognosis, particularly given only standard drug abuse counseling. This prognosis was supported by the results of his first 3 months of treatment. On the ASI, Rick reported increased drug use and family and social problems compared with baseline scores. Although he also reported fewer legal and employment problems, these changes were probably related to his being on unsupervised probation and having slightly improved work attendance. He reported no changes in medical problems, alcohol use, or psychiatric problems. The results of urine drug tests during the first 3 months of treatment clarified his self-reported increase in drug use. Of the eight urine specimens provided, six (75%) were positive for drug use. Specifically, five of the six specimens were positive for morphine and two were positive for cocaine.

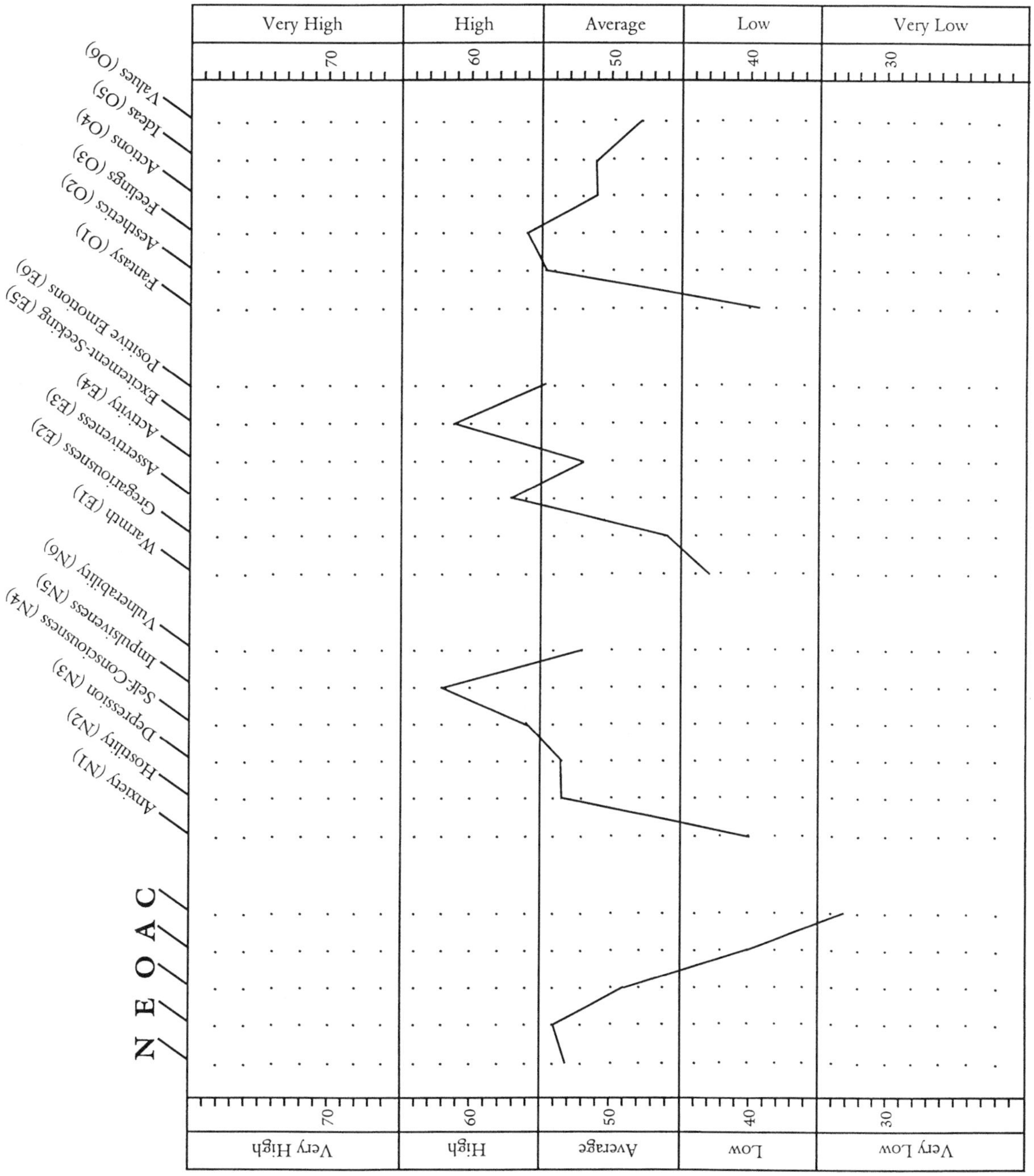

FIGURE 15.3. NEO Personality Inventory (NEO-PI) profile of Rick, a pure antisocial personality disordered (ATS) abuser. N = Neuroticism; E = Extraversion; O = Openness to Experience; A = Agreeableness; C = Conscientiousness. From the *NEO Personality Inventory*, by P. T. Costa, Jr., and R. R. McCrae, Copyright 1978, 1985, 1989, 1992 by PAR, Inc. Further reproduction is prohibited without permission of PAR, Inc. Reproduced by special permission of the publisher, Psychological Assessment Resources, Inc., 16204 North Florida Avenue, Lutz, FL 33549.

Case Report 2: AVD Opioid Abuser

Persephone was a 22-year-old single White woman who was admitted for treatment of opioid dependence. At the time of admission, she was 4 months pregnant with her third child. Persephone's family history was significant for alcohol and drug problems in both parents and her two siblings. In fact, her parents had both been treated for substance abuse, with her father having multiple treatment episodes. Persephone was born prematurely, only weighing 3 pounds at birth. The first 3 months of her life were spent in the hospital for treatment of bronchial pneumonia and other medical complications. She reported an otherwise healthy childhood but attained developmental milestones later than expected. For example, she began walking at 3 years of age. The family had chronic, severe financial problems and moved frequently during her childhood. The parents separated when Persephone was 11 years old. A maternal uncle began living with them but was removed after attempting to rape her. The mother married a second time to an opioid drug abuser who had been in several different treatment programs.

Persephone's school history was remarkable for frequent truancy and several failed years, and she dropped out after she completed the seventh grade. She reported "good" relationships with teachers but was "a loner" and had frequent fights with peers. She had a very limited work history. Her only job had been that of a house painter at age 19. She quit this job after several months because of "child care problems" and no "motivation." She had relied on social services and her boyfriend for financial support. Her legal history was negative for any arrests.

Persephone had become sexually active at age 14 and reported having had a total of three sexual partners, including her present boyfriend with whom she had been with for 8 years. In fact, this boyfriend was also the father of her two children (4 and 6 years old) and her unborn baby. She had her first child at age 16 and her second child at age 18. The boyfriend was a truck driver who abused heroin and other drugs and had one brief unsuccessful treatment episode. Although she reported that their relationship was "good," they argued frequently, and he had physically abused her on several occasions.

Persephone's medical history was unremarkable, and her admission history and physical was normal. Her social life had been extremely limited. She denied having friends with the exception of her boyfriend, had no "social life," and had no specific life goals. In fact, she reported being unable to "imagine" what goals to even set. She began using heroin at the age of 20 when her boyfriend "talked me into doing it with him." The drug abuse history was otherwise negative, with the exception of "social drinking." Prior to admission, she reported 1 year of continuous heroin use, ranging from three times a day to "as much as I could get." This was her first drug abuse treatment episode. She denied a history of other psychiatric treatment. On a mental state examination, she was fully oriented, and her talk was both logical and directed. She reported recurrent brief periods of anxiety, irritability, and depression but denied problems with self-attitude or vital sense and was negative for thoughts of self-harm. She was also negative for delusions, hallucinations, obsessions or compulsions, or phobias.

Persephone's personality profile is presented in Figure 15.4. Compared with the NEO-PI normative sample, Persephone scored in the high range of Neuroticism; the low ranges of Extraversion, Openness, and Conscientiousness; and the very low range of Agreeableness.

Her high Neuroticism and low Extraversion scores indicated a tendency toward emotional distress and instability combined with considerable introversion. The low Openness to Experience score indicated that she was extremely closed to new experiences. Her very low Agreeableness and low Conscientiousness scores pointed to a great deal of interpersonal antagonism and mistrust and an absence of structure, direction, or life goals. The high Neuroticism and low Extraversion scores were both consistent with the conceptual formulation of the AVD diagnosis. These personality traits were also consistent with several aspects of her life (e.g., recurring dysphoria, lack of friends, and lack of social interest). The low Openness to Experience score was somewhat surprising but was perhaps generally related to her lack of formal education. It was certainly consistent with her poor academic performance and her inability to imagine what she might "do in life." In

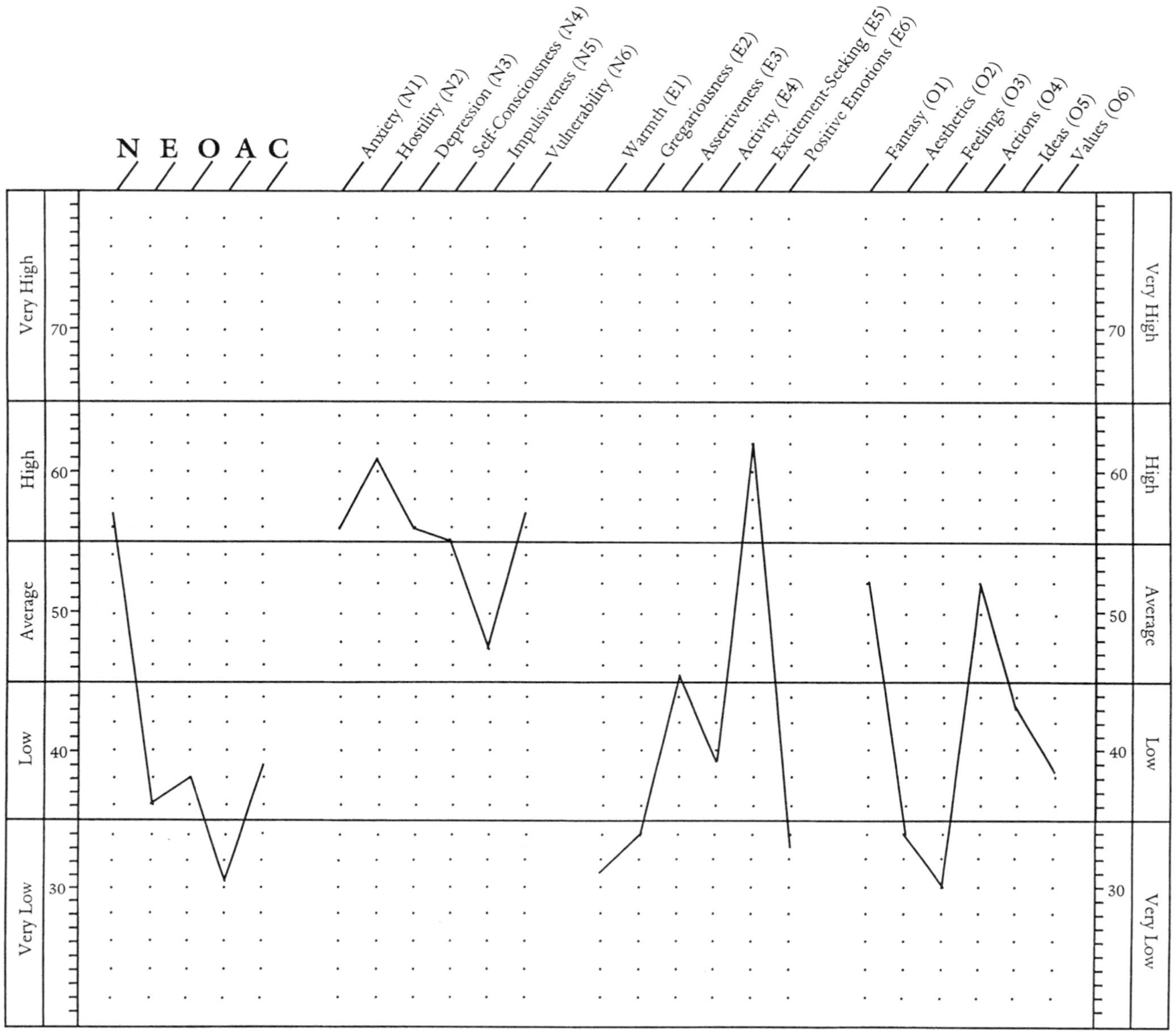

FIGURE 15.4. NEO Personality Inventory (NEO-PI) profile of Persephone, a pure avoidant personality disordered (AVD) abuser. N = Neuroticism; E = Extraversion; O = Openness to Experience; A = Agreeableness; C = Conscientiousness. From the *NEO Personality Inventory*, by P. T. Costa, Jr., and R. R. McCrae, Copyright 1978, 1985, 1989, 1992 by PAR, Inc. Further reproduction is prohibited without permission of PAR, Inc. Reproduced by special permission of the publisher, Psychological Assessment Resources, Inc., 16204 North Florida Avenue, Lutz, FL 33549.

fact, she reported being very content with her status as an untrained, unemployed mother on social assistance. Very low Agreeableness and low Conscientiousness scores are not conceptually related to AVD but are characteristic of a drug abuse disorder. These traits were also consistent with prominent aspects of her behavior (e.g., frequent fights in school and with her boyfriend, poor school attendance, poor interpersonal relationships, and lack of direction or life goals).

More detailed information on the personality characteristics of Persephone was provided by an examination of her NEO-PI facet scores. Specifically, her Neuroticism facet scores indicated a marked tendency toward anxiety, anger, depression, vulnerability to stress, and self-consciousness. These traits are strongly associated with AVD, with the exception of high hostility, and correlated with her complaints of periodic intense dysphoria. We speculated that the high hostility was related to her interpersonal antagonism, frequent arguments, and fights with others.

Persephone's scores on the Extraversion facets were also interesting. Her low scores on the Warmth, Gregariousness, and Activity scales were all consistent with AVD. She was extremely distant from others, preferred to be left alone, and was slow and deliberate in her actions. She had no close personal friends or confidants other than her boyfriend, which is consistent with these traits. Although low Assertiveness and Positive Emotions scale scores are not conceptually related to AVD, these traits were consistent with her lack of autonomy and her tendency toward dysphoria. The high Excitement Seeking scale score was characteristic of her drug abuse disorder. Finally, her scores on facets of the Openness to Experience domain indicated an experiential style that was generally closed to new ideas, with a rather narrow-minded and rigid set of moral beliefs.

Given this personality profile, her treatment prognosis was guarded. Although Persephone's marked tendency toward emotional distress and instability could have motivated treatment involvement, her extremely high level of introversion and interpersonal antagonism and her low Conscientiousness were compromising features. This prognosis was supported by the mixed results of her first 3 months of treatment. At baseline, she obtained a high ASI severity score (1.00) for employment problems and a relatively low severity score (0.07) for drug problems; all other ASI problem domains were rated as nonproblematic (0.00). There were no changes in any of the ASI domain scores at Month 3 with the exception of a slight increase in problem alcohol use (0.01). Thus, she appeared to have derived little benefit from treatment. However, it should be noted that the ASI's failure to detect more of her problems at baseline (e.g., lack of friends, social interests or activities, occupational skills, life goals) reflects the instrument's inability to adequately assess psychosocial functioning. It is possible that a more sensitive psychosocial measure may have shown greater change.

In contrast to the ASI data, only 2 of 13 (15%) urine specimens were positive for drugs or alcohol. The first positive sample was obtained shortly following admission, the second 1 week after the birth of her child. Thus, the rate of drug and alcohol use was relatively low over the initial 3 months of treatment. Of course, it is possible that being pregnant helped her exert greater control over her drug abuse. Regardless of the reason for her reduced drug abuse, these data indicated a positive response to treatment, despite the lack of change in other life areas.

Case Report 3: BDL Opioid Abuser

Nancy was a 40-year-old single White woman who was admitted for treatment of opioid dependence. Her family history was positive for alcohol problems in both of her parents and in one of her two brothers. She reported having a "bad experience" growing up and marked conflict with both parents and one of her brothers. In fact, she "ran away" from home on several occasions beginning at age 16 and was finally placed in reform school, where she remained until her 18th year.

Nancy provided limited information about her school attendance or academic performance. She had completed the 10th grade and denied frequent truancy or school suspensions. In reform school, she had studied cosmetology. Between the ages of 18 and 30, she had more than 20 different jobs including assistant commercial artist, cocktail waitress, telephone solicitor, cosmetologist, and cashier. Since age 30, her main sources of income had included frequent prostitution, sale of illicit drugs, and social service support.

Nancy became sexually active at age 16 and denied a history of sexual abuse. Although never married, she reported having five "serious" relationships, each with a chronic drug abuser. She had been with her current boyfriend for 10 years, and they had a 3-year-old daughter. Her boyfriend was unemployed and abused heroin and other drugs. She described the relationship as chronically unstable and "unhealthy." In fact, she reported that each of her "important" relationships had been "intense and abusive," describing them as "codependent drug relationships." She reported having sexual relations with other men during each of her "long-term" relationships. Aside from frequent "one-night stands," she had been engaged in prostitution for more than 10 years. As a result of these practices, she estimated having had sexual relations with more than 200 different people. She denied condom use throughout much of this activity and had only recently begun to use them consistently. Despite a history of high-risk sexual behavior and intravenous drug use, she reported two consecutive (over a 6-month period), recent negative HIV-1 test results.

Her legal history was remarkable for multiple arrests on a variety of charges and frequent activities that escaped detection (e.g., prostitution, drug sales, theft, and shoplifting). At age 16, she was arrested three times for running away from home. She was sent to reform school for 3 months following the second occasion and was returned there until she was 18 years of age after the third episode. At age 20, she was arrested for selling LSD and was placed on unsupervised probation. Between the ages of 29 and 37, she was arrested six times for shoplifting and was fined for each offense. At age 37, she was arrested for prostitution and was court ordered to a long-term residential treatment program where she stayed for 2 years.

Her medical history was also remarkable. At age 21, she contracted hepatitis from intravenous drug use, and at age 23 she contracted gonorrhea for the first time. She was hospitalized at age 24 for treatment of a skull fracture sustained in a fall, had three hospitalizations for treatment of "seizures" during

sedative withdrawal, and at age 31 had three fingers amputated due to gangrene from multiple drug injections. Finally, she had four abortions between the ages of 23 and 39. Nancy first began abusing substances at age 15, starting with solvents (e.g., sniffing glue) and followed by alcohol and intravenous use of heroin by age 16. At age 19, she began using marijuana, stimulants, and sedatives on a regular basis. On admission, she reported using heroin intravenously up to four times per day. Her treatment history was remarkable for multiple inpatient and outpatient admissions, representing more than 14 episodes of care. She denied treatment for other psychiatric problems. On a mental state examination, she was fully oriented, and her talk was both logical and directed. Although she complained of brief periods of intense anxiety, depression, and anger, she denied a change in self-attitude or vital sense. She was also negative for delusions, hallucinations, true obsessions or compulsions, or phobias.

Nancy's personality profile is presented in Figure 15.5. Compared with the NEO-PI normative sample, she scored in the very high range of Neuroticism and Openness to Experience, in the average range of Extraversion and Agreeableness, and in the very low range of Conscientiousness.

The very high Neuroticism and Openness to Experience scores indicated a strong tendency toward extreme emotional distress and instability, combined with a marked interest in new experiences. Her remarkably low Conscientiousness score indicated a lack of consistent structure, direction, or life plan. The extremely high score on Neuroticism was consistent with both the conceptual formulation of the BDL diagnosis and with much of her life history (e.g., intense periods of dysphoria and extreme affective instability, chronically unstable relationships, and self-damaging behaviors).

Although her high score on the Openness domain was not predicted, it was consistent with major aspects of her life history (e.g., varied employment positions, sexual relations with many people, and use of hallucinogens). Her extremely low standing on the Conscientiousness domain was also not predicted but was consistent with prominent aspects of her behavior and with the clinical impression of a large number of similar patients (e.g., running away

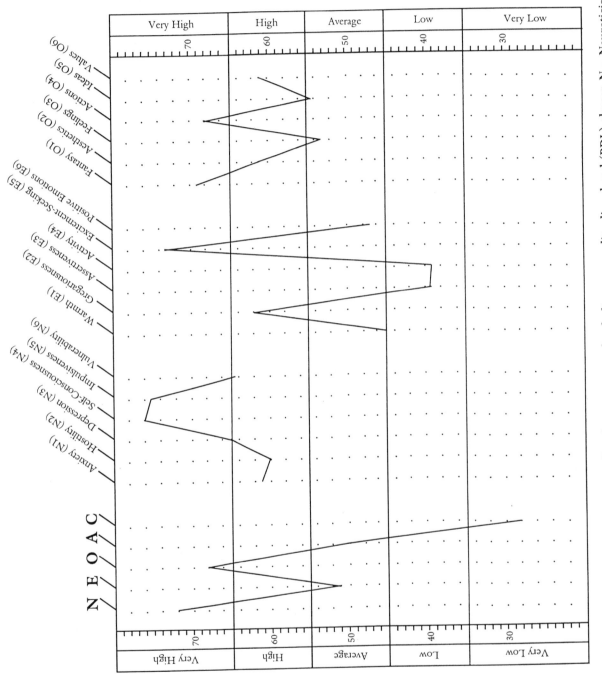

FIGURE 15.5. NEO Personality Inventory (NEO-PI) profile of Nancy, a pure borderline personality disordered (BDL) abuser. N = Neuroticism; E = Extraversion; O = Openness to Experience; A = Agreeableness; C = Conscientiousness. From the *NEO Personality Inventory*, by P. T. Costa, Jr., and R. R. McCrae, Copyright 1978, 1985, 1989, 1992 by PAR, Inc. Further reproduction is prohibited without permission of PAR, Inc. Reproduced by special permission of the publisher, Psychological Assessment Resources, Inc., 16204 North Florida Avenue, Lutz, FL 33549.

from home, reform school, frequent shoplifting, chronic prostitution, severe drug abuse, multiple failed treatment episodes, lack of direction and marked opposition to structure, and no consistent life goals). Many of her medical problems may also have been associated with her low standing on Conscientiousness. For example, she reported only limited condom use, despite having had over 200 sexual partners, and a good knowledge of the risks associated with her behavior. In addition, her score on Conscientiousness was certainly consistent with a drug abuse disorder.

More detailed information on Nancy's personality characteristics was provided by an examination of her NEO-PI facet scores. Specifically, she obtained high scores on each of the facets of the Neuroticism domain. Thus, she was highly prone to pervasive emotional distress. She scored especially high on the Self-Consciousness and Impulsiveness facet scales. Thus, embarrassment or shyness was a problem for her when dealing with strangers and was consistent with her life history. She had great difficulty controlling her impulses and desires.

In terms of the Extraversion facets, she scored high on Gregariousness and Excitement Seeking scales and low on Assertiveness and Activity scales. Thus, she tended to seek out people and enjoyed excitement, stimulation, and thrills (e.g., her sexual contacts). Both of these personality traits are consistent with the repeated behavior of many BDL patients to avoid being alone or to avoid experiencing boredom. Her high score on Excitement-Seeking scale is also characteristic of a drug abuse disorder. Her low Assertiveness may have been related to a fear of abandonment and marked vulnerability to stress common among BDL patients. Her low level of activity may have been associated with her strong tendency toward dysphoria. In terms of experiential style, she was remarkably open to new experiences. She had a vivid imagination and active fantasy life, enjoyed new and different activities, and was liberal in her social and moral beliefs.

Given her personality profile, Nancy's treatment prognosis was guarded, particularly because she was receiving only standard counseling. Although her marked tendency toward emotional distress and general Openness would have suggested a good progno-

sis, her very low standing on Conscientiousness clearly represented a major problem. This prognosis was generally supported by the results of her first 3 months of treatment. Her baseline ASI scores indicated severe employment problems (i.e., chronic unemployment), moderate family and social problems (i.e., unstable relationship with current boyfriend and strained family relations), and a modest problem with drugs and alcohol. There were few changes in any of these problem areas at follow-up, and she had developed a moderate medical problem (0.49). A similar picture emerged from her drug test records. First, although eight tests were scheduled, she provided urine specimens for only five. Three (60%) of the five urine specimens were positive, primarily for sedative drugs (e.g., alprazolam).

CONCLUSION

The data presented in this chapter are useful for understanding the relation of opioid drug abuse and personality disorder to the FFM of normal personality. First, all patients obtained low scores on the NEO-PI domains of Agreeableness and Conscientiousness and high scores on the Excitement-Seeking facet scale of Extraversion. In fact, the high interpersonal antagonism (i.e., low Agreeableness), high disregard for established social rules and conventions (i.e., low Conscientiousness), and high excitement seeking reported by these patients were remarkably consistent with clinical impressions and provide additional insight into many of the therapeutic problems common in the treatment of opioid abusers. Second, the NEO-PI also showed clear differences in the personality traits of opioid abusers. For example, high Neuroticism was characteristic only of those patients who also had a personality disorder. Third, support was obtained in the study for several hypotheses regarding the relations between the FFM and specific personality diagnoses discussed in chapter 6 by Widiger et al. Specifically, most of the defining personality features predicted for patients with ATS, AVD, and BDL were confirmed. Finally, the case histories showed the potential benefit of the FFM in predicting response to drug abuse treatment. Taken together, these data provide new information about the relation of the FFM of normal personality to opioid abuse with and without comorbid personality disorder and support new research on the implications of the FFM for improving patient–treatment matching.

References

Alterman, A. L., & Cacciola, J. S. (1991). The antisocial personality disorder diagnosis in substance abusers: Problems and issues. *Journal of Nervous and Mental Disease, 179,* 401–409.

American Psychiatric Association. (1987). *Diagnostic and statistical manual of mental disorders* (3rd ed., rev.). Washington, DC: Author.

Blume, S. B. (1989). Dual diagnosis: Psychoactive substance dependence and the personality disorders. *Journal of Psychoactive Drugs, 21,* 139–144.

Brooner, R. K., Herbst, J. H., Schmidt, C. W., Bigelow, G. E., & Costa, P. T., Jr. (1993). Antisocial personality disorder among drug abusers: Relations to other personality diagnoses and the five-factor model of personality. *Journal of Nervous and Mental Disease, 181,* 313–319.

Costa, P. T., Jr., & McCrae, R. R. (1985). *The NEO Personality Inventory manual.* Odessa, FL: Psychological Assessment Resources.

Costa, P. T., Jr., & McCrae, R. R. (1989). *The NEO-PI/NEO-FFI manual supplement.* Odessa, FL: Psychological Assessment Resources.

Craig, R. J. (1988). Psychological functioning of cocaine free-basers derived from objective psychological tests. *Journal of Clinical Psychology, 44,* 599–606.

Kadden, R. M., Cooney, N. L., Getter, H., & Litt, M. D. (1989). Matching alcoholics to coping skills or interactional therapies: Post-treatment results. *Journal of Consulting and Clinical Psychology, 57,* 698–704.

Khantzian, E. J., & Treece, C. (1985). DSM-III psychiatric diagnosis of narcotic addicts: Recent findings. *Archives of General Psychiatry, 42,* 1067–1071.

Kilmann, P. R. (1974). Personality characteristics of female narcotic addicts. *Psychological Reports, 35,* 485–486.

Kosten, T. A., Kosten, T. R., & Rounsaville, B. J. (1989). Personality disorders in opiate addicts show prognostic specificity. *Journal of Substance Abuse Treatment, 6,* 163–168.

Kosten, T. R., Rounsaville, B. J., & Kleber, H. D. (1982). *DSM-III* personality disorders in opiate addicts. *Comprehensive Psychiatry, 23,* 572–581.

McLellan, A. T., Luborsky, L., Woody, G. E., & O'Brien, C. P. (1980). An improved evaluation instrument for substance abuse patients. *Journal of Nervous and Mental Disease, 168,* 26–33.

Miller, T. R. (1991). The psychotherapeutic utility of the five-factor model of personality: A clinician's experience. *Journal of Personality Assessment, 57,* 415–433.

Reith, G., Crockett, D., & Craig, K. (1975). Personality characteristics in heroin addicts and nonaddicted prisoners using the Edwards Personality Preference Schedule. *International Journal of the Addictions, 10,* 97–112.

Rounsaville, B. J., Weissman, M. M., Kleber, H. D., & Wilber, C. H. (1982). The heterogeneity of psychiatric diagnosis in treated opiate addicts. *Archives of General Psychiatry, 39,* 161–166.

Spitzer, R. L., Williams, J. B. W., Gibbon, M., & First, M. B. (1988). *Instruction manual for the Structured Clinical Interview for DSM-III-R (SCID).* New York: New York State Psychiatric Institute, Biometrics Research Department.

Sutker, P. B., Patsiokas, A. T., & Allain, A. N. (1981). Chronic illicit drug abusers: Gender comparisons. *Psychological Reports, 49,* 383–390.

Widiger, T. A., Trull, T. J., Clarkin, J. F., Sanderson, C., & Costa, P. T., Jr. (1994). A description of the *DSM-III-R* and *DSM-IV* personality disorders with the five-factor model of personality. In P. T. Costa, Jr., & T. A. Widiger (Eds.), *Personality disorders and the five-factor model of personality* (pp. 41–56). Washington, DC: American Psychological Association.

Woody, G. E., McLellan, A. T., Luborsky, L., & O'Brien, C. P. (1985). Sociopathy and psychotherapy outcome. *Archives of General Psychiatry, 42,* 1081–1086.

CHAPTER 16

THE NEO PERSONALITY INVENTORY AND THE MILLON CLINICAL MULTIAXIAL INVENTORY IN THE FORENSIC EVALUATION OF SEX OFFENDERS

Gregory K. Lehne

Forensic evaluations are conducted in a variety of different settings using psychological instruments that are oriented toward diagnosing psychopathology or personality disorders or describing personality factors. The personality characteristics of sex offenders have been investigated using many different instruments (see Levin & Stava, 1987). Sex offenders are an appropriate population in which to empirically investigate the nature of the relationship between personality disorders and personality factors, as measured by the Millon Clinical Multiaxial Inventory (MCMI; Millon, 1983) and the NEO Personality Inventory (NEO-PI; Costa & McCrae, 1985). The relationship between personality disorders and personality factors has been studied only in nonclinical samples, from which significant and sensible patterns of correlations were found (Costa & McCrae, 1990; Wiggins & Pincus, 1989).

Sex offenders who were undergoing forensic evaluation at the Johns Hopkins Hospital (Baltimore, MD) Sexual Disorders Clinic were given the MCMI and NEO-PI. The correlations were determined between their scores on these two inventories. In this clinical sample, personality disorders and personality factors were related in ways similar to those found in other research with nonclinical samples (Costa & McCrae, 1990). An actual case history illustrates the types of information provided by the MCMI and NEO-PI in an initial evaluation and retesting 4 months later. Consistencies between the two testings with the NEO-PI and differences in results from the testings with the MCMI raise issues for forensic evaluations and the conceptualization of personality dis-

orders and personality factors. I conclude this chapter with a discussion of my personal experience in evaluating personality disorders and related traits among forensic populations.

PERSONALITY EVALUATION OF SEX OFFENDERS

The research literature on personality variables and sex offenders most frequently uses the Minnesota Multiphasic Personality Inventory (MMPI; Hathaway & McKinley, 1967; (Dahlstrom, Welsh, & Dahlstrom, 1972), or occasionally the MCMI, to assess personality disorders. Other studies use inventories like the Edwards Personal Preference Schedule (EPPS; Edwards, 1959), the Eysenck Personality Questionnaire (EPQ; Eysenck & Eysenck, 1975), or the Sixteen Personality Factor Questionnaire (16PF; Cattell, Eber, & Tatsuoka, 1970) to examine the personality traits of sex offenders. Much of this literature was reviewed by Levin and Stava (1987).

In general, the literature fails to confirm any direct or clear association between personality disorders and sex offenders. With reference to 27 studies that they reviewed using the MMPI, Levin and Stava (1987) concluded that the resultant knowledge was sparse and that "negative or inconsistent findings outweigh those of a positive nature" (p. 69). They reported that the most consistent findings are that sex offenders who use force may be more likely to show elevations on the MMPI Schizophrenia scale or show a 48/84 high-point pairs profile characterized by social alienation, chronic hostility, and peculiarities of thought. No tests were able to differentiate particular groups of sex offenders from other populations. Some groups of sex offenders, such as exhibitionists, produced normal MMPI results in most studies, despite predictions from the literature that they would be passive or schizoid personality disordered.

The MCMI is available with a special computer-generated forensic clinical interpretation, but the scoring is the same with forensic subjects as with other clinical populations. The MCMI was used in several studies to categorize personality disorders among sex offenders. Unlike the MMPI, the MCMI is specifically normalized to provide a typology of personality disorders in categories that roughly correspond to disorders of the third edition, revised, of the *Diagnostic and Statistical Manual of Mental Disorders* (*DSM-III-R*; American Psychiatric Association, 1987). The MCMI uses a base-rate (BR) scale score cut-off point of 85 or greater to indicate the probable presence of a disorder, with a score of 75–84 indicating the presence of a related trait. Only high scores are interpreted, not low scores or scores in the average range, so the test does not provide a measure of normal personality factors in nonclinical samples.

In one study, 101 men who had been incarcerated as "sexually dangerous persons," primarily rapists and child molesters, were administered the MCMI (Bard & Knight, 1987). Despite the pathological nature of the sample, none of the sample means were greater than 75 (which would have indicated the prevalence of a personality trait or disorder). In fact, 25% of the men had no elevations on any of the scales of the MCMI. The remaining men could be clustered into three groups.

The first group, called the detached type, included both rapists and child molesters who had elevated scores on the Avoidant scale (*M* = 87), with lesser mean elevations on the Schizoid (Asocial; *M* = 76) and Dependent (Submissive; *M* = 74) scales. The second group showed the most typical criminal sample characteristics, with elevations on the following scales: Narcissistic (*M* = 90), Antisocial (aggressive; *M* = 85), and Histrionic (gregarious; *M* = 78). This group included mostly (82%) rapists. The third group had MCMI elevations on the Antisocial (ag-

gressive; *M* = 81) and Passive-Aggressive (negativistic; *M* = 76) scales. This group seemed to be more generally dangerous, in ways that were not only sexual.

Thus, in this study, sex offenders could not be defined by any one personality type or by any combination of sex offense and personality type. However, individual sex offenders showed elevations on a variety of clinical scales designed to assess the presence of personality disorders. They could be classified into groups with similar personality patterns but not with the same sex offenses.

In another study, Neuman (1981) compared rapists and child molesters on the MCMI and found some differences but no clear profile for either group. Rapists were scored as more extraverted, gregarious, and active than were child molesters. Rapists were also found to have a more active ambivalent personality style compared with a more passive ambivalent style for child molesters. But in general, it was difficult to find results with the MCMI (or the MMPI, which was also used in this study) that supported predictions from the literature about the personality characteristics of sex offenders.

Because sex offenders showed a variety of personality disorders in both studies that used the MCMI, they were deemed to be an appropriate clinical sample in which to examine the relationship between personality disorders and personality factors. Sex offenders are not characterized by any single pattern of personality disorders that would tend to bias the results of a correlational study.

Personality factors have been studied in sex offenders using the EPPS (Fisher, 1969; Fisher & Howell, 1970; Fisher & Rivlin, 1971; Langevin, Paitich, Freeman, Mann, & Handy, 1978; Scott, 1982), the 16PF (Langevin et al., 1978), the EPQ (Wilson & Cox, 1983), the Comrey Personality Scale (Smukler & Schiebel, 1975), and the California Psychological Inventory (Forgac & Michaels, 1982). Findings from assessments that used personality factor inventories showed differences among types of offenders on personality characteristics such as introversion, abasement, aggression, deference, succorance, and nurturance (Levin & Stava, 1987). The difficulty in interpreting the results of these studies is that the personality factors that were derived varied among the different instruments, and the research studies were performed within different populations. Nevertheless, the studies do suggest that research on the personality factors of sex offenders is appropriate and likely to show significant differences.

RELATIONSHIP BETWEEN PERSONALITY DISORDERS AND PERSONALITY FACTORS

The relationship between personality disorders and the five-factor model (FFM) of personality was studied by Costa and McCrae (1990) and Wiggins and Pincus (1989). Costa and McCrae (1985) correlated results from the MCMI and the NEO-PI in two separate normal populations with no noted propensities toward personality disorders. Their analysis of the results suggested that personality factors, as measured by the NEO-PI, were related in fairly clear and specific ways to the personality disorders as defined by the MCMI. For example, the MCMI Schizoid scale scores were negatively correlated with scores on the NEO-PI Extraversion scale, and the MCMI Avoidant scale scores were correlated negatively with Extraversion and positively with Neuroticism scores on the NEO-PI. Both MCMI Histrionic and Narcissistic scales were positively correlated with Extraversion and Openness to Experience on the NEO-PI but differed in their correlations with other factors. The results of Wiggins and Pincus, who used a different methodology but a normal population, are generally consistent with the findings from Costa and McCrae (1990).

Costa and McCrae (1990) interpreted the overall pattern of findings as indicating that the NEO-PI is measuring underlying factors that are part of personality disorders as assessed by the MCMI. Thus, personality disorders could be conceptualized as extreme or dysfunctional combinations of normal personality factors. However, the empirical findings can be faulted for the use of a nonclinical sample, for which the MCMI was not strictly appropriate and which probably had a low frequency of personality disorders.

The conceptual relationship among personality factors and disorders has not been studied in forensic or sex-offending populations. In general, clinical tests of personality disorders, like the MCMI, are used with clinical populations and are not normalized in a way that makes them valid with nonclinical populations. So Costa and McCrae's (1990) findings of correlations between the NEO-PI and the MCMI may not hold up in a clinical population. However, tests of normal personality factors, like the NEO-PI, can be used with clinical populations without compromising their validity. There is little data available to relate the results of such testing to possible personality disorders or pathology.

Thus, it is not known whether a clinical forensic population, such as sex offenders, would show a similar pattern of correlations on the personality disorder scales of the MCMI and the five factors of personality as measured by the NEO-PI. Also unexplored is the relative usefulness of evaluating sex offenders using clinical tests of personality disorders compared with more normative inventories of personality factors. These are the issues that are examined in the present study that tested a clinical forensic group of sex offenders with the MCMI and the NEO-PI.

PRESENT STUDY

Procedures

Men who were undergoing evaluation or treatment at the Sexual Disorders Clinic of the Johns Hopkins Hospital were the subjects for the study of the correlation between MCMI and NEO-PI test scores. The population of the Sexual Disorders Clinic tends to be sexually compulsive with multiple offenses and has typically offended against victims outside the family. Thus, this group is a primary forensic population as well as a clinical population. All of the men had admitted to engaging in inappropriate sexual behavior and were charged with or convicted of at least one sex offense. Mentally retarded men and men with reading difficulties were excluded from the study

Each man underwent a complete psychiatric evaluation and was diagnosed according to *DSM-III-R* criteria. The Axis I psychiatric diagnosis judged most directly related to the sexual offense was designated as the primary diagnosis. Ninety-nine men completed the evaluation process and produced valid test results on both the MCMI and the NEO-PI. In most cases ($n = 81$), the primary diagnosis was a sexual disorder or paraphilia (pedophilia, $n = 44$; exhibitionism, $n = 8$; other paraphilias, involving adolescent or adult-oriented behavior, $n = 29$). In 18 cases, the inappropriate sexual behavior was not associated with a sexual disorder. There were 9 cases of transitory adjustment disorders, 4 cases related to alcohol or substance abuse or conduct disturbance, 1 case with an atypical psychotic episode, and 4 cases with no psychiatric diagnoses.

The evaluated sex offenders were tested with both the MCMI and the NEO-PI, either at the time of their initial evaluation or at the time of a group psychotherapy session. Testing was done using the paper-and-pencil versions of the MCMI and the NEO-PI. Tests were scored according to the published manuals, with no deviations from standard procedures, and using the appropriate adjustments and normative tables (Costa & McCrae, 1985; Millon, 1983). The results of the testing were not used in making diagnoses of the patients or clinical recommendations.

Results

On the MCMI, a score of 85 or greater was taken as evidence for the presence of a personality disorder. Among the 99 men, 33% had no MCMI scores greater than 85, 28% had one scale score above 84, 23% had two or three scale scores above 84, and 15% had four to six scale scores above 84. Scale scores of 75–84 indicate the presence of a personality trait related to the more extreme disorder. Scores below 75 should not be interpreted in individual cases. Table 16.1 shows the frequency of scores in this population of sex offenders. All of the means are below a score of 75. Thus, no individual trait or combination of personality traits and disorders is characteristically descriptive of this population of sex offenders. Dependent (50% of sample) and passive–aggressive (36%) are the most common personality disorder scale elevations, and anxiety (47%) and dysthymia (44%) are the most prevalent clinical symptom syndromes.

With reference to the NEO-PI, Table 16.2 shows the means and standard deviations for the sample. Unlike the MCMI, which uses BR cut-off scores, all

TABLE 16.1

Descriptive Statistics for Millon Clinical Multiaxial Inventory (MCMI) Personality Disorder Scales in a Sex Offender Sample

MCMI scale (trait)	Disorder (%)	Trait (%)
Schizoid (asocial)	18	12
Avoidant	23	8
Dependent (submissive)	34	16
Histrionic (gregarious)	9	10
Narcissistic	9	17
Antisocial (aggressive)	11	8
Compulsive (conforming)	3	9
Passive–Aggressive (negativistic)	27	9
Schizotypal (schizoid)	2	5
Borderline (cycloid)	5	10
Paranoid	7	6
Anxiety	30	17
Somatoform	5	14
Hypomanic	2	2
Dysthymic	28	16
Alcohol Abuse	3	8
Drug Abuse	6	12
Psychotic Thinking	1	4
Psychotic Depression	1	5
Psychotic Delusions	4	3
None	33	13

Note. N = 99 men; base-rate scale scores for disorders ≥85; base-rate scale scores for traits = 75–84.

scores on the NEO-PI can be interpreted. Thus, the NEO-PI means of the sample can be interpreted as providing a descriptive profile of this group of sex offenders, in comparison to a normal, nonclinical population. A higher mean score would indicate a greater presence of that personality factor in the sex offender sample, and a lower score would correspond to a smaller presence of that factor. Whether significant deviations in either direction correspond in a meaningful way to psychopathology is a question that is examined empirically in the correlational analysis of the NEO-PI and the MCMI.

This sex offender sample's mean scores were at least one-half a standard deviation higher than the normal population on all facets of the Neuroticism domain—anxiety and depression (which were also elevated on the MCMI) as well as hostility, self-consciousness, impulsiveness, and vulnerability. The

TABLE 16.2

Descriptive Statistics for NEO Personality Inventory (NEO-PI) Scales in a Sex Offender Sample

NEO-PI scale	*M*	Range
Domain		
Neuroticism	60.9	High
Extraversion	53.0	Average
Openness to Experience	49.0	Average
Agreeableness	45.2	Average
Conscientiousness	46.3	Average
Neuroticism facet		
Anxiety	57.2	High
Hostility	55.7	High
Depression	62.0	High
Self-consciousness	57.6	High
Impulsiveness	56.5	High
Vulnerability	58.5	High
Extraversion facet		
Warmth	49.1	Average
Gregariousness	52.8	Average
Assertiveness	48.2	Average
Activity	52.8	Average
Excitement seeking	57.1	High
Positive emotions	51.5	Average
Openness facet		
Fantasy	50.0	Average
Aesthetics	50.8	Average
Feelings	52.3	Average
Actions	49.0	Average
Ideas	48.0	Average
Values	46.3	Average

Note. N = 99 men.

mean score on the Excitement-Seeking facet scale of Extraversion was also higher than in the general population. All other scores were within the average range, corresponding to a typical normal population sample.

The group means are consistent with apparently honest and candid responding to the inventory questions. There was no evidence that suggested that responses were distorted in a socially desirable direction, for example, producing artificially low scores on the facets of hostility, impulsiveness, or excitement seeking or high scores on the Agreeableness or Conscientiousness domains.

The results of testing sex offenders in this sample with the MCMI and the NEO-PI show that it is a population that produces results in the clinically significant range. The sample population shows a high level of Neuroticism, which would be expected for clinical samples, and a variety of personality traits and disorders. Yet there is no homogeneous pattern in the findings because the sample is not characterized by the prevalence of any one particular personality trait, disorder, or cluster of traits.

Correlations between the BR scores on the MCMI and the scale scores for the five factors on the NEO-PI are provided in Table 16.3. The pattern of these correlations is compared, in Table 16.4, with the correlations reported in Costa and McCrae (1990) for a normal sample of 207 men and women. This comparison is not strictly equivalent because Costa and McCrae included both men and women, whereas the present sample involved only men. Also Costa and McCrae used raw scores for the MCMI, whereas the present sample used BR scores. Nevertheless, the patterns of correlations are remarkably similar. Of the 55 correlational cells (11 MCMI disorders × 5 NEO-PI factors), there is agreement in the direction of significant correlations or the absence of a correlation in 36 cells (65%). There were no cases of disagreement in the direction of a correlation. In 10 cells (18%), there are significant correlations only for the sex offender sample. In 9 cells (16%), there are significant correlations only for the normal sample; with only three exceptions, these noncorresponding correlations were lower than 0.5.

The correlations in the sample of sex offenders also replicate the basic pattern of findings from normal populations found by Wiggins and Pincus (1989), which was also replicated by Costa and McCrae (1990). In all of these studies, Extraversion was strongly and negatively correlated with schizoid and avoidant personality disorders and positively correlated with histrionic and narcissistic disorders. In addition, negative correlations were found in all of the studies between Agreeableness and antisocial and paranoid personality disorders. Conscientiousness was positively correlated with compulsive personality disorder in all the studies. Neuroticism was positively correlated with avoidant and borderline personality disorders in all three studies. A negative correlation between Openness and schizotypal personality disorder was also replicated in these studies.

TABLE 16.3

Correlations of Millon Clinical Multiaxial Inventory (MCMI) and NEO Personality Inventory (NEO-PI) Scale Scores in a Sex Offender Sample

MCMI scale	NEO-PI domain				
	N	E	O	A	C
Schizoid	0.54**	−0.56**	−0.33**	−0.47**	−0.28**
Avoidant	0.63**	−0.57**	−0.26*	−0.43**	−0.23*
Dependent	0.20*	−0.19	−0.21*	0.19	−0.10
Histrionic	−0.18	0.63**	0.42**	0.04	0.02
Narcissistic	−0.30**	0.57**	0.25*	−0.05	0.28**
Antisocial	0.09	0.13	−0.05	−0.49**	−0.01
Compulsive	−0.63**	0.21*	−0.09	0.58**	0.36**
Passive–Aggressive	0.69**	−0.32**	−0.01	−0.50**	−0.31**
Schizotypal	0.44**	−0.63**	−0.30**	−0.18	−0.22*
Borderline	0.49**	−0.29**	0.00	−0.16	0.13
Paranoid	0.02	0.09	−0.08	−0.31**	0.18
Anxiety	0.45**	−0.46**	−0.07	−0.21*	−0.26**
Somatoform	0.12	−0.22*	−0.05	0.10	0.04
Hypomanic	0.26**	0.33**	0.26**	−0.29**	0.03
Dysthymic	0.50**	−0.49**	−0.04	−0.14	−0.28**
Alcohol Abuse	0.48**	−0.06	−0.01	−0.35**	−0.19
Drug Abuse	0.16	0.43**	0.21*	−0.32**	0.03
Psychotic Thinking	0.56**	−0.41**	−0.24*	−0.49**	−0.18
Psychotic Depression	0.64**	−0.38**	−0.16	−0.41**	−0.19
Psychotic Delusions	0.14	−0.08	−0.20*	−0.27**	0.14

Note. N = 99 men. N = Neuroticism; E = Extraversion; O = Openness to Experience; A = Agreeableness; C = Conscientiousness.   *p < .05.   **p < .01.

A positive correlation between Openness and histrionic personality disorder was also replicated.

In addition, the sex offender sample replicates the findings from Costa and McCrae's (1990) normal sample for much of the pattern for both the Neuroticism and Extraversion factors. In both studies, Neuroticism is positively correlated with avoidant, passive–aggressive, schizotypal, and borderline personality disorders and negatively correlated with narcissistic and compulsive personality disorders. For the Extraversion factor, there is replication of negative correlations with schizoid, avoidant, schizotypal, and borderline personality disorders and positive correlations with histrionic and narcissistic disorders.

Neuroticism and Extraversion are the factors that have the most consistent correlational relationships with personality disorders in the different samples. Except as previously mentioned, the Openness, Agreeableness, and Conscientiousness factors had less consistent agreements in correlations between the two studies.

In the sex offender sample, not all of the personality disorders as measured by the MCMI could be uniquely differentiated on the basis of the patterns of correlations with the NEO-PI. For example, scores for the MCMI Antisocial and Paranoid scales had negative correlations with NEO-PI Agreeableness scores and no other significant correlations. Essentially, both of these personality disorders share an interpersonal antagonism, which is an essential part of low Agreeableness. It is important to remember that the sex offender population had a diversity of scores and evidence of few clinical traits or disorders on the MCMI Antisocial (19% > 75 BR) and Paranoid (13% > 75 BR) scales.

In the sex offender sample, there were no correlations between dependent personality characteristics and any NEO-PI factors. This is remarkable because the dependent personality disorder was the most fre-

TABLE 16.4

Comparison of Significant Correlations of Millon Clinical Multiaxial Inventory (MCMI) Personality Disorder Scales With NEO Personality Inventory (NEO-PI) Factors

MCMI scale and sample	NEO-PI factors				
	N	E	O	A	C
Schizoid					
Normal		—			
Sex offenders	++	—	-	-	-
Avoidant					
Normal	+	—			
Sex offenders	++	—	-		
Dependent					
Normal	+		-	+	
Sex offenders					
Histrionic					
Normal		++	+		-
Sex offenders		++	+		
Narcissistic					
Normal	-	+	+	-	
Sex offenders	-	++			+
Antisocial					
Normal	-		+	-	
Sex offenders				-	
Compulsive					
Normal	-		-		+
Sex offenders	—			++	+
Passive–Aggressive					
Normal	++				
Sex offenders	++	-		—	-
Schizotypal					
Normal	+	-	-		
Sex offenders	+	—	-		
Borderline					
Normal	++	-			
Sex offenders	+	-			
Paranoid					
Normal				-	
Sex offenders				-	

Note. N = Neuroticism; E = Extraversion; O = Openness to Experience; A = Agreeableness; C = Conscientiousness. All correlations at $p < .01$ level of significance. ++ and — indicate positive and negative correlations, respectively, that are $\geq .5$; + and - indicate positive or negative correlations, respectively, that are $< .5$. Normal sample: $N = 207$ men and women from Costa and McCrae (1990), correlations based on raw scores. Sex offender sample: $N = 99$ men, present study sample, correlations based on base-rate scores.

quently elevated scale on the MCMI in the sex offender sample (50% > 75 BR).

Discussion

The MCMI and the NEO-PI were developed from different theoretical perspectives. The MCMI was developed using Millon's theory of personality and pathology, which ultimately goes back to a conceptualization of people's sources of reinforcements and activity levels in pursuing those reinforcements (Millon, 1981). Pathology results from extremes in personality styles and personality decompensation under situations of marked stress. The MCMI is loosely related to *DSM-III-R* categories, which also incorporate a historical psychiatric typology of personality disorders. The NEO-PI is based on factor analytic research on personality in both the natural language and theory-based personality inventories.

The correlation of the results from testing a sample of sex offenders with the MCMI and the NEO-PI shows that the two tests produced findings that generally could be interpreted in mutually consistent ways. Neuroticism and Extraversion are the two factors most consistently linked in theory, research, and common parlance to personality disorders. Both positive and negative correlations between these factors and different personality disorders have been shown in several studies.

Neuroticism, as a general indicator of distress and negative affectivity, is positively correlated with borderline, passive–aggressive, schizotypal (and possibly schizoid), and avoidant personality disorders. Individuals with these types of disorders are commonly perceived by others as negative and discontented. A negative correlation with Neuroticism was found for the narcissistic and compulsive personality disorders; these types of individuals do not typically describe themselves as discontented, which is consistent with low Neuroticism.

Similarly, the correlations among Extraversion and various personality disorders closely correspond to the definitional qualities of the disorders. For example, histrionic and narcissistic individuals are by definition outgoing and oriented toward influencing others with their personality styles. Avoidant, schizoid, schizotypal, and borderline personality disorders involve deficiencies in the ability to relate interpersonally. The other disorders do not present such defining characteristics with reference to Extraversion.

Thus, the correlation of the results from the MCMI and NEO-PI provides support for the idea that there are common personality factors that underlie the personality disorders. But the tests do not say the same things. The magnitude of the correlation or agreement between the different studies and tests decreases for factors such as Openness, Agreeableness, and Conscientiousness.

There is no clear formula or pattern that allows the direct translation of findings on one test to be translated into the language of the other. In the present study, it was not possible to identify each or all of the different personality disorders in terms of specific NEO-PI profiles. Nor do the results of either of the tests directly translate into the *DSM-III-R* categories of personality disorders. Despite the typology of MCMI scale names that appear to correspond to the discrete personality disorders in the *DSM-III-R,* the actual results of testing with the MCMI tend to produce patterns of scores with two or three scale elevations as often as they produce a single scale elevation. This implies that the MCMI personality disorders are not mutually exclusive syndromes. Thus, interpreting the results of testing on the MCMI and the diagnosis of personality disorders according to the *DSM-III-R* criteria requires skilled, professional clinical expertise.

It may be that discriminability of personality disorders can be improved in the future with new versions of tests (e.g., the MCMI-II; Millon, 1987) or by more analysis of facets of specific personality factors, such as the facets of the NEO-PI. The MCMI-II was not available at the time of the testing of sex offenders, and the sample size was too small to allow for a reliable correlational analysis of NEO-PI facet scores.

But it also may be that the present conceptualization of personality disorders is part of the problem of discriminability. Personality disorders may be historical artifacts of the intellectual-domain bias of psychiatry, clinical psychology, and social work. Many other fields of human services, such as industrial and occupational psychology, career consulting and guidance, and pastoral counseling typically use models of personality other than *DSM-III-R* personality disorders.

The criminal justice and forensic fields are presently split between using personality disorder models and other approaches to analyze the personality characteristics of individuals in their purview. Thus, forensic evaluators are caught in the middle in their attempts to evaluate individuals in terms that are mutually understandable to clinically trained personnel and others who are involved in the criminal justice system (e.g., attorneys, judges, juries, and probation officers) with no background in clinical psychology. The case example that follows illustrates some of the issues of forensic evaluation in using concepts of personality disorders on the basis of assessment with the MCMI compared with using the NEO-PI factors.

CASE EXAMPLE

Ron was a 35-year-old man who was referred by his doctor for evaluation after he was legally charged with exposing himself to a young adolescent girl in the food mall of a public shopping center. He was first seen 4 days after his arrest and was then seen a week later, at which time he was tested with the MCMI and the NEO-PI. After 4 months of weekly individual psychotherapy, he was retested. He was not a subject in the previously described research sample.

Ron reported an extensive history of exposing himself to teenage and adult females, and he reported one prior arrest. He also had been frequently involved with prostitutes and had frequently attended strip bars, either alone or with friends, at which times he drank prodigious quantities of alcohol. He drank only rarely otherwise in social situations and never to excess. He had no other history of inappropriate sexual behavior. His legal history also included arrests for shoplifting. He had previously undergone psychiatric treatment for his sexual behavior and depression. His first suicide attempt was at age 12. He was suicidally depressed following his previous arrest for indecent behavior.

He was morbidly obese, with medical complications of diabetes and high blood pressure, and had no prior success in losing weight. He was happily married to a Vietnamese woman whom he met while he was in the U.S. armed services, and they had a 10-year-old son. He and his wife reported some difficulties in communication but no other marital or sexual problems. He was well regarded in his career and was socially popular among his peers at work. Outside of work, he reported no social friendships or hobbies.

At the time of the initial evaluation, Ron was significantly depressed with suicidal plans and feared the loss of his marriage and job as a consequence of his arrest. He had almost no appetite, had lost 25 pounds, and had problems sleeping. His physical hygiene was appropriate. His speech was clear, coherent, and task oriented. Despite being intermit-

tently overcome with tears, he repeatedly made jokes during the evaluation session, some of which were self-deprecating. He had a dramatic storytelling style and seemed prone to exaggeration or overstatement. He reported a history of being class clown and office joker.

The initial diagnoses were exhibitionism and major depression (recurrent). The diagnosis of a personality disorder was deferred. The impression was that he suffered from some personality disorders but that he did not meet a sufficient number of criteria for any one *DSM-III-R* diagnosis.

Ron's history of adolescent shoplifting, illicit sexual behavior that continued during his marriage, and recklessness in drinking and driving, along with self-justification and disregard for the effects of his illegal behavior on others, suggested antisocial personality disorder features. Borderline personality disorder features included his instability of mood accompanied with suicidal plans and poor self-esteem; his excessive impulsiveness in sexuality, shoplifting, and drinking; and concerns about abandonment by his wife and family. His personality style seemed excessively emotional and attention seeking in a clowning way, which is suggestive of histrionic characteristics. Dependent personality disorder features were also present in his seeking affirmation from others and his hypersensitivity to possible disapproval, his preoccupation and imagined devastation if his wife and son abandoned him, and a tendency to allow his wife to make all the major decisions for the family. One of the difficulties in the diagnosis of a possible personality disorder was that many of these characteristics might be more related to his other diagnoses of depression or exhibitionism rather than indicative of an independent personality disorder.

Initial testing with the MCMI showed significant elevations on the scales measuring passive–aggressive (96) and dependent (88) personality disorders, with scores in the trait range on the scales measuring borderline (82) and avoidant (77) personality disorders. The MCMI Anxiety and Depression scales each had scores over 100, but no other scales were elevated. The complete scores for the MCMI scales are provided in the first column of Table 16.5. The MCMI computer-generated interpretative

TABLE 16.5

Case Example: Millon Clinical Multiaxial Inventory (MCMI) Base-Rate Scores

MCMI scale (trait)	1st test	2nd test
Schizoid (asocial)	60	51
Avoidant	77	46
Dependent (submissive)	88	80
Histrionic (gregarious)	71	85
Narcissistic	47	67
Antisocial (aggressive)	45	45
Compulsive (conforming)	54	63
Passive–Aggressive (negativistic)	93	47
Schizotypal (schizoid)	53	68
Borderline (cycloid)	81	69
Paranoid	49	69
Anxiety	102	76
Somatoform	66	72
Hypomanic	52	60
Dysthymic	99	84
Alcohol Abuse	79	55
Drug Abuse	67	64
Psychotic Thinking	60	60
Psychotic Depression	71	43
Psychotic Delusions	62	57

Note. The MCMI was administered to the patient in the first evaluation session (1st test) and then re-administered 4 months later (retest).

report suggested the following diagnoses: generalized anxiety disorder, dysthymic disorder, alcohol abuse, and borderline personality disorder (with prominent dependent and passive–aggressive traits).

The text of the MCMI interpretive report did not correspond to Ron's initial presentation. He depicted himself as much more disturbed and emotionally unstable and likely to act out in hostile ways than he appeared. Nor did the elevated personality disorder scales and suggested diagnoses correspond to the clinical impressions of the patient. For example, he neither met any of the *DSM-III-R* criteria nor gave the impression of a passive–aggressive personality disorder, although his highest MCMI scale score was for this disorder.

This pattern of scores on the MCMI is not unusual among sex offenders. In the previously described research sample, as in Ron's results, the two most frequently occurring scale scores over 85

were for the Dependent (34% of the sample) and Passive–Aggressive (27%) scales, along with similarly high frequencies for elevations on the scales for anxiety (30%) and dysthymia (28%).

Incorporating the results of the MCMI testing into the diagnostic process, it was decided that Ron probably suffered from a mixed personality disorder, with dependent, passive–aggressive, and histrionic features. The results of the NEO-PI were not used to make a clinical diagnosis but were included in the forensic evaluation report to describe his "premorbid" personality.

Ron's results on the NEO-PI are given in Table 16.6. He scored in the very high range on Neuroticism, in the very low range on Conscientiousness, and in the low range on Agreeableness. He obtained average scores on Extraversion and Openness. This pattern is more extreme and varied than the group means for sex offenders in the previously described research sample, for which the Neuroticism domain was in the high range and the other domains were in the average range.

Other than the very high Neuroticism score, the domain scores and text of the computer-generated NEO-PI report did not appear to be consistent with Ron's initial presentation and history. He appeared more extraverted and socially agreeable, with his joking style, than did most patients. He had a solid record of achievement in his career as well as a stable family life, which did not appear to be consistent with his very low level of conscientiousness.

Interpretation of Ron's test scores must consider that at the time of testing, Ron was experiencing extreme depression as a result of being arrested. Thus, both the MCMI and the NEO-PI showed high scores for depression and anxiety, some of which may be associated with a transitory adjustment reaction but which may also reflect aspects of Ron's general personality style. The MCMI is designed to be used on individuals who are experiencing difficulties, and it is particularly designed to be used during the early phases of assessment and treatment. The NEO-PI was not designed to be used in times of distress or to identify transitory stress-induced reactions.

Ron's depression decreased significantly after his legal problems were satisfactorily resolved. Although he continued to report feeling depressed, his depres-

TABLE 16.6

Case Example: NEO Personality Inventory (NEO-PI) Scores

NEO-PI scale	1st test		Retest	
	T score	Range	*T* score	Range
Domain				
Neuroticism	70	Very high	70	Very high
Extraversion	46	Average	55	Average
Openness to Experience	47	Average	51	Average
Agreeableness	40	Low	44	Low
Conscientiousness	25	Very low	32	Very low
Neuroticism facet				
Anxiety	72	Very high	64	High
Hostility	55	Average	48	Average
Depression	65	Very high	75	Very high
Self-Consciousness	56	High	66	Very high
Impulsiveness	57	High	69	Very high
Vulnerability	86	Very high	60	High
Extraversion facet				
Warmth	57	High	55	Average
Gregariousness	46	Average	48	Average
Assertiveness	46	Average	53	Average
Activity	41	Low	56	High
Excitement Seeking	61	High	61	High
Positive Emotions	33	Very low	48	Average
Openness facet				
Fantasy	61	High	63	High
Aesthetics	43	Low	47	Average
Feelings	54	Average	49	Average
Actions	45	Average	45	Average
Ideas	41	Low	51	Average
Values	45	Average	45	Average

Note. The NEO-PI was administered to the patient in the first evaluation session (1st test) and then re-administered 4 months later (retest).

sion was masked by a jovial style and there was no fearfulness or reports of suicidal intentions. He was retested on the MCMI and the NEO-PI 4 months after the initial testing (see Tables 16.5 and 16.6).

The pattern of results on the MCMI was quite different from that of the initial testing. The only two significant personality scale elevations were on the Histrionic (85) and Dependent (80) scales. The score on the Passive–Aggressive scale dropped from 96 to 47. Anxiety and depression scores dropped significantly, although Ron continued to be depressed and still scored in the clinical range (84, down from 101). The suggested diagnoses were dysthymic disorders, generalized anxiety disorder, and dependent personality disorder with prominent his-

trionic traits. The computer-generated MCMI clinical interpretive report depicted Ron in totally different, and generally positive, terms as a passive and dependent individual who strived to be socially accommodating.

The change from a dangerous, social menace to a socially conforming person did not appear to be related to any personality changes produced in psychotherapy. Instead, an analysis of changes in item responses between the two testings showed that most of the changes were on items measuring state depression, which were also incorporated into the MCMI personality disorder scales such as the Passive–Aggressive and Borderline scales.

Retesting Ron with the NEO-PI resulted in essentially the same pattern of scores as the previous test results from the initial assessment (see Table 16.6). After 4 months of therapy, which predominantly addressed the depression and anxiety and some aspects of the sexual disorder, it was not evident that Ron's personality had changed. However, the therapist's impressions of Ron began to correspond to the description of his personality, as described in the computer-generated NEO-PI report, which had not seemed particularly accurate at the time of the initial assessment.

For example, Ron had initially appeared to be highly agreeable because of his joking style, his expressions of gratitude, and his willingness to do whatever was recommended to help his situation. But later in the therapy process, it was clear that he was not actually an agreeable person. It was hard for him to feel or express concern for his wife or son, although earlier he had cried with gratitude because they had not rejected him. Later, he seemed to be generally unable to initiate positive behaviors toward them and, in fact, offended them in thoughtless ways. He became critical of professionals involved with his care, expressing (often unjustified) negative or hostile evaluations. For example, he antagonistically stated that his previous therapy was mostly "b__s__" and boasted how he had lied to his doctors in the past. By implication, he was expressing similar beliefs about his present therapy. The issues of low Agreeableness and low concern for others became important in therapy to help him understand the effects of his inappropriate behavior on others. He never expressed concern about this and thus lacked one of the tools for helping control his behavior.

As his mood improved during treatment, his low Conscientiousness became evident. He had created the impression of Conscientiousness through his unblemished work record. Although tardiness and irresponsibility did not appear to be work issues, the nature of his job did not make it a good test of Conscientiousness. He became more lax about appointments, rescheduling or canceling them or arriving late. He was also less conscientious in bringing forth relevant material in sessions; he became compliant rather than being conscientious or responsible in examining himself and his situation. He began to

carelessly disregard rules that he had observed earlier in therapy (e.g., avoiding situations in which he might have exposed himself). Earlier he had brought up subjects for discussion, whereas later he only presented less favorable material in response to direct inquiries.

These changes in my conceptualization of him might appear to be related to changing issues in the course of therapy, such as transference. But the similar results of the two testings with the NEO-PI indicate that these personality factors were present at the start of therapy and did not change. So the NEO-PI testing actually provided information that was not readily apparent in all of the dramatics of the initial presentation—aspects of Ron's "normal" personality that were somewhat masked by the presenting problems of depression, compulsive sexual behavior, and all of the stresses associated with the arrest and forensic processes.

PERSONAL EXPERIENCE

The purpose of a forensic psychological evaluation is to provide an accurate and understandable description of relatively enduring characteristics of an individual that can then be used by criminal justice personnel. The forensic evaluation is written primarily to determine the disposition of a case or to develop sentencing recommendations, including making predictions about future behavior and rehabilitation planning. Except in cases that involve criminal responsibility or insanity, psychiatric diagnoses, particularly of personality disorders, are not critical. Presentence investigation reports, for example, are the most common type of forensic evaluation, and psychiatric diagnoses were rarely incorporated.

My experience in clinical services, including work within the medical model in a hospital setting, has led me to put an emphasis on personality disorders and related traits when conducting evaluations. As such, I might incorporate into an evaluation the results of testing with instruments such as the MMPI or the MCMI, both of which have special interpretations available for forensic settings. When the test results show clinical elevations that are consistent with my understanding of a patient, I feel comfortable incorporating this information into my reports.

Diagnosing a distinct personality disorder is difficult, even with *DSM-III-R*-explicit criteria, and forensic patients tend not to fit neatly into the diagnostic categories.

The resultant descriptions of personality disorders and related traits often require elaborate explanations and interpretations for criminal justice personnel, who sometimes have little patience with clinical nuances of the diagnosis. The clinical disorders also sound very judgmental and negativistic. The diagnostic labels are often subjected to even more negative re-interpretations by criminal justice personnel who have associations that are different from the *DSM-III-R* psychopathological criteria. In court, there is often little interest in personality disorder labels, and in trials, there might be disagreements with other professionals about the specific diagnosis of personality disorder. (Diagnosing personality disorders is, after all, part clinical skill and part art.) I justify the continued use of personality disorder diagnostics because it makes sense to me and appears to have prognostic utility in predicting future adjustment as well as the effectiveness of different types of therapy.

When one does psychological testing as part of a forensic evaluation, one is ethically obligated to report the results of all testing. Although I might choose to re-interpret the results, I cannot pretend that the results from any given test do not exist. In the case example of Ron, the diagnosis of exhibitionism instead of pedophilia was an important factor in the sentencing. Also important, however, was the unstable and negative characterization of Ron as a result of personality disorder testing with the MCMI. As it turned out, much of the negativism was derived from his more transitional and extreme depressive state following his arrest than being a characteristic personality disorder or trait.

In my role as an academic psychologist and researcher, I am aware of the limitations of the concepts of personality disorders, particularly as applied to forensic populations like sex offenders. The concepts of personality traits or factors, without the baggage of clinical disorders, are interesting because they are so generalizable. But they do not seem appropriate for clinical or forensic evaluations, despite their stability and prognostic utility. Somehow, they seem to predict more normal behavior, not psychopathology. I have found it hard to use the concepts of personality factors in conceptualizing treatment plans other than in a straightforward, somewhat commonsense cognitive–behavioral plan.

When I first started using the NEO-PI with sex offenders for research purposes and in my clinical practice, I was initially surprised to find that the offenders usually seemed to understand and agree with the resultant descriptions of their personality. Some of the NEO-PI reports are quite negative sounding, particularly for people who are low in Agreeableness or Conscientiousness, yet the subjects rarely disagree or object to the characterization. When I incorporate the resultant analyses into evaluation reports (as a premorbid or general description of personality), the people reading them generally do not have difficulty understanding the material, nor do they tend to question or disagree with it. Typical feedback is that they feel it is useful in giving an impression of what the person was like. There are usually some implications that it is not "real" psychology because they share the same impression of the individual as a result of their own interactions and interviews.

The case example only raises issues, and one must be cautious not to overgeneralize. However, I was very surprised at the differences between the retesting in the case example with the MCMI and the NEO-PI. I rarely retest patients because I tend to assume that the results of testing remain stable. I had not expected so much change on the MCMI, and I did not really believe that the NEO-PI would be so consistent. To be fair to the MCMI, the manual does not hide the dual loading of depression and other state factors with personality disorder scales (Millon, 1983). Also Millon's theory (1981) predicts that in situations of moderate to severe stress, personality disorders decompensate into other personality disorders of greater severity (e.g., borderline personality disorder in the case example). But this type of knowledge is, frankly, a little esoteric for the typical forensic consumers of the concepts of personality disorders and the results of testing.

Perhaps the whole concept of personality disorders is too esoteric for use in forensic evaluations. Unlike other types of psychological evaluations, which are written to transmit information to professional clinicians, forensic evaluations are primarily prepared for nonclinicians. I wonder whether pathologizing personalities as disorders appropriately describes and respects one's clients and provides useful information for the readers of one's forensic reports. Descriptions of personality factors, which have consensual validity and reliability, may turn out to be more fair and useful. Personality factors, as described on inventories like the NEO-PI, at least have a basis in natural language that makes them more easily understood by nonclinicians.

What is needed is more research looking at personality factors in forensic populations. Are certain patterns of personality factors more associated with certain problems in living or more likely to change as a result of different types of rehabilitative experiences? Research examining personality disorders in sex offending populations (or in forensic populations) has not been particularly productive. Perhaps future research on personality factors may provide information that is useful in understanding forensic clients and rehabilitation planning.

References

American Psychiatric Association. (1987). *Diagnostic and statistical manual of mental disorders* (3rd ed., rev.). Washington, DC: Author.

Bard, L. A., & Knight, R. A. (1987). Sex offender subtyping and the MCMI. In C. Green (Ed.), *Conference on the Millon Clinical Inventories* (pp. 133–137). Minneapolis, MN: National Computer Systems.

Cattell, R. B., Eber, H. W., & Tatsuoka, M. M. (1970). *The handbook for the Sixteen Personality Factor Questionnaire.* Champaign, IL: Institute for Personality and Ability Testing.

Costa, P. T., Jr., & McCrae, R. R. (1985). *The NEO Personality Inventory manual.* Odessa, FL: Psychological Assessment Resources.

Costa, P. T., Jr., & McCrae, R. R. (1990). Personality disorders and the five-factor model of personality. *Journal of Personality Disorders, 4,* 362–371.

Dahlstrom, W. G., Welsh, G. S., & Dahlstrom, L. E. (1972). *An MMPI handbook: Vol. 1. Clinical interpretation* (rev. ed.). Minneapolis: University of Minnesota Press.

Edwards, A. L. (1959). *Edwards Personal Preference Schedule manual.* New York: Psychological Corporation.

Eysenck, H. J., & Eysenck, S. B. G. (1975). *Manual of the Eysenck Personality Questionnaire.* London, England: Hodder & Stoughton.

Fisher, G. (1969). Psychological needs of heterosexual pedophiles. *Disease of the Nervous System, 30,* 419–421.

Fisher, G., & Howell, L. M. (1970). Psychological needs of homosexual pedophiles. *Disease of the Nervous System, 31,* 623–625.

Fisher, G., & Rivlin, E. (1971). Psychological needs of rapists. *British Journal of Criminology, 11,* 182–185.

Forgac, G. E., & Michaels, E. J. (1982). Personality characteristics of two types of male exhibitionists. *Journal of Abnormal Psychology, 91,* 287–293.

Hathaway, S. R., & McKinley, J. C. (1967). *Minnesota Multiphasic Personality Inventory manual.* New York: Psychological Corporation.

Langevin, R., Paitich, D., Freeman, R., Mann, K., & Handy, L. (1978). Personality characteristics and sexual anomalies in males. *Canadian Journal of Behavioral Sciences, 10,* 222–238.

Levin, S. L., & Stava, L. (1987). Personality characteristics of sex offenders: A review. *Archives of Sexual Behavior, 16,* 57–79.

Millon, T. (1981). *Disorders of personality:* DSM-III, Axis II. New York: Wiley.

Millon, T. (1983). *Millon Clinical Multiaxial Inventory manual* (3rd ed.). Minneapolis, MN: Interpretive Scoring Systems.

Millon, T. (1987). *Manual for the MCMI-II* (2nd ed.). Minneapolis, MN: National Computer Systems.

Neuman, C. J. (1981). *Differentiation between personality characteristics of rapists and child molesters: A validation study of the Millon Clinical Multiaxial Inventory.* Unpublished doctoral dissertation, University of Miami, Miami, FL.

Scott, R. L. (1982). Analysis of the needs systems of twenty male rapists. *Psychological Reports, 51,* 1119–1125.

Smukler, A. J., & Schiebel, D. (1975). Personality characteristics of exhibitionists. *Diseases of the Nervous System, 36,* 600–603.

Wiggins, J. S., & Pincus, A. L. (1989). Conceptions of personality disorders and dimensions of personality. *Psychological Assessment: A Journal of Consulting and Clinical Psychology, 1,* 305–316.

Wilson, G. D., & Cox, D. N. (1983). Personality of pedophile club members. *Personality and Individual Differences, 4,* 323–329.

CHAPTER 17

A CASE OF BORDERLINE PERSONALITY DISORDER

Stephen Bruehl

Betty was a 45-year-old White, divorced woman. Her original complaint when she entered therapy 4 years earlier was that she was experiencing discipline problems with her daughter and difficulties in adjusting to her recent divorce. She had been married three times and had divorced her most recent husband shortly before entering therapy. She had two children from her first marriage, a 24-year-old son and a 20-year-old daughter. Two months before Betty began her therapy, her daughter was arrested on drug possession charges and was suspended from high school. Betty was quite distraught about her inability to control her daughter's behavior. She also felt somewhat responsible for her daughter's problems, believing that her marriage to her second husband had been a selfish decision that had irreparably damaged her relationship with her daughter. Her daughter entered into court-ordered therapy concurrently with Betty's therapy. Betty had participated in predominately insight-oriented psychotherapy weekly for the next 4 years.

Betty presented as a moderately overweight woman, well groomed and dressed neatly on most occasions. Her speech was grammatically precise, she enunciated clearly, and she reflected a high level of intelligence. She often spoke rapidly and intensely, clearly exhibiting her predominate affect at the time. Her body language was frequently theatrical, and she punctuated her words with elaborate arm gestures and facial expressions (e.g.,

clenched teeth, exaggerated smiles). When experiencing high levels of anxiety or anger, she wrung her hands and, on occasion, would get out of her chair and pace the room. Her affect was quite intense and variable, ranging from near manic excitement to sobbing and screaming. Her emotions could change rapidly during the course of a session, and she sometimes appeared unable to modulate her affect.

Betty was the second of four children, with one older brother and two younger brothers. Her parents and her siblings were all currently living. Betty's relationship with her parents had been strained for a number of years. This strain had increased in the past year following Betty's telling her parents of her sexual abuse by a relative when she was a child. Betty reported that her mother's response was denial that the abuse could have happened. As indicated by this incident, Betty felt that her mother had not always been supportive of her. She stated that despite this perceived lack of support, she had always respected and looked up to her mother, although her mother had always been quite domineering. She described her father in somewhat more positive terms, noting a warm relationship, but also indicated that she resented the fact that he allowed her mother to dominate him. Betty described her relationships with her siblings as moderately close, and these relationships appeared to be less filled with tension than her rela-

The preparation of this chapter was supported, in part, by National Institute of Mental Health Training Grant MH15730-12.

tionship with her mother. She had contact with her parents and her siblings approximately every 2 months.

Betty initially described her childhood as ideal. However, over the course of 2 years of therapy, she gradually revealed evidence of childhood sexual abuse perpetrated by an uncle who had lived next door. She initially had few specific memories of this abuse other than an incident at age 11 in which her uncle put his hand on her buttocks in a suggestive way. At that time, she recalled telling her uncle to stop. During the course of therapy, Betty began recovering additional memories of this abuse by her uncle dating back to approximately age 2. Her earliest memory of abuse was of looking out of her crib at a bloody penis near her face. She remembered later incidents of being forced to perform oral sex, which were associated with intense nausea.

Not surprisingly, given her history, Betty's relationships with men had been problematic. She dated in high school but had no steady relationships. Her first experience of sexual intercourse was in college and resulted in intense feelings of disgust toward herself. She reported one incident of attempted date rape in college, which she successfully repelled.

Each of her marriages had been characterized by intense emotionality and a high level of conflict. Betty first married when she was age 20 an East Indian man with very conservative views. Betty attempted to adopt a traditional role, allowing her husband to hold the power in the relationship. However, she later began to assert herself, which contributed to increased conflict. Betty had extramarital affairs during this marriage, and it ended after 5 years, primarily because of the power struggles that could not be resolved. Four years later, she married her second husband, who was emotionally abusive to her and sexually abused her daughter. Again, Betty experienced ongoing conflict regarding who would control the marriage. This marriage ended 4 years later. Six years after the termination of her second marriage, she remarried a third time. This marriage ended after 2 years, shortly before Betty entered therapy. She was not currently involved in a close relationship with a man, although she had dated over the past 4 years.

Betty had always had few close friends, most of them women. These relationships had tended to be emotionally intense but transient and superficial and had often ended abruptly as a result of interpersonal conflict. For example, a roommate stated, "you may be able to control your kids' lives but not mine," and then proceeded to ask Betty to move out. Her closest relationships appeared to be with immediate family members.

Betty attended 2 years of college beginning at age 18 but withdrew as a result of motivational problems associated with depression. Despite a long history of depressed mood, she reported no previous psychological care prior to her current therapy. She returned to college after 1 year of therapy and had recently graduated. Betty had been employed throughout much of the past 10 years. At one time, she was trained as an emergency medical technician (EMT) but worked in this job for only a short time. She had most frequently worked in retail business settings. She was currently employed full time in retail sales.

Betty's Axis I symptoms at the time of entering therapy indicated a diagnosis of major depression, reflected in sleep problems, appetite disturbance, anhedonia, social withdrawal, concentration problems, and depressed mood. The most appropriate Axis II diagnosis was borderline personality disorder (BDL). The criteria set included a pattern of unstable and intense relationships, impulsive behavior, affective instability, marked and persistent identity disturbance, and chronic feelings of emptiness and boredom.

PERSONALITY DESCRIPTION

The clinician's evaluation of Betty's personality traits as measured by the revised NEO Personality Inventory (NEO-PI-R; Costa & McCrae, 1992) are presented in Table 17.1. Betty scored high on Neuroticism and Openness to Experience, average on Conscientiousness, and low on Extraversion and Agreeableness. Analysis of the facets of each of these factors provided a more detailed description of her personality.

Neuroticism

Within the Neuroticism domain, Betty scored high on every facet. She exhibited high levels of anxiety,

TABLE 17.1

Revised NEO Personality Inventory Personality Profile

Scale	Range	Clinical implications
Neuroticism	Very high	
Anxiety	High	Nervous–ruminative
Angry hostility	Very high	Rageful–bitter
Depression	Very high	Gloomy–despondent
Self-Consciousness	High	Insecure–ashamed
Impulsiveness	High	Spontaneous–unpredictable
Vulnerability	High	Overwhelmed-defenseless
Extraversion	Low	
Warmth	Low	Cold
Gregariousness	Low	Shy–withdrawn
Assertiveness	Average	
Activity	Average	
Excitement Seeking	High	Adventurous
Positive Emotions	Low	Placid–disinterested
Openness	High	
Fantasy	Very high	Imaginative–dissociative
Aesthetics	Average	
Feelings	Average	
Actions	Average	
Ideas	High	Cognitively flexible
Values	High	Open minded
Agreeableness	Low	
Trust	Low	Cynical–suspicious
Straightforwardness	Low	Deceptive–manipulative
Altruism	Average	
Compliance	Low	Aggressive–oppositional
Modesty	Average	
Tender-Mindedness	Average	
Conscientiousness	Average	
Competence	High	Perfectionistic
Order	Average	
Dutifulness	Low	Unreliable–irresponsible
Achievement Striving	High	Driven
Self-discipline	Average	
Deliberation	Low	Hasty

expressing ongoing worries regarding her relationship with her daughter, her finances, her dissatisfaction with her career, her problems in relationships with men, and her perceived personal deficits. These were her anxious thoughts at the time, but she described herself as always having been anxious and ruminative. She noted high levels of tension, resulting in painful muscular "trigger points" in her back. She was also quite apprehensive regarding the intentions of men with whom she had interpersonal con-

tact, reflecting not only her general level of anxiety but also her self-consciousness and antagonistic suspiciousness.

Betty's very high score on the Angry–Hostility facet scale was seen in her frequent experience of and readiness to experience anger and bitterness, especially when provoked by sexually aggressive men. For example, on a date with a man with whom she had gone out only several times, she experienced extreme irritation to the point of anger and rage in response to his inadvertently touching her buttocks. Her antagonistic aggressiveness then contributed to the threatening manner in which she expressed this anger, warning him that "the last man who did that I ripped his ear off!" This extreme verbal response reflected her low threshold for both experiencing and expressing anger. Certainly, unwelcome sexual advances would elicit rebuke from almost anyone, but the extreme nature of her response reflected as well her particularly high level of hostility and Antagonism.

Her proclivity to experience and express anger was reflected in her fantasies as well. Once when Betty was swimming in a creek, men in a passing truck made comments about her appearance. This prompted a variety of "Thelma and Louise" fantasies of running to get a gun and waiting for the men to return so that she could shoot them when they reappeared (these fantasies were generated prior to the appearance of the movie). Clearly, this fantasy also reflected her Antagonism.

Betty also scored high on the Depression facet scale of Neuroticism. She had always felt generally hopeless that she could ever improve her life situation. She described herself as having enjoyed little in her life. She indicated that her choices of husbands and boyfriends had been in part a resignation to what was available rather than a real attraction. Her mood was frequently blue, with only temporary positive moods that attempted to mask an underlying negative affect. Betty felt guilty that she had let down herself and her family by not being engaged in a high-prestige career. She also displayed a sense of low self-esteem that was inconsistent with her actual abilities. Even though she had done well in college, she felt that that had been a fluke and was not attributable to her intelligence. This low self-esteem was also noted during an intellectual evaluation. Despite the fact that her performance was in the very superior range, she displayed an extreme lack of confidence about her intellectual abilities, repeatedly stating "I'm no good at this" during testing. Although the Depression and Anxiety facets of Neuroticism do not correspond to criteria of the third edition revised of the *Diagnostic and Statistical Manual of Mental Disorders* (*DSM-III-R*; American Psychiatric Association, 1987) for Axis I mood disorders, her

standing on these two facets might suggest a personality predisposition to experience major depression and various anxiety disorders.

Betty's profile showed a high score on the Self-Consciousness facet scale of Neuroticism, indicating a sense of insecurity around others. Betty had been intensely ashamed of her abuse history. Although she possessed some clear memories of abuse on entering therapy, she did not reveal this to anyone for 2 more years, nor did she reveal these experiences to her therapist until 1 year ago. She was also ashamed of the fact that she frequently felt depressed and consistently attempted to "put on a smiling face" when having contact with others, despite her negative mood. Betty reported that she felt that if others knew she was depressed, they would realize her weakness.

She also scored high on the Impulsiveness facet scale of Neuroticism. This level of Impulsiveness reflected an inability to control her urges. When Betty's chronically elevated levels of depression and anxiety become exacerbated by situational factors, she attempted to reduce these feelings through overuse of alcohol. This, along with her low tolerance for frustration and inability to resist cravings (high Impulsiveness), resulted in a tendency toward alcohol binges. For example, in the past 2 years, she had experienced situational stressors including being forced out of two living arrangements she enjoyed because of conflict with female roommates and conflict with her parents regarding her informing them of her childhood abuse. Betty began her binge drinking on weekends. She had also used food as a means of trying to regulate her mood and, as with alcohol, tended to binge rather than eat moderately. Because of her concern about her weight, a pattern of bingeing and purging had developed, at times reaching clinically significant levels (i.e., meeting the *DSM-III-R* criteria for bulimia nervosa).

In addition to impulsive drinking and eating, she had also engaged in impulsive sex. For example, after experiencing a high level of anger toward her abuser during a therapy session, she impulsively had unprotected sex with a bisexual man with whom she had previously been a platonic friend. Betty described this friend as a person who jokingly made passes at her on a regular basis that she always turned down. On this particular occasion, when he made a pass, she "resisted" by grabbing him and wrestling him to the floor. After gaining control of him, they proceeded to have sex. This sexual impulsiveness was perhaps an attempt to manage her feelings of anger by re-enacting a situation of sexual powerlessness in which, unlike her childhood abuse, she was able to get control. Despite her concerns following this event that she may have been exposed to the AIDS virus, she impulsively had unprotected sex with this same individual on later occasions when she was experiencing intense emotional dysphoria.

Because of chronically overwhelmed coping resources, she had difficulties dealing with high stress levels (i.e., a facet scale of Vulnerability). For example, each time examinations approached in college, Betty expressed increased feelings that "I just don't know whether I can handle it" and would become so disrupted that she would have great difficulty completing her work. High levels of stress either at work or at school consistently resulted in increasing social withdrawal and an expressed desire to "hole up and rest." Her feelings of depression and anxiety also increased dramatically during these periods.

Extraversion

Betty's personality with respect to Extraversion was interesting because she had traits of both Extraversion and introversion. This complexity of her personality was evident from scores on the Extraversion facets. For example, she was elevated on Excitement Seeking, a facet evident in her bungee jumping, sky diving, and other life choices. Several years ago, Betty entered training to become an EMT. She actually worked as an EMT for only a short time. Although she found it exciting, she also found it too stressful, possibly reflecting her high Vulnerability. Despite her tendency to seek out excitement, Betty's level of Positive Emotions was low. When involved in exciting activities, she experienced temporary increases in positive mood. However, as a personality disposition, the dysphoria reflected in the facets of Neuroticism was more characteristic.

She scored in the average range on the facets of Assertiveness and Activity but in the low range of the facet of Warmth. Although in public Betty often made an effort to smile and act warmly toward others, her interpersonal warmth was quite shallow. Betty was too absorbed in her own difficulties to extend herself and make deeper contact with others. It is interesting that although Betty described herself as high on Warmth in her self-report NEO-PI-R, a more objective rating placed her as low on Warmth. This discrepancy appeared attributable to Betty considering her ability to put on a front of friendliness as an ability to be genuinely warm. This example is indicative of important discrepancies that may be observed between the self-perceptions of certain patient types and the evaluations of independent observers.

Consistent with Betty's low level of Warmth was her low level of Gregariousness. Betty made little effort to get to know individuals with whom she had regular contact, such as coworkers. Her low levels of Warmth and Gregariousness, combined with high levels of Hostility, clearly contributed to her lack of close friends as well as her chronic difficulties in intimate relationships.

Openness to Experience

Within the Openness domain, Betty scored highest on the facet of Fantasy. Betty described herself as always having a "very active fantasy life." Because of the emotional impact of ongoing sexual abuse as a child, Betty felt a great need to escape and used fantasy as a way of doing this. As a child, she remembered frequently looking out the windows of her house, "spacing out," and imagining that she was somewhere else. This pattern of withdrawal into fantasy as an escape from stress continued into adulthood. For example, she stated that she sometimes imagined that she was a hermit in a cave, isolated from all the problems of interpersonal relationships. Betty found her tendency to withdraw into fantasy a problem, noting that this dissociation from reality had resulted in difficulty attending to and remembering emotionally aversive incidents in her life. She complained of having very few memories of actual childhood events and remembered instead frequently staring off into space and imagining being in a safer situation.

Although most of the characteristics of the *DSM-III-R* diagnosis of BDL are reflected in the facets of

287

Neuroticism (Costa & McCrae, 1990), one particular characteristic of BDL may be reflected in high scores on the Openness to Ideas facet scale. Individuals who score high on Openness to Ideas possess a variety of ways of seeing themselves. At pathological levels, this "flexibility" may reflect a lack of certainty or clarity regarding identity (i.e., identity diffusion). In Betty's case, a maladaptive flexibility of ideas may have been exhibited in her sexual identity confusion. She identified herself as heterosexual but had often questioned this identity and had engaged in sexual relations with a woman on at least one occasion. Her most clear statement was that she was just uncertain regarding her sexual orientation. In addition to uncertainty about sexual identity, Betty was also uncertain about her career goals. As mentioned earlier, she had worked in a variety of sales jobs and as an EMT and had contemplated careers in medicine and social work. In general, she tended to be dissatisfied with all of her jobs and seemed uncertain regarding the direction of her future life. Betty scored high on the facet of Values. She was generally open minded regarding what behavior she felt was acceptable, as evidenced by her close friendship and sexual relations with a bisexual man and her first marriage to an East Indian man. Betty scored in the average range on the remaining Openness facets scales of Aesthetics, Feelings, and Actions.

Agreeableness

Betty scored in the low range of the Agreeableness domain (i.e., Antagonism). This was reflected in her low levels of Trust, Straightforwardness, and Compliance. Betty stated that she had always had her "guard up" to protect herself from others, especially men. For example, when an old male friend who wanted to develop an intimate relationship with Betty visited her at her workplace, she put him off, stating that she was busy but that he could come back when she got off work. Betty accidentally "forgot" that the man was coming back and left, leaving the friend alone. A similar incident happened shortly thereafter, and consequently, the man did not attempt to see her again. Betty felt that this forgetting was purposeful and protective. She generally appeared to be suspicious of the motives of any men who were interested in developing an intimate rela-

tionship with her. Her low level of Trust could be seen even more vividly in her perceptual distortions and misinterpretations. Betty had on a number of occasions reported seeing men behind her (e.g., through peripheral vision or while looking in the rearview mirror of a car), only to turn around and find no one there. She also had noted irrational fears at night that someone was outside of her home trying to get in. This typically caused her to turn on all of the lights inside and outside of her house. The source of this characteristic level of mistrust and suspicion from her childhood experiences of abuse was self-evident.

Betty also scored low on the Straightforwardness facet of Agreeableness. Rather than discussing her concerns about living arrangements with her roommates, she surreptitiously manipulated the situation, prompting one of her roommates to state that "you may be able to control your kids' lives but not mine." When Betty became concerned about her impulsive sex with her bisexual friend (who was also a coworker), she intentionally short changed him on a commission on a sale with the hope that he would become angry and refuse any further contact with her. Thus, she attempted to manipulate the situation rather than openly discuss her difficulties with her friend. Her manipulations and power struggles had also been interpreted in therapy as an effort to avoid being abused and exploited again by others. She felt she needed to outmaneuver others to avoid being taken advantage of.

Betty scored low on the Compliance facet scale of Agreeableness. She displayed a tendency to be somewhat oppositional in interactions with authority figures. For example, her first marriage to an East Indian man reflected not only flexibility of values but also opposition to her mother's expressed dislike of the man. Her consistent marital difficulties were also related to her low Compliance. Betty initially acted in a way that suggested that she wanted her husbands to take responsibility for making decisions related to finances, discipline of the children, and division of labor. However, when each husband attempted to do this, Betty covertly resisted by taking actions to undercut the husband's decisions. This behavior led to chronic but covert power struggles within the marriage. She received average scores on the Altruism, Modesty, and Tender-Mindedness facet scales of Agreeableness.

Conscientiousness

Betty's overall scores on Conscientiousness were in the low range. However, inspection of the various facets of this factor revealed a more complex picture. Betty scored in the average range on the facet scales of Order and Self-Discipline but in the high range on the facet scales of Competence and Achievement Striving. Betty's desire for competence was reflected subtly in her very precise speech patterns as well as in her strong desire to do well in college despite her fears that she was incapable of doing so. In Betty's case, her desire to do well and appear competent seemed to be motivated by her perception of her family members as quite competent and accomplished individuals whom she continually must struggle to equal. This perception also seemed to motivate her high need for achievement. In college, she set her goals quite high, for example, seeking a 4.0 grade point average. Since graduating, she had expressed a desire to become a physician, in large part because of the prestige this would bring to herself and her family. Thus, she set high expectations for herself, striving to achieve to gain acceptance from her family.

Despite her high level of intelligence and striving, Betty had failed to achieve what she desired in terms of her career because of changeable goals and a low level of Dutifulness. She perceived herself as quite committed to her responsibilities at work and school. However, throughout her college career she had consistent problems with procrastination. These problems were severe enough that she often had to stay up throughout an entire night to complete assignments on time. Although she procrastinated, she was still able to do well in school because of her high level of intelligence. Betty's low level of Dutifulness was also exhibited at work. For example, she had on a number of occasions called in sick to obtain a day off from work when she was not actually ill. Her low level of Dutifulness conflicted with her ability to achieve. On the one hand, she wanted to achieve and be competent to gain respect, but on the other hand, she did not follow through on the responsibilities required to gain that respect. Thus,

she became quite angry at herself for "sabotaging" her own goals. During the course of therapy, Betty complained that her tendency to sabotage herself was one of the things she would most like to change about herself.

Betty also scored low on the Deliberation facet scale of Conscientiousness. In conjunction with her high impulsiveness, her low level of Deliberation had caused problems in her life. During her second year of therapy, Betty was living alone and feeling quite lonely and depressed. When an opportunity arose to share a house with her two children, she immediately agreed, without considering the likelihood of problems as a result of her enmeshment with them. Rather than taking the time to consider possible outcomes, Betty grasped a chance to decrease her loneliness. As might have been predicted, this living arrangement did not work out, and several months later, just as hastily as she moved in, Betty moved out.

In summary, Betty's personality was characterized primarily by very high levels of Neuroticism, high levels on particular facets of Extraversion and Openness, and low levels of the facets of Agreeableness and Conscientiousness. Betty's elevated Neuroticism and low Agreeableness were consistent with what would be expected based on the *DSM-III-R* criteria for BDL. Her elevated Neuroticism was characterized by elevations on each of the six facet scales of Neuroticism, with negative affect prominent. Although Betty exhibited many of the profile characteristics that would be expected of BDL based on both the *DSM-III-R* criteria and the clinical literature, her profile was not entirely prototypic. Perhaps, like most cases of BDL, Betty was not prototypic. Her low Warmth, Gregariousness, Deliberation, and Dutifulness scale scores were also very important in understanding the difficulties she had had in life and in therapy.

PERSONALITY IMPLICATIONS FOR TREATMENT

The strength of the psychotherapeutic relationship was slow to develop because of Betty's low levels of Warmth and Trust. Betty was quite wary initially, and for several months, she attempted to minimize the seriousness and impact of her difficulties. During this period, she presented consistently with a happy face, but as described earlier, this happy face appeared to be a "false face," masking her underlying dysphoria. Her hesitation in trusting the therapist was evident in the fact that what emerged as a central issue of therapy, namely, her sexual abuse as a child, was not mentioned until 2 years into the therapy, despite a powerful memory of abuse of which she was aware at the onset of therapy.

The transference issues observed in therapy related primarily to Betty's low Trust and high hostility. As might be expected given her low Straightforwardness, she expressed her anger and lack of trust passively. During the first 2 years of therapy, there were few problems regarding scheduling issues and missed appointments. However, as the therapeutic relationship became closer and more emotionally laden, her underlying hostility toward men and her lack of trust resulted in problems in maintaining the structure of therapy. Over the past 6 months of therapy, there had been ongoing issues related to the scheduling of sessions. Betty had moved to a new job and stated that the previous appointment time would no longer work. When given several scheduling options, Betty insisted that her new schedule would not allow her to have a set appointment, and therefore, she requested that she schedule her appointments on a week-to-week basis. Given her previously good history of scheduling, this new arrangement was attempted. However, Betty began missing appointments or simply not calling to set up appointments. Betty insisted that her manager was refusing to keep her on a regular schedule and that, therefore, it was quite difficult for her to set up appointments. There was some truth to her explanations, but they were also reminiscent of the barriers she had placed in all of her past adult relationships. It was therefore important to interpret her scheduling problems as an expression of resistance and fears of trusting the therapist.

Finally, Betty was given the option of either accepting a standing appointment time or suspending treatment. Although she then chose to remain in treatment, she manipulated the therapist to accept a time she knew was inconvenient for him, and she expressed her anger by being 20 minutes late for the next two sessions, each time calling at the scheduled time to let the therapist know she would be coming (i.e., low Straightforwardness). At the following session, the therapist told Betty that she would have to choose a different time. Betty complained that there were no other possible times because of her schedule but later admitted that she had never discussed the possibility of schedule changes with her manager for fear that it would make her look bad in the eyes of her employer (high Self-Consciousness). Eventually, these scheduling issues were resolved, and therapy continued to become more intense and focused on issues related to her past abuse.

Betty's low Compliance suggested that it was important to watch for control issues in therapy. On the few occasions when therapeutic "homework" assignments were attempted and agreed on, Betty failed to complete them. The effects of low Compliance could also be seen within a single session. On several occasions when therapy became unfocused and bogged down, the therapist attempted to direct therapy to issues in which Betty had expressed an interest in addressing, but each time Betty resisted by changing the direction of treatment to tangential issues. Her low Compliance seemed to interact with her low Trust and high Hostility to cause interpersonal difficulties in therapy. These same issues were responsible for her problems in previous intimate relationships with close friends, family members, and husbands.

As Betty's scheduling problems were resolved and the affective intensity of sessions increased, her high level of Vulnerability became an important issue. Her susceptibility to stress combined with her history of perceptual distortions suggested the possibility of decompensation when her work in therapy became too intense. Betty's vulnerability to stress was reflected dramatically in an incident that occurred in her ongoing therapy. While vividly experiencing the affect associated with her childhood abuse that had been repressed, Betty began stuttering and eventually was totally unable to talk. She also began shaking physically and appeared to squeeze her hands together tightly as if attempting to hold herself together. These symptoms lasted approximately 1 hour, but Betty felt quite fragile for the next several weeks. Betty later expressed the feeling that she was splitting apart into different parts of herself as she was experiencing these symptoms.

Each of these examples focuses on the negative

implications for therapy of particular personality characteristics. However, information provided by the NEO-PI-R also suggested strengths that improved treatment prognosis. Betty's high level of Openness to Ideas did reflect in part pathological aspects, but it also reflected an ability to be more cognitively flexible, encouraging the use of insight-oriented treatment. Although she had difficulty addressing and confronting her conflicts (high Vulnerability), she was very open to looking at her problems in different ways and considering alternative ways for understanding and addressing these problems. For example, Betty's initial focus in therapy was on her problems in her relationship with her daughter. Much of this early therapeutic work focused on increasing Betty's understanding of the dynamics of their relationship and working on better ways of handling her interactions with her daughter. Betty was able to engage in these tasks quite effectively, in part, because of her openness to self-insight and problem-solving alternatives.

Information from her personality profile also suggested a potential effectiveness for other particular therapeutic techniques. In Betty's case, her openness to fantasy enhanced her responsiveness to gestalt techniques that were used to address her anger. For example, encouraging Betty to confront her deceased uncle using the empty chair technique resulted in a vivid cathartic experience. Betty immediately began talking to her uncle, engaging in an increasingly heated dialogue with him, eventually kicking and hitting the floor (where his image lay). She then suddenly stopped her activity, stating "he's gone."

Betty continued therapy, and her progress was significant. Her symptoms of depression lifted, and she reported feeling more stable. Her wide variations in emotion became less extreme, and instances of impulsive behavior became more rare. Although changes in her manner of relating interpersonally were subtle, she reported feeling more positive emotionally when interacting with others. She was not involved in an intimate relationship with a man, reflecting continued distrust, although in therapy her level of trust currently appeared moderately high. Betty made progress in therapy, and with continued therapy, prognosis for further progress was good.

References

American Psychiatric Association. (1987). *Diagnostic and statistical manual of mental disorders* (3rd ed., rev.). Washington, DC: Author.

Costa, P. T., Jr., & McCrae, R. R. (1990). Personality disorders and the five-factor model of personality. *Journal of Personality Disorders, 4,* 362–371.

Costa, P. T., Jr., & McCrae, R. R. (1992). *Revised NEO Personality Inventory and the NEO Five-Factor Inventory professional manual.* Odessa, FL: Psychological Assessment Resources.

CHAPTER 18

NARCISSISM FROM THE PERSPECTIVE OF THE FIVE-FACTOR MODEL

Elizabeth M. Corbitt

Narcissistic personality disorder (NAR) is defined in the third edition, revised, of the *Diagnostic and Statistical Manual of Mental Disorders* (*DSM-III-R*; American Psychiatric Association, 1987) as "a pervasive pattern of grandiosity (in fantasy and behavior), lack of empathy, and hypersensitivity to the evaluation of others, beginning by early adulthood and present in a variety of contexts" (p. 351) and is diagnosed on the basis of the presence of at least five of the nine criteria indicating these traits. Such attributes may also be conceptualized as extreme, dysfunctional variants of certain personality traits described by the five-factor model (FFM) of normal personality, such as conceit, tough mindedness, and self-consciousness. This chapter outlines the principles just described and uses a case study to illustrate the utility of the FFM in describing and conceptualizing narcissism.

The primary dimension of normal personality (as defined by the FFM) that relates to narcissism is antagonism (the polar opposite of Agreeableness). Widiger, Trull, Clarkin, Sanderson, and Costa (see Table 6.1) suggest that NAR criteria primarily involve extremely low variants of the Agreeableness facets of modesty (indicating arrogance and conceit), altruism (indicating self-centeredness, selfishness, and exploitation), and tender mindedness (indicating lack of empathy), with the clinical literature also suggesting low straightforwardness (e.g., manipulativeness). Furthermore, these investigators determine that the criteria also suggest high variants of openness to fantasy (e.g., "fantasies of unlimited success, power, brilliance, beauty, or ideal love"; American Psychiat-

ric Association, 1987, p. 351) and the Neuroticism facets of self-consciousness (hypersensitivity to evaluations) and hostility (rage).

However, such predictions of the NAR patient's presentation on an inventory of normal personality may not be as straightforward as direct extrapolations from the *DSM-III-R* criteria suggest. A complication that is likely to arise in the evaluation of NAR patients is suggested by the criterion "reacts to criticism with feelings of rage, shame, or humiliation (*even if not expressed*)" (American Psychiatric Association, 1987, p. 351, emphases added). The ambiguity of the NAR patient's response to criticism is even more explicit in the third edition of *DSM* (*DSM-III*), in which it is stated that these individuals may display a "cool indifference" to criticism, rejection, or defeat by others (American Psychiatric Association, 1980, p. 317). In fact, this item was deleted in the fourth edition of the *DSM* (*DSM-IV*; American Psychiatric Association, 1994) in part because of the ambiguity and complexity of its assessment (Gunderson, Ronningstam, & Smith, 1991). NAR patients are very vulnerable and self-conscious, but they at times express this through a complete denial of any faults or insecurities (Kernberg, 1984). Thus, NAR patients may deny the existence of their own vulnerability, self-consciousness, and hostility. On the sole basis of the *DSM-III-R* criteria for NAR, it may be predicted that NAR patients will score high on the Neuroticism facets of self-consciousness and vulnerability. However, NAR patients may deny feelings of shame and inferiority and thereby produce average or even low scores on these facet scales.

Costa and McCrae (1990) supported this supposition, finding significant negative correlations among the Minnesota Multiphasic Personality Inventory (MMPI) and the Millon Clinical Multiaxial Inventory (MCMI) scales for NAR and the NEO Personality Inventory (NEO-PI; Costa & McCrae, 1985) Neuroticism scale. Similarly, in a combined factor analysis of the five factors and several personality disorder scales, Wiggins and Pincus (1989) found that both the MMPI and the Personality Adjective Check List (PACL) Narcissistic scales loaded negatively on Neuroticism. Trull (1992) likewise found a significant negative relation between the MMPI Narcissistic scale and NEO-PI Neuroticism in a clinical population of personality disordered individuals, further supporting the contention that NAR patients tend to present themselves as psychologically healthy rather than vulnerable to emotional weakness.

An additional complication of this issue involves the NAR patient's reasons for seeking treatment. Although theoretically one would predict a lack (or at least a denial) of depression and anxiety in patients with NAR, clinical experience suggests that they seek treatment in response to overwhelming discomfort brought about by the failure of their typical modes of defense against precisely these feelings of depression and anxiety. In such cases, it is likely that elevations will occur on these facets of Neuroticism, at least in the early stages of treatment. In other words, a poorly defended person with NAR may produce elevations on Neuroticism (an accurate portrayal of his or her vulnerability), whereas a rigidly defended person with NAR may produce extremely low scores (reflecting a defensive denial of vulnerability).

The following case illustration further clarifies both the expected relation between NAR and the FFM and the additional issues that may ensue from both the patient's denial of traits evident to others and his or her temporary state-related symptoms.

CASE ILLUSTRATION: PATRICIA

Presenting Complaint

Patricia was a 41-year-old married woman who presented at an outpatient mental health clinic complaining of interpersonal difficulties at work and re-

curring bouts of depression. She described a series of jobs in which she had experienced considerable friction with coworkers, stating that people generally did not treat her with the respect she deserved. She attributed her depression to the recent suspicion that perhaps people did not like her because of her behavior; she indicated that she wished to explore this possibility further in therapy to discover how to act with others so that they would not continue to be hostile toward her. The immediate reason for her entrance into treatment was her recent failure to succeed in a supervisory position at the bank at which she was employed—a failure that she said was very damaging to her self-esteem.

History and Clinical Description

Patricia was an only child. She described her parents as reserved to the point of coldness, stating that both were busy with their jobs and disapproved of displays of affection. Patricia said that she always felt that she was not appreciated for herself but only for what she accomplished. As an adult, Patricia had few friendships and had had only three romantic relationships, including her marriage at the age of 35. At the time she entered treatment, she reported having little time for friendships because of her long hours at work. She described her marriage as unsatisfying, stating for example that her husband was very childish (e.g., referring to his sentimentality on anniversaries as "adolescent").

Patricia reported a long history of banking jobs in which she had experienced interpersonal discord. Shortly before her entrance into treatment, Patricia was demoted from a supervisory capacity at her current job because of her inability to effectively interact with those she was supposed to supervise. She described herself as always feeling out of place with her coworkers and indicated that most of them failed to adequately appreciate her skill or the amount of time she put in at work. She reported that she was beginning to think that perhaps she had something to do with their apparent dislike of her. However, even during the initial treatment sessions, her descriptions of her past and current job situations quickly and inevitably reverted to defensive statements concerning others' mistreatment and lack of appreciation of her. Despite her stated goal of changing her own behavior to be better liked, it quickly became clear that her actual wish was to cause her coworkers and supervisors to realize her superiority and to treat her accordingly. Patricia stated several times, for example, that the tellers at the bank were jealous of her status and abilities as a loan officer and that this made them dislike her.

Five-Factor Description

Figure 18.1 provides Patricia's description of herself in terms of the domain and facet scales of the Revised NEO Personality Inventory (NEO-PI-R; Costa & McCrae, 1992b). This section describes the salient features of Patricia's self-description, especially those pertaining to narcissism, and gives examples of situations or statements that illustrate each extreme score.

As stated earlier, Agreeableness is the dimension most central to narcissism. Patricia described herself as low on five of the six facets of the Agreeableness domain. Her very low score on the facet of modesty suggested grandiosity and arrogance about her own abilities compared with others'. Patricia often made condescending remarks about coworkers working under her, indicating that they were inferior to her in intelligence and abilities and thus had little or nothing to offer her. For example, she described one incident in which she was assigned an assistant whom she was expected to train but who could also help her with her duties. Instead of accepting such help, Patricia told her boss and the assistant that she did not see how someone so much younger and less skilled than herself could be anything but a drain on her time and energy.

Her low level of altruism, indicating perhaps selfishness and exploitation, was evidenced in her manipulation of her work situation so that others were required to do tasks she considered beneath her while leaving more desirable tasks for herself. In one such situation, Patricia pretended to have a back injury as an excuse to avoid sales work, thus forcing the other employees to do this less pleasant job while she was given more prestigious loan accounts. Lack of empathy was suggested by Patricia's low score on the tender-mindedness facet scale. For example, she reported one incident in which a friend had agreed to meet her for dinner but was late be-

cause her child was ill; Patricia was highly offended and irritated by what she referred to as her friend's "lack of consideration" in being late. She felt no compassion for her friend or the child.

The remaining facets of Agreeableness are less central to the construct of narcissism but were additional aspects of Patricia's personality. Her tendency toward suspiciousness, as indicated by her low trust score, was exemplified by her belief that others did not like her and conspired against her to make her job harder (e.g., by "purposely" failing to get necessary paperwork to her on time). Finally, her low score on the compliance scale suggested uncooperativeness; this was perhaps illustrated by her tendency not to follow instructions at work and to refuse to cooperate with her husband at home. For example, although her boss had asked Patricia not to stay at the bank after hours because of security considerations, she often stayed late to work, saying that the boss's request was "stupid and restrictive." Furthermore, she regularly ignored her husband's request that she do at least some of the housework, for which he did in fact take most of the responsibility despite also pursuing a career in law.

On the Neuroticism domain, Patricia described herself as both depressed and anxious. As mentioned earlier, this pattern may be expected in NAR patients when their defensive systems are poor, particularly on first entering treatment. Although mood states do not generally affect the assessment of normal personality, clinical depression is often manifested on personality inventories in the area of Neuroticism (Costa & McCrae, 1992a). More specifically, elevations on Neuroticism tend to occur when patients are depressed and tend to decrease on their recovery from depression. This was the case with Patricia.

Patricia also exhibited an elevation on the angry–hostility facet scale, which was apparent in her tendency to become enraged when criticized or "treated badly." However, she described herself as low on vulnerability and self-consciousness, the former indicating an ability to deal well with stress and the latter suggesting feelings of security, poise, and an absence of feelings of inferiority or embarrassment. As noted earlier, this issue is complicated by the distinction between the patient's self-report and others'

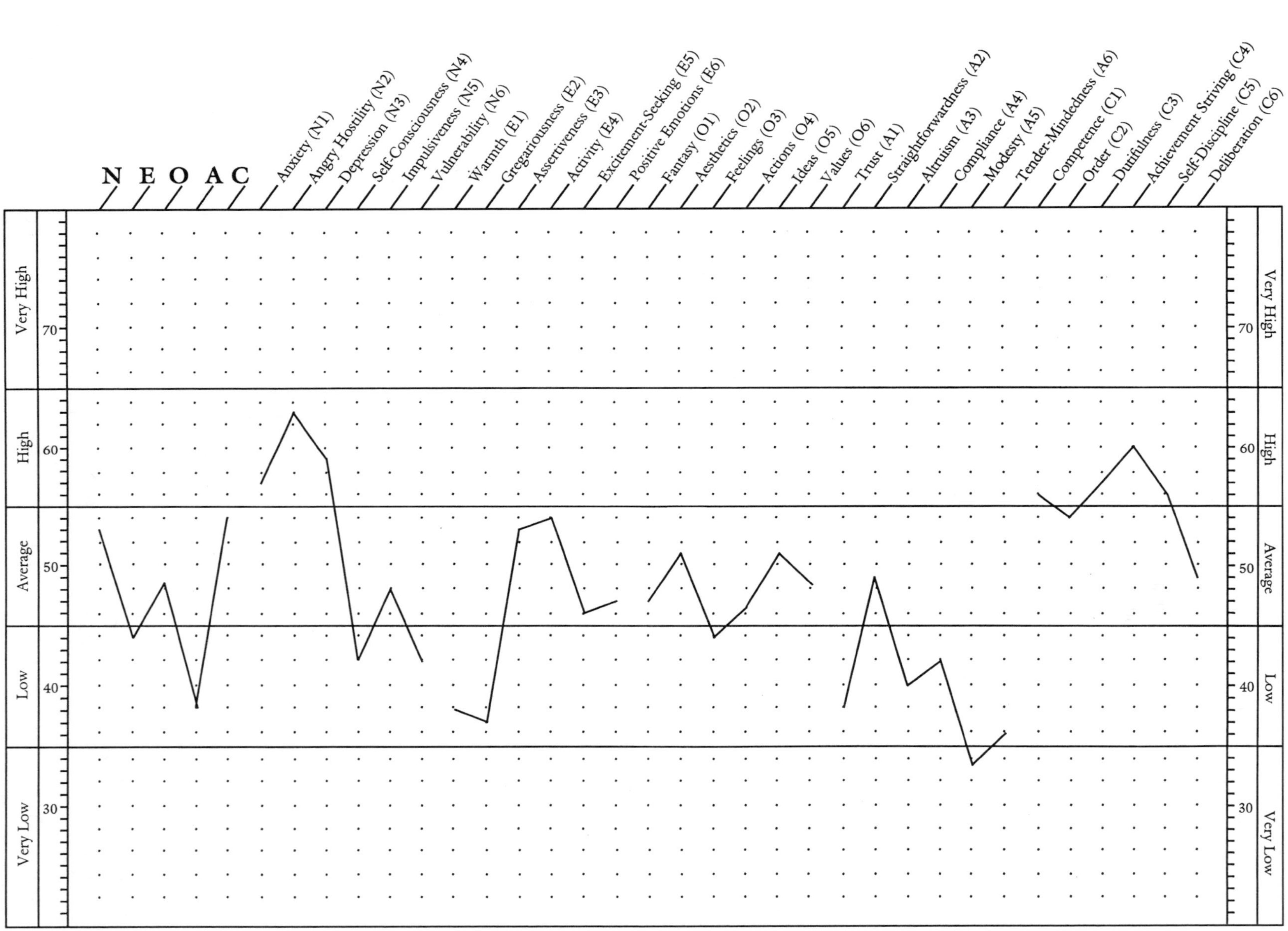

FIGURE 18.1. Revised NEO Personality Inventory profile of Patricia. From the *NEO Personality Inventory—Revised*, by Paul T. Costa, Jr., and Robert R. McCrae. Copyright 1978, 1985, 1989, 1992 by PAR, Inc. Reproduced by special permission of the publisher, Psychological Assessment Resources, Inc., 16204 North Florida Avenue, Lutz, FL 33549. Further reproduction is prohibited without permission of PAR, Inc.

view of him or her. Although Patricia denied feelings of humiliation and insecurity, such feelings were evident in her behavior and reactions toward others. For example, when criticized, Patricia would blush and either defensively make excuses for her behavior ("They can't expect me to work any harder than I already work!") or negate the criticism through a narcissistic stance ("She's just envious of me because I'm smarter than she is"). This behavior would be interpreted by many clinicians as a defensive reaction to deep-seated insecurity, regardless of the denial of such feelings.

Patricia described herself as low on Extraversion, specifically on the facets of warmth and gregariousness. Although the Extraversion domain is not theoretically central to narcissism, in Patricia's case her low scores on these facets seemed to be almost secondary to her narcissistic qualities. For example, low warmth implies coldness and distance from others. This was exemplified in Patricia by the infrequency with which others called her or visited with her to talk about their problems; when they did, she responded with intellectual advice usually delivered in a condescending manner, such as, "When you're older, you'll understand better how things are." Furthermore, her solitary nature in having few friends, not seeking out social groups, and keeping to herself at work was indicative of low gregariousness but may in fact have resulted in part from actual rebuffs from others in response to her antagonistic behavior.

A final interesting aspect of Patricia's self-description involved her elevations on several facets of the Conscientiousness domain. She perceived herself as accomplished, persistent, strongly committed to standards of conduct, and tending to strive for excellence. These elevations may indicate a classic narcissistic inflation of self-image, especially given that she was, even by her own report, having considerable difficulties at work.

TREATMENT

Knowledge of Patricia's levels on the five broad domains of the FFM and their facets was an aid to the conceptualization of her case in terms of personality pathology. Certain aspects of such pathology may either contribute to or constitute difficulties in treatment. Awareness of these aspects can be invaluable to the clinician in formulating treatment issues. In Patricia's case, her long-standing pattern of antagonism made the formation of a therapeutic relationship difficult. Patricia was often condescending toward and critical of her therapist, refusing at times to believe that anyone could understand her problems or help her in any way. Her lack of trust interfered with treatment as well; she was slow to develop confidence in her therapist's benevolent intent. Patricia's low compliance was also evident in treatment, as might be expected, through lateness or missed sessions as well as noncompliance with payment.

Patricia's depression and anxiety, however, were motivating factors in entering and continuing treatment. Her low levels of vulnerability and self-consciousness alerted the clinician to a potential tendency toward a defensive denial. As treatment progressed, the feelings of depression and anxiety decreased, whereas her awareness of her vulnerability and self-consciousness increased. Patricia gradually began to realize that she often felt unable to deal with stresses at work and that she reacted to possibly imagined criticism and lack of respect with rage and shame, perhaps because of her feeling as a child that nothing she did was "good enough" for her parents.

References

American Psychiatric Association. (1980). *Diagnostic and statistical manual of mental disorders* (3rd ed.). Washington, DC: Author.

American Psychiatric Association. (1987). *Diagnostic and statistical manual of mental disorders* (3rd ed., rev.). Washington, DC: Author.

American Psychiatric Association. (1994). *Diagnostic and statistical manual of mental disorders* (4th ed.). Washington, DC: Author.

Costa, P. T., Jr., & McCrae, R. R. (1985). *The NEO Personality Inventory manual*. Odessa, FL Psychological Assessment Resources.

Costa, P. T., Jr., & McCrae, R. R. (1990). Personality disorders and the five-factor model of personality. *Journal of Personality Disorders, 4,* 362–371.

Costa, P. T., Jr., & McCrae, R. R. (1992a). Normal personality assessment in clinical practice: The

NEO Personality Inventory. *Psychological Assessment, 4,* 5–13.

Costa, P. T., Jr., & McCrae, R. R. (1992b). *Revised NEO Personality Inventory and the NEO Five-Factor Inventory professional manual.* Odessa, FL: Psychological Assessment Resources.

Gunderson, J. G., Ronningstam, E., & Smith, L. E. (1991). Narcissistic personality disorder: A review of data on DSM-III-R descriptions [Special Series: DSM-IV and personality disorders]. *Journal of Personality Disorders, 5,* 167–177.

Kernberg, O. F. (1984). *Severe personality disorders.* New Haven, CT: Yale University Press.

Trull, T. J. (1992). *DSM-III-R* personality disorders and the five-factor model of personality: An empirical comparison. *Journal of Abnormal Psychology, 101,* 553–560.

Wiggins, J. S., & Pincus, A. L. (1989). Conceptions of personality disorders and dimensions of personality. *Psychological Assessment: A Journal of Consulting and Clinical Psychology, 1,* 305–316.

CHAPTER 19

PERSONALITY OF THE PSYCHOPATH

Timothy J. Harpur, Stephen D. Hart, and Robert D. Hare

In contemplating the five-factor model of personality (FFM) along side the two-factor model of psychopathy described here, it is worth highlighting some arresting contrasts and similarities. The FFM and psychopathy share venerable histories, the former traced to the 1930s (Wiggins & Trapnell, 1997) and the latter to the early 1800s (Pichot, 1978). However, they provide contrasting historical trajectories: The former is now presented as the most comprehensive system in the sphere of personality theory (Digman, 1990; John, 1990), whereas the latter is the distillate of a once far-ranging category that "at some time or other and by some reputable authority . . . has been used to designate every conceivable type of abnormal character" (Curran & Mallinson, 1944, p. 278). We might stretch the analogy a little further and suggest that both share an interrupted history, the former because of the vagaries of publication sources (Wiggins & Trapnell, 1997) and the latter because of the emergence of the third edition of the *Diagnostic and Statistical Manual of Mental Disorders* (*DSM-III*; American Psychiatric Association [APA], 1980) and its criminally oriented approach to psychopathy. Regardless of whether these comparisons are appropriate, we are left with two structural models, one comprehensive, the other highly specific; each may help to clarify and organize thinking in its respective field. This chapter considers what we know, or might guess, about the relations between these models.

We first examine some historical views of the psychopathic personality as well as more conceptualizations represented by the *DSM-III*'s antisocial personality disorder (ATS) and an alternative set of criteria for assessing psychopathy: the Psychopathy Checklist (PCL). We then review research on psychopathy using two structural models of normal personality: Eysenck's three-factor model and the FFM. Finally, we discuss how the two-factor PCL relates to the FFM and explore some implications for the use of the FFM in the field of personality disorders.

THE PSYCHOPATHIC PERSONALITY

Historically, the psychopathic personality represented an all-encompassing category of mental disorder that was distinct from, but on the same level of specificity as, psychosis and neurosis. Thus, Schneider (1958) referred to psychopathic personalities in much the same way that the field now refers to personality disorders. He identified 10 varieties of psychopathy, only 1 of which bears much resemblance to the term as it is currently used in North America. A similar use is apparent in the first edition of the *DSM* (APA, 1952). The term *personality disorder* was used for the most general classification of personality disturbances, of which four types were identified: personality pattern disturbances, personality trait disturbances, sociopathic personality disturbances,

We thank Stephan Ahadi, Jerry Clore, Ed Diener, Aaron Pincus, Paul Trapnell, and the editors of this book for their helpful comments on an earlier version of this chapter.

and special symptom reactions. Sociopathic personality disturbances were further divided into four subtypes: the antisocial reaction, the dyssocial reaction, the sexual deviation, and the addictions. In the second edition of the *DSM* (*DSM-II*; APA, 1968), the category "sociopathic personality, antisocial reaction" was retained to describe a personality type that would be recognizable to most clinicians today. The prominent features included failure to profit from experience and punishment; a lack of loyalty to any person, group, or code; callousness, hedonism, and emotional immaturity; a lack of responsibility and judgment; and an ability to rationalize behavior so that it appears warranted, reasonable, and justified.

From this brief summary, one might discern at least two types of confusion (see Pichot, 1978, for a discussion of some other sources of confusion). The first is that the term *psychopathic* has been applied to personality disturbances at different levels of generality. This has ceased to be an issue in North American nosology, although it continues to present a problem in England (Pichot, 1978). The second source of confusion concerns the descriptive content of the specific category that is termed either ATS (APA, 1980, 1987) or *psychopathy*.

Nevertheless, writings have been remarkably consistent in the description of the personality characteristics of the psychopath. Beginning with Cleckley (1941) and continuing with A. H. Buss (1966), Craft (1965), Hare (1970), Karpman (1961), McCord and McCord (1964), and Millon (1981), among others, clinicians and researchers have appeared to agree in general about the personality and behavioral attributes that are relevant to the construct. These have typically included, with varying emphases and orders of importance, impulsivity; a lack of guilt, loyalty, or empathy; an incapacity to form deep or meaningful interpersonal relationships; a failure to learn from experience or punishment; profound egocentricity and superficial charm; a persistent antisocial and criminal behavior without any evidence of remorse for the harm done to others; and a predisposition to aggression, particularly under the influence of alcohol.

Although different writers have argued about specific criteria, there has been general agreement about the breadth and content of the category for nearly

50 years (see Curran & Mallinson, 1944; Davies & Feldman, 1981; Gray & Hutchison, 1964; and Livesley & Jackson, 1986). This conception of the disorder, by whatever name it is known, has been reflected in the definitions of the corresponding categories designated by the American Psychiatric Association and the World Health Organization (WHO) in the *DSM* and *DSM-II* and the *International Classification of Diseases—9* and *—10* (WHO, 1977, 1993), respectively.

Antisocial Personality Disorder

The definition of ATS included in the *DSM-III* departs quite markedly from this consensus. In keeping with the policy of creating fixed and explicit criteria for the identification of psychopathology, a definition of ATS was created that consisted largely of determining whether the subject had participated in a number of criminal or antisocial acts in childhood and in adulthood (APA, 1980). Although the advent of the *DSM-III* undeniably boosted the reliability of psychiatric diagnosis in general, in the case of ATS, it is widely believed that this increase in reliability has been at the expense of validity (Frances & Widiger, 1986; Gerstley, Alterman, McLellan, & Woody, 1990; Hare, 1983; Hare, Hart, & Harpur, 1991; Harpur, Hare, & Hakstian, 1989; Millon, 1981; Morey, 1988a; Widiger, Frances, Spitzer, & Williams, 1988). Robins (1978), whose research had a profound influence on the *DSM-III* definition, justified the reliance on solely behavioral criteria as follows:

> *We can get reasonably good agreement on behaviours typifying the disorder, but little agreement on why they occur. There are many who feel that the essence of antisocial personality is inability to love, lack of anxiety, or inability to feel guilt. Yet there are people whom these same diagnosticians would agree are psychopaths who claim to love someone (particularly their mothers), who say they feel nervous and fearful, and who say that they are sorry for their behaviour. To maintain a conviction about the nature of the psychological substrate in these cases requires believing that these*

*psychopaths do not really feel the way they
claim to feel. . . . Yet the grounds for dis-
counting the psychopath's claim to love,
anxiety, and guilt, is always his behaviour.
. . . Since we rely on behaviour to infer the
psychological substrate anyhow, I find it
more parsimonious to stick to behaviour
and skip the inferences until such time as
we have a way to validate them independently of behaviour. (p. 256)*

Although the logic of Robins's (1978) claim is
valid, reliance on the specific behaviors listed in the
DSM-III (or its revision [*DSM-III-R*]) is problematic.
In the first place, it is not clear that the behaviors
chosen are the most appropriate for assessing the
traits that even Robins acknowledged underlie the
disorder. For instance, impulsivity is assessed by determining whether the individual travels from place
to place without a prearranged job or plan or lacks
a fixed address for at least a month. Although these
behaviors are relevant to impulsivity, they are clearly
not the only behaviors relevant to the trait and are
probably not the most prototypical. Theoretical advances in the use of behavioral acts in the assessment of dispositional constructs (e.g., D. M. Buss &
Craik, 1983) could be brought to bear on this issue
(D. M. Buss & Craik, 1986; but see also Block,
1989).

In the second place, without a more sophisticated use of behavioral indicators, it will not be possible to measure accurately the subtleties of which
Robins (1978) spoke (e.g., the inability to form
meaningful relationships despite verbal claims of the
opposite). The inability to maintain a totally monog-
amous relationship for more than 1 year (ATS Criterion C9) is presumably intended, in part, to tap this
characteristic.

The criteria for ATS (and its revision) are out of
step not only with historical conceptions of the disorder but also with the other sets of criteria included in Axis II of the *DSM-III*. No other personality disorder is defined by a closed-ended checklist of
behaviors that must be used to infer the characteris-

tics or symptoms in question. For other disorders,
both personality traits and specific characteristics are
elaborated in general terms, using typical but not
necessary examples. Histrionic personality disorder
Criterion B2, for example, reads "egocentric, self-
indulgent, and inconsiderate of others." Schizotypal
personality disorder Criterion A5 reads "odd speech
(without loosening of associations or incoherence),
e.g., speech that is digressive, vague, overelaborate,
circumstantial, metaphorical" (APA, 1980). In the
DSM-III-R, this difference between these two criteria
remains marked and is best illustrated by the language used to describe the adult ATS criteria: Eight
of the ten criteria contain the phrase "as indicated
by," followed by a list of specific behaviors. Every
other criterion listed on Axis II is a general descriptive phrase, sometimes followed by "e.g."

One might view the specificity of the ATS criteria
as a sign of sophistication, suggesting a better understanding of this disorder than of the others. We
think that a more accurate assessment of this difference is given by Lilienfeld (1994), who suggested
that *DSM-III*'s definition treats psychopathic traits as
closed concepts, allowing the diagnostician to consider only a fixed and limited set of indicators of a
trait. As a result, many other behaviors or attributes
that may be highly relevant to the trait in question
are considered inadmissible as diagnostic information. Conceptualizing traits as closed concepts ignores the fact that traits are dispositions to act in a
variety of trait-relevant ways across a variety of situations and that any one behavior is likely to be mul-
tiply determined.

The Psychopathy Checklist
At approximately the same time that the criteria for
ATS were being finalized, Hare (1980; Hare & Frazelle, 1980) developed an alternative criterion set for
assessing psychopathy in male criminal populations.
The instrument was aimed at assessing the construct
as defined by Cleckley (1976), incorporating many
of the trait concepts omitted from the *DSM-III*. In
addition, the PCL[1] treated most of the constructs it

[1] The PCL was revised in relatively minor ways (see Hare et al., 1990). The properties of the scale and the constructs measured are essentially unchanged by this revision, so for the purposes of this chapter, we do not distinguish between the two versions.

measured as open, giving typical examples of the kinds of behaviors indicative of, say, a lack of empathy but not strictly circumscribing the behaviors that would be considered in making a judgment regarding each trait.

A detailed review of the PCL is beyond the scope of this chapter, but reviews of its development and scoring are available in Hare (1991) and Hart, Hare, and Harpur (1992). The PCL consists of the 20 items shown in Exhibit 19.1, each scored on a 0–2 scale according to the extent to which the item applies to the individual. Subjects are interviewed, and a source of collateral information, usually a prison

or forensic psychiatric file, is reviewed. Items are scored after considering both sources of information. Although the item titles are representative, more specific operationalizations given in the scoring manual are followed when rating each one. The scale is highly reliable, as demonstrated by its use in several different laboratories (Hare et al., 1990; Harpur, Hakstian, & Hare, 1988; Kosson, Smith, & Newman, 1990; Ogloff, Wong, & Greenwood, 1990; Schroeder, Schroeder, & Hare, 1983; Smith & Newman, 1990; Wong, 1988) and is readily administered by anyone familiar with the construct of psychopathy and experienced with the populations in which it is assessed.

Considerable evidence has accrued attesting to the construct validity of the PCL. That is, the expected pattern of relations has been obtained with diagnoses of ATS and psychopathy-related self-report scales (Hare, 1985; Harpur & Hare, 1991b; Harpur et al., 1989; Hart, Forth, & Hare, 1991; Hart & Hare, 1989; Kosson et al., 1990; Newman & Kosson 1986) as well as with a variety of demographic, behavioral, and experimental variables (for reviews, see Hare, 1991; Hare, Williamson, & Harpur, 1988; Harpur & Hare, 1990; Harpur et al., 1989; Hart et al., 1992; Newman & Wallace, 1993; Wong, 1984). Moreover, the PCL appears to be superior to the ATS criteria in predicting, criminal behaviors and accounting for the results of laboratory research (Hare et al., 1991; Hart et al., 1992).

Factor analysis reveals two highly replicable factors underlying the PCL items (Hare et al., 1990; Harpur et al., 1988; see Exhibit 19.1). Factor 1 measures a selfish, callous, and remorseless use of others and contains most of the personality characteristics considered central to the traditional clinical conception of the disorder. Factor 2 measures social deviance, as manifested in a chronically unstable and antisocial lifestyle. The items defining this factor tend to be scored more on the basis of explicit behaviors than inferred traits. In the 11 samples examined to date, these two factors have shown a consistent correlation of .50, indicating a strong relation but by no means an identity between these two constructs.

A variety of evidence is available attesting to the discriminant validity of these two factors. Factor 1 is

---

EXHIBIT 19.1

Items in the Revised Psychopathy Checklist

Factor 1

1. Glibness–superficial charm
2. Grandiose sense of self-worth
4. Pathological lying
5. Conning–manipulative
6. Lack of remorse or guilt
7. Shallow affect
8. Callous–lack of empathy
16. Failure to accept responsibility for actions

Factor 2

3. Need for stimulation–proneness to boredom
9. Parasitic lifestyle
10. Poor behavioral controls
12. Early behavior problems
13. Lack of realistic, long-term goals
14. Impulsivity
15. Irresponsibility
18. Juvenile delinquency
19. Revocation of conditional release

Items not included in the factor scores

11. Promiscuous sexual behavior
17. Many short-term marital relationships
20. Criminal versatility

more strongly related to global ratings of psychopathy and to Cleckley's (1976) criteria than is Factor 2, whereas the reverse is true for diagnoses of ATS (Harpur et al., 1989). A variety of self-report instruments commonly used to assess psychopathy are moderately related to Factor 2 but fail to measure the egocentric, callous, and manipulative traits captured by Factor 1. An exception to this trend are assessments of narcissism, which share with Factor 1 features of egocentricity, grandiosity, and a lack of empathy (Harpur et al., 1989; Harpur & Hare, 1991b; Hart et al., 1991; Hart & Hare, 1989). Evidence that the two factors may be distinguished in terms of their relations with age, social class, cognitive abilities, alcohol and drug abuse or dependence, violent behavior, and recidivism may be found in Harpur and Hare (1991a, 1994), Harpur et al. (1989), Hart and Hare (1989), and Smith and Newman (1990).

The identification of two factors underlying our assessments of psychopathy has helped to clarify the relation between the PCL and ATS criteria. Correlations among the two are shown in Table 19.1. It is apparent from these correlations that the strong relation between the PCL and ATS criteria reported by Hare (1985) is mediated largely by Factor 2. Conversely, one could say that the PCL conception of psychopathy differs from the *DSM-III*'s conception of ATS by virtue of the former's inclusion of Factor 1. In fact, Factor 1 is more related to current conceptions of narcissism (or NAR) than to ATS (see Table 19.1). Our contention is that those pathological characteristics of narcissism measured by Factor 1 in fact covary with a more general trait of social deviance and that together they form the higher order construct of psychopathy. Arguments and evidence for this position, in addition to that provided by structural analyses of the PCL, can be found in Gerstley et al. (1990); Harpur, Hare, Zimmerman, and Coryell (1990); and Morey (1988a, 1988b).

This research places psychopathy in a unique position among the personality disorders as a construct for which there exist both a highly reliable assessment procedure and substantial evidence for its construct validity. In addition, detailed knowledge of the structure of this disorder provides a firm criterion with which to compare dimensional models of normal personality. Unfortunately, the data currently available are meager. This is largely because adequate assessments of psychopathy, as we conceptualize it, require the application of detailed and time-consuming procedures. The use of available self-report questionnaires or 10-minute interviews do not provide an adequate basis for assessing the personality characteristics that are crucial in the psychopath. In addition, the inclusion of ATS in the official diagnostic taxonomy of APA directs many research efforts toward use of this category, despite its lesser homogeneity and predictive power.

TABLE 19.1

Correlations Among the Psychopathy Checklist (PCL), Assessments of Antisocial Personality Disorder (ATS), and Narcissistic Personality Disorder (NAR)

Assessment	*N*	PCL	Factor 1	Factor 2
Diagnoses				
ATS	319	.56	.42	.55
	180[a]	.55	.37	.61
	387	.63	.49	.58
	114	.58	.39	.57
	80[b]	.45	.21[c]	.59
ATS-R	176[a]	.54	.32	.63
Prototypicality ratings				
ATS	80[b]	.71	.40	.83
NAR	80[b]	.39	.49	.24

Note. ATS-R = antisocial personality disorder—revised. Superscript a and b indicate identical or overlapping samples. All *p*s < .05, except [c]. From *The Hare Psychopathy Checklist—Revised,* by R. D. Hare, 1991, Toronto, Ontario, Canada: Multi-Health Systems. Copyright 1991 by Multi-Health Systems. Adapted with permission.

PSYCHOPATHY AND MODELS OF NORMAL PERSONALITY

Given the long history of this disorder, it is not surprising that the relation between psychopathy and dimensions of normal personality has been the subject of research (and speculation) for many years. Here, we review research using two structural models of normal personality: Eysenck's three-factor model and the FFM, as assessed by Wiggins's interpersonal adjective scales and the NEO Personality Inventory (NEO-PI).

Eysenck's Three-Factor Model

Eysenck produced not only a seminal body of theory on the structure of personality (Eysenck, 1967, 1970; Eysenck & Eysenck, 1976) but an extension of that theory to account for criminal behavior (Eysenck, 1977; Eysenck & Gudjonsson, 1989). Although his research represents a major contribution to the literature on crime and personality, it is not entirely clear how applicable his theory is to the understanding of the psychopathic personality. In the model's original formulations (Eysenck, 1964, 1977; Eysenck & Eysenck, 1978), the distinction between the psychopath and the criminal was ignored on the grounds that considerable overlap was assumed to exist between them. Although such an assumption may be justified when using ATS as a diagnostic category, it is clearly not appropriate when psychopathy is defined using the PCL. Base rates for ATS may be as high as 75% in Canadian correctional facilities, but base rates for PCL-defined psychopathy are about 30% (Correctional Service of Canada, 1990; Hare, 1983; Harpur & Hare, 1991a; Hart & Hare, 1989; Wong, 1984).

Eysenck and Gudjonsson (1989) acknowledged the need to distinguish criminality in general from psychopathy:

> *Psychopathy and criminality are not to be identified, although both are characterized by antisocial behavior, psychopaths are not necessarily criminals in the legal sense, and criminals may not be psychopathic in their behavior. Nevertheless, both share the trait of antisocial behavior, and it seems likely that they will also share personality traits related to this type of behavior.* (p. 48)

Eysenck's theory predicts that psychopaths should be characterized by high scores on all three of his personality dimensions, Extraversion (E), Neuroticism (N), and Psychoticism (P), with "primary" psychopaths characterized chiefly by high P scores and "secondary" psychopaths characterized by high E and N scores. Although there is considerable evi-

dence for the relation between these dimensions and criminal behavior (for a review, see Eysenck & Gudjonsson, 1989), the researchers who have compared PCL-defined psychopathy with the Eysenck Personality Questionnaire (EPQ) have found only partial support for the predicted relations. Hare (1982) reported moderate correlations between these scales and the PCL in a sample of 173 inmates from a medium-security Canadian institution. Statistically significant but marginal correlations were reported with scores on P ($r = .16$) and Lie ($r = -.14$). Furthermore, zone analysis using median splits on E, N, and P revealed no significant differences in the level of psychopathy for subjects classified within any of the eight personality octants. Kosson et al. (1990) reported a somewhat higher correlation between the PCL and P ($r = .34$) but only for White inmates. The correlations with E and N, however, were negligible. A different pattern of correlations was reported for Black inmates, psychopathy being correlated with E but not with P or N. This difference must be interpreted with caution, however, in light of the limited information available on the use of the PCL with Black inmates (see Kosson et al., 1990).

Harpur et al. (1989) examined the relation between E, N, and P and the PCL factors using the sample described by Hare (1982) plus an additional 49 subjects. The correlations with total PCL scores, shown in Table 19.2, remained very small. However, it was apparent that P was solely related to Factor 2 and was completely orthogonal to the cluster of personality attributes measured by Factor 1. A second theoretically interesting result emerged: N was positively correlated with Factor 2 but negatively correlated with Factor 1. A similar divergent pattern of correlations between the PCL factors and anxiety was replicated using a variety of other measures of trait anxiety (mean $r = -.21$ and .03 for Factors 1 and 2, respectively; Harpur et al., 1989).

A number of artifactual explanations for these modest correlations must be considered before examining more substantive explanations. Most obviously, either limitations in the range of scores or dissimulation might have contributed to attenuating the correlations. The first possibility can be discounted by comparison of the standard deviations obtained

TABLE 19.2

Correlations Among the Psychopathy Checklist (PCL) and Eysenck Personality Questionnaire (EPQ) Scales

EPQ scale	PCL	Factor 1	Factor 2
Extraversion	0.11	0.08	0.10
Neuroticism	0.02	−0.17*	0.16*
Psychoticism	0.14*	0.01	0.22*
Lie	−0.17*	−0.03	−0.22*

Note. N = 222.   *p < .05. From "Two-Factor Conceptualization of Psychopathy: Construct Validity and Assessment Implications," by T. J. Harpur, R. D. Hare, and A. R. Hakstian, 1989, *Psychological Assessment: A Journal of Consulting and Clinical Psychology, 1,* p. 11–12. Copyright 1989 by the American Psychiatric Association. Adapted with permission.

in our samples with published norms. Only P showed a slight reduction (12%) compared with normal subjects (Hare, 1982).

Although one defining feature of the psychopath is pathological lying, several arguments can be made against the possibility that dissimulation plays a role in this correlation. In the first place, the kind of information that the inmates are asked to reveal, even when completing scales for P and socialization, is far less probing than is the interview that the inmate has already completed, usually on videotape, as part of the PCL assessment. It seems unlikely that an inmate would be unwilling to admit to the kinds of behaviors examined by the P scale, having very likely already discussed far more serious criminal and antisocial acts on tape. Furthermore, the questionnaire is always administered as part of a research project for which there is no strong or obvious benefit to the inmate for impression management. In situations with significant outcomes for the inmate (e.g., parole hearings), psychopaths might be expected to display considerable care in their self-disclosure, although it cannot be assumed that this is generally the case. Finally, several scales designed to measure impression management (e.g., faking good or bad, dissimulation) have been administered to inmates over the years, and their relation with psychopathy has always been zero or negative. In our data, the EPQ Lie scale was as highly correlated

with Factor 2 as was P but in the direction opposite to that predicted if psychopaths were dissimulating.

Assuming then that these results are not artifactual, what implications do they have for the understanding of the personality of the psychopath? In a large sample of carefully assessed inmates, the relations between psychopathy and Eysenck's dimensions were small. If we examine separately the two factors measured by the PCL, the picture is clarified somewhat. Factor 2, a measure of extreme social deviance and antisocial behavior, did show the expected pattern of positive correlations with all three EPQ dimensions, although the size of the correlations was modest at best. Factor 1 of the PCL shows a relation only with anxiety, and in this case, it was in the direction opposite to that predicted by Eysenck.

To provide as comprehensive a test of Eysenck's hypothesis as possible and in light of the hypothesis discussed later in this chapter, we conducted a further analysis using the sample described by Harpur et al. (1989). We examined whether the interaction of the E, N, and P dimensions might provide a stronger link with psychopathy than had been found for the zero-order correlations. Although to our knowledge such an interactive model has not been explicitly endorsed by Eysenck, it is implicit in his use of quadrant or octant analysis. In a hierarchical multiple regression, the main effects of the three dimensions, the three two-way interactions between pairs of dimensions, and the three-way interaction term were regressed on each of the PCL factor scores. In each case, the analysis proceeded by entering all main effects, then testing the change in R^2 when the block of two-way effects was added, and finally testing for the three-way term (see Cohen & Cohen, 1983).

The results did not support the hypothesis that an interactive combination of E, N, and P would improve on the main effects of these dimensions. For Factor 1, the multiple correlation after entry of the main effects failed to reach significance (R^2 = .03, $p < .07$), and an addition of the two- or three-way interaction terms failed to produce a significant increment in this value. The squared multiple correlation with all terms entered reached .05.

Not surprisingly, the main effects for E, N, and P

were significantly related to PCL Factor 2 scores (R^2 = .08, $p < .001$), with all three variables contributing to the relationship. Inclusion of the interaction terms did not boost this relationship significantly, producing a R^2 of .09 for the full model.

Having attempted to relate psychopathy to Eysenck's model of personality in a variety of ways, we see no reason to alter the opinion expressed by Hare (1982) that "high scores on the P scale may be more a reflection of criminal and antisocial tendencies and behavior than of the inferred psychological constructs ... that are essential for the diagnosis of psychopathy" (p. 41). These psychological constructs were largely being measured by PCL Factor 1. It must be acknowledged that E, N, and P do share the predicted relations with the trait of social deviance measured by Factor 2, and somewhat less clearly by ATS criteria, but in combination, they accounted for less than 10% of the variance of Factor 2 scores and none of the variance of Factor 1 scores. Even allowing for unreliability and the different measurement methods, considerable variance in psychopathy is unaccounted for within this three-dimensional model.

The Five-Factor Model

Although Eysenck's measurement of E and N is largely congruent with conceptions of five-factor theorists, his dimension of P combines elements of low Conscientiousness (C) and low Agreeableness (A), traits considered orthogonal within the FFM (Costa, McCrae, & Dye, 1991). In addition, although he acknowledged the importance of intelligence as an aspect of personality relevant to behavior (Eysenck & Gudjonsson, 1989), he did not measure it in any form in the EPQ. In view of the inadequacy of three factors in predicting our assessments of psychopathy and particularly because the controversial P dimension is the dimension most strongly related to the PCL, it is clearly necessary to determine whether the separation of A and C and the measurement of Openness to Experience (O) can provide a more comprehensive characterization of the nature of the two psychopathy constructs.

Most of the dimensions of personality measured to date have been selected for their theoretical relevance to psychopathy rather than for their interpretability within a comprehensive structural model of personality. In particular, scales from clinical assessment instruments, such as the Minnesota Multiphasic Personality Inventory (MMPI; Hathaway & McKinley, 1967) and the Millon Clinical Multiaxial Inventory (MCMI; Millon, 1983, 1987), Zuckerman's Sensation Seeking Scale (Zuckerman, 1978), the Socialization scale of the California Psychological Inventory (Gough, 1969) as well as scales relating to Machiavellianism, empathy, and impulsiveness, have been administered. Although interpretively ambiguous with respect to the FFM, these scales often show the most robust correlations with psychopathy. In addition, myriad clinical descriptions of the psychopath provide a rich source of information allowing us to develop a more detailed picture of the personality profile of the psychopath. In this section, we discuss these findings and present new data using instruments designed more specifically to measure the FFM.

Psychopaths are prototypically thrill seeking, impulsive, lacking in anxiety, unable to sustain long-term plans or relationships, cynical, egocentric, manipulative, Machiavellian, cold hearted, and callous. A rough translation of these characteristics within the organizing framework of the FFM produces a descriptive profile of the psychopath: high on E and low on N, O, A, and C (relative to a normative sample). In fact, this characterization may hide as much as it reveals. In the first place, there is strong evidence for the existence of two distinct constructs underlying our conception of psychopathy. Second, the mapping of these characteristic traits onto the framework of the FFM is not straightforward, given that a single, consensual description of the five factors has yet to emerge (John, 1990). Third, the specific traits listed earlier and expanded on in the clinical literature tend to be at a lower level of generality than are the broad dimensions that form the framework for the FFM. Finally, in many cases, the traits characteristic of psychopathy are the same traits that generate the greatest disagreement concerning their place within this organizing framework. Bearing these difficulties in mind, we now examine the available data.

We have several sources of data pertinent to conceptions of the FFM. Although the sample sizes are in some cases small and the data derive from diverse samples, we present them here as a spur to future, more comprehensive data collection efforts and as a structure on which to hang our (sometimes speculative) thinking. We rely on the reader to weigh the relative importance of different results based on the nature and size of each sample.

Samples.   Research using the PCL has been conducted almost exclusively in criminal populations. Most of the results reported here follow this pattern, both because of the higher prevalence of the disorder among incarcerated criminals and because the PCL was developed (and validated) on a male forensic population.

Nevertheless, the need to extend the applicability of the PCL to other populations is widely recognized. For this reason, we have begun to examine how the PCL performs in nonforensic populations. Data from one of these samples, 50 undergraduate volunteers (25 men, 25 women), included self-report personality measures as well as PCL assessments.

Psychopathy assessments on criminal samples were performed as described in an earlier section. Several important differences should be noted about the assessments carried out on the students. For obvious reasons, no historical records were readily available for these subjects, so PCL items were completed entirely on the basis of an interview. Also because none of the subjects admitted to having a criminal record, several of the items on the PCL, mostly from Factor 2, could not be scored because they are based largely or wholly on criminal activity. When necessary, such items were omitted, and the PCL total and factor scores were prorated. The absence of overt antisocial behavior among students may have made it more difficult to score Factor 2 for this group, leading perhaps to lower reliabilities for coding this factor (unfortunately, reliabilities are not available yet for this sample). Alternatively, because these items had to be scored on the basis of different information, the construct actually measured by the PCL Factor 2 in noncriminal samples

may have differed slightly from that measured in criminal samples.

Most important, of course, the students scored on average far lower (and in a narrower range) on the total PCL and both factors than did the prison inmates. The mean scores (and standard deviations) for the 50 students for the total PCL, Factor 1, and Factor 2 were 6.7 (5.5), 1.7 (2.0), and 4.3 (3.7), respectively.[2] This compares with mean scores for prison inmates of 23.6 (7.0), 8.7 (4.0), and 11.4 (4.0), respectively (Hare, 1991). In fact, of the 50 students assessed, only 1 scored above the mean score obtained for prison populations, and none would have been diagnosed as a psychopath by our usual cut-off, a total score of 30 or above. The range of scores on the PCL for the student and inmate samples used for the present study were almost entirely different: Only 3 inmates scored below 17 on the total PCL, and only 2 students out of 50 scored above this value.

Because of these differences, it would not be appropriate to consider the two samples to be equivalent. Although we would hope that strong relations between personality variables would hold across the range of PCL scores, it is quite possible that the relations between the PCL and external criteria are nonlinear. These are largely speculations, but they emphasize the fact that dissimilarity between pairs of nominally comparable correlations in the two samples should be interpreted with caution and should not be assumed to constitute a replication failure.

Measures.   In the student sample and in the inmate samples, we and other investigators have made use of a variety of assessment devices. The two with the clearest relation to the FFM are the Revised Interpersonal Adjective Scales (IAS-R; Wiggins, Trapnell, & Phillips, 1988), its extension to the FFM (the Big 5 version [IASR-B5]; Trapnell & Wiggins, 1991), and the NEO-PI.

We obtained self-report data on the IAS-R for 113 inmates from a study by Foreman (1988) and for 47 student subjects. The students also completed

---

[2] There were marked sex differences in scores on the PCL. Means for the total PCL, Factor 1, and Factor 2 were 8.5, 2.6, and 5.3, respectively, for men and 4.8, 0.7, and 3.4, respectively, for women. Differences for the total PCL and Factor 1 scores were significant. The only personality measure significantly differentiating the sexes was the dimension of Love, on which women scored higher than men.

the NEO-PI, as did 28 of the inmates. Finally, we obtained a set of ratings on each of the FFM dimensions made by observers watching videotaped PCL assessment interviews. Tapes from 12 inmates and 12 students were rated independently by two research assistants using the adjective scales of the IASR-B5. The raters were blind to the subjects' PCL scores and had, in fact, never been trained in the assessment of psychopathy. These ratings, made on an 8-point scale, were then averaged and converted to scores on each dimension (see Trapnell & Wiggins, 1991).

The Interpersonal Circumplex. The IAS-R assesses interpersonal dispositions within a circumplex spanned by the major dimensions of Love and Dominance. These dimensions correspond closely to E and A as measured, for instance, by the NEO-PI, although the precise alignment of these pairs of dimensions within the circumplex differs (McCrae & Costa, 1989; Wiggins & Pincus, chapter 7, this volume; Wiggins & Trapnell, 1997). Unlike data from the EPQ, these data can provide a measure of A independent of C.

Harpur et al. (1989) reanalyzed part of Foreman's (1988) data to examine the location of the two PCL factors in relation to self-reported interpersonal style. The correlations between the PCL and these dimensions are shown in Table 19.3. A strong negative relation between both factors and Love was apparent, as was a positive relation between Dominance and Factor 1. Factor 2 was unrelated to Dominance as measured by the IAS-R. These data provide a strong reason to think that A is a dimension relevant to psychopathy but independent of C.

The data for the student sample are also presented in Table 19.3. A strong convergence is apparent for the dimension of Love, although the relation appears to be dominated by PCL Factor 1 in the student data. The relation between the PCL and Dominance was negligible in this sample, however. Perhaps in the low range of PCL scores present in the student sample, the importance of Dominance in scoring the PCL items is lessened. In any case, the data for both samples confirm the long-standing view that psychopathy is characterized, above all, by a cold, callous, and antagonistic personality, but they once again present a slightly mixed message with respect to E-Dominance.

The NEO Personality Inventory. For a more detailed understanding of the relation between psychopathy and the FFM, we administered the NEO-PI to inmates assessed on the PCL. The NEO-PI provides domain scales with excellent psychometric properties for measuring each of the five dimensions as well as six facet scales underlying the dimensions of N, E, and O. Unfortunately, data are currently available for only 28 subjects.

Means and standard deviations for psychopathic and nonpsychopathic inmates (PCL total scores >30 and <30, respectively) are shown in Table 19.4. Mean values for the domain and facet scales are also presented in Figure 19.1, plotted as *T*-score profiles based on a normal adult sample (Costa & McCrae, 1989). These profiles reveal that the nonpsychopathic inmates showed relatively little deviation from the normative sample. A moderate elevation in N, attributable mostly to increased depression and feelings of inferiority and shame (measured by the self-consciousness facet), is apparent.

Psychopaths, however, showed a distinctive personality profile, with a moderate elevation on N, a moderate depression on C, and an extreme depression on A.[3] It should be emphasized that these values are group means. On the basis of these data,

[3] The personality profile for psychopaths shown in Figure 19.1 probably underestimates their low scores on A and C. Current norms for the NEO-PI are based on subjects from the Baltimore Longitudinal Study on Aging (see McCrae & Costa, 1987). This sample was drawn largely from managerial, professional, and scientific occupations, and it overrepresents subjects from higher educational and socioeconomic levels. Differences between the normative sample and the criminals considered here would be quite marked. Psychological Assessment Resources has circulated revised norms for the Five-Factor Inventory (a short form of the NEO-PI domain scales) based on a new normative sample that matches more closely the age and race (and presumably education and socioeconomic status, although this is not stated explicitly) of the U.S. population. Comparison of these norms with those for this sample provide some estimate of the bias that might be present in the profiles in Figure 19.1. Mean Five-Factory Inventory scores for adult men on N, E, and C were approximately .1 to .2 standard deviations higher in the newly collected normative sample. Both criminal groups' corresponding *T* scores would be expected to be slightly lower if based on these more representative norms. The mean level of A in the new sample was approximately .75 standard deviations higher. This substantial difference means that the *T* score for psychopaths in Figure 19.1, already very low, would be lowered even further, probably by a substantial amount.

TABLE 19.3

Correlations Among the Psychopathy Checklist (PCL) and the Revised Interpersonal Adjective Scales (IAS-R)

IAS-R scale	PCL		Factor 1		Factor 2	
	In	St	In	St	In	St
Dominance	.19*	−.03	.35*	.08	−.01	−.17
Love	−.30*	−.32*	−.26*	−.42*	−.29*	−.25

Note. In = Inmate sample, $N = 113$; St = student sample, $N = 47$. $*p < .05$.

about 50% of psychopaths would receive a T score of 35 or lower, and few, if any, would score over 50 on this dimension.

Correlations among the PCL, its factors, and the five domain scales for this sample are shown in Table 19.5. The correlations mirror the mean differences observed for the two groups: Those for E and N were in line with results obtained using the EPQ, although the broader domain encompassed by the NEO-PI N dimension eliminated the negative correlation with Factor 1. As expected, A, C, and O were all negatively correlated with the PCL, but only the negative correlation with A reached statistical significance. It is interesting to note that both factors cor-

related about equally with A—a result that is consistent with the projection of the PCL factors and the NEO-PI A scale on the interpersonal circumplex (Harpur et al., 1989; McCrae & Costa, 1989).

Also included in Tables 19.4 and 19.5 are comparable statistics for the student sample. The students' mean scores on the NEO-PI domain scales were similar to those reported for a normative college sample (Costa & McCrae, 1989). The relations between the PCL and the five factors were broadly consistent with those for the inmate sample. The correlation between psychopathy and C was stronger for the student sample than for the inmate sample,

TABLE 19.4

Means and Standard Deviations for NEO Personality Inventory (NEO-PI) Domain Scales for Psychopaths, Nonpsychpaths, and Students

NEO domain scale	Psychopaths		Nonpsychopaths		Male students		Female students		Adult males[a]	
	M	SD	M	SD	M	SD	M	SD	M	SD
Neuroticism	83.8	17.3	80.9	22.6	83.9	24.7	91.1	24.7	73.0	19.3
Extraversion	106.3	19.9	98.1	20.0	113.7	17.6	112.4	15.2	102.6	18.0
Openness	110.5	12.1	110.8	18.3	127.8	20.0	125.3	19.7	109.2	17.4
Agreeableness	39.8	5.7	47.1	10.2	43.8	9.1	47.0	7.7	48.4	6.1
Conscientiousness	46.2	10.0	48.4	6.7	43.2	12.4	48.0	6.9	49.8	8.2

Note. Psychopaths, $N = 12$; nonpsychopaths, $N = 16$; male students, $N = 24$; female students, $N = 23$; adult males, $N = 502$.
[a]From *NEO-PI/FFI Manual Supplement* (p. 3), by P. T. Costa, Jr., and R. R. McCrae, 1989, Odessa, FL: Psychological Assessment Resources. Copyright 1989 by Psychological Assessment Resources.

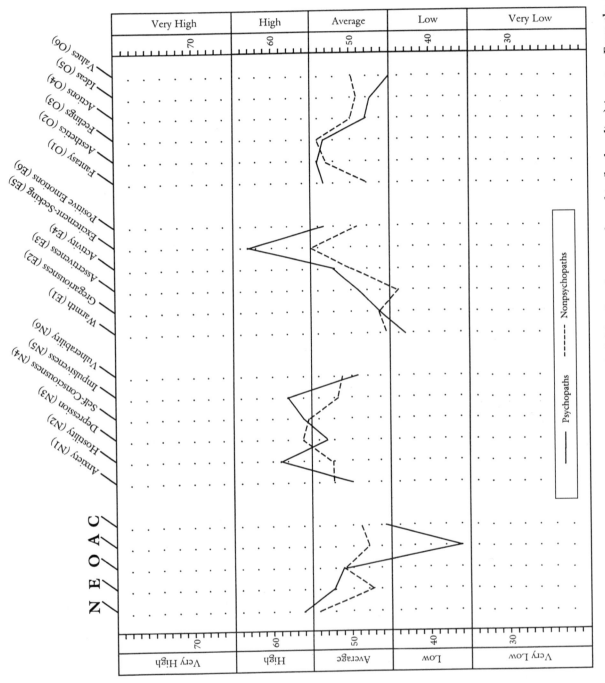

FIGURE 19.1. Mean NEO Personality Inventory profiles for psychopathic (solid line) and nonpsychopathic (broken line) inmates. From the *NEO Personality Inventory*, by Paul T. Costa, Jr., and Robert R. McCrae. Copyright 1978, 1985, 1989, 1992 by PAR, Inc. Reproduced by special permission of the publisher, Psychological Assessment Resources, Inc., 16204 North Florida Avenue, Lutz, FL 33549. Further reproduction is prohibited without permission of PAR, Inc.

TABLE 19.5

Correlations Among the Psychopathy Checklist (PCL) and NEO Personality Inventory (NEO-PI) Domain Scales

NEO domain scale	PCL		Factor 1		Factor 2	
	In	St	In	St	In	St
Neuroticism	.14	.10	.06	.05	.15	.11
Extraversion	.07	.05	−.10	.17	.16	−.17
Openness to Experience	−.13	.19	−.17	.20	.01	.05
Agreeableness	−.47*	−.26	−.35	−.41*	−.36	−.18
Conscientiousness	−.12	−.38*	−.07	−.33*	−.15	−.38*

Note. In = Inmate sample, $N = 28$; St = student sample, $N = 47$. $*p < .05$.

perhaps because of the greater range of scores on this dimension ($SDs = 10.3$ and 8.1 for students and inmates, respectively).[4] In addition, O related positively to the PCL for the students but negatively for the inmates.

The breadth of the domain tapped by three of the five dimensions of the NEO-PI is ensured by the inclusion of six facet scales. A more detailed picture of the relation between the PCL factors and the domains of E, N, and O may be obtained by examining these more specific traits. Although the numbers of subjects are small, we include these correlations in Table 19.6. We now turn to each of the five major dimensions in more detail.

Neuroticism. The trait of N has historically provoked the greatest debate in relation to psychopathy. On the one hand, an absence of anxiety has been considered a necessary component of the disorder (see Spielberger, Kling, & O'Hagan, 1978). On the other hand, Robins (1966) reported a positive correlation between the number of psychopathic and neurotic symptoms. This conflicting picture has been clarified by the realization that the two PCL factors differ in their relation to anxiety and that the definitions of psychopathy used by theorists on ei-

ther side of this debate have emphasized one or the other of these components of the disorder (Harpur et al., 1989). The clinical prototype of the psychopath represented by Factor 1 is moderately related to low anxiety, whereas the trait of social deviance tapped by Factor 2, ATS, and Robins's (1966) earlier definition of the psychopath is largely uncorrelated with anxiety. Furthermore, the relation between somatic complaints and chronic negative affect in the general population is probably mediated by alcoholism, drug abuse, and other behaviors that increase health risks (Costa & McCrae, 1987). The fact that psychopaths use drugs and alcohol to an excessive degree and that this use is related solely to PCL Factor 2 (Smith & Newman, 1990) may account entirely for reports that they demonstrate many somatic symptoms, regardless of level of anxiety.

A second source of confusion may stem from varied conceptions of anxiety. The consistent relation between the PCL factors and anxiety just described has been found for many different instruments (Harpur et al., 1989). However, these instruments all had in common a relatively narrow conception of the trait. The N dimension of the NEO-PI, on the other hand, incorporates both a hostility scale that

[4] As noted in Footnote 2, there were reliable sex differences in scores on the PCL. Although the gender differences for mean scores on N, E, and C were not statistically significant, they were nevertheless substantial. These differences might have artifactually obscured the relations between the PCL and the personality measures. However, analyzing the data separately for the two sexes would have reduced the sample sizes substantially. For this reason, results are reported for the whole sample. Nevertheless, separate-sex analyses were run, with results that were mostly consistent with those reported. For the male students, correlations of the PCL with the NEO-PI domain scales were larger than those reported in Table 19.5 for N, A, and C (.34, −.40, and −.40, respectively). Similar increases were seen for correlations with the PCL factors. The very limited range of PCL scores obtained for the female students makes interpretation of these correlations difficult, although they were generally similar to those reported for the combined sample.

TABLE 19.6

Correlations Among the Psychopathy Checklist (PCL) and NEO Personality Inventory (NEO-PI) Facet Scales

NEO facet scale	PCL		Factor 1		Factor 2	
	In	St	In	St	In	St
N1: Anxiety	.00	−.14	.07	−.14	−.05	−.13
N2: Hostility	.41*	.12	.14	.17	.48*	.09
N3: Depression	−.11	.14	−.05	.07	−.14	.14
N4: Self-consciousness	.02	.06	.15	.02	.00	.09
N5: Impulsiveness	.33	.25	.05	.15	.44*	.21
N6: Vulnerability	.02	.12	−.06	.01	.03	.19
E1: Warmth	−.15	−.08	−.14	−.07	−.08	−.12
E2: Gregariousness	.03	.09	.02	.22	−.03	.02
E3: Assertiveness	.15	.08	−.02	.27	.21	−.14
E4: Activity	−.07	−.02	−.18	−.05	.00	−.16
E5: Excitement seeking	.42*	.17	.22	.24	.38	.00
E6: Positive emotions	−.05	−.05	−.28	−.03	.20	−.15
O1: Fantasy	.25	.16	.15	.22	.27	.06
O2: Aesthetics	−.03	.23	−.18	.15	.21	.13
O3: Feelings	−.08	−.03	−.10	.04	.01	−.17
O4: Actions	−.21	.14	−.26	.04	−.14	.14
O5: Ideas	−.15	.20	−.13	.29*	−.05	.06
O6: Values	−.29	.01	−.07	.00	−.46*	−.05

Note. In = Inmate sample, N = 28; St = student sample, N = 47.   *p < .05.

emphasizes short temperedness and an impulsiveness scale oriented toward a lack of control over cravings and temptation—both traits would be expected to show positive relations with psychopathy. In fact, these two traits show strong relations with the PCL: Psychopaths' profiles for N facets show peaks in the high range for these scales, whereas their scores on the remaining four facets are equal to or lower than those for nonpsychopaths (see Figure 19.1). As expected, both impulsivity and hostility related most strongly to Factor 2.

Because of the inclusion of impulsiveness and hostility, a negative correlation between Factor 1 and the NEO-PI domain scale could hardly be expected. However, the more specific facet of anxiety also failed to show the expected negative correlation. Whether this was attributable to sampling error or the nature of the NEO-PI anxiety facet is unclear at present.

Extraversion. As discussed in relation to Eysenck's theory, E should be positively related to

psychopathy. The data, however, failed to confirm prediction. A substantial relation was visible with only a single facet, excitement seeking, and this correlation was considerably weaker in the student sample than in the inmate sample. This relation is consistent with the empirical and theoretical link between sensation seeking (Zuckerman, 1978) and psychopathy (Hare & Jutai, 1986; Harpur et al., 1989; Zuckerman, 1978), and its specific nature may help explain why the broad domain scale was only marginally related to the PCL.

In addition to sensation seeking, the trait of impulsivity is one of the dimensions that shows a robust relation with the PCL and its factors (Hare & Jutai, 1986; Harpur & Hare, 1991b; Harpur et al., 1989; Kosson et al., 1990; Newman & Kosson, 1986). However, the position of impulsivity within the FFM is controversial. Eysenck initially identified impulsivity as a component of E but later incorporated it, along with elements of sensation seeking, into his P dimension. Costa and McCrae (1985), as noted, considered impulsiveness (a failure to inhibit urges and impulses) to be a facet of N, excitement seeking to be a facet of E, and the more cognitive dimensions of self-discipline ("the ability to continue with a task despite boredom"; p. 888) and deliberation ("caution, planning, and thoughtfulness" and quick decision making; p. 889) to be facets of C (Costa et al., 1991; McCrae & Costa, 1985). John's (1990) consensual adjectival markers for the five dimensions place "assertive" and "adventurous" at the pole of surgency and "planful" and "painstaking" at the pole of Conscientious but identify no clear place for cognitive or behavioral impulsivity.

Despite conceptual arguments in favor of the taxonomic distinctions included in the NEO-PI (e.g., Costa, McCrae, & Dembroski, 1989; Costa et al., 1991), empirical results are less clear cut. For instance, excitement seeking, impulsiveness, and hostility, the facet scales correlating substantially with the PCL, all show complex loadings (.30) in a factor analysis of the NEO-PI (Costa et al., 1991). Both impulsiveness and excitement seeking share strong negative loadings on C, whereas hostility loads as highly on the A dimension as it does on N. In the revision of the NEO-PI, the facet scales of self-discipline and deliberation also share with impulsiveness substantial loadings on both N and C (Costa & McCrae, 1992).

However this controversy is resolved, the fact remains that psychopathy is consistently related to these various aspects of impulsivity, broadly defined. We leave it to others to decide whether it is more parsimonious to consider these as individual facets of several dimensions within the FFM or as elements of a unitary, biologically based dimension of temperament (e.g., Zuckerman, 1989).

One further, interesting relation was suggested by the opposite correlations of the PCL factors with positive emotions in the inmate sample. Factor 1 includes an item measuring lack of empathy, but no formal measure of positive (or negative) affectivity has been used with psychopaths. The failure of psychopaths (or of subjects scoring high on Factor 1) to experience positive emotions would be an interesting extension of the growing literature linking psychopathy and affective insensitivity (see Williamson, Harpur, & Hare, 1991). Although the effect

was absent in the student sample, this may not rule out its relevance in the inmate sample (as discussed earlier).

Openness to Experience. The dimension of O has the most limited research base of the five factors. The most important component of this dimension with respect to psychopathy is that of openness of attitudes and values. Its converse has been characterized by McCrae and Costa (1985) as authoritarianism and dogmatism—both characteristics one should not be surprised to see in a psychopath. This impression is supported by the negative correlation seen for inmates with the NEO-PI O domain scale, particularly with the values facet (see Tables 19.5 and 19.6). The strong negative correlation with the values scale, which includes items measuring dogmatic moralism and intolerance, confirms the clinical impression that psychopaths are capable of verbalizing dogmatic ethical and moral views, despite their flagrant failure to abide by these same precepts.

The marked divergence of results between the inmate and student samples is probably related to the vast differences in socioeconomic status, education, and background that separates the undergraduates from the criminals in general. These differences might be expected to show up in this domain more than others because exposure to artistic, literary, and culinary diversity is undoubtedly greater at a university than in a prison (of course, these differences would be present for these two populations long before they had contact with either prison or higher education). In this domain at least, it would seem likely that the inmate data should be given precedence.

The O facet scales also suggest some detailed differences among the scales. In particular, a positive relation was apparent with fantasy (daydreaming, active imagination, etc.) despite a negative relation with the remaining scales.

Agreeableness. Perhaps the greatest consensus would be found for the contention that psychopaths are prototypically low on the trait of A. All of our data confirm that the PCL identifies individuals who are extremely hostile, aggressive, antagonistic, cynical, and manipulative. As shown, this places them at one pole of the IAS-R measure of this dimension, and this is confirmed by the correlations of the PCL with the NEO-PI A domain for both students and inmates. Historical characterizations of the psychopath (e.g., Leary, 1957; Wiggins, 1982) as well as conceptions of the negative pole of the dimension of A fit well with this finding. Adjectives defining the negative pole of A include ruthless, selfish, callous, antagonistic, manipulative, and proud (Costa et al., 1989; but see John, 1990, for an alternative list); all of them are likely to appear in anyone's description of the prototypical psychopath. Other aspects of this dimension emphasized by Costa et al. are its similarity to Machiavellianism, the accompanying cognitive attitude of mistrust and cynicism, and the affective components of contemptuousness and callousness. It is important to note that some of these negative traits are potentially adaptive in certain circumstances.

Further empirical evidence for the link between the PCL and low A comes from studies using the MMPI. Although attempts have been made to recover the FFM dimensions using the MMPI item content (e.g., Costa, Busch, Zonderman, & McCrae, 1986), studies of psychopathy only report correlations of the PCL with the MMPI clinical scales.[5] These studies consistently report moderate correlations between the PCL and the MMPI Psychopathic Deviate and Hypomania scales (Hare, 1985; Harpur et al., 1989). Of the MMPI clinical scales, these are the two with the strongest (inverse) relation with self-reported and peer-rated A (Costa et al., 1989).

In the same manner, the MCMI-II (Millon, 1987) can be used to "triangulate" the PCL. The largest correlation is, not surprisingly, between the PCL and MCMI-II antisocial personality scale ($r = .45$; Hart et al., 1991). This scale, in turn, correlates substantially with both A ($r = -.42$) and C ($r = -.40$) as measured by the NEO-PI. The MCMI-II Aggressive-sadistic scale, which correlates negatively ($-.46$) with Agreeableness but negligibly with the remaining four NEO-PI dimensions, also correlates positively (.36) with the PCL. Other studies pertinent to A–antagonism collected measures of Machiavellianism

(Christie & Geis, 1970) and empathy (Davis, 1983). Moderate correlations were found between the PCL and both measures (Harpur & Hare, 1991b).

Although these findings are consistent, they disguise several more subtle relations. Other scales in the MCMI-II correlated moderately with the PCL. In addition, the two PCL factors were differentially related to these scales. The highest correlation of Factor 1 with any MCMI-II scale (in an inmate sample) was only .28. Factor 2 correlated .30 or above with Passive–Aggressive, Schizotypal, Borderline, and Paranoid scales as well as with Antisocial and Aggressive–sadistic scales. Whereas the Antisocial and Aggressive scales primarily share a negative relation with A and C, the Passive–Aggressive, Schizotypal, and Borderline scales have in common a robust positive relation with N (Costa & McCrae, 1990; see also Wiggins & Pincus, chapter 7, this volume). This pattern confirms the earlier contention that psychopathy represents a pattern of deviation across several of the FFM dimensions. Again, however, the presence of the two factors in the PCL complicates the picture. Although the correlations were small, Factor 1 showed a consistently negative relation with anxiety, correlating with narcissism, which in turn is negatively related to NEO N (Costa & McCrae, 1990) as well as with MCMI-II Anxiety ($r = -.22$ and $-.07$ for Factors 1 and 2, respectively; Hart et al., 1991).

This picture may undoubtedly be clarified with the introduction of the NEO-PI facet scales for A, permitting finer discriminations to be made within this domain. The domain is differentiated with respect to trust (vs. suspicion), straightforwardness (vs. Machiavellianism), altruism (vs. selfish egocentricity), compliance (vs. quarrelsomeness or anger expression), modesty (vs. arrogance), and tender mindedness (vs. tough mindedness or callousness). Given their extremely low standing on the broad dimension, psychopaths would be expected to score at the antagonistic pole of each of these facets. However, some differences, particularly with respect to the PCL factors might emerge. Manipulativeness,

---

[5] Of course, many studies have simply used these scales to classify subjects as psychopathic—a procedure that clearly fails to identify the same subjects assessed as psychopaths using the PCL.

egocentricity, and grandiosity are prominent features of PCL Factor 1, leading us to predict the strongest relation between this factor and the facets of trust, straightforwardness, altruism, and modesty. Factor 2, characterized by anger and tough mindedness, should correlate most strongly with compliance and tender mindedness.

Conscientiousness. C must also rank as a dimension on which all practitioners would agree that psychopaths should score low. Few self-report data, other than those already reviewed, are available to confirm this hypothesis, but a careful examination of the scoring criteria for the PCL (Hare, 1985, 1991) and for the *DSM-III-R* criteria for ATS (APA, 1987) reveals that behaviors characteristic of irresponsibility, undependability, a lack of deliberation, and a lack of persistence are prominent features of the disorder. However, examination of the breadth of traits subsumed under the dimension of C also reveals characteristics that are less central to psychopathy. John (1990) reported that disorderliness, frivolousness, and forgetfulness are considered prototypical of low C, and Costa et al. (1991) included competence ("the sense that one is capable"; p. 889) and order ("the tendency to keep one's environment tidy"; p. 889) in their six facets of C. Our impression is that neither competence nor order is inherently related to psychopathy. If anything, psychopaths might consider themselves to be exceptionally competent, in line with other inflated and unrealistic views of their own abilities, resulting in a positive correlation with this facet.

Self-discipline and deliberation, which we already discussed in relation to impulsivity, are both characteristics lacking in the psychopath. In scoring the PCL, behaviors indicative of this deficit throughout the subject's life (e.g., being bored by schoolwork, quitting jobs out of boredom after 1 or 2 days, having inadequate or unrealistic plans after release from prison) are used to score PCL Items 3 (need for stimulation–proneness to boredom) and 13 (lack of realistic long-term plans). Both of these items load on Factor 2, suggesting that these facets, and perhaps the C domain in general, relate most strongly to psychopaths' impulsive and antisocial characteristics.

The correlations in Table 19.5 seem to support

the suggestion that psychopathy is negatively related only to certain facets of C. The correlations with the domain scale are generally small, consistent with there being a strong relation with only a few subtraits within the domain. In addition, the magnitude of the correlation is slightly larger for Factor 2 than for Factor 1. It is unclear why, in this instance, the students demonstrated a correlation of larger magnitude than that of the inmates.

Data concerning the psychopathy–C relation are also available from a variety of studies making use of the Socialization Scale (Gough, 1969). This scale has a proven empirical relation with PCL assessments (Hare, 1985; Newman & Kosson, 1986), although it is much more strongly related to Factor 2 of the PCL but does little to measure Factor 1.

Five-Factor Model Ratings. A final source of data is available that may be useful as a counterbalance to the preponderance of self-report measures already discussed. Ratings of the five factors, based on videotapes of an interview used to assess psychopathy, were completed using the IASR-B5 (Trapnell & Wiggins, 1991). Ratings were obtained for 12 students and 12 inmates assessed on the PCL. Because the inclusion of both students and inmates resulted in a very high correlation between the PCL factors ($r = .93$), we present only analyses of the total PCL score.

Strong relations among the PCL and each of the FFM dimensions were obtained. These correlations are presented in Table 19.7 for the entire sample and for the 12 criminal and 12 noncriminal subjects separately. Despite the small numbers, the pattern of results for the entire sample was largely duplicated in each group. This is important because combining criminal and noncriminal subjects introduces a confound between level of psychopathy and a number of other variables (e.g., criminality, social class, education) that differentiate criminals from college students. For example, the IASR-B5 adjectives for O emphasize artistic, literary, and philosophical dispositions, with relatively little emphasis on other facets of this domain such as dogmatic values and openness to feelings. These aspects of O might particularly characterize students (who score low on the PCL but not criminals (who score higher).

The pattern of results confirmed the profile of re-

TABLE 19.7

Correlations Among the Psychopathy Checklist (PCL) Total Scores and the Shortened Revised Interpersonal Adjective Scale–Big Five (IASR-B5) Scale Ratings

IASR-B5 scale	PCL		
	Inmates	**Students**	**All**
Dominance	.55	.67*	.66*
Love	−.73*	.27	−.82*
Neuroticism	−.52	−.59*	−.44*
Openness	−.52	.35	−.76*
Conscientiousness	−.77*	−.49	−.83*

Note. Inmates, N = 12; students, N = 12; all, N = 24.
*p < .05.

lations we expected between psychopathy and the five factors. However, several features of this study should be noted before the results are taken at face value. The ratings were performed on interviews gathered for other reasons and were not specifically designed to elicit behavior relevant to the dimensions subsequently rated. This procedure could lead to the underestimation of certain characteristics because of a lack of data or the undesirable sharing of method variance between FFM and PCL ratings (for which the interviews were specifically designed). The latter possibility would seem to be more likely in view of the fact that four of the five correlations for the entire sample exceeded the estimated reliability of the averaged FFM ratings (ranging from .54 to .77, based on the intraclass correlation coefficient and use of the Spearman–Brown Prophecy formula). Nevertheless, whatever the magnitude of the correlations, the pattern conformed closely to the expected profile.

PSYCHOPATHY, FIVE-FACTOR PROFILES, AND INTERACTIONS

From the results reviewed here, it is possible to get a reasonable picture of how the two-factor model of psychopathy embodied in the PCL relates to the FFM. The factor of social deviance (PCL Factor 2) is related in predictable ways to four of the five dimensions: positively to E and N and negatively to A

and C. If one thinks of P as the converse of the latter two dimensions combined, this accords well with Eysenck's theoretical treatment of criminality in general. It must be said, however, that the magnitude of these relations is not large and that a multiple correlation accounting for less than 10% of the variance of Factor 2 (based on Eysenck's scales) leaves much variance unaccounted for.

The construct measured by Factor 1 of the PCL showed a substantial relation with the A facet of the NEO-PI, as it does with the related scales of Dominance, Machiavellianism, and Empathy. A modest but consistently negative correlation has been found with various measures of anxiety other than the NEO-PI. However, for the most part, self-report questionnaires seem to measure quite poorly the characteristics identified by the interview-based assessments using the PCL.

What are the implications of these observations and findings for either psychopathy or the FFM? We think there are several. First, it is worth considering again the fact that the personality scales most strongly related to the PCL have frequently been those that bear a complex relation to the FFM. In several instances, the prototypical characteristics of the psychopath combine several dimensions of the FFM. As an example, psychopaths are typically hostile and aggressive, as manifested in their violent and abusive behavior, their cold and callous affective reactions, and their contemptuous and cynical attitudes. These characteristics form a unified whole when seen in a psychopathic inmate but are represented by distinct dimensions in the FFM. The facet of N termed hostility measures anger and low frustration tolerance ("hot-blooded" hostility; Costa et al., 1989), and not surprisingly, this scale correlates substantially with the PCL (Factor 2). "Cold-blooded" hostility is hypothesized, however, to appear as an antagonistic orientation to other people and to be measured best as a facet of A. Similar arguments can be made about the various manifestations of impulsiveness, which form a coherent cluster when considered as elements of psychopathy but are represented in the domains of E, N, and C in the FFM framework.

This raises a major question facing FFM theorists: What are the developmental origins of the factors, and what kind of causal model can be developed to explain them (John, 1990; see also D. M. Buss, 1991)? With respect to psychopathy, an unbiased observer might conclude that the most likely lines of causal influence do not lie along the five dimensions to which this volume is devoted but along dimensions of hostility, impulsiveness, and sensation seeking that bear a complex relation with the major domains. Needless to say, the resolution of this issue will have to accommodate a far broader range of data than is considered here (e.g., D. M. Buss, 1991; John, 1990; Zuckerman, 1991).

These observations also have implications for how the FFM may be used as an organizing framework for examining personality disorders in general, as advocated by, for instance, Costa and McCrae (1990) and Wiggins and Pincus (chapter 7, this volume). To date, these approaches have used self-report measures of personality disorder dimensions administered to nonclinical populations. One rationale for this has been that the poor empirical basis for current operationalizations of personality disorders and the unreliability inherent in their assessment lead to a "criterion problem" when measures of personality dimensions, based on far more extensive bodies of empirical research, are used as predictors (Wiggins & Pincus, 1989). Although this is true, it makes moot the question of whether the empirical relations uncovered by these analog studies mirror those that would be seen in a clinically disordered population. Psychopathy represents perhaps the single exception to this criterion problem.

It is troubling, then, that none of the self-report measures demonstrates very strong empirical relation to the PCL. Given the evidence attesting to the PCL's reliability and validity, this failure cannot simply be ascribed to the use of a poor criterion. Other than for A, the relations are also too small to be accounted for solely on the grounds of nonshared method variance between the measures.

The FFM profile of the psychopath is considerably more complex than that envisaged for several other personality disorders. The simplest relation proposed is one in which an extreme position on a single major dimension places one at risk for a specific disorder (e.g., extreme O may characterize schizotypal personality disorder). More complex

linear relations have also been considered (e.g., the profile for psychopathy given in Figure 19.1). However, the traits that make up our description of psychopathy appear to be more than this linear combination in two distinct ways. First, perhaps with the exception of A–antagonism, the broad level description of the five factors does not represent the most appropriate level at which to describe traits that define the psychopath. In each instance, one subtrait or facet may relate to the disorder, but another facet of the same dimension may manifest an opposite relation. Indeed, the present data indicate that discrimination of psychopathic from nonpsychopathic inmates is best achieved using specific facets, not general domain scales.

Second, the prototypical characteristics of the psychopath appear, both phenomenologically and possibly statistically, to be more than mere linear combinations of the five dimensions. Someone extremely low on C and openness to values is not, we contend, very close to being a psychopath. Even the addition of a low score on A does not, it seems to us, push the person much closer to the diagnosis. Even in the absence of, say, Dominance, excitement seeking, and impulsivity, the syndrome fails to take on its distinctive form: One might see a shiftless authoritarian person but not a psychopath.

These speculations are open to empirical testing in at least two ways. The most obvious is that an interactive combination of the five factors (or perhaps of a subset of facet scales) should be able to predict clinical assessments. This interactive model was tested earlier using Eysenck's dimensions, with little success. However, the addition of the remaining dimensions, or measurement of the less broadband facet scales, may provide a combination of normal traits that produces the clinical picture. Although the data we have are not adequate in terms of sample sizes, we decided to try a partial test of this hypothesis using the data from students and inmates on the NEO-PI domain scales.

Psychopathy and Five-Factor Interactions

The primary data for examining the interaction hypothesis were the NEO-PI domain scores gathered from 47 students. As was done for the EPQ scales, the main effects and interaction terms for the five scales were entered into a hierarchical multiple regression equation predicting subjects' PCL and Factor 1 and Factor 2 scores. Because of the small sample size, it was not possible to test anything more than the two-way interactions between the scales. The five main effects were entered first to test the magnitude of the combined linear relations between the five factors and the PCL. Next, the 10 two-way interactions were entered, and the increase in multiple correlation was tested.

The main effects of the five factors significantly predicted the PCL total scores, $R^2 = 0.26$, $F(5, 41) = 2.82$, $p < .03$, and Factor 1 scores, $R^2 = 0.38$, $F(5, 41) = 4.95$, $p < .01$, but not Factor 2 scores, $R^2 = .20$, $.08 < p < .09$. In both instances, the beta weights for C and A were negative and significant. The addition of the two-way terms increased the multiple correlations to .52 for the PCL total, to .60 for Factor 1, and to .49 for Factor 2, although none of these increases reached significance (all $ps > .10$), largely because of the reduction in the degrees of freedom resulting from the addition of the 10 two-way terms. Nevertheless, the introduction of the interaction terms increased the multiple correlations considerably, accounting for between 49% and 60% of the variance of PCL ratings. Inspection of the beta weights for the full models revealed an interesting consistency: Beta weights for two interaction terms were significantly related to the total PCL and to both factors, and no other interaction terms even approached significance. The two interactions were

A × N and A × C; in each case, the resulting beta was large and negative.

On the basis of this observation, the regression was run once more, entering the five main effects at Step 1, followed by the 2 two-way interactions of A × N and A × C at Step 2. Using these seven terms produced multiple correlations of .42, .50, and .37, respectively, for the full model (all $ps < .01$). The standardized regression equations for these models are shown in Exhibit 19.2, where the nature of the interaction becomes apparent. In every case, the beta weights indicated a substantial positive contribution made to the prediction of psychopathy by the main effects of N, C, and A, but an even stronger negative contribution was made by the interaction of A × N and A × C. Because these latter terms were made simply by the multiplication of the component scales, we are led to the interpretation that the role of A in predicting psychopathy ratings is moderated by a subject's score on both N and C. Furthermore, an extreme score on the PCL would only be expected if someone scored particularly low on all three traits.

Because the preceding analyses were based on a student sample with a small sample size and seven independent variables, they of course cannot be trusted very far. In addition, the possibility of capitalizing on chance findings by selecting only these two interactions is great (Cohen & Cohen, 1983). Nevertheless, the theoretical importance of these two interactions is apparent from the literature reviewed

---

EXHIBIT 19.2

Standardized Regression Equations Relating the Five-Factor Model to the Psychopathy Checklist (PCL) Total and Factor Scores

PCL total = 0.13*E + 1.89*N + 1.62*C + 0.18*O + (2.46 − 1.93*N − 2.55*C)*A

Factor 1 = 0.24*E + 1.69*N + 0.84*C + 0.19*O + (1.55 − 1.80*N − 2.48*C)*A

Factor 2 = −0.08*E + 1.79*N + 1.89*C + 0.08*O + (2.75 − 1.87*N − 2.91*C)*A

Note. N = Neuroticism, E = Extraversion, O = Openness to Experience, A = Agreeableness, C = Conscientiousness.

in this chapter, suggesting that something more than chance is at work.

It seemed worthwhile, therefore, to explore this finding further using the remaining data on the NEO-PI gathered on 28 inmates. A cross-validation using this sample would seem to provide as challenging a test as possible of the validity of these findings, given that the new sample was from an entirely different population, was entirely male, and scored in a completely different range on the dependent variables. Despite this, we computed predicted PCL, Factor 1, and Factor 2 scores on the basis of the regression equations given in Exhibit 19.2 and NEO-PI scores standardized within the prison sample. Correlations between the predicted PCL total and Factor 1 and Factor 2 scores and the inmates' actual ratings were .52, .47, and .29, respectively, the first two significant at $p < .02$, even with only 28 subjects.

The interactive model developed on students apparently did a remarkable job of predicting PCL scores on carefully assessed inmates. The cross-validated correlation of .52 is as high as has been obtained with any self-report scales designed specifically to assess this disorder. Whether this value would be maintained with a larger sample remains to be seen, but it seems likely that more accurate prediction could be achieved by developing the regression weights on a similar criminal sample.

PSYCHOPATHY AND THE FIVE-FACTOR MODEL: SOME IMPLICATIONS

The data reviewed in this chapter have a number of implications for use of the FFM in the field of personality disorders. Clinical lore and empirical literature present a fairly clear picture of where psychopathy should fit in the FFM, and some of the additional data we presented contribute further to this picture. The question of the relation between personality disorders and dimensions of personality being presently debated continues to be framed in terms of the most straightforward, linear relations possible: Extremity on one dimension puts one at risk for pathology; at best, several dimensions contribute to that risk. There is good reason for maintaining this simplicity. Nonlinear effects frequently

fail to cross-validate, and when combined with criteria of dubious reliability (and perhaps even more dubious validity), the likelihood of capitalizing on sample-specific findings is great. Nevertheless, it would be foolish not to consider the possibility that more complex relations may be necessary to model the complexity of the real world.

Psychopathy as assessed by the PCL is perhaps the most reliable and well-validated diagnostic category in the field of personality disorders. Our data suggest that it is also a good candidate for demonstrating a possible interactive relation between dimensions of normal personality and personality disorder.

A second implication concerns the strategy for creating a taxonomy suitable for classification of personality disorders. A clinical approach to this advocates operationalizing clinical knowledge, developing adequate assessment procedures, and performing research using clinically diagnosed individuals as the main database. A more parsimonious strategy might be to begin with a well-developed taxonomy of normal functioning and to search for extreme variants of these normal dimensions, namely, individuals likely to display pathology of some kind. Both strategies are likely to provide some useful information, but if psychopathy is to serve as an example, one would have to conclude that it would take a great many years using the latter strategy to arrive at a pathological variant of the FFM combined in the profile that is apparent in psychopathy. It would take even longer if the disorder turns out to be a truly interactive combination of traits.

Third, the question remains whether the five broad-band factors are, in fact, sufficient (in whatever linear or nonlinear combination) to "produce" the personality of the psychopath. Although the linear relation between the five broad-band dimensions and the PCL are not large, the interactive model, cross-validated on a small sample, accounted for 27% of the PCL variance. Even with method variance removed and optimal weights developed on a comparable criminal sample, there still may remain unexplained variance in the assessment of psychopathy.

What kinds of characteristics might be left out? One possibility is that the FFM is not, in fact, comprehensive. Grove and Tellegen (1991), for instance, suggested that the dimensions of excellence (feeling oneself remarkable or unique) and evilness (feeling oneself fundamentally bad) have been omitted from previous taxonomies because of the exclusion of evaluative adjectives from earlier word lists. The former dimension would most certainly be relevant to the psychopath's seemingly indestructible self-esteem. The latter dimension might reveal an interesting discrepancy between self- and peer-report.

It may also be unreasonable to expect the five broad-band factors to be the best predictors of this disorder. In general, predictive power is greater using traits measured at the more specific facet levels, and as we emphasized throughout, it is mostly specific facet scales, not the broad domain scales, that demonstrate strong relations with the PCL. Although we could not test this with the present data, we expect that a combination of selected facet scales would provide a stronger relation with the PCL than the domain scales examined here.

Our concentration on the domain scales may also account for the relative lack of differentiation of the two PCL factors in our data. At the level of the facet scales, however, several of the correlations were far stronger with Factor 2 than with Factor 1. Despite ample evidence attesting to the discriminant validity of these two components of psychopathy, few self-report measures successfully assess the egocentric, manipulative, and callous characteristics assessed by Factor 1. Those that do so most successfully are scales measuring dominance, narcissism, Machiavellianism, and a lack of empathy (Harpur & Hare, 1994; Hart et al. 1991). These traits were not well represented by the NEO-PI data, but they should be better captured by the forthcoming facet scales for A and C.

Another possibility is the emergence of a new or distinct type of personality organization that is qualitatively different from that seen in nonpathological subjects. A specific five-factor profile might certainly represent a risk factor for developing this type of personality organization, but it may require additional experiences or attributes that lie outside the traditional sphere of personality research for its full emergence. This speculation need not be entirely abstract, however. Current conceptions of personality organization make frequent use of cognitive concepts and processes as mediating factors in the expression of personal dispositions in behavior. Psychopaths, as a group, display a puzzling set of abnormalities in several basic cognitive functions involved in attention (Harpur, 1991; Harpur & Hare, 1990; Kosson & Newman, 1986), impulse control (Newman & Wallace, 1993), and the processing of affect and language (Hare et al., 1988; Williamson et al., 1991). These may represent critical additional risk factors for the development of the disorder in addition to, or in combination with, the underlying personality structure.

References

American Psychiatric Association. (1952). *Diagnostic and statistical manual of mental disorders.* Washington, DC: Author.

American Psychiatric Association. (1968). *Diagnostic and statistical manual of mental disorders* (2nd ed.). Washington, DC: Author.

American Psychiatric Association. (1980). *Diagnostic and statistical manual of mental disorders* (3rd ed.). Washington, DC: Author.

American Psychiatric Association. (1987). *Diagnostic and statistical manual of mental disorders* (3rd ed., rev.). Washington, DC: Author.

Block, J. (1989). Critique of the act frequency approach to personality. *Journal of Personality and Social Psychology, 56,* 234–245.

Buss, A. H. (1966). *Psychopathology.* New York: Wiley.

Buss, D. M. (1991). Evolutionary personality psychology. *Annual Review of Psychology, 42,* 459–491.

Buss, D. M., & Craik, K. H. (1983). The act frequency approach to personality. *Psychological Review, 90,* 105–126.

Buss, D. M., & Craik, K. H. (1986). Acts, dispositions, and clinical assessment: The psychopathology of everyday conduct. *Clinical Psychology Review, 6,* 387–406.

Christie, R., & Geis, F. L. (1970). *Studies in Machiavellianism.* New York: Academic Press.

Cleckley, H. (1941). *The mask of sanity.* St. Louis, MO: Mosby.

Cleckley, H. (1976). *The mask of sanity* (5th ed.). St. Louis, MO: Mosby.

Cohen, J., & Cohen, P. (1983). *Applied multiple re-*

gression/correlation analysis for the behavioral sciences (2nd ed.). Hillsdale, NJ: Erlbaum.

Correctional Service of Canada. (1990). *Forum on corrections research, 2*(1). Ottawa, Ontario, Canada: Author.

Costa, P. T., Jr., Busch, C. M., Zonderman, A. B., & McCrae, R. R. (1986). Correlations of MMPI factor scales with measures of the five-factor model of personality. *Journal of Personality Assessment, 50,* 640–650.

Costa, P. T., Jr., & McCrae, R. R. (1985). *The NEO Personality Inventory manual.* Odessa, FL: Psychological Assessment Resources.

Costa, P. T., Jr., & McCrae, R. R. (1987). Neuroticism, somatic complaints, and disease: Is the bark worse than the bite? *Journal of Personality, 55,* 301–316.

Costa, P. T., Jr., & McCrae, R. R. (1989). *NEO-PI/FFI manual supplement.* Odessa, FL: Psychological Assessment Resources.

Costa, P. T., Jr., & McCrae, R. R. (1990). Personality disorders and the five-factor model of personality. *Journal of Personality Disorders, 4,* 362–371.

Costa, P. T., Jr., & McCrae, R. R. (1992). *Revised NEO Personality Inventory (NEO-PI-R) and NEO Five-Factor Inventory (NEO-FFI) professional manual.* Odessa, FL: Psychological Assessment Resources.

Costa, P. T., Jr., McCrae, R. R., & Dembroski, T. M. (1989). Agreeableness versus antagonism: Explication of a potential risk factor for CHD. In A. W. Siegman & T. M. Dembroski (Eds.), *In search of coronary-prone behavior beyond type A* (pp. 41–63). Hillsdale, NJ: Erlbaum.

Costa, P. T., Jr., McCrae, R. R., & Dye, D. A. (1991). Facet scales for Agreeableness and Conscientiousness: A revision of the NEO Personality Inventory. *Personality and Individual Differences, 12,* 887–898.

Craft, M. J. (1965). *Ten studies into psychopathic personality.* Bristol, UK: Wright.

Curran, D., & Mallinson, P. (1944). Psychopathic personality. *Journal of Mental Science, 90,* 266–286.

Davis, M. H. (1983). Measuring individual differences in empathy: Evidence for a multidimensional approach. *Journal of Personality and Social Psychology, 44,* 113–126.

Davies, W., & Feldman, P. (1981). The diagnosis of psychopathy by forensic specialists. *British Journal of Psychiatry, 138,* 329–331.

Digman, J. M. (1990). Personality structure: Emer-gence of the five-factor model. *Annual Review of Psychology, 41,* 417–440.

Eysenck, H. J. (1964). *Crime and personality.* London, England: Routledge & Kegan Paul.

Eysenck, H. J. (1967). *The biological basis of personality.* Springfield, IL: Charles C Thomas.

Eysenck, H. J. (1970). *The structure of human personality.* London, England: Methuen.

Eysenck, H. J. (1977). *Crime and personality* (3rd ed.). London, England: Routledge & Kegan Paul.

Eysenck, H. J., & Eysenck, S. B. G. (1976). *Psychoticism as a dimension of personality.* London, England: Hodder & Stoughton.

Eysenck, H. J., & Eysenck, S. B. G. (1978). Psychopathy, personality and genetics. In R. D. Hare & D. Schalling (Eds.), *Psychopathic behavior: Approaches to research* (pp. 197–223). New York: Wiley.

Eysenck, H. J., & Gudjonsson, G. H. (1989). *The causes and cures of criminality.* New York: Plenum Press.

Foreman, M. (1988). *Psychopathy and interpersonal behavior.* Unpublished doctoral dissertation, University of British Columbia, Vancouver, British Columbia, Canada.

Frances, A. J., & Widiger, T. (1986). The classification of personality disorders: An overview of problems and solutions. In A. J. Frances & R. E. Hales (Eds.), *American Psychiatric Association annual review* (Vol. 5, pp. 244–257). Washington, DC: American Psychiatric Press.

Gerstley, L. J., Alterman, A. L., McLellan, A. T., & Woody, G. E. (1990). Antisocial personality disorder in substance abusers: A problematic diagnosis? *American Journal of Psychiatry, 147,* 173–178.

Gough, H. G. (1969). *Manual for the California Psychological Inventory.* Palo Alto, CA: Consulting Psychologists Press.

Gray, K. C., & Hutchison, H. C. (1964). The psychopathic personality: A survey of Canadian psychiatrists' opinions. *Canadian Psychiatric Association Journal, 9,* 452–461.

Grove, W. M., & Tellegen, A. (1991). Problems in the classification of personality disorders. *Journal of Personality Disorders, 5,* 31–41.

Hare, R. D. (1970). *Psychopathy: Theory and research.* New York: Wiley.

Hare, R. D. (1980). A research scale for the assessment of psychopathy in criminal populations. *Personality and Individual Differences, 1,* 111–117.

Hare, R. D. (1982). Psychopathy and the personality dimensions of Psychoticism, Extraversion and Neuroticism. *Personality and Individual Differences, 3,* 35–42.

Hare, R. D. (1983). Diagnosis of antisocial personality disorder in two prison populations. *American Journal of Psychiatry, 140,* 887–890.

Hare, R. D. (1985). Comparison of procedures for the assessment of psychopathy. *Journal of Consulting and Clinical Psychology, 53,* 7–16.

Hare, R. D. (1991). *The Hare Psychopathy Checklist —Revised.* Toronto, Ontario, Canada: Multi-Health Systems.

Hare, R. D., & Frazelle, J. (1980). *Some preliminary notes on the use of a research scale for the assessment of psychopathy in criminal populations.* Unpublished manuscript, University of British Columbia, Department of Psychology, Vancouver, British Columbia, Canada.

Hare, R. D., Harpur, T. J., Hakstian, A. R., Forth, A. E., Hart, S. D., & Newman, J. P. (1990). The Revised Psychopathy Checklist: Reliability and factor structure. *Psychological Assessment: A Journal of Consulting and Clinical Psychology, 2,* 338–341.

Hare, R. D., Hart, S. D., & Harpur, T. J. (1991). Psychopathy and the proposed *DSM-IV* criteria for antisocial personality disorder. *Journal of Abnormal Psychology, 100,* 391–398.

Hare, R. D., & Jutai, J. W. (1986). Psychopathy, stimulation seeking, and stress. In J. Strelau, F. H. Farley, & A. Gale (Eds.), *The biological bases of personality and behavior* (Vol. 2, pp. 175–184). Washington, DC: Hemisphere.

Hare, R. D., Williamson, S. E., & Harpur, T. J. (1988). Psychopathy and language. In T. E. Moffitt & S. A. Mednick (Eds.), *Biological contributions to crime causation* (pp. 68–92). Dordrecht, The Netherlands: Martinus Nijhoff.

Harpur, T. J. (1991). *Visual attention in psychopathic criminals.* Unpublished doctoral dissertation, University of British Columbia, Vancouver, British Columbia, Canada.

Harpur, T. J., Hakstian, A. R., & Hare, R. D. (1988). Factor structure of the Psychopathy Checklist. *Journal of Consulting and Clinical Psychology, 56,* 741–747.

Harpur, T. J., & Hare, R. D. (1990). Psychopathy and attention. In J. Enns (Ed.), *The development of attention: Research and theory* (pp. 429–444). Amsterdam, The Netherlands: North-Holland.

Harpur, T. J., & Hare, R. D. (1991a, August). *Psychopathy and violent behavior: Two factors are better than one.* Paper presented at the 99th Annual Convention of the American Psychological Association, San Francisco, CA.

Harpur, T. J., & Hare, R. D. (1991b). *Self-report correlates of psychopathy: Narcissism, Machiavellianism, and empathy.* Unpublished manuscript, University of British Columbia, Vancouver, British Columbia, Canada.

Harpur, T. J., & Hare, R. D. (1994). Assessment of psychopathy as a function of age. *Journal of Abnormal Psychology, 103,* 604–609.

Harpur, T. J., Hare, R. D., & Hakstian, A. R. (1989). Two-factor conceptualization of psychopathy: Construct validity and assessment implications. *Psychological Assessment: A Journal of Consulting and Clinical Psychology, 1,* 6–17.

Harpur, T. J., Hare, R. D., Zimmerman, M., & Coryell, W. (1990, August). *Dimensions underlying DSM-III personality disorders: Cluster 2.* Paper presented at the 98th Annual Convention of the American Psychological Association, Boston, MA.

Hart, S. D., Forth, A. E., & Hare, R. D. (1991). The MCMI-II and psychopathy. *Journal of Personality Disorders, 5,* 318–327.

Hart, S. D., & Hare, R. D. (1989). Discriminant validity of the Psychopathy Checklist in a forensic psychiatric population. *Psychological Assessment: A Journal of Consulting and Clinical Psychology, 1,* 211–218.

Hart, S. D., Hare, R. D., & Harpur, T. J. (1992). The Psychopathy Checklist: An overview for researchers and clinicians. In P. McReynolds & J. Rosen (Eds.), *Advances in psychological assessment* (Vol. 8, pp. 103–130). New York: Plenum Press.

Hathaway, S. R., & McKinley, J. C. (1967). *Manual for the Minnesota Multiphasic Personality Inventory.* New York: Psychological Corporation.

John, O. P. (1990). The "Big Five" factor taxonomy: Dimensions of personality in the natural language and in questionnaires. In L. A. Pervin (Ed.), *Handbook of personality: Theory and research* (pp. 66–100). New York: Guilford Press.

Karpman, B. (1961). The structure of neurosis: With special differentials between neurosis, psychosis, homosexuality, alcoholism, psychopathy, and criminality. *Archives of Criminal Psychodynamics, 4,* 599–646.

Kosson, D. S., & Newman, J. P. (1986). Psychopathy and allocation of attentional capacity in a divided-attention situation. *Journal of Abnormal Psychology, 95,* 257–263.

Kosson, D. S., Smith, S. S., & Newman, J. P. (1990). Evaluation of the construct validity of psychopathy in Black and White male inmates: Three preliminary studies. *Journal of Abnormal Psychology, 99*, 250–259.

Leary, T. (1957). *Interpersonal diagnosis of personality.* New York: Ronald Press.

Lilienfeld, S. O. (1994). Conceptual problems in the assessment of psychopathy. *Clinical Psychology Review, 14*, 17–38.

Livesley, W. J., & Jackson, D. N. (1986). The internal consistency and factorial structure of behaviors judged to be associated with *DSM-III* personality disorders. *American Journal of Psychiatry, 143*, 1473–1474.

McCord, W., & McCord, J. (1964). *The psychopath: An essay on the criminal mind.* Princeton, NJ: Van Nostrand.

McCrae, R. R., & Costa, P. T., Jr. (1985). Openness to experience. In R. Hogan & W. H. Jones (Eds.), *Perspectives in personality* (Vol. 1, pp. 145–172). Greenwich, CT: JAI Press.

McCrae, R. R., & Costa, P. T., Jr. (1987). Validation of the five-factor model of personality across instruments and observers. *Journal of Personality and Social Psychology, 52*, 81–90.

McCrae, R. R., & Costa, P. T., Jr. (1989). The structure of interpersonal traits: Wiggins's circumplex and the five-factor model. *Journal of Personality and Social Psychology, 56*, 586–595.

Millon, T. (1981). *Disorders of personality:* DSM-III, *Axis II.* New York: Wiley.

Millon, T. (1983). *Millon Clinical Multiaxial Inventory manual* (3rd ed.). Minneapolis, MN: National Computer Systems.

Millon, T. (1987). *Millon Clinical Multiaxial Inventory manual* (2nd ed.). Minneapolis, MN: National Computer Systems.

Morey, L. C. (1988a). The categorical representation of personality disorder: A cluster analysis of *DSM-III* personality features. *Journal of Abnormal Psychology, 97*, 314–321.

Morey, L. C. (1988b). A psychometric analysis of the *DSM-III-R* personality disorder criteria. *Journal of Personality Disorders, 2*, 109–124.

Newman, J. P., & Kosson, D. S. (1986). Passive avoidance learning in psychopathic and nonpsychopathic offenders. *Journal of Abnormal Psychology, 95*, 252–256.

Newman, J. P., & Wallace, J. (1993). Psychopathy and cognition. In K. S. Dobson & P. C. Kendall (Eds.), *Psychopathology and cognition* (pp. 293–349). San Diego, CA: Academic Press.

Ogloff, J. P. R., Wong, S., & Greenwood, A. (1990). Treating criminal psychopaths in a therapeutic community program. *Behavioral Sciences and the Law, 8*, 81–90.

Pichot, P. (1978). Psychopathic behaviour: A historical overview. In R. D. Hare & D. Schalling (Eds.), *Psychopathic behavior: Approaches to research* (pp. 55–70). New York: Wiley.

Robins, L. N. (1966). *Deviant children grown up.* Baltimore: Williams & Wilkins.

Robins, L. N. (1978). Aetiological implications in studies of childhood histories relating to antisocial personality. In R. D. Hare & D. Schalling (Eds.), *Psychopathic behavior: Approaches to research* (pp. 255–271). New York: Wiley.

Schneider, K. (1958). *Psychopathic personalities.* Springfield, IL: Charles C Thomas.

Schroeder, M. L., Schroeder, K. G., & Hare, R. D. (1983). Generalizability of a checklist for the assessment of psychopathy. *Journal of Consulting and Clinical Psychology, 51*, 511–516.

Smith, S. S., & Newman, J. P. (1990). Alcohol and drug abuse/dependence disorders in psychopathic and nonpsychopathic criminal offenders. *Journal of Abnormal Psychology, 99*, 430–439.

Spielberger, C. D., Kling, J. K., & O'Hagan, S. E. J. (1978). Dimensions of psychopathic personality: Antisocial behaviour and anxiety. In R. D. Hare & D. Schalling (Eds.), *Psychopathic behavior: Approaches to research* (pp. 23–46). New York: Wiley.

Trapnell, P. D., & Wiggins, J. S. (1991). Extension of the Interpersonal Adjective Scales to the Big Five dimensions of personality. *Journal of Personality and Social Psychology, 59*, 781–790.

Widiger, T. A., Frances, A. J., Spitzer, R. L., & Williams, J. B. W. (1988). The *DSM-III-R* personality disorders: An overview. *American Journal of Psychiatry, 145*, 786–795.

Wiggins, J. S. (1982). Circumplex models of interpersonal behavior in clinical psychology. In P. C. Kendall & J. N. Butcher (Eds.), *Handbook of research methods in clinical psychology* (pp. 183–221). New York: Wiley.

Wiggins, J. S., & Pincus, A. L. (1989). Conceptions of personality disorders and dimensions of personality. *Psychological Assessment: A Journal of Consulting and Clinical Psychology, 1*, 305–316.

Wiggins, J. S., & Trapnell, P. D. (1997). Personality structure: The return of the Big Five. In S. R. Briggs, R. Hogan, & W. H. Jones (Eds.), *Handbook of personality psychology* (pp. 737–765). San Diego, CA: Academic Press.

Wiggins, J. S., Trapnell, P., & Phillips, N. (1988). Psychometric and geometric characteristics of the Revised Interpersonal Adjective Scales (IAS-R). *Multivariate Behavioral Research, 23,* 517–530.

Williamson, S., Harpur, T. J., & Hare, R. D. (1991). Abnormal processing of affective words by psychopaths. *Psychophysiology, 28,* 260–273.

Wong, S. (1984). *Criminal and institutional behaviors of psychopaths: Program's branch users report.* Ottawa, Ontario, Canada: Ministry of the Solicitor-General of Canada.

Wong, S. (1988). Is Hare's Psychopathy Checklist reliable without an interview? *Psychological Reports, 62,* 931–934.

World Health Organization. (1977). *Manual of the international classification of diseases, injuries, and causes of death* (9th rev.). Geneva, Switzerland: Author.

World Health Organization. (1993). *The ICD-10 classification of mental and behavioral disorders: Diagnostic criteria for research.* Geneva, Switzerland: Author.

Zuckerman, M. (1978). Sensation seeking and psychopathy. In R. D. Hare & D. Schalling (Eds.), *Psychopathic behavior: Approaches to research* (pp. 165–185). New York: Wiley.

Zuckerman, M. (1989). Personality in the third dimension: A psychobiological approach. *Personality and Individual Differences, 10,* 391–418.

Zuckerman, M. (1991). *Psychobiology of personality.* New York: Cambridge University Press.

CHAPTER 20

PSYCHOPATHY FROM THE PERSPECTIVE OF THE FIVE-FACTOR MODEL OF PERSONALITY

Donald R. Lynam

The term psychopathy has been around for well over 100 years. Although it was originally used to denote "all mental irregularities," in the last 50 years it has come to be used much more narrowly (Millon, Simonsen, & Birket-Smith, 1998). If not the first description of psychopathic individuals, Cleckley's (1941/1988) was certainly the richest. He described 15 men and women that he thought were "psychopaths," by which he meant individuals who seemed sane, intelligent, and competent but who were clearly disturbed. Because they seemed sane but were clearly disordered, Cleckley said these individuals wore "masks of sanity." Since Cleckley's original writings, other clinicians and researchers (Buss, 1966; Hare, 1970; Karpman, 1941; McCord & McCord, 1964) have been remarkably consistent in their descriptions of the psychopath. At this point, one can describe psychopathy as a form of personality disorder. Behaviorally, the psychopath is an impulsive, risk taker involved in a variety of criminal activities. Interpersonally, the psychopath has been described as grandiose, egocentric, manipulative, forceful, and cold hearted. Affectively, the psychopath displays shallow emotions; is unable to maintain close relationships; and lacks empathy, anxiety, and remorse. Given this description, it is not surprising that the psychopath poses great harm and exacts great costs from the society in which he or she lives.

The psychopathic offender is among the most prolific, versatile, and violent of offenders (Hare, McPherson, & Forth, 1988; Kosson, Smith, & Newman, 1990; Rice, Harris, & Quinsey, 1990; Serin, 1991). Psychopathic individuals also use substances at high rates; in several studies, researchers have found elevated rates of alcohol and drug use, abuse, and dependence[1] among psychopathic offenders (Hemphill, Hart, & Hare, 1994; Smith & Newman, 1990). Unfortunately, the psychopathic individual also appears to be relatively resistant to efforts of treatment and rehabilitation; psychopathic offenders are more likely to recidivate when released from prison (Salekin, Rogers, & Sewell, 1996) and benefit less from psychiatric treatment than nonpsychopathic offenders (Ogloff, Wong, & Greenwood, 1990). In summary, the monetary, emotional, and interpersonal costs exacted by the psychopathic individual from those around him or her far outweigh his or her representation in the population.

Up to this point, most of the research aimed at understanding psychopathy operates from the perspective that psychopathy is a relatively homogeneous condition that is qualitatively distinct from normal functioning. This perspective has channeled the research into two distinct areas. First, it has led to a strong focus on assessment issues (see Lilienfeld, 1994, 1998). Second, it has led to substantial efforts to identify a pathology that is distinct or unique to people with psychopathy that explains their inexplicable behavior (Sutker, 1994). I wish to offer a

---

[1]*Use* refers to the amount and variety of substances used, whereas *abuse* and *dependence* refer to different levels of maladaptive patterns of use that lead to impairment or distress (APA, 1994).

slightly different perspective on psychopathy that understands the disorder as a collection of personality traits that exists on a continuum with normal functioning. More specifically, I believe that psychopathy can be understood from the perspective of the five factor model of personality (FFM; McCrae & Costa, 1990). In the pages that follow, I outline the FFM conceptualization, provide supporting evidence, review the advantages offered by this perspective, and attempt to answer in advance several anticipated objections.

THE FIVE-FACTOR MODEL CONCEPTUALIZATION

Working from descriptions of constructs from the Hare Psychopathy Checklist—Revised (PCL-R; Hare, 1991), Widiger and I (Widiger & Lynam, 1998) translated the PCL-R description of psychopathy into the language of the FFM on an item-by-item basis. The comprehensiveness of the FFM makes this translation possible. The FFM consists of five broad domains of personality, each of which is comprised of more specific and narrow facets. Table 20.1 provides the facets underlying each broad domain and provides descriptors for each pole. The description of psychopathy in the PCL-R is an excellent place to begin because the PCL-R is arguably the best validated measure of psychopathy for use in forensic settings (Hare et al., 1990; Harpur, Hakstian, & Hare, 1988; Harpur, Hare, & Hakstian, 1989; Kosson et al., 1990). The instrument is a symptom construct rating scale in which 20 items are scored by an examiner on the basis of a semistructured interview and review of institutional records. The PCL-R shows an arguably stable factor structure, good interrater and test-retest reliability, and predictive relations with important outcomes (e.g., recidivism, violence). In the next several pages, following Widiger and Lynam (1998), I discuss how each of the constructs assessed by the PCL-R maps onto the domains and facets of the FFM.

1. **Glib and superficial charm.** This item captures the psychopath's tendency to be smooth, verbally facile, charming, and slick. It is a clear indicator of the absence of self-consciousness—a facet of Neuroticism that captures the tendency

of an individual to experience social anxiety, shame, and embarrassment (Costa & McCrae, 1992). As Lykken (1995) noted, "the unafraid, unabashed, uninhibited psychopath always has his wits about him, does not get rattled, [and] does not draw a blank when trying to think of something to say" (p. 136).

2. **Grandiose sense of self-worth.** This item assesses the psychopath's high level of self-assuredness, cockiness, and inflated self-regard. It maps directly onto the arrogance (vs. modesty) facet of Antagonism. Individuals high in arrogance "believe they are superior people and may be considered conceited or arrogant by others" (Costa & McCrae, 1992, p. 18).

3. **Need for stimulation and proneness to boredom.** Despite the straightforward name, this item is complex in its FFM representation. Nominally, it is equivalent to the excitement seeking facet of Extraversion. High scorers on this facet "crave excitement and stimulation" (Costa & McCrae, 1992, p. 17). However, this item also includes the inability to complete routine, monotonous, or uninteresting tasks and is assessed by the repeated starting and stopping of activities (e.g., school, jobs). In this way, this item maps onto Conscientiousness, particularly low self-discipline, which involves "the ability to begin tasks and carry them through to completion despite boredom and other distractions" (p. 18).

4. **Pathological lying.** This item describes an individual for whom lying is a typical part of everyday discourse. It is well captured by the deception (vs. straightforwardness) facet of Antagonism. Individuals at the extreme are characteristically deceptive, unscrupulous, manipulative, and dishonest.

5. **Conning/manipulative.** Similar to the previous item, this item is concerned with the use of deception to cheat, con, defraud, and manipulate others for personal gain (Hare, 1991). As such, it represents a combination of deception and exploitation (vs. altruism), which are both facets of Antagonism. As Hare (1991) indicated, the scams are often carried off without any concern or consideration for the victim. This item would

TABLE 20.1

Five-Factor Model of Personality: Domains and Facets

Domain	Facet	Description
Neuroticism	Anxiousness	Fearful, apprehensive vs. relaxed, unconcerned, cool
	Angry hostility	Bitter, angry vs. even tempered
	Trait depression	Pessimistic, glum, despondent vs. optimistic
	Self-consciousness	Timid, embarrassed vs. self-assured, glib, shameless
	Impulsiveness	Tempted, reckless vs. controlled, restrained
	Vulnerability	Fragile, helpless vs. stalwart, brave, fearless
Extraversion (vs. introversion)	Warmth	Affectionate, attached vs. cold, aloof, reserved, indifferent
	Gregariousness	Sociable, outgoing vs. withdrawn, isolated
	Assertiveness	Enthusiastic, forceful vs. unassuming, quiet, resigned
	Activity	Active, energetic, vigorous vs. passive, lethargic
	Excitement seeking	Adventurous, rash vs. cautious, monotonous, dull
	Positive emotions	High spirited vs. placid, anhedonic
Openness vs. closedness to Experience (or unconventionality)	Fantasy	Imaginative, dreamer, unrealistic vs. practical, concrete
	Aesthetic	Aesthetic vs. unaesthetic
	Feelings	Emotionally responsive, sensitive vs. unresponsive constricted
	Actions	Novelty seeking, eccentric vs. routine, habitually stubborn
	Ideas	Curious, odd, peculiar, strange vs. pragmatic, rigid
	Values	Broad minded, tolerant vs. traditional, dogmatic, biased
Agreeableness (vs. Antagonism)	Trust	Trusting, gullible vs. skeptical, cynical, suspicious, paranoid
	Straightforwardness	Honest, confiding vs. cunning, manipulative, deceptive
	Altruism	Giving, sacrificial vs. selfish, stingy, greedy, exploitative
	Compliance	Cooperative, docile vs. oppositional, combative, aggressive
	Modesty	Self-effacing, meek vs. confident, boastful, arrogant
	Tender mindedness	Concerned, compassionate, empathic vs. callous, ruthless
Conscientiousness	Competence	Efficient, perfectionistic vs. lax, negligent
	Order	Organized, methodical, ordered vs. disorganized, sloppy
	Dutifulness	Dutiful, reliable, rigid vs. casual, undependable
	Achievement striving	Purposeful, ambitious, workaholic vs. aimless
	Self-discipline	Industrious, devoted, dogged vs. negligent, hedonistic
	Deliberation	Reflective, thorough, ruminative vs. careless, hasty

Note. Derived in part from Costa and McCrae (1992) and Tellegen and Waller (in press).

seem to encompass an additional facet of Antagonism, namely, tough mindedness (vs. tender mindedness). Tough-minded individuals are described as ruthless, callous, and lacking pity (Costa & McCrae, 1992).

6. **Lack of remorse or guilt.** This item represents an explicit assessment of the psychopath's lack of concern for the losses, pain, and suffering of his or her victims. This item would seem to describe the extreme variant of tough mindedness, as described above.

7. **Shallow affect.** This item may be the most difficult to understand and assess; it is certainly one of the most difficult to place within the FFM. If the item is understood as emotional poverty, it can be taken as an indicator of anhedonia (vs. high positive emotions) or indifference (vs. interpersonal warmth), which are both facets of Extraversion. However, the typical assessment of this item is more consistent with facets of Antagonism. For example, the interviewer is directed to look at an individual's de-

gree of involvement with family and friends. As such, this item might be taken as an indicator of tough mindedness or exploitation (vs. low altruism). It is interesting to note that other FFM theorists (e.g., John, 1990) have placed interpersonal warmth within the domain of Antagonism and that the NEO-PI-R's warmth scale has a substantial secondary loading on the Antagonism factor (Costa & McCrae, 1992).

8. **Callousness or lack of empathy.** More easily mapped onto the FFM, this item reflects a disregard for the feelings, rights, and welfare of others and an extreme egocentricity (Hare, 1991). As such, it maps clearly onto the tough mindedness and arrogance facets of Antagonism.

9. **Parasitic lifestyle.** This item is complex, representing facets of Antagonism and low Conscientiousness. On the one hand, the item refers to a selfish, manipulative, coercive, and exploitive financial dependence on others; as such, it reflects multiple facets of Antagonism (i.e., deception, exploitation, aggression, arrogance, and tough mindedness). On the other hand, a parasitic lifestyle may reflect a lack of ambition (vs. achievement striving), low self-discipline, or both, which are facets of Conscientiousness.

10. **Poor behavior controls.** Concerned with the expression of irritability, annoyance, impatience, threats, and aggression, this item represents a complex mixture of Neuroticism, Antagonism, and low Conscientiousness. One aspect of poor behavioral controls emphasizes an inadequate control of anger that would correspond to the angry hostility facet of Neuroticism or the aggression facet of Antagonism. However, the assessment of poor behavioral controls also includes consideration of whether assaults are sudden, spontaneous, and unprovoked. To the extent that sudden, spontaneous assaults reflect a failure to consider future consequences, acting hastily, or acting first and thinking later, they reflect low deliberation, which is a facet of Conscientiousness. As Costa and McCrae (1992) noted, "at best, low scorers [on deliberation] are spontaneous and able to make snap decisions" (p. 18).

11. **Promiscuous sexual behavior.** This item repre-

sents a mixture of low Conscientiousness and Antagonism. On the one hand, Hare (1991) described promiscuous sexual behavior as consisting of frequent, brief, casual interludes with an indiscriminate selection of partners. In this way, promiscuous sexual behavior reflects a lack of Conscientiousness, primarily the carelessness of low deliberation, the hedonism of low self-discipline, and the moral casualness of low dutifulness. On the other hand, PCL-R promiscuous sexual behavior includes frequent infidelities and exploitive, coercive, and aggressive sexual behavior. From this view, promiscuous sexual behavior is more reflective of deception, exploitation, aggression, arrogance, and tough mindedness, which are all facets of Antagonism.

12. **Early behavior problems, 18. juvenile delinquency, and 20. criminal versatility.** These three PCL-R items assess explicitly antisocial behavior, differing in the ages at which the behavior referenced occurs. Each item includes a variety of different acts, ranging from lying and bullying to assault, theft, rape, and murder. As such, they are really behavioral descriptions more than personality traits. Nonetheless, I believe that all of these behaviors are reflections of Antagonism and low Conscientiousness. Although the specific facets involved may depend on the specific act, the facets include almost all facets of Antagonism (i.e., deception, exploitation, aggression, arrogance, and tough mindedness) and several facets of low Conscientiousness (i.e., low deliberation, low self-discipline, and low dutifulness). High Antagonism reflects the antipathetic nature of crime, whereas low Conscientiousness reflects its opportunistic and impulsive character. This analysis is consistent with other theoretical (e.g., Moffitt, 1993) and empirical (e.g., Miller & Lynam, in press) work that links antisocial behavior with these two personality domains.

13. **Lack of realistic long-term goals.** This item describes an individual who lives primarily day to day, gives little thought to the future, is uninterested in a steady job, and may even lead a nomadic existence. This item corresponds to low scores on several facets of Conscientious-

ness, particularly achievement striving, self-discipline, and deliberation.

14. **Impulsivity.** Nominally, this PCL-R item, which refers to the tendency to act without premeditation or forethought, corresponds to the FFM impulsiveness facet of Neuroticism. However, neurotic impulsiveness has more to do with the experience of strong cravings and an inability to resist temptations, frustrations, and urges. For this reason, it seems that PCL-R impulsiveness better maps onto the deliberation facet of Conscientiousness. Low scorers on deliberation are "hasty and often speak or act without considering the consequences" (Costa & McCrae, 1992, p. 18). An identification of impulsivity with Conscientiousness is consistent with alternative descriptions of the FFM. For example, Tellegen and Waller (1994) identified this domain as constraint rather than Conscientiousness to emphasize a lack of control.

15. **Irresponsibility.** Hare (1991) described the irresponsible individual as one who has little sense of duty or loyalty to family, friends, or employers and who habitually fails to fulfill obligations in a variety of areas. This item provides an excellent description of low scorers on Conscientiousness, primarily the facet of dutifulness. Low scorers on dutifulness are described as casual about ethical principles, undependable, and unreliable (Costa & McCrae, 1992).

16. **Failure to accept responsibility for one's own actions.** At first glance, this item may seem a straightforward indicator of low dutifulness, which is a facet of Conscientiousness. However, the PCL-R assessment of this item places more emphasis on an unwillingness to accept responsibility and a shifting of blame to others rather than neglectful irresponsibility. For example, Hare (1991) suggested the presence of this characteristic when individuals baldly deny responsibility in the face of overwhelming evidence to the contrary. Taken this way, this item better maps onto opposition (vs. compliance), tough mindedness, or deception, which are all facets of Antagonism.

17. **Many short-term marital relationships.** This item overlaps substantially with promiscuous sexual behavior but may be more reflective of low Conscientiousness than high Antagonism. This item lacks the flavor of exploitation and deception present in the description for promiscuous sexual behavior. Rather, it seems to reflect primarily an inability to make a commitment to a long-term relationship, which is more likely a reflection of low Conscientiousness, primarily low dutifulness.

19. **Revocation of conditional release.** This item assesses whether an individual has escaped from an institution or violated a conditional release through a technical but noncriminal infraction or through the commission of a new criminal act (Hare, 1991). The item, similar to the frankly antisocial items described above, seems to be a blend of Antagonism and low Conscientiousness. The commission of a new criminal act reflects the traits associated with antisocial behavior, high Antagonism (i.e., deception, exploitation, aggression, arrogance, and tough mindedness), and low Conscientiousness (i.e., low deliberation, low self-discipline, and low dutifulness). Technical violations, however, may be more reflective of low Conscientiousness, particularly the facets of low order (i.e., haphazard and disorganized), low self-discipline, and low deliberation.

From the descriptions above (and Table 20.2), two omissions become obvious. First, despite the fact that many consider it a cardinal characteristic (Lykken, 1995), low anxiety, a facet of Neuroticism, does not appear in our FFM translation of the PCL-R. As Costa and McCrae (1992) noted, "low scorers [on anxiety] are calm and relaxed. They do not dwell on things that might go wrong" (p. 16). Second, all facets of Antagonism are represented in multiple PCL-R items except for the suspiciousness (vs. trust) facet, which contrasts a disposition to believe that others are honest and well intentioned with the tendency to be cynical and to assume that others may be dishonest or dangerous (Costa & McCrae, 1992). These omissions are due to the fact that Widiger and I restricted ourselves to the description of the psychopath provided by the PCL-R, which has itself been criticized for its omission of an

---

TABLE 20.2

Five-Factor Model (FFM) Description of the Hare Psychopathy Checklist—Revised (PCL-R)-Defined Psychopathy

FFM factor and facet	PCL-R items
Neuroticism	
High angry hostility	10
Low self-consciousness	1
High impulsiveness	14
Extraversion (vs. Introversion)	
Low warmth	7
High excitement seeking	3
Low positive emotions	7
Antagonism (vs. Agreeableness)	
High deception (vs. straightforwardness)	4, 5, 9, 11, 12, 16, 18, 19, 20
High exploitation (vs. altruism)	5, 7, 9, 11, 12, 18, 19, 20
High aggression (vs. compliance)	9, 10, 11, 12, 16, 18, 19, 20
High arrogance (vs. modesty)	2, 8, 9, 11, 12, 18, 19, 20
High tough mindedness (vs. tender mindedness)	5, 6, 7, 8, 9, 11, 12, 16, 18, 19, 20
Conscientiousness	
Low dutifulness	11, 12, 15, 16, 17, 18, 19, 20
Low achievement striving	9, 13
Low self-discipline	3, 9, 11, 12, 13, 18, 19, 20
Low deliberation	10, 11, 12, 13, 14, 18, 19, 20

Note. Based on an analysis by Widiger and Lynam (1998).

explicit assessment of anxiety (e.g., Lilienfeld, 1994). Similarly, despite the fact that psychopaths are likely to be among the least trusting of other people, suspiciousness is not directly assessed by the PCL-R.

EVIDENCE FOR THE FIVE-FACTOR MODEL CONCEPTUALIZATION

In an effort to be sure that the FFM description of psychopathy above was not the result of idiosyncracies in the PCL-R or in the FFM translation, my students and I have undertaken several studies. In the first two, we have asked other psychopathy experts to describe the personalities of prototypic psychopaths. From these ratings, prototypic descriptions of the psychopathic individual can be generated and compared with the FFM translation of the PCL-R. Such a description is useful because it brings out in stark contrast the aspects on which experts agree and blunts the idiosyncratic elements of each description. Additional studies take a more traditional approach of empirically examining the relations be-

tween the FFM and psychopathy. To the extent that the FFM description presented above is obtained across ratings, measures, and methods, one can have confidence in the representation.

Expert Ratings: NEO-PI-R and Common Language Q-Sort

In the first expert study, Miller, Lynam, Widiger, and Leukefeld (2001) wrote to 23 nationally known psychopathy researchers and asked each to "rate the prototytpical, classic Cleckley psychopath" on each of 30 bipolar scales that correspond to the 30 facets of the FFM. For example, to assess the Antagonism facet of deception, experts were asked "to what extent is the male [or female] psychopath honest, genuine, and sincere versus deceptive and manipulative?" (p. 260). Response choices ranged from 1 (*extremely low*) to 5 (*extremely high*). Experts were asked to rate a prototypic male and prototypic female psychopath; however, because results were similar across ratings, I present only results for the prototypic male psychopath.

Sixteen experts returned the ratings. There was remarkable agreement in their descriptions of the prototypic psychopath. The experts' mean rating on each of the facets as well as the standard deviations and ranges are given in Table 20.3; the graphical profile is provided in Figure 20.1. According to the standard deviations and ranges, agreement was good. Fifty percent of items had standard deviations less than 0.70, and only 17% had standard deviations greater than 1.00. Similarly, almost two-thirds of the items had ranges of two or less. Agreement is equally good when raters are compared with each other. The average inter-rater reliability for each rater (i.e., the average correlation of one rater's profile

TABLE 20.3

Expert-Generated Five-Factor Model Psychopathy Prototype

Factor and facet	M	SD	Range	Approximate NEO-PI-R T score
Neuroticism				
Anxiety	` 1.47	0.52	1–2	31
Angry hostility	3.87	0.64	3–5	74
Depression	1.40	0.51	1–2	33
Self-consciousness	1.07	0.26	1–2	20
Impulsiveness	4.53	0.74	3–5	80
Vulnerability	1.47	0.52	1–2	36
Extraversion				
Warmth	1.73	1.10	1–5	20
Gregariousness	3.67	0.62	3–5	60
Assertiveness	4.47	0.52	4–5	75
Activity	3.67	0.98	2–5	59
Excitement seeking	4.73	0.46	4–5	87
Positive emotions	2.53	0.92	1–4	33
Agreeableness				
Trust	1.73	0.80	1–3	20
Straightforwardness	1.13	0.35	1–2	20
Altruism	1.33	0.62	1–3	20
Compliance	1.33	0.49	1–2	20
Modesty	1.00	0.00	1–1	20
Tender mindedness	1.27	0.46	1–2	20
Conscientiousness				
Competence	4.20	1.00	1–5	60
Order	2.60	0.51	2–3	36
Dutifulness	1.20	0.78	1–4	20
Achievement striving	3.07	1.20	1–5	44
Self-discipline	1.87	0.83	1–4	20
Deliberation	1.60	1.10	1–4	20
Openness to Experience				
Fantasy	3.07	0.88	2–4	50
Aesthetics	2.33	0.62	1–3	39
Feelings	1.80	0.86	1–4	20
Actions	4.27	0.59	3–5	77
Ideas	3.53	1.10	1–5	50
Values	2.87	0.99	1–4	37

Note. T values were obtained by subtracting 1 from the mean of the expert ratings and multiplying by 8 to put the scores on the same scale as the Revised NEO Personality Inventory (NEO-PI-R) facets. The scores are only approximate because the T scores were derived from a normative sample and depend on the actual SDs of the eight-item facet scales, but the experts rated only a single item for each scale.

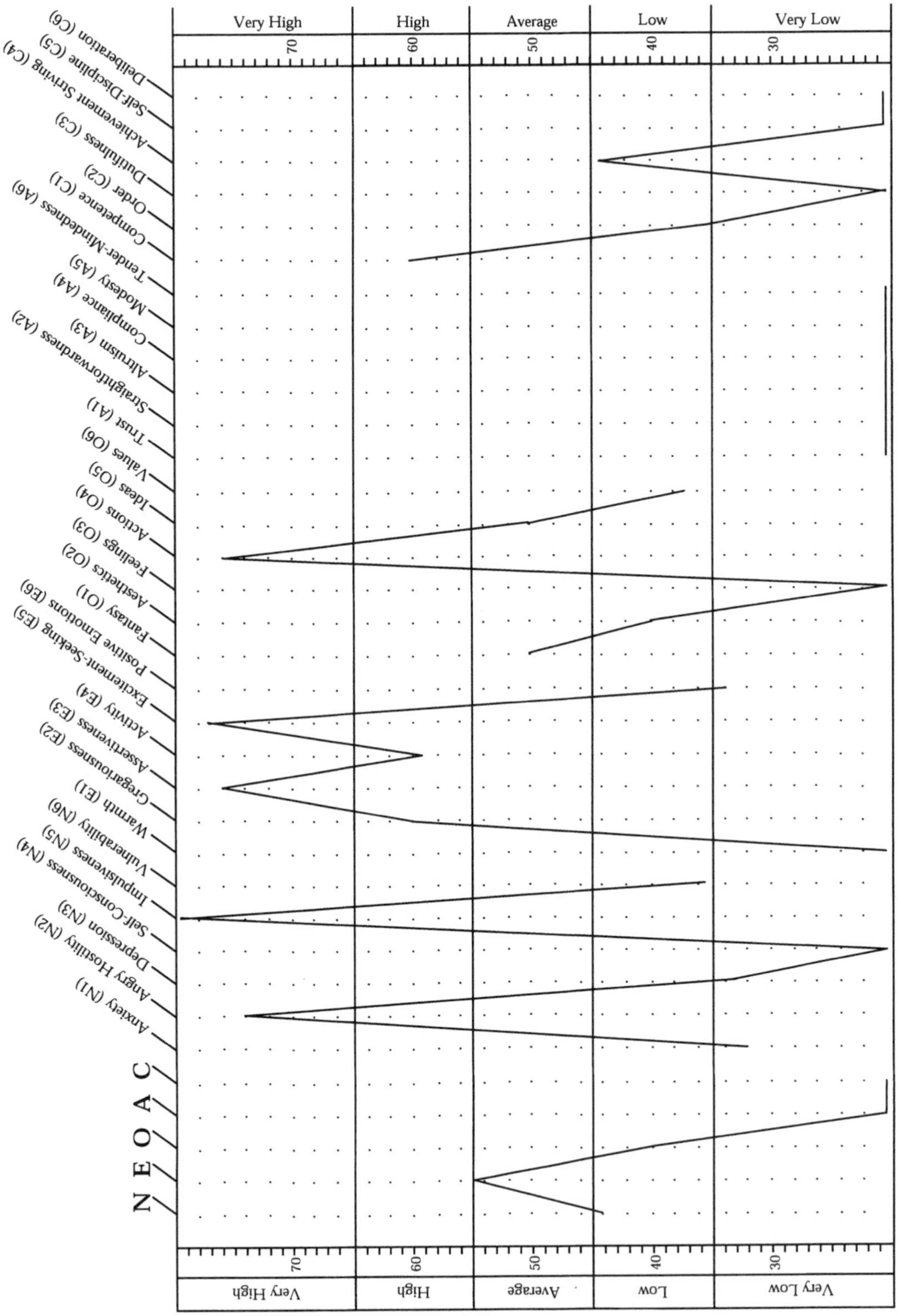

FIGURE 20.1. *Revised NEO Personality Inventory* (NEO-PI-R) profile of prototypic psychopathy based on approximate NEO-PI-R T scores of expert's ratings from Table 20.3. From the *NEO Personality Inventory*, by Paul T. Costa, Jr., and Robert R. McCrae, Copyright 1978, 1985, 1989, 1992 by PAR, Inc. Reproduced by special permission of the publisher, Psychological Assessment Resources, Inc., 16204 North Florida Avenue, Lutz, FL 33549. Further reproduction is prohibited without permission of PAR, Inc.

with every other rater's profile) ranged from 0.61 to 0.84, with a mean of 0.75, which can be taken as the reliability of the composite profile.

What does the prototypic psychopath look like? Taking any facet with a mean score lower than 2 (low) or higher than 4 (high) as characteristic, the profile is similar to the one provided by Widiger and Lynam (1998). As with that profile, the psychopath is low in self-consciousness, warmth, all facets of Agreeableness, dutifulness, self-discipline, and deliberation and high in impulsiveness and excitement seeking. Additionally, unconstrained by the definition inherent in the PCL-R, Miller et al.'s (2001) expert raters indicated that the psychopath is low in anxiety, depression, vulnerability, trust, and openness to feelings but high on assertiveness, openness to actions, and, perhaps surprisingly, competence. With the exception of psychopaths being characterized as high in competence, the additional traits included by the experts make good sense. I already discussed why one would expect the psychopath to be low in anxiety and high in suspicious (i.e., low in trust). It is also easy to see why the psychopath would be characterized as low scoring on the two additional facets of Neuroticism, depression and vulnerability. Costa and McCrae (1992) described low scorers on depression as rarely experiencing "feelings of guilt, sadness, hopelessness, and loneliness" (p. 16). Low scorers on vulnerability are described as being capable of handling themselves in difficult situations; extremely low scores on vulnerability might suggest the fearlessness seen in prototypic cases of psychopathy emphasized by Lykken (1995). Additionally, the elevation on assertiveness makes sense given the description of high scorers as "dominant, forceful, and socially ascendant" (Costa & McCrae, 1992, p. 17).

Although Widiger and I did not include any facets of Openness to Experience in our description, the experts' characterization of the psychopath as high in openness to actions and low in openness to feelings is also understandable. Costa and McCrae (1992) described high scorers on openness to actions as preferring "novelty and variety to familiarity and routine" (p. 17). Low scorers on openness to feelings are described as having somewhat blunted affect and not believing that feeling states have much importance (Costa & McCrae, 1992). At first

blush, the most difficult aspect of the experts' rating to understand is the characterization of the psychopath as high in competence. If ever an individual were lax and negligent (i.e., low in competence), it would seem to be the psychopath. This mystery is solved, however, when one recognizes that NEO-PI-R assessed competence is, in part, a self-assessment of efficacy. In the single-item description of the facet, Miller et al. (2001) asked raters "to what degree does the psychopath feel capable, sensible, and effective versus feeling unsure, unprepared, and inept?" This description is in line with Costa and McCrae's (1992) rendering of the construct; in fact, they acknowledged that "of all the C [Conscientiousness] facet scales, competence is most highly associated with self-esteem" (p. 18). There is, therefore, an interesting dissociation among the facets of Conscientiousness in psychopathic individuals; they see themselves as competent, but their life history belies them.

Besides the facet of competence, three other facets (i.e., angry hostility, low positive emotions, and low achievement striving) that Widiger and Lynam (1998) identified within the PCL-R were not conceived as essential to the construct of psychopathy by the expert raters. All three were rated as being neither high nor low. The rating for angry hostility, however, almost surpassed our somewhat arbitrary criterion. Additionally, ratings for positive emotions and achievement striving were among the most disagreed on; both had standard deviations above 0.90, and the 1.20 standard deviation for achievement striving was the highest for all items. Finally, low positive emotions was represented only by the most troublesome PCL-R item, namely, shallow affect.

A second expert study reveals that the impressive agreement between the expert raters and the FFM translation of the PCL-R was not due to constraining our raters to the 30 facets of the FFM. Similar results were obtained by having psychopathy experts rate the prototypical fledgling psychopath using the 100 items of the Common Language Version of the California Child Q-Set (CLQ, Caspi et al., 1992; CCQ, Block & Block, 1980). The CLQ does not represent any one theoretical viewpoint; instead, it reflects a general language for describing variations in children's personalities. Therefore, replication of the FFM description of psychopathy using the CLQ should be especially convincing.

As in the previous study, nationally recognized researchers of psychopathy were contacted and asked to provide descriptions of the fledgling psychopath using the CLQ. Specifically, raters were asked to describe the fledgling psychopath by placing a specified number of items into each of nine categories, which ranged from "Category 9: Extremely Characteristic" to "Category 1: Extremely Uncharacteristic." Items that were neither characteristic nor uncharacteristic were placed in the middle categories (i.e., Categories 4, 5, and 6). Raters were provided with a deck of cards that contained the 100 items and a sorting guide that forced a "normal" distribution on the item placements (i.e., few items at the extremes but many in the middle).

Eight of 14 experts returned their Q sorts of the fledgling psychopath, which were used to construct a prototype by averaging across raters for each of the 100 items. Agreement among the returned Q sorts was excellent. Fifty-eight percent of the items had standard deviations less than 1.0 and 88% had standard deviations less than 1.5; fully 73% of the items had a range of 3 or less. Agreement was also excellent when raters were compared with each other. The average inter-rater reliability for each rater (i.e., the average correlation of one rater's profile with every other rater's profile) ranged from .61 to .87, with a mean of .73, which can be taken as the reliability of the composite profile.

The 10 items most characteristic and the 10 items most uncharacteristic of the fledgling psychopath are provided in Table 20.4. It is important that I need not rely on my interpretation of these items to find out how they map onto the FFM. Two studies already identify how the CLQ maps onto the FFM. In both studies, Q sorts from mothers of over 400 13-year-old boys from the Pittsburgh Youth Study were examined for their relations to the FFM. In the first study, John, Caspi, Robins, Moffitt, and Stouthamer-Loeber (1994) developed Big Five scales for the CLQ. They began by rationally categorizing items into one of the Big Five domains. These rational scales were then refined through item analyses and factor analyses. The final scales contained 48 of the 100 CLQ items. In a second study, Robins,

John, and Caspi (1994) provided information on how the remaining 52 items map onto the Big Five. They found that most of the remaining items (73%) represented blends of two or three of the Big Five dimensions.

Using results from these studies, Table 20.4 also provides the FFM mapping of each CLQ item. From this mapping, it can be seen that the prototype obtained from the Q sort is similar to that obtained using the FFM. Ten of the defining items are relatively clear indicators of a single Big Five dimension; of these, 5 were indicators of Antagonism, 3 were indicators of low Conscientiousness, and 2 were indicators of low Neuroticism. The remaining 10 items were interstitial items that assessed both Antagonism and low Conscientiousness. Importantly, these interstitial items were strongly related to both dimensions; the multiple squared correlations between the Big Five scales and the items ranged from .37 to .67, with a mean of .56 (Robins, John, & Caspi, 1994). In summary, the psychopath, described using the atheoretical Q sort, is high in Antagonism, low in Conscientiousness, and low in Neuroticism.

Empirical Relations Between the Five-Factor Model and Psychopathy

A more traditional approach to describing psychopathy in FFM terms would be to look at the relations between measures of psychopathy and measures of the FFM. Several studies have been conducted using the PCL-R. In these studies, researchers have found psychopathy to be most strongly related, negatively, to the dimensions of Conscientiousness and Agreeableness (Forth, Brown, Hart, & Hare, 1996; S. Hart & Hare, 1994). I recently collected data from two samples that allow for an examination of the relations among the FFM and the Levenson Self-Report Psychopathy Scale (LSRP; Levenson, Kiehl, & Fitzpatrick, 1995; Lynam, Whiteside, & Jones, 1999). This scale has good reliability and validity as a self-report measure of psychopathy; it also has a replicable two-factor structure that seems to map onto the two factors of the PCL-R. This is important because Widiger and Lynam (1998) argued that the FFM conception of psychopathy might bring clarity to the two-factor structure frequently obtained in analyses of the PCL-R.

TABLE 20.4

Common Language Q-Sort (CLQ) Items Describing the Fledgling Psychopath

CLQ item	M	SD	Range	FFM scale
Characteristic items				
11. He tries to blame other people for things he has done.	9.0	0.00	9–9	A–, C–
22. He tries to get others to do what he wants by playing up to them. He acts charming to get his way.	8.5	0.76	7–9	A–
65. When he wants something, he wants it right away. He has a hard time waiting for things he wants and likes.	8.5	0.53	8–9	A–, C–
20. He tries to take advantage of other people.	8.4	0.74	7–9	A–, C–
13. He tries to see how much he can get away with. He usually pushes the limits and tries to stretch the rules.	8.3	0.71	7–9	A–, C–
21. He tries to be the center of attention.	8.0	1.07	6–9	A–, C–
85. He is aggressive.	8.0	0.76	7–9	A–, C–
10. His friendships don't last long; he changes friends a lot.	7.6	1.69	4–9	A–, C–
91. His emotions don't seem to fit the situation.	7.6	0.92	6–9	A–, C–
93. He's bossy and likes to dominate other people.	7.6	0.74	6–8	A–
Uncharacteristic Items				
76. He can be trusted; he's reliable and dependable.	1.3	0.46	1–2	C+
15. He shows concern about what's right and what's wrong.	1.9	0.99	1–4	A+, C+
62. He is obedient and does what he is told.	1.9	0.83	1–3	A+, C+
99. He thinks about his actions and behavior; he uses his head before doing or saying something.	1.9	0.83	1–3	C+
9. He makes good and close friendships with other people.	2.0	0.76	1–3	A+
67. He plans things ahead; he thinks before he does something; he "looks before he leaps."	2.0	0.93	1–3	C+
23. He is nervous and fearful.	2.3	0.89	1–3	N+
77. He feels unworthy; he has a low opinion of himself.	2.4	1.19	1–4	N+
2. He is considerate and thoughtful of other people.	2.5	1.60	1–5	A+
3. He is a warm person and responds with kindness to other people.	2.5	1.07	2–5	A+

Note. He is used because the data were collected within the context of an all-boys study. FFM = five-factor model; A = Agreeableness; C = Conscientiousness; N = Neuroticism.

In the first study, Lynam et al. (1999) examined the relation between scores on the LSRP and scores on the Big Five Inventory (John, 1995) in a sample of 739 male and female undergraduates. Although the LSRP assesses both primary and secondary psychopathy, only results for the total score are presented; results for the subscales are discussed later. The total score was moderately negatively correlated with both Agreeableness ($r = -.48$) and Conscientiousness ($r = -.39$), slightly negatively correlated with Openness ($r = -.07$) and Extraversion ($r = -.12$), and slightly positively correlated with Neuroticism ($r = .12$). The latter correlation is likely due to the saturation of self-report scales with negative affect (Lilienfeld, 1994; Lynam et al., 1999).

In a more recent study, I examined the relation between psychopathy and the 30 facets of the FFM. Data were collected from 481 men and women, aged 20 to 22, who are participating in the Lexington Longitudinal Study—an ongoing, longitudinal study examining antisocial behavior and related outcomes. Participants completed the LSRP and the entire NEO-PI-R. Because this study included the full NEO-PI-R, it is possible to examine the relations at the facet level. Although Table 20.5 provides the correlations for the total score and both subscales, I concentrate on the results for the total scale and discuss the results for each subscale in the section dealing with implications of the FFM understanding of psychopathy.

TABLE 20.5

Correlations Between Levenson Self-Report Psychopathy Scale (LSRP) Scores and Revised NEO Personality Inventory (NEO-PI-R) Facets

NEO-PI-R domain and facet	Total	LSRP Scale 1	Scale 2
Agreeableness			
Trust	−.47	−.38	−.44
Straightforwardness	−.59	−.60	−.37
Altruism	−.51	−.48	−.38
Compliance	−.47	−.36	−.47
Modesty	−.19	−.31	.04
Tender-mindedness	−.32	−.37	−.14
Conscientiousness			
Competence	−.43	−.25	−.54
Order	−.16	−.02	−.29
Dutifulness	−.41	−.32	−.40
Achievement striving	−.34	−.18	−.47
Self-discipline	−.35	−.17	−.49
Deliberation	−.44	−.26	−.52
Neuroticism			
Anxiousness	.07	−.07	.25
Angry hostility	.47	.28	.57
Trait depression	.34	.12	.53
Self-consciousness	.15	.00	.31
Impulsiveness	.29	.14	.41
Vulnerability	.25	.06	.42
Extraversion			
Warmth	−.46	−.38	−.40
Gregariousness	−.14	−.08	−.17
Assertiveness	−.10	.02	−.21
Activity	−.13	−.06	−.20
Excitement seeking	.17	.16	.13
Positive emotions	−.39	−.27	−.40
Openness to Experience			
Fantasy	−.14	−.13	−.10
Aesthetic	−.17	−.17	−.13
Feelings	−.26	−.31	−.10
Actions	−.07	−.04	−.11
Ideas	−.13	−.06	−.18
Values	−.08	−.02	−.13
Adjusted R^2	.54	.46	.56

The correlations between LSRP psychopathy and Antagonism were in line with results from other studies. All facets of Antagonism were positively related to scores on the LSRP. Except for the relation to arrogance, all correlations were at least moderate in size. Results for Conscientiousness were similarly encouraging. Psychopathy was at least moderately negatively correlated with all facets of Conscien-tiousness except for order, in which case the correlation was negative and small. Not unexpectedly, given the saturation of the LSRP with negative affect, the correlations for Neuroticism were all positive; however, interesting patterns emerged within these correlations. The highest positive correlation was between psychopathy and angry hostility, whereas the lowest correlations were for anxiety and self-consciousness. For Extraversion, results were consistent with other analyses. Psychopathy was negatively related to warmth and positive emotions but positively related to excitement seeking. Finally, psychopathy was negatively related to openness to aesthetics and openness to feelings. Importantly, relations between psychopathy and the facets were relatively strong; taken together, the facets accounted for 57% of the variation in total psychopathy scores.

In summary, whether one translates a psychopathy inventory into the language of the FFM, asks experts to describe the prototypical psychopath, or examines the empirical relations among the FFM and measures of psychopathy, results are remarkably consistent. The psychopath is high in all facets of Antagonism; he or she is suspicious, deceptive, exploitive, aggressive, arrogant, and tough minded. The psychopath is also low in the dutifulness, self-discipline, and deliberation facets of Conscientiousness. There was disagreement about the psychopath's standing on competence and achievement striving, however. The description of the psychopath in terms of Neuroticism and Extraversion was complex and interesting. In terms of Neuroticism, the psychopath appears to be low in anxiety, self-consciousness, and perhaps vulnerability and depression; however, the psychopath is high on the remaining facets of Neuroticism, namely, impulsiveness and angry hostility. In terms of Extraversion, the psychopath is high in excitement seeking, but low in warmth and perhaps positive emotions. There was also good agreement across methods regarding the facets of Openness; the only facet to be consistently related to psychopathy was closedness to feelings.

CLARIFICATIONS OF THE LITERATURE

Besides providing a potentially more accurate and more specific picture of the psychopath than the traditional categorical approach, the FFM perspective on psychopathy provides several clarifications of the findings from the field. Specifically, the FFM clarifies (a) the PCL-R factor structure, (b) the litany of psychopathic deficits, (c) the concept of successful psychopathy, and (d) the patterns of comorbidity. In the next section, I describe these contributions.

The Psychopathy Checklist—Revised Factor Structure

Several factor analyses of the PCL-R and its predecessor identify a robust two-factor solution (Harpur et al., 1988, 1989), which is provided in Table 20.6. The interpretations of the two factors, however, are somewhat unclear and confusing. One interpretation, dropped in more recent writings, is that the two factors are primarily method factors. On the one hand, the scoring of Factor 1 items relies primarily on clinical judgment and inference from interview impressions, whereas Factor 2 items are scored on the basis of file information (Harpur et al., 1988, p. 745). A second interpretation is that the first factor represents the "a constellation of interpersonal and affective traits commonly considered to be fundamental to the construct of psychopathy" (Hare, 1991, p. 38), whereas the second reflects a "chronically unstable, antisocial, and socially deviant lifestyle" (p. 38). Although the latter interpretation is more substantive than the former, it has several shortcomings. It raises and leaves unanswered the question of what psychopathy is. As Lilienfeld (1994) asked, "is an individual with very high scores on the first PCL-R factor (who, according to Harpur et al., possess the major personality traits of psychopathy), but with very low scores on the second PCL factor, a psychopath?" (p. 28). Additionally, the personality–behavior dichotomy into which this interpretation frequently slips is simplistic. This interpretation overlooks the fact that Factor 2 explicitly includes several personality dimensions, such as impulsivity, irresponsibility, and sensation seeking (Rogers & Bagby, 1994).

I agree with Lilienfeld (1994) when he suggested that "both PCL factors represent personality traits, but the traits assessed by the second factor are more highly associated with antisocial behavior" (p. 28). Furthermore, I suggest that clarity is provided by the FFM interpretation. As can be seen in Table 20.6, when the PCL-R factor structure is examined according to the FFM re-interpretation, a clear distinction between factors emerges. Factor 1 appears to be confined largely to facets of Antagonism, with minimal representations of low Neuroticism and low Extraversion. Factor 2 is dominated by items that are mixtures of low Conscientiousness and Antago-

TABLE 20.6

Factors of the Psychopathy Checklist—Revised (PCL-R) From the Perspective of the Five-Factor Model (FFM)

PCL-R item	FFM domain
Factor 1 items	
1. Glibness–superficial charm	Low Neuroticism
2. Grandiose sense of self-worth	High Antagonism
4. Pathological lying	High Antagonism
5. Conning–manipulative	High Antagonism
6. Lack of remorse or guilt	High Antagonism
7. Shallow affect	High Antagonism, low Extraversion
8. Callous–lack of empathy	High Antagonism
16. Failure to accept responsibility	High Antagonism
Factor 2 items	
3. Need for stimulation	High Extraversion, low Conscientiousness
9. Parasitic lifestyle	Low Conscientiousness, high Antagonism
10. Poor behavioral controls	Low Conscientiousness, high Antagonism, high Neuroticism
12. Early behavior problems	Low Conscientiousness, high Antagonism
13. Lack of realistic, long-term goals	Low Conscientiousness
14. Impulsivity	Low Conscientiousness, high Neuroticism
15. Irresponsibility	Low Conscientiousness
18. Juvenile delinquency	Low Conscientiousness, high Antagonism
19. Revocation of conditional release	Low Conscientiousness, high Antagonism

Note. Data from Widiger and Lynam (1998).

nism, with minimal representations of high Neuroticism and high Extraversion. This interpretation provides a substantive rather than methodological interpretation of the factors, acknowledges the presence of "personality" in both factors of the PCL-R, and does not suggest that one element is more central to psychopathy than another. Additionally, the FFM interpretation accounts for the correlation between factors, which is typically about .50 (Hare, 1991); the factors are moderately correlated because both include facets of Antagonism.

Data from the two studies discussed above are also relevant to this issue. Lynam et al. (1999) found that Scale 1 of the LSRP, which is conceptually related to PCL-R Factor 1, was moderately negatively correlated with Agreeableness ($r = -.41$) and slightly negatively correlated with Conscientiousness ($r = -.20$), Extraversion ($r = -.08$), and Neuroticism ($r = -.05$). Scale 2, which is conceptually related to PCL-R Factor 2, was moderately negatively correlated with both Agreeableness ($r = -.42$) and Conscientiousness ($r = -.59$), slightly negatively

correlated with Extraversion ($r = -.15$), and positively correlated with Neuroticism ($r = .37$). Correlations with Scale 1 were significantly different than correlations with Scale 2 for both Conscientiousness and Neuroticism.

Data from Table 20.5 provide additional support. The relations between the FFM and scores on the two LSRP subscales were, for the most part, in line with predictions. The facets of Antagonism were strongly related to both scales of the LSRP, although arrogance and tough mindedness were related only to Scale 1. For Conscientiousness, all facets were strongly negatively related to Scale 2 and only slightly related to Scale 1; except for dutifulness, all facets of Conscientiousness were more strongly related to Scale 2 than to Scale 1. As discussed earlier, results for the facets of Neuroticism were more complex. Scale 2 was positively related to all facets of Neuroticism, whereas Scale 1 was significantly related only to the angry hostility facet; furthermore, angry hostility was significantly more strongly related to Scale 2 than to Scale 1. Given the saturation of the LSRP with negative affect, the failure of Scale 1 to correlate negatively with anxiousness and vulnerabilty is understandable, and the absence of significant positive correlations is remarkable. The correlations between the scales and the facets of Extraversion were also supportive of the hypothesis. Both scales were negatively related to warmth and positive emotions and positively related to excitement seeking, but the anticipated differential pattern for the scales was not present.

Final support is provided by a factor analysis of the two LSRP scales and the 16 FFM facets into which I parsed the PCL-R. When the 18 variables are entered into a factor analysis and a two-factor solution is extracted, the pattern of loadings is in line with predictions. One factor had high loadings on Scale 1 of the LSRP (positive), warmth (negative), positive emotions (negative), and all facets of Antagonism (positive). The other factor had high loadings on Scale 2 of the LSRP (positive), the five facets of Conscientiousness (all negative), angry hostility, impulsiveness, and several facets of Antagonism (positive). The only substantial departures from the hypothesized structure was the presence of high vulnerability on Factor 2 (rather than low vulnerability on Factor 1) and the failure of excitement seeking to relate to either factor.

Psychopathic Deficits

Much of the effort in psychopathy research over the past 50 years has been directed at identifying a specific pathology that is unique to people with psychopathy. However, researchers in this effort have failed to identify a single psychopathic deficit. Rather, the search for the fundamental psychopathic deficit has generated a litany of diverse candidates and resulted in occasional Procrustean re-interpretations of all psychopathic traits in terms of a single underlying deficit. The list of candidate traits is long (see Table 20.7) and includes deficits in role-taking ability (Gough, 1948), fearlessness (Lykken, 1957), chronic underarousal and subsequent sensation seeking (Quay, 1965), electrodermal hyporeactivity (Fowles, 1980), semantic aphasia (Hare & McPherson, 1984), poor response modulation (Newman, 1987), deficient defensive emotional response (Patrick, 1994), deficits in psychopathic constraint

TABLE 20.7

The Proposed Psychopathic Deficits and Their Five-Factor Model (FFM) Mappings

Deficit	FFM mapping
Role-playing	High Antagonism
Fearlessness	Low Neuroticism
Chronic underarousal	Low Extraversion
Electrodermal hyporeactivity	Low Neuroticism
Semantic aphasia	High Antagonism
Poor response modulation	Low Conscientiousness
Deficient defensive emotional response	Low Neuroticism
Deficient psychopathic constraint	Low Conscientiousness
Callous–unemotional temperament	High Antagonism

(Lynam, 1996), and callous–unemotional temperament (Frick, 1998). The FFM conceptualization of psychopathy posits that these pathologies are on a continuum with normal personality functioning and that the litany of deficits is due to the fact that different investigators are examining different domains of the FFM's representation of psychopathy. Although space allows for only the discussion of a few of these deficits and their FFM reinterpretations, Table 20.7 provides my speculations regarding the FFM mapping of the deficits given above.

Poor Fear Conditioning–Electrodermal Hypoarousal–Deficient Defensive Emotional Response. Whether one refers to it as poor fear conditioning, electrodermal hypoarousal, or deficient defensive emotional response, I believe that all three of these terms refer to a similar phenomenon and are best understood as underlying the domain of Neuroticism and particularly the facets of low anxiousness and low vulnerability (see also Lykken, 1995).

In the first demonstration, Lykken (1957) used a classical conditioning paradigm with electric shock as the unconditioned stimulus and electrodermal responses as the conditioned response. He found that Cleckley psychopaths displayed smaller electrodermal responses (EDRs) to the conditioned stimuli than those displayed by normal (noninmate) controls and concluded that primary sociopaths were deficient in the ability to develop anxiety responses.

Since Lykken's original study, dozens of replications have been published (see Fowles, 1993) using conditioning paradigms (Hare, 1965a), countdown procedures (Hare, 1965b; Ogloff & Wong, 1990; Schmauk, 1970), and the presentation of stimuli with inherent aversive signal value. The conclusion from these studies is fairly clear: When strong, usually aversive, stimuli are involved, psychopaths frequently manifest EDR hyporeactivity during a time period prior to an anticipated stressor.

Patrick, Bradley, and Lang (1993) provided a demonstration of this hyporeactivity using a measure different from the EDR, namely, the fear-potentiated startle response. These authors found that nonpsychopathic subjects showed the greatest startle magnitude in response to probes when viewing unpleasant slides (e.g., mutilations), the next greatest magnitude when viewing neutral slides (e.g., household objects), and the least startle in response to probes when viewing positive slides (e.g., opposite-sex nudes). In contrast, psychopathic subjects showed less startle in response to probes when viewing unpleasant slides than when viewing neutral slides. Results were taken to indicate an abnormality in the processing of emotional stimuli by psychopaths, and it was argued that psychopaths are deficient in their fear response.

Although Fowles and Missel (1994) attempted to argue that this "pathology" maps onto Antagonism, it seems to more clearly map onto the domain of Neuroticism, particularly the facets of low anxiousness and low vulnerability. This interpretation is supported by looking at the Activity Preference Questionnaire (APQ; Lykken, 1995), which was designed to assess this pathology. On the APQ, respondents choose between two negative events that were equal in general unpleasantness but differed in their degree of threat or danger (e.g., being sick to one's stomach for 24 hours or being chosen as the target for a knife throwing act). According to Lykken (1995), individuals low in fearfulness should find "the frightening experiences preferable to the onerous but nonfrightening alternatives" (p. 146). Although Lykken attempted to argue that fearlessness as assessed by the APQ is distinct from the FFM's Neuroticism, it seems that this distinction is the result of Neuroticism being a broader domain than

fearlessness. In the end, fearlessness seems to be similar to the facets of low anxiousness and low vulnerability. In fact, Patrick (1994) seemed to agree with my mapping of this pathology on the domain of Neuroticism. Citing the research of Cooke, Stevenson, and Hawk (1993), who found reduced startle potentiation during unpleasant imagery among low negative emotionality subjects, Patrick (1994) suggested that "the observed absence of startle potentiation in psychopaths (Patrick et al., 1993) may reflect a temperamental deficit in the capacity for negative affect" (p. 325).

Response Modulation. Patterson and Newman (1993) developed a theory of psychopathy that targets the processes underlying the regulation of immediate response inclinations. According to these authors, the psychopath has a deficit in response modulation that involves suspending a dominant response set in order to assimilate environmental feedback. Recently, they placed more emphasis on the role of shifting attention from the organization and implementation of behavior to its evaluation. In either case, this pathology should be manifest in low scores on Conscientiousness, particularly the facets of self-discipline and deliberation.

Patterson and Newman (1993) offered a four-stage model to explicate the response modulation process: (Stage 1) establishment of a dominant response set, (Stage 2) reaction to an aversive event, (Stage 3) subsequent behavioral adaptation, and (Stage 4) consequences of reflection or lack thereof. They traced the problems of the psychopath to a bias for disinhibition over reflectivity at Stage 3, which hinders learning from experience. Several studies support this conclusion. Newman, Patterson, and Kosson (1987) demonstrated that psychopaths, relative to comparison subjects, perseverated in a dominant response set on a card-playing task, whose odds grew worse across time. However, when the researchers forced participants to be reflective by imposing a mandatory, 5-second, feedback-viewing period, the psychopathic deficit was erased. In another study, Newman, Patterson, Howland, and Nichols (1990) used a discrimination task in which a subject had to use feedback following a response to determine whether a given stimulus resulted in reward or punishment. These authors found that psychopathic offenders, in comparison with nonpsychopathic offenders, paused less after punishment and committed more passive–avoidance errors (i.e., failure to withhold a response to a negative stimulus). In general, because they do not pause and reflect, psychopathic individuals have difficulty making use of "peripheral" information that might helpfully influence their goal-directed behavior.

Patterson and Newman (1993) also discussed the individual-difference variables that are operative at various stages. The important variable at Stage 3 is the response modulation bias; individuals with such a bias "fail to alter their response set in accordance with changing environmental events and contingencies: they do not pause, process, and then go on" (Patterson & Newman, 1993, p. 721). Patterson and Newman indicated that the "disinhibited individuals' lack of retrospective reflection is central to their enduring impulsive style" (p. 722). This description is similar to that of individuals who are low in deliberation and who are "hasty and often speak or act without considering the consequences" (Costa & McCrae, 1992, p. 18).

Semantic Dementia–Abnormal Affective Processing. In his classic description of the psychopath, Cleckley (1941/1988) hypothesized that the underlying deficit of the psychopath was a failure to process the emotional meaning of language, a deficit he called "semantic dementia." I believe this description best maps onto the domain of Antagonism, particularly the facet of tough mindedness or the inability to experience empathy.

Several investigators have pursued this hypothesis using psychophysiological and behavioral methods. When Williamson, Harpur, and Hare (1990) asked psychopathic and nonpsychopathic subjects to group the two words from a triad that were closest in meaning, they found that psychopathic offenders made less use of affective meaning than did nonpsychopathic offenders. Additionally, in a task that required matching clauses or pictures on inferred emotional meaning, psychopathic offenders confused emotional polarity (good vs. bad). Williamson, Harpur, and Hare (1991) examined the psychopathic offender's use of the connotative aspects of language in a lexical decision task that required indicating, as quickly as possible, whether a letter string formed a word. Although most people make the lexical decision more quickly when the letter string is an emotional word than when it is a neutral word, psychopathic offenders did not show this advantage. Additionally, psychopathic offenders' event-related potentials to the emotional words were not different from their potentials to the neutral words. More recently, Patrick, Cuthbert, and Lang (1994) examined psychopathic offenders' cardiac, electrodermal, and facial muscle responses to imagined fearful and neutral scenes in a cued sentence-processing task. Psychopathic offenders showed smaller heart rate, electrodermal, and facial response changes during fear imagery, relative to neutral imagery, than did nonpsychopathic offenders. Because there were no differences in the self-reports of emotional experience, the authors concluded that semantic and emotional processes are dissociated in psychopaths.

As noted earlier, I believe that this pathology maps most closely onto the domain of Antagonism, particularly the facet of tough mindedness. Patrick et al. (1994) suggested that emotional imagery mediates between perceptual or conceptual processes and action. They speculated that "an affective imagery deficit would be manifested as a failure to review the harmful consequences of one's actions and as an inability to entertain new behavioral strategies" (p. 533). The idea of a "failure to review the harmful consequences of one's actions" is a fairly good descriptor of the tough-minded individual.

Social Information Processing Deficits. Models of social information processing describe how individuals encode, represent, and process social (e.g., interpersonal) circumstances. Although the social information processing of psychopaths has not been examined explicitly, social information processing difficulties and deficits have been found among incarcerated violent offenders (Slaby & Guerra, 1988), severely aggressive adolescents (Dodge, Price, Bachorowski, & Newman, 1990), aggressive boys in residential treatment (Nasby, Hayden, & DePaulo, 1979), and aggressive school children (Dodge & Frame, 1982). Given the positive relation between psychopathy and aggression (Hare, 1991), it seems likely that psychopaths may demonstrate deficits in social information processing. It also seems likely that the problems of social information processing will map directly onto the domain of Antagonism, particularly the facets of deception, exploitation, aggression, and tough mindedness.

Dodge and colleagues have described a five-stage social information-processing model of aggression (Dodge & Crick, 1990); results of dozens of studies demonstrate that aggressive individuals have biases at each stage of the model. At Stage 1, aggressive individuals attend to fewer cues generally and selectively attend to aggressive cues (Dodge, Petit, Bates, & Valente, 1995). At Stage 2, aggressive individuals are biased to interpret ambiguous and benign situations in aggressive ways (Dodge, 1980). Aggressive individuals generate fewer competent responses (Deluty, 1981) and more manipulative and aggressive responses (Waas, 1988) at Stage 3. At Stage 4, aggressive individuals evaluate the outcomes of their possible responses less fully (Slaby & Guerra, 1988) and expect more positive instrumental and intrapersonal outcomes and fewer sanctions for aggressive responses (C. H. Hart, Ladd, & Burleson, 1990). The attention to hostile cues, hostile attributional bias, and generation of manipulative and aggressive responses describe the Antagonism facets of suspicion, deception, and aggression, whereas the apparent lack of concern for others implies tough mindedness.

In summary, multiple psychopathic deficits emerge because psychopathy is a multifaceted construct. Although there is insufficient evidence available to evaluate the claim, I believe that so-called "specific pathologies" may be found to map onto specific FFM domains. The inclusion of assessments of the FFM within these traditional laboratory-based research paradigms would help to clarify and integrate the findings across the studies.

Successful Psychopathy

A third issue to which the FFM conceptualization brings clarification is that of "successful" psychopathy, which is meant to refer to individuals who possess the core personality traits of psychopathy but who are not criminals (or at least are without arrest histories). In several studies, researchers have attempted to examine successful psychopaths (Belmore & Quinsey, 1994; Widom, 1977); unfortunately, all have found extremely high rates of criminality

among their participants. For example, in Widom's first study of successful psychopaths, recruited through an advertisement in a counterculture newspaper, she found that of the 28 participants, 46% reported a history of heavy drinking, 90% reported using illegal drugs, 65% had been arrested (mean number of arrests for sample = 1.86), and 50% had been incarcerated. Despite this lack of success, theorizing about the successful psychopath goes on. I believe that all of the exemplars provided are best understood as individuals who score high on some FFM domains or facets of psychopathy but not on others.

Hare (1993) wrote that

> many psychopaths never go to prison or any other facility. They appear to function reasonably well—as lawyers, doctors, psychiatrists, academics, mercenaries, police officers, cult leaders, military personnel, business people, writers, artists, entertainers, and so forth—without breaking the law, or at least without being caught and convicted. (p. 113)

At one point, Hare indicated that if he could not study psychopathy in prison settings, his next choice would "very likely be a place like the Vancouver Stock Exchange" (p. 119). The individuals Hare described are clearly deceptive, exploitive, arrogant, and callous (i.e., high in Antagonism). However, these individuals frequently obtain advanced degrees and move far in their fields, and they seem to lack other important characteristics possessed by the prototypic psychopath such as unreliability, aimlessness, and poor impulse control (i.e., low Conscientiousness). Thus, it seems odd to call them psychopaths. Hare's successful psychopaths are simply people who possess some of the FFM facets of psychopathy (particularly from the domains of Antagonism and low Neuroticism) but lack others (particularly the facets of low Conscientiousness) that are likely to contribute to occupational failures or arrests.

The case is similar to Lykken's (1982) descriptions of the "hero" whom he saw as closely related to the psychopath. He wrote *that the hero and the psychopath are twigs from the same branch. Both are relatively fearless. . . . Had Chuck Yeager had slightly different parents (not necessarily bad parents, just more ordinary ones), he might have become a con man or a Gary Gilmore. (p. 22).*

Again, Lykken's description focuses on only one FFM domain of psychopathy, low Neuroticism. He neglected the fact that Yeager lacks the high Antagonism (i.e., deceptiveness, exploitiveness, aggressiveness, arrogance, and callousness) and low Conscientiousness (i.e., unreliability, aimlessness, negligence, and carelessness) that Gilmore possessed. In short, Yeager may share the characteristic of low fear with Gilmore, but there are more elements to prototypic psychopathy than low fear.

Comorbidity

Finally, the FFM conceptualization of psychopathy provides an understanding of the patterns of comorbidity surrounding psychopathy. Psychopathy should covary with other disorders to the extent that they share FFM elements. For example, psychopathy is highly positively correlated with the fourth edition of the *Diagnostic and Statistical Manual of Mental Disorders* (*DSM-IV*; American Psychiatric Association, 1994) diagnosis of antisocial personality disorder (ATS), positively correlated in some studies with narcissistic personality disorder (NAR), relatively uncorrelated with *DSM-IV* borderline personality disorder (BDL), and strongly negatively correlated with *DSM-IV* dependent personality disorder (DEP; Hare, 1991). These patterns can be understood by examining the other disorders in terms of the FFM (Costa & McCrae, 1990; Trull, 1992; Widiger & Trull, 1992). From an FFM perspective, ATS consists of slightly elevated scores on Neuroticism, very high scores on Antagonism, and low scores on Conscientiousness; the positive correlation with psychopathy is driven by the shared aspects of Antagonism and low Conscientiousness, but this correlation is somewhat attenuated by the divergence of Neuroticism across the two disorders. Similarly, NAR shares with psychopathy the facets of Antagonism (low altruism, tough-minded lack of empathy, and arrogance) but

lacks the facets of low Conscientiousness. BDL consists of very high scores on Neuroticism, slightly elevated scores on Antagonism, and slightly low scores on Conscientiousness; the lack of correlation with psychopathy can be understood to reflect the divergence of Neuroticism and the convergence of Antagonism and low Conscientiousness. Finally, DEP is comprised of very high scores on Neuroticism, low scores on Antagonism, and slightly low scores on Conscientiousness; the divergence in relations to Antagonism and Neuroticism for DEP and psychopathy likely account for the negative relation between the two disorders.

OBJECTIONS TO THE FIVE-FACTOR MODEL CONCEPTUALIZATION

There are likely several objections to the FFM conceptualization of psychopathy presented here. Almost all of these revolve around the dimensional perspective inherent in this conceptualization. That is, some people may challenge my rejection of the idea that psychopathic individuals are qualitatively distinct from nonpsychopathic individuals. I imagine that these objections take one of four forms.

First, some individuals may rightly point out that since the 18th-century conception of moral insanity, people (e.g., lawyers, doctors) have recognized that certain individuals seem to have little control over their actions. On this basis, these individuals may ask how can such a disorder be a collection of facets? Is this not evidence for the distinctiveness of psychopathy? I believe it is not evidence for the taxonicity of psychopathy. Instead, I believe that psychopathy consistently comes to the attention of mental health professionals and criminal justice workers because it is such a virulent collection of traits. If I asked someone to "build" the most dangerous person that he or she could imagine, that someone would probably build the psychopath. The collection of traits seen in psychopathy—high Antagonism, low Conscientiousness, and low anxiety—is an extremely consequential one. It reveals a lack of control that can lead to nothing but trouble. In its most full-blown form, the psychopathic individual is not restrained by fear, concern for others, or the ability to reflect on the longer term outcomes of his or her behavior. This is why the psychopathic offender has always held such specific interest, attention, and concern.

Second, some individuals may cite a study purported to be a demonstration of the taxonicity of psychopathy. In this study, Harris, Rice, and Quinsey (1994) applied several taxometric methods to data collected from over 600 offenders. Although frequently cited, I do not believe this study constitutes strong evidence for the taxonicity of psychopathy (see also Lilienfeld, 1998). The authors did find evidence for a taxon underlying the PCL-R Factor 2 antisocial lifestyle items and for childhood antisocial behavior items, but they found no evidence for the taxonicity of Factor 1 items. Given the failure to find a taxon underlying the items that are frequently argued to constitute the core of psychopathy (and certainly to distinguish it from ATS), it seems there is little need to reject the FFM conceptualization on the basis of this study.

Third, criticism of the FFM conceptualization might indicate that psychopathy is associated with a variety of deficits in conditioning, emotional reactivity, and psychophysiology; furthermore, one might ask how can such a collection of problems be understood from the FFM perspective? In response, I would first question the notion of "deficit" in the sense of a discontinuity with normal functioning. Instead, I think all of the differences observed between psychopathic and nonpsychopathic individuals are matters of degree rather than differences in kind. Many researchers of psychopathy agree with me on this point. For Lykken (1995), fearlessness, which he believed underlies the psychopathic individual's poor passive–avoidance learning, is clearly a matter of degree, not an all-or-nothing phenomenon. Fowles (1980) argued that some of the psychophysiological indices on which psychopaths have been found to differ from nonpsychopaths are reflections of the strengths (not the presence or absence) of two underlying motivational systems. Although Patterson and Newman (1993) suggested that the psychopathic offender has a deficit in response modulation, they write about the response modulation bias as an individual difference variable. Finally, Patrick (1994) explicitly argued that the abnormal affective response shown by psychopathic offenders "may rep-

resent an extreme variation of normal temperament" (p. 319). Therefore, finding differences between psychopathic and nonpsychopathic individuals does not constitute evidence for the categorical nature of psychopathy.

Next, methodological issues should make one question the idea that psychopathy is related to deficits in the areas above. An important methodological point not adequately appreciated is that in no study have researchers examined multiple deficits in the same sample. That is, one cannot say whether the individuals who show electrodermal hyporeactivity are the same ones who show problems in response modulation. Even if such a study was available, one would have to question the conclusion given the standard extreme group approach used in most studies of this kind. Although selecting the highest and lowest scoring PCL-R groups while discarding those in the middle range is understandable from a scarce resources perspective, it may have several unintentional negative consequences. It exaggerates the degree of relation between psychopathy and whatever individual difference variable is examined. It leads to groups that are high or low in all FFM facets of psychopathy, which can make more specific differentiations difficult, if not impossible.

In fact, the FFM conceptualization might be the best way to make sense of all of these so-called deficits. Psychopathy is related to such a diverse set of correlates because psychopathy is itself a collection of diverse traits. If psychopathy were comprised of only high Antagonism, only low anxiousness or vulnerability, or only low Conscientiousness, its list of correlates would be far smaller. Psychopathy, however, is comprised of high Antagonism, low anxiousness, and low Conscientiousness; as such, psychopathy is related to the correlates of each of these individual traits.

A fourth and final objection might take the form of granting that the FFM can describe the psychopath, but doubting whether such a description truly constitutes psychopathy. I think this is a reasonable question, and more research needs to be done to examine it. The results of a recently completed study (Miller et al., 2001), however, suggest that the FFM conceptualization may indeed capture the essence of psychopathy. In this study of 481 young adults from the Lexington Longitudinal Study, Miller et al. (2001) examined how well psychopathy assessed through the FFM could reproduce the nomological network surrounding PCL-R-defined psychopathy. They assessed psychopathy through the degree of resemblance between an individual's NEO-PI-R profile and the expert-generated psychopathy prototype described earlier. FFM psychopathy was strongly related to all of their validation measures. Besides bearing the predicted relations to scores on the facets of the NEO-PI-R, FFM psychopathy was strongly positively correlated with scores on the LSRP; the number of symptoms of ATS and substance abuse and dependence taken from a diagnostic interview; and the variety and frequency of delinquent acts committed since the fourth grade. Additionally, FFM psychopathy was negatively correlated with internalizing symptoms. All of these relations replicate those obtained in other studies using incarcerated, PCL-R-defined psychopathic offenders.

CONCLUSION

I believe that psychopathy is best understood as a collection of personality traits that exists on a continuum with normal functioning. I also believe that the FFM provides a specific representation of psychopathy. In terms of Agreeableness and Conscientiousness, the picture is straightforward; psychopathy consists of extremely high Antagonism and very low Conscientiousness, particularly the facets of dutifulness, self-discipline, and deliberation. The picture is more complex for Neuroticism and Extraversion. In terms of Neuroticism, psychopathy consists of low anxiety, low self-consciousness, and low vulnerability but high angry hostility and high impulsiveness. In terms of Extraversion, psychopathy consists of low warmth and low positive emotions but high excitement seeking. This conceptualization helps to make sense of four enduring issues in the psychopathy literature: (a) the PCL-R factor structure, (b) the diversity of psychopathic deficits, (c) the concept of successful psychopathy, and (d) the patterns of comorbidity surrounding psychopathy. Finally, I believe that the FFM conceptualization of psychopathy presented here holds the potential for being generative and moving forward the understanding of psychopathy.

References

American Psychiatric Association (1994). *Diagnostic and statistical manual of mental disorders* (4th ed.). Washington, DC: American Psychiatric Association.

Belmore, M. F., & Quinsey, V. L. (1994). Correlates of psychopathy in a noninstitutional sample. *Journal of Interpersonal Violence, 9,* 339–349.

Block, J. H., & Block, J. (1980). *The California Child Q-Set.* Palo Alto, CA: Consulting Psychologists Press.

Buss, A. H. (1966). *Psychopathology.* New York: Wiley.

Caspi, A., Block, J., Block, J. H., Klopp, B., Lynam, D., Moffitt, T. E., & Stouthamer-Loeber, M. (1992). A "common language" version of the California Child Q-Set (CLQ) for personality assessment. *Psychological Assessment, 4,* 512–523.

Cleckley, H. (1988). *The mask of sanity.* St. Louis, MO: Mosby. (Original work published 1941)

Cooke, E. W., Stevenson, V. E., & Hawk, L. W. (1993, October). *Enhanced startle modulation and negative affectivity.* Paper presented at the annual meeting of the Society for Research in Psychopathology, Chicago, IL.

Costa, P. T., Jr., & McCrae, R. R. (1990). Personality disorders and the five-factor model of personality. *Journal of Personality Disorders, 4,* 362–371.

Costa, P. T., Jr., & McCrae, R. R. (1992). *Revised NEO Personality Inventory (NEO-PI-R) and NEO Five-Factor Inventory (NEO-FFI) professional manual.* Odessa, FL: Psychological Assessment Resources.

Deluty, R. H. (1981). Alternative-thinking ability of aggressive, assertive, and submissive children. *Cognitive Therapy and Research, 5,* 309–312.

Dodge, K. A. (1980). Social cognition and children's aggressive behavior. *Child Development, 51,* 162–170.

Dodge, K. A., & Crick, N. R. (1990). Social information processing bases of aggressive behavior in children. *Personality and Social Psychology Bulletin, 16,* 8–22.

Dodge, K. A., & Frame, C. L. (1982). Social cognitive biases and deficits in aggressive boys. *Child Development, 53,* 620–635.

Dodge, K. A., Petit, G. S., Bates, J. E., & Valente, E. (1995). Social information processing patterns partially mediate the effect of early physical abuse on later conduct problems. *Journal of Abnormal Psychology, 104,* 632–643.

Dodge, K., Price, J., Bachorowski, J., & Newman, J.

(1990). Hostile attributional biases in severely aggressive adolescents. *Journal of Abnormal Psychology, 99,* 385–392.

Forth, A. E., Brown, S. L., Hart, S. D., & Hare, R. D. (1996). The assessment of psychopathy in male and female noncriminals: Reliability and validity. *Personality and Individual Differences, 20,* 531–543.

Fowles, D. (1980). The three-arousal model: Implications of Gray's two-factor learning theory for heart-rate, electrodermal activity, and psychopathy. *Psychophysiology, 17,* 87–104.

Fowles, D. (1993). Electrodermal activity and antisocial behavior: Empirical findings and theoretical issues. In J. C. Roy, W. Boucsein, D. Fowles, & J. Gruzelier (Eds.), *Progress in Electrodermal Research* (pp. 223–237). London: Plenum Press.

Fowles, D. C., & Missel, K. A. (1994). Electrodermal hyporeactivity, motivation, and psychopathy: Theoretical issues. In D. Fowles, P. Sutker, & S. Goodman (Eds.), *Psychopathy and antisocial personality: A developmental perspective. Vol. 18. Progress in experimental personality and psychopathology research* (pp. 263–283). New York: Springer.

Frick, P. J. (1998). Callous-unemotional traits and conduct problems: A two-factor model of psychopathy in children. In R. D. Hare, J. Cooke, & A. Forth (Eds.), *Psychopathy: Theory, research and implications for society* (pp. 161–187). Amsterdam, The Netherlands: Kluwer Academic.

Gough, H. G. (1948). A sociological theory of psychopathy. *American Journal of Sociology, 53,* 359–366.

Hare, R. D. (1965a). Acquisition and generalization of a conditioned fear response in psychopathic and nonpsychopathic criminals. *Journal of Psychology, 59,* 367–370.

Hare, R. D. (1965b). Temporal gradient of fear arousal in psychopaths. *Journal of Abnormal Psychology, 70,* 442–445.

Hare, R. D. (1970). *Psychopathy: Theory and practice.* New York: Wiley.

Hare, R. D. (1991). *The Hare Psychopathy Checklist —Revised.* Toronto, Ontario, Canada: Multi-Health Systems.

Hare, R. D. (1993). *Without conscience: The disturbing world of the psychopaths among us.* New York: Pocket Books.

Hare, R. D., Harpur, T. J., Hakstian, A. R., Forth, A. E., Hart, S. D., & Newman, J. P. (1990). The Revised Psychopathy Checklist: Reliability and factor structure. *Psychological Assessment, 2,* 338–341.

Hare, R. D., & McPherson, L. M. (1984). Psychopathy and perceptual asymmetry in semantic processing. *Personality and Individual Differences, 9,* 329–337.

Hare, R. D., McPherson, L. M., & Forth, A. E. (1988). Male psychopaths and their criminal careers. *Journal of Consulting and Clinical Psychology, 56,* 710–714.

Harpur, T. J., Hakstian, A. R., & Hare, R. D. (1988). Factor structure of the Psychopathy Checklist. *Journal of Consulting and Clinical Psychology, 56,* 741–747.

Harpur, T., Hare, R., & Hakstian, A. (1989). Two-factor conceptualization of psychopathy: Construct validity and assessment implications. *Psychological Assessment, 1,* 6–17.

Harris, G. T., Rice, M. E., & Quinsey, V. L. (1994). Psychopathy as a taxon: Evidence that psychopaths are a discrete class. *Journal of Consulting and Clinical Psychology, 62,* 387–397.

Hart, C. H., Ladd, G. W., & Burleson, B. (1990). Children's expectations of the outcomes of social strategies: Relations with sociometric status and maternal disciplinary styles. *Child Development, 61,* 127–137.

Hart, S., & Hare, R. (1994). Psychopathy and the Big 5: Correlations between observers' ratings of normal and pathological personality. *Journal of Personality Disorders, 8,* 32–40.

Hemphill, J. F., Hart, S. D., & Hare, R. D. (1994). Psychopathy and substance use. *Journal of Personality Disorders, 8,* 169–180.

John, O. P. (1990). The "Big Five" factor taxonomy: Dimensions of personality in the natural language and questionnaires. In L. A. Pervin (Ed.), *Handbook of personality: Theory and research* (pp. 66–100). New York: Guilford.

John, O. P. (1995). *Big Five Inventory.* Berkeley: University of California, Berkeley, Institute of Personality and Social Research.

John, O. P., Caspi, A., Robins, R. W., Moffitt, T. E., & Stouthamer-Loeber, M. (1994). The "Little Five": Exploring the nomological network of the five-factor model of personality in adolescent boys. *Child Development, 65,* 160–178.

Karpman, B. (1941). On the need for separating psychopathy into two distinct clinical types: Symptomatic and idiopathic. *Journal of Criminology and Psychopathology, 3,* 112–137.

Kosson, D. S., Smith, S. S., & Newman, J. P. (1990). Evaluating the construct validity of psychopathy on Black and White male inmates: Three preliminary studies. *Journal of Abnormal Psychology, 99,* 250–259.

Levenson, M., Kiehl, K., & Fitzpatrick, C. (1995). Assessing psychopathic attributes in a noninstitutional population. *Journal of Personality and Social Psychology, 68,* 151–158.

Lilienfeld, S. O. (1994). Conceptual problems in the assessment of psychopathy. *Clinical Psychology Review, 14,* 17–38.

Lilienfeld, S. O. (1998). Methodological advances and developments in the assessment of psychopathy. *Behaviour Research and Therapy, 36,* 99–125.

Lykken, D. T. (1957). A study of anxiety in the sociopathic personality. *Journal of Abnormal and Clinical Psychology, 55,* 6–10.

Lykken, D. T. (1982, September). Fearlessness. *Psychology Today,* pp. 20–28.

Lykken, D. T. (1995). *The antisocial personalities.* Hillsdale, NJ: Erlbaum.

Lynam, D. R. (1996). The early identification of chronic offenders: Who is the fledgling psychopath? *Psychological Bulletin, 120,* 209–234.

Lynam, D. R., Whiteside, S., & Jones, S. (1999). Self-reported psychopathy: A validation study. *Journal of Personality Assessment, 73,* 110–132.

McCord, W., & McCord, J. (1964). *The psychopath: An essay on the criminal mind.* Princeton, NJ: Van Nostrand.

McCrae, R. R., & Costa, P. T., Jr. (1990). *Personality in adulthood.* New York: Guilford.

Miller, J. D., & Lynam, D. R. (in press). Structural models of personality and their relation to antisocial behavior: A meta-analytic review. *Criminology.*

Miller, J. D., Lynam, D. R., Widiger, T., & Leukefeld, C. (2001). Personality disorders as extreme variants of common personality dimensions: Can the five-factor model adequately represent psychopathy? *Journal of Personality, 69,* 253–276.

Millon, T., Simonsen, E., & Birket-Smith, M. (1998). Historical conceptions of psychopathy in the United States and Europe. In T. Millon, E. Simonsen, M. Birket-Smith, & R. D. Davis (Eds.), *Psychopathy: Antisocial, criminal, and violent behaviors* (pp. 3–31). New York: Guilford.

Moffitt, T. E. (1993). Adolescence-limited and life-course persistent antisocial behavior: A developmental taxonomy. *Psychological Review, 100,* 674–701.

Nasby, W., Hayden, B., & DePaulo, B. B. (1979). Attributional bias among aggressive boys to interpret unambiguous social stimuli as displays of hostility. *Journal of Abnormal Psychology, 89,* 459–468.

Newman, J. P. (1987). Reaction to punishment in extraverts and psychopaths: Implications for the impulsive behavior of disinhibited individuals. *Journal of Research in Personality, 21,* 464–480.

Newman, J. P., Patterson, C., Howland, E., & Nichols, S. (1990). Passive avoidance in psychopaths: The effects of reward. *Personality and Individual Differences, 11,* 1101–1114.

Newman, J. P., Patterson, C. M., & Kosson, D. S. (1987). Response perseveration in psychopaths. *Journal of Abnormal Psychology, 96,* 145–148.

Ogloff, J., & Wong, S. (1990). Electrodermal and cardiovascular evidence of a coping response in psychopaths. *Criminal Justice and Behavior, 17,* 231–245.

Ogloff, J., Wong, S., & Greenwood, A. (1990). Treating criminal psychopaths in a therapeutic community program. *Behavioral Sciences and the Law, 8,* 181–190.

Patrick, C. J. (1994). Emotion and psychopathy: Startling new insights. *Psychophysiology, 31,* 319–330.

Patrick, C. J., Bradley, M. M., & Lang, P. J. (1993). Emotion in the criminal psychopath: Startle reflex modulation. *Journal of Abnormal Psychology, 102,* 82–92.

Patrick, C. J., Cuthbert, B. N., & Lang, P. J. (1994). Emotion in the criminal psychopath: Fear image processing. *Journal of Abnormal Psychology, 103,* 523–534.

Patterson, M. C., & Newman, J. P. (1993). Reflectivity and learning from aversive events: Toward a psychological mechanism for the syndromes of disinhibition. *Psychological Review, 100,* 716–736.

Quay, H. C. (1965). Psychopathic personality as pathologic stimulation seeking. *American Journal of Psychiatry, 122,* 180–183.

Rice, M. E., Harris, G. T., & Quinsey, V. L. (1990). A follow-up of rapists assessed in a maximum security psychiatric facility. *Journal of Interpersonal Violence, 5,* 435–448.

Robins, R. W., John, O. P., & Caspi, A. (1994). Major dimensions of personality in early adolescence: The Big Five and beyond. In C. F. Halverson, G. A. Kohnstamm, & R. P. Martin (Eds.), *The developing structure of temperament and personality from infancy to adulthood* (pp. 267–291). Hillsdale, NJ: Erlbaum.

Rogers, R., & Bagby, M. (1994). Dimensions of psychopathy: A factor analytic study of the MMPI antisocial personality scale. *International Journal of Offender Therapy and Comparative Criminology, 19,* 21–31.

Salekin, R. T., Rogers, R., & Sewell, K. W. (1996). A review and meta-analysis of the Psychopathy Checklist and Psychopathy Checklist—Revised: Predictive validity of dangerousness. *Clinical Psychology: Science and Practice, 3,* 203–215.

Schmauk, F. J. (1970). Punishment, arousal, and avoidance learning in sociopaths. *Journal of Abnormal Psychology, 76,* 325–335.

Serin, R. C. (1991). Psychopathy and violence in criminals. *Journal of Interpersonal Violence, 6,* 423–431.

Slaby, R. G., & Guerra, N. G. (1988). Cognitive mediators of aggression in adolescent offenders: I. Assessment. *Developmental Psychology, 24,* 580–588.

Smith, S., & Newman, J. (1990). Alcohol and drug abuse–dependence disorders in psychopathic and nonpsychopathic criminal offenders. *Journal of Abnormal Psychology, 99,* 430–439.

Sutker, P. B. (1994). Psychopathy: Traditional and clinical antisocial concepts. In D. Fowles, P. Sutker, & S. Goodman (Eds.), *Psychopathy and antisocial personality: A developmental perspective. Vol. 18. Progress in experimental personality and psychopathology research* (pp. 73–120). New York: Springer.

Tellegen, A., & Waller, N. G. (1994). Exploring personality through test construction: Development of the Multidimensional Personality Questionnaire. In S. R. Briggs & J. M. Cheek (Eds.), *Personality measures: Development and evaluation.*

(Vol. 1, pp. 136–161). Greenwich, CT: JAI Press.

Trull, T. J. (1992). *DSM-III-R* personality disorders and the five-factor model of personality: An empirical comparison. *Journal of Abnormal Psychology, 101,* 553–560.

Waas, G. A. (1988). Social attributional biases of peer-rejected and aggressive children. *Child Development, 59,* 969–992.

Widiger, T. A., & Lynam, D. R. (1998). Psychopathy and the five-factor model of personality. In T. Millon, E. Simonsen, M. Birket-Smith, & R. D. Davis (Eds.), *Psychopathy: Antisocial. criminal, and violent behaviors* (pp. 171–187). New York: Guilford.

Widiger, T. W., & Trull, T. J. (1992). Personality and psychopathology: An application of the five-factor model. *Journal of Personality, 60,* 363–393.

Widom, C. S. (1977). A methodology for studying noninstitutionalized psychopaths. *Journal of Consulting and Clinical Psychology, 45,* 674–683.

Williamson, S., Harpur, T. J., & Hare, R. D. (1990). *Sensitivity to emotional polarity in psychopaths.* Paper presented at the 98th Annual Convention of the American Psychological Association, Boston, MA.

Williamson, S., Harpur, T. J., & Hare, R. D. (1991). Abnormal processing of affective words by psychopaths. *Psychophysiology, 28,* 260–273.

PART IV

DIAGNOSIS AND TREATMENT USING THE FIVE-FACTOR MODEL

FURTHER USE OF THE NEO-PI-R PERSONALITY DIMENSIONS IN DIFFERENTIAL TREATMENT PLANNING

Cynthia Sanderson and John F. Clarkin

In this chapter, we examine the potential contribution of a dimensional model of personality (i.e., the five-factor model [FFM]) to the planning and application of psychological interventions. Contrary to popular perception, personality disorders are not untreatable. Treatment is unlikely to remove fully all vestiges of a personality disorder, but there is compelling empirical support to indicate that clinically meaningful responsivity to treatment will occur (Linehan, 1993; Linehan & Kehrer, 1993; Perry, Banon, & Ianni, 1999; Sanislow & McGlashan, 1998). Treatment of borderline personality disorder (BDL, e.g.) is unlikely to result in the development of a fully healthy or ideal personality (many significant aspects of the personality disorder often remain after effective treatment has occurred; Linehan, Tutek, Heard, & Armstrong, 1994), but treatment can result in the removal of the more harmful, damaging, or debilitating components of the disorder and may at times even result in enough change that the person would no longer meet the fourth edition of the *Diagnostic and Statistical Manual of Mental Disorders* (*DSM-IV*; American Psychiatric Association [APA], 1994) diagnostic criteria for BDL.

There also continues to be growing interest, both in clinical practice (APA, 1989; Beutler & Clarkin, 1990; Frances, Clarkin, & Perry, 1984; Miller, 1991) and research (Beutler & Clarkin, 1991; Harkness & Lilienfeld, 1997; Shoham-Salomon, 1991), to match patients with a treatment that is tailored to the specific needs of the individual. There is also a recognition that Axis II personality disorders modify treatment outcome of Axis I disorders (e.g., Reich &

Vasile, 1993; Shea, Widiger, & Klein, 1992), but here we make a more general point. We suggest that broad personality dimensions, whether abnormal or not, contribute to and influence both the choice of and process of treatment intervention (e.g., Blatt, Quinlan, Pilkonis, & Shea, 1995; Blatt, Zuroff, Quinlan, & Pilkonis, 1996). We suggest that rather than of academic interest alone, the power of personality dimensions is substantial and that therapy focus, alliance, and outcome all relate to personality dimensions.

A major stimulus for the examination of the contribution of the FFM to treatment planning and, in particular, the Revised NEO Personality Inventory (NEO-PI-R; Costa & McCrae, 1992) is the incompleteness of the *DSM-IV* in reference to this clinical task. Of course, the *DSM-IV* system was not meant to be a treatment planning document but simply an organizing schema for the acquisition for such a process (APA, 1989). However, it is used as such, and the inadequacies of the *DSM* for differential treatment planning are related to the following considerations.

First, a total picture of personality strengths, excesses, deficits, and dysfunction is needed to plan treatment intervention for the individual patient, regardless of whether he or she complains of Axis I symptomatic syndromes or Axis II disturbed interpersonal relations. Although the Axis I disorders describe common symptomatic patterns, the treatment of these conditions is always modified by the personality characteristics of the individual, none of which are noted in the Axis I diagnostic criteria themselves. Treatment efforts that only focus on strengths or, worse yet, focus on the deficits without attention to the assets of the individual's personality are shortsighted. The third edition of the *DSM* (*DSM-III*; APA, 1980) suggests that one does not treat the person but rather the disorder that the person is manifesting. While this statement may have some validity when dealing with syndromal symptom patterns on Axis I that have a clear onset and course, this is not so with the personality disorders on Axis II. The personality disorders concern traits that form the very fabric of the individual. When treating personality disorders, one is addressing the "whole" individual, and one must consider both the pathological and the nonpathological attributes.

Second, both medical and social treatments are focused on particular constellations of behavior, attitudes, moods, and traits, not on diagnostic categories. We argue in this chapter that psychosocial treatment is focused on the trait level. It is at the construct–trait level that one plans medical treatment. For example, in the medication treatment of BDL patients, the targets are impulsivity, mood dyscontrol, and thought disorder that are characteristic of long-term functioning (Cowdry, 1987; Sanislow & McGlashan, 1998; Soloff, 1987).

Third, the personality disorders as defined in the *DSM-IV* Axis II have problematic construct validity (Clark, Livesley, & Morey, 1997). Empirical data suggest that the internal consistency of the disorders is often poor (Morey, 1988) and many of the disorders include several different constructs (Livesley, 1998). In addition, because the Axis II disorders are polythetic, the group of patients who meet the diagnosis are not homogeneous even in the defining characteristics (Clarkin, Widiger, Frances, Hurt, & Gilmore, 1983; Widiger et al., 1990). Furthermore, Axis II does not cover the total universe of personality problems (Westen, 1997; Widiger, 1993). It has been pointed out, for example, that only half of the interpersonal circle is covered by Axis II (Kiesler, 1986).

Fourth, the categorical nature of Axis I and Axis II is inadequate if not misleading in regard to treatment planning. In the clinical situation, many patients come for therapy who do not meet the criteria for the categorization of any one personality disorder but seek treatment for troubling and disruptive personality traits or patterns (Paris, 1998; Westen, 1997; Widiger, 1993). Diagnostically, these individuals may be accurately put in the category of personality disorder not otherwise specified (PDNOS), the catch-all diagnosis for patients with a personality disorder that do not meet the criteria for any existing diagnostic category (APA, 1994). In many settings, PDNOS is the most prevalent Axis II condition. Alternatively, many patients meet the criteria for more than one personality disorder, so that the clinician cannot plan treatment intervention around each disorder independently but rather must conceptualize the person and the multiple foci of intervention in an organized and hierarchical pattern tailored to the individual.

DIFFERENTIAL TREATMENT DECISIONS

For each patient, many different kinds of treatment decisions must be made. In this chapter, we present some important dimensions of treatment and suggest ways in which insights that are gained from a patient's NEO-PI-R profile can help the therapist tailor the components of treatment to the individual's needs. First, we discuss four fundamental or macrotreatment decisions that are made at the initial evaluation stage (Frances et al., 1984). These are the selection of (a) treatment setting (i.e., inpatient, day hospital, outpatient); (b) treatment format (i.e., family, marital, group, individual); (c) strategies and techniques (i.e., psychodynamic, cognitive, behavioral); and (d) duration and frequency (i.e., brief or longer term treatments), frequency of sessions—a fifth and equally important macrotreatment decision is the potential use of medications. In the second half of the chapter, we discuss important microtreatment decisions that are relevant to the moment to moment in-session and between-session decisions, such as degree of therapist directiveness, depth of therapy experience, and breadth of treatment goals (Beutler & Clarkin, 1990). Several clinical vignettes illustrate our observations. Although there is much interdependence between the various dimensions of treatment planning, we have found it pedagogically helpful to separate them for illustrative purposes.

Macrotreatment Decisions

Setting. The settings of treatment have remained somewhat constant in the last several decades: inpatient, day hospital, outpatient clinic, private office, treatment in the family home, and sessions at the site of the disorder (e.g., systematic desensitization in vivo). The accessibility of these treatment settings, however, has changed dramatically in the era of cost containment. Inpatient care has become much more restricted in terms of who obtains it (the most severely disturbed patients in acute distress) and for how long a period of time (the length of stay is becoming much shorter). This constriction of resources has forced clinicians to be more creative in using alternatives to hospitalization in crisis situations, such as day hospital settings and crisis intervention.

Format. The treatment format is the interpersonal context within which the intervention is conducted. The choice of a particular treatment format (i.e., individual, group, family–marital) is determined by the perspective from which a presenting problem is initially defined by the patient–family, the clinician, or both. For example, from the clinician's point of view, the treatment of the spouse with depression can vary depending on whether it is viewed as a current adaptation to a larger problem involving the family unit (suggesting a need for family intervention) or as the patient's personal symptomatic adaptation to a unique biological, social, and historical situation (in which case individual or group treatment is more likely to be indicated). The mediating and final goals of treatment vary accordingly.

The individual treatment format is one in which the patient and therapist meet in privacy, and the individual is seen as the focus of intervention. The relationship between the therapist and patient is fostered and used as the framework for the application of a multitude of therapeutic techniques to assist the individual in coping with symptoms and resolving interpersonal conflicts through their replay with the therapist. The individual format has advantages in addressing problems achieving intimacy, the striving for autonomy in adolescents and young adults, and issues that are of such private nature, embarrassing nature, or both that the confidentiality of the individual format is required at least for the beginning phase.

The group treatment format is one in which a small number of patients meet with one or several therapists on a regular basis for the goal of treating the disorders of the group members. The group treatment format provides an economic mode of treatment delivery, an effective means of reducing or circumventing the resistances expressed in individual therapy, and adjunctive support or ancillary therapists in the form of other patients. Group therapy also creates a setting in which interactional forces can be manifested and examined. Group treatments can be classified as heterogeneous or homogeneous in membership. Although this distinction is not supported by controlled research, it has been used extensively in clinical practice.

In heterogeneous groups, individual patients differ widely in their problems, strengths, ages, socioeconomic backgrounds, and personality traits. Treatment in heterogeneous groups fosters self-revelation of one's inner world in an interpersonal setting where sharing and feedback are encouraged. The group provides a context in which interpersonal behavior patterns are re-experienced, discussed, and understood and in which patients experiment with new ways of relating. There are two general indications for heterogeneous group therapy. First, the patient's most pressing and salient problems occur in current interpersonal relationships. Second, prior individual therapy formats have failed for various reasons (e.g., the patient has a strong tendency to actualize interpersonal distortions in individual therapy formats, or the patient is excessively intellectualized). The enabling factors for heterogeneous group therapy include a capacity to participate in the group treatment as evidenced by openness to influence from others, willingness to participate in the group process, and willingness and ability to protect group norms. The patient's motivation for group treatment must be sufficiently adequate to foster participation.

Homogeneous groups are self-help or professionally led groups in which all members share the same symptom or set of symptoms that are the primary if not sole focus of the intervention and change. The type of group is usually highly structured and provides a social network for the patient who previously may have felt alone and isolated with the target symptom. The sense of commonality in jointly combating a shared problem provides support and self-validation. Homogeneous groups tend to avoid techniques of psychological interpretations and use group inspiration, didactics, modeling, and advice because the goal is not insight but behavioral change.

The indication for homogeneous group treatment is that the patient's most salient problem or chief complaint involves a specific disorder for which a homogeneous group is available. These problems fall into four general categories: (a) specific impulse disorders, such as, obesity, alcoholism, drug addiction, gambling, and violence; (b) problems adjusting to and coping with medical disorders, such as cardiac ailments, ileostomy, terminal illness, chronic pain, and others; (c) problems of a particular developmental phase, such as childhood, adolescence, childrearing, and aging; and (d) specific mental disorders or symptom constellations, such as agoraphobia, somatoform disorders, BDL, and schizophrenia.

The family treatment format is one in which various subgroups of a family (a nuclear family, a couple, or a couple with a family of origin) meet on a regular basis with a therapist. The family format was derived in large part from an emphasis on the contextual origins of the presenting problems. Recently, family and marital treatments have been applied more broadly, with greater emphasis on their practical utility rather than solely or primarily on the hypothesized role of the family dyad in the problem's generation, maintenance, or both. Hence, family- and marital-based treatments are used for various medical (e.g., hypertension) and psychiatric disorders (e.g., agoraphobia, schizophrenia, BDL), wherein the spouse or family member is enlisted to provide social support to the patient.

The mediating goals of family and marital treatments are to change the repetitive and often rigid interpersonal interchanges by family members that are in themselves the focus of complaint or are hypothesized to be related to the symptoms of one or more individuals. In addition to the use of the usual range of strategies and techniques, the use of the family format allows direct therapeutic assessment and impact on these behaviors because they operate in predictable sequences in the family setting.

The relative indications for family–marital formats include (a) family–marital problems presented as such without any one family member designated as the identified patient; (b) a family presents with current structured difficulties in intrafamilial relationships, with each person contributing collusively or openly to the reciprocal interaction problems, or symptomatic behaviors are experienced almost predominantly within the family–marital system; or (c) a family is unable to cope adequately with the behavior of a particular family member, such as adolescent acting-out behavior (promiscuity, drug abuse, delinquency, vandalism, violent behavior) or a chronic mental illness of one family member.

The NEO-PI-R, in combination with a clinical interview, can be helpful in the choice of treatment format in two ways. First, the NEO-PI-R helps describe the predominant interpersonal patterns of the patient and suggest areas of difficulty needing treatment, whether these interpersonal problem areas could be addressed in individual, family, or group formats. For example, although the NEO-PI-R profile is not directly related to the choice of family–marital treatment format (because it is an instrument concerned with characteristics of the individual as a self-contained unit), the NEO-PI-R can suggest how that individual relates to others, including family members.

Second, the NEO-PI-R can help individuals who could effectively use a particular treatment format. For example, the NEO-PI-R could indicate which individuals could use a group format, those who would likely need the privacy of individual treatment, or those who may have difficulty accepting group treatment. Those who are particularly antagonistic (e.g. suspicious, critical, unempathic) or introverted (low warmth, low gregariousness) may not be suitable for group therapy. The NEO-PI-R can also be useful in anticipating conflicts and problems among the group members (e.g., antagonistic people may take advantage of the excessively trusting or passive patient).

Strategies and Techniques.   There seems to be a consensus in the clinical literature that the differences between treatments—differences seen as crucial for outcome—are captured at the level of treatment strategies and techniques. We would question this assumption as far from complete and suggest that psychotherapy has advanced in its specificity, not through investigation of techniques but through research on the disorders themselves. As the disorders have become more clearly differentiated, the treatments have become more focused. For example, the family treatment of schizophrenia has flourished since the concept of expressed emotion (EE) and its influence on the course of the disorder was explicated. Treatments have been formulated with the explicit focus of reducing EE through the use of various strategies and techniques. The implication is that no treatment strategy–technique can be considered in isolation, but its value lies in its usefulness in achieving the mediating goals of treatment for the specific problem diagnosis.

Treatment manuals are now being written to guide research and training in the techniques of the various schools (dynamic, behavior, cognitive) for diverse patient populations, for example anxiety (Beck & Emery, 1985), depression (Beck, Rush, Shaw, & Emery, 1979), schizophrenia (Falloon, Boyd, & McGill, 1984), interpersonal problems (Luborksy, 1984; Strupp & Binder, 1984), and BDL traits (Linehan, 1993). Clinical research indicates which strategies–techniques are effective with which specific patient problem areas.

Paradoxically, although treatment manuals that define treatment packages for all individuals with a common diagnosis or syndrome are growing in number, at the same time there is a concerted effort to assign the individual patient to the most optimal treatment. In this chapter we suggest that the NEO-PI-R has the potential for utility at the very intersection of manuals for specific disorders as applied to the individual.

In addition to using the strategies and techniques common to the various schools of therapy, the clinician must consider the use of more specific approaches that might be appropriate for the particular case. In this process, one considers most carefully the mediating goals of treatment and those strategies and techniques that might be instrumental in reaching those goals. The selection of specific techniques is related to the (a) nature of the problem–disorder (e.g., etiology, causes, stressors), (b) breadth of therapy goals, (c) depth of therapy goals, and (d) reac-

tance level of the patient. In rare instances, specific strategies and techniques have shown superiority over competing ones in comparison studies. The clinician must determine individual mediating goals for each patient, given his or her unique diagnosis, social environmental situation, and personality assets and liabilities. For example, psychodynamic techniques have the mediating goal of insight and conflict resolution; behavioral techniques, the mediating goals of specific behavioral changes; cognitive techniques, the mediating goals of change in conscious thought processes; and experiential–humanistic techniques, the mediating goals of increased awareness that is more fully integrated into the patient's personality.

Although the NEO-PI-R does not relate directly to the mediating goals of the treatment of the individual case, information from this instrument can be of assistance in choosing strategies and techniques for the treatment of the individual. This occurs mainly through the consideration of the patient's problem complexity, coping styles, and reactance level, which is considered in detail later in this chapter.

Duration and Frequency of Treatment.   Treatment duration is multifaceted. The concept can refer to (a) the duration of a treatment episode, (b) the duration of a treatment element (e.g., hospitalization) within a single treatment episode, or (c) the succession of treatment episodes in a virtually lifetime treatment of a chronic disorder such as schizophrenia. The major reference is to the duration of the treatment episode, that is, the time from evaluation to termination of a particular treatment period.

A number of factors make the relationship between duration of a treatment episode and outcome relatively unpredictable. The duration of the treatment episode and the frequency of sessions are related to the amount of effort and length of time needed to achieve the mediating and final goals of the intervention, which in turn are related to the nature of the disorder and symptoms under treatment. In general, the greater the breadth of goals and depth of experience of the treatment, the longer the treatment. Alternatively, when the goals of treatment are circumscribed, treatment can be brief. Setting the duration for a brief treatment can assist in ensuring that the goals will be reached more quickly than leaving the duration open ended.

Brief Therapy. Psychologists may be in an era in which brief psychotherapies are the predominant form of treatment for many patients. Whether it is planned in advance or not, most patients engage in psychotherapy for only a short period of time. Patients seeking clinical outpatient psychotherapy generally expect it to last no more than 3 months, and a very high percentage of patients actually remain in treatment for fewer than 12 sessions. Most therapy has always been brief; what is new is the notion of time-limited therapy by design.

The first step in planning for treatment duration is to decide whether to recommend a brief or longer term outpatient intervention. Some clinicians offer brief therapy as the initial treatment for all patients, except those few who have already had an unsuccessful experience with it or those who present with clear motivation and indications for long-term treatment. Because it is difficult to predict from one or two interviews which patients require and can benefit from longer interventions, a trial of brief therapy is often useful as an extended evaluation or role induction.

Brief psychotherapies differ among themselves in goals, treatment techniques, strategies, format (group, family, or individual), setting (inpatient, day hospital, outpatient), and selection criteria. In fact, the different models of brief therapy are as diverse as those applied in longer treatments. However, certain essential features characterize the brief therapies: establishing a time limit, achieving a focus with clear and limited goals, achieving a workable patient–therapist alliance rapidly, and having an active therapist.

The indications for brief therapy, of whatever model, include (a) a definite focus, precipitating event, or target for intervention must be present; (b) the patient's overall motivation and goals may be limited but must be sufficient for cooperation with the brief treatment; (c) the patient must be judged to be capable of separation from treatment; (d) the patient's usual level of functioning is adequate and does not require the level of change usually brought about only by long-term or maintenance treatment; (e) limited financial or time resources on the part of the patient or the delivery system may incline toward brief treatment; and (f) brief treatment may be chosen in preference to longer treatment to avoid secondary gain, negative therapeutic reactions, unmanageable therapeutic attachments, or other iatrogenic effects.

An important consideration in making the decision for brief treatment is the potential usefulness of one of the brief therapies for a specific patient problem area. Difficulties brought by patients can be broadly conceptualized as either symptomatic or conflictual in nature (Beutler & Clarkin, 1990). Brief treatments have been articulated for symptoms (e.g., depression, anxiety), unrecognized feelings, behaviors (e.g., phobias), and interpersonal conflicts (Clarkin & Hull, 1991; Hollon & Beck, 1986; Koss & Beutler, 1986).

The NEO-PI-R can help clinicians choose which brief-focused treatments might be the most beneficial in two ways: (a) by indicating the breadth of problem and (b) by indicating the interpersonal assets that would foster a rapid alliance with the therapist and the acceptance of the therapist's assistance. Thus, the ideal patient for planned brief treatment from the NEO-PI-R would show isolated but significant elevations on Neuroticism, high openness to activities and ideas, high warmth (for rapport), and high Agreeableness.

Long-Term Psychotherapy. Regardless of technique, the rationale for treatment of long-term duration is that some problems are so ingrained, complex, and extensive that an extended period of time is necessary for their dissection and resolution and for the patient to assimilate and apply new solutions to daily life. Because regularly scheduled long-term psychotherapy is expensive and is minimally supported by available research, the prescription of this duration requires the most thoughtful assessment of indications, contraindications, and enabling factors.

A poor or insufficient response to brief treatment is an empirical demonstration of the need for further intervention. Whereas most psychotherapy research studies deal with brief therapy, these studies are impressive in the number of patients who do not respond to the brief intervention. The overuse and limitations of brief therapies have been described elsewhere (Clarkin & Hull, 1991). Patient factors that tend to lengthen the treatment include the diagnosis of chronic mental disorders (e.g., schizophrenia, bipolar disorder), multiple problem areas, poor patient enabling factors for treatment, and relatively poor premorbid functioning and adjustment.

Prescription for No Treatment. Evaluation only, or the prescription of no treatment for the individual following evaluation, is the briefest intervention. Clinicians are not inclined to recommend no treatment and rarely do so for patients applying for help in a clinical setting (Frances & Clarkin, 1991). For treatment planning purposes, it is helpful to distinguish (a) patients likely to improve without treatment (spontaneous remission, i.e., healthy individuals in crisis); (b) patients who are likely not to respond (nonresponders, i.e., antisocial, malingering, or factitious illness, iatrogenically infantilized patients, or poorly motivated patients without incapacitating symptoms); (c) those at risk for a negative response to treatment (i.e., severe masochistic, narcissistic, and oppositional patients; patients who enter treatment wanting to justify a legal claim or disability); and (d) those for whom the recommendation of no treatment is an intervention in itself aimed at their resistance (i.e., oppositional patients refusing treatment; Frances et al., 1984).

Combined with a careful history, the NEO-PI-R may be of assistance in isolating those patients for whom treatment is contraindicated or for whom engagement, change, or both in treatment is unlikely. A conceptualization of this parameter early in the patient's assessment enables the clinician to save valuable time and effort from a foredoomed treatment or provides information to be used in confronting the patient with the potential roadblocks, hence resulting in effective treatment from the first evaluation.

Spontaneous Remission. A relatively healthy individual caught in the throes of a crisis is a likely candidate for spontaneous remission. The NEO-PI-R for such an individual would show strengths in terms of, at most, an isolated and only moderate elevation in Neuroticism and good contact with others (i.e., Agreeableness and Extraversion). In particular, the profile would emphasize strengths in the area of Conscientiousness. The individual might present with a profile that is not substantially problematic

(e.g., moderate on Neuroticism and at worst high or low on Extraversion). The patient's problems may be situational and transient, and the patient may have the personality strengths to overcome these problems on his or her own (e.g. high in Conscientiousness and openness to ideas and activity). The best approach might then be to recommend no treatment because the patients can call on their own resources.

Clinical Vignette of a Likely Case for Spontaneous Remission. Christine was a 29-year-old single woman who presented to a hospital outpatient clinic complaining of problems in relationships with men. In this clinical setting, a screening battery was designed to provide suggestions for treatment planning, with information on functioning (Social Adjustment Schedule [SAS]), symptom distress (Symptom Checklist 90 [SCL-90]; Beck Depression Inventory [BDI]) and personality traits (NEO-PI). The relative elevation of symptoms (SCL-90) to interpersonal difficulties (scales of the NEO-PI) provided information on treatment focus.

Christine's SCL-90 was quite low with scaled scores in the 20–30 range ($M = 50$), indicating little symptom distress. Likewise, the BDI was below average. The SAS-SR indicated adaptive functioning in all areas, with some minor difficulties in finances and social functioning. Her NEO-PI was average for Neuroticism; very high in Extraversion, Openness, and Agreeableness; and high in Conscientiousness. She appeared to be extraverted, open to experience, agreeable in her relationships, and conscientious in her behavior. Her distress level, on both the SCL-90 (more of a state measure) and NEO-PI Neuroticism (more of a trait measure), was not significantly elevated.

In the clinical setting, Christine was assigned to brief individual therapy. She, however, discontinued treatment after a few sessions in which she discussed some difficulties with a current boyfriend. On hindsight, this patient probably could have been assigned by the clinical team for evaluation only or at least scheduled from the beginning for a limited number of sessions. She was not substantially symptomatic and she presented with many strengths, so the assessment could have been presented to her in an optimistic way. With the clinician relating to her many strengths, she could have been advised in a positive way that she did not need extensive or perhaps even any therapy.

Nonresponders.   Some individuals are not likely to benefit from treatment. Two subgroups of nonresponders are important to note. One group is composed of individuals low in Conscientiousness and very high on Neuroticism. They are in tremendous pain, but they drop out of treatment quickly. An individual in this group may have a history of being in and out of psychotherapy. Regrettably (or understandably) extremely high scores on Neuroticism coupled with low scores on Conscientiousness are often seen in people with personality disorders, particularly BDL, antisocial, and passive–aggressive personality disorders. A second group is composed of individuals low in Conscientiousness and very low in Neuroticism. Individuals in this group may bother other people with their behavior but not particularly be bothered by their own behavior. Consequently, they have little motivation to change. These individuals may express mild interest but may find various reasons for why they cannot continue treatment.

Patients at Risk for a Negative Response to Treatment.   We are also concerned here with individuals who get into a hostile, possibly psychotic transference. In psychodynamic terms, some of these patients manifest a negative therapeutic reaction. Some people who meet the *DSM-IV* criteria for BDL would fit into this group.

On the NEO-PI-R, these patients score very low on openness to actions. If the therapist tries to encourage them to do something, they may try to improve their life only slightly, they may not try at all, or they may do so only in a cursory manner. The therapist may assign them homework or practice, but somehow it never works out. These patients are also likely to be low on Conscientiousness. They are not diligent or responsible in their efforts. People high on openness to fantasy are adaptively responsive to speculation and introspection, but people who are very high on openness to fantasy can be weak in their reality testing. Low scores on Agreeableness suggest that a person is suspicious, oppositional, and resistant. Nothing that the therapist offers is considered useful or valuable. What the therapist suggests is either perceived as deficient or

has been tried with no success. Such individuals are unlikely to work well in a team or a group, even though they may be very high on Neuroticism. Low scores on Agreeableness often (but not always) seen in people diagnosed with a personality disorder, particularly BDL and antisocial personality disorder.

No Treatment as an Intervention for Resistance.   Some patients who apply for treatment are, at the same time, motivated to escape treatment at any possible turn. For example, individuals sent to treatment by others (e.g., mates sent by spouses, adolescents and early adults sent to treatment by parents, employees sent by employers, or those sent by the courts) fall into this category. They may experience little dysphoria or distress (e.g., average score on Neuroticism). If they are really in trouble (i.e., they are treatment resisters, yet they need treatment, which they then impulsively reject), one might expect high scores on Impulsiveness and Hostility. However, the particularly resistant people are low on Openness and low on Agreeableness. They resist anyone "telling them what to do" because they are not open to change and are antagonistic to the suggestions of others.

Clinical Vignette of the Initial Evaluation Process.   The patient was a 25-year-old woman, Abigail, who was an executive within a major telecommunication corporation. Never in psychotherapy before, she was evaluated and referred by a colleague at work because she had been engaged in promiscuous relationships. She presented with the complaint that she had very few friends, despite appearing as an engaging and friendly person. On the NEO-PI, Abigail came out as fairly well adjusted in most areas. She was average on Extraversion, high on Conscientiousness (a high-achieving woman), high on Agreeableness, and high on Openness. On Neuroticism, Abigail was very high on the Hostility facet scale.

Her difficulties were seen as conflict focused rather than simple, habitual symptoms. Therefore, the treatment goals included conflict resolution, especially those conflicts that were expressed within her interpersonal relationships. Her coping style was somewhat repressive, while she still maintained an active internal life. In many ways, she had some qualities of internalization because she was open to ideas. She was very intellectual, thought about things, read, and was open to considering other people's points of view. By relating to her repressive and internalized coping style, the clinician was able to plan a therapy experience with depth that included exploration of thoughts, feelings, motives, and drives.

Her reactance potential was high, as manifested by her very high hostility score within the domain of Neuroticism. However, she was also high on Agreeableness and high on Conscientiousness. High hostility on the NEO-PI immediately suggests to the therapist to use a cautious approach. Because of the characteristic hostility, the therapist assumed that it would not be a good idea to confront her. Rather, the therapist would have to take a slower course, speculating with her why these events were taking place in her life and slowly introducing the idea that she had a part in it (i.e., appeal to her openness to ideas). Thus, a confrontational brief therapy was not deemed as promising. The patient's level of Conscientiousness, however, boded well for an ability to remain involved in a more long-term treatment.

Abigail was assigned to open-ended individual psychodynamic treatment. What emerged over the course of the psychotherapy, however, was that despite this woman's friendly, agreeable presentation, she had a troubling high degree of hostility. She was oriented toward other people and was generally agreeable, but she had difficulties controlling her temper and anger. Invariably this anger led to a number of interpersonal conflicts. The NEO-PI had uncovered this information immediately, whereas the interview did not. The initial interviewer was struck more by her strengths (i.e., her Conscientiousness and Agreeableness). Her difficulties with anger, temper, and hostility were hidden by her effort to be agreeable and conscientious.

When the therapist introduced an idea to Abigail about herself that might be a problem behavior (e.g., she pushes people away with her hostility), Abigail would react with impulsive anger. The main way her hostility was exhibited in the transference was that she would state how much she liked the therapist, that the therapist was wonderful, and that she was so lucky to have the therapist. But if the therapist was late by a minute or if the therapist was momentarily unavailable (e.g., one time the therapist

had to answer the phone during the session because someone was calling in crisis), she became extremely angry and at times even enraged. However, Abigail was conscientious and agreeable enough to keep the angry reaction to herself, at least until the next session when she would again attack the therapist. Over the course of time, however, Abigail was able to integrate these interventions. She would go home and think about the content of her therapy session (i.e., high Openness), and she was able to make real gains, including the cessation of promiscuous relationships and the initial motivation for treatment. Subsequent to treatment, Abigail married and has since been very successful in establishing several meaningful friendships.

Microtreatment Decisions

In contrast to the macrotreatment decisions made at evaluation that set the course for the major parameters of treatment, numerous microtreatment decisions are made by the therapist throughout the course of treatment. Beutler and Clarkin (1991) postulated that key patient characteristics help the clinician decide about moment-to-moment decisions regarding breadth of treatment goals, depth of therapy experience, and degree of directiveness in the treatment assumed by the patient. We suggest that decisions around these parameters of treatment should be based on patient characteristics of problem complexity, characteristic coping styles, and reactance level.

Problem Complexity and Breadth of Treatment Goals. It is therapeutically useful to distinguish between simple or habitual symptoms and complex symptom patterns. Habitual or simple symptoms are isolated, environmentally specific, currently supported by reinforcing environments, and bear a clearly discernible relationship to their original adaptive form and etiology (Beutler & Clarkin, 1990). In contrast, underlying conflicts can be inferred when the symptoms have departed from their original and adaptive form and are elicited in environments that bear little relationship to the originally evoking situations.

Matched with the patient's problem complexity is the breadth of treatment goals. We distinguish between conflict-focused goals and simple symptom-focused goals. Somatic treatments by definition are symptom focused; likewise, behavioral and cognitive psychotherapies are directed most specifically to altering simple symptom presentations. In contrast, interpersonal, experiential, and psychodynamic therapies are more broadly focused on symptomatic change as related to change in internal characteristics of the patient. Manuals for the cognitive treatment of anxiety (Beck & Emery, 1985) and depression (Beck et al., 1979; Klerman, Weissman, Rounsaville, & Chevron, 1984) are useful for guiding an individual's treatment focused on the cognitive and interpersonal underpinnings of both of these troubling affects. Manuals for conflict-focused psychotherapies are illustrated by defining a conflict-oriented therapeutic focus. Experiential (Daldrup, Beutler, Engle, & Greenberg, 1988), interpersonal (Klerman et al., 1984), psychodynamic (Strupp & Binder, 1984), and family (Minuchin & Fishman, 1981) all formulate treatment foci and mediating goals that are beyond the simple symptom focus itself.

The NEO-PI-R measures neither the acuteness of symptoms nor direct conflicts. Rather, "trait" symptoms such as depression and anxiety are measured on the Neuroticism scale. The NEO-PI-R is useful in detecting the presence of single or multiple symptom patterns (e.g., one facet elevated in Neuroticism vs. many). The clinical interview is useful to ascertain if the symptom is simple or complex and of conflict organization. The dimensions of Neuroticism and Extraversion (and their facets) provide indications of the spread of symptoms that the individual typically experiences. Conflicts might be indicated or have fertile ground in those individuals with high self-consciousness and high vulnerability facet scores in combination with signs of distress (e.g., high scores on hostility, depression, and anxiety).

The breadth of goals (e.g., behavioral and conflict-resolving change) may not always coincide with depth of therapy experience. For example, underlying conflicts do not have to be addressed directly in therapy to be resolved. Behavioral change may result in conflict change without directly addressing the conflicts in the treatment. This is especially true in patients with real strengths (Global Assessment of Functioning Scale score of 71–100; APA, 1994).

Thus, the depth of therapy experience does not have a one-to-one relationship with breadth of therapy goals, at least from an outcome perspective. The depth of therapy experience is limited by (a) the coping styles of the patient (i.e., as defensiveness goes up, depth goes down) and (b) the capability of the patient to handle disturbing material (e.g., exploring conflicts with schizophrenia patients can be counterproductive).

Coping Styles and Depth of Treatment Experience. The coping style of the patient, in addition to the focus of difficulty, is central to treatment planning. There is no definitive method of categorizing patient coping styles. Three fundamental coping styles are internalization, repression, and externalization (Beutler & Clarkin, 1990).

Internalizing. An internalized coping style involves preferential use of defenses such as undoing, self-punishment, intellectualization, isolation of affect, and emotional overcontrol and constriction. Individuals with this coping style often present with blunted or constricted affect (low positive emotions) and with constrained interpersonal relationships (low Extraversion).

A patient who is using internalization as a coping style, however, probably has a very active inner life. This would appear on NEO-PI-R Openness, with openness to ideas and fantasy and possibly openness to aesthetics. The individual may be low on openness to feelings. This person often engages in excessive ideation to control conflicted or painful feelings. People using internalization present with symptoms; they are aware of an intrapsychic conflict, which causes anxiety and depression that they might intellectualize in therapy. Thus, some elevation on the Neuroticism score is to be expected. But the scores on Openness, especially relatively high scores on openness to ideas combined with low scores on openness to feelings and low Extraversion, might identify their propensity to internalization.

Externalizing. In contrast to internalizers, externalizers present with defensive acting out and projection. They limit and curtail anxiety by assigning responsibility for their behavior onto external sources and discharge anxiety by action rather than thought. Interpersonally, these individuals move against others and act against the environment. They keep intense feelings at a distance. Their symptoms are ego syntonic.

Those who use externalization would be high on Extraversion, low on Neuroticism, and low on Conscientiousness. These individuals do not internalize or experience much psychological discomfort. Hostility may be their one spike within the domain of Neuroticism. They do not express much anxiety or depression. Impulsivity may be slightly elevated, indicating that they act rather than reflect (although this may also be evident by their low scores on Conscientiousness). Again, as they externalize blame, they may indicate some elevations on hostility. It is unlikely that they would be high scorers on Openness because they do not reflect much or consider widely diverse opinions. They may feel free to criticize others (low Agreeableness), but as low scorers on Neuroticism, they deny any pain of their own.

Repressive. Reliance on repression and denial, such as denial of negative feelings, reaction formation, repression of the content that arouses uncomfortable experiences, negation of the meaning of negative social stimuli, and insensitivity to one's impact on others, are characteristic of a repressive coping style.

On the NEO-PI-R, such people may report a degree of intrapsychic pain on Neuroticism, but they would be particularly low on openness to ideas, emotion, and fantasy. This person does not want to think about things very much and may repress feelings and thoughts. Moreover, this person may also be very low on Neuroticism because he or she does not want to admit that anything is wrong. In summary, if the individual is low on Neuroticism and very low on Openness (especially to ideas, fantasy, and feelings), the individual may not be interested in opening up or reflecting on any psychological issues.

Their scores on Agreeableness could also be moderate to high. This kind of individual goes along with others' suggestions and directions, avoiding conflicts because they repress and deny uncomfortable feelings including anger. Such an individual joins in, does what is expected, and does not address conflict. This makes treatment difficult because there is a willingness to agree and join with the therapist in confluence with a lack of openness to thinking about one's life or experience.

Depth of Experience Addressed in the Treatment. The foci or targets for treatment intervention can be conceptualized as involving four areas of functioning on a dimension of levels of experience (Beutler & Clarkin, 1990): (a) behaviors of excess and insufficiency, (b) dysfunctional cognitive patterns, (c) unidentified feelings and sensory experiences, and (d) unconscious conflicts. There is a progression in this conceptualization from behaviors to cognitions to feelings and motivations, recognized and unrecognized. Whereas most treatments usually touch on all these areas either inadvertently or by design, emphasis on one or more areas of experience can vary considerably depending on the patient and his or her concerns and the therapist's orientation and focus of treatment intervention.

It is important to match the dominant coping style of the patient with the depth of experience addressed by the treatment procedures. Most specifically, patients who are prone to externalize their distress are probably best matched with behaviorally oriented therapies targeted to external behavior rather than those that focus on unconscious processes. The externalizing patient resists nondirective, exploratory psychotherapy. If the externalizing individual comes for therapy, it may be because of some circumscribed complaint or because a significant other (spouse or boss) insists on behavioral change. Thus, in treatment, one would want to work with strict contingencies for changes in behavior. In extreme cases, where the patient is very low on Neuroticism (lacking much internal motivation for change) but is high on Extraversion and Agreeableness, the therapist might work at a hierarchy of concrete rewards that have intrinsic meaning to the patient.

The externalizing patient's social acting out and avoidance of responsibility would be reflected in a low score on Conscientiousness. The lower the patient's score on Conscientiousness, the more difficult the therapist's task. This is especially true if the patient is relatively high on Extraversion and average on Agreeableness; the patient presents as a "hail fellow, well met" who may tend to give superficial and affable agreement in sessions, without having the slightest intention of following through in the treatment contract. Likewise, patients who internalize should be matched with therapies that address the level of their unrecognized–unconscious motives and fears.

Reactance Level and Degree of Therapy Directiveness. Reactance is defined as the individual's likelihood of resisting threatened loss of interpersonal control (Beutler & Clarkin, 1990). The high reactance person seeks direction from within rather than from outside resources for solutions or answers. High reactivity would be reflected on the NEO-PI-R by moderate to high levels of openness to ideas and fantasy. It might also be reflected in average to high Conscientiousness because the high reactance individual feels in control and takes responsibility for outcomes. The high reactance person is probably seen as moderate to low on Agreeableness. This individual would not want other people to make decisions for them. However, evidence of inner resources would be reflected in openness to ideas. One might think of the high reactance person as fairly introverted, scoring low on Extraversion. By contrast, the low reactance person accepts and possibly gravitates to direction from other people, as reflected in higher scores on Agreeableness and Extraversion, and viewed as real joiners who like to be a part of groups. He or she prefers to be a part of groups, a member of cooperative efforts. Consensus with others is valued. However, the individual who is low in reactance might not have a particular openness to ideas or be high in openness to fantasy life and one's internal world. There might be openness to action, such as one would undertake in a cognitive-behavior treatment (Linehan, 1989). In summary, high reactance can reflect a variety of personality profiles; one value of the FFM is providing a means by which to obtain a more specific and differentiated understanding of the patient than is provided by a simple reference to being high in reactance.

The individual high on Extraversion, Agreeableness, and openness to ideas probably would be an ideal candidate for both individual and group cognitive-behavioral treatment (Miller, 1991). High

reactance and low reactance have not only to do with the modality of the treatment but whether it is supportive or exploratory. The NEO-PI-R might be used to make decisions about group versus individual psychotherapy. The high reactance person would be screened away from those treatments where there is direct advice giving. The NEO-PI-R would also be helpful in the selection of group members. It might be helpful in the matching together of group members in one particular way, so that there would be a balance of Extraversion–introversion, Agreeableness, and reactance levels. The more introverted (low Extraversion) and the less agreeable (low Agreeableness) the individual, the more the therapist would want to be extremely careful about forming a treatment alliance. Patients who are quite introverted may shy away if confronted with too much warmth or friendliness from the therapist.

Clinical Vignette of a High-Reactance Patient. A 32-year-old single, male tax attorney, Tony, appeared for treatment complaining of anxiety. Constant irritability and hostility were manifested in interpersonal relations. In the initial evaluation, he reported just recently realizing he had many psychological difficulties, as exemplified by his anger and explosive temper on the job, especially toward women. He was dating a young woman and felt anxious about how the relationship was proceeding. The woman, he feared, might be getting serious about him. The clinical diagnosis was depression in the context of PDNOS (features of paranoid and self-defeating personality disorder traits). He was given the NEO-PI as part of an evaluation. He obtained clinically interpretable (above $T = 65$) elevations on Neuroticism (including the hostility and vulnerability facets) and a very low score on Agreeableness. Extraversion was in the average range, and Conscientiousness was in the high average range. At the macro level of treatment planning, it was decided to recommend individual therapy for the patient, with treatment duration undetermined at the initiation of treatment.

The patient's current difficulties stemmed from a long history of troubled relationships with a contradictory mother and a brutal stepfather. This man carried a history of conflict, with a marked tendency to see others as hostile, stupid, and difficult to deal with. Theoretically, this patient needed a treatment that had a breadth of treatment goals including conflict resolution.

This man's rigid defenses, including projection, rationalization, splitting, and devaluation, were aligned in such a way as to make treatment slow and to limit the depth of experience available to the treatment. Even though conflict stemming from the past seemed to control his present behavior, the patient was not inclined to even discuss the past. At times, he could relate present fear of women to the hatred of his mother, but in general, he wanted to focus on his present behavior. He asked the therapist for key phrases he could use to control his impulsive, angry responses to clients. He talked of himself as "damaged," with little hope of change through therapy, but sought for a change in his environment. Clearly, the depth of experience and breadth of treatment goals were limited by the patient's coping style.

This patient was highly reactant, as evidenced by his high scores on the hostility and vulnerability facets of Neuroticism, and his high Conscientiousness and low Agreeableness scores, as measured by the NEO-PI. Even though he recognized his need for help, he feared any loss of control and did not want to place himself in the hands of another. Aware of this dilemma, the therapist let the patient guide the discussion for the most part. Only tentatively did the therapist suggest connections (e.g., his intense reaction to a minor incident in the present as related to his past). Only when the patient directly asked for advice and suggestions did the therapist provide them.

Feedback concerning his NEO-PI profile was introduced early in the treatment to focus the intervention, educate the patient about his difficulties, and anticipate possible treatment alliance snags (Harkness & Lilienfeld, 1997). The patient was convinced that he was "crazy," so this test with its norms was reassuring. The particular combination of high vulnerability and hostility was reviewed carefully with the patient, and a focus of treatment was on how his feelings of vulnerability (related to his past including harsh treatment by a stepfather and neglect from mother) in current interpersonal relations led repetitively to hostile attack on the patient's part.

The treatment provided to the patient was similar to interpersonal psychotherapy for depression. It focused on his symptoms of anger and depression and their relationship to interpersonal conflict at work and in his intimate relationships. There were several episodes of brief treatment because the patient saw the need for therapy only under acute distress.

ASSESSMENT

A practical question concerns the choice of procedures to use in the initial assessment of patients to foster differential treatment plans. The clinical interview is the most direct method in assessing the chief complaint, diagnosis, information concerning explicit behavioral dysfunctions, and environmental stressors and supports. The NEO-PI-R, inexpensive in clinician time, is useful in providing information on patient personality variables relevant to treatment selection as well as related diagnostic and problem area information. The NEO-PI-R alone, however, cannot inform the clinician totally on the foci for intervention. Acute distress—both acute symptomatic distress (Axis I disorders) and environmental stressors (marital disputes, loss of job, etc.)—is not assessed by the NEO-PI-R. Rather, the NEO-PI-R provides a background to the figure created by the current distress. This framework of the individual's more enduring orientation and proclivities informs the clinician to the focus of intervention but does not totally predict or pinpoint it.

We propose that the NEO-PI-R, in combination with the standard clinical evaluation interview, can be of great assistance in making decisions in the therapeutic selection process. The NEO-PI-R provides vital information on patient dimensions that are central for treatment planning. We also suggest that a small battery of screening tests, as used in one of our clinical cases (the case of Christine), might be of assistance in furthering the treatment assignment task. A screening battery that gathers data on current functioning (SAS-SR), symptom distress (SCL-90, BDI) and personality traits (NEO-PI-R) provides a three-pronged approach for treatment planning. High functioning, moderate to low symptom distress, and interpersonal difficulties bodes well for brief individual therapy. Poor functioning, high symptom distress, and difficulties in relating indicate a more symptom-focused, supportive, longer term intervention.

It remains to be seen what will be the most frequent and characteristic profiles of individuals who apply for intervention. The manner in which the profiles relate to *DSM-IV* diagnoses provide the clinician with two coordinates in an attempt to locate the individual in treatment planning space. The NEO-PI-R provides data on the typical personality traits, and the *DSM-IV* provides behavioral and symptomatic information in terms of the diagnostic categories.

CLINICAL ILLUSTRATIONS

To amplify several major themes of this chapter, we use three clinical examples with background data on the NEO-PI or the NEO-PI-R. All three of our patients carried a primary diagnosis of BDL. The first patient was treated by a clinician with a predominately psychodynamic orientation (Kernberg, 1984; Waldinger, 1987), the latter two patients were treated by clinicians using dialectical behavior therapy (Linehan, 1993). As with other Axis II disorders, BDL describes a group of patients who are often very heterogeneous, not only with respect to the particular diagnostic criteria that are prominent but also with respect to other important traits not included within the *DSM-IV* criteria set. Diagnosing each of these patients with BDL was not specific or individualized enough to adequately describe their personality strengths nor their personality deficits and liabilities. Although each of these three patients met the *DSM-III-R* and *DSM-IV* criteria for BDL, they differed in a number of clinically significant ways. We think that the heterogeneity of people with the broad diagnostic category of BDL are evaluated most effectively for treatment planning using · the NEO-PI-R.

We collected NEO-PI data on carefully diagnosed female BDL patients with other comorbid Axis II conditions seen at Cornell University Medical Center (Ithaca, NY; Clarkin, Hull, Cantor, & Sanderson, 1993). These individuals presented with impulsive acting out, usually involving food, sex, and drugs and more direct suicidal behavior. The mean

NEO-PI profiles across these 64 female BDL patients is presented in Figure 21.1. In the spirit of this chapter, we are less interested in whether borderline patients have profiles that are distinct from other Axis II groups than in how the profiles, in conjunction with the Axis II diagnosis, can be helpful for treatment planning.

As expected (see also Widiger et al., chapter 6, this volume), BDL patients as a group are extremely high on Neuroticism. All facets of Neuroticism—Anxiety, Depression, Vulnerability, Self-consciousness, and Impulsiveness, especially—are high in the BDL group. The BDL patients are also characterized by extremely low Conscientiousness (aimless lack of goal direction, a lax and negligent orientation) and low Agreeableness (cynical, suspicious, uncooperative, vengeful, irritable, manipulative). Major treatment foci would be the elevated levels of Neuroticism and the uncooperative, manipulative interpersonal behavior. However, it is important to emphasize that there is substantial heterogeneity within the borderline diagnostic category with respect to personality traits that have an important impact on treatment responsivity. Within these general parameters, the individual patient's treatment should be tailored according to specific dimensions and severity as indicated by his or her specific NEO-PI-R profile.

NEO-PI for Ruth, a 26-Year-Old Borderline Patient

Consider, for example, treatment planning for a 26-year-old single woman, Ruth, who met criteria for Axis II BDL. Ruth had had numerous hospitalizations for suicidal behavior, alcohol abuse, eating dyscontrol, and mood lability; several times she received the Axis I diagnosis of major depression. She was a social worker by training and had worked for periods between hospitalizations. However, in many respects, she was not a typical borderline patient; this became evident in her NEO-PI profile.

During the course of outpatient individual treatment, Ruth completed the NEO-PI (the broken line on Figure 21.1). She was much lower on Neuroticism than other borderline patients. In terms of facet scores of the Neuroticism domain, she was impulsive but less anxious, hostile, depressed, and vulner-

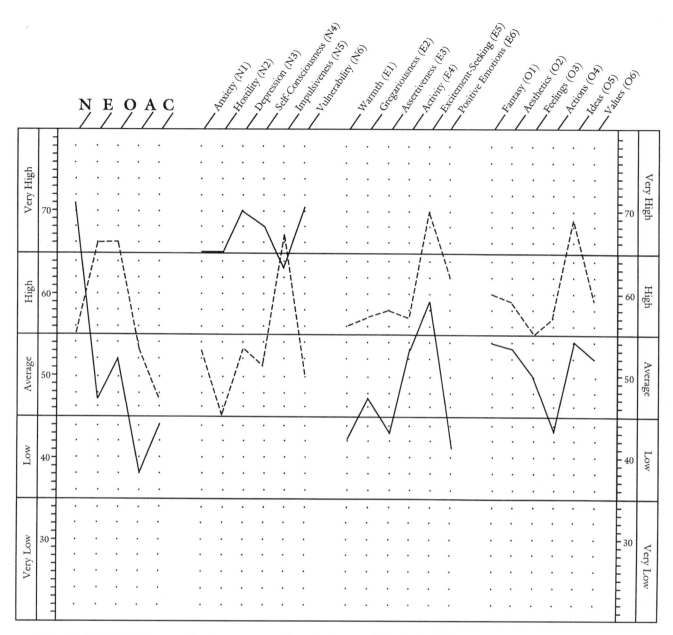

FIGURE 21.1. NEO Personality Inventory profiles of a group of female borderline personality disorder (BDL) patients (solid line; *n* = 64) and Ruth, a 26-year-old female BDL patient (broken line). From the *NEO Personality Inventory,* by Paul T. Costa, Jr., and Robert R. McCrae, Copyright 1978, 1985, 1989, 1992 by PAR, Inc. Reproduced by special permission of the publisher, Psychological Assessment Resources, Inc., 16204 North Florida Avenue, Lutz, FL 33549. Further reproduction is prohibited without permission of PAR, Inc.

able, nor was she was especially antagonistic (although we suspect that she might have obtained low scores on particular facets of Agreeableness if the NEO-PI-R had been available at that time). She did at times suffer from mood disorders, but she was not characteristically anxious or depressed. Her borderline pathology was confined largely to her im-

pulse dyscontrol. She also showed relative strengths on the Extraversion, Openness, Agreeableness, and Conscientiousness scales. Using normative data from this test, these scaled scores would indicate that she would approach psychotherapy with enthusiasm and approach the therapist with openness and cooperation (Miller, 1991; Waldinger, 1987; Waldinger &

Gunderson, 1987). She would be conscientious in carrying out the tasks of the treatment in a serious way. It is clinical wisdom that BDL patients with antisocial characteristics (low Conscientiousness) have poor treatment prognosis (Kernberg, 1984; Kernberg, Selzer, Koenigsberg, Carr, & Applebaum, 1989; Robins, 1986). Ruth's relatively high levels of Conscientiousness and Agreeableness (average but high compared with the other BDL patients) bode well for a therapeutic involvement that was responsible and not corrupted by manipulation or deceit.

Ruth tended toward externalization and acting out. On the NEO-PI, this was manifested on the Extroversion domain scale and the Excitement-seeking facet scale. However, this extraverted orientation was moderated by her Openness. The reactance level of Ruth seemed relatively low, manifested on the NEO-PI by high Agreeableness and high warmth. It appeared that she might enter into a productive therapeutic relationship in which she could accept guidance from another. At first, she mistrusted the therapist but quickly overcame her doubts and uncertainty.

Across 1½ years of individual psychodynamic psychotherapy, she responded remarkably well, and treatment was ended by mutual agreement. Of the 31 borderline patients that we have followed in outpatient psychodynamic treatment, she had shown one of the most successful responses (Clarkin et al., 1992). All of the behavioral impulsivity and self-destructive behavior that she had shown previously (eating binges, alcohol abuse, sexual promiscuity, and suicidal behavior) ceased for over 1 year. She also became engaged in full-time productive work. Equally important, she had a new male friend who, contrary to former mates, was not abusive and destructive toward her. Her enthusiasm in treatment and her ability to work in and out of sessions all seem correlated with her NEO-PI profile, which suggested substantially more optimism regarding her treatment success than had been suggested by her original BDL diagnosis. Her responsivity to treatment and her disposition to become successfully involved in a satisfying relationship and productively employed were not suggested by her BDL diagnosis but were suggested by her level of Conscientiousness and Agreeableness on her NEO-PI profile.

NEO-PI-R for Marta, a 37-Year-Old Borderline Patient

Marta was a 37-year-old married, Hispanic woman, with 3 children and a bachelor's degree in nursing. She had been on psychiatric disability from her job at an area hospital for the past 2 years. Raised in the Catholic church, Marta felt very guilty about her reliance on public benefits. Her husband was a moderately successful businessman in a family-owned company. He worked more than 70 hours a week and his schedule, as well as his history of bipolar disorder Type II, was a significant source of anxiety and anger for Marta.

Marta had done very well in school, obtaining average to high grades in her classes, but she had often gotten into trouble for oppositional, rebellious, and defiant acts. She was at times a mystery to her teachers because she appeared to be a bright child who worked very hard on her assignments but would at times explode in a mean-spirited, hostile anger. She never received any major disciplinary sanctions at school, other than repeated scoldings, staying after school, letters home to the parents, and other relatively minor sanctions. However, her closest friends were children who did poorly in school and got into substantial disciplinary trouble. Marta denied using drugs or engaging in risky sexual behaviors during adolescence but acknowledged "taking a few chances now and then."

Marta was the second child and first daughter of a family with 8 children, wherein there was severe corporal punishment for most misdeeds. Whenever her parents discovered that she had been disciplined at school, she was severely disciplined at home, which would at times reach the level of bruises, wounds, and scars, along with various atonements for the apparent shame that they felt she should feel in the eyes of her church. When she reached the age of 14, Marta was repeatedly sexually abused by a friend of the family—a fact rarely acknowledged by her mother and treated largely as a shameful secret by her father and her other siblings. Marta was in fact viewed as the troublemaker by her siblings and father, not for the accusations of sexual abuse but for other behaviors and problems that arose prior to and after the episodes of abuse. She was as times referred to as the "lost one" by her father, who apparently suggested to her younger siblings that they not follow Marta's path. Marta felt that she was often singled out for blame and punishment primarily to warn or to even scare the younger children into submission. As the second oldest child, she had substantial household responsibilities, including babysitting and child care that she took quite seriously. However, she acknowledged that she did often do things that warranted punishment or rebuke by her parents, particularly for staying out late, smoking, or having a "bad attitude." She stated that she would often get into verbal arguments with her father, which were often resolved by her being slapped and sent to her room. She described having severely mixed feelings toward her mother. She felt very guilty for "letting her down" because she would at times find her mother crying or praying for her "lost soul." However, she would also feel angry and bitter toward her mother for passively standing by whenever she was wrongfully or excessively punished by her father.

Marta did not receive any formal clinical treatment during her childhood but was often within treatment after she left home. She had been in psychotherapy and treated with various psychotropic medications since her early 20s. She had been hospitalized seven times for suicide attempts and major depression prior to her admission into a dialectical behavior therapy (DBT) treatment program (Linehan, 1993). Her most serious attempt was at age 29, when she took a near lethal overdose and was only discovered accidentally when her husband returned home uncharacteristically early from work. She stated that she often wanted to just die to end a constant pain, anger, fearfulness, and emptiness that pervaded her life. Marta had received a variety of diagnoses throughout her clinical history, primarily posttraumatic stress disorder (delayed onset), major depressive disorder (recurrent, severe without psychotic features), and generalized anxiety disorder, along with BDL. At times, she reported symptoms of obsessive–compulsive anxiety disorder, but it was unclear whether she ever met enough criteria for this diagnosis. She denied any history of clinically significant alcohol or substance abuse.

After entry to the hospital, Marta completed the NEO-PI-R (see Figure 21.2). The profile was intriguing for a number of reasons. On the one hand, she revealed many of the traits often seen in patients with BDL. She obtained very high scores on all but one of the facets of Neuroticism, namely, angry hostility, self-consciousness, depression, anxiety, and vulnerability (she was "only" high for level of impulsivity); these traits would often compel her to seek treatment but were rarely helped by the treatment. She also obtained average low scores on the two facets of Agreeableness that are often seen in patients with BDL (compliance and straightforwardness), along with severe feelings of mistrust and suspicion (low trust). However, inconsistent with these expressions of antagonism were elevations on the Agreeableness facets of modesty and altruism. Marta was often defiant, oppositional, and angry, particularly toward people in authority, but she was also very self-sacrificial, self-denying, and self-deprecating. She would often get into verbal fights and arguments, but these arguments were also coupled with sincere feelings of warmth and concern toward others.

Equally informative were her elevations on the facets of Conscientiousness. Marta was very high with respect to achievement striving. It could be said that she had achieved little in her life but, given her childhood experiences, upbringing, inadequate peer support, and many psychiatric problems, perhaps one should say that she had achieved a great deal (e.g., bachelor's degree, steady employment). In any case, she clearly did aspire to be successful and competent in all that she did. She described herself as being low on competence not because she did not value being competent but because she considered herself to be incompetent. She was also highly elevated on the facets of dutifulness, self-discipline, and deliberation. Marta took her responsibilities seriously, even sacrificing and denying pleasures to achieve her goals (perhaps at times primarily to please others). Elevations on facets of Conscientiousness are not usually seen in patients with a BDL, but they bode well for a potential responsivity to the rigors and demands of the DBT program.

Complicating treatment were her average to low scores on facets of Openness. Marta had a strong, committed, and unwavering perspective on many matters of life, including herself. She was very self-critical in a self-deprecatory, depressive way but was

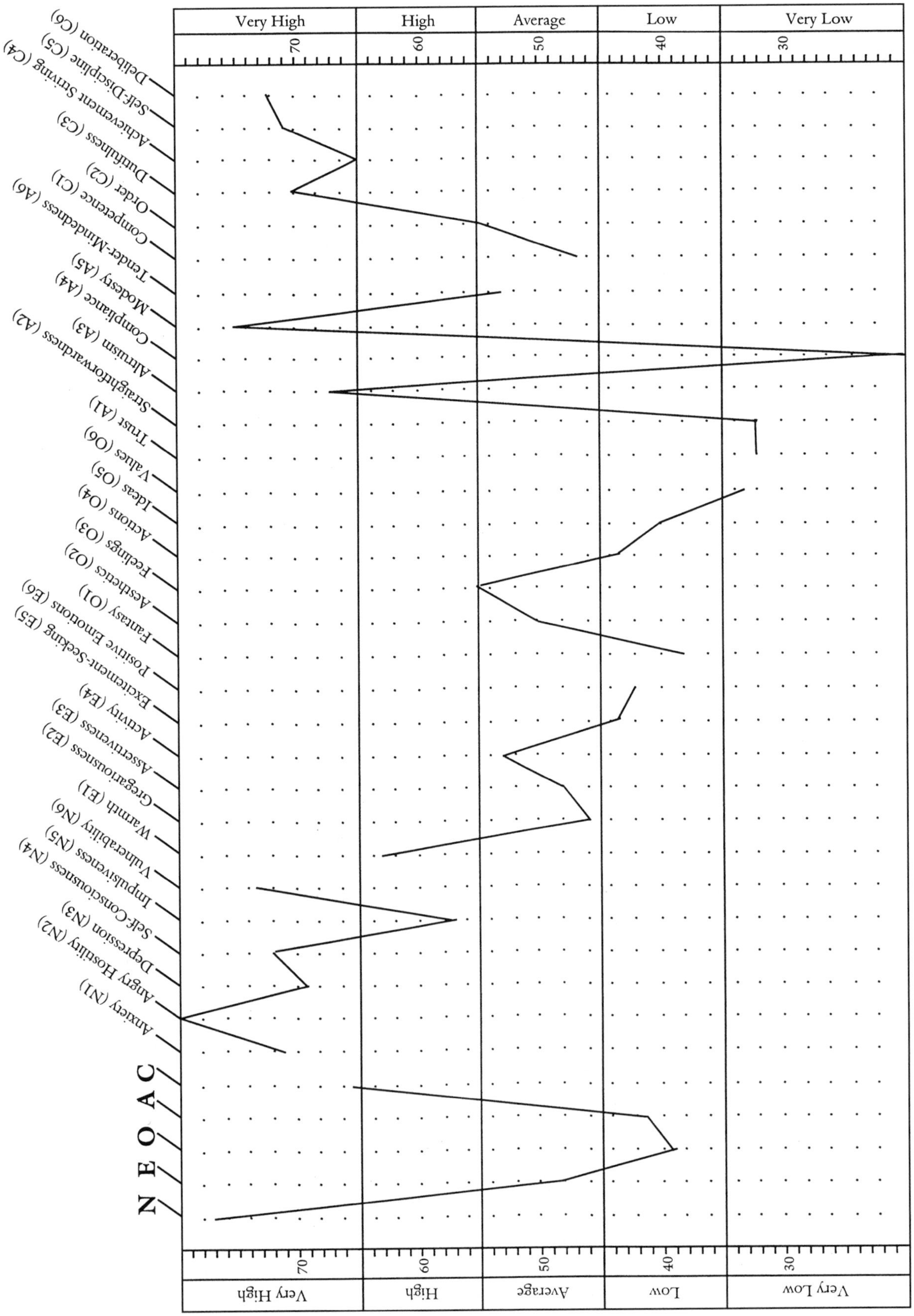

FIGURE 21.2. Revised NEO Personality Inventory profile of Marta, a 37-year-old borderline personality disorder patient. From the *NEO Personality Inventory*, by Paul T. Costa, Jr., and Robert R. McCrae, Copyright 1978, 1985, 1989, 1992 by PAR, Inc. Reproduced by special permission of the publisher, Psychological Assessment Resources, Inc., 16204 North Florida Avenue, Lutz, FL 33549. Further reproduction is prohibited without permission of PAR, Inc.

nevertheless highly resistant to questioning this self-criticism. She had a strong sense of religion, values, and moral expectations. However, she was open and sensitive to how she felt about things and did recognize the harmful and problematic nature of her feelings of guilt, suffering, and depression. She was very open to questioning and addressing her feelings of anger; in time, she became more open to questioning her feelings of guilt and depression.

Marta was transferred from the inpatient hospital to the partial hospital because she continued to present with a high and chronic risk of suicide. On the surface, she was easily engaged in the partial hospital DBT program. She attended all scheduled sessions, groups, and activities. Furthermore, Marta volunteered for extra responsibilities, such as being a member of the patient government. Unlike most of the other clients, she often stayed late to help clean the public areas used by staff and clients for breakfast and lunch. However, Marta strongly disliked a number of the other clients in the program, particularly those who had different cultural and religious backgrounds from her own, which is consistent with her low openness to values that predisposes her to being relatively intolerant of those who are different from her. Also she did not like aspects of the treatment that in any way challenged her rigidly held ideas about right and wrong. Marta's therapists liked working with Marta initially, but then they reported feeling increasingly frustrated over her defiance, objections, and apparent lack of change. Marta seemed unmoveable in her conviction that she was "weak, bad, and a burden" and undeserving of the sympathy and efforts of the treatment team. She viewed her problems as moral in origin, despite the efforts of the team to educate her about the biological and social aspects of her problems.

Nevertheless, Marta took well to the social skills group, where she excelled in the completion of assignments and tasks that increased her ability to control her feelings of anger, to understand more accurately what others were really saying to her, and to no longer assume or expect that others were being critical of or abusive toward her. Marta's strengths were tapped by the group leader by giving her more assignments in which she could experience greater success and accomplishments. She eventually became almost a mentor to the younger patients and felt it was her responsibility to better herself if she was to be a successful "mentor" to them. She offered them rides home, lent them money, allowed them to "crash" at her house when they were in trouble, and defended them to the group leader when they had broken the rules. Her involvement in their problems was helpful to her, although it would at times become excessive. To help her rebalance her involvement with other patients, the group leader established specific limits and goals for each relationship.

Marta's individual therapist eventually abandoned her effort to confront or challenge Marta's strong moral attitudes, focusing instead on an effort to get Marta to forgive those who had abused, wronged, or mistreated her (Sanderson & Linehan, 1999). Marta found this approach to be more acceptable to her religious and spiritual values, and she worked hard at exploring the sources and roots for her feelings of anger and bitterness. Progress was slow, due largely to her continued rigidity in her view of others and herself, but enough progress did occur such that she established substantially better control of her feelings of anger and depression. She did not leave treatment feeling any peace of mind, but she did leave feeling more confident in her potential ability to eventually obtain it.

NEO-PI-R for Dayna, a 20-Year-Old Borderline Patient

Dayna was a 20-year-old White woman, born in Germany, who had been living with her father and three sisters in the United States since leaving her mother at age 13. According to Dayna, parental conflict and spousal abuse (on both parents' parts) led to the disintegration of the marriage. She had few distinct memories of the early fights but did recall witnessing screaming tirades, vicious accusations, and physical assaults. Both Dayna's parents completed a university in Germany, but their careers were compromised by their mutually severe alcohol dependence. Her mother's alcohol dependence was a major reason that the children went with their father, although Dayna also wondered whether her father may have forced the decision of separation by the move to the United States. Dayna reported that she had always felt closer to her father than to her mother, due in part to her mother's unavailability and withdrawal, particularly when she was intoxicated. Nevertheless, Dayna said that she missed her mother "all the time" and always wanted "to get close to her again." Her mother, however, had rarely made any effort to contact Dayna or the other children and had shown no apparent interest in spending more time with them.

Dayna was remarkably fluent in both German and English, without a trace of an accent, and most of her friends were unaware that she had spent any time, let alone grew up, in another country. Dayna identified herself as bisexual since puberty, with most of her sexual relationships having been with girls or women. Dayna was drinking alcohol prior to the age of 10 when still living in Germany and used alcohol and marijuana heavily with her childhood and adolescent friends in the United States. She also described having intensive and rapid mood shifts and would at times superficially cut herself during periods of high stress. She stated that she often felt empty and dysphoric and would at times seriously ponder killing herself to "get out of all this pain." She stated that she was never upset about anything in particular but just felt that life itself was "an empty waste of time." She was not a severe problem at school, managing to maintain a B– average. On her report cards, her teachers made comments like "easy to have in class," "not working up to her potential," "well liked," and "at times rebellious, sarcastic, and angry." Dayna reported having a number of close friends who, like her, were seen as "strange," "freaks," or "outcasts" by the more socially mainstream and popular teenagers in her school. However, Dayna and her friends were active in a number of art and political clubs. Dayna was recognized in the school for her talent in photography and for a comic strip she drew for the school's alternative newspaper. In contrast to Marta, Dayna showed a high openness to values, which was expressed in terms of her artistic and unconventional behaviors (e.g., liberal political clubs).

Since the age of 16, Dayna held a variety of minimum wage jobs, such as waiting tables or working as a clerk in a video rental store. She reported having few difficulties with these jobs and chose them largely because they demanded little so she could

get away with doing even less. She continued to live with her father and two of her sisters in rural Connecticut after she graduated from high school and attended college part time. Dayna's two older sisters drank moderately as adolescents and adults but apparently not to the extent that it interfered with their functioning; both were married and steadily employed. Dayna's younger sister objected to and abstained entirely from alcohol use and was an active member of a conservative Christian church. Dayna stated that she got along well with her older sisters but could not tolerate her younger sister's conservatism.

Dayna's college attendance was sporadic and largely unsuccessful, making little progress toward ever obtaining a degree. She first attempted to attend a large university, having obtained good aptitude scores on the entrance examinations. However, she drank heavily, skipped classes, failed to complete most of her assignments, and left after the first semester. She was seen briefly by a counselor at the college who recommended psychotherapy and a trial of medication, but Dayna refused the recommendations, stating that she could solve her problems by herself. Dayna next attended a smaller college, designed for students interested in liberal arts. She felt like she fit in better with these students but continued to feel depressed, abuse alcohol, and at times cut herself superficially "to relieve stress." After one particular drinking binge, she passed out in her dorm room, hit her head on her desk, and needed three stitches to close the gash in her forehead. At this point, a college counselor insisted that she see a psychologist in the community as a condition of remaining in school. Dayna was diagnosed by this counselor with alcohol abuse, major depression (recurrent, moderate, without psychotic features) and BDL. She attended only three sessions of treatment.

Dayna, however, was hospitalized the following year (at age 20) after an attempted overdose of over-the-counter medications, coupled with alcohol. She was treated for 6 days on a general, acute psychiatric inpatient unit and was referred for follow-up outpatient psychotherapy. Her father insisted she enter this treatment, and he threatened to cut off all financial support if she failed to comply. As part of the standard assessment battery provided at the outpatient clinic, Dayna completed the NEO-PI-R. Dayna did meet the *DSM-IV* diagnostic criteria for BDL and evidenced most of the traits seen in patients with this disorder. Her NEO-PI-R profile is provided in Figure 21.3.

Dayna obtained substantial elevations on all but one of the facets of Neuroticism. Dayna displayed the very high depression, anxiety, impulsivity, angry hostility, and vulnerability seen in patients with a BDL. However, she denied substantial feelings of self-consciousness (which may not in fact be a cardinal trait of this disorder). Dayna felt highly vulnerable, insecure, and unstable, not so much with respect to the perceptions or feelings of others. She indicated that she often cared little for how others felt about her and would at times show behavior that both evoked (evocative) and provoked (provocative) the perceiver. Dayna was not as gregarious or interpersonally involved as our other DBT patients, and we were concerned about her motivation (or ability) to make much use of the group therapy and social skills component of the DBT program. However, her high level on warmth did suggest potential for establishing a strong rapport with her individual DBT counselor.

Dayna also obtained low scores on most of the facets of Conscientiousness. We are not surprised by the low scores in some of the facets of Conscientiousness for our borderline patients, particularly the facets of self-discipline and achievement striving. Dayna's scores, however, were so consistently low on most of them that we also expected an added difficulty in sticking with the demanding treatment regimen. On the more positive side were Dayna's elevations on facets of Openness. Dayna enjoyed exploring alternative belief systems and would perhaps be motivated or at least willing to explore and question her past and current perceptions, beliefs, and behaviors. Her high Openness scores led to good test scores despite her poor study habits and grades.

Dayna was placed by the clinic with a DBT psychologist experienced in treating depression and alcohol abuse in the context of BDL. The therapist recommended that Dayna attend Alcoholics Anonymous (AA) meetings, individual psychotherapy once a week, and DBT skills training group once a week and start taking antidepressant medication. Dayna agreed to the latter three conditions of treatment but refused AA after twice attending a local chapter. She said that she "hated" the AA atmosphere and felt that she was "way too young" to be at the meetings. The therapist agreed to let Dayna avoid this component of her treatment, at least temporarily, given Dayna's propensity to want to control her treatment. Instead, she agreed that Dayna would monitor her use of alcohol on a daily diary card and to commit to reducing and eliminating her use of alcohol during the first year of treatment. Dayna agreed that if she could not reduce her use of alcohol during the first 6 months of treatment or if she had another episode of passing out, she would attend AA. She also agreed not to drive while intoxicated.

During the first 2 months of treatment, Dayna's compliance was poor. She nearly quit several times, and she failed to take her medications as prescribed. When she attended groups, she sat on the periphery, refusing to join in. She stated she did not trust the therapist but revealed within individual therapy that she was afraid she would get too close to the therapist and would eventually be abandoned, just as her mother had abandoned her. Dayna missed a number of the group sessions but found the explorations of her past and current problems within the individual therapy sessions to be very helpful. These sessions focused in particular on her feelings of mistrust and suspiciousness. When Dayna was gently confronted about her poor attendance and told she could not continue in the program unless it improved, she began to attend group regularly and her use of alcohol also began to decline. She slowly developed stronger feelings of trust toward the other group members and to the group leader. She was particularly responsive to their indications that her rebelliousness and outcast demeanor were not being met with criticism or rejection, and she appreciated learning about their life histories and comparable struggles.

Treatment goals were eventually adjusted to include better performance at college, and she established herself as a solid student, although initially it required very close monitoring of her class attendance and homework assignments by the group staff and other group members. The skills training sessions were instrumental in helping her approach

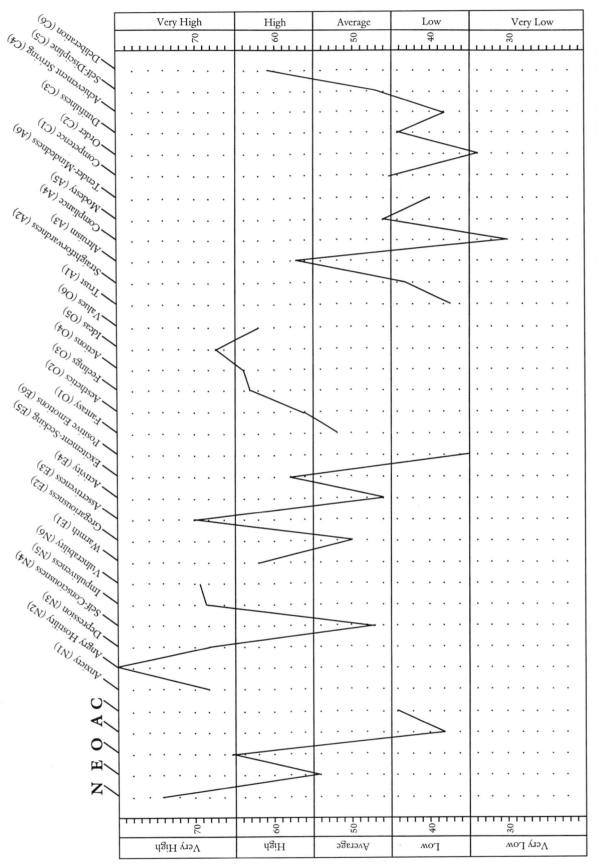

FIGURE 21.3. Revised NEO Personality Inventory profile of Dayna, a 20-year-old borderline personality disorder patient. From the *NEO Personality Inventory*, by Paul T. Costa, Jr., and Robert R. McCrae, Copyright 1978, 1985, 1989, 1992 by PAR, Inc. Reproduced by special permission of the publisher, Psychological Assessment Resources, Inc., 16204 North Florida Avenue, Lutz, FL 33549. Further reproduction is prohibited without permission of PAR, Inc.

others more effectively. She met more and more students like herself—individuals who had struggled with psychiatric problems but who now were sober and making good grades. After 14 months of therapy, Dayna began her second year of college with a B+ average, reduced her use of alcohol significantly, and joined a number of school organizations that fit her values and interests. She was not "mainstream" and appeared rebellious in her dress and jewelry, but she was functioning well and was committed to improving her life. She described her relationship with her treatment team as "the best thing that had ever happened to me."

References

American Psychiatric Association. (1980). *Diagnostic and statistical manual of mental disorders* (3rd ed.). Washington, DC: American Psychiatric Association Press.

American Psychiatric Association. (1989). *Treatments of psychiatric disorders: A task force report of the American Psychiatric Association.* Washington, DC: American Psychiatric Association.

American Psychiatric Association. (1994). *Diagnostic and statistical manual of mental disorders* (4th ed.). Washington, DC: American Psychiatric Association.

Beck, A. T., & Emery, G. (1985). *Anxiety disorders and phobias: A cognitive perspective.* New York: Basic Books.

Beck, A. T., Rush, A. J., Shaw, B. F., & Emery, G. (1979). *Cognitive therapy of depression.* New York: Guilford Press.

Beutler, L. E., & Clarkin, J. F. (1990). *Systematic treatment selection: Toward targeted therapeutic interventions.* New York: Brunner/Mazel.

Beutler, L. E., & Clarkin, J. F. (1991). Future research directions. In L. E. Beutler & M. Crago (Eds.), *Psychotherapy research: An international review of programmatic studies* (pp. 329–334). Washington, DC: American Psychological Association.

Blatt, S. J., Quinlan, D. M., Pilkonis, P. A., & Shea, M. T. (1995). Impact of perfectionism and need for approval on the brief treatment of depression: The National Institute of Mental Health Treatment of Depression Collaborative Research Program revisited. *Journal of Consulting and Clinical Psychology, 63,* 125–132.

Blatt, S. J., Zuroff, D. C., Quinlan, D. M., & Pilkonis, P. A. (1996). Interpersonal factors in brief treatment of depression: Further analyses of the National Institute of Mental Health Treatment of Depression Collaborative Research Program. *Journal of Consulting and Clinical Psychology, 64,* 162–171.

Clark, L. A., Livesley, W. J., & Morey, L. (1997). Personality disorder assessment: The challenge of construct validity. *Journal of Personality Disorders, 11,* 205–231.

Clarkin, J. F., & Hull, J. W. (1991). Brief therapies. In M. Hersen, A. E. Kazdin, & A. S. Bellack (Eds.), *The clinical psychology handbook* (3rd ed., pp. 780–796). Elmsford, NY: Pergamon Press.

Clarkin, J. F., Hull, J. W., Cantor, J., & Sanderson, C. (1993). Borderline personality disorder and personality traits: A comparison of SCID-II BPD and NEO-PI. *Psychological Assessment, 5,* 472–476.

Clarkin, J. F., Koenigsberg, H., Yeomans, F., Selzer, M., Kernberg, P., & Kernberg, O. (1992). Psychodynamic psychotherapy of the borderline patient. In J. F. Clarkin, E. Marziali, & H. Munroe-Blum (Eds.), *Borderline personality disorder: Clinical and empirical perspectives* (pp. 268–287). New York: Guilford.

Clarkin, J. F., Widiger, T. A., Frances, A. J., Hurt, S. W., & Gilmore, M. (1983). Prototypic typology and the borderline personality disorder. *Journal of Abnormal Psychology, 92,* 263–275.

Costa, P. T., Jr., & McCrae, R. R. (1985). *The NEO Personality Inventory manual.* Odessa, FL: Psychological Assessment Resources.

Costa, P. T., Jr., & McCrae, R. R. (1992). *Revised NEO Personality Inventory (NEO-PI-R) and NEO Five-Factor Inventory (NEO-FFI) professional manual.* Odessa, FL: Psychological Assessment Resources.

Cowdry, R. W. (1987). Psychopharmacology of borderline personality disorder: A review. *Journal of Clinical Psychiatry, 48,* 15–22.

Daldrup, R. J., Beutler, L. E., Engle, D., & Greenberg, L. S. (1988). *Focused expressive psychotherapy: Freeing the overcontrolled patient.* New York: Guilford.

Falloon, I. R. H., Boyd, J. L., & McGill, C. W. (1984). *Family care of schizophrenia.* New York: Guilford.

Frances, A., & Clarkin, J. F. (1991). No treatment as the prescription of choice. *Archives of General Psychiatry, 38,* 542–545.

Frances, A., Clarkin, J. F., & Perry, S. (1984). *Differential therapeutics in psychiatry: The art and science of treatment selection.* New York: Brunner/Mazel.

Harkness, A. R., & Lilienfeld, S. O. (1997). Individual differences science for treatment planning: Personality traits. *Psychological Assessment, 9,* 349–360.

Hollon, S. D., & Beck, A. T. (1986). Cognitive and cognitive–behavioral therapies. In S. L. Garfield & A. E. Bergin (Eds.), *Handbook of psychotherapy and behavior change* (3rd ed., pp. 443–482). New York: Wiley.

Kernberg, O. F. (1984). *Severe personality disorders: Psychotherapeutic strategies.* New Haven, CT: Yale University Press.

Kernberg, O. F., Selzer, M. A., Koenigsberg, H. W., Carr, A. C., & Applebaum, A. H. (1989). *Psychodynamic psychotherapy of borderline patients.* New York: Basic Books.

Kiesler, D. J. (1986). The 1982 interpersonal circle: An analysis of *DSM-III* personality disorders. In T. Millon & G. L. Klerman (Eds.), *Contemporary directions in psychopathology: Toward the DSM-IV* (pp. 571–597). New York: Guilford.

Klerman, G. L., Weissman, M. M., Rounsaville, B., & Chevron, E. (1984). *Interpersonal psychotherapy of depression.* New York: Basic Books.

Koss, M. P., & Butcher, J. N. (1986). Research on brief psychotherapy. In S. L. Garfield & A. E. Bergin (Eds.), *Handbook of psychotherapy and behavior change* (3rd ed., pp. 627–670). New York: Wiley.

Linehan, M. M. (1989). Cognitive and behavior therapy for borderline personality disorder. In R. E. Hales & A. J. Frances (Eds.), *American Psychiatric Association: Annual review* (Vol. 8, pp. 84–102). Washington, DC: American Psychiatric Press.

Linehan, M. M. (1993). *Cognitive–behavioral treatment of borderline personality disorder.* New York: Guilford Press.

Linehan, M. M., & Kehrer, C. A. (1993). Borderline personality disorder. In D. H. Barlow (Ed.), *Clinical handbook of psychological disorders: A step by step treatment manual* (2nd ed., pp. 396–441). New York: Guilford Press.

Linehan, M. M., Tutek, D. A., Heard, H. L., & Armstrong, H. E. (1994). Interpersonal outcome of cognitive behavioral treatment for chronically suicidal borderline patients. *American Journal of Psychiatry, 151,* 1771–1776.

Livesley, W. J. (1998). Suggestions for a framework for an empirically based classification of personality disorder. *Canadian Journal of Psychiatry, 43,* 137–147.

Luborsky, L. (1984). *Principles of psychoanalytic psychotherapy: A manual for supportive–expressive treatment.* New York: Basic Books.

Miller, T. R. (1991). The psychotherapeutic utility of the five-factor model of personality: A clinician's experience. *Journal of Personality Assessment, 57,* 415–433.

Minuchin, S., & Fishman, H. C. (1981). *Family therapy techniques.* Cambridge, MA: Harvard University Press.

Morey, L. (1988). The categorical representation of personality disorder: A cluster analysis of *DSM-III-R* personality features. *Journal of Abnormal Psychology, 97,* 314–321.

Paris, J. (1998). Psychotherapy for the personality disorders: Working with traits. *Bulletin of the Menninger Clinic, 62,* 287–297.

Perry, J. C., Banon, E., & Ianni, F. (1999). Effectiveness of psychotherapy for personality disorders. *American Journal of Psychiatry, 156,* 1312–1321.

Reich, J. H., & Vasile, R. G. (1993). Effect of personality disorders on the treatment outcome of Axis I conditions: An update. *Journal of Nervous and Mental Disease, 181,* 475–484.

Robins, L. (1986). Epidemiology of antisocial personality disorder. In R. Michels & J. Cavenar (Eds.), *Psychiatry* (Vol. 3, pp. 1–14). Philadelphia: Lippincott.

Sanderson, C. J., & Linehan, M. M. (1999). Acceptance and forgiveness. In W. Miller (Ed.), *Integrating spirituality into treatment* (pp. 199–216). Washington, DC: American Psychological Association.

Sanislow, C. A., & McGlashan, T. H. (1998). Treatment outcome of personality disorders. *Canadian Journal of Psychiatry, 43,* 237–250.

Shea, M. T., Widiger, T. A., & Klein, M. H. (1992). Comorbidity of personality disorders and depression: Implications for treatment. *Journal of Consulting and Clinical Psychology, 60,* 857–868.

Shoham-Salomon, V. (1991). Client–therapy interaction research [Special section]. *Journal of Consulting and Clinical Psychology, 59,* 203–244.

Soloff, P. H. (1987). Neuroleptic treatment in the borderline patient: Advantages and techniques. *Journal of Clinical Psychiatry, 48,* 26–35.

Strupp, H. H., & Binder, J. L. (1984). *Psychotherapy in a new key.* New York: Basic Books.

Waldinger, R. J. (1987). Intensive psychodynamic therapy with borderline patients: An overview. *American Journal of Psychiatry, 144,* 267–274.

Waldinger, R. J., & Gunderson, J. (1987). *Effective psychotherapy with borderline patients: Case stud-*

ies. Washington, DC: American Psychiatric Press.

Westen, D. (1997). Divergences between clinical and research methods for assessing personality disorders: Implications for research and the evolution of Axis II. *American Journal of Psychiatry, 154,* 895–903.

Widiger, T. A. (1993). The *DSM-III-R* categorical personality disorder diagnoses: A critique and an alternative. *Psychological Inquiry, 4,* 75–90.

Widiger, T. A., Frances, A. J., Harris, M., Jacobsberg, L. B., Fyer, M., & Manning, D. (1990). Comorbidity among Axis II disorders. In J. Oldham (Ed.), *Axis II: New perspectives on validity* (pp. 163–194). Washington, DC: American Psychiatric Press.

CHAPTER 22

USING PERSONALITY MEASUREMENTS IN CLINICAL PRACTICE

K. Roy MacKenzie

This chapter describes the use of structured instruments for assessing psychotherapy candidates. Two clinical applications are discussed: feedback procedures that help to prepare patients for psychotherapy and intervention strategies chosen on the basis of test results. One goal of this chapter is to encourage ways by which clinicians can integrate diverse theoretical approaches in a planned manner to maximize therapeutic effect. Most of the described measures are also well suited to measuring change over time, so they can also be used for clinical outcome trials or service delivery evaluation studies.

The perspective of this chapter is from experience in a general hospital outpatient setting; however, the principles apply to most clinical services. The program offers the usual spectrum of services: crisis intervention of up to 6 sessions, time-limited therapy falling into the range of 12–25 sessions, and longer term approaches lasting up to 1 year or more. The detailed assessment approach described in this chapter is used only for patients who need more than crisis intervention.

The assessment techniques are equally applicable to psychodynamic, interpersonal, and cognitive therapies. They are also suitable for patients entering either individual or group modalities. The study of outcome in randomized clinical trials indicates that the results of group therapy are equivalent to those of individual treatment that uses the same theoretical model (Budman et al., 1988; Pilkonis, Imber, Lewis, & Rubinsky, 1984; Piper, Debanne, Bienvenu, & Garant, 1984). The pressures of cost containment are likely to promote group over individual approaches in the future. As is described later, the use of more sophisticated assessment techniques has some unique advantages for patients entering group therapy.

There is a long history of the use of psychological testing in the assessment of patients for psychotherapy. However, this type of formal assessment seems to have fallen somewhat out of favor. Although no hard figures are available, it is probably safe to say that most patients who enter psychotherapy receive only a general clinical assessment, without augmentation by formal structured assessment procedures. A number of factors may be at work in clinical situations to explain this.

Clinicians tend to make global assessment decisions and often speak of their intuitive sense of understanding the nature of the patient's pathology. They resist the restrictions of formal diagnostic procedures. Indeed, most clinicians probably use categories of the third edition, revised, of the *Diagnostic and Statistical Manual of Mental Disorders* (*DSM-III-R*; American Psychiatric Association, 1987) in a nonprecise manner. There is widespread and understandable skepticism with the specific diagnostic criteria listed for each condition. Clinicians have to face situations on a daily basis in which patients do not neatly fit into a specific category, even though a clinical diagnosis is warranted on the basis of significant dysfunction. Often a patient meets the criteria for several categories simultaneously. This is particularly true in the anxiety and mood disorder areas. This diagnostic fragmentation often seems to the clinician to obscure rather than clarify the problems of the individual. A formal diagnostic decision may be useful in ruling out particular treatments but often has limited use in prescribing the optimum approach. For example, most comparative treatment studies of the depressive and anxiety disorders indicate limited differential effect among psychopharmacological, psychodynamic, and cognitive approaches (Elkin et al., 1989).

These problems with the official nomenclature are multiplied when the focus shifts to Axis II of the *DSM-III-R*. Numerous studies indicate high rates of overlap between Axis II categorical diagnoses. Although this is most evident among the conditions in a given cluster, overlap also occurs even between diagnoses from different clusters. For the clinician, this induces a degree of doubt as to the validity and usefulness of the concepts being assessed. The idea of neurotic problems is still widely used, even though the word is not officially sanctioned. This diagnostic language uses intrapsychic rather than interpersonal terminology and therefore is subject to even more complex diagnostic dilemmas. It is common to find not only divergence of opinions but also directly contradictory conclusions about the same patient. There appears to be a general trend to integrate what used to be the terrain of psychodynamic conceptualization into a broader approach of personality description. The distinction between conflict-based psychodynamic diagnostic terms and description-based personality features has become increasingly blurred.

Psychological testing has tended to be concerned primarily with formal diagnostic issues that often add only marginally to a clinical diagnostic evaluation. Such measures may be of interest to the clinician but are of limited value in providing guidance for the actual therapeutic approach. The traditional tests have usually used a variety of scales, often with esoteric names that needed to be translated into meaningful concepts for the clinician. Few clinicians are cognizant of the theoretical background from which test scales are derived. They therefore feel unprepared to interpret the results for their patients. These factors have made clinicians reluctant to use formal testing results and have often bred outright antagonism to the very idea. This may take the form of concern that the individuality of the patient, the

patient's sense of self, may be lost by applying predetermined concepts. This conveniently ignores the fact that all clinicians operate on theoretical assumptions whether they are easily described or are understood in the same manner by one's professional peers.

The results of psychological testing have been seen to be of value primarily to the professional. There has not been an emphasis on translating such information into a form that is readily understandable to the average patient. This reinforces the role of the clinician as the director of therapy, operating on the basis of privileged information. This chapter describes an approach to the use of psychological testing that actively incorporates the patient into the application of test results. It also shows how a small number of basic dimensions can be effectively used by the clinician in helping to determine therapeutic choices. This material is based on an underlying belief in the importance of active collaboration between clinician and patient in designing treatment conditions.

PERSONALITY TRAITS IN PERSPECTIVE

The concept of personality represented by the five-factor (referred to as the "Big Five") model (FFM) of personality offers one hopeful alternative to some of the problems just mentioned. To apply it, the clinician must first come to grips with the need for a major paradigm shift. The FFM approach is based on dimensions, that is, taxonomic traits that are descriptive, not etiological, in nature. Most clinicians have been trained to think of dysfunctional patterns as stemming from unfortunate early learning experiences. The psychodynamic clinician conceptualizes these as centering on conflictual issues or failure to master developmental tasks. The cognitive clinician thinks in terms of learned patterns of thinking about self and others. It is somewhat of a culture shock to consider personality as something that one simply has and must live with, like being excessively tall.

For a given personality trait, there is as much likelihood of dysfunction with too much of a given trait as with too little. That is, traits tend to have a normal distribution in the population, and pathology lies at both extremes, like blood pressure. This contrasts with usual diagnostic methods that assume if one has a diagnosis, then one is ill; if not, then one is healthy. Similarly, many of therapeutic approaches tend to assume that better function lies only in one direction. For example, it might be thought that the ability to use fantasy and dream material is more "healthy" than a more prosaic attention to pragmatic issues. Thus, a low score on openness to fantasy would be taken to mean a failure to come to grips with understanding one's inner self. Such a position ignores the dysfunctional effects of disorganization and scatter that accompanies high Openness scores. An extraverted, engaging interpersonal style might be assumed to be "better" than a quiet and reserved pattern, which might be seen as defensive and reflective of low self-esteem. However, a patient with extraverted characteristics tends to have difficulty with intimate relationships and may need stimulation so that self-destructive patterns do not emerge.

There is a danger that the clinician may experience a strong pull to select patients who meet the therapist's concept of the ideal psychotherapy candidate. This commonly means patients with evident features of Extraversion, Openness, Agreeableness, and Conscientiousness. The treatments applied are usually based on the theory or technique of the therapist's favored treatment method. Unfortunately, this results in a patient receiving that which the clinician is prepared to offer more so than what the patient really needs. The use of personality trait concepts may bring some helpful perspectives to the clinical setting (Miller, 1991).

First, the use of personality trait language encourages the clinician to be a neutral observer. The trait approach considers the individual to have a particular predisposition that goes back into earliest childhood and probably has genetic origins. It is not seen to be the result of learning experiences per se. What is of greater interest is how such characteristics have interacted with both the patient's rearing environment and current interpersonal world to produce more-or-less effective functional adaptation. The emphasis is on how the patient can learn to adapt more successfully. This can be helpful in allowing the clinician to differentiate between the long-standing style and the person underneath who

must mediate between the style and the particular circumstances. This way of conceptualizing psychopathology is not exclusive of other theoretical positions. The value of the addition of a personality style viewpoint is to encourage therapeutic efforts to manage a style and resolve a conflict.

Second, an understanding of how the patient "is" in terms of trait terminology helps the clinician to understand the individual's inner reality. Trait descriptions provide a model of how the patient is internally influenced to interact with others. This approach falls into the original meaning of phenomenological, that is, how the patient experiences his or her personal psychological world. Such an understanding is likely to enhance empathy as the patient recognizes that the view of self is understood by the clinician. This idea of understanding the patient's perspective is closely aligned with personal construct theory (Kelly, 1955). Constructs are seen as the criteria by which individuals assess their interpersonal worlds. This orientation provides a bridge linking personality dimensions with the use of cognitive strategies and interpersonal theory.

Third, the application of trait theory provides the clinician with another vantage point from which to conceptualize how the present circumstances have produced distress or dysfunction. The interface between personal patterns or styles and specific types of people or circumstances can be seen in descriptive terms rather than with an evaluation of personal pathology.

Fourth, the recognition of trait qualities may contribute to the choice of therapeutic strategies. In particular, it may be of considerable value in determining the mix of the less structured approaches that fall under the psychodynamic–interpersonal label and the cognitive–behavioral self-control techniques that use a more structured approach. This is not to say that various techniques cannot be used in a combined manner, but the trait perspective may be illuminating on how to balance the mix.

Fifth, trait theory offers a useful way of predicting various aspects of the therapeutic alliance. This may alert the therapist to issues likely to arise in treatment, so that preventive measures can be considered at an early point. To be forewarned is to be forearmed.

Sixth, the trait perspective also may temper the clinician's judgment as to what is likely to change during the course of therapy. Traits are not going to disappear or turn into their opposites, however much the clinician and the patient may want this to happen. In practice, patients usually find it helpful to know that they are not going to have to stop being themselves. The task, rather, is how to come to grips with being more adaptive with what they have to work with.

A BASIC CHANGE-MEASURES PACKAGE

This section describes a systematic application of psychological assessment that is compatible with most service settings. The principles outlined by Pfeiffer, Heslin, and Jones (1976) have been kept in mind. These investigators identified 10 benefits of structured assessment:

1. Encourages client involvement in the treatment process.
2. Fosters open reaction to personal feedback.
3. Clarifies client goals and facilitates contracting for new behavior.
4. Increases objectivity of measuring client change.
5. Provides for comparisons of individual clients with normative groups.
6. Facilitates longitudinal assessment of therapeutic change (i.e., before, after, follow-up).
7. Sensitizes clients and therapists to the multifaceted nature of therapeutic change.
8. Gives clients the sense that their therapist is committed to effective treatment.
9. Improves communication between clients and therapists.
10. Allows the therapist to focus and control therapy more effectively.

The procedure requires a minimum of two assessment interviews. This is not an unreasonable time expectation for most service settings, especially when the outcome is a decision to enter the patient into a treatment program that entails a significant expenditure of time and energy, to say nothing of expense.

The patient is first assessed in a standard diagnostic interview that is approximately 1-hour long.

From this, a *DSM-III-R* diagnosis is established and a general formulation is developed, thereby pulling together past development, current stress, and relevant psychological issues. On the basis of this interview, the patient is accepted into the treatment program.

The second meeting is also approximately 1-hour long and consists of a detailed feedback session based on a series of questionnaires completed between the two interviews. This basic change-measures package was developed in accord with the principles of multiple measures, multiple areas, and multiple perspectives (MacKenzie & Livesley, 1986). It provides an evaluation of symptoms and interpersonal behaviors in general and in relation to specific significant others, the FFM, and a general assessment of psychosocial functioning. Perspectives are obtained from the patient, the clinician, and a significant other (see Table 22.1). The package presently consists of the following instruments:

1. Symptom Checklist—Revised (SCL-90-R)
2. Inventory of Interpersonal Problems (IIP-B5)
3. Dimensional Assessment of Personality Pathology (DAPP)
4. NEO Personality Inventory (NEO-PI)
5. Structural Analysis of Social Behavior (SASB)
6. Global Assessment of Functioning Scale (GAFS)
7. Target Goals

This list has some redundancy in regard to the FFM, particularly between the IIP-B5 and the NEO-PI. The DAPP adds several scales not found in either of these instruments.

Symptom Checklist 90—Revised

This 90-item self-report symptom inventory is the latest version of the original psychological symptom portion of the Cornell Medical Index (Derogatis, 1977). There is a high degree of correlation between the SCL-90-R subscale scores and comparable Minnesota Multiphasic Personality Inventory dimensions. Results are expressed on nine symptom dimensions: somatization, obsessive–compulsive, interpersonal sensitivity, depression, anxiety, hostility, phobic anxiety, paranoid ideation, and psychoticism. The Global Severity Index gives an overall measure of symptom

TABLE 22.1

A Model for Developing a Change-Measures Battery With Examples

	Source of information			
Type of information	Patient	Clinician	Significant other	Clinical record
Demographic–statistics				Data sheet service use
Symptoms	SCL-90-R			
Interpersonal	IIP, SASB		SASB	
Personality	DAPP, NEO-PI		DAPP	
Target goals	Target goals	Target goals		
Global functioning		GAFS		

Note. SCL-90-R = Symptom Checklist-90—Revised; IIP = Inventory of Interpersonal Problems; SASB = Structural Analysis of Social Behavior; DAPP = Dimensional Assessment of Personality Pathology; NEO-PI = NEO Personality Inventory; GAFS = Global Assessment of Functioning Scale.

status. This is the most widely used standard measure of general psychopathology.

Inventory of Interpersonal Problems— Big 5

This is an adaptation of the original instrument developed by Horowitz, Rosenberg, Baer, Ureno, and Villasenor (1988). The wording of the questions is particularly well suited to a clinical population. The question stems are either "It is hard for me to . . . (be assertive)" or "I am too . . . (controlling)." It contains 148 items of which 64 are taken from the original IIP. These items measure 8 problem clusters that form a circumplex pattern based on the 2 major axes of Dominance and Nurturance (Alden, Wiggins, & Pincus, 1990). A vector is calculated that offers the best representation of the two-dimensional space. In addition, conflict scores are calculated for each of the four pairs of opposite segments. A positive conflict score indicates that the patient has an elevated score on conceptually opposite qualities, such as Dominance and submission. The instrument has been expanded by adding items that tap into the domains of Neuroticism, Openness to Experience, and Conscientiousness (Pincus, 1991). The Dominance score is taken to represent Extraversion, and the Nurturance score is taken to represent Agreeableness. Thus, the IIP-B5 results in scores representing the Big Five personality traits and a circumplex model.

Dimensional Assessment of Personality Pathology

The DAPP is a new instrument consisting of 290 items developed from a systematic study of the dimensions in the personality literature (Livesley, Jackson, & Schroeder, 1989; Schroeder, Wormworth, & Livesley, 1992). Each dimension has been operationalized into specific behavior expressions. Eighteen dimensions are rated by the DAPP, most of which can also be clustered into five principle areas that generally correspond to the FFM. (Further information regarding this instrument is found in chapter 9 of this volume.)

NEO Personality Inventory

This 181-item instrument is the original measure of the FFM (Costa & McCrae, 1985), plus an addendum of an additional 74 items for further facet scales of Agreeableness and Conscientiousness (Costa, McCrae, & Dye, 1991). Each dimension has several facets based on item subsets.

Structural Analysis of Social Behavior

This instrument is based on a unique circumplex model of interpersonal functioning (Benjamin, 1987) and comprises two axes. The first axis runs from positive affiliation (loving, approaching) to negative affiliation (attacking, rejecting), whereas the other goes from high independence (autonomy) to high interdependence (enmeshment). This conceptual space may be applied to relationships (how one acts toward the other, how one reacts to the other) or to a view of one's self (introject). The measure is applied to best–worst–ideal views of self and to eight intimate relationships drawn from the patient's life over time. These include mother, father, and the parental relationship itself, as seen during preadolescent years. The measure that was used in this study was the SASB questionnaire, a 16-item form used to rate each relationship in each direction: the other to me, me to the other. The results of the 288-item SASB provide a view of specific relationship patterns rather than a global description of personality dimensions.

Global Assessment Functioning Scale

This is Axis V of the *DSM-III-R* (American Psychiatric Association, 1987), which was developed from the original Health–Sickness Rating Scale as a general measure of psychosocial functioning (Luborsky, 1975).

Target Goals

Three target goals are developed by the initial assessment clinician in collaboration with the patient (Battle et al., 1966). They are based on the combined information from the clinical assessment interview and the results of the questionnaires. When possible, target goals are connected with specific scores from the assessment battery. Each target goal is rated for severity by the patient before treatment begins. At later administrations, the goals are rated for severity, relevance to what has been worked on in therapy, and improvement. The same goals are also rated by the clinician. Goals may be altered as treatment progresses and thus form a record of deepening self-understanding.

Demographics–Statistics

Basic patient demographic information is collected on the registration sheet, including age, sex, marital status, education, and employment status. When possible, data concerning use of both health and mental health services before and after treatment provide a powerful measure of effectiveness.

INTRODUCING STRUCTURED ASSESSMENTS IN A CLINICAL SETTING

The manner in which questionnaires are introduced to the patient is crucial for ensuring compliance and reliable results. A systematic attempt is made to legitimize the use of the measurement instruments. The relevance of each measure to the therapeutic experience itself is emphasized. This is done by briefly introducing each measure and explaining the target area it focuses on: for example, psychological symptoms such as anxiety (SCL-90-R), how one sees one's self (SASB), interpersonal problems such as trouble being intimate (IIP-B5), personality qualities such as extraversion–introversion that may lead to problems (DAPP, NEO-PI), and the nature of specific relationships that have been important to the patient (SASB). This information is given in as direct and open a manner as possible, with the patient's questions and concerns being addressed throughout the process. This serves a double purpose: to motivate the patient to answer the questionnaire carefully and thoughtfully and to decrease response anxiety.

The words *research* or *test* are not used. The structured assessments are properly referred to as part of the clinical assessment procedure and as being of value in program evaluation. Patients are encouraged to view the completion of the questionnaire as the beginning of their therapy and as an opportunity to think seriously about themselves and their relationships. With this simple but systematic approach, patient compliance has been extremely high.

The second clinical interview to review the results takes place before the patient begins therapy. This interview is also carefully constructed (Dies, 1983). The patient is reassured that there is no magic to the scoring process of the questions that they have answered. The results are described as being simply "their own words" coming back to them in a different form. Emphasis is placed on their role in defining the issues of importance. The patient receives a handout with his or her personal scores rated from very low to average to very high. He or she also receives a sheet of "scale descriptions" that briefly define what qualities the various dimensions are trying to capture. All results are presented in a tentative manner, inviting discussion, elaboration, and examples. Most patients are able to quickly move into a more in-depth discussion of the issues raised by the results.

> *One woman responded to her high Agreeableness score by acknowledging that she was forever getting into relationships in which she felt used. She could never drop her smiling acquiescent behavior until the situation got so bad that she had to flee it impulsively. These problematic issues were never directly discussed with her partner. She then went on to identify a recent situation in which she found herself going out of her way specifically to find a man whom she identified as a low-Agreeableness person. The clinician commented aloud that it sounded as if she were trying to complement an area of problem for herself by finding someone who had just the opposite set of qualities. She elaborated with further thoughts about how comfortable and "right" it always seems at the start of such relationships until the control imbalance, a component of the Agreeableness dimension, begins to emerge.*

Patients are deeply interested in how they describe important relationships on the SASB questions. Generally, there is prompt acknowledgment and elaboration on the patterns revealed. It is of particular interest to find identical patterns in the descriptions of parental relationships as seen in childhood and current adult relationships. The SASB ratings are unique because they probe actual relationships, not generalized descriptions of the self. This specificity regarding person complements the specificity regarding interpersonal behavioral style that comes from the other personality instruments.

> *A man with difficulties in a series of relationships with women was shocked to the point of being upset at his results. He described his relationships with these partners as one of outward pleasant passivity*

accompanied by inner rage at what he saw as their controlling behavior. Eventually, the anger would build up to the point where he would either precipitate a fight (sometimes with a physical attack) or abruptly terminate the relationship. He had always harbored strong negative reactions to his controlling and critical father in childhood. What shocked him was that his own adult response patterns were modeled on those of his mother toward his father. He had always felt that she had not protected him adequately from his father's attacks and left when he needed her most. This realization stimulated a gradual reassessment of the nature of his parental images.

The clinician must be careful not to make absolute interpretive statements. All results are described in bland and somewhat technical language that encourages a cognitive exploration of the issues raised. The onus is placed on the patient to take the self-generated information and apply it to attitudes or patterns regarding him- or herself or others. The feedback material is couched in terms of raising ideas or perspectives that should not be accepted immediately but might be pursued further within the context of therapy.

The clinician might also use the scores to highlight for the patient some aspects of the treatment program that would match issues generated from the questionnaires. For example, patients with very high Neuroticism scores are encouraged to use the stress management and relaxation portions of the day program. Extraverts are alerted to the value of sitting with their reactions and experiencing them rather than translating them immediately into impulsive action. Patients with very low Openness scores are reassured that they will find the cognitive therapy sessions helpful but that they will have to work hard at making sense of the interpersonal groups. High Agreeableness patients are forewarned that they do not have to believe everything they hear and will need to concentrate on thinking through and discussing their personal opinions. For patients with low Conscientiousness scores, discussion centers on their struggle to allow themselves to follow through on treatment programs. Such people are usually aware of their tendency to drop out of therapy prematurely and recognize this as a pervasive pattern that interferes with how they can find more satisfaction in their lives. The likelihood of finding themselves experiencing a desire to terminate therapy before it is finished is therefore explicitly reviewed along with their ideas about how they might try to counteract this tendency. Most patients talk of revealing their concerns early in the sessions and making a commitment to put such ideas into words as soon as they arise later.

Most patients welcome this direct and candid discussion of core issues that are related to their dysfunctional patterns. The fact that it is generated directly from their own responses to the questionnaires makes the information even more acceptable. Most express relief that key issues are not going to be skirted. They acknowledge that they have known for a long time that they would have to tackle the sorts of concerns that they identified. Sometimes new, or at least unacknowledged, perspectives are opened up by this process. It seems that patients often have an awareness, perhaps only a hunch, about what needs to be changed but have never actually put it into words before. The assessment procedures help to make these implicit understandings more explicit. By the end of the feedback interview, areas of concern are transformed into target goals.

The feedback process appears to be an effective mechanism for promoting the rapid development of a therapeutic alliance between patient and therapist. To some extent, this undercuts the power imbalance that is inevitable in the clinical context. The process of rapid engagement is particularly important in the use of time-limited approaches for which a fast start leaves more time for working on the most salient material. For example, in a time-limited group psychotherapy program, patients are encouraged to introduce themselves to the group in the first session by recounting what they have just found out about themselves during the preceding feedback session. This process stimulates rapid universalization mechanisms in the group as patients hear each other describing recognizable issues. It also provides a psychological language for discussing interpersonal

matters. There is no time lost in general unfocused introductions.

The early disclosure, even if handled relatively superficially, puts the issues on the table. They can then be legitimately reintroduced by the therapist or by other patients if in a group. Thus, when a patient starts to stray from a focus on core issues or begins to enact the very patterns that had been discussed earlier, a prompt identification can be made. Such focusing or reflective interventions are accepted with less resistance because of their correspondence to what the patient has already said about themselves. Hearing such feedback from other group members draws the focus of psychological work directly into the here-and-now of group interaction and thereby promotes a powerful correctional emotional experience. This process applies not only to the recipient of feedback but also to the person giving it, which lends additional therapeutic power from group work compared with that available in the traditional dyadic therapy context (MacKenzie, 1990).

USING STRUCTURED ASSESSMENTS TO SELECT INTERVENTION STRATEGIES

The approach of administering psychotherapy varies greatly among practitioners. A great deal of this divergence is related to the unidimensional nature of many training programs. The most basic divide is between structured approaches based on cognitive–behavioral techniques and relatively unstructured exploratory techniques of psychodynamic–interpersonal methods. Within each of these traditions are many variations, but there is a general agreement about the basics. Between them, however, there is a vast gulf of misunderstanding and antagonism. The discussion that follows concerning intervention strategies implies that every clinician should be competent to provide a diversity of theoretical approaches or at least to be sympathetically knowledgeable about them.

Outcome studies clearly show that careful application of a treatment regimen results in a large common therapeutic effect. The more stringent the study in terms of suitable control conditions, randomization, and monitoring of the treatment process, the less differential in outcome. The field has not yet come to grips with methods to select patients effectively for specific types of treatment. However, inherent in the dimensional trait literature are some important clues as to how this might be accomplished. Some examples follow, all given in the acknowledged absence of substantial direct empirical evidence at this time.

Example 1

Patients with high Neuroticism scores seem likely to benefit from management strategies that help them establish some control over their emotional reactivity. Such patients often respond to stress with an escalating spiral of anxiety and disorganization that becomes self-sustaining. Trying to deal with conflictual issues or interpersonal misperceptions when in such a highly aroused state is difficult. Affect control methods and relaxation exercises may help to interrupt this sequence. These procedures may allow the level of anxiety to drop down into a range where the patient can use other therapeutic components more effectively.

> *A young man found himself paralyzed with doubts when faced with situations he interpreted as demanding a high level of performance. The more he tried to think of ways to calm himself and not appear tremulous, the more his anxiety escalated. He learned the effective use of deep breathing relaxation techniques that gave him an opportunity to reassess the true nature of the situation. Getting some sense of mastery over his reactivity allowed him to begin to address psychological issues connected with the roots of his low self-esteem.*

Example 2

Patients with low Neuroticism scores respond positively if the clinician pays attention to their pragmatic problems and physical symptoms. They see little point in addressing psychological issues if their symptoms are not acknowledged. I have found that group methods are particularly useful in helping such patients make the transition from a symptom–problem-based orientation to a psychological–

interpersonal perspective. A group can provide powerful interpersonal support while exerting pressure to reconceptualize the locus of difficulty.

> *A 40-year-old man was asked to describe his relationship with his parents as a child using the SASB questions, but he stated that he had no recall of any childhood memories before the age of 18. His descriptions of his reaction to a variety of significant people all showed no directionality. His Neuroticism and Openness scores were very low, with the exception of the Openness to Ideas facet scale, which was quite high. Conscientiousness was also very high. Review of these patterns led to a discussion of his almost total lack of contact with emotionality. Everything was handled in a purely cognitive mode, including the discussion of this material. He was surprised to see that he described himself in these terms. He had always been puzzled when others told him he needed to loosen up. He considered himself the successful professional, which he was. He began to acknowledge that he led an extremely lonely personal life but had never wondered why and thought that was something he might ponder. This intellectual approach allowed him to countenance the idea of looking at relationship issues. By the 4th week in an intensive psychotherapy day program, he was able to detect emotional reactions in himself and to have fragmentary memories of childhood events including the ability to visualize his parents.*

Example 3

Patients with high Extraversion scores may need help to refrain from translating arousal or anxiety into direct action. For them, the ability to delay responding for long enough to appreciate the issues they are experiencing is important. Many patients with components of the borderline syndrome find it helpful to understand that they can tolerate their inner states without having to do something about it. Intervention techniques taken from a self-psychology orientation are often helpful. The therapist carefully does not react to the intrusive demands that something be done. By calmly tolerating these expectations and not feeling the need to respond, the therapist is sending a transactional message that the patient's inner state can be lived with. This promotes a more consolidated sense of self that is independent from the interaction with others.

> A 27-year-old woman presented with high Neuroticism, Extraversion, and Openness scores. Her SASB relationship patterns were replete with conflict scores of both a Control Double-Bind Nature and Ambivalent Attachment. She had a history of tumultuous relationships of a highly enmeshed nature. In therapy, she was alternatively angrily critical and tearfully demanding. Her intrusive behaviors were handled in an accepting but noncontrolling manner. They were reflected back to her as dilemmas that she must experience as being quite upsetting. The various facets of her reactions were gently explored for clarification. With time, she was able to tolerate her extremes by saying in effect: "There I go again. I'm angry for no good reason. With time, I'll cool down."

Example 4

Patients falling into the introversion spectrum usually have control, perhaps too much control, over their reactions. Structured cognitive approaches may only reinforce this tendency. Interpersonal approaches that focus on acceptance of self and the establishment of relationships are likely to be of greater benefit.

> A 35-year-old librarian presented with a major depression triggered by apprehension over concerns that her common-law partner was paying little attention to her and seemed attracted to another. She had tried many methods of trying to accommodate her partner's expressed needs without success. Now she felt hopeless and at an impasse. Her only positive coping method was to take long walks by herself where

she could commune with nature. She had a small group of like-minded friends but did not feel that she should burden them with her misery. She paid close attention in her feedback session to her self-descriptions, particularly how she avoided others and exerted tight control over her own reactions. She actively applied this information to her work in an outpatient group and in conversations with her partner. By the end of a 16-week time-limited group, she reported an improvement in mood and self-esteem and emerged as more spontaneous in the group. She had clarified the issues with her partner and was considering a more stimulating job. In the final session of the group, she volunteered her belief that the most important therapeutic effect was connected to the process of being accepted in the group. This had alerted her to the damaging effects of her reclusive style and strengthened her belief in herself.

Example 5

Patients with high Openness tend to become overloaded with ideas or fantasies to the point where they become disorganized or scattered. They often respond to cognitive techniques that help them master this scattering effect. This can often be accomplished by a soothing approach and the encouragement to restate the issues and look realistically at the options. These patients find themselves taking on too many responsibilities simultaneously and then descending into a frantic whirl trying to keep up with them all. Planned efforts to structure their lives with more control are helpful.

> A 42-year-old teacher scored very high on Openness. She described herself as becoming overly stimulated in new situations and feeling overwhelmed with creative ideas. She would begin many projects at the start of each school year that positively engaged her students. But shortly into the year, she found herself feeling burnt out and unable to keep on top of them all. This cycled into a self-critical mode and a sense of disen-

gagement from her class that was severe enough to put her job into jeopardy. She was encouraged to place particular emphasis on cognitive therapy groups. At 1-year follow-up, she reported that her patterns were much improved and that she regularly repeated the cognitive structured organizing exercises she had developed in the program.

Example 6

Low scores on Openness suggest that the patient is able to use structured approaches more easily. Such patients may need to have special preparation and support if they are to adapt successfully to unstructured therapeutic settings. Piper, McCallum, and Azim (1992) found that patients who score low on psychological mindedness—a concept closely related to Openness—tend to drop out of time-limited groups at a high rate. However, those who remain do just as well as high psychological mindedness patients on outcome measures. Others have reported that low Openness patients do better with biofeedback than imagery techniques for relaxation training (Kelso, Anchor, & McElroy, 1988).

Example 7

The Agreeableness trait is related to control–submission issues that are central to autonomy–enmeshment problems. Patients who fall at either extreme on the Agreeableness dimension are appropriate candidates for dynamic therapies that focus on interpersonal issues. At the high end, the patient's vulnerable predisposition to interpersonal abuse must be addressed directly. This generally involves poor self-esteem and associated difficulty in personal assertion. The example earlier in this chapter exemplified some of these issues.

Example 8

Patients at the low end of Agreeableness must address the issues of suspiciousness and lack of trust that generally underlie their sarcastic, distancing interpersonal style. It has been my impression that dyadic therapy is likely to inflame this quality. The leadership dilution found in therapy groups gives the patient more room to try out a more positive approach to others without losing face to an authority figure.

A 42-year-old man described a childhood of high achievement in academic and sports activities. These elevated levels were in response to being criticized from his father and being ignored by his mother. In his late teens, he realized that his efforts were to no avail. This precipitated a dysthymic state that had persisted ever since. He viewed the world as an unforgiving place where effort was not rewarded and success was futile. His attitude and tone of voice were bitter and sarcastic, and his demeanor had an adolescent quality. His participation in an intensive psychotherapy group was minimal, but he attended regularly. After several months, it became apparent that he was involved with some of the members outside of the group. This was an unusual level of socialization for him, even though it was primarily only meeting for coffee. He remained suspicious of the male group leader, although he clearly paid very close attention to him. Efforts at an empathic connection were repeatedly rebuffed. Finally, one of the female members with whom he would socialize blurted out with tears that she "could not stand to see him gradually dying within himself." This was echoed by other group members and slowly led to his increased participation. At about the 12-month point, he was able to begin to deal with his fear of rejection because he felt better about the leader.

Example 9

A patient who scores low on Conscientiousness finds it hard to consistently address the tasks of therapy. Modest goals are best established at the beginning of treatment, so that the patient is not set up for an experience of recurrent failure. As mentioned earlier in this chapter, attention to motivational issues should form a continuing theme in treatment.

A 35-year-old man was referred for outpatient treatment because of a sense of being stuck in his life. He had a graduate degree, acquired after a decade of intermittent studies, but he had never put it to use. He worked itinerant construction jobs to make ends meet. He considered himself a musician but worked only sporadic gigs and resolutely refused to learn how to read music. He had started many relationships, but they all dwindled away as he became involved in other interests. He stated that he was now ready to make changes in his life. The assessment interviewer pressed him on motivational issues. This led to an acknowledgment of concern about starting now because it was spring to look for a summer job, which would do him good. He was repeatedly offered the opportunity to make a commitment to the program and finally agreed to do so, saying he realized he had no alternative, that his life was going nowhere. The next week he phoned to say that he had found a job and knew that would be best for him right now.

Example 10

Highly conscientious patients tend to be reliable and consistent in their therapeutic involvement. They often win the admiration of their therapist for their efforts in the session and in following through on homework. However, these features may mask underlying difficulties. The hard work may be approached with a sense of duty and compulsiveness that translates the potential achievements into earnest and perhaps restrictive routines. If anything, these people need an experience in spontaneously not following through. Providing detailed structure to the therapeutic task must therefore be regarded with caution.

A woman in her early 30s, who was married to a professional and was finishing a graduate-level course, was seen as a leader in an intensive day program. She edited an information bulletin, organized activities, and was helpful in interpreting issues for others. Despite this involvement, she reported continuing hopelessness and intermittent active suicidal ideation. It was only after the level of her helpfulness was challenged by the group that she began to reveal her internal sense of desperate futility if she had nothing to do. This highly charged response allowed her to begin effective personal introspection.

Some general trends are evident in the just-mentioned discussion regarding the decision to use high versus low structure. Patients who are low on Neuroticism, Extraversion (or Introversion), Openness, and Conscientiousness take to structured approaches more readily. Conversely, high scores on all four suggest that the patient feels comfortable with unstructured and more novel techniques. In short, with an accumulation of these predictors, an increasingly strong warning is issued about the type of treatment to which the patient is likely to be receptive. This is not the same thing as predicting what type of treatment will be more effective. As Piper et al. (1992) found out, the low psychological mindedness patients did well if they completed therapy. The problem was that they did not take to it very well and therefore terminated before they had a dose sufficient to produce an effect.

It appears reasonable, at the very least, for the clinician to use these indicators to be forewarned and to institute appropriate pretherapy preparation procedures. Most dropouts tend to occur within the first six sessions. The group literature demonstrates the effectiveness of pretherapy "role induction" techniques in lowering the rate of these early dropouts (Piper & Perrault, 1989). The preparation, done with handouts and discussion, concentrates on giving patients an appreciation of how the therapy works and how they can get the most out of it. This practice could be emulated by therapists seeing patients individually. Such systematic preparation material can be unobtrusively inserted into early sessions.

These ideas of low and high structure may also be incorporated into the sequencing of treatment components. In general, the more unstructured dynamic–interpersonal techniques emphasize personal disclosure and expect a degree of spontaneity and initiative from the patient. They involve a greater attention to the process of psychotherapy than the overt content. This produces a more interpersonally threatening environment that is seen as particularly dangerous to patients who are low on Neuroticism, Extraversion, and Openness. Many treatment programs begin with structured psychoeducational techniques to engage the patient. For example, inpatient units focus on education about how to recognize an emerging relapse, how to stay out of the hospital, how to use medication information, how to use community resources, and so on. Eating disorder programs routinely begin with psychoeducational material and anticipate that a significant number of patients will find this adequate to master their symptoms. Many self-help groups provide a structured approach that fits the needs of the target population (Lieberman, 1990). In all of these examples, the structured initial approach also acquaints the patient with the idea of talking about his or her problems and indirectly lays the groundwork for more exploratory psychotherapy for those still in need. Because most of the structured programs tend to be brief in nature, they are able to retain the low Neuroticism, Extraversion, and Openness people but not turn off the high Neuroticism, Extraversion, and Openness people.

In more complex therapeutic settings such as day programs, two therapeutic tracks might be considered: one that focuses on control and mastery and one that focuses on self-exploration. I have found it important to clarify for patients that these two approaches are complementary, not in competition. By dampening reactivity through self-mastery techniques, the patient is able to deal constructively with internal and interpersonal issues. Interpersonal therapy also helps to explore the roots of the issues that trigger reactive responses. Clearly, such a dual-track program is only possible when there is goodwill and respect among the clinicians providing each modality.

CONCLUSION

Many of the examples used in this chapter referred to group psychotherapy. Almost by definition, per-

sonality pathology is manifested in disturbed interpersonal relationships. Such problems seem particularly well suited to a group approach. Indeed, a case can be made that a well-functioning therapy group is more likely to provide an arena in which entrenched patterns can be effectively challenged. The power of group engagement and the resulting collective normative expectations for change can be used to augment technical therapeutic interventions.

Given the equivalency of outcome, it would seem appropriate to expect that clinicians might be called on to justify the use of individual therapy for patients with major personality disorders.

References

Alden, L. E., Wiggins, J. S., & Pincus, A. L. (1990). Construction of circumplex scales for the Inventory of Interpersonal Problems. *Journal of Personality Assessment, 55,* 521–536.

American Psychiatric Association. (1987). *Diagnostic and statistical manual of mental disorders* (3rd ed., rev.). Washington, DC: Author.

Battle, C. C., Imber, S. D., Hoehn-Saric, R., Stone, A. R., Nash, E. H., & Frank, J. (1966). Target complaints as a criteria of improvement. *American Journal of Psychotherapy, 20,* 184–192.

Benjamin, L. S. (1987). Use of the SASB dimensional model to develop treatment plans for personality disorders: I. Narcissism. *Journal of Personality Disorders, 1,* 43–70.

Budman, S. H., Demby, A., Redondo, J. P., Hannan, M., Feldstein, M., Ring, J., & Springer, T. (1988). Comparative outcome in time-limited individual and group psychotherapy. *International Journal of Group Psychotherapy, 38,* 63–86.

Costa, P. T., Jr., & McCrae, R. R. (1985). *The NEO Personality Inventory manual.* Odessa, FL: Psychological Assessment Resources.

Costa, P. T., Jr., McCrae, R. R., & Dye, D. A. (1991). Facet scales for Agreeableness and Conscientiousness: A revision of the NEO Personality Inventory. *Personality and Individual Differences, 12,* 887–898.

Derogatis, L. R. (1977). *SCL-90 administration, scoring and procedures manual: 1.* Baltimore: Johns Hopkins University Press.

Dies, R. R. (1983). Bridging the gap between research and practice in group psychotherapy. In R. R. Dies & K. R. MacKenzie (Eds.), *Advances in group psychotherapy* (pp. 1–26). New York: International Universities Press.

Elkin, I., Shea, M. T., Watkins, J. T., Imber, S. D., Sotsky, S. M., Collins, J. F., Glass, D. R., Pilkonis, P. A., Leber, W. R., Docherty, J. P., Fiester, S. J., & Parloff, M. B. (1989). National Institute of Mental Health Treatment of Depression Collaborative Research Program: General effectiveness of treatments. *Archives of General Psychiatry, 46,* 971–982.

Horowitz, L. M., Rosenberg, S. E., Baer, B. A., Ureno, G., & Villasenor, V. S. (1988). Inventory of Interpersonal Problems: Psychometric properties and clinical applications. *Journal of Consulting and Clinical Psychology, 56,* 885–892.

Kelly, G. A. (1955). *The psychology of personal constructs.* New York: Norton.

Kelso, H., Anchor, K., & McElroy, M. (1988). The relationship between absorption capacity and electromyographic biofeedback relaxation training with a male clinical sample. *Medical Psychotherapy, 1,* 51–63.

Lieberman, M. A. (1990). A group therapist perspective on self-help groups. *International Journal of Group Psychotherapy, 40,* 251–278.

Livesley, W. J., Jackson, D. N., & Schroeder, M. L. (1989). A study of the factorial structure of personality pathology. *Journal of Personality Disorders, 3,* 292–306.

Luborsky, L. (1975). Clinician's judgments of mental health: Specimen case descriptions and forms for the Health–Sickness Rating Scale. *Bulletin of the Menninger Clinic, 39,* 448–480.

MacKenzie, K. R. (1990). *Introduction to time-limited group psychotherapy.* Washington, DC: American Psychiatric Press.

MacKenzie, K. R., & Livesley, W. J. (1986). Out-come and process measures in brief group psychotherapy. *Psychiatric Annals, 16,* 715–720.

Miller, T. R. (1991). The psychotherapeutic utility of the five-factor model of personality: A clinician's experience. *Journal of Personality Assessment, 57,* 415–433.

Pfeiffer, J. W., Heslin, R., & Jones, J. E. (1976). *Instrumentation in human relations training* (2nd ed.). La Jolla, CA: University Associates.

Pilkonis, P. A., Imber, S. D., Lewis, P., & Rubinsky, P. (1984). A comparative study of individual, group, and conjoint psychotherapy. *Archives of General Psychiatry, 41,* 431–437.

Pincus, A. L. (1991, August). Extending interpersonal problems to include the "Big Five" personality dimensions. In L. E. Alden (Chair), *Assessment of interpersonal problems: Implications for treatment and research.* Symposium conducted at the 99th Annual Convention of the American Psychological Association, San Francisco, CA.

Piper, W. E., Debanne, E. G., Bienvenu, J. P., & Garant, J. (1984). A comparative study of four forms of psychotherapy. *Journal of Consulting and Clinical Psychology, 52,* 268–279.

Piper, W. E., McCallum, M., & Azim, H. F. A. (1992). *Adaptation to loss through short-term group psychotherapy.* New York: Guilford Press.

Piper, W. E., & Perrault, E. L. (1989). Pretherapy preparation for group members. *International Journal of Group Psychotherapy, 39,* 17–34.

Schroeder, M. L., Wormworth, J. A., & Livesley, W. J. (1992). Dimensions of personality disorder and their relationships to the Big Five dimensions of personality. *Psychological Assessment: A Journal of Consulting and Clinical Psychology, 4,* 47–53.

CHAPTER 23

IMPLICATIONS OF PERSONALITY INDIVIDUAL DIFFERENCES SCIENCE FOR CLINICAL WORK ON PERSONALITY DISORDERS

Allan R. Harkness and John L. McNulty

Personality individual differences science represents the successful union of dispositional approaches to personality, psychometrics, and behavior genetics. This science has profound implications for human psychology and puts many of the classic views of human nature into question. This science evidences increasing links with the best of general law psychology (see, e.g., Zuckerman, 1994), neuropsychology (e.g., Depue, 1996; Gray, 1982; Zuckerman, 1991), and related disciplines. Over the last several decades, personality individual differences science has seen advances in trait theory (e.g., Harkness & Hogan, 1995; McCrae & Costa, 1995; Meehl, 1986; Messick, 1981; Tellegen, 1988, 1991; Wiggins, 1996) and greater focus and clarity in structural issues (e.g., Almagor, Tellegen, & Waller, 1995; Block, 1995, and rejoinders; Digman, 1990; Harkness & McNulty, 1994; McCrae & Costa, 1997; Watson, Clark, & Harkness, 1994; Zuckerman, Kuhlman, Joireman, & Teta, 1993), coupled with behavior genetic advances in theory (e.g., Lykken, McGue, Tellegen, & Bouchard, 1992; Plomin, DeFries & Loehlin, 1977; Rowe, 1994; Scarr & McCartney, 1983), methods (e.g., the genetic analysis of correlations, DeFries, Kuse, & Vandenberg, 1979; for general advances in analysis, see Neale & Cardon, 1992), and findings (e.g., Bouchard, Lykken, McGue, Segal, & Tellegen, 1990; Loehlin, 1992; Riemann, Angleitner, & Strelau, 1997; Tellegen et al., 1988). Further growth of this science will be evidenced in the development of further connections with evolutionary perspectives (e.g., Buss, Haselton, Shackelford, Bleske, & Wakefield, 1998). Evolutionary perspectives clarify the origin and teleology of the purposeful people researchers and clinicians study and treat. Maturity will be evidenced by a greater understanding of the intertwining of genetics and environment in the causal web and by an increasing understanding of personality development (e.g., Ahadi & Rothbart, 1994; Goldsmith, Buss, & Lemery, 1997; Rothbart, Derryberry, & Posner, 1994).

Personality individual differences science now offers alternative viewpoints on many classic issues in psychopathology and the accepted diagnostic systems (e.g., Clark, 1993; Clark, Watson, & Mineka, 1994; Cloninger, Svrakic, & Przybeck, 1993; Livesley, Jang, & Vernon, 1998; Schroeder, Wormsworth, & Livesley, 1992; Trull, 1992; Watson et al., 1994; Widiger, 1993; Widiger & Trull, 1992), explaining the massive and coherent comorbidities found not only in Axis II but also in Axis I (Clark & Watson, 1999). McCrae (1994) and MacKenzie (1994; chapter 22, this volume) offered bold, perhaps even radical, reconceptualizations of clinical work based on personality individual differences science.

Harkness and Lilienfeld (1997) offered a primer of basic concepts of this individual differences science of personality such as current trait theory, essential concepts and findings in the behavior genetics of personality, and an explication of the clinical significance of the distinction between basic tendency and characteristic adaptation (McCrae & Costa, 1995). Harkness and Lilienfeld concluded that if the individual differences science of personality were brought to bear on clinical problems, four major benefits would be realized: (a) a better understanding of where to focus clinical intervention efforts, (b) realistic expectations for degree of clinical change, (c) matching treatment to patient personality to optimize engagement and retention and to minimize adverse reactions, and (d) the development of higher regulatory structures of personality (i.e., the self) through the use of nomothetic test results.

Clinical application of the last several decades of individual differences science holds great promise, but the work has only begun. In this chapter, we offer a reconceptualization of the links among personality traits and the personality disorders (PDs). We then offer the outlines of a new psychotherapeutic approach based on personality individual differences science. We explore how trait psychology can be translated into clinical intervention.

PERSONALITY INDIVIDUAL DIFFERENCES SCIENCE TRAITS AND THE PERSONALITY DISORDERS

How do traits derived from the structural models of personality individual differences science relate to the PDs of the *Diagnostic and Statistical Manual of Mental Disorders* (*DSM*; American Psychiatric Association, e.g., 1987, 1994)? The PDs are descriptive, not etiological, categories descended from a variety of historical traditions (see, e.g., Frances & Widiger, 1986; Lenzenweger & Clarkin, 1996; Mack, 1975; and Millon, 1981) and then shaped by committee (schizotypal PD may be an exception; see Meehl, 1990). In a sense, the PDs of the fourth edition of the *DSM* (*DSM-IV*; American Psychiatric Association, 1994) are 10 impact craters left by the collision of fuzzy sets of people with various institutions: For example, people with antisocial PD collide with the legal system; those with borderline personality disorder (BDL) owe some lineage to "borderline analyzability," that is, people who collide with the analytic

couch (see, e.g., Knight, 1953). These impact craters were then refined somewhat by offering diagnostic criteria (which do not in any practical way specify measurement operations and thus should not be called operational).

Hence, the PDs found in the *DSMs* do not offer strong science, but they do offer codified clinical experience, describing major recurring problems in life patterns that have come to professional attention. The first edition of this book (Costa & Widiger, 1994) provided an extensive theoretical and empirical examination of the links among five-factor model personality traits and PDs. Authors from widely varied perspectives within individual differences science have considered the links between personality traits and PDs (e.g., Clark & Watson, 1999; Depue, 1996; Grove & Tellegen, 1991; Lykken, 1995). In this section, we add to the discussion of the mechanisms by which personality traits link with the PDs of the *DSMs*. We emphasize two major points. The first is that the distinction between basic tendencies and characteristic adaptations (McCrae, 1993; McCrae & Costa, 1995) is a key to understanding the link between traits and PDs. The second provides an important caveat: Clinical work may require examination of the complete trait hierarchy and may even include unique traits.

Traits and Personality Disorders: The Importance of Characteristic Adaptations

McCrae (1993) and McCrae and Costa (1995) offered a highly useful distinction between basic tendencies and characteristic adaptations.[1,2] Basic tendencies are essentially traits construed in the tradition of Allport (1937). They are dispositions arising from the operation of real and relatively stable biological–psychological systems. Characteristic adaptations represent the distilled products of living a life with a particular set of dispositions within a

---

[1] The term *adaptation* is not being used as an evolutionary term.

[2] Although the basic tendency–characteristic adaptation distinction has been linked historically to Cattell's (1950) source–surface distinction, we avoid that terminology for the theoretical reason that the *R*-factor hierarchy (based on correlations of tests, homogeneous item clusters, facets, or factored homogeneous item dimensions within a population) is the structure to which Cattell attached the source–surface distinction. Although real traits in people can give rise to *R* factors, *R* factors are first mathematical descriptions of trait dimensions (population structures), not traits (Block, 1995). Cattell's terminology tends to obscure a critical inferential step; on such habits rises or falls the clarity of theorizing in the field. We prefer McCrae's (1993) framing of the distinction to Cattell's.

web of social and cultural forces. As McCrae (1993) described them, characteristic adaptations are "the concrete habits, attitudes, roles, relationships, and goals that result from the interaction of basic tendencies with the shaping forces of the social environment" (p. 584).

Characteristic adaptations vary in the length of the causal path leading to them from the traits. Some characteristic adaptations lie causally close to the traits; others are more remote. Characteristic adaptations themselves exert causal power over behaviors further downstream. They are not fully determined by the traits, but the traits are one important path in the cause of characteristic adaptations. Characteristic adaptations are thus in part enactments of traits, the behavioral realizations of traits, but not traits themselves. Characteristic adaptations may be destructive or growth promoting. They may impair or foster relationships.

An Example of a Hypothetical Borderline Personality Disorder Patient

Table 23.1 shows a common trait pattern found in BDL patients, typical phenomenology, and two alternative patterns of characteristic adaptations. Because of emerging standards in the use of case material, we chose to illustrate the concepts with a hypothetical BDL patient (we describe the patient as female; however, some of the same features in a male would tend to be described as antisocial PD). Traits are shown in the far lefthand column of Table 23.1. Assume our patient was tested using the Revised NEO

Personality Inventory (NEO-PI-R; Costa & McCrae, 1992) or the Minnesota Multiphasic Personality Inventory—2 (MMPI-2) incorporating the Personality Psychopathology Five (PSY-5) scales (Harkness, McNulty, & Ben-Porath, 1995). Suppose the results suggest prominent traits of high Neuroticism (N) and low Agreeableness (A; elevated Aggressiveness on the PSY-5). Good assessment is the key to establishing the leftmost column for a given patient. Note, however, many people have high N and low A without meeting the BDL criteria. The left column should contain the full constellation of important traits for the patient. If the patient were to have an additional trait emphasis such as high sensation seeking (Zuckerman, 1994) or disconstraint (Watson & Clark, 1993), that could color the dynamic expression of N and A (Allport, 1937).

The next column, Typical Phenomenology, indicates some psychological products of traits that are very close to the traits in the causal chain. For a patient with traits of high N and low A, a typical phenomenology results, with a few example elements described in Table 23.1, such as a low expectation of the capacity to provide for one's own needs; experiencing a negative affect when alone, identified as loneliness, to which the patient has become sensitized; and expecting untrustworthy behavior on the part of dating partners. Some aspects of typical phenomenology may be influenced predominantly by a single trait, whereas others are influenced by Allport's (1937) dynamic constellation of several traits. Typical phenomenology is the source from which

TABLE 23.1

Description of a Hypothetical Patient With Borderline Personality Disorder

Traits	Typical phenomenology	Borderline characteristic adaptations	Nonborderline characteristic adaptations
High Neuroticism	Low expectation of own capacity to meet needs	Picks flawed boyfriend "who will take me"	Learns to attend to realistic danger signals in potential mate
	Sensitization to pain of loneliness	Attempts to make boyfriend jealous by cheating	Learns to combat loneliness through a mix of romantic and social affiliations
Low Agreeableness	Expectation of untrustworthy behavior in dating partner	Begins following boyfriend, stimulates jealousy	Exercises caution in choice of future mates

test items are usually drawn. Test items have to be screened to avoid factorial complexity. Cognitive and psychodynamic analyses of the patient often begin with a listing of elements from the Typical Phenomenology column, without linking them to the column of traits on the left.

As we move to the next column to the right, the causal chain lengthens a bit more, and we arrive at the column describing BDL-like characteristic adaptations. Partly in response to expecting untrustworthy behavior on the part of dating partners and stemming from strong discomfort with unmet needs, and acute sensitivity to loneliness, the patient develops certain adaptations. For example, one BDL-like adaptation is to pick flawed partners in the hope that they "will take me." In response to expectations from the current phenomenology of distrust and from probable experiences of real untrustworthiness of boyfriends picked using this strategy, our patient develops a new characteristic adaptation: following her boyfriend to check up on him. She might also attempt to keep him by engaging his jealousy through cheating; the additional contact provided by such a liaison may serve to transiently reduce loneliness. The volatility that cheating adds to the relationship is not adequately anticipated by the patient. These behaviors are not random, trial-and-error operants: They owe part of their cause to the traits and pre-existing characteristic adaptations. However, once emitted, their future is controlled by their consequences, consequences that are in part the creation of the typical phenomenology of the patient. The typical phenomenology of a person high in N may create a fertile soil for negative reinforcement of behaviors that produce transient reductions in the negative affect of the moment. Attack, avoidance, escape, and self-medication are broad response classes offering temporary reduction of negative affectivity, and thus often appear as BDL-like characteristic adaptations. Behavioral analyses often begin in this third column of characteristic adaptations, without making the connections to the columns to the left.

As we consider characteristic adaptations with longer causal chains, more causally distal from the traits, the "fungible" nature of basic dispositions becomes clear. *Fungibility* refers to the transformability of a commodity such as money. If one has a high

level of negative emotionality or N and thus a disposition to worry, one might spend one's worry dollars on the possibility of nuclear war, the possibility of economic collapse, concern over the fitness of bolts in the bridge one is driving over, or over the fate of one's favorite basketball team. Fungibility applies across all the dispositions. For example, Zuckerman (1994) pulled together evidence indicating that although criminals do indeed have higher average sensation seeking scores than college students, their levels are comparable with firefighters. The findings are consistent with a central thesis of Lykken's (1995) fascinating work *The Antisocial Personalities*: Even children with very difficult temperaments can be steered toward nondestructive, alternative adaptations. Lykken's idea is central to the clinical approach proposed in this chapter: As characteristic adaptations contain more causal distance between themselves and the traits, a less destructive trait-enacting characteristic adaptation may be substituted for the more pathological presenting adaptation.

Thus, the pathological characteristic adaptations of the Borderline column of Table 23.1 are not the only possible trait enacting adaptations for this patient. For example the patient's sensitivity to danger signals, so characteristic of high N, might be engaged for purposes of mate selection: With proper education about the importance of character, the patient might undergo a strategic shift in her approach to picking boyfriends. Working through the patient's past choices and the role played by her pattern of mate choices in creating her environment could yield a strong clinical contribution to her growth and health. Learning to combat loneliness not only through romantic affiliation but also social affiliation may also serve the patient.

Table 23.1 illustrates one major feature of the linkage between personality traits and PDs. Diagnostic criteria sets generally do not describe personality traits or even typical phenomenology; instead, PD criteria sets tend to be comprised of particular and problematic downstream characteristic adaptations. Harkness and Lilienfeld (1997) noted a major implication of McCrae's (1993) distinction: "Hence, relatively pure dispositional measures may show only moderate relations with diagnostic categories" (Harkness & Lilienfeld, 1997, p. 355). Later in the chapter, we describe a therapeutic approach that plays on the fungibility of the basic dispositions, attempting to shift the patient from problematic adaptations to more promising adaptations. First, however, we continue to explicate the links between the concepts of personality individual differences science and the PDs.

Full Exploration of the Personality Hierarchy Plus Unique Traits

Many current structural models of traits are hierarchical (e.g., Goldberg, 1980; Harkness, 1992; Watson et al., 1994). At the top of the hierarchy are a small number of traits of great breadth. Below this level, we find traits with narrower behavioral implications. These lower level traits enact some of the themes of the higher order traits, but they also contain some specific features not shared with the higher level or with other traits at this lower level. Further lower levels could be added to reflect more narrow width traits. From the highest levels of broad personality traits down to those of narrower bandwidth, a consistent behavior genetic picture appears to emerge.

Some impressive research on this topic has been conducted with the NEO-PI-R, which has an explicit hierarchical structure: 30 facet level constructs nested within the five domains of the five-factor model (Costa & McCrae, 1992). Jang, McCrae, Angleitner, Riemann, and Livesley (1998) conducted a cross-cultural behavior genetic study of the hierarchical personality model underlying the NEO-PI-R. The focus of their study was on the facet level. Jang et al. examined the behavior genetics of the specific variance of the facets, that is, the variance left after the five broad factors have been partialled out. For example, they studied the skeletal remains of the positive emotions facet after the flesh of the broad N, Extraversion, Openness to Experience, A, and Conscientiousness domains had been removed. From German and Canadian samples, they concluded that the specific variance of 26 of the 30 facets had a significant heritable component. Using test–retest data, they showed that the specific variance of facets had a reliable component and that "nearly half the reliable specific variance is heritable" (Jang et al., 1998, p. 1564).

The Jang et al. (1998) results suggest that there is a consistent and distributed genetic architecture throughout the personality hierarchy. At each level, from global factors down to narrower facets, the data seem to suggest the same pattern of genetic–environmental influence: There is substantial genetic influence, predominantly of an additive nature (more searching tests of nonadditive genetic models require other types of data than Jang et al. used); environmental influence is virtually all unshared. If this pattern turns out to be a reflection of reality and not a yet undeduced artifact of current methods, it has profound clinical implications. Some of these implications are discussed later in this chapter.

Clinically, there may even be another important level that is "below" the facet level. Our psychometric science captures what Allport (1937) referred to as "common traits." These are the traits for which each person has a status along a population trait dimension; for example, each person has a degree of tallness. Factor analytic solutions seek major basis vectors of common trait variation across a population. As a scientific agenda, quite reasonably, the field has focused first on these common traits. But Allport asserted that there are not only common traits but also "unique traits."

What are unique or "idiographic" traits? These are traits of such uniqueness that they have very low base rates in populations. Without much variance in a population, they are not found in a correlation matrix, so they cannot define common factors. For any individual, an Allportian possibility is that some major determining tendencies, not well captured by the major common traits that characterize populations, are wielding potent causal influence of adaptive significance. Allport's (1937) contention was that major causal horsepower in personality extends beyond the common traits, and thus important features might be lost in a purely nomothetically based assessment and therapy regimen.

Unique traits are not qualitatively different from common traits. Consideration of unique traits is really an extension of the thinking that values facets as providing information not deducible from the broad factors. The principle is that narrow does not mean unimportant or devoid of adaptive implications. Low base rate does not necessarily imply narrow, but generally one expects the two go together. To make clear the concept of the individual, unique trait, we use an example from normal psychology, in this case, the life of a psychologist. Starke Hathaway was a distinguished professor at the University of Minnesota, where he served as doctoral advisor to a number of well-known psychologists, including Paul Meehl. Hathaway is probably most widely known as the first author of the MMPI. In 1973, Hathaway participated in an extensive filmed interview conducted by James Butcher. During the course of the interview, Hathaway recalled incidents that illuminated a strong and unique determining tendency: He was drawn to build electronic apparatuses, especially if the apparatus could be used in research with an unknown outcome. This unique determining tendency appears to have played a role in Hathaway's shift of academic major from electrical engineering to psychology when he was a student at Ohio University. He strongly disliked an engineering class in which another student was in charge of the apparatuses and in which he was required to run "experiments" in which he already knew what would happen. Professor Porter, in Ohio University's psychology department, allowed him to build and use apparatus in real research. Hathaway noted that he later first attained some notoriety demonstrating vacuum tube lie detectors that he built and sold. The lie detection demonstrations involved Starke examining test subjects to solve a problem through lie detection, such as locating an object (again the link between apparatus and an unsolved problem). While at Minnesota, he developed a working relationship with the neurologist J. B. McKinley. By Hathaway's account, his ability to design and build apparatus for measuring neural potentials caught McKinley's attention and opened the door to a collaboration that would result in the MMPI.

It is an open question whether Hathaway's narrative personal history resulted from extensive Freudian "secondary revision," that is, the cleaning up of fragments in his life memory to assemble them into a narrative of greater coherence and direction than his real life warranted. Nevertheless, it seems possible that this seemingly narrow determining tendency (love of apparatus for unsolved problems) could have had important adaptive implications because of

its sheer power and behavioral penetrance. The point is illustrated in a thought experiment: Suppose one could leave untouched Hathaway's nomothetic traits (whether from, e.g., Costa & McCrae, 1992; Eysenck & Eysenck, 1985; Harkness et al., 1995; Tellegen & Waller, in press; or Zuckerman et al., 1993) and simply remove his "love of apparatus for unsolved problems." Our contention is that major adaptations and life course would have been significantly different because this one unique determining tendency was powerful for Hathaway. This narrow determining tendency seems hard to conceptualize as an effect of general Openness or even to a combination of broad higher order traits. Rather, "love of apparatus for unsolved problems" seems to have been a powerful determining tendency in its own right.

In fact, some observations suggest that genetic influence may penetrate to these lower levels, where one deals with very narrow, even unique, traits. In the course of the Minnesota Twin Study of Twins Reared Apart (Bouchard et al., 1990), monozygotic and dizygotic twins who had been separated and raised by adoptive families were extensively observed and tested. Great breakthroughs often come from having just the right phenomenon on the experimental bench, before the eyes of the scientist. Some of the informal observations of monozygotic twins reared apart (MZA) in these studies may alter the way humans look at themselves. One aspect of these observations is the existence of similarities that seem unique to the twin pair:

> While videotaping an interview with one twin, we discovered that he was an accomplished raconteur with a fund of amusing anecdotes, so, while interviewing the cotwin, we asked him if he knew any funny stories. "Why sure," he said, leaning back with a practiced air, "I'll tell you a story" and proceeded to demonstrate his concordance. A pair of British MZAs, who had met for the first time as adults just a month previously, both firmly refused in their separate interviews to express opinions on controversial topics; since long before they discovered each other's existence,

each had resolutely avoided controversy. Another pair were both habitual gigglers, although each had been raised by adoptive parents whom they described as undemonstrative and dour, and neither had known anyone who laughed as freely as she did until finally she met her twin. Both members of another pair independently reported that they refrained from voting in political elections on the principle that they did not feel themselves well enough informed to make wise choices. A pair of male MZAs, at their first adult reunion, discovered that they both used Vademecum toothpaste, Canoe shaving lotion, Vitalis hair tonic, and Lucky Strike cigarettes. After that meeting, they exchanged birthday presents that crossed in the mail and proved to be identical choices, made independently in separate cities (Lykken et al., 1992, p. 1565).

The authors noted that dizygotic twins, regular siblings born at the same time but reared apart, do not show a similar level of unusual and specific similarities. This study laid on the laboratory bench, for our view, a truly remarkable phenomenon, namely, the MZAs. The informal observations of the study suggest that MZAs end up with impressive but rather unusual similarities and that less genetically related (dizygotic) twins, while resembling their relatives much more than strangers, do not possess the same level of "eerie" coincidences. These coincidences seem to occur across all levels of adaptive significance, from toothpaste choices on one end to broader career and life trajectories on the other. If correct about the level of unique similarity of MZAs, these observations shake the foundations of one's views of oneself, from ancient philosophies to present musings. Of course, the "if correct" is a big "if." The MZA coincidences are the more informal results of the study, and the biggest science lesson of psychology is that no human nervous system is immune to theory guiding the categorization that guides the counting. So *coincidences* must be defined and metrified, and the observations must be confirmed and replicated (Wyatt, 1993). Nevertheless, if

they stand (and knowing the scientists, we place our bet that they do stand), they are the most provocative observations on human personality of the 20th century. Not just every personality psychologist but every person must now wonder: What would another genetic copy of me be like? Even if one does not have an identical twin who was reared in another family, as a human imagines what one's twin would have been like, we must give up some romantic fantasies about our human nature and personality.

Just because one does not have an MZA, one is not exempt from the guiding forces, the determining tendencies, and the personality traits that produce the eerie coincidences in MZAs. To return to Starke Hathaway, even though he had no MZA cotwin, his narrative makes one think of the famous Charles Addam's cartoon, often found in introductory psychology texts, depicting twins encountering each other at the patent attorney's office, with matching apparatuses perched on their knees, bearing the caption, "separated at birth, the Mallifert twins meet accidentally." If correct, these observations call for some renewed scientific optimism because the pernicious power of the "random walk" (Meehl, 1978) may be less than one feared. But the specific and unusual nature of the MZA coincidences force psychologists to look again at the challenges raised by Allport against the completeness of nomothetic traits.

Thus, there may be important genetically influenced determining tendencies at all levels of trait breadth, from broad common traits, to narrow facets, to unique traits. The clinical lesson is that personality problems could arise from traits and patients' adaptations to them at all levels of trait breadth. For example, the NEO-PI-R not only provides assessment at the five-factor level but also provides information from narrower facets. Such facet-level information may be critical for a particular patient. The clinical picture may also require that one detects unique determining tendencies. Unique traits are not beyond the reach of scientific method. The highly individuating interview approaches of Fischer (1985) and Finn (1996) could be coupled with nomothetic personality trait assessment strategies such as the MMPI-2-based PSY-5 or NEO-PI-R.

As noted in the *American Psychological Association's Personality Assessment Working Group Report, Part I* (Meyer et al., 1998, p. 12), multimethod–multitrait methodological concepts could in principle be applied to unique traits.

To summarize this section, we focused on two important features of the connection between the personality traits of individual differences science and the PDs of the *DSMs*. First, PD criteria tend to be causally downstream from the traits; they generally reflect characteristic adaptations. Second, traits exist at all levels of breadth, and characteristic adaptations are probably erected around them at all levels. This becomes an important caveat for all assessment-based clinical intervention. Nomothetic tests may act like a sieve. What the sieve catches, common personality traits, is essential for treatment planning (Harkness & Lilienfeld, 1997; Miller, 1991). But that which slips through the sieve, very narrow or even unique traits, may also be critical elements in the clinical picture of the patient.

Numerous other issues in the trait-PD link are beyond the scope of this chapter, for example, the choice of the most appropriate trait model (Clark, 1993; Watson et al., 1994; Widiger, 1993, 1994; Widiger & Trull, 1992), the impact of trait configuration, assessments that capture all the necessary ranges of the traits (Harkness & McNulty, 1994; Rouse, Finger, & Butcher, 1999), the role of evaluative traits (Almagor et al., 1995), and the importance of taxonomic subcategories (Meehl, 1995). Nevertheless, we hope we have convinced the reader that personality individual differences science offers a new vantage point for conceptualizing the PDs. We also believe that personality individual differences science offers a new approach to psychotherapeutic intervention for patients with personality-based problems.

OUTLINES OF A NEW PSYCHOTHERAPEUTIC STRATEGY

The major current strategies for psychotherapeutic intervention—cognitive, behavioral, and dynamic—were all developed without benefit of the conceptual power arising from the last several decades of progress in the individual differences science of personality. To take this new science from journal pages and walk into the consulting room to face troubled people and bring them new understanding, solutions, relief, and opportunities for growth is to face fully the problems of integrating science and practice. The background science promises great potential, but without a fresh plan for clinical intervention informed by this science, the integration will not occur. Emerging professional standards require that therapeutic interventions be sufficiently defined so as to allow testing (Chambless, 1995). In this chapter, we do not provide a treatment manual; however, we do suggest the outlines of a treatment, informed by personality individual differences science, that could be manualized. Our outline of treatment is broad; a number of different structural models of personality could be used within this framework. The treatment we describe would be applicable when the problems entail long-term patterns of adjustment that are reflected across a variety of situations—problems classified by Beutler (1986) as "complex."

We owe much for the outlined intervention to McCrae's (1994) contribution to the first edition of this volume, Miller's (1991) concept of therapeutic tailoring, Lykken's (1995) ideas on intervention with difficult children, and Finn's (1996; Finn & Tonsager, 1992) therapeutic assessment approach. Finn, in turn, was influenced by Fischer's (1985) work on individualized assessment. Finn (1996) offered an assessment-based intervention approach with a number of explicit stages, generally conducted in two meetings with testing sandwiched between them. In the first meeting, a collaborative therapeutic alliance is formed. The assessment approaches to be used are introduced, and questions are solicited from the client: What does the client want to learn from the assessment? Then the assessment is conducted, and feedback is planned, organized around the questions generated by the client. In a feedback session, the client-generated questions are answered. Finn's outstanding contribution is a model of a brief assessment consultation with therapeutic effects (Finn & Tonsager, 1992; Newman & Greenway, 1997).

In this section, we incorporate the concept of alternative characteristic adaptations, integrate the behavior genetics concept of active genotype–

environment correlations, and extend Finn's approach to offer a model of a complete course of therapy. This clinical intervention involves learning about the links among the client's personality traits, presenting problems, life patterns, typical environments, and major characteristic and alternative adaptations. Therapy is not an abstract lecture to the patient by the therapist. Rather, it involves "working through." That is, therapy is accomplished over a series of sessions in which the individual brings in fresh life examples of new concerns, recurring problems, adaptive challenges, and environmental presses. Across these sessions, the clinician uses the fruits of personality individual differences science to guide the development of the client's increased self-knowledge, new adaptive skills, and increased power over selecting, evoking, and creating situations. Here is our outline of the procedures of such a treatment:

1. Establish and maintain a collaborative working alliance. In the domain of PDs, this involves continual monitoring and intervention.
2. During intake, develop an understanding of the problem areas encapsulated as "presenting complaint"; also develop an understanding of major adaptive challenges related to long-standing patterns. Through open-ended interviewing, examine for highly individuating determining tendencies. Instruct the patient on major nomothetic dimensions of personality and describe contemplated assessment procedures. Following Finn's (1996) suggestion, solicit patient questions to be answered by the assessment. As questions are developed, explore links between major problem areas and adaptive challenges resulting from personality. Sensitively add therapist-generated questions that may further engage the patient and offer insight into the connections between personality and life adaptation patterns.
3. Conduct formal assessment. Gain a comprehensive understanding of the patient's status on major nomothetic traits. Recommendations of the *American Psychological Association's Board of Professional Affairs Psychological Assessment Work Group Report, Part I* (Meyer et al., 1998) include the use of multiple methods (e.g., self-report questionnaire, structured interviews) and multiple data sources (e.g., self-reports, peer reports, spousal–partner reports). Various assessment instruments have different foci (Widiger & Trull, 1997) that can guide test selection to target suspected problem areas. To interpret, have an extensive knowledge of the constructs of major personality individual differences traits. On the basis of this knowledge, prepare answers to patient and therapist questions connecting the patient's personality with current concerns, clinical problems, life patterns, major adaptive challenges, and the patient's typical environments.

4. Over an adequate but time-limited series of therapy sessions, "work through" those answers by demonstrating the links between personality and the fresh concerns brought in by the patient to each session. In each session, demonstrate the links among personality, current concerns, life patterns, clinical problems, major adaptive challenges and choices, and especially the environments the patient selects, evokes, and creates (Buss, 1987; Plomin et al., 1977; Scarr, 1996; Scarr & McCartney, 1983). Collaboratively develop a treatment plan exploring the existence of problematic characteristic adaptations the patient has fashioned around his or her personality dispositions. Explore options for the development of new characteristic adaptations that are consonant with the patient's personality. For symptom relief, select specific techniques drawn from the best of general law psychology. Select interventions to match the personality and problems of the patient. Thus, the introvert is not asked to star in a psychodrama, and the person of high boredom susceptibility is not asked to keep extensive journals (Miller, 1991).
5. Prepare homework involving the selection, evocation, and creation of environments. Frame change as alterations of characteristic adaptations. Provide hope and expectation for change by describing others who have extreme personality traits but who have fashioned nondestructive, nonpathological adaptations. Thus, couple hope and expectation for change with self-understanding and self-acceptance of that which is difficult to change.
6. Explain the origin of personality traits based up behavior genetics research, honestly describing

the limits of psychology's current knowledge. For example, parents are not a focus of blame for the patient's personality (this is a central feature of many therapies unsupported by solid evidence; extremes of parental behavior receive no such exemption, of course; see Scarr, 1996). Focus not on the past but on finding new adaptations and finding healthier ways to realize one's strengths and dispositions.

7. Terminate with plans in place for continued development. Make contingency plans for "relapse" and crisis. Schedule annual check-ups to review self-understanding and the evolution of characteristic adaptations.

The central activities of this intervention are uniquely tied to personality individual differences science: They involve active working through of presenting problems, adaptive styles, clinical patterns, current concerns, typical environments, and the exploration of new options, all guided by an understanding of the client's personality. Such work is empowering but realistic. It educates the patient about his or her capacity to control environments, while retaining realism about the stability of the patient's basic dispositions. This is not a mere knock-off of cognitive, behavioral, or dynamic approaches, although it draws techniques from each. Personality individual differences science clearly suggests the promise of such an intervention. In therapy derived from individual differences science, great emphasis is placed on exploring the typical environments of the patient to determine the extent to which they are characteristic adaptations, that is, downstream trait enactments. To what extent has the person selected, evoked, or created those environments (Buss, 1987) in ways that flow from basic dispositions? Personality individual differences science differs from other therapeutic approaches in that it does not regard operants, cognitions, or environments as originating randomly. Rather, operants, cognitions, and environments tend to be characteristic adaptations; these trait enactments are then also sculpted by the pre-existing pattern of other characteristic adaptations.

Personality individual differences science represents the successful union of dispositional approaches to personality, psychometrics, and behavior genetics. It is a science that is ready to move from journal pages to the consulting room. We believe that the therapy outlined here can make a fresh contribution to clinical intervention when the problems involve the patient's personality (Beutler's, 1986, "complex" category). To integrate this science with practice, the field must fully appreciate the implications of individual differences science for clinical work on PDs and other problems devolving from the patient's personality. If the field does less, then psychology fails to integrate this science into practice.

References

Ahadi, S. A., & Rothbart, M. K. (1994). Temperament, development, and the big five. In C. F. Halverson, Jr., G. A. Kohnstamm, & R. P. Martin (Eds.), *The developing structure of temperament and personality from infancy to adulthood* (pp. 189–207). Hillsdale, NJ: Erlbaum.

Allport, G. W. (1937). *Personality: A psychological interpretation.* New York: Holt.

Almagor, M., Tellegen, A., & Waller, N. G. (1995). The big seven model: A cross-cultural replication and further exploration of the basic dimensions of natural language trait descriptors. *Journal of Personality and Social Psychology, 69,* 300–307.

American Psychiatric Association. (1987). *Diagnostic and statistical manual of mental disorders* (3rd ed., rev.). Washington, DC: Author.

American Psychiatric Association. (1994). *Diagnostic and statistical manual of mental disorders* (4th ed.). Washington, DC: Author.

Beutler, L. E. (1986). Systematic eclectic psychotherapy. In J. C. Norcross (Ed.), *Handbook of eclectic psychotherapy* (pp. 94–131). New York: Brunner/Mazel.

Block, J. (1995). A contrarian view of the five-factor approach to personality description. *Psychological Bulletin, 117,* 187–215.

Bouchard, T. J., Lykken, D. T., McGue, M., Segal, N. L., & Tellegen, A. (1990). Sources of human psychological differences: The Minnesota Study of Twins Reared Apart. *Science, 250,* 223–228.

Buss, D. M. (1987). Selection, evocation, and manipulation. *Journal of Personality and Social Psychology, 53,* 1214–1221.

Buss, D. M., Haselton, M. G., Shackelford, T. K., Bleske, A. L., & Wakefield, J. C. (1998). Adaptations, exaptations, and spandrels. *American Psychologist, 53,* 533–548.

Cattell, R. B. (1950). *Personality: A systematic, theoretical, and factual study.* New York: McGraw.

Chambless, D. (1995). Training and dissemination of empirically validated psychological treatment: Report and recommendations. *The Clinical Psychologist, 48,* 23.

Clark, L. A. (1993). Personality disorder diagnosis: Limitations of the five-factor model. *Psychological Inquiry, 4,* 100–104.

Clark, L. A., & Watson, D. (1999). Personality, disorder, and personality disorder: Towards more rational conceptualization. *Journal of Personality Disorders, 13,* 142–151.

Clark, L. A., Watson, D., & Mineka, S. (1994). Temperament, personality, and the mood and anxiety disorders. *Journal of Abnormal Psychology, 103,* 103–116.

Cloninger, C. R., Svrakic, D. M., & Przybeck, T. R. (1993). A psychobiological model of temperament and character. *Archives of General Psychiatry, 50,* 975–990.

Costa, P. T., Jr., & McCrae, R. R. (1992). *NEO-PI-R: Professional manual.* Odessa, FL: Psychological Assessment Resources.

Costa, P. T., Jr., & Widiger, T. A. (Eds.). (1994). *Personality disorders and the five-factor model of personality.* Washington, DC: American Psychological Association.

DeFries, J. C., Kuse, A. R., & Vandenberg, S. G. (1979). Genetic correlations, environmental correlations, and behavior. In J. R. Royce & L. P. Mos (Eds.) *Theoretical advances in behavior genetics* (pp. 389–421). Alphen aan den Rijn, Netherlands: Sijthoff Noordhoff International.

Depue, R. A. (1996). A neurobiological framework for the structure of personality and emotion: Implications for personality disorders. In J. F. Clarkin & M. F. Lenzenweger (Eds.), *Major theories of personality disorder* (pp. 347–390). New York: Guilford.

Digman, J. M., (1990). Personality structure: Emergence of the five-factor model. *Annual Review of Psychology, 41,* 417–440.

Eysenck, H. J., & Eysenck, M. W. (1985). *Personality and individual differences: A natural sciences approach.* New York: Plenum Press.

Finn, S. E. (1996). *Manual for using the MMPI-2 as a therapeutic intervention.* Minneapolis: University of Minnesota Press.

Finn, S. E., & Tonsager, M. E. (1992). Therapeutic effects of providing MMPI-2 test feedback to college students awaiting therapy. *Psychological Assessment, 4,* 278–287.

Fischer, C. T. (1985). *Individualizing psychological assessment.* Hillsdale, NJ: Erlbaum.

Frances, A. J., & Widiger, T. A. (1986). The classification of personality disorders: An overview of problems and solutions. In A. J. Frances & R. E. Hales (Eds.), *The American Psychiatric Association annual review* (pp. 240–257). Washington, DC: American Psychiatric Press.

Goldberg, L. R. (1980, May). *Some ruminations about the structure of individual differences: Developing a common lexicon for the major characteristics of human personality.* Meeting of the Western Psychological Association, Honolulu, HI.

Goldsmith, H. H., Buss, K. A., & Lemery, K. S. (1997). Toddler and childhood temperament: Expanded content, stronger genetic evidence, and new evidence for the importance of environment. *Developmental Psychology, 33,* 891–905.

Gray, J. A. (1982). *The neuropsychology of anxiety.* New York: Oxford University Press.

Grove, W. M., & Tellegen, A. (1991). Problems in the classification of personality disorders. *Journal of Personality Disorders, 5,* 31–42.

Harkness, A. R. (1992). Fundamental topics in the personality disorders: Candidate trait dimensions from lower regions of the hierarchy. *Psychological Assessment, 4,* 251–259.

Harkness, A. R., & Hogan, R. (1995). Theory and measurement of traits: Two views. In J. N. Butcher (Ed.), *Clinical personality assessment: Practical approaches* (pp. 28–41). New York: Oxford University Press.

Harkness, A. R., & Lilienfeld, S. O. (1997). Individual differences science for treatment planning: Personality traits [Invited article]. *Psychological Assessment, 9,* 349–360.

Harkness, A. R., & McNulty, J. L. (1994). The Personality Psychopathology Five (PSY-5): Issue from the pages of a diagnostic manual instead of a dictionary. In S. Strack & M. Lorr (Eds.), *Differentiating normal and abnormal personality* (pp. 291–315). New York: Springer.

Harkness, A. R., McNulty, J. L., & Ben-Porath, Y. S. (1995). The Personality Psychopathology Five (PSY-5): Constructs and MMPI-2 scales. *Psychological Assessment, 7,* 104–114.

Jang, K. L., McCrae, R. R., Angleitner, A., Riemann, R., & Livesley, W. J. (1998). Heritability of facet-level traits in a cross-cultural twin sample: Support for a hierarchical model of personality. *Jour-*

nal of Personality and Social Psychology, 74, 1556–1565.

Knight, R. P. (1953). Borderline states. *Bulletin of the Menninger Clinic, 17,* 1–12.

Lenzenweger, M. F., & Clarkin, J. F., (1996). Personality disorders: History, classification, and research issues. In J. F. Clarkin & M. F. Lenzenweger (Eds.), *Major theories of personality disorder* (pp. 1–35). New York: Guilford.

Livesley, W. J., Jang, K. L., & Vernon, P. A. (1998). Phenotypic and genetic structure of traits delineating personality disorder. *Archives of General Psychiatry, 55,* 941–948.

Loehlin, J. C. (1992). *Genes and environment in personality development.* Newbury Park, CA: Sage.

Lykken, D. T. (1995). *The antisocial personalities.* Hillsdale, NJ: Erlbaum.

Lykken, D. T., McGue, M., Tellegen, A., & Bouchard, T. J., Jr. (1992). Emergenesis: Genetic traits that may not run in families. *American Psychologist, 47,* 1565–1577.

Mack, J. E. (1975). Borderline states: An historical perspective. In J. E. Mack (Ed.), *Borderline states in psychiatry* (pp. 1–27). New York: Grune & Stratton.

MacKenzie, K. R. (1994). Using personality measurements in clinical practice. In P. T. Costa, Jr., & T. A. Widiger (Eds.), *Personality disorders and the five-factor model of personality* (pp. 237–250). Washington, DC: American Psychological Association.

McCrae, R. R. (1993). Moderated analyses of longitudinal personality stability. *Journal of Personality and Social Psychology, 65,* 577–585.

McCrae, R. R. (1994). A reformulation of Axis II: Personality and personality-related problems. In P. T. Costa, Jr., & T. A. Widiger (Eds.), *Personality disorders and the five-factor model of personality* (pp. 303–309). Washington, DC: American Psychological Association.

McCrae, R. R., & Costa, P. T., Jr. (1995). Trait explanations in personality psychology. *European Journal of Personality, 9,* 231–252.

McCrae, R. R., & Costa, P. T., Jr. (1997). Personality trait structure as a human universal. *American Psychologist, 52,* 509–516.

Meehl, P. E. (1978). Theoretical risks and tabular asterisks: Sir Karl, Sir Ronald, and the slow progress of soft psychology. *Journal of Consulting and Clinical Psychology, 46,* 806–834.

Meehl, P. E. (1986). Trait language and behaviorese. In T. Thompson & M. D. Zeiler (Eds.), *Analysis and integration of behavioral units* (pp. 315–334). Hillsdale, NJ: Erlbaum.

Meehl, P. E. (1990). Toward an integrated theory of schizotaxia, schizotypy, and schizophrenia. *Journal of Personality Disorders, 4,* 1–99.

Meehl, P. E. (1995). Bootstraps taxometrics: Solving the classification problem in psychopathology. *American Psychologist, 50,* 266–275.

Messick, S. (1981). Constructs and their vicissitudes in educational and psychological measurement. *Psychological Bulletin, 89,* 575–588.

Meyer, G. J., Finn, S. E., Eyde, L. D., Kay, G. G., Kubiszyn, T. W., Moreland, K. L., Eisman, E. J., & Dies, R. R. (1998). *Benefits and costs of psychological assessment in healthcare delivery: Report of the Board of Professional Affairs Psychological Assessment Work Group, Part 1.* Washington, DC: American Psychological Association.

Miller, T. R. (1991). The psychotherapeutic utility of the five-factor model of personality: A clinician's experience. *Journal of Personality Assessment, 57,* 415–433.

Millon, T. (1981). *Disorders of personality: DSM-III, Axis II.* New York: Wiley.

Neale, M. C., & Cardon, L. R. (1992). *Methodology for genetic studies of twins and families.* Dordrecht, The Netherlands: Kluwer.

Newman, M. L., & Greenway, P. (1997). Therapeutic effects of providing MMPI-2 test feedback to clients at a university counseling service: A collaborative approach. *Psychological Assessment, 9,* 122–131.

Plomin, R., DeFries, J. C., & Loehlin, J. C. (1977). Genotype–environment interaction and correlation in the analysis of human behavior. *Psychological Bulletin, 84,* 309–322.

Riemann, R., Angleitner, A., & Strelau, J. (1997). Genetic and environmental influences on personality: A study of twins reared together using the self- and peer-report NEO-FFI scales. *Journal of Personality, 65,* 449–475.

Rothbart, M. K., Derryberry, D., & Posner, M. I. (1994). A psychobiological approach to the development of temperament. In J. E. Bates & T. D. Wachs (Eds.) *Temperament: Individual differences at the interface of biology and behavior* (pp. 83–116). Washington, DC: American Psychological Association.

Rouse, S. V., Finger, M. S., & Butcher, J. N. (1999). Advances in clinical personality measurement: An item response theory analysis of the MMPI-2 PSY-5 scales. *Journal of Personality Assessment, 72,* 282–307.

Rowe, D. C. (1994). *The limits of family influence: Genes, experience, and behavior.* New York: Guilford Press.

Scarr, S. (1996). How people make their own environments: Implications for parents and policy makers. *Psychology, Public Policy, and Law, 2,* 204–228.

Scarr, S., & McCartney, K. (1983). How people make their own environments: A theory of genotype-environment effects. *Child Development, 54,* 424–435.

Schroeder, M. L., Wormsworth, J. A., & Livesley, W. J. (1992). Dimensions of personality disorder and their relationship to the Big Five dimensions of personality. *Psychological Assessment, 4,* 47–53.

Tellegen, A. (1988). The analysis of consistency in personality assessment. *Journal of Personality, 56,* 621–663.

Tellegen, A. (1991). Personality traits: Issues of definition, evidence, and assessment. In D. Cichetti & W. Grove (Eds.), *Thinking clearly about psychology: Essays in honor of Paul Everett Meehl* (pp. 10–35). Minneapolis: University of Minnesota Press.

Tellegen, A., Lykken, D. T., Bouchard, T. J., Wilcox, K. J., Segal, N. L., & Rich, S. (1988). Personality similarity in twins reared apart and together. *Journal of Personality and Social Psychology, 54,* 1031–1039.

Tellegen, A., & Waller, N. G. (in press). *Exploring personality through test construction: Development of the Multidimensional Personality Questionnaire.* Minneapolis: University of Minnesota Press.

Trull, T. J. (1992). *DSM-IV-R* personality disorders and the five-factor model of personality: An empirical comparison. *Journal of Abnormal Psychology, 101,* 553–560.

Watson, D., & Clark, L. A. (1993). Behavioral disinhibition versus constraint: A dispositional perspective. In D. M. Wegner & J. W. Pennebaker (Eds.), *Handbook of mental control* (pp. 506–527). New York: Prentice Hall.

Watson, D., Clark, L. A., & Harkness, A. R. (1994). Structures of personality and their relevance to psychopathology. *Journal of Abnormal Psychology, 103,* 18–31.

Widiger, T. A. (1993). The *DSM-III-R* categorical personality disorder diagnoses: A critique and an alternative. *Psychological Inquiry, 4,* 75–90.

Widiger, T. A. (1994). Conceptualizing a disorder of personality from the five-factor model. In P. T. Costa, Jr., & T. A. Widiger (Eds.), *Personality disorders and the five-factor model of personality* (pp. 311–317). Washington, DC: American Psychological Association.

Widiger, T. A., & Trull, T. J. (1992). Personality and psychopathology: An application of the five-factor model. *Journal of Personality, 60,* 363–393.

Widiger, T. A., & Trull, T. J. (1997). Assessment of the five-factor model of personality. *Journal of Personality Assessment, 68,* 228–250.

Wiggins, J. S. (Ed.). (1996). *The five-factor model of personality: Theoretical perspectives.* New York: Guilford.

Wyatt, W. J. (1993). Identical twins, emergenesis, and environments. *American Psychologist, 48,* 1294–1295.

Zuckerman, M. (1991). *Psychobiology of personality.* New York: Cambridge University Press.

Zuckerman, M. (1994). *Behavioral expressions and biosocial bases of sensation seeking.* New York: Cambridge University Press.

Zuckerman, M., Kuhlman, D. M., Joireman, J., & Teta, P. (1993). A comparison of three structural models for personality: The big three, the Big Five, and the alternative five. *Journal of Personality and Social Psychology, 65,* 757–768.

CHAPTER 24

TREATMENT OF PERSONALITY DISORDERS FROM THE PERSPECTIVE OF THE FIVE-FACTOR MODEL

Michael H. Stone

Very few patients come to members of the mental health profession for help who do not manifest and experience difficulties in living from various peculiarities of personality. Often enough, these peculiarities are widespread enough and intense enough to amount, in the eyes of the clinician, to a "disorder" of personality. It is common currency to speak of such people as "suffering" from this or that personality disorder. But in reality and because personality is ego syntonic (i.e., in harmony with each person's self-conception and not a source of anguish), those with distinctly disordered personalities seldom suffer themselves; rather, they make others—coworkers, family members, acquaintances—suffer.

As a case in point, the famous art critic of 19th-century England, John Ruskin, was as cruel to his wife as he was keen as a connoisseur of the painted canvas. Compulsive, stuffy, prudish, he was unable to consummate their marriage and, apparently to externalize the problem on her, tormented her unceasingly with rebukes, humiliating remarks, and criticisms. With her he became a verbal bully, even as he was being lionized by genteel society. When, after some years, she finally sued for annulment (and left him for his best friend, the painter–protégé Everett Millais), he seemed to have had a moment of self-realization. What had all his life up to that point been ego syntonic became suddenly dystonic: He saw that he had been needlessly harsh and degrading toward her and had driven her away. Only then did Ruskin suffer from his—what would one call it

now?—obsessive–compulsive–sadistic personality disorder. The one who suffered beforehand was Mrs. Ruskin (Kemp, 1983).

The fact is, one cannot characterize the personality of a complex man like Ruskin with just a few terms lifted from the sparse shelf of descriptors in the category-based *DSM-IV* (fourth edition of the *Diagnostic and Statistical Manual of Mental Disease*; American Psychiatric Association, 1994). One only has 10 choices (in the *DSM* of 1980, there were 11) to describe the personality disorders of a patient, which is itself the most serious problem one now confronts in the domain of abnormal personality and its treatment. One is asked, in effect, to sketch the 15–20% of humanity (now numbering 6 billion and belonging to numberless cultures and subcultures) who show markedly aberrant or irritating personalities with a palette of less than a dozen hues. This is analogous to insisting one relies on a vocabulary of *red, yellow, blue, violet, orange, green,* and *purple* to describe the myriad variations of color that actually exist in nature (Widiger, 1997).

CATEGORY VERSUS DIMENSION: TWO APPROACHES TO THE TAXONOMY OF PERSONALITY

Although descriptions of different "character types" go back to the time of Aristotle's pupil Theophrastus and of temperament types, to the still earlier time of Hippocrates, *personality* as a term is comparatively new, hardly being encountered until the end of the

19th century. In France, Théodule Ribot envisioned a continuum spanning the normal and pathological ranges in personality—the term he used in 1885. Influenced by Charles Darwin, he stressed the importance of heredity in shaping individual characteristics. Pierre Janet wrote a monograph on personality in 1929, although he did not give a systematic typology. In Germany, Kraepelin (1915) described both varieties of temperament (depressive, manic, irritable, and cyclothymic—all related to manic-depressive psychosis and its attenuated forms in close relatives) and varieties of personality. He used the term *psychopathische Persönlichkeiten* (psychopathic personalities) to mean mentally ill (psycho + pathic) or abnormal. *Psychopathic* did not take on its current meaning (as an especially intense type of antisocial personality with glibness, deceitfulness, and callousness) until the mid-20th century when the label "psychopath" was redefined and popularized by Hervey Cleckley (1941). Yet for the most part, Kraepelin's taxonomy emphasized the disagreeable and antisocial. He spoke mainly of such types as the *erregbar* (irritable), *haltlos* (unstable), *Triebmensch* (impulse-ridden person), *verschroben* (eccentric), *Gesellschaftsfeinde* (enemy of the people), and the *streitsüchtig* (combative). Kraepelin also added some "subtypes" within his categories: Among the antisocial *Gesellschaftsfeinde,* for example, one may encounter instances of *Zechprällerei* (skipping out of restaurants without paying the bill).

In keeping with the universal tendency in science to describe the extreme and the dramatic before turning attention to the subtle, categories of personality (and here I include the two main compartments: *temperament,* the inborn aspects, and *character,* the environmentally acquired aspects) appeared first in the literature. The contributors to this area were mostly psychiatrists who were primarily interested in the illness or disease of personality and its treatment, hence resulting in the medical-based approach. This was true not only of Kraepelin and Janet but also of Freud, whose character types accorded with his theory of early development (e.g., oral–depressive, anal–obsessive–compulsive, phallic–narcissistic). Likewise, the typology of Kurt Schneider (1923/1950) was category based and included 10 types, only half of which map easily onto

the current *DSM-IV* Axis II categories: anankastic = obsessive–compulsive; fanatic = paranoid; attention seeking = hysteric–histrionic; affectionless = antisocial; and weak willed = dependent.

The obvious advantages of a category-based taxonomy are ease of use (a palette with only a dozen colors or so) and utility when dealing with the more extreme aberrations—where the medical bias of such a taxonomy seems more justifiable. The obvious disadvantages involve the incompleteness of such an approach, when one considers the totality of personality, normal and abnormal (which would require a palette of hundreds of colors, as it were: the mauves, the heliotropes, the beiges, and all the other subtle mixtures), and the rigidity of a narrow categorical system. Because real people are so different from the category "prototypes"—each person, especially each "disordered" person, being a *Gemisch* [mixture] of traits belonging to several categories and to qualities not even addressed in the categories—it became obvious that something different was needed if one were to make any sense of the true complexity of personality. This need gave rise—I think it is fair to say—to the lexical approach and to the related dimensional approaches.

These approaches were pursued and championed primarily by psychologists, in as much as their primary concern was not the medical study and treatment of diseases but the meticulous research into and rigorous description of all mental phenomena, normal and abnormal alike. Among the pioneers in these endeavors were Gordon Allport and Henry Odbert (1936), from whose "psycholexical" study out of Harvard University's Psychological Laboratory came a gigantic list of about 18,000 words, culled from an unabridged dictionary, that pertained to personality. Many of these words are, to be sure, either quaint and archaic or slangy. Thus, one finds *fable monger, sciolous* (knowing only superficially), *lethiferous* (death dealing—not a bad word for Miloševic, only no one knows it), and *sulphitic* (acid natured?—it is not in my unabridged dictionary) and the slangy *fat-brained, geezer,* and *screwy.* One also finds pairs of words with precisely the same meaning: one in common use (*insubordinate*) and the other a "hifalutin" word (*contumacious*) used by those manifesting the traits of affectedness or preciosity (aspects of narcissism). The great achievement of Allport and Odbert consists of their complete vocabulary of personality, out of which everyone—from the normal to the grossly maladaptive or repugnant —could be adequately described.

The next step in the development of the lexical approach was to reduce this vast and unwieldy dictionary to something with more manageable proportions. Absent the archaic, the slangy, and the lengthy "$5 words" only pedants use, the trait dictionary can be boiled down to less than 1,000 words. Over the next 50 years, many psychologists, pursuing factor analytic approaches, created either briefer lexical lists (viz., those of Goldberg [1982] and Gough [Gough & Heilbrun, 1983]) or else factor sets comprised of about 20–50 groupings of similar personality trait adjectives into which the lexical lists could conveniently and meaningfully be compartmentalized. I discussed a number of these in an earlier publication (Stone, 1993), including the 16 shadings of interpersonal behavior resulting from blends of the two dimensions Extraversion and Agreeableness in the circumplex model of Wiggins (1982), the 24 factors of Tyrer and Alexander (1988), and the 79 dimensions of Livesley (1987). Livesley, for example, united common descriptors of the schizoid personality disorder (SZD)—loner, detached, withdrawn, seclusive—into a dimension that he named "low affiliation."

With respect to the newer and briefer lexical lists —some of which have been developed in other countries, reflecting other cultures (viz., Yang & Bond, 1990, for the Chinese language and culture) —vocabularies with from 300 terms (Gough & Heilbrun, 1983) to 5–600 terms (Goldberg, 1982; Stone, 1990b; Yang & Bond, 1990) are sufficient. My revised list (Stone, 1993, pp. 100–103) contains 625 negative or unflattering traits and 101 positive traits. This lopsidedness does not represent pathological focus on the abnormal, but instead the fact that in all the languages known to me, there are simply more negative than positive descriptors. I believe this is a reflection of the human tendency, now embedded in languages, to pay more attention to the ways in which certain people bother or endanger others than to the ways they may please them. Evolutionarily speaking, this has survival value.

There are synonyms for *honest* (fair, virtuous, just, respectable) but not nearly as many as for *deceitfulness* (treacherous, cunning, machiavellian, devious, dishonest, sly, deceptive, false, tricky, cheating, slippery, untrustworthy—one could go on). It is important to be able to convey specific warning signs regarding the threats to one's welfare others may expose one to, hence the proliferation of trait words with negative valence.

Meantime, still other psychologists have carried on the search for larger hierarchies, embracing all the important factors (and thereby all the traits in everyday usage), that might constitute an irreducible set of personality-related umbrella concepts. Eysenck (1947) proposed a three-dimensional model where Extraversion, Neuroticism, and Psychoticism were the orthogonal (in a three-dimensional space) umbrella concepts. Earlier, McDougall (1932) suggested that personality may be analyzed into five separate factors—the first proposal of what has come to be recognized as the five factor model (FFM). Tupes and Christal (1961/1992) developed the model further, with the ingredients consisting of surgency, emotional stability, Agreeableness, dependability, and culture and their opposites. (Currently, it has become more common to speak of Extraversion, Neuroticism, Agreeableness, Conscientiousness, and Openness to Experience and their opposites.) Extraversion versus introversion, terms derived from Jung's 1921 monograph, depict schizoid (inwardly withdrawn) versus manic (outgoing) people. Neuroticism covers the range from comfortable normalcy to anxious, fearful people. Agreeableness, allied both to normalcy and (when excessive) to dependent people, has its opposite, Antagonism, which takes in, at the extremes, sadistic and antisocial–psychopathic people. Conscientiousnes covers aspects both of normalcy and of obsessive–compulsive people and its opposite, negligence, those who are careless, aimless, undependable, and so forth. Openness refers to being open to new ideas as opposed to people who are "closed" to new ideas, such as narrow-minded, biased, or rigid people.

In recent years, Cloninger and his colleagues (Cloninger, 1986; Cloninger & Svrakic, 1993; Cloninger, Skravic, & Przybeck, 1993) have proposed a biopsychosocial model of personality, in which they strove to find correspondence among certain major dimensions and alterations in brain chemistry that may underlie these dimensions. In this model, the overarching concepts of Novelty Seeking, Harm Avoidance, and Reward Dependence are assumed to reflect individual differences in the activities of the neurotransmitters, dopamine, serotonin, and norepinephrine, respectively. Because people can vary from "high" to "low" along these three dimensions, eight personality configurations, answering to eight of the DSM-personality types, can be described. Thus, someone who is antisocial is likely to be high in Novelty Seeking, low in Harm Avoidance, and low in Reward Dependence. Several new superfactors have been added by Cloninger's group: Persistence (deficiencies in this are found across the board in all people with a DSM Axis II disorder), Self-Directedness, Cooperativeness, and Self-Transcendence. These new dimensions are not closely linked with various neurotransmitters. They can, however, be subsumed under several of the FFM components. Cooperativeness, for example, is an aspect of compliance, a facet of the FFM factor Agreeableness.

Advantages of the Dimensional Approach in the Therapy of Personality Problems

Unlike the category-based taxonomy of the DSM (or of the International Classification of Diseases in its various editions; World Health Organization, 1977) that constitute so many islands in a vaster sea of personality variation, the dimensional approach not only has (as was said of the Greek language) a "word for everything" but can deal easily with the complexity of a personality. It does so by assigning different weights, usually in the form of numbers on a scale, to all aspects of a given personality that seem noteworthy from a clinical standpoint, both the negative and the positive. This capacity helps one to get around the problem of whether to classify a particular patient as having borderline personality disorder (BDL) with narcissistic personality disorder comorbidity or narcissistic personality disorder with BDL comorbidity, if there are about equally prominent traits present from both these categories. In actual practice, dilemmas of this sort are resolved often enough by the personal predilections or bias of

the investigator or therapist. Thus, Kernberg (1967), in that hypothetical 50–50 situation, because of his special expertise in (BDL) might diagnose such a patients as having BDL with narcissistic personality disorder comorbidity. Elsa Ronningstam (1997), with her special expertise in narcissistic might conclude narcissistic personality disorder with borderline comorbidity. But a diagnosis should be free of observer bias of this sort. It would be more useful to be able to piece together a complete profile of the patient's personality. In this way, a therapist could see the peaks and valleys along all relevant dimensions, the better to avoid leaving some important personality feature unattended and to give due therapeutic attention to the most prominent and worrisome aspects of the total personality.

Instruments that create a profile of personality have been available for many years: The most widely used is the Minnesota Multiphasic Personality Inventory—2 (MMPI-2; Greene, 1980), with its 10 major dimensions. But the dimensional systems of Tyrer and Alexander or Livesley also lend themselves to this purpose. The Revised NEO Personality Inventory (NEO-PI-R; Costa & McCrae, 1992) is organized around the FFM. For each of the five factors, six important subfactors of smaller breadth are also provided. Using this model, one can generate a personality profile based on FFM descriptors. Furthermore, the ratings for each person (or patient, if made within a clinical context) can be compared with the norms for the particular personality disorders (viewed categorically) that person is suspected of showing. This process is akin to the use of the vertical 0–100 scale when scoring the MMPI-2: The pathological range extends from 70 and up. Several years ago, I proposed a similar schema (Stone, 1993, p. 96) using the Aristotelian concept of the "golden mean." This schema consisted of five rows of personality traits, arranged with the normal or ideal traits in the middle. On either side were two rows of other trait adjectives representing mild–moderate and extreme exaggerations of the ideal traits in either direction to show too little or too much of the golden mean or ideal trait.

An example of this schema, showing only 15 ideal traits and their positive and negative exaggerated counterparts is shown in Table 24.1. One could

TABLE 24.1

The Golden Mean Schema for Personality Traits

Very low	Low	Average	High	Very high
Abrasive	Tactless	**Polite**	Courtly	Obsequious
Stingy	Tight	**Thrifty**	Generous	Prodigal
Unfeeling	Cold	**Sympathetic**	Oversensitive	Maudlin
Vampish	Seductive	**Receptive**	Coy	Prudish
Paranoid	Suspicious	**Trusting**	Naive	Gullible
Ruthless	Exploitative	**Fair**	Deferential	Meek
Chaotic	Sloppy	**Neat**	Meticulous	Fussbudget
Vengeful	Bitter	**Forgiving**	Philosophic	Altruistic
Aggressive	Hostile	**Agreeable**	Friendly	Ingratiating
Bigoted	Dogmatic	**Open**	Easily Swayed	"As-if"
Extraverted	Outgoing	**At ease**	Shy	Reclusive
Unscrupulous	Devious	**Honest**	Scrupulous	Overscrupulous
Pretentious	Affected	**Modest**	Humble	Self-effacing
Obnoxious	Disagreeable	**Likeable**	Charming	Charismatic
Boorish	Philistine	**Cultured**	Mannered	Precious

Note. Words in boldface represent the ideal or normal.

extend this process out to 30, 40, or more of such ideal traits to permit greater inclusiveness. In the analysis of a given subject, a marker can be placed somewhere in each row, designating the spot along the continuum (each row constituting a continuum from its middle ideal trait) that seems appropriate to the diagnostician. This yields a zig-zag vertical line similar to the zig-zag horizontal line generated by the FFM facets of the NEO-PI-R. The places where the markers deviate from the middle column in my schema represent those aspects of the personality that stand out: Some are acceptable or laudable, not in need of therapeutic intervention; others represent maladaptive, unpleasant deviations or outright aberrations, thus those very much in need of therapeutic work.

These instruments—one a direct outgrowth of the FFM, the other derived from a large trait list and rearranged to show graded departures from a hypothetical ideal—are lexical in origin and dimensional in operation. Both aim at the assessment of all possible personality attributes: the adaptive, the somewhat exaggerated, and the clearly pathological. Many of the traits on the "plus" side of the golden mean, for example, although deviations or exaggerations of the ideal, do not lead to serious difficulties in living

either for the person in question or for those whose lives are affected by that person. Someone who is prudish, self-effacing, and overscrupulous may be noticeable in the eyes of acquaintances for specifically those qualities, but he or she is not likely to seek treatment nor be admonished by others to do so because such quirks are not usually sufficiently bothersome. Quite different, the person who is vengeful, aggressive, and unscrupulous is also unlikely to seek treatment but is much more urgently in need of a drastic change in personality. A person with these characteristics, however, is not likely to benefit from therapy—these are some of the attributes of antisocial or psychopathic people, many of whom remain beyond the reach of currently available treatment methods.

PERSONALITY ANALYSIS THROUGH A LEXICAL LIST

Related to the FFM facets approach and the golden mean schema is the use of a raw and complete lexical list, not as yet broken into trait groupings or factors. Therapists working with a patient after 1 month or 2 usually get to know the particularities of that patient's personality well enough to fill out such a checklist. Although I have subsequently reduced my original list of negative traits from 625 to 500 (and have kept the list of positive traits at 101), the more exhaustive list in my 1993 book can be used to get a rough idea of how "dense" the personality is with respect to either the maladaptive or adaptive traits. It is particularly instructive to carry out this exercise when dealing with borderline patients, who almost invariably manifest many traits that belong (in *DSM*-category language) to other disorders plus many traits that lie outside the range of the *DSM* traits. The personality section of the current edition of *DSM* actually uses only about 64 trait words, along with several "items" (e.g., ideas of reference, suicidal gestures, lack of close friends) that are not personality traits at all. The *DSM* descriptions of schizotypal, antisocial, and borderline personality disorders, in particular, are all conglomerations of a few true trait words, along with several symptom descriptors that belong more correctly in Axis I.

For didactic purposes, I filled out the longer checklist as it would apply to several of my borderline patients (all meeting *DSM-IV* criteria). The sheer number of pertinent items is itself instructive. A few examples are provided below.

One patient currently in treatment is a woman in her mid-40s with a history of depression, suicide gestures, bulimia, dissociative identity disorder, and, in her early years, an incestuous relationship with an older male relative. A talented artist, she is married and the mother of two children. At the beginning of treatment, she was remarkably moody and irritable but also perseverant and highly motivated for treatment. From the checklist, 44 maladaptive traits and 20 positive traits are applicable.

Another patient, also currently in treatment, is a woman in her late 40s, married with two grown children, who made suicide gestures in connection with an unhappy marital situation. She had major depression but no other comorbid symptom disorders. During the early part of her adolescent years, she had endured an incestuous relationship with an older male relative. Much more calm and generally cheerful but often dodging discussion of the more painful aspects of her past, she had at the beginning been frequently tearful and depressed. She makes a great effort to appear poised and untroubled and is sociable with an excellent, if mordant, sense of humor. Only 10 of the maladaptive traits but 53 of the positive traits are applicable in her case.

A third patient, who abruptly quit therapy after 4 months, was a single woman in her mid-20s who made suicide threats (which were never carried out) when confronted by her parents after she had stolen their credit cards and run up many thousands of dollars' worth of clothing and jewelry to "keep up" with her much wealthier friends. Seductive and superficially charming at first acquaintance, she rapidly showed her dark side, bursting into abusive language and explosive tantrums when a meeting was arranged with her parents. When her parents made it clear that they were barring her from their home (where she had stolen many items to pawn, besides taking the credit cards) and would (on my recommendation) not "bail her out" the next time she were to run up unauthorized bills (she had also been running up monthly bills of a thousand dollars by speaking for hours at a time to a mystic "healer" from California), she flew into a rage, threatening to kill her parents and me if we did not "get off her back" and start sympathizing with her (stagey and ungenuine) depression. From a *DSM* standpoint, she met the criteria for all four Cluster B personality disorders: narcissistic, antisocial, borderline, and histrionic. She also met the criteria for Hare's Factor I psychopathic traits (Hare et al., 1990). As for the lexical list, 98 maladaptive traits but only 3 of the positive traits were applicable.

Without even a list of all the particular traits that were applicable, it is clear that the first patient had a fair sprinkling of negative and positive traits. Average people usually have less than 20 of the negative traits and more than 20 of the positive ones. Borderline patients generally have about 40–70 of the negative traits. The second woman would have scored much higher on the FFM scale for Agreeableness and was seldom angry once her depression had largely lifted; she continued to maintain her cheerful, almost breezy, facade. After 6 months of (analytically oriented and supportive) therapy, it would no longer have been possible to diagnose her as borderline by *DSM* standards. She had no more of the maladaptive traits than would be found in a well-functioning nonpatient in the community. Prognostically, this mixture of few negative and many positive traits augurs well for her long-term adjustment.

The third woman presents a combination of borderline and antisocial personality disorders. Although she was referred to me by a colleague as a borderline patient, she was more distinctly antisocial (six of the seven *DSM* items) than borderline (six of the nine items), not just through a raw count of the *DSM* items but because her life course from early adolescent was that of an antisocial person constantly in trouble with her parents and the authorities. Several months after she quit treatment, she was arrested for credit card fraud. The profusion of negative traits was in keeping with one's overall impression of her, namely, a person with a very high score on the FFM Antagonism scale (i.e., the opposite of Agreeableness). She was, for example, manipulative, deceptive, greedy, aggressive, arrogant, and callous. To make matters worse, she was not motivated for therapy in the sense of wanting to make changes for the better and to get her life in order; she was willing to come only insofar as she felt she could get me to "protect" her from her parents' limit setting and indignation at her for making their life miserable. When it became clear to her that I would not join forces with her in such an unjustified plan, she screamed at me, slammed the door, and left.

The Usefulness of a Combined Diagnostic Approach With Borderline Patients

From the standpoint of personality diagnosis, one can view the categories of *DSM* as a "coarse lens," such as one uses in microscopy, to get a gross picture of the subject at hand. Such a picture tells little about the subject's prognosis. Some antisocial people, for example, get better as they get older, even without treatment; some dependent personality disordered people remain incapacitated all their lives. The polythetic system of personality disorder diagnosis allows for hundreds of combinations of item sets that trigger the same diagnosis. In the case of BDL, there are patients who are primarily moody, others primarily angry, still others mostly identity disordered, and so forth. The focus in their treatment should not all be the same. More than the other disorders, BDL is generally commingled with

two or three "comorbid" personality disorders or even more (Oldham, Skodol, Kellman, Rosnick, & Davies, 1992; Stone, 1990a), sometimes as many as six or seven others. Certainly it is not unusual to encounter borderline patients whose personality profile meets the criteria for the other three Cluster B disorders, as was the case with the patient in the last example. The therapeutic approach and the prognosis depend to a considerable extent on which "secondary" diagnoses are applicable. This remains true if one widens the lens to include personality configurations not included in the *DSM*, such as depressive–masochistic, explosive–irritable, hypo–manic, passive–aggressive, and sadistic. The combination of BDL and depressive–masochistic (the latter term used often in psychoanalytic circles) has generally a much better prognosis than does BDL and passive–aggressive, let alone BDL and antisocial personality disorder.

Given this state of affairs, there is much to gain by supplementing the coarse lens picture with a finer lens in the form of a dimensional system, such as the one used by Costa and Widiger (1994) and based directly on the FFM or the one I constructed reflecting the golden mean concept. The rating methods used in both are similar: The FFM personality description relies on scores from 0 to 100 (most occurring in the 30–70 range); the scores lower than 50 represent "too little" or "less than average" of an FFM descriptor, those above 50, "too much" or "more than average." Thus, Agreeableness can be average (50), somewhat less than average (40; i.e., mildly disagreeable), or distinctly less than average (30; i.e., aggressive, repugnant, obnoxious). Or a person can be a little or a great deal more than average, namely, generous or all the way to self-sacrificing and altruistic. Granted, one can assign intermediate numbers; in ordinary practice, the scale can be graded "30, 40, 50 (the mean), 60, 70," resembling my 5-point golden mean scale, which is essentially a "−2, −1, 0 (the mean), +1, +2" system. These systems, in any event, force the diagnostician or the therapist evaluating a new patient to address several dozen personality variables that are not found in the *DSM*. Both systems draw attention to positive traits (Agreeableness, Conscientiousness, and their finer lexical branches), which must be added into the reckoning alongside the maladaptive ones, if one is to make a more accurate prognostic appraisal. I would go a step further and recommend one pays attention to each prospective patient's salient, most prominent trait, namely, the defining feature that most people who know the patient immediately think of as that person's "ID tag." In addition, one should try to assess certain variables not ordinarily attended to in one's task of personality evaluation. One such variable is what I called "spirituality" (akin to Cloninger's Self-Transcendence), which I feel plays an important role in determining which patients, especially which borderline patients, will do well and which will not (Stone, 2000b).

The usefulness of a combined diagnostic approach for borderline patients has already been recommended by Clarkin, Hull, Cantor, and Sanderson (1993). In their study, clinically diagnosed borderline inpatients at New York Hospital–Westchester were evaluated by both the Structural Clinical Interview for *DSM-III-R* (Spitzer, Williams, Gibbon, & First, 1990) and by the FFM-based NEO-PI. Clarkin et al. concluded, in regard to the NEO-PI, that the Neuroticism and Agreeableness scales picked up the pathological aspects of the borderline patients (as did the *DSM* items), but the Extraversion, Conscientiousness and Openness scales yielded important information about the constituent facets of those three scales, which addressed issues of perseverance at work, social abilities, and openness to new ideas (related probably to the self-reflective function; Fonagy et al., 1995). These qualities, or their comparative deficiencies, play a vital role in determining amenability to therapy, capacity for attachment to significant others (including the therapist), and the probability for a successful lifecourse in the long run.

Whereas I recommend a combined categorical–dimensional approach to the assessment of patients in general who present with personality problems including well-functioning patients in psychoanalysis, this recommendation goes double for borderline patients. They constitute the largest group of personality disordered patients at most clinics and hospitals, and they present with the most difficult challenge for therapists among patients who are still amenable to psychotherapy. Patients who are psy-

chopathic are of course more "challenging" but are, as I discuss later in this chapter, usually outside the domain of treatability. At this point, I would like to show the usefulness of the NEO-PI-R in relation to a number of borderline patients with whom I have worked.

THE NEO-PI-R AS A DIMENSIONAL SCALE APPLICABLE TO BORDERLINE PATIENTS

The way in which the NEO-PI-R may be used as a medium–fine lens in the inspection of borderline patients can be illustrated with a side-by-side comparison of ratings for several patients (see Table 24.2). I chose nine patients with whom I have worked using a largely analytically oriented psychotherapy (supplemented when necessary or practical with supportive interventions), rating each with a number from 0 to 100 for each of the 30 facets of the NEO-PI-R (six facets for each of the five factors: Neuroticism, Extraversion, Openness, Agreeableness, and Conscientiousness). In this scale, the relevant ratings are very high, high, average, low and very low. Brief sketches of the nine patients, numbered 1–9 across Table 24.2, follow.

Patient 1. An 18-year-old high school student. She was referred for therapy following a suicide attempt that led to a brief hospitalization. Following the death of her mother in a car accident when she was 9 years old, she and her sister were raised by their father, whom they experienced as a "Jekyll and Hyde" figure: cordial with outsiders but tyrannical and hypercritical with them. Nothing she did was "right" in his eyes; he would often strike her or throw things at her for failing to keep her room perfectly neat. She tried to escape his wrath by living with friends for as long as they would let her and had begun to feel, as she put it, like "Cinderella with no prince in sight." She lost all ambition, was falling behind in her schoolwork, began abusing marijuana and engaging in casual sex with boys she barely knew, and, finally feeling depressed and hopeless, took an overdose

TABLE 24.2

Revised NEO Personality Inventory (NEO-PI-R) Facet Scale Ranges for Borderline Cases

NEO-PI-R facet	Case number								
	1	2	3	4	5	6	7	8	9
N1: Anxiety	Very high	Very high	Average	Average	Very high	Very high	Very high	Average	Average
N2: Angry–hostility	High	Average	Very high	High	Very high	Average	Very high	Very high	Very high
N3: Depression	Very high	Very high	Average	Very high	High	Very high	Very high	Very high	High
N4: Self-consciousness	Very high	Very high	Low	Average	High*	Average	High	Low	Very low
N5: Impulsiveness	Very high	Average	Low	Very high	Very high	Low	Very low*	Very high	Very low
N6: Vulnerability	High	Average	Average	High	Very high	Average	Very high	Average	High
E1: Warmth	Average	Very high	Average	Very high	Very high*	High	Low	Average*	Average*
E2: Gregariousness	Low	Average	Average	High	Very low	Average	Very low	Low	Very high
E3: Assertiveness	Low	Average	Average	High	High	Average	Average	High	High
E4: Activity	Average	Average	High	High	High	Average	Average	High	Average
E5: Excitement seeking	High	Average	High	High	Very high	Low	Very low	Average	Very high
E6: Positive emotions	Low	Average	Very high	High	High*	Average	Very low	Average	Very high
O1: Fantasy	Very high	Average	Low	Average	High	Low	Low	Average	Very high
O2: Aesthetics	Average	Average	Average	Average	Very high	Average	Average	Average	Average
O3: Feelings	High	High	Average	High	Very high	High	Very high	Average	Very high
O4: Actions	High	Average	Average	High	Very high	Average	Very low	Average	Very high
O5: Ideas	Average	Average	Low	Average	Very high	Average	High	Very low	High
O6: Values	Very high	Very high	High	Very high	Average	Average	Average	Very low	Low
A1: Trust	Average	Average	Average	Low	Very low*	Low	Very low	Very low	Very low
A2: Straightforwardness	Average	Very high	Average	Very high	High*	Low	Average	Very low	Very low
A3: Altruism	Average	High	Average	High	High*	High	Average	Average	Very low
A4: Compliance	High	Average	Low	High	Average	Low	Low	Very low	Very low
A5: Modesty	Very high	Very high	Low	Average	Average	Average	Average	Low	Very low
A6: Tender mindedness	High	Very high	Average	High	Average	Average	Average	Low	Very low
C1: Competence	Very low	Average	High	High	Average	High	High	Average	Low
C2: Order	Very low	Average	High	Average	High	Average	Average	Average	Very low
C3: Dutifulness	Very low	Average	High	High	High	High	Very high	Average	Very low
C4: Achievement striving	Very low	Average	Very high	Average	Low	Low	High	Average	Low
C5: Self-discipline	Very low	Average	Very high	Average	Low	Low	High	High	Very low
C6: Deliberation	Low	High	High	Average	Average	Average	Very high	Low	Very low

Note. N = Neuroticism; E = Extraversion; O = Openness to Experience; A = Agreeableness; C = Conscientiousness. Very low (*T* = 34 and lower); low (*T* = 35 to 44); average (*T* = 45 to 55); high (*T* = 56 to 65); very high (*T* = 66 and higher). * = a rating based on the patient's customary state (not taking psychotropic medications).

of the antidepressants she had received from a doctor she had seen at the school psychologist's suggestion. During the 6 months I worked with her, she seldom came on time and often "forgot" appointments altogether, necessitating my calling around town to various friends with whom she might be staying the night. Finally, she dropped out altogether; although less depressed than before, she still had no plan for what to do with the rest of her life. She moved to Italy where her mother's relatives resided. This patient's NEO-PI-R profile is shown in Figure 24.1.

Patient 2. The next patient is the elder sister of Patient 1. She sought help for depression following the breakup of a romantic relationship 2 years after her younger sister quit treatment. She had felt suicidal, saw her life as going nowhere, and was convinced people thought she was "worthless" and "stupid." More committed academically than her sister, she had nearly completed college. Living at home had become unbearable because her father constantly criticized her for being "dirty" or "bad smelling," even after she had just showered. Although she was actually the more attractive of his two very attractive daughters, he missed no opportunity to make sarcastic remarks about her looks or her clothes. She had lost self-confidence to the point where it was painful to be among friends because she assumed that they felt she was as much of a "nothing" as her father did.

In the course of her therapy, she revealed what her sister had never mentioned; namely, that their mother had been indifferent to them and had spent much of her time away from the family with a lover (in whose car she had died). Her father would sometimes wander into the bathroom undressed when she was there, "unaware" she was still in the shower. Although he had never molested

her sexually, it became clear to her that there was another side to the story of his criticism: He seemed to be defending himself against his own attraction to her by devaluing her as an "ugly good-for-nothing." As she began to understand her father, her depression lifted and she grew more self-confident.

Patient 3. Hospitalized at 16 because of a suicide gesture, this woman had come from a family where her parents were in continual battle with one another and her mother was critical, rejecting, and hostile toward the patient and her younger sister. Her father, a surgeon, was possessive toward her, was intolerant of any boyfriend she might introduce to the family, and went so far as to do pelvic exams on her after a date, ostensibly to make sure she had not "done anything wrong." Sensing this exaggerated affection for his daughter and aware that he had crossed the line into a form of sexual molestation, her mother grew intensely jealous, hence part of the reason for her venomous anger. While at the hospital, the patient oscillated between moods of suicidal depression and extreme irritability. Therapy consisted of analytically oriented therapy four times a week. Because the home environment was so destructive, the hospital's plan was to keep her for 1 year until she could go to college directly from the unit. An outstanding student, she got accepted to a major university. From there she went on to obtain a medical degree and become a surgeon like her father. Married now with two children, she is still noticeably moody and has a biting, often sarcastic, way of talking. This patient's NEO-PI-R profile is shown in Figure 24.2.

Patient 4. This patient is the younger sister of Patient 3. She entered therapy 10 years after her sister had left the hospital. The problem was a deteriorating marriage. Her husband had grown inattentive and

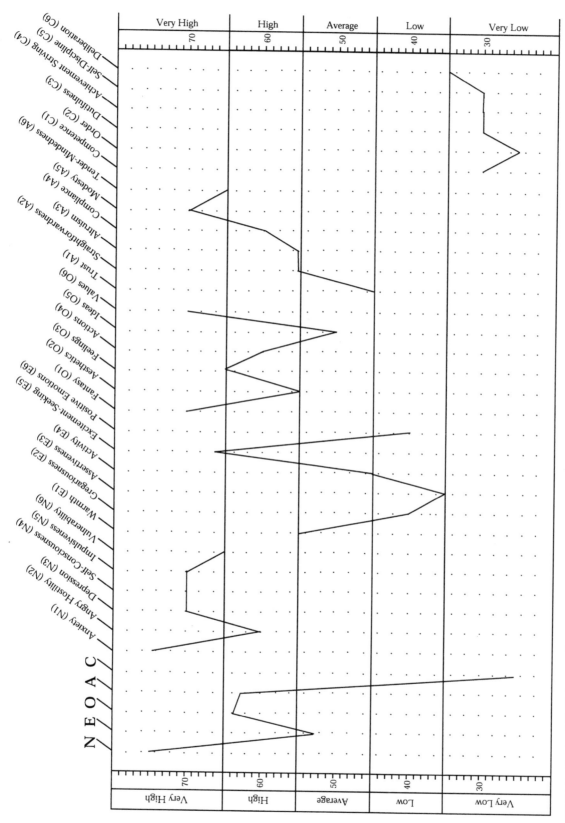

FIGURE 24.1. Revised NEO Personality Inventory (NEO-PI-R) profile of Patient 1. N = Neuroticism; E = Extraversion; O = Openness to Experience; A = Agreeableness; C = Conscientiousness. From the *NEO Personality Inventory—Revised*, by Paul T. Costa, Jr., and Robert R. McCrae. Copyright 1978, 1985, 1989, 1992 by PAR, Inc. Reproduced by special permission of the publisher, Psychological Assessment Resources, Inc., 16204 North Florida Avenue, Lutz, FL 33549. Further reproduction is prohibited without permission of PAR, Inc.

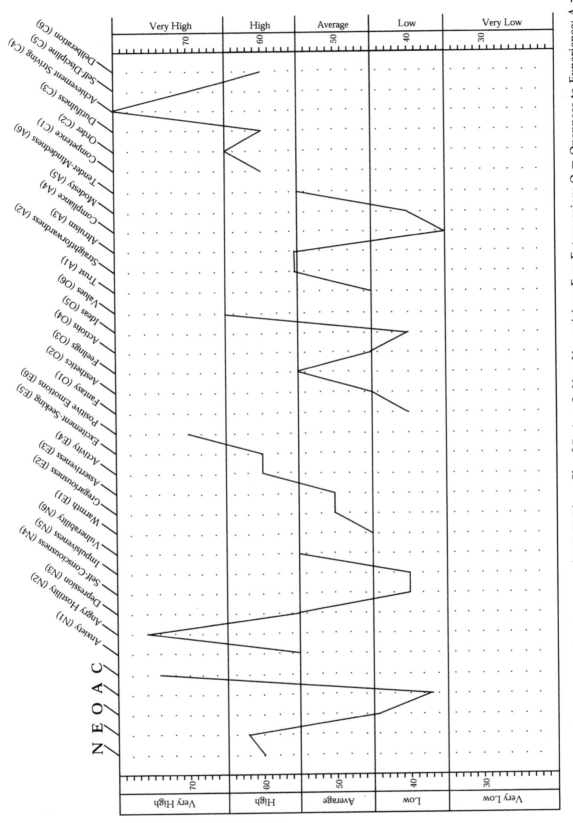

FIGURE 24.2. Revised NEO Personality Inventory (NEO-PI-R) profile of Patient 3. N = Neuroticism; E = Extraversion; O = Openness to Experience; A = Agreeableness; C = Conscientiousness. From the *NEO Personality Inventory—Revised*, by Paul T. Costa, Jr., and Robert R. McCrae. Copyright 1978, 1985, 1989, 1992 by PAR, Inc. Reproduced by special permission of the publisher, Psychological Assessment Resources, Inc., 16204 North Florida Avenue, Lutz, FL 33549. Further reproduction is prohibited without permission of PAR, Inc.

almost totally uncommunicative. She became depressed and often thought of suicide, although she had not as yet engaged in self-destructive behavior. Outwardly more integrated than her sister had been, she soon revealed material that called into question just how emotionally healthy she was. One of her first dreams she told me, for example, involved mutilation: "I am in the recovery room after surgery. All my vital organs are arranged at the sides of, and just outside, my body: the liver and kidneys to the right, my spleen and a lung to the left. An obviously drunk surgeon waves goodbye to me as he leaves the room, saying with slurred speech, 'Don' chu worry, you're gonna be OK.'" This was a tipoff to the transference: She viewed me as an unreliable person into whose hands she should not place her secrets and her life. This was also a reflection of the fact that her father had been an alcoholic and had died when she was in her teens. She affiliated herself frequently with men who mistreated and neglected her. More attractive than her sister, she had actually been her father's favorite, only to draw even more fire from her jealous mother than had been directed at her sister. This seemed to be the key to her masochistic style: She could have relationships with men but only if (as she assumed her mother would want it) she suffered. She finally divorced her husband but then became alcoholic herself and began to drive at high speeds on the highway. She was hospitalized at this point for 2 months and treated with mood stabilizers and antidepressants before returning to therapy. Having worked through the mechanisms of her disastrous choices of men during the next 2 years, she eventually met a much more suitable man, whom she married. Unlike many borderline patients, she had always been highly focused and perseverant.

Patient 5. At age 30 when she entered thrice-weekly therapy, this woman, a mother of three, had been unhappily married to a man she considered a boorish philanderer. She was pathologically jealous about his having affairs—on one occasion she actually caught him in the act. She grew depressed and suicidal, thought of hurling herself off the roof of her house, but was persuaded to come to a hospital instead. Between the ages of 6 and 15, she had been the "secret wife" of her father, who subjected her to performing oral sex on him as if to "work off" the punishments she had "deserved" for any number of minor "offenses," such as not finishing her vegetables at dinner. She cut her wrists when a teenager and finally told her mother what had been going on. Her mother promptly divorced her father and moved away with her daughter. The patient married early to escape her past but ended up with a man who was in many ways a carbon copy of her father: domineering, seductive, and exploitative. Toward the end of the marriage, she took on some of these qualities herself, going to bars to pick up men and using an assumed name. Although she did not have a dissociative disorder, she did shift rapidly, especially after her divorce, between two states: one in which she was dependent, docile, and affectionate toward the new men in her life; the other in which she tormented them with her jealousy, used her beauty as a weapon, drawing men to her, on whom she could then avenge herself (symbolically) for the wrong done to her by her father. She developed some insight into this mechanism during her therapy, although the jealousy did not diminish for several years. She remained highly anxious when alone and, like many borderline patients, was unable at such times to stifle her anxiety through vocational activities. She was a skilled sculptress but was unable to pursue her craft unless things were going well. Around the time of her divorce, she began to abuse alcohol but refused to go to Alcoholic Anonymous. She was unable to conquer the problem until several years later when her life stabilized after entering a less destructive marital relationship.

Patient 6. At age 26 when she began therapy with me, this woman had been in psychiatric hospitals three times before, starting when she was in college. There, she made a serious suicide attempt with hypnotics after a love affair had ended. She had been in analytically oriented therapy with two previous therapists, and each time she had become erotomanically attached to the therapist and consumed with jealousy about the therapist's wife. The same pattern repeated itself with me. Merely seeing my wife in the hallway of our apartment building (where I also have my office) sent her into such despondency that she made a suicide gesture and had to be rehospitalized briefly.

Her early life had been traumatic. An older sister had been crazily jealous of her (the patient had been her mother's favorite) and had tried to stab her with a kitchen knife on several occasions. Her father was a successful professional man, a "workaholic" who was uncomfortable around his children and had time only for his wife. He was mercilessly critical of the patient and, during her teen years, derogated her boyfriends—one sign among many of his thinly veiled sexual attraction to her. The patient became bulimarexic while at college, a tendency which became exaggerated around the time of her menstrual period.

Dynamically, the jealousy toward the wives of her therapists hid a deeper layer of (now sexualized) longing for closeness toward another woman. This was a layer she could never reach in her treatment. She was still terrified of her sister and

worried that if she found happiness with a man, her sister would finish the job she had started years earlier and kill her (a totally unlikely scenario because the sister was now married with children of her own). The thrust of therapy changed after 2 years to a more supportive mode, where the emphasis was on enabling her to date men again (she had not done so for 10 years). Eventually, she met a suitable man, married, continued her work, and had a child. She was no longer symptomatic.

Patient 7. A woman in her late 40s had been in analytic psychotherapy for a number of years with a colleague of mine, who referred her to me because the work had reached an impasse. A professional woman, she was married for the second time but felt trapped in a joyless marriage to a man whom she experienced as irritable; he was more interested in the television than in her. She had obsessive–compulsive personality disorder, with a prominent cancer phobia. In addition, she suffered from marked anxiety in social situations and bouts of depression. Just as irritable as her husband, she argued with him almost daily, mostly about his inertia and uncooperativeness around the house. During her early years, her mother, a highly narcissistic woman, had humiliated her about her appearance and was generally aloof. Her father alternated between being affectionate and being frighteningly irascible and physically punitive. Extraordinarily dependent and importunate, she wore out other people's (and her therapists') patience with frequent phone calls begging for reassurance. When she had to undergo a minor surgical procedure for a benign condition, she became panicky and threatened suicide, claiming she could not endure waiting over a weekend to receive the official report of a biopsy, although the surgeon had already told her by phone that the lesion was benign. Life for her was an unending series of catastrophes (as she envisioned them) that never occurred. In addition, she remained embittered over her past in such a way as to render her impatient, sour, and critical with others, often destroying friendships in the process.

Patient 8. A woman of 48 years came for treatment at the urging of her husband. Their marriage, which had been satisfying for many years, had begun to deteriorate rapidly. She had become explosively irritable, suicidal, and abusive. At times she would snatch the newspaper away that her husband had been reading, throw his dinner at him from across the table, or smash down the screen of his laptop computer. She had grown to hate his "indifference" yet said she would kill herself if he ever divorced her. Her children twice rescued her from suicide gestures, on one occasion grabbing her at the last minute as she was about to jump off the roof of their house. At our first meeting, she announced that she was going to buy a gun, kill her husband, and then herself. When I reminded her of the law requiring me to warn her husband, she simply added me to the hit list. Meeting with her daily for a while helped defuse the situation. She grew calmer, although she was still enraged at her husband for his lack of attention. She was convinced he had a mistress. Having discovered that he had been renting a small apartment in the city, ostensibly to escape for some "peace and quiet," she threatened to wreck it. Such an act would certainly lead to his divorcing her, I warned her, but she sneaked into his apartment anyway and reduced it to a shambles. He called his lawyer about divorce. She then quit treatment, wrote me a nasty note, and moved to Europe for several months. After her return, she cut her wrists and was hospitalized briefly. I did not hear how the story ended until recently when I learned that in the intervening 10 years, the couple had divorced, both had remarried, and were now happier. The patient herself had become more stable and was no longer aggressive nor out of control. Always tempestuous in her earlier years, she became borderline during her menopausal years, only to become calmer (to where BDL was no longer applicable as a diagnosis) in her late 50s.

This woman's situation illustrates one of the peculiarities of the *DSM* definition of BDL. The definition is based more on symptomatic behaviors (e.g., self-damaging acts, stormy relationships, brief psychotic episodes) than on true traits of personality (e.g., demandingness, unreasonableness, vehemence, manipulativeness, changeableness; all of which are encountered often in those diagnosed with BDL). But because symptoms can often be diminished or eliminated with medications and therapy—whereas real personality traits are much more tenacious—clinicians may sometimes treat a woman in her midlife who is passing through what proves to be a 4- or 5-year timeframe of appearing to be borderline by the *DSM* criteria. Some women, of course, during the menopausal years show a resurgence of symptomatic behaviors that were characteristic of them in their 20s and 30s and who were correctly diagnosed with BDL in their earlier years. I gave several examples of the latter in my book on the long-term follow-up of borderline patients (Stone, 1990a).

Patient 9. This patient, described on pages 410–411 in the section on the use of the lexical checklist, got into problems with credit card debt, among other things; 98 of the maladaptive traits were applicable.

As for the salient characteristics of these nine borderline patients, one could sum up their personalities in a few words, the maladaptive aspects of which point to the main areas of focus for psychotherapy (second column); the positive aspects of which point to their main strengths or "saving graces" (third column).

Patient 1	Chaotic, a "lost soul"	Appealing, sympathetic
Patient 2	Un-self-confident, mournful	Reflective, sweet
Patient 3	Rebellious, contemptuous	Ambitious, brilliant
Patient 4	Masochistic, impulsive	Undemanding, pleasant
Patient 5	Jealous, manipulative	Seductive, refined
Patient 6	Erotomanic, envious	Sympathetic, perseverant
Patient 7	Bitter, "catastrophizing"	Independent minded, free of prejudice
Patient 8	Vengeful, abusive	Devoted, passionate
Patient 9	Exploitative, unscrupulous	Seductive, high spirited

From an inspection of the NEO-PI-R profiles, as outlined in Table 24.2, several interrelationships become apparent. All the patients were above average on the N1, N2, and N3 (Neuroticism) scales for anxiety, anger, and depressiveness, respectively. This is consistent with data customary for a group of borderline patients. Most showed "vulnerability" as well, although not as many were impulsive. On the Extraversion and Openness scales, the ratings were less consistent and less often at the extremes. On the Agreeableness scale only Patient 2 was even averagely "trusting"; all the others were less so (and some were extremely untrusting). Seven of the nine patients could be rated as adequate or better on the Conscientiousness scale, whereas Patients 1 and 9 scored distinctly below average. Many of these patients ultimately did well, even the woman who threatened to kill me. These seven patients scored at least average or better on the Conscientiousness scale (akin to Cloninger's Persistence and self-discipline, which is self-embodied in the NEO-PI-R scale and to which I drew attention in my follow-up study, concerning borderline patients who did better than average; Stone 1990a). The two whose Conscientiousness ratings were uniformly low were Patient 1, who was poorly motivated and disorganized, and Patient 9, who had strong psychopathic features. The virtue of the NEO-PI-R is that it draws attention to the prognostically important variables having

to do with Conscientiousness and Openness (which addresses artistic sensibilities). These variables are ignored in the *DSM*-category approach, which focuses on illness, not on areas of wellness.

For several of the patients, I added an asterisk to their rating (see Table 24.2) to indicate the patient's customary state (not taking psychotropic medication): Patients 7, 8, and 9 but especially Patient 5. Patient 7 was ordinarily the antithesis of impulsivity. But when she was on a serotonin reuptake inhibitor antidepressant, she became transitorily hypo-manic and was given to overspending. Patient 8 had usually displayed a good degree of emotional warmth, but this quality disappeared during the time I worked with her when her hostility level was maximal. The same was true of Patient 9, who could show warmth toward others when she was younger and even recently toward a few key friends during the time she was otherwise in a fury for being reprimanded because of the credit card theft. Patient 5, as with many borderline patients at the height of their illness, showed a markedly unintegrated personality. She could "turn on a dime," switching from friendly to hostile, pampering to abusive, trusting to delusionally jealous, fun loving and sensation seeking to despondent, from one moment to the next, depending on what was happening in her social life. It was therefore not possible to give her ratings for several of the facets of the scale that would be valid across long-time stretches. Oldham and Morris (1990) referred to these emotional oscillations in borderline patients as their "mercuriality"—a useful term and one that underlines the difficulty in assigning consistent ratings to this behavior. This mercurial quality is another indication of how the *DSM* definition of BDL belongs more to the sphere of symptom disorders than to the domain of true personality disorders—extreme lability of mood being more of a symptom, strictly speaking, than a personality trait.

I chose the two pairs of sisters (Patients 1 and 2, Patients 3 and 4) to highlight the influence of genetic-constitutional factors and of nonshared environment on the emerging personalities of siblings raised in the same family. These differences may affect amenability to therapy and long-term prognosis. For example, although exposed to the same abusive harshness of their father as was her sister and to the traumatic loss of their mother during their younger years and although equally attractive and intelligent, Patient 1 was more impulsive, less outgoing, more sensation seeking, less reflective or straightforward and candid, more of a nonfocused "dreamer," and much less self-disciplined than was her older sister. The latter persevered with her treatment and has begun to make genuine progress, whereas the younger sister drifted away and remains in shakier circumstances.

The second pair were less different, yet the differences were important: Patient 3 was more driven, ambitious, angry, less impulsive (at least as she got into her 20s), and not as emotionally warm. She was even more self-disciplined than her younger sister. These probably innate differences help account for her having become a surgeon, whereas her sister chose a more conventional, less challenging path.

Among the salient or defining traits of the patients in the nine vignettes, several were from a therapeutic standpoint particularly difficult to deal with. The last five patients, for example, were described (along with their other traits) as jealous, envious, bitter, vengeful, and unscrupulous, respectively. Of course, almost any patient with a maladaptive trait exhibited to an extreme presents major hurdles to a therapist. But certain traits, when present at all, are routinely challenging, constituting a nearly impenetrable "character armor" (the term is from Wilhelm Reich's, 1933/1949, celebrated monograph). Patient 3, for example, displayed a fair degree of contemptuousness when I first worked with her. She always had an abrasive facade and does so to this day. But her contemptuousness melted away after the first few months of our work and thus did not become an impediment to the therapy nor to her maturation. Beyond a certain level, nevertheless, this trait —in a highly narcissistic personality disorder person with little motivation for change and with a strong tendency to devalue the therapist's efforts—can easily sabotage treatment. Such patients generally drop out of therapy prematurely.

In my book on abnormalities of personality (Stone, 1993), I devoted the last two chapters to traits "less amenable to or not amenable to therapy" and to people who were beyond the reach of therapy altogether; namely, people who are psychopathic

and who commit heinous acts short of or including murder. Some of the case illustrations in the first of those chapters concern traits similar to those of the last five vignettes mentioned above. I gave examples of a man who was extraordinarily cheap, so much so that he would make a scene in a restaurant where he had invited a new "date" to dinner, humiliating her by loudly accusing the waiter of overcharging him a dime. I mentioned another who was a "plastic" company man (i.e., so disposed to parrot back the sentiments and opinions of his superiors and to mouth platitudes that he seemed to have no personality of his own, just a kind of cerebral "play dough" that could be molded at will). As a third example, a breathtakingly callous robber's bullet paralyzed the policeman who was trying to arrest him who then squawked that he could not get a fair trial because the policeman's wife wheeled her paraplegic husband into the courtroom to give his testimony and "all the sympathy went to the cop!" For a sensation-seeking example, a bank executive had been carrying on a torrid affair with a much younger and extremely tempestuous woman. Their life together oscillated rapidly between days of wild love making and days of raucous, alcohol-fueled arguments that ended in assaults and the damage of each other's property.

On the distaff side, an indiscreet nanny, when accompanying the family she worked for on their vacation in Europe, ordered caviar for lunch while the family merely had sandwiches. She talked cheerily to the family's two young boys about her homosexual brother who had been jailed for "sucking penises in the subway bathrooms" while the father tried to negotiate hairpin turns in the south of France. She cuddled naked with the 11-year-old boy in bed, ostensibly to "warm him up" after a swim, during which she had held his head underwater for a time, terrifying him, as a punishment for not coming promptly to lunch.

For bitterness, I chose the example of the divorced technician in her 40s whose mental life was dominated by preoccupations with all the wrongs done her when she was young and with everything that was miserable about her current life. She complained of loneliness, yet she ensured this state by wearing out the patience of friends and relatives.

Friends that were married were intolerable to her because "they have each other" (which stirred up her envy), but single friends were no good either because "they're in the same boat I'm in." When treating her if I took notes (as I customarily do when patients report dreams), she would "twit" me with "all you seem to care about are those notes!" If I was not taking notes on another day, I would hear, "you're not making notes—does this mean I don't matter to you?" Her bitterness and suicidality grew particularly intense around the time of her mother's birthday: She felt that was a good time to do herself in, "to teach the bitch what she did to me." Once when she became seriously suicidal after a brief absence on my part, I felt very worried about her and took her myself to a emergency ward, preparatory to her being admitted to a psychiatric unit. Enraged, she yelled at me, "who told you to save my fucking life?"

Curiously, the story ends better than it began. When I called her 10 years after the hospitalization (and 6 years after my book appeared), she was happy to hear from me and mentioned how she had remained ill and embittered over the next 3 years and unable to work but then was able to work through certain childhood trauma with the therapist she had met while at the hospital. Now almost 60 years old, she was more at peace, able to work again, and had gathered around her a circle of friends, whom she no longer alienated with her complaints as in the old days. In her case, the bitterness proved not to be insuperable, although it had scarred her life for half a century. Patient 5, in contrast, remains embittered (also for half a century); it is not yet clear whether a similar kind of mellowing will take place later on.

For vengefulness, the example I provided was that of Betty Broderick, the divorcee who sneaked into the apartment of her former husband and his fiancée and shot them to death. The lurid details of her life just before the murders is told by her biographer, Taubman (1992). Broderick is an interesting case study because she was raised in a nurturing well-to-do home, never abused sexually or physically, was attractive and intelligent, and married a man with degrees in both medicine and law. The divorce settlement left her with custody of their four children, their large house, and an allowance of

$16,000 per month. Despite all this, she became so enraged as to burn his clothes with gasoline in front of the children, ram her car into her ex-husband's new house, smash his windows, and spray paint his walls. Urged by her friends to get psychiatric help, she adamantly refused, saying that this would be proof that she was "crazy" and she would lose custody of her children. This refusal certainly ensured that her vengefulness would remain untreatable.

These scarcely treatable and outright untreatable personality traits are noteworthy for their virtual absence in the DSM. It is true that the DSM-IV description of obsessive–compulsive personality disorder does include "adopts a miserly spending style toward self and others" (APA, 1994). Yet the man whose cheapness I mentioned (here and in my book) showed none of the other obsessive–compulsive personality disorder traits. Even if he did meet the criteria for obsessive–compulsive personality disorder, to refer to him just by that diagnostic term would gloss over this most striking characteristic—one that inevitably became the focal point of his treatment. Callousness is not even included in the DSM definition of antisocial personality disorder. In contrast, the FFM model, and the lexical lists from which the FFM was originally abstracted, can readily find a place for these challenging traits— which certainly deserve a home in any personality nomenclature of use to clinicians.

One can add to this list numerous other traits. Although the depressive–masochistic personality type within the domain of BDL often has a more favorable prognosis (Kernberg, 1967) compared with hypo–manic and paranoid types—one sometimes encounters more firmly entrenched cases of this type. Kernberg (1984) wrote of them under the heading Self-Destructiveness as Triumph Over the Analyst (p. 291). Masochistic patients of this type carry out their emotionally and at times physically self-destructive tendencies, not in an uncontrolled rageful state but with a "calm, determined, even elated attitude" (p. 292). For example, a depressive–masochistic woman in her 40s, whom I briefly treated, had had to work hard all her life to support herself and had nothing saved for the future. She had been married for a few years in her 20s, but after that ungratifying relationship, she had been living in an odd arrangement for over 15 years, married to a wealthy older man who kept a separate apartment, was rarely actually with her, and for whom she did a great deal of decorating work for his chain of restaurants. For this she received no pay, was sometimes invited to join him on trips, but mostly lived apart; as he reminded her, she was not included in his will. She could never summon the courage to confront him about this, nor could she bring herself to divorce him in hopes of finding a man who would treat her less shabbily. She could acknowledge to me that she had some "worries" about the future, given the "somewhat insecure" situation she had been enduring for so many years. When I confronted her about the perilousness of her circumstances and the frustrating quality of having a husband that was not a husband, she quit treatment.

There is another trait that poses difficulties in both treatment and terminology. The trait is perhaps a blend of a few simpler qualities such as overdramatic, disorganized, or scatter brained. People usually cover this blend by the colloquial word *flakey* (referring to the unpredictable zig-zag course a snowflake follows as it descends to earth), for want of a more conventional term. I had an occasion to treat a remarkably flakey woman in her late 50s, who had married and divorced twice. She had a daughter by her first marriage, a budding artist with some promise, who died of a drug overdose when she was 23 years old. There were two children by the second marriage. The patient had never worked, having inherited a fortune from her parents. She fancied herself a choreographer, for which she had some experience, less talent, and no success. Although whimsical, articulate, and humorous, she had no close friends; they gave up on her after tolerating a number of spoiled luncheon appointments, theater dates, and the like, which she somehow forgot about. The same trouble cropped up in our meetings: She would forget her session times, wander off to a different city, give only vague possibilities for when she could come for the next appointment, and that only after I did some investigative work to track down where she was. Eccentric, like Giraudoux's "Mad Woman of Chaillot," and full of impractical plans for "making her name" in the dance world or in writing, she mostly frittered away her time doing nothing.

What propelled her into therapy was her newest infatuation with a bellhop she had met at a resort who had some aspirations as a violinist. She took him under her wing, imagined him the next Isaac Stern, and became totally infatuated with him, buying him expensive presents and in general making him as dependent on her as she had become dependent on him. Her children resented this relationship, which was so consuming as to marginalize them. They insisted she seek help. Reluctantly she did so, but there was no consistency to our work because of all the missed appointments. It was clear she was not motivated to explore the meaning of her relationship with the young man, namely, that it gave her surcease from her loneliness or that he was a stand in for her dead (and same-aged) daughter. They could not be seen in public because of the age difference, which rationalized her wish of having him all to herself. Therapy threatened this wish, and after a few months, she broke off the treatment.

Sadistic and Other Essentially Untreatable, Highly Destructive People

As one moves further toward the limits of treatability, one encounters people with personality configurations dominated by destructiveness, usually in the form of sadism, either of a primarily verbal sort (the "psychological" sadism of betraying loved ones, crushing the self-esteem of others, humiliating others in public situations, etc.) or of a violent, physical sort. Not all such people meet the criteria for antisocial personality disorder nor for psychopathy (which I focus on in the next section). Mainly they are found as the cruel parents or spouses, known all too well to their families but scarcely at all to the authorities. Or they may be seen as the "bosses from hell" who make life miserable for their underlings in the workplace but who never cross the line over into grossly illegal, indictable behavior. Sadistic personality disorder (SDS) itself, largely for political reasons, is no longer even recognized in the *DSM* (Stone, 1998b; Widiger, 1996). The elimination of SDS from the *DSM* was not a reflection of its disappearance from the body social, however. Sadism is alive and well. In addition, there is a place for it in the FFM, namely, at the far end of the scale for Antagonism (i.e., the opposite of Agreeableness) on the facet for (the opposite of) tender mindedness, where there are such traits as callous and ruthless. Below, I describe a few examples of this kind of callous and ruthless behavior—behavior that led Shengold (1989) to coin the term "soul murder."

A psychologist of my acquaintance told me of a 9-year-old boy he had been treating for symptoms akin to posttraumatic stress disorder and depression. These conditions had been set in motion by his father, who had poured boiling water on his son's penis and had then proceeded to strap a "cherry bomb" (a powerful type of firecracker) under the boy's new puppy and blow the animal to bits. Because the boy was still alive and because of the "sacredness" of the family—where acts short of attempted (or actual) murder rarely reach the light of day—the man was not arrested and imprisoned.

I served as an expert witness in a case involving a bitter custody battle between the divorced parents of two teenage children. The mother, an untreated bipolar manic, had become progressively more out of control over the preceding 6 years. She arrived several hours late to pick up her daughter at the airport on her return from boarding school, whereon the father went to get her and bring her to his home. The mother flew into a rage at the girl, as though the girl had "stood her mother up." When the girl later paid her mother a visit, her mother threw a large flower pot at her and then chased her around the dining room table with a kitchen knife. Shortly thereafter, her son was to participate in an important religious ceremony. On the way to the ceremony, as he was sitting next to her in the limousine, she cut her wrist with a razor, cut his necktie in two, and spread some blood from her wrist on his shirt, thus ruining his desire to participate in the ceremony.

Earlier I cited many examples of this sort from biographies of famous (and infamous) people (Stone, 1993, p. 451). One of these examples concerned the father of Edie Sedgwick, the actress (Stein & Plimpton, 1982). Her father was an intensely narcissistic man who sponged off his heiress wife and paraded around the family mansion in a bikini. He violated Edie incestuously when she was an adolescent, pre-

cipitating a long series of psychiatric hospitalizations. Despite her transitory fame as an Andy Warhol protégé, she never really recovered, committing suicide shortly after her wedding. Of the remaining seven children, two of her brothers had been repeatedly humiliated and mocked by their father, and they too ultimately committed suicide.

The essence of sadism is the conscious scheming to inflict suffering or pain on another, often as part of an urge to assert absolute dominance over the victim. Wilson and Seaman (1992) drew attention to this phenomenon as a manifestation of the "Roman Emperor syndrome," referring to the likes of Nero and Caligula who took delight in the torture of others. As for torture, it would seem that its attraction derives from the knowledge that so long as the victim is alive and conscious of the pain being inflicted on him or her, the torturer is vividly aware of being "top dog."

More subtle forms of torture are encountered in the workplace, such as when certain bosses taunt an employee about a shortcoming in front of coworkers or burdens an employee with impossible assignments, with the failure to complete resulting in dismissal.

This century has witnessed too many sadistic tyrants to require enumeration here, although it can be said that some were sadistic "at a distance," ordering others to mete out the torture (Milošević, Lenin, Ceauçescu), whereas others enjoyed direct participation in the sadistic acts (Lavrentia Beria, Stalin, Saddam Hussein).

Having the protection of a powerful parent can at times convert a person with narcissistic personality disorder who feels like a nonentity into a person with confirmed SDS, such as the case with Nicolae Ceauçescu's son Niku. As Pacepa (1987) told the story, on one occasion, Niku presided over a banquet honoring the promotion of an army officer. It chanced that oysters were served as an appetizer. Niku asked a waiter if there was a sauce for this dish. After being told "no," Niku hopped up on the table, urinated on the tray of oysters, and then commanded that the assembled guests feast on the oysters. From this and numerous other anecdotes in the book, one gains the impression that Niku was psychopathic and sadistic. It is possible to be one without the other, just as one can be described as antisocial (by *DSM* terms) without meeting the criteria for SDS as described in the appendix of the third edition of the *DSM* (*DSM-III*; APA 1980). The existence of any one of these heightens the likelihood that one or both of the other personality configurations will also be present, but none of them implies the simultaneous presence of the other(s). Niku's example serves, at all events, as an introduction to the topic of psychopathy, to which I now turn.

PSYCHOPATHY: ON THE FAR SIDE OF TREATABILITY

The concept of antisocial personality disorder as embedded in the *DSM* and as alluded to above, remains confusing; it is a mixture of true personality traits and certain behaviors. Admittedly, the definition in the *DSM-IV* is better in this regard (emphasizes traits more than does the *DSM-III*) but still falls short of what would be most useful clinically. The Psychopathy Checklist—Revised (PCL-R) of Hare et al. (1990) represents an improvement in this regard, especially because one of the factors that emerged from the analysis of the 20 items—Factor I—is defined exclusively in traits terms. Glibness, grandiosity, manipulativeness, cunning, callousness, lack of remorse or compassion, mendacity, and the refusal to accept responsibility for one's harmful actions (which translates into a kind of haughty contemptuousness or what the French call *je-m'en-fichisme* [having the attitude of "I don't give a damn"]) all represent the extreme of narcissistic personality disorder, namely, self-centeredness combined with ruthlessness and contempt.

More to the point, Hare's concept of psychopathy has proven itself a powerful predictor of recidivism when applied to offenders in either prisons or forensic hospitals (Cooke, Forth, & Hare, 1998; Harris, Rice, & Cormier, 1991) and an actual predictor of higher rates of recidivism in treated (vs. untreated) psychopaths (Rice, Harris, & Cormier, 1992), owing, it seems, to the proclivity of the treated psychopath to use the lessons transmitted in the therapy to "con" the staff more effectively, win release, and reoffend with greater bravado. Hare (1998) spoke of the psychopath, in evolutionary language, as the "intra-

species predator who uses charm, manipulativeness, intimidation and violence to control others and to satisfy his own selfish needs" (p. 196)—a person "lacking in conscience and in feelings for others, who can do as he pleases without the slightest sense of guilt or regret" (p. 196). Furthermore, neurophysiological researchers have recently established correlations between the presence of psychopathy, as defined by a PCL-R score >29 (each of the 20 items can be scored 0, 1, or 2, yielding a maximum score of 40), and a diminished evoked potential response to emotionally shocking words, which elicit stronger responses from people who are not psychopathic (Williamson, Harpur, & Hare, 1991). Similarly, the psychopath's startle response to noxious stimuli is significantly less pronounced when assessed by evoked potential than is the response of nonpsychopathic people (Patrick, Bradley, & Lang, 1993). Elsewhere, I reviewed other data bearing on the reliability and validity of the psychopathy concept (Stone, 2000a).

Because psychopathy at the lower PCL-R scores (e.g., in the range of 5–15) reflects personality configurations that blend into the "normal" population, there are many "subclinical" cases, such as people who scarcely ever come to the attention of the law and people who cheat, bamboozle, and manipulate others, thanks to their charm, convincing insincerity, and forceful "come on." Others succeed through their harsh domineering attributes that take advantage of weak, dependent, and gullible people. One knows them as shady used car salesmen, corrupt but charismatic politicians, seductive golddiggers, and the like. Most of the latter stay this side of the law, but occasionally, for example, one murders her rich husband or other prey, such as in the case of the recently captured "grifter" Sante Kimes (Havill, 1999), who insinuated her way into the home of a wealthy New York widow and then murdered her.

In recent years, I have seen in consultation or have attempted to treat seven patients with significant psychopathic traits, including those of the true personality portion (Factor-I items). In addition to Patient 9 of the vignettes above, a young man in his late 20s would make repeated phone calls to women he knew as acquaintances of his family and badger them for dates. Routinely rebuffed, he would then adopt a more threatening tone. This would be brought to the attention of his mother, who finally had to warn him she would notify the police if he continued "stalking" these women. He had a low-paying job at a large company whose director was his father's close friend. He did no useful work, came in late, stole important papers, and was eventually fired—only to carry on in a similar way at another company whose president owed his father a favor. After his father died, he took to spiriting away valuable books from his father's antiquarian collection to sell for supplementing his meager income. He took money from his mother's purse and from his brother's wallet, until finally the family put locks on all the doors of their sprawling apartment, locking the bedroom door when they went to the bathroom and then the bathroom door before returning to the bedroom.

My "treatment" of this obviously psychopathic but (thus far) nonviolent man was to urge the mother to change the apartment door locks when he was at work and leave a note with the doorman containing a week's worth of money and the address of the hotel where she had reserved him a room and shipped his belongings. I had met with the mother and her son to explain why I felt this was the only recourse; they accepted this plan, not without regrets at having to recognize the immutability of the man's character aberrations. Once implemented, they lived (separately) with a sense of freedom and security such as they had not experienced in the 6 years since his behavior had become so intolerable.

In another case, I treated for about 1 year a 39-year-old woman who had been married for a few years, during which time she was involved with another man by whom she had a boy, now 4 years old. The exhusband knew he was not the father, so he refused to pay child support; the actual father knew she had told the boy her "ex" was the father to obviate the stigma of illegitimacy. He balked about paying any support, knowing that she would not take him to court, lest the truth be exposed. Meantime, she worked sporadically at various menial jobs, getting fired from each because of lateness, missing items, and so forth. Her wealthy father, an alternatingly irascible and indulgent man, could be relied on to pick up the tab, until, that is, after I

arranged a family meeting with the patient, her father, two brothers, and their wives about how best to handle the situation. At that meeting, she stole a watch and some money from the purse of one of her sisters-in-law. That was the last straw. The family sent her to another city where she had a distant relative willing to take her and the child in. Her father henceforth refused to "throw good money after bad" and cut off her allowance. She had been a seductive, idle, and larcenous charmer ever since she was in her teens, causing great trouble to the family. Until the stolen watch episode, they had used their wealth and connections to keep her out of trouble, so she had no arrest record and no delinquency record. Therefore, her PCL-R score was artificially low. As for the year of psychotherapy with me and the years of therapy earlier on with several other therapists, this left intact her manipulativeness, deceitfulness, and penchant for petty thievery.

THE UNTREATABLE AND THE DANGEROUS: THE VIOLENT PSYCHOPATH

Some of the patients alluded to above, those with moderate PCL-R scores, came from families with strong histories of bipolar manic–depression. Risk genes for this condition are associated with novelty seeking, impulsivity, irascibility, and sometimes emotional insensitivity. These are characteristics of psychopathy, and it is no surprise that there is a degree of overlap between bipolar manic–depression and psychopathic traits. In my study of murderers, I attempted to situate them on a spectrum I called the "gradations of evil" (Stone, 1993, p. 453; Stone, 1998b, p. 348). I enumerated 22 gradations, starting with cases of justified homicide (which is not murder) and ending with psychopathic torture, namely, murderers where torture was prolonged. Beginning with the 9th gradation, psychopathy is part of the personality profile. The 9th gradation is reserved for "jealous lovers with psychopathic features." Many of these people are bipolar manic–depressives: Ira Einhorn (Levy, 1988), Richard Minns (Finstad, 1991), and Buddy Jacobson (Haden-Guest, 1981).

As one moves toward the end of the spectrum, toward the region of people subjecting others to torture, serial sexual homicide, or both, manic–

depression is no longer a noticeable feature. Instead, the personality profiles, besides full-blown psychopathy, include the traits of SZD. Of the serial killers in my biography series (now numbering 87), 40% were comorbid for SZD and SDS (as defined in the appendix of the *DSM-III-R*). Those with psychopathy and SDS include Fred and Rose West from the English Midlands (Sounes, 1995) and Angelo Buono (the "leader" of the two Hillside Stranglers in Los Angeles, CA; O'Brien, 1985). Those with psychopathy and SZD include Jeffrey Dahmer (Schwartz, 1992) and Gary Heidnick (Englade, 1988).

Although there seems to be no absolute bottom to human depravity—no case of torturous maltreatment more grotesque than all other examples (I limit myself to people operating in peacetime; the atrocities of the Nazis and the recent Serbian soldiers in Bosnia and Kosovo are another story)—there are some remarkable candidates. Two of these I described in some detail elsewhere (Stone, 1998b, pp. 352–353): Theresa Knorr (Clarkson, 1995) and Paul Bernardo (Burnside & Cairns, 1995). Knorr was predominantly sadistic, burning her daughters' arms with cigarettes and shooting one daughter in the chest and then (when the girl failed to die) extracting the bullet to hide the incident from the authorities. She finally, with the help of her sons, took the girl to the foothills of California's Sierra mountains, where they burned her alive and left her to die. Knorr was motivated by a crazy jealousy of her daughters, whom she subjected to tortures and imprisonment for years (e.g., chaining one inside a closet and leaving her without food) before murdering two of the three.

Toronto-born Bernardo was a "classic" psychopath of the charmer–con artist type. He became obsessed with sex, power, and rape fantasies, especially after finding out that his mother's husband was not his real father. He married Karen Homolka, used this easily intimidated young woman, whom he had completely subjugated, as an accomplice in his torture–murders of young women, including Karen's younger sister. Bernardo had built a secret room in their house where he carried out the tortures and forced Karen to have lesbian sex with two women, which he videotaped to ensure that she would not dare tell the authorities about him. Burnside and

Cairns (1995) outlined the progression of the typical sexual sadist, as he moves from choosing a vulnerable and easily exploited woman, then charming her with his "loving and considerate" manner (none of it was genuine), next inducing her to indulge in sexual practices far beyond what is customary (use of bondage, dildoes, etc.), progressing to possessiveness and jealousy, isolating the woman from all her friends, and finally transforming her into a helpless object for his physical and psychological abuse (Burnside & Cairns, 1995, p. 551).

Spirituality: The Opposite Extreme From Psychopathy and a Positive Prognostic Factor

In the same way that psychopathy within the FFM model represents the extreme of Antagonism, spirituality may be said to represent the extreme of Agreeableness. More specifically, psychopathy is a step beyond narcissistic personality disorder. There are vain, self-centered (i.e., narcissistic) people who are not psychopathic. There are, likewise, agreeable people who show little spirituality, the latter being a step beyond the merely agreeable. Spirituality implies a general other orientedness, a predisposition to minimize one's own troubles, emphasizing instead serenity and one's obligation to the whole human community. Such altruism is not limited to selfless acts on behalf only of one's immediate circle. The term and the concept behind it are seldom discussed in psychiatry. There is an allusion to something closely akin to spirituality in Cloninger et al.'s (1993) personality factor that he called Self-Transcendence, as mentioned above.

What made me aware of this trait—perhaps it is best thought of as a superordinate or composite trait (and thus akin to a factor)—was my work with Patient 7 of the vignettes. What seemed to differentiate her dramatically from other depressed patients I have treated was her near total lack of the qualities that go to make up this attribute of spirituality. It was this deficiency that, at the same time, made her a much greater suicide risk than other patients who suffer considerably worse depressions yet retain a good measure of spirituality. This latter attribute thus appears to differentiate rather well the highly suicide-prone patients from the not-very-suicide-prone patients, who in other respects seem to have the clinical picture one associates with suicidality. By spirituality, I do not mean absorption within a religious group nor any profound belief in a deity. Of course, many profoundly religious people do, in addition, have a great deal of this quality.

What I feel comes under the heading of spirituality are such traits and attitudes as the following, which I have gathered into a scale (Stone, 2000b): hopefulness, forbearance, humility, oriented toward others, faith in self and others, self-acceptance, resignation, serenity, forgiveness, compassion, uncomplainingness, self-transcendence, dignity, and a sense of mission oriented toward the repair of the world along with a sense of responsibility to do something positive for the world, coupled with a concern for the suffering of others. In my scale (which has 20 items and their opposites), each of these qualities can be envisioned on a visual analog scale with a high degree of the quality at one end of the line and the high degree of its opposite at the other end. The opposite traits–attitudes include despair, impatience, false pride, self-centeredness, disillusion, self-pity, bitterness, grudge holding, meanspiritedness, cynicism, and a lack of respect for others.

Many of the facets of Agreeableness, as enumerated in the NEO-PI-R, overlap with these positive spiritual qualities: trustingness, giving and sacrificial, cooperative, self-effacing, and concerned–compassionate. It is my impression, however, that there is something to be gained by drawing attention to the array of these positive traits under the rubric of spirituality because of their prognostic implications. I believe attention to these qualities will help in alerting therapists to suicide risk where spirituality is lacking and to a diminished risk where they are present in abundance, independent of the other known risk factors such as a family history of depression, low cerebrospinal fluid–serotonin, and the demographic variables associated with suicide risk.

CONCLUSION

I hope to have demonstrated with the examples throughout this chapter the utility and indeed the superiority of the FFM approach to the diagnosis of personality and as a guide to what is treatable and what is not. Allied to the lexical system for detailing all aspects of personality including both the negative maladaptive traits and the positive traits, the FFM is also a dimensional model that permits greater subtlety of diagnosis than what can be derived from a category-based system, such as that of the *DSM*. The NEO-PI-R allows the clinician or the prospective therapist to set down in a convenient way all the relevant strong and weak points of the personality in someone being considered for treatment. Because psychopathy has a place within the FFM schema as the furthest outpost of "Antagonism," the schema is also useful in drawing the boundary line demarcating the kinds of personality aberrations that are still amenable to therapy from those that are not amenable or which, if Rice's (Rice et al., 1992) study can be replicated in future studies, may even be made worse by treatment. The one area where I believe the FFM needs some modification is in dealing with the "mercuriality" of the typical borderline patient, whose rapid changes of mood make it difficult to give but one rating on a number of facets.

Because the FFM lends itself so well to the inclusion of both negative traits like those related to psychopathy and positive traits like those associated with spirituality, its use should be encouraged as a guide whether to begin (or not to begin) one's therapeutic work: who are likely to be amenable to treatment (those with high spirituality), who are likely to be intermediate in this regard, and who are most unlikely to respond with favorable outcomes to psychotherapy (those meeting the criteria for psychopathy).

References

Allport, G. W., & Odbert, H. S. (Eds.). (1936). Trait names: A psycholexical study [Whole issue]. *Psychological Monographs, 47.*

American Psychiatric Association. (1980). *Diagnostic and statistical manual of mental disorders* (3rd ed.). Washington, DC: American Psychiatric Press.

American Psychiatric Association. (1994). *Diagnostic and statistical manual of mental disorders* (4th ed.). Washington, DC: American Psychiatric Press.

Burnside, S., & Cairns, A. (1995). *Deadly innocence: The true story of Paul Bernardo, Karen Homolka, and the Schoolgirl Murders.* New York: Times Warner.

Clarkin, J. F., Hull, J. W., Cantor, J., & Sanderson, C. (1993). Borderline personality disorder and personality traits: A comparison of SCID-II and NEO-PI. *Psychological Assessment, 5,* 472–476.

Clarkson, W. (1995). *Whatever mother says: A true story of a mother, madness, and murder.* New York: St. Martin's Press.

Cleckley, H. (1941). *The mask of sanity.* St. Louis, MO: Mosby.

Cloninger, C. R. (1986). A unified biosocial theory of personality and its role in the development of anxiety states. *Psychiatric Developments, 3,* 167–226.

Cloninger, C. R., & Svrakic, D. M. (1993). Personality dimensions as conceptual framework for explaining variations in normal, neurotic, and personality-disordered behavior. In G. D. Burrows & M. Roth (Eds.), *Handbook of anxiety* (pp. 79–104). Amsterdam, The Netherlands: Elsevier.

Cloninger, C. R., Svrakic, D. M., & Przybeck, T. R. (1993). A psychobiological model of temperament and character. *Archives of General Psychiatry, 50,* 975–990.

Cooke, D. J., Forth, A. E., & Hare, R. D. (1998). *Psychopathy: Theory, research and implications for society.* Dordrecht, The Netherlands: Kluwer Academic.

Costa, P. T., Jr., & McCrae, R. R. (1985). *The NEO Personality Inventory manual.* Odessa, FL: Psychological Assessment Resources.

Costa, P. T., Jr., & McCrae, R. R. (1992). *Revised NEO Personality Inventory (NEO-PI-R) and NEO Five-Factor Inventory (NEO-FFI) professional manual.* Odessa, FL: Psychological Assessment Resources.

Costa, P. T., Jr., & Widiger, T. A. (Eds.). (1994). *Personality disorders and the five-factor model of personality.* Washington, DC: American Psychological Association.

Englade, K. (1988). *Cellar of horrors.* New York: St. Martin's Press.

Eysenck, H. J. (1947). *The dimensions of personality.* London, England: Kegan Paul, Trench & Trubner.

Finstad, S. (1991). *Sleeping with the devil.* New York: Morrow.

Fonagy, P., Steele, M., Steele, H., Leigh, T., Kennedy, R., Mattoon, G., & Target, M. (1995). Attachment, the reflective self and borderline states: The predictive specificity of the Adult Attachment Interview and pathological emotional development. In S. Goldberg, R. Muir, & J. Kerr (Eds.), *Attachment theory* (pp. 233–278). Hillsdale, NJ: Analytic Press.

Goldberg, L. R. (1982). From ace to zombie: Some explorations in the language of personality. In C. Spielberger & J. Butcher (Eds.), *Advances in personality assessment* (pp. 203–234). Hillsdale, NJ: Erlbaum.

Gough, H. G., & Heilbrun, A. B., Jr. (1983). *Adjective Checklist manual.* Palo Alto, CA: Consulting Psychologists Press.

Greene, R. L. (1980). *The MMPI: An interpretive manual.* New York: Grune & Stratton.

Haden-Guest, A. (1981). *Bad dreams: A true story of sex, money and murder.* New York: Ballantine Books.

Hare, R. D. (1998). Psychopaths and their nature. In T. Millon, E. Simonsen, M. Birket-Smith, & R. D. Davis (Eds.), *Psychopathy: Antisocial, criminal and violent behavior* (pp. 188–212). New York: Guilford Press.

Hare, R. D., Harpur, T. J., Hakstian, A. R., Forth, A. E., Hart, S. D., & Newman, J. P. (1990). The Revised Psychopathy Checklist: Reliability and factor structure. *Psychological Assessment, 2,* 338–341.

Harris, G. T., Rice, M. E., & Cormier, C. A. (1991). Psychopathy and violent recidivism. *Law and Human Behavior, 15,* 625–637.

Havill, A. (1999). *The mother, the son and the socialite: The true story of a mother–son crime spree.* New York: St. Martin's Press.

Janet, P. (1929). *L'évolution Psychologique de la personnalité* [The psychological evolution of the personality]. Paris, France: Chahine.

Jung, K. (1921). *Psychologische typen.* Zürich, Switzerland: Rascher.

Kemp, W. (1983). *The desire of my eyes: The life and work of John Ruskin.* New York: Farrar, Straus & Giroux.

Kernberg, O. F. (1967). Borderline personality organization. *Journal of the American Psychoanalytic Association, 15,* 641–685.

Kernberg, O. F. (1984). *Severe personality disorder.* New Haven, CT: Yale University Press.

Kraepelin, E. (1915). *Psychiatrie: Ein Lehrbuch für Studierende und Ärzte: Vol. IV. Die psychopathische Persönlichkeiten* [Psychiatry: A Textbook for Students and Physicians: Vol. IV. The psychopathic personalities]. Leipzig, Germany: Barth Verlag.

Levy, S. (1988). *The unicorn's secret: Murder in the Age of Aquarius.* New York: Prentice Hall.

Livesley, W. J. (1987). A systematic approach to the delineation of personality disorders. *American Journal of Psychiatry, 144,* 772–777.

McDougall, W. (1932). Of the words character and personality. *Character and Personality, 1,* 3–16.

O'Brien, D. (1985). *Two of a kind: The Hillside Stranglers.* New York: New American Library.

Oldham, J. M., & Morris, L. B. (1990). *The personality self-portrait*. New York: Bantam.

Oldham, J. M., Skodol, A. E., Kellman, H. D., Rosnick, L., & Davies, M. (1992). Diagnosis of *DSM-III* personality disorders by two structured interviews: Patterns of comorbidity. *American Journal of Psychiatry, 149*, 213–220.

Pacepa, I. M. (1987). *Red horizons: The true story of Nicolae and Elena Ceauçescu's crimes, life-style and corruption*. New York: Regenery Gateway.

Patrick, C. J., Bradley, M. M., & Lang, P. J. (1993). Emotion in the criminal psychopath: Startle reflex modulation. *Journal of Abnormal Psychology, 102*, 82–92.

Reich, W. (1933/1949). *Character analysis* (1st & 3rd eds.). New York: Farrar, Straus, Giroux.

Rice, M. E., Harris, G. T., & Cormier, C. A. (1992). An evaluation of a maximum security therapeutic community for psychopaths and other mentally disordered offenders. *Law and Human Behavior, 16*, 399–411.

Ronningstam, E. F. (Ed.). (1997). *Disorders of narcissism*. Washington, DC: American Psychiatric Press.

Schneider, K. (1950). *Psychopathic personalities*. London, England: Cattell. (Original work published 1923)

Schwartz, A. (1992). *The man who could not kill enough: The secret murders of Milwaukee's Jeffrey Dahmer*. New York: Carol.

Shengold, L. (1989). *Soul murder: The effects of child abuse and deprivation*. New Haven, CT: Yale University Press.

Sounes, H. (1995). *Fred and Rose: The full story of Fred and Rose West and the Gloucester house of horrors*. London, England: Warner Books.

Spitzer, R. L., Williams, J. B. W., Gibbon, M., & First, M. B. (1990). *User's guide for the Structural Clinical Interview for DSM-III-R (SCID)*. Washington, DC: American Psychiatric Press.

Stein, J., with Plimpton, G. (Eds.). (1982). *Edie: An American biography*. New York: Knopf.

Stone, M. H. (1990a). *The fate of borderlines*. New York: Guilford Press.

Stone, M. H. (1990b). Toward a comprehensive typology of personality. *Journal of Personality Disorders, 4*, 416–421.

Stone, M. H. (1993). *Abnormalities of personality: Within and beyond the realm of treatment*. New York: Norton.

Stone, M. H. (1998a). The personalities of murderers: The importance of psychopathy and sadism. In A. Skodol (Ed.), *Psychopathology and violent crime: Annual review of psychiatry* (pp. 29–52). Washington, DC: American Psychiatric Press.

Stone, M. H. (1998b). Sadistic personality in murderers. In T. Millon, E. Simonsen, M. Birket-Smith, & R. D. Davis (Eds.), *Psychopathy: Antisocial, criminal and violent behavior* (pp. 346–355). New York: Guilford Press.

Stone, M. H. (2000a). *The gradations of antisociality. Annual review: The American Psychiatric Association*. Washington, DC: American Psychiatric Press.

Stone, M. H. (2000b). Wesentliche prognostische Faktoren für die borderline Persönlichkeitsstörung [Essential prognostic factors for the borderline personality disorder]. In B. Dulz, O. F. Kernberg, & U. Sachsse (Eds.), *Handbuch der Borderline-störungen* [Handbook of borderline disorders]. Stuttgart, Germany: Schattauer Verlag.

Taubman, B. (1992). *Hell hath no fury: A true story of wealth and passion, love and envy, and a woman driven to the ultimate act of revenge*. New York: St. Martin's Press.

Tupes, E. C., & Christal, R. E. (1992). Recurrent personality factors based on trait ratings. (U.S. Air Force ASD Tech. Rep. No. 61-97). *Journal of Personality, 60*, 225–251. (Original work published 1961)

Tyrer, P., & Alexander, J. (1988). Personality assessment schedule. In P. Tyrer (Ed.), *Personality disorders: Diagnosis, management and course* (pp. 43–62). London, England: Wright.

Widiger, T. A. (1996, May 9). *Aggression: Within and beyond the DSM-IV*. Paper presented at the 149th annual meeting of the American Psychiatric Association, New York.

Widiger, T. A. (1997). Personality disorder as maladaptive variants of common personality traits: Implications for treatment. *Journal of Contemporary Psychotherapy, 27*, 265–282.

Wiggins, J. (1982). Circumplex models of interpersonal behavior in clinical psychology. In P. C. Kendall & J. N. Butcher (Eds.), *Handbook of research methods in clinical psychology* (pp. 183–221). New York: Wiley.

Williamson, S., Harpur, T. J., & Hare, R. D. (1991). Abnormal processing of affective words by psychopaths. *Psychophysiology, 28*, 260–273.

Wilson, C., & Seaman, D. (1992). *The serial killers*. New York: Simon & Schuster.

World Health Organization. (1977). *International classification of diseases* (9th ed.). Geneva, Switzerland: Author.

Yang, K. S., & Bond, M. H. (1990). Exploring implicit personality theories with indigenous or imported constructs: The Chinese case. *Journal of Personality and Social Psychology, 58*, 1087–1095.

CHAPTER 25

A PROPOSAL FOR AXIS II:
DIAGNOSING PERSONALITY
DISORDERS USING THE
FIVE-FACTOR MODEL

Thomas A. Widiger, Paul T. Costa, Jr., and Robert R. McCrae

In chapter 6 of this text, Widiger, Trull, Clarkin, Sanderson, and Costa describe how each of the 10 officially recognized personality disorders (PDs) in the American Psychiatric Association's (APA) *Diagnostic and Statistical Manual of Mental Disorders* (*DSM-IV*, APA, 1994; *DSM-IV*, text revised [*DSM-IV-TR*], APA, 2000) can be understood from the perspective of the five-factor model (FFM) of personality functioning. This translation is helpful to those who are familiar with the *DSM-IV* constructs and wish to understand how a person with one or more of these diagnoses would be described in terms of the FFM constructs. However, they do not indicate how one would diagnose a disorder of personality solely on the basis of the FFM. If the FFM is to provide a viable alternative to the *DSM-IV* diagnostic categories, one must understand how to diagnose a PD using the FFM. The purpose of this chapter is to indicate how this might be done.

We begin with a brief description of how PDs are diagnosed by *DSM-IV*, followed by a more detailed discussion of how they could be diagnosed with the FFM. Our process for the diagnosis of a PD includes four cumulative steps, not all of which are in fact necessary, because stopping at any one of the first three steps provides a substantial amount of clinically relevant and useful information.

Step 1. Provide a description of the person's personality traits with respect to the 5 domains and 30 facets of the FFM.

Step 2. Identify the problems, difficulties, and impairments that are secondary to each trait.

Step 3. Determine whether the impairments are clinically significant.

Step 4. Determine whether the constellation of FFM traits matches sufficiently the profile for a particular PD pattern.

PERSONALITY DISORDER DIAGNOSES THROUGH THE *DSM-IV*

For certain legal, medical, and administrative purposes, it is necessary to obtain a formal *DSM-IV* diagnosis. The initial step toward the provision of a PD diagnosis in the *DSM-IV* is to evaluate the general diagnostic criteria (APA, 2000; see Exhibit 25.1). The general diagnostic criteria do not indicate whether a particular PD is present; they determine instead whether any PD could be present. Most of the general diagnostic criteria are concerned primarily with the determination of whether there are pervasive and enduring personality traits; only one general diagnostic criterion is actually concerned explicitly with the maladaptivity of these traits. As indicated in Exhibit 25.1, the general diagnostic criteria include the determination of whether there is an enduring pattern of inner experience and behavior that deviates markedly from the expectations of the individual's culture and that this enduring pattern is manifested in two or more of the following ways: (a) cognitively, (b) affectively, (c) interpersonally, and (c) through impulse dyscontrol.

One must also determine whether the enduring pattern is inflexible and pervasive across a broad range of personal and social situations; the enduring pattern leads to clinically significant distress or im-

---

EXHIBIT 25.1

DSM-IV-TR **General Diagnostic Criteria for Personality Disorders**

A. An enduring pattern of inner experience and behavior that deviates markedly from the expectations of the individual's culture. This pattern is manifested in two (or more) of the following areas:
   1. Cognition (i.e., ways of perceiving and interpreting self, other people, and events)
   2. Affectivity (i.e., the range, intensity, lability, and appropriateness of emotional response)
   3. Interpersonal functioning
   4. Impulse control.
B. The enduring pattern is inflexible and pervasive across a broad range of personal and social situations.
C. The enduring pattern leads to clinically significant distress or impairment in social, occupational, or other important areas of functioning.
D. The pattern is stable and of long duration, and its onset can be traced back at least to adolescence or early adulthood.
E. The enduring pattern is not better accounted for as a manifestation or consequence of another mental disorder.
F. The enduring pattern is not due to the direct physiological effects of a substance (e.g., a drug of abuse, a medication) or a general medical condition (e.g., head trauma).

Note. From the fourth edition, text revised, of the *Diagnostic and Statistical Manual of Mental Disorders* (*DSM-IV-TR*, 2000; p. 689), by the American Psychiatric Press, Washington, DC: Author. Copyright 2000 by the American Psychiatric Press. Reprinted with permission.

---

pairment in social, occupational, or other important areas of functioning; the enduring pattern is indeed stable, of long duration, and can be traced back at least to adolescence or early adulthood; the enduring pattern is not better accounted for as a manifestation or consequence of another mental disorder; and the enduring pattern is not due to the direct physiological effects of a substance or medical condition, such as head trauma. If all of these criteria are met, then a PD diagnosis can be provided.

The *DSM-IV* provides two general options for the particular PD diagnosis (or diagnoses) that would be provided. One general option is to provide one or more of the 10 officially recognized individual diagnoses (e.g., borderline [BDL], histrionic, antisocial, paranoid). Exhibit 25.2 provides the *DSM-IV-TR* diagnostic criteria set for a schizoid personality disorder (SZD; APA, 2000). As indicated in Exhibit 25.2, this disorder is diagnosed by determining whether four of the set of seven diagnostic criteria are present as well as by ruling out the presence of a mood disorder with psychotic features, a pervasive developmental disorder, and other Axis I mental disorders. If four or more of the diagnostic criteria are present, then the person is diagnosed as having SZD; if three or fewer of the criteria are present, then the diagnostic judgment is that the person does not have SZD.

"When (as is often the case) an individual's pattern of behavior meets criteria for more than one Personality Disorder, the clinician should list all relevant Personality Disorder diagnoses in order of importance" (APA, 2000, p. 686). Determining which of the multiple PD diagnoses should be provided requires an assessment of at least most of the diagnostic criteria for each PD; therefore, the standard procedure used by most researchers is to administer all of the diagnostic criteria. The assessment of all 80 *DSM-IV* PD diagnostic criteria (94 if the depressive and passive–aggressive PDs are assessed) requires 2–4 hours, if each diagnostic criterion is indeed systematically assessed (Rogers, 1995; Segal, 1997;

EXHIBIT 25.2

DSM-IV-TR **Criteria for Schizoid Personality Disorder**

A. A pervasive pattern of detachment from social relationships and a restricted range of expression of emotions in interpersonal settings, beginning by early adulthood and present in a variety of contexts, as indicated by four (or more) of the following:

    (1) neither desires nor enjoys close relationships, including being part of a family

    (2) almost always chooses solitary activities

    (3) has little, if any, interest in having sexual experiences with another person

    (4) takes pleasure in few, if any, activities

    (5) lacks close friends or confidants other than first-degree relatives

    (6) appears indifferent to the praise or criticism of others

    (7) emotional coldness, detachment, or flattened affectivity.

B. Does not occur exclusively during the course of schizophrenia, a mood disorder with psychotic features, another psychotic disorder, or a pervasive developmental disorder and is not due to the direct physiological effects of a general medical condition.

    Note: If criteria are met prior to the onset of schizophrenia, add "pre-morbid," (e.g., "schizoid personality disorder [pre-morbid]").

Note. From the fourth edition, text revised, of the *Diagnostic and Statistical Manual of Mental Disorders* (*DSM-IV-TR*, 2000; p. 697), by the American Psychiatric Press, Washington, DC: Author. Copyright 2000 by the American Psychiatric Press. Adapted with permission.

Widiger & Saylor, 1998; Zimmerman, 1994). It is not surprising then that most clinicians fail to assess all 80 diagnostic criteria, focusing their interview instead on only one or two PDs that they believe are likely to be present (Gunderson, 1992). However, a number of studies indicate that the failure to provide a comprehensive assessment of the full range of PD symptomatology results in a substantial loss of clinically important information, notably the presence of additional maladaptivity that is likely to have an important impact on the understanding and treatment of the patient (Westen, 1997; Widiger, 1993).

The second general option for an individual PD diagnosis is to provide the diagnosis of personality disorder not otherwise specified (PDNOS), which may in fact be the most frequently used PD diagnosis in clinical practice (Fabrega, Ulrich, Pilkonis, & Mezzich, 1991; Kass, Skodol, Charles, Spitzer, & Williams, 1985; Koenigsberg, Kaplan, Gilmore, & Cooper, 1985; Loranger, 1990; Morey, 1988; Zimmerman & Coryell, 1989). The diagnosis of PDNOS is provided when the person meets the general diagnostic criteria for a PD (see Exhibit 25.1), but the relevant PD symptomatology fails to meet the diagnostic criteria for any 1 of the 10 officially recognized PD diagnoses. A PDNOS diagnosis therefore requires the administration of the general diagnostic criteria (to indicate the presence of a PD) and the administration of the diagnostic criteria for all of the 10 officially recognized diagnoses (to rule out the presence of any 1 of the 10 officially recognized PDs).

The diagnosis of PDNOS can be used in a variety of ways. PDNOS can be used in cases in which the person fails to meet the diagnostic criteria for any 1 of the 10 officially recognized diagnoses yet has enough of the features from more than 1 of them "that together cause clinically significant distress or impairment in one or more important areas of functioning (e.g., social or occupational)" (APA, 2000, p. 729). The specific title for this PDNOS diagnosis is often given as "mixed," followed by a specification of the particular symptomatology that is present (e.g., 301.9 [*ICD* code number], PDNOS, mixed, with borderline, avoidant, and dependent features). It is important to note that if the person fails to have features from more than one PD but did have some of the diagnostic criteria for one of them (e.g., three of the nine BDL criteria), the diagnosis of PDNOS cannot be provided because a clinically significant level of impairment is not said to occur unless the specified threshold for the diagnosis is obtained (i.e., five or more of the nine BDL criteria). The PDNOS mixed diagnosis is for those (commonly occurring) instances in which the person fails to meet the criteria for a particular PD but has enough symptoms from a variety of different PDs that together results in a clinically significant level of impairment (e.g., a person with only three BDL criteria but also three avoidant, two histrionic, and three dependent would probably have as much clinically significant impairment or distress as a person with five BDL diagnostic criteria).

A second option for PDNOS is "when the clinician judges that a specific Personality Disorder that is not included in the Classification is appropriate" (APA, 2000, p. 729). This could include diagnoses that had received official or unofficial recognition (e.g., sadistic or self-defeating), that currently receive unofficial recognition (i.e., depressive or passive–aggressive), or even those that have never received any official or unofficial recognition (e.g., delusional dominating, pleonexic, abusive, or aggressive). The availability of this option is in recognition of the fact that the *DSM-IV* fails to cover all of the possible ways in which one might have a PD (Clark, Watson, & Reynolds, 1995). If one has a diagnostic term that adequately describes the particular constellation of personality traits, then this term should be provided (e.g., 301.9, PDNOS, sadistic). However, if there is no specific term available for that particular constellation of maladaptive personality traits, then a generic, nondescript term is typically provided (e.g., 301.9, PDNOS, atypical).

Note that clinicians can diagnose PDNOS along with 1 or more of the 10 officially recognized PDs. As the *DSM-IV* states, PDNOS "is for disorders of personality functioning . . . that do not meet criteria for any specific personality disorder" (APA, 2000, p. 729). This statement has been interpreted by some

clinicians and researchers to mean that PDNOS is only used when a person fails to meet the criteria for any 1 of the 10 officially recognized PDs. However, PDNOS is used to diagnose a particular set or constellation of PD symptomatology that fails to meet the criteria for any 1 of the 10 officially recognized PDs, and this symptomatology could co-occur with 1 or more of the 10 officially recognized PDs. For example, a patient could be given the diagnoses of antisocial (301.7) and abusive (301.9); antisocial (301.7) and mixed (301.9, with borderline, paranoid, and narcissistic features); or antisocial (301.7), histrionic (301.5), and mixed (301.9, with borderline and abusive features). How often clinicians do in fact diagnose PDNOS along with 1 of the 10 officially recognized diagnoses is unknown.

An additional option, beyond the provision of an officially recognized diagnosis or PDNOS, is to indicate the presence of specific maladaptive personality traits that together are below the threshold for an officially recognized, mixed, or atypical diagnosis. "Specific maladaptive personality traits that do not meet the threshold for a Personality Disorder may also be listed on Axis II" (APA, 2000, p. 687). These are instances in which the clinician has determined that the person does not have a PD but does have maladaptive personality traits. "In such instances, no specific code should be used" (p. 687) because the judgment is that there are maladaptive personality traits, but no PD is present. One instance in which this occurs is when a person has features of one or more PDs that are below the threshold for any one of them and below the threshold for a mixed PD (i.e., these features together result in maladaptivity but not clinically significant maladaptivity). In this instance, the clinician might record, for example, "V71.09, no diagnosis on Axis II, histrionic personality traits" (p. 687). A second possibility is when the clinician observes the presence of personality traits that are not included within the 10 officially recognized diagnoses; these traits would be maladaptive, but they again fail to result in a clinically significant level of maladaptivity. One might record in such an instance, "V71.9, no diagnosis on Axis II, introverted and overcontrolled personality traits."

In summary, it is apparent that a *DSM-IV* PD diagnosis is neither simple nor straightforward. As indicated above, researchers typically require 2–4 hours to determine whether one or more of the 10 officially recognized PDs are present. Most semistructured interviews and systematic empirical studies fail to even consider the presence of PDNOS, yet it is perhaps the most common diagnosis in clinical practice (Fabrega et al., 1991, Koenigsberg et al., 1985; Loranger, 1990) and the most frequent diagnosis when considered in empirical studies (Kass et al., 1985; Morey, 1988; Zimmerman & Coryell, 1989). Most patients meet the criteria for more than one *DSM-IV* PD diagnosis (Clark, Livesley, & Morey, 1997; Oldham et al., 1992; Widiger & Sanderson, 1995; Widiger & Trull, 1998), yet clinicians typically fail to assess systematically each of the 80 diagnostic criteria, providing instead only one diagnosis to represent the diverse and complex array of PD symptomatology (Gunderson, 1992). It is also unclear if clinicians consider the general diagnostic criteria when they provide the PDNOS diagnosis. Most semistructured interviews fail to include a systematic assessment of the general diagnostic criteria (e.g., Diagnostic Interview for *DSM-IV* Personality Disorders by Zanarini, Frankenburg, Sickel, & Yong, 1996; International Personality Disorder Examination by Loranger, Sartorius, & Janca, 1997; Personality Disorder Interview—IV by Widiger, Mangine, Corbitt, Ellis, & Thomas, 1995; Structured Clinical Interview for *DSM-IV* Axis II Personality Disorders by First, Gibbon, Spitzer, Williams, & Benjamin, 1997; and the Structured Interview for *DSM-IV* Personality Disorders by Pfohl, Blum, & Zimmerman, 1997). It could be argued that the general diagnostic criteria are embedded within the diagnostic criteria for the individual PDs (e.g., see Exhibits 25.1 and 25.2), but this representation is at best unsystematic and inconsistent (Clark, 1997).

FIVE-FACTOR MODEL PERSONALITY DISORDER DIAGNOSIS

If the clinician or researcher is interested in understanding and treating the problems that are caused by a client's personality, then *DSM-IV* diagnoses may not be optimal. As clinicians and researchers within this volume and elsewhere have argued, official diagnoses are substantially arbitrary, often unreliable,

overlapping, and incomplete and have only a limited utility for treatment planning (Clark et al., 1997; Livesley, 1998; McCrae, 1994; Westen & Arkowitz-Westen, 1998; Widiger, 1993). The FFM provides a better basis for personality assessment (John & Srivastava, 1999; McCrae & Costa, 1999). We now discuss how it can be used to diagnose PDs.

The process we recommend for the provision of a PD diagnosis from the perspective of the FFM consists of four integrated and cumulative steps:

Step 1. Provide a description of the person's personality traits with respect to the 5 domains and 30 facets of the FFM.
Step 2. Identify the problems, difficulties, and impairments that are secondary to each trait.
Step 3. Determine whether the impairments are clinically significant.
Step 4. Determine whether the constellation of FFM traits matches the profile for a particular PD pattern.

As we indicated earlier, one does need to complete all of the steps (or follow them in order) to obtain clinically useful information.

PERSONALITY-RELATED PROBLEMS

One approach to the application of the FFM is to limit oneself to just the first two steps: assess traits and identify associated problems. A distinct advantage of confining oneself to the first two steps is that one obtains all of the detail regarding the personality traits that can be obtained from the FFM and the problems in living associated with them, without arbitrarily diagnosing a proportion of people as having a mental disorder (McCrae, 1994). This approach might be particularly well suited in counseling psychology or other contexts in which a diagnosis of PD is not desired or required.

The 30 facets of the FFM can be assessed within a variety of instruments, including self-reports, informant ratings, and clinical interviews (Costa & McCrae, 1992; Trull & Widiger, 1997), and the results provide a reasonably comprehensive and precise description of the personality of any particular person (John & Srivastava, 1999; McCrae & Costa, 1990, 1999; Wiggins, 1996). The FFM description covers all of the personality traits included within the *DSM-IV* (see chapter 6, this volume) and many additional traits (adaptive and maladaptive) not covered by the *DSM-IV* (see, e.g., Stone, chapter 24, this volume). One of the more consistent criticisms of the categorical system of diagnosis used by the *DSM-IV* is that many patients have personality-related problems that are not covered by the current nomenclature (Westen, 1997) because they are either outside the realm of personality functioning covered by the 10 diagnostic categories or below the threshold for existing diagnoses (Widiger, 1993). "Because the full range of personality traits is covered [by the FFM], problems may be noted that would otherwise have gone unnoticed" (McCrae, 1994, p. 307).

A distinct advantage of personality description in terms of the FFM, relative to the existing *DSM-IV* categorical diagnoses of PD, is that the FFM description also includes beneficial, adaptive traits that will likely facilitate decisions concerning treatment and the treatment itself. "The last 40 years of individual differences research require the inclusion of personality trait assessment for the construction and implementation of any treatment plan that would lay claim to scientific status" (Harkness & Lilienfeld, 1997, p. 349). A description of the patient from the perspective of the FFM has considerable value as a scientifically based description of personality that informs clinicians of the personality traits of particular relevance to treatment decisions. "The explicit assessment of all five factors [and facets] would call attention to features of personality that may have implications for prognosis and treatment, even if they are unrelated to diagnosis" (McCrae, 1994, p. 307). "Because therapies differ dramatically in degree of structure, directedness, introspective demands, required verbal productivity, emotional precipitation, patient initiative, and depth of interpersonal interaction, rich opportunities exist for matching treatment to personality" (Harkness & Lilienfeld, 1997, p. 356). The clinical relevance and value of a comprehensive FFM description of a patient has been illustrated in numerous case studies (e.g., Ellis, 1994; Fagan, 1994; T. R. Miller, 1991; Piedmont, 1998; Widiger, 1997), including those cases in this text (see Bruehl, chapter 17; Corbitt, chapter 18, Sander-

son & Clarkin, chapter 21, and Stone, chapter 24, all in this volume).

An illustrative example of an FFM profile is provided in Figure 25.1. This profile was obtained from a patient, "Donna," seen in the private practice of Widiger (1997). Donna's FFM profile describes her as having maladaptive levels of angry–hostility (N2; in Neuroticism); cynicism, mistrust, and skepticism that border on suspiciousness (A1; in Agreeableness); and argumentativeness (A4). She also had problematic levels of self-consciousness (N4) and depressiveness (N3). These problematic traits, however, were offset to some extent by her adaptive levels of empathy (A6), gregariousness (E2; in Extraversion), warmth (E1), sociability (E2), generosity (A3), and concern for others (A6). She wanted to get along with others and to develop close, intimate relationships, but she inevitably complicated these relationships by her bitterness, resentment, anger, mistrust, and suspiciousness. However, an excellent indication for a potential responsivity to treatment was her openness to an exploration of her feelings (O3; in Openness to Experience), fantasies (O1), and ideas (O5). She was indeed reflective, open minded, and receptive to change. She harbored substantial feelings of cynicism, skepticism, and mistrust, but she was still open to reviewing, questioning, and changing her characteristic attitudes. She was also adaptively conscientious. She was quite deliberative (C6; in Conscientiousness), at times to the point of being overly ruminative. She was generally responsible (C3), organized (C2), and oriented toward successfully completing her goals (C4). (For more details regarding Donna, see Widiger, 1997.)

In addition to an FFM profile description, however, one might also wish to specify the problems, difficulties, and impairments that are secondary to these traits. McCrae (1994) provided a list of problems typically associated with each pole of the domains of the FFM. Trull and Widiger (1997) provided a somewhat expanded list of typical problems associated with each pole of the FFM facets. Exhibit 25.3 provides an integrative summary of both of these descriptions. The list of possible problems that may occur secondary to each of the domains and facets of the FFM calls attention to the kinds of problems people with particular traits are likely to

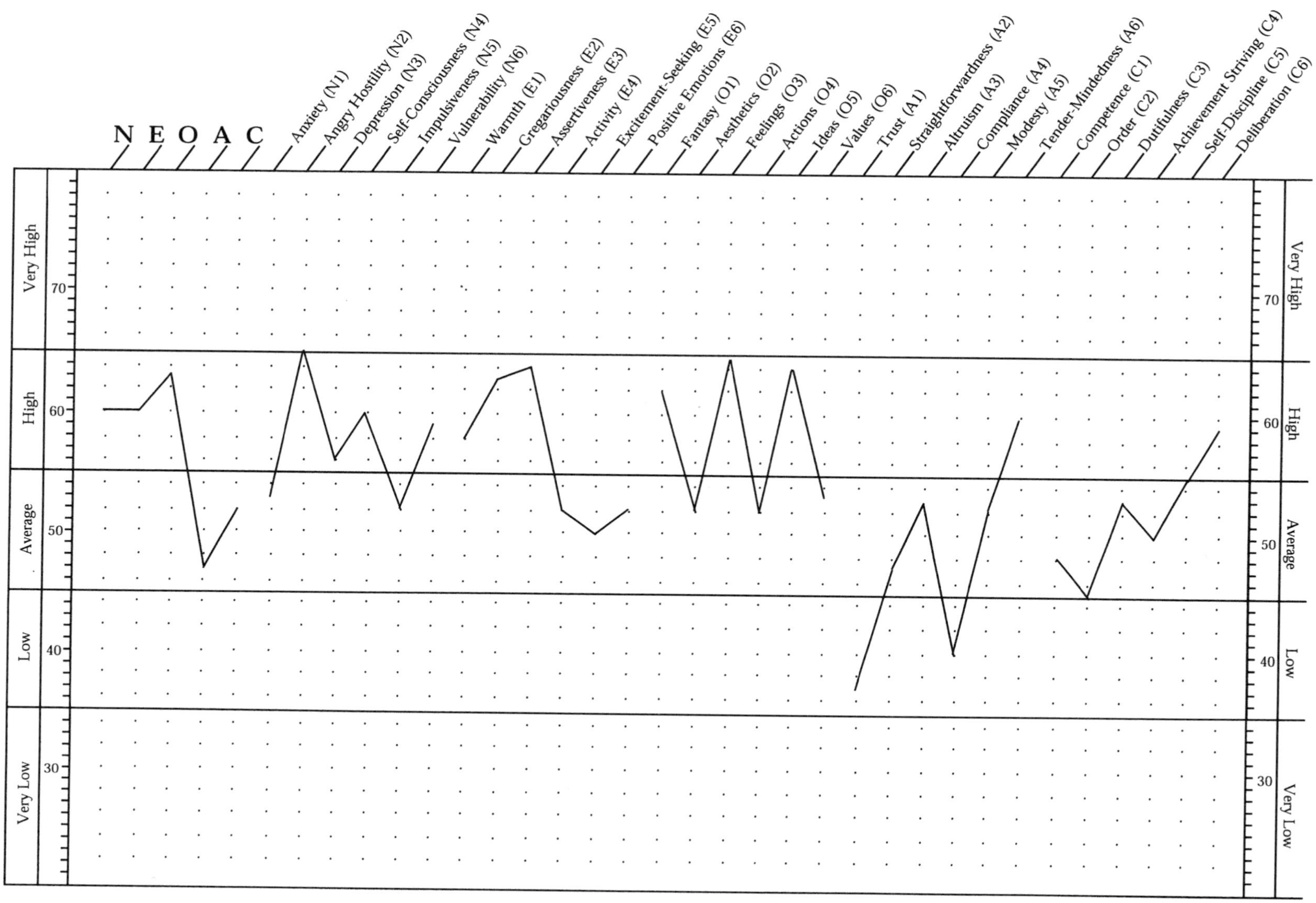

FIGURE 25.1. Revised NEO Personality Inventory (NEO-PI-R) profile of "Donna." From the *NEO Personality Inventory—Revised*, by Paul T. Costa, Jr., and Robert R. McCrae. Copyright 1978, 1985, 1989, 1992 by PAR, Inc. Reproduced by special permission of the publisher, Psychological Assessment Resources, Inc., 16204 North Florida Avenue, Lutz, FL 33549. Further reproduction is prohibited without permission of PAR, Inc.

EXHIBIT 25.3

Potential Problems Associated With the Domains and Facets of the Five-Factor Model of Personality

---

NEUROTICISM

High: Shows chronic negative affect, including anxiety, fearfulness, tension, irritability, anger, dejection, hopelessness, guilt, and shame; has difficulty in inhibiting impulses, for example, to eat drink, smoke, or spend money; has irrational beliefs, for example, unrealistic expectations, perfectionistic demands on self, and unwarranted pessimism; has unfounded somatic complaints; is helpless and dependent on others for emotional support and decision making.

Low: Lacks appropriate concern for potential problems in health or social adjustment; shows emotional blandness.

Anxiousness

High: Is extremely nervous, anxious, tense, or jittery; is excessively apprehensive, prone to worry, inhibited, and uncertain.

Low: Lacks significant or appropriate feelings of anxiety or apprehension; fails to expect, anticipate, or appreciate normal, obvious, or readily apparent dangers, risks, threats, or consequences.

Angry–Hostility

High: Has episodes of intense and out of control rage and fury; is hypersensitive and touchy; easily reacts with anger and hostility toward annoyances, rebukes, criticisms, rejections, frustrations, or other minor events; hostility may provoke arguments, disputes, and conflicts.

Low: Suppresses appropriate feelings of anger or hostility; does not even become annoyed or angry when confronted with substantial provocation, exploitation, abuse, harm, or victimization.

Depressiveness

High: Is continually depressed, gloomy, hopeless, and pessimistic; feels worthless, helpless, and excessively guilty; may at times be suicidal.

Low: Fails to appreciate actual costs and consequences of losses, setbacks, and failures; has difficulty soliciting or maintaining support and sympathy from others after sustaining a loss.

Self-Consciousness

High: Has intense feelings of chagrin and embarrassment; feels mortified, humiliated, ashamed, or disgraced in the presence of others.

Low: Is indifferent to opinions or reactions from others; often commits social blunders, insults, and indiscretions; lacks feelings of shame, even for socially egregious acts; appears glib and superficial.

Impulsiveness

High: Eats or drinks to excess; is troubled by debts secondary to overspending; is susceptible to cons, tricks, and poor business decisions; impulsively engages in a variety of harmful acts, including binge eating, excessive use of drugs and alcohol, excessive gambling, and suicidality or self-mutilation.

Low: Is excessively restrained or restricted; life is dull or uninteresting; lacks spontaneity.

Vulnerability

High: Is easily overwhelmed by minor stress; responds with panic, helplessness, and dismay to even minor stressors; is prone to dissociative, psychotic, anxiety, and/or mood disorder symptomatology when experiencing stress.

Continued on next page

EXHIBIT 25.3 (*continued*)

Low: Feels unrealistically invulnerable or invincible to danger; fails to recognize his or her own limitations; fails to take appropriate precautions or obtain necessary support or assistance; fails to recognize or appreciate signs of illness, failure, or loss.

EXTRAVERSION

High: Talks excessively, leading to inappropriate self-disclosure and social friction; has an inability to spend time alone; is attention seeking; shows overly dramatic expressions of emotions; shows reckless excitement seeking; inappropriately attempts to dominate and control others.

Low: Is socially isolated and interpersonally detached and lacks support networks; shows flattened affect; lacks joy and zest for life; is reluctant to assert his or her self or assume leadership roles even when qualified; is socially inhibited and shy.

Warmth

High: Develops inappropriate, problematic, and harmful attachments to others; develops and expresses excessive feelings of affection in situations in which more formal, neutral, and objective feelings are necessary or preferable.

Low: Has difficulty developing or sustaining personal, intimate relationships.

Gregariousness

High: Is unable to tolerate being alone; has an excessive need for the presence of others; may place more emphasis on the quantity of relationships (or developing new relationships) than the depth and quality of existing relationships.

Low: Is socially isolated; has no apparent social support network due to his or her own social withdrawal.

Assertiveness

High: Is domineering, pushy, bossy, dictatorial, or authoritarian.

Low: Is resigned and ineffective; has little influence or authority at work and for decisions that affect his or her own personal life.

Activity

High: Is driven, often overextended, frenzied, frantic, distractible, and at times burned out; feels driven to keep busy, filling spare time with numerous and at times trivial or pointless activities and rarely taking time off to relax and do nothing; is annoying, frustrating, or exhausting to friends and colleagues.

Low: Is inactive, idle, sedentary, and passive; appears apathetic, inert, and lethargic.

Excitement Seeking

High: Engages in a variety of reckless and even highly dangerous activities; behavior is rash, foolhardy, and careless.

Low: Activities and apparent pleasures are habitual, mechanical, and routine; life is experienced as dull, monotonous, and in a rut.

Positive Emotions

High: Is overemotional and overreactive to minor events; loses control of emotions during major events; tends to be giddy and may appear to others as euphoric or manic.

Low: Is severe, austere, solemn, or stern; appears unable to enjoy himself or herself at happy events; remains grim and humorless.

Continued on next page

EXHIBIT 25.3 (*continued*)

OPENNESS TO EXPERIENCE

High: Is preoccupied with fantasy and daydreaming; lacks practicality; has eccentric thinking (e.g., belief in ghosts, reincarnation, UFOs); has a diffuse identity and unstable goals, for example, joining a religious cult; is susceptible to nightmares and states of altered consciousness; shows social rebelliousness and nonconformity that can interfere with social or vocational advancement.

Low: Has difficulty adapting to social or personal change; shows a low tolerance or understanding for different points of view or lifestyles; shows emotional blandness and an inability to understand and verbalize his or her own feelings; is alexythymic; has a constricted range of interests; is insensitive to art and beauty; excessively conforms to authority.

Fantasy

High: Is often distracted by or preoccupied with fantasies; may often confuse reality and fantasy; appears to be living in a dream world; may have dissociative or hallucinatory experiences.

Low: Lacks any interest in fantasy or daydreams; imagination tends to be sterile; fails to enjoy activities that involve fantasy or imagination.

Aesthetics

High: Is preoccupied with aesthetic interests or activities to the detriment of social and occupational functioning; is "driven" or "obsessed" with some form of unusual, peculiar, or aberrant aesthetic activity.

Low: Has no appreciation of aesthetic or cultural pursuits; is unable to communicate with or relate to others due to an absence of appreciation for cultural or aesthetic interests (e.g., artwork "just looks like a bunch of colors to me").

Feelings

High: Is excessively governed by or preoccupied with his or her emotionality; may experience self as continuously within an exaggerated mood state, and may be excessively sensitive or responsive to transient mood states.

Low: Is oblivious to the feelings within him or herself and within other people; may seldom experience substantial or significant feelings; appears highly constricted.

Actions

High: Is unpredictable in his or her plans and interests; may switch careers and jobs numerous times.

Low: Avoids any change to his or her daily routine; establishes a set routine in his or her daily activities, and keeps to this routine in a repetitive, habitual manner.

Ideas

High: Is preoccupied with unusual, aberrant, or strange ideas; reality testing can be tenuous.

Low: Fails to appreciate or recognize new solutions; rejects new, creative, or innovative ideas as too strange or "crazy"; repeatedly applies old, failed solutions to new problems; does better with straightforward problems and concrete solutions; is rigidly traditional, old fashioned, and resistant to new, alternative perspectives or cultures.

Values

High: Continually questions and rejects alternative value systems; lacks any clear or coherent guiding belief system or convictions; is adrift and lost when faced with moral, ethical, or other significant life decisions; can be excessively unconventional and permissive.

Low: Is dogmatic and closed minded with respect to his or her moral, ethical, or other belief system; rejects and is intolerant of alternative belief systems; may be prejudiced and bigoted.

Continued on next page

EXHIBIT 25.3 (*continued*)

AGREEABLENESS

High: Is gullible; shows indiscriminant trust of others; shows excessive candor and generosity to the detriment of self-interest; has an inability to stand up to others and fight back; easily taken advantage of.

Low: Shows cynicism and paranoid thinking; has an inability to trust even friends or family; is quarrelsome; is too ready to pick fights; is exploitative and manipulative; lies; rude and inconsiderate manner alienates friends and limits social support; lacks respect for social conventions, which can lead to troubles with the law; shows an inflated and grandiose sense of self; is arrogant.

Trust

High: Has a tendency to be gullible, "green," "dewy eyed," or naive; fails to recognize that some people should not be trusted; fails to take realistic or practical cautions with respect to property, savings, and other things of value.

Low: Is paranoid and suspicious of most people; readily perceives malevolent intentions within benign, innocent remarks or behaviors; is often involved in acrimonious arguments with friends, colleagues, associates, or neighbors due to unfounded belief or expectation of being mistreated, used, exploited, or victimized.

Straightforwardness

High: Naively and indiscriminately reveals personal secrets, insecurities, and vulnerabilities to others, thereby exposing him- or herself to unnecessary exploitation, loss, or victimization; is unable to be clever, secretive, cunning, or shrewd.

Low: Is continually deceptive, dishonest, and manipulative; cons or deceives others for personal profit, gain, or advantage; other people may quickly or eventually recognize that this person cannot be trusted; may engage in pathological lying.

Altruism

High: Is excessively selfless and sacrificial; is often exploited, abused, or victimized due to a failure to consider or be concerned with his or her own needs or rights.

Low: Has little to no regard for the rights of others; is greedy and stingy; is exploitative or abusive.

Compliance

High: Is acquiescent, yielding, docile, and submissive; is often exploited, abused, or victimized as a result of a failure to protect or defend oneself.

Low: Is argumentative, defiant, resistant to authority, contentious, contemptuous, belligerent, combative, and obstructive; may bully, intimidate, and even be physically aggressive.

Modesty

High: Is meek and self-denigrating; fails to appreciate or is unable to acknowledge his or her talents, abilities, attractiveness, or other positive attributes.

Low: Is conceited, arrogant, boastful, pretentious, and pompous; feels entitled to special considerations, treatment, and recognition that are unlikely to be provided.

Tender Mindedness

High: Is soft hearted, mawkish, or maudlin; becomes excessively depressed, tearful, and overwhelmed in the face of pain and suffering of others; feelings of pity and concern are exploited by others.

Low: Is callous and coldhearted, and, at times, even merciless and ruthless toward others; experiences no concern, interest, or feelings for the pain and suffering of others.

Continued on next page

EXHIBIT 25.3 (*continued*)

CONSCIENTIOUSNESS

High: Overachieves; shows workaholic absorption in his or her job or cause to the exclusion of family, social, and personal interests; is compulsive, including excessively clean, tidy, and attention to detail; has rigid self-discipline and an inability to set tasks aside and relax; lacks spontaneity; is overscrupulous in moral behavior.

Low: Underachieves; does not fulfill intellectual or artistic potential; has a poor academic performance relative to ability; disregards rules and responsibilities, which can lead to trouble with the law; is unable to discipline him- or herself (e.g., stick to a diet or exercise plan), even when required for medical reasons; shows personal and occupational aimlessness.

Competence

High: Shows perfectionism, emphasizing or valuing competence to the detriment of most other activities and interests; fails to be successful or even adequate in tasks, assignments, and responsibilities due to excessive perfectionism.

Low: Is lax, disinclined, incapable, and unskilled, despite a potential to be highly or at least adequately skilled.

Order

High: Is preoccupied with order, rules, schedules, and organization; undermines leisure activities; tasks remain uncompleted due to a rigid emphasis on proper order and organization; friends and colleagues are frustrated by this preoccupation.

Low: Is disorganized, sloppy, haphazard, and slipshod.

Dutifulness

High: Shows rigid adherence to rules and standards, fails to appreciate or acknowledge ethical and moral dilemmas; places duty above all other moral or ethical principles.

Low: Is undependable, unreliable, and at times immoral and unethical.

Achievement Striving

High: Is excessively devoted to career, work, or productivity to the detriment of other important areas of life; is a workaholic, sacrificing friends, family, and other relationships for achievement or success.

Low: Is aimless, shiftless, and directionless; has no clear goals, plans, or direction in life; drifts from one job, aspiration, or place to another.

Self-Discipline

High: Shows single-minded doggedness for trivial, inconsequential, impossible, or even harmful tasks or goals.

Low: Employment is unstable and marginal; is negligent at work; is excessively hedonistic and self-indulgent.

Deliberation

High: Has ruminations and excessive ponderings of all possible consequences to the point that decisions fail to be made on time, effectively, or at all.

Low: Is a hasty and careless decision maker with harmful to dire consequences; fails to consider consequences and costs, even for important life decisions.

Note. Adapted from McCrae (1994) and Trull and Widiger (1997).

have; the list can serve as a guide to systematic assessment of the client's problems in living.

For example, the particular problems evident in the illustrative case of Donna (see Figure 25.1) were episodes of explosive anger and bitter tirades, along with weekly (sometimes daily) expressions of bitterness and resentment. Frustrations and disappointments, which are inevitable within any relationship and would only be annoying inconveniences to most people, were perceived by Donna as outrageous mistreatments or exploitations. Even when she recognized that they did not warrant a strong reaction, she still had tremendous difficulty stifling her feelings of anger and resentment. Her tendency to misperceive innocent remarks as being intentionally inconsiderate (at times even malevolent) further exacerbated her propensity to anger. She acknowledged that she would often push, question, and test her friends and lovers so hard for signs of disaffection, reassurances of affection, or admissions of guilt, that they would become frustrated and exasperated and might eventually lash out against her. She would often find herself embroiled in fruitless arguments that she subsequently regretted. She had no long-standing relationships, but there were numerous people who remained embittered toward her. Three marriages had, in fact, all ended in acrimonious divorce.

An advantage to confining the application of the FFM to these first two steps is that they do not force a clinician to make arbitrary distinctions that some people have clinically significant maladaptive personality traits, whereas other people do not. "There is no requirement that some minimum number or particular configuration of personality-related problems be noted to justify a diagnosis, as is currently the case with personality disorder diagnosis" (McCrae, 1994, p. 307). Because no arbitrary point of demarcation is provided between normal and abnormal personality functioning in this application of the FFM, the personality-related problems of people below any existing diagnostic thresholds would still be identified and addressed. All of the personality-related problems identified by the diagnostic categories of the *DSM-IV* would be identified, plus many additional personality-related problems not covered by the existing categories (e.g., alexythymia), with-

out the arbitrary distinctions and stigmatization of categorizing a subset of people as having a PD.

Separating the description of the personality traits from the problems that have arisen from them is also advantageous because it encourages the recognition that treatment can focus on altering or adjusting the situations or contexts in which the person has been ineffectively attempting to function rather than necessarily trying to alter the personality traits themselves (see Harkness & McNulty, chapter 23, this volume). This is not to say that clinically significant and meaningful changes to personality structure cannot occur. On the contrary, numerous studies indicate effective and meaningful treatment of maladaptive personality traits through a variety of psychotherapeutic and pharmacologic approaches (Linehan, 1993; Perry, Banon, & Ianni, 1999; Piedmont, 1998; Sanislow & McGlashan, 1998). Nevertheless, PDs are among the more difficult to treat, due in part to the chronicity of the maladaptive behavior pattern; the integration of any particular trait, symptom, or feature of the disorder within a complex array of interacting traits; the ego-syntonic nature of many of the components of personality; and the complex biogenetic–psychosocial etiology of personality dispositions (Costa & McCrae, 1994; McCrae & Costa, 1999; Millon et al., 1996). "The single greatest misconception that patients (and perhaps some therapists) hold about therapy is the expectation that a high-negative affectivity person can be turned into a low-negative affectivity person" (Harkness & Lilienfeld, 1997, p. 356).

One useful goal of treatment is helping people develop realistic expectations for change, focusing their efforts more productively on what is changeable or resolvable. For example, the goal of marital therapy is at times to help couples recognize that a spouse is unlikely to change. If marital success is to be achieved, it would require improvements in the ability of both spouses to accept and tolerate the problematic dispositions of their partner. Or with the appreciation that the spouse is unlikely to change, each person needs to recognize that future growth, happiness, or fulfillment lies elsewhere. "Finding new adaptations, with less personal and social cost and greater potential for growth, which are also consonant with the patients' basic tendencies, poses an exciting new clinical challenge" (Harkness & Lilienfeld, 1997, p. 356).

CUT-OFF POINTS AT CLINICALLY SIGNIFICANT LEVELS OF IMPAIRMENT

Many clinicians have a valid need for providing a formal, authoritative distinction between the presence and absence of a PD, which might be codified as a *DSM-IV* diagnosis of PDNOS. If so, the clinician would need to proceed to the third step in FFM PD diagnosis, namely, determine whether the person exceeds a cutoff point that indicates the presence of a clinically significant level of impairment. There are two considerations to make such a determination, corresponding to the first two steps of FFM diagnosis: (a) Personality traits must exceed a specified level to be considered sufficiently present, and (b) problems in living must be deemed sufficiently serious to warrant a diagnosis. Both of these concerns have parallels in current *DSM* decision rules.

Critical Levels of Maladaptive Traits

A useful model for the FFM method of classification is provided by the diagnosis of mental retardation (Widiger, 1997). Intelligence, like personality, concerns a characteristic level of functioning that is relatively stable throughout most people's lives (Neisser et al., 1996). This level of functioning, like personality, is evident within everyday behavior and has important implications to successes (adaptivity) and failures (maladaptivity) across a variety of social and occupational contexts (Ross, Begab, Dondis, Giampiccolo, & Meyers, 1985). Intelligence, also like personality, is a multifactorial construct, including many varied but correlated and interacting components of cognitive functioning that have resulted from a variety of complexly interacting etiologies. In addition, intelligence, like personality, is best described as a continuous variable with no discrete break in its distribution that would provide a qualitative distinction between normal and abnormal levels. A qualitatively distinct disorder may be evident in some people with mental retardation, but the disorder in such cases is not mental retardation; it is a physical disorder (e.g., Down syndrome) that can be traced to a specific biological event. Mental retardation, in contrast, is a mental disorder for which "there are more than 200 recognized biological syndromes . . . entailing disruptions in virtually any sector of brain biochemical or physiological functioning" (Popper & Steingard, 1994, p. 777).

A clinically significant degree of maladaptive intelligence is currently defined in large part as the level of intelligence below an IQ of 70 (APA, 1994, 2000). This point of demarcation does not carve nature at a discrete joint, distinguishing the presence versus absence of a discrete pathology. It is an arbitrary point of demarcation along a continuous distribution of cognitive functioning. This is not to say that any point of demarcation chosen along a continuum of functioning would have to be determined randomly or would be necessarily meaningless, inappropriate, or unreasonable. On the contrary, a substantial amount of thought and research supports the selection of an IQ of 70 as providing a meaningful and reasonable point at which to characterize lower levels of intelligence, thus resulting in a clinically significant level of impairment that warrants professional intervention (American Association on Mental Retardation, 1992; Reschly, 1992).

PDs can likewise be diagnosed at that point on the continuum of personality functioning that indicates a clinically significant level of impairment (Widiger, 1994). For example, individuals with *T* scores of 70 or above on standard measures of Neuroticism or with *T* scores of 30 or less on measures of trust or self-discipline often qualify for a PD diagnosis (although see further discussion below). Identifying the optimal point of demarcation would be difficult, as it is for the diagnosis of mental retardation (Hodapp & Dykens, 1996; Szymanski & Wilska, 1997). However, the discussion, consideration, and research that would have to occur to determine a meaningful point of demarcation would itself represent a substantial improvement over the virtual absence of any research or rationale to justify the current diagnostic thresholds for the dependent, avoidant, histrionic, obsessive–compulsive, narcissistic, SZD, PDNOS, and other PDs (Widiger & Corbitt, 1994).

Such a cutoff would be required for the diagnosis of a PD because a problem in living could not be reasonably attributed to a personality trait if the client did not have a distinctive level of the trait. "Patients with average scores would be precluded from receiving a diagnosis of problems related to that factor" (McCrae, 1994, p. 305). *T* scores above 55 or below 45 might then be considered a necessary condition for assigning a PD diagnosis, although future research might suggest more stringent (or perhaps even less stringent) cutoff points that may also vary across the domains and facets of the FFM.

The point of demarcation along the continuum of personality functioning at which a diagnosis of a PD would be provided might not be consistent across the domains and facets of the FFM because "each domain of personality functioning will not have equivalent implications with respect to maladaptivity" (Widiger, 1994, p. 314). As indicated in Exhibit 25.3, there are maladaptive correlates for every pole of every facet and domain, but "elevations on neuroticism are clearly more suggestive of dysfunction than are elevations on extraversion or conscientiousness and are perhaps more suggestive of dysfunction than are comparable elevations on antagonism or introversion" (p. 314). Thus, more extreme scores might be needed on Extraversion or Conscientiousness than are needed on Neuroticism to suggest a PD (Widiger & Costa, 1994).

Establishing a uniform, consistent cutoff point across the domains and facets of the FFM that correspond to a particular degree of deviation from a normative mean would be consistent with the procedures used for interpretations of elevations on other personality instruments, such as the Minnesota Multiphasic Personality Inventory—2 (Butcher & Williams, 1992). A respondent's score on this scale is considered to be clinically significant when it is 1.5 standard deviations from the normative mean. However, statistical deviance from a mean might not be an adequate or compelling basis for determining when the degree of elevation suggests the presence of a mental disorder or a clinically significant impairment (Gorenstein, 1984; Lilienfeld & Marino, 1995, 1999; Wakefield, 1992, 1999), particularly in the absence of the same prevalence rate for each PD within the population (Millon, Millon, & Davis, 1994). PDs should be diagnosed when the personality traits result in a clinically significant impairment, not when a particular prevalence rate is obtained for their diagnosis. What should be consistent across the PDs is not their prevalence but the level of impairment required for their diagnosis. The thresholds for diagnosis would then be uniform and, at least in this respect, less arbitrary (Funtowicz & Widiger, 1999; Widiger & Corbitt, 1994).

Significant Levels of Impairment

Personality trait levels themselves, no matter how extreme, may not justify a diagnosis. It is stated in the *DSM-IV* that it is "only when personality traits . . . cause significant functional impairment or subjective distress do they constitute Personality Disorders" (APA, 2000, p. 686). An assessment would need to be made of the severity of the personality-related problems to warrant a diagnosis of PD.

A useful model for this point of demarcation is already provided in *DSM-IV-TR* by the Global Assessment of Functioning Scale presented on Axis V. "Axis V is for reporting the clinician's judgment of the individual's overall level of functioning" (APA, 2000, p. 32). The clinician is instructed to "consider psychological, social, and occupational functioning on a hypothetical continuum of mental health–illness" (p. 32) and to indicate the current level of functioning along a scale that ranges from 1–10 (persistent danger of severely hurting self or others, persistent inability to maintain minimal personal hygiene, or a serious suicidal act with clear expectation of death) to 91–100 (superior functioning in a range of activities, life's problems never seem to get out of hand, sought out by others because of many positive qualities, and no symptoms of mental disorder). Exhibit 25.4 provides a complete summary of the *DSM-IV-TR* Global Assessment of Functioning Scale.

It is apparent from Exhibit 25.4 that a 71+ level of functioning would be within a normal range of functioning (i.e., problems are transient and expectable reactions to stressors, with no more than slight impairments), whereas a 60– level of functioning would be within a range that could be reasonably considered to represent a clinically significant level of impairment (i.e., moderate symptoms, e.g., flat affect; or moderate difficulty in social or occupational functioning, e.g., having few friends or significant conflicts with coworkers). A level of functioning from 61 to 70 would be the range of functioning in

EXHIBIT 25.4

Global Assessment of Functioning Scale

Consider psychological, social, and occupational functioning on a continuum of mental health–illness. Do not include impairment in functioning due to physical or environmental limitations.

1–10: Persistent danger of severely hurting self or others (e.g., recurrent violence); persistent inability to maintain minimal personal hygiene, serious suicidal act with clear expectation of death.

11–20: Some danger of hurting self or others (e.g., suicide attempts without clear expectation of death or infrequently violent); occasional failure to maintain minimal personal hygiene (e.g., smears feces); or gross impairment in communication (e.g., largely incoherent, mute).

21–30: Behavior is considerably influenced by delusions or hallucinations; serious impairment in communication or judgment (e.g., is sometimes incoherent, acts grossly inappropriately, or has suicidal preoccupation); or inability to function in almost all areas (e.g., stays in bed all day; no job, home, or friends).

31–40: Some impairment in reality testing or communication (e.g., speech is at times illogical, obscure, or irrelevant); major impairment in several areas, such as work, school, family relations, judgment, thinking, or mood (e.g., a depressed person avoids friends, neglects family, and is unable to work).

41–50: Serious symptoms (e.g., suicidal ideation, severe obsessional rituals, frequent shoplifting) or any serious impairment in social, occupational, or school functioning (e.g., no friends, unable to keep a job).

51–60: Moderate symptoms (e.g., flat affect, circumstantial speech, occasional panic attacks) or moderate difficulty in social, occupational, or school functioning (e.g., few friends, conflicts with peers or coworkers).

61–70: Some mild symptoms (e.g., depressed mood, mild insomnia) or some difficulty in social, occupational, or school functioning (e.g., occasional truancy or theft within the household) but generally well functioning; some meaningful interpersonal relationships.

71–80: If symptoms are present, they are transient and expectable reactions to psychosocial stressors (e.g., difficulty concentrating after a family argument); no more than slight impairment in social, occupational, or school functioning (e.g., temporarily falling behind in schoolwork).

81–90: Absent or minimal symptoms (e.g., mild anxiety before an exam), good functioning in all areas, interested and involved in a wide range of activities, socially effective, generally satisfied with life, no more than everyday problems or concerns (e.g., an occasional argument with family members).

91–100: Superior functioning in a wide range of activities; life's problems never seem to get out of hand; sought out by others because of his or her many positive qualities; no symptoms of mental disorder.

Note. From the fourth edition, text revised, of the *Diagnostic and Statistical Manual of Mental Disorders* (2000), by the American Psychiatric Association, Washington, DC: Author. Copyright 2000 by the American Psychiatric Association. Adapted with permission.

which the provision of a diagnosis would be tentative or provisional (i.e., mild symptoms, with some difficulties in social or occupational functioning but generally functioning pretty well). In summary, a diagnosis of PD could be made when the overall level of functioning associated with the problems and impairments identified in Step 2 (see Exhibit 25.3) is below a level of 60 on Axis V; a provisional or tentative diagnosis when the level is between 61 and 70.

Donna's score on the Global Assessment of Functioning Scale was 52 (moderate symptoms), which is above the threshold for clinically significant symptomatology and within the range for a PD diagnosis. Donna did have repeated conflicts with peers and coworkers that significantly impaired her career aspirations; she had no sustained relationships; and she had three marriages that ended in divorce due in large part to conflicts secondary to her personality traits. A consideration was in fact given to a more impaired rating of 45–50 (serious symptoms) because of the absence of any long-standing friendships and three failed marriages. However, she was able to develop friendships and currently did have close, intimate friends. Her personality conflicts did impair her ability to advance in her career, but she had always maintained steady and successful employment.

Requiring both a particular elevation on a domain or facet of the FFM and a clinically significant level of impairment is again consistent with the procedure for the diagnosis of mental retardation. A diagnosis of mental retardation is not based simply on the presence of impairment or a particular level of intelligence. One must document that there are both "concurrent deficits or impairments in present adaptive functioning (i.e., the person's effectiveness in meeting the standards expected for his or her age by his or her cultural group)" (APA, 2000, p. 49) and a "significantly subaverage intellectual functioning" (p. 49). Requiring that the clinician document the presence of adaptive impairments, in addition to a subaverage level of intelligence, is helpful to ensure that the low level of intelligence has in fact resulted in clinically significant impairments that warrant professional intervention and assistance. A low level of intelligence in the absence of any clinically signif-

icant impairments would not warrant a diagnosis of mental retardation or at least would not warrant professional intervention (Spitzer & Williams, 1982). The same principle would apply for the diagnosis of PDs. The presence of a particular elevation or constellation of personality traits would not result in a diagnosis of PD, unless there is also documentation that there is a clinically significant level of impairment secondary to these traits.

The assessment of level of impairment, along with levels of personality functioning, also provides a flexibility that can have substantial benefit to clinicians faced with different types of decisions and concerns. A limitation of the categorical diagnoses of *DSM-IV* is that the thresholds for diagnosis may not be optimal for any particular clinical decision, let alone the variety of clinical, social, and scientific decisions that need to be informed by a diagnosis. As, for example, the primary authors of *DSM-IV* noted,

> *the significance of Axis V has increased greatly in recent years for several reasons. First, the threshold for determining who is and who is not entitled to mental health benefits cannot generally be based strictly on the individual's psychiatric diagnosis because, for most conditions, there is a wide variability in severity of impairment and need for treatment. Increasingly, eligibility is determined by some combination of the presence of a specific diagnosis and the presence of sufficient functional impairment as indicated by a low score on Axis V. Second, decisions regarding the particular type of treatment (e.g., inpatient versus outpatient) and the frequency and duration of the treatment (e.g., length of stay) are also increasingly dependent on standardized measures of functioning. Third, it is often necessary to determine the level of functioning below which an individual is entitled to disability payments. Finally, it is becoming increasingly important to document treatment outcomes not only with symptom rating scales but also with scales measuring changes in functioning.* (Frances, First, & Pincus, 1995, p. 74)

Different cutoff points can be established along the personality and impairment scales for different social and clinical concerns. For example, simply the presence of a PD might not be sufficient justification for the obtainment of disability benefits; disability coverage might require a more severe level of impairment than would be required for outpatient treatment or perhaps even for inpatient hospitalization. Admission to a particular group therapy program might require elevations above a particular threshold on Agreeableness or at least the absence of a particular threshold on certain facets of antagonism (Soldz, Budman, Demby, & Merry, 1993); admission to a particular drug treatment program might likewise require a particular level of Conscientiousness (see Ball, chapter 11, this volume). Similarly, the particular degree of maladaptive Agreeableness that results in a liability for the onset of depression might be different from the degree of maladaptive Agreeableness that is associated with a family history of depression (Kendler, 1990) or that justifies the provision of a diagnosis of clinically significant dependent personality traits (Overholser, 1991). It is evident that the ability of researchers to identify the optimal thresholds for different clinical and social decisions and the ability of clinicians to tailor the diagnostic system for their optimal and particular needs should be improved by the provision of FFM personality functioning and impairment scales.

PROFILE MATCHING FOR PERSONALITY DISORDER PATTERNS

One of the purported advantages of a categorical model is the ability to summarize a particular constellation of maladaptive personality traits with a single diagnostic label. "There is an economy of communication and vividness of description in a categorical name that may be lost in a dimensional profile" (Frances, 1993, p. 110). The most specific, accurate, and individualized description of a person's constellation of adaptive and maladaptive personality traits is provided by an FFM profile description. No single word can adequately describe any particular person's personality, nor can any single word adequately describe the many ways in which his or her

traits are maladaptive. Nevertheless, many people prefer the simplification obtained by and the ease of communication provided by the use of diagnostic categories and typological descriptions.

There may also be particular constellations of personality traits that are worth identifying with a single diagnostic term, such as the BDL FFM profile (e.g., Gunderson, 1984; Kernberg, 1975; Linehan, 1993; Paris, 1994) or the psychopathic FFM profile (e.g., Cooke, Forth, & Hare, 1998; Hare, 1993; Lykken, 1995). These constellations of personality traits may have particular theoretical significance, clinical interest, or social implications. In the context of an FFM PD, these constellations are called patterns; they may or may not correspond to *DSM-IV* diagnostic categories. Patterns are prototypic personality profiles that can be used to describe people; there is no implication that they refer to a category of people with a distinct disorder.

Researchers and clinicians may wish to assess for or research patterns that have particular theoretical significance, clinical interest, or social implications. For example, as indicated by Lynam (see chapter 20, this volume), if one asked members of a population to describe the most dangerous or harmful constellation of personality traits, they would probably provide the FFM profile for psychopathy.

> *The social and clinical interest in this particular collection of personality traits is understandable, as one could hardly construct a more virulent constellation of traits. . . . Persons with this constellation will invariably be of immediate and substantial concern to other members of society, as they will be irresponsible, hedonistic, aggressive, exploitative, ruthless, unempathic, deceptive, fearless, and un-self-conscious.* (Widiger & Lynam, 1998, p. 185)

It is not surprising that this particular constellation of traits has been of tremendous interest and concern to society for many years (Cleckley, 1941; Hare, 1993). Identifying this particular constellation of traits with a particular descriptive label, such as psychopathy, does have value, utility, and meaning for the many scientific, social, governmental, and clinical professionals concerned with the havoc, destruction, exploitation, and harm committed by people with constellations of traits that resemble closely the FFM prototypic profile for psychopathy. Rather than summarize all of the scale elevations or trait terms included within this constellation of traits, one can communicate the entire constellation of the prototypic profile by simply providing a single diagnostic label, namely, the psychopathy pattern (Frances, 1993).

The BDL diagnosis has a similar utility. People who are at the highest elevations of anxiousness, depressiveness, vulnerability, impulsivity, and angry hostility of Neuroticism; have the antagonism of high deceptive manipulativeness and low compliance; and have a highly assertive, emotional, and intensely involved Extraversion are clearly among the most difficult patients to treat (Gunderson, 1984; Kernberg, 1975; Linehan, 1993; Paris, 1994). They are the most in need of treatment because they are the most vulnerable, anxious, and depressed; they are among the most intensely involved with other people and with their therapists; but they are also among the most difficult to sustain a working, therapeutic alliance due to their intense angry hostility, impulsivity, deception, and manipulation (see Sanderson & Clarkin, chapter 21, this volume). The BDL FFM profile is a particularly volatile constellation of traits. It is not surprising then that clinicians have identified this constellation with a diagnostic label that conveys nicely the instability and fragility of the personality structure.

The provision of single diagnostic terms to characterize a particular syndrome or constellation of personality traits is not at all incompatible with the FFM approach presented in this chapter. Single diagnostic terms for particular constellations of personality traits are readily obtained by implementing all four steps for diagnosing PDs, as identified earlier. The identification of a PD pattern with which to characterize the constellation of FFM traits of an individual person is the fourth, optional step in FFM diagnosis. It can be done informally by a simple examination of FFM scores or by statistical techniques of pattern analysis. In either case, the pattern is detected by noting the resemblance to a prototype.

This FFM procedure is in many respects consistent with that in the *DSM-IV* to obtain individual

PD diagnoses. The third edition of the *DSM* (*DSM-III*; APA, 1980) required for some of the PDs that all of the defining features be present. However, it soon became evident that this threshold for diagnosis was too stringent and that many of the people who did warrant a particular PD diagnosis varied in the extent to which they resembled a prototypic case (Livesley, 1985; Widiger & Frances, 1985). The authors of the third edition, revised, of the *DSM* (*DSM-III-R*; APA, 1987) therefore converted all of the criteria sets to a polythetic format in which a set of optional diagnostic criteria were provided, only a subset of which were necessary for the diagnosis (Spitzer & Williams, 1987; Widiger, Frances, Spitzer, & Williams, 1988). Prototypic cases of each respective PD have all of the diagnostic criteria (Blashfield, Sprock, Pinkston, & Hodgin, 1985), but the threshold for diagnosis is the presence of only a subset of criteria that provide a sufficient resemblance to the prototypic case.

> *The prototypal approach to the use of categories serves to bridge the categorical and dimensional approaches and eases the application of the categorical approach to the "fuzzy set" problem of psychiatric diagnosis. The prototypal approach recognizes the fuzzy boundaries and heterogeneity within the DSM-IV criteria sets. Definitions are seen as the prototypal forms of the disorder, and individual class members are expected to vary greatly in the degree to which they resemble one or another prototypal category. Sorting is based on the probabilistic estimation of the resemblance of an individual member to the prototypes. (Frances et al., 1995, p. 19)*

The FFM approach to the diagnosis of a PD, as described in this chapter, retains the detailed, precise description of the adaptive and maladaptive traits of the individual patient through the provision of the FFM profile. Broad summary terms, however, can be added through a comparison of an individual's profile with a prototypic profile. If the individual's FFM profile is sufficiently close to the prototypic FFM profile, then one could describe the personality profile of the individual client with that pattern, keeping in mind that the person probably did not in fact match entirely or precisely the prototypic profile.

For example, Donna's substantial elevation on the antagonism facet of trust (see Figure 25.1) suggests the presence of paranoid personality traits, but her overall profile of FFM traits might be matched more closely with the constellation of traits characteristic of BDL, particularly the elevations on the three facets of Neuroticism and the two facets of antagonism. However, there are also notable discrepancies from the prototypic BDL profile, particularly the absence of impulsivity (N5), manipulativeness (A2), and low Conscientiousness (C3, C4, and C5). In addition, the elevations on Neuroticism and antagonism were not nearly as high as they would occur in prototypic cases of BDL. Her clinical diagnosis would likely be PDNOS, with BDL and paranoid traits (Widiger, 1997).

Two statistical approaches to FFM pattern assessment have been used (McCrae et al., 2001; J. D. Miller, Lynam, Widiger, & Leukefeld, 2001). J. D. Miller et al. generated an FFM profile for a prototypic case of psychopathy through a survey of 15 nationally recognized psychopathy experts. Figure 20.1 in chapter 20 by Lynam provides this FFM profile. The prototypic FFM expert-based psychopathy profile closely matched the profile generated earlier by Widiger and Lynam (1998) based on their review of the diagnostic criteria for psychopathy generated by Hare (1991). J. D. Miller et al. obtained the intraclass Q correlations between the prototypic psychopathy FFM profile and each of 481 subjects' Revised NEO Personality Inventory (NEO-PI-R) FFM profiles. The subjects were participating in a longitudinal study of people at risk for substance-related disorders (additional aspects of their study are summarized by Lynam, chapter 20, this volume). For the male participants, the correlations ranged from −.57 to .42, with a mean of .08 (SD = .17); for the female participants, the correlations ranged from −.97 to .37, with a mean of −.22 (SD = .18). A maximal correlation of .42 is not particularly high. However, it is important to keep in mind that the intraclass Q correlation assesses for consistency in both elevation and profile shape across all 30 facets of the FFM. In addition, given the rarity of

true prototypic cases, high correlations with prototypic profiles are not expected. Only a few of the men in the study by J. D. Miller et al. would have even met the Revised Psychopathy Checklist threshold for a diagnosis of psychopathy; none of them were likely to have been prototypic cases of psychopathy.

McCrae et al. (2001) adopted a different approach to detecting PD patterns. They used the description of each of the *DSM-III-R* PDs in Appendix A (this volume) as the basis for prototypic profiles for each of the *DSM-III-R* PDs—a choice justified by numerous studies that confirm most of the hypothesized relationships of the FFM to these PDs (e.g., Axelrod, Widiger, Trull, & Corbitt, 1997; Costa & McCrae, 1990; Dyce & O'Connor, 1998; O'Connor & Dyce, 1998; Soldz et al., 1993; Trull, 1992; Trull, Widiger, & Burr, 2001; Wiggins & Pincus, 1989; for details regarding the research by O'Connor and Dyce, see chapter 14, this volume). Resemblance to each of these prototypes was calculated using McCrae's (1993) coefficient of profile agreement; base rates of these coefficients in a normal sample were used to determine cutoff points. For example, patients were considered to have the BDL pattern if their coefficient of profile agreement with the BDL prototype exceeded that of 90% of the control volunteers. For most disorders, these FFM pattern assignments were significantly associated with *DSM-IV* diagnoses based on a self-report PD questionnaire and clinical interviews (McCrae et al., 2001).

People with sufficiently high Q correlations (J. D. Miller et al., 2001) or profile agreement coefficients (McCrae et al., 2001) with a respective prototypic FFM profile pattern could be provided the term for that pattern (e.g., psychopathy, borderline, or antisocial), although further research is needed to address a number of important issues, including the magnitude of agreement that should be necessary to provide the respective term. In most instances, the prototypic profile does not provide the most accurate or precise description of the personality profile for a particular patient. We expect that in most instances, there are no close matches with any one prototypic profile, given that most people only have a family resemblance to any particular prototype. As McCrae et al. indicated, the search for a single diagnostic label for a particular patient could be a "fool's errand" because no single term can adequately describe the particular constellation of traits that are present within any particular patient, unless that person is indeed one of the rare prototypic cases. It is expected that many patients have moderate correlations with more than one prototypic profile, just as many patients meet the *DSM-IV* criteria sets for more than one PD. The complexity and individuality of any particular individual's personality are most likely best described by that person's specific FFM profile rather than by any single term describing the profile of a prototypic case.

CONCLUSION

In this chapter, we provided a four-step process by which one can clinically apply the FFM. We believe that the process of FFM PD diagnosis described in this chapter can provide the clinician with valuable information regarding the patient and his or her problems, which will ultimately prove to be more clinically useful than the standard *DSM-IV* PD diagnoses. However, it is important to note that the two systems are not mutually exclusive or incompatible. For example, clinicians who proceed through Step 3 of FFM diagnosis and find clinically significant personality-related problems have sufficient information to code Axis II as PDNOS, which may suffice.

Those who continue through Step 4 and identify patterns associated with the official *DSM-IV* PDs cannot automatically assign the respective *DSM-IV* diagnoses because the PD patterns identify constellations of traits associated with particular disorders and do not guarantee that the specific *DSM-IV* diagnostic criteria for that disorder have in fact been met. However, the magnitude of agreement identifies the *DSM-IV* PDs that the patient is most likely to have. Clinicians who are unable to assess all 80 *DSM-IV* diagnostic criteria might then find Step 4 useful in directing them toward the specific *DSM-IV* PD diagnostic criteria sets that should receive more systematic assessment before confirmation.

FFM diagnoses, however, may also proceed independent of the *DSM-IV* diagnostic system, in which case one need not complete all of the steps, depending on one's clinical interests, needs, or perspective.

For example, one might be interested only in the FFM profile of a person. Many clinical applications of the FFM currently stop at this point. This would then be the description of the personality structure with respect to the FFM that provides a substantial amount of useful information for treatment planning. However, one might also wish to consider further the problems or impairments associated with the personality traits identified by the FFM. A list of likely impairments associated with each domain and facet of the FFM is provided in Exhibit 25.3. One can stop at this point if one does not need or desire a PD diagnosis. However, a diagnosis of PD could be provided when there is a clinically significant level of impairment secondary to the maladaptive personality traits. A scale for determining the level of impairment is provided in Exhibit 25.4. One can stop at this point if one is comfortable with the specificity and detail provided by the FFM profile description. However, one can also determine, through clinical judgment or a statistical algorithm, if the profile is sufficiently close to the prototypic FFM profile for one (or more) particular personality pattern.

The specific methods by which this process is implemented have not yet been established. There are instruments for the assessment of the FFM profile (e.g., Costa & McCrae, 1992; Trull & Widiger, 1997) and for the assessment of problems and impairments in functioning associated with various levels of clinical significance (Funtowicz & Widiger, 1995; Goldman, Skodol, & Lave, 1997; Turner & Dudek, 1997). However, there are limitations to all of these instruments, and further details and even fundamental issues have not been resolved. For example, expert-based FFM profiles for various PDs and syndromes are currently in the process of being developed. It is unclear if the optimal prototypic FFM profile is obtained by modeling the FFM profiles on existing diagnostic criteria sets. Pincus (see chapter 12) indicates substantial limitations of the *DSM-IV*-based FFM profile for dependent PD; Lynam (see chapter 20) makes comparable points with respect to the Revised Psychopathy Checklist-based FFM profile for psychopathy. In addition, there is no specific magnitude of Q correlation or profile agreement that indicates that an individual's

FFM profile is sufficiently close enough to a proto-typic profile to warrant a particular diagnosis. The descriptions of each point of demarcation along the Axis V Global Assessment of Functioning Scale should also be expanded to provide more range and specificity of social and occupational impairments (Goldman et al., 1997; Williams, 1998).

Further research is also needed for determining an optimal point of demarcation for identifying a clinically significant level of impairment (Spitzer & Wakefield, 1999; Strack & Lorr, 1994; Widiger & Clark, 2000; Widiger & Corbitt, 1994). Finally, there is ongoing controversy over whether any particular point of demarcation between normal and abnormal psychological is appropriate or meaningful (Bergner, 1997; Lilienfeld & Marino, 1995, 1999; Wakefield, 1992, 1999; Widiger, 1997; Widiger & Sankis, 2000). However, we do suggest that there has been sufficient empirical support for an FFM of PDs to at least encourage researchers to pursue the development of the specifics of these additional steps and issues in future research.

References

American Association on Mental Retardation. (1992). *Mental retardation: Definition, classification, and systems of supports.* Washington, DC: Author.

American Psychiatric Association. (1980). *Diagnostic and statistical manual of mental disorders* (3rd ed.). Washington, DC: Author.

American Psychiatric Association. (1987). *Diagnostic and statistical manual of mental disorders* (3rd ed., rev.). Washington, DC: Author.

American Psychiatric Association. (1994). *Diagnostic and statistical manual of mental disorders* (4th ed.). Washington, DC: Author.

American Psychiatric Association. (2000). *Diagnostic and statistical manual of mental disorders* (4th ed., text revised). Washington, DC: Author.

Axelrod, S. R., Widiger, T. A., Trull, T. J., & Corbitt, E. M. (1997). Relationships of five-factor model antagonism facets with personality disorder symptomatology. *Journal of Personality Assessment, 67,* 297–313.

Bergner, R. M. (1997). What is psychopathology? And so what? *Clinical Psychology: Science and Practice, 4,* 235–248.

Blashfield, R. K., Sprock, J., Pinkston, K., & Hodgin, J. (1985). Exemplar prototypes of per-sonality disorder diagnoses. *Comprehensive Psychiatry, 26,* 11–21.

Butcher, J. N., & Williams, C. L. (1992). *Essentials of MMPI-2 interpretation.* Minneapolis: University of Minnesota Press.

Clark, L. A. (1997, December). *Values in personality concepts: Normal and disordered* [Invited address]. Values in Psychiatric Nosology: A Conference for Philosophers and Mental Health Professionals, Dallas, TX.

Clark, L. A., Livesley, W. J., & Morey, L. (1997). Personality disorder assessment: The challenge of construct validity. *Journal of Personality Disorders, 11,* 205–231.

Clark, L. A., Watson, D., & Reynolds, S. (1995). Diagnosis and classification of psychopathology: Challenges to the current system and future directions. *Annual Review of Psychology, 46,* 121–153.

Cleckley, H. (1941). *The mask of sanity.* St. Louis, MO: Mosby.

Cooke, D. J., Forth, A. E., & Hare, R. D. (Eds.). (1998). *Psychopathy: Theory, research, and implications for society.* Dordrecht, The Netherlands: Kluwer.

Costa, P. T., Jr., & McCrae, R. R. (1990). Personality disorders and the five-factor model of personality. *Journal of Personality Disorders, 4,* 362–371.

Costa, P. T., Jr., & McCrae, R. R. (1992). *Revised NEO Personality Inventory (NEO-PI-R) and NEO Five-Factor Inventory (NEO-FFI) professional manual.* Odessa, FL: Psychological Assessment Resources.

Costa, P. T., Jr., & McCrae, R. R. (1994). "Set like plaster"? Evidence for the stability of adult personality. In T. Heatherton & J. Weinberger (Eds.), *Can personality change?* (pp. 21–40). Washington, DC: American Psychological Association.

Dyce, J. A., & O'Connor, B. P. (1998). Personality disorders and the five-factor model: A test of facet-level predictions. *Journal of Personality Disorders, 12,* 31–45.

Ellis, C. G. (1994). Bulimia nervosa within the context of maladaptive personality traits. In P. T. Costa, Jr., & T. A. Widiger (Eds.), *Personality disorders and the five-factor model of personality* (pp. 205–209). Washington, DC: American Psychological Association.

Fabrega, H., Ulrich, R., Pilkonis, P., & Mezzich, J. (1991). On the homogeneity of personality disorder clusters. *Comprehensive Psychiatry, 32,* 373–386.

Fagan, P. J. (1994). Treatment case: A couple with sexual dysfunction and paraphilia. In P. T. Costa, Jr., & T. A. Widiger (Eds.), *Personality disorders and the five-factor model of personality* (pp. 251–257). Washington, DC: American Psychological Association.

First, M., Gibbon, M., Spitzer, R. L., Williams, J. B. W., & Benjamin, L. S. (1997). *User's guide for the Structured Clinical Interview for DSM-IV Axis II Personality Disorders.* Washington, DC: American Psychiatric Press.

Frances, A. J. (1993). Dimensional diagnosis of personality—Not whether, but when and which. *Psychological Inquiry, 4,* 110–111.

Frances, A. J., First, M. B., & Pincus, H. A. (1995). DSM-IV *guidebook.* Washington, DC: American Psychiatric Press.

Funtowicz, M. N., & Widiger, T. A. (1995). Sex bias in the diagnosis of personality disorders: A different approach. *Journal of Psychopathology and Behavioral Assessment, 17,* 145–165.

Funtowicz, M. N., & Widiger, T. A. (1999). Sex bias in the diagnosis of personality disorders: An evaluation of the *DSM-IV* criteria. *Journal of Abnormal Psychology, 108,* 195–202.

Goldman, H. H., Skodol, A. E., & Lave, T. R. (1997). Revising Axis V for *DSM-IV:* A review of measures of social functioning. In T. A. Widiger, A. J. Frances, H. A. Pincus, R. Ross, M. B. First, & W. Davis (Eds.), DSM-IV *sourcebook* (Vol. 3, pp. 439–458). Washington, DC: American Psychiatric Press.

Gorenstein, E. (1984). Debating mental illness. *American Psychologist, 39,* 50–56.

Gunderson, J. G. (1984). *Borderline personality disorder.* Washington, DC: American Psychiatric Press.

Gunderson, J. G. (1992). Diagnostic controversies. In A. Tasman & M. B. Riba (Eds.), *Review of psychiatry* (Vol. 11, pp. 9–24). Washington, DC: American Psychiatric Press.

Hare, R. D. (1991). *The Revised Psychopathy Checklist.* Toronto, Ontario, Canada: Multi-Health Systems.

Hare, R. D. (1993). *Without conscience: The disturbing world of the psychopaths around us.* New York: Simon & Schuster.

Harkness, A. R., & Lilienfeld, S. O. (1997). Individual differences science for treatment planning: Personality traits. *Psychological Assessment, 9,* 349–360.

Hodapp, R. M., & Dykens, E. M. (1996). Mental retardation. In E. J. Mash & R. A. Barkley (Eds.), *Child psychopathology* (pp. 362–389). New York: Guilford Press.

John, O. P., & Srivastava, S. (1999). The Big Five trait taxonomy: History, measurement, and theoretical perspectives. In L. A. Pervin & O. P. John (Eds.), *Handbook of personality: Theory and research* (2nd ed., pp. 102–138). New York: Guilford.

Kass, F., Skodol, A. E., Charles, E., Spitzer, R. L., & Williams, J. B. W. (1985). Scaled ratings of *DSM-III* personality disorders. *American Journal of Psychiatry, 142,* 627–630.

Kendler, K. S. (1990). Toward a scientific psychiatric nosology: Strengths and limitations. *Archives of General Psychiatry, 47,* 969–973.

Kernberg, O. F. (1975). *Borderline conditions and pathological narcissism.* New York: Aronson.

Koenigsberg, H. W., Kaplan, R. D., Gilmore, M. M., & Cooper, A. M. (1985). The relationship between syndrome and personality disorder in *DSM-III:* Experience with 2,462 patients. *American Journal of Psychiatry, 142,* 207–212.

Lilienfeld, S. O., & Marino, L. (1995). Mental disorder as a Roschian concept: A critique of Wakefield's "harmful dysfunction" analysis. *Journal of Abnormal Psychology, 104,* 411–420.

Lilienfeld, S. O., & Marino, L. (1999). Essentialism revisited: Evolutionary theory and the concept of mental disorder. *Journal of Abnormal Psychology, 108,* 400–411.

Linehan, M. M. (1993). *Cognitive–behavioral treatment of borderline personality disorder.* New York: Guilford Press.

Livesley, W. J. (1985). The classification of personality disorder: I. The choice of category concept. *Canadian Journal of Psychiatry, 30,* 353–358.

Livesley, W. J. (1998). Suggestions for a framework for an empirically based classification of personality disorder. *Canadian Journal of Psychiatry, 43,* 137–147.

Loranger, A. W. (1990). The impact of *DSM-III* on diagnostic practice in a university hospital. *Archives of General Psychiatry, 47,* 672–675.

Loranger, A. W., Sartorius, N., & Janca, A. (Eds.). (1997). *Assessment and diagnosis of personality disorders: The* ICD-10 *International Personality Disorder Examination (IPDE).* Cambridge, England: Cambridge University Press.

Lykken, D. T. (1995). *The antisocial personalities.* Hillsdale, NJ: Erlbaum.

McCrae, R. R. (1993). Agreement of personality profiles across observers. *Multivariate Behavioral Problems, 28,* 13–28.

McCrae, R. R. (1994). A reformulation of Axis II: Personality and personality-related problems. In P. T. Costa, Jr., & T. A. Widiger (Eds.), *Personality disorders and the five-factor model of personality* (pp. 303–309). Washington, DC: American Psychological Association.

McCrae, R. R., & Costa, P. T., Jr. (1990). *Personality in adulthood*. New York: Guilford.

McCrae, R. R., & Costa, P. T., Jr. (1999). A five-factor theory of personality. In L. A. Pervin & O. P. John (Eds.), *Handbook of personality. Theory and research* (2nd ed., pp. 139–153). New York: Guilford.

McCrae, R. R., Yang, J., Costa, P. T., Jr., Dai, X., Yao, S., Cai, T., & Gao, B. (2001). Personality profiles and the prediction of categorical personality disorders. *Journal of Personality, 69,* 155–174.

Miller, J. D., Lynam, D. R., Widiger, T. A., & Leukefeld, C. (2001). Personality disorders as extreme variants of common personality dimensions— Can the five-factor model adequately represent psychopathy? *Journal of Personality, 69,* 253–276.

Miller, T. R. (1991). The psychotherapeutic utility of the five-factor model of personality: A clinician's experience. *Journal of Personality Assessment, 57,* 415–433.

Millon, T., Davis, R. D., Millon, C. M., Wenger, A., Van Zullen, M. H., Fuchs, M., & Millon, R. B. (1996). *Disorders of personality: DSM-IV and beyond* (2nd ed.). New York: Wiley.

Millon, T., Millon, C., & Davis, R. (1994). *MCMI-III manual*. Minneapolis, MN: National Computer Systems.

Morey, L. C. (1988). Personality disorders in *DSM-III* and *DSM-III-R*: Convergence, coverage, and internal consistency. *American Journal of Psychiatry, 145,* 573–577.

Neisser, U., Boodoo, G., Bouchard, T. J., Boykin, A. W., Brody, N., Ceci, S. J., Halpern, D. F., Loehlin, J. C., Perloff, R., Sternberg, R. J., & Urbina, S. (1996). Intelligence: Knowns and unknowns. *American Psychologist, 51,* 77–101.

O'Connor, B. P., & Dyce, J. A. (1998). A test of models of personality disorder configuration. *Journal of Abnormal Psychology, 107,* 3–16.

Oldham, J. M., Skodol, A. E., Kellman, H. D., Hyler, S. E., Rosnick, L., & Davies, M. (1992). Diagnosis of *DSM-III-R* personality disorders by two semistructured interviews: Patterns of comorbidity. *American Journal of Psychiatry, 149,* 213–220.

Overholser, J. C. (1991). Categorical assessment of the dependent personality disorder. *Journal of Personality Disorders, 5,* 243–255.

Paris, J. (1994). *Borderline personality disorder: A multidimensional approach*. Washington, DC: American Psychiatric Press.

Perry, J. C., Banon, E., & Ianni, F. (1999). Effectiveness of psychotherapy for personality disorders. *American Journal of Psychiatry, 156,* 1312–1321.

Pfohl, B., Blum, N., & Zimmerman, M. (1997). *Structured Interview for* DSM-IV *Personality Disorders*. Washington, DC: American Psychiatric Press.

Piedmont, R. L. (1998). *The Revised NEO Personality Inventory: Clinical and research applications*. New York: Plenum Press.

Popper, C. W., & Steingard, R. J. (1994). Disorders usually first diagnosed in infancy, childhood, or adolescence. In R. E. Hales, S. C. Yudofsky, & J. A. Talbott (Eds.), *Textbook of psychiatry* (2nd ed., pp. 729–832). Washington, DC: American Psychiatric Press.

Reschly, D. J. (1992). Mental retardation: Conceptual foundations, definitional criteria, and diagnostic operations. In S. R. Hynd & R. E. Mattison (Eds.), *Assessment and diagnosis of child and adolescent psychiatric disorders: Vol. 11. Developmental disorders* (pp. 23–67). Hillsdale, NJ: Erlbaum.

Rogers, R. (1995). *Diagnostic and structured interviewing: A handbook for psychologists*. Odessa, FL: Psychological Assessment Resources.

Ross, R. T., Begab, M. J., Dondis, E. H., Giampicolo, J., & Meyers, C. E. (1985). *Lives of the retarded: A forty-year follow-up study*. Stanford, CA: Stanford University Press.

Sanislow, C. A., & McGlashan, T. H. (1998). Treatment outcome of personality disorders. *Canadian Journal of Psychiatry, 43,* 237–250.

Segal, D. L. (1997). Structured interviewing and DSM classification. In S. M. Turner & M. Hersen (Eds.), *Adult psychopathology and diagnosis* (pp. 24–57). New York: Wiley.

Soldz, S., Budman, S., Demby, A., & Merry, J. (1993). Representation of personality disorders in circumplex and five-factor space: Explorations with a clinical sample. *Psychological Assessment, 5,* 41–52.

Spitzer, R. L., & Wakefield, J. C. (1999). The *DSM-IV* diagnostic criterion for clinical significance: Does it help solve the false positives problem? *American Journal of Psychiatry, 156,* 1856–1864.

Spitzer, R. L., & Williams, J. B. W. (1982). The definition and diagnosis of mental disorder. In W. Gove (Ed.), *Deviance and mental illness* (pp. 15–31). Beverly Hills, CA: Sage.

Spitzer, R. L., & Williams, J. B. W. (1987). Revising

DSM-III: The process and major issues. In G. Tischler (Ed.), *Diagnosis and classification in psychiatry* (pp. 425–434). New York: Cambridge University Press.

Strack, S., & Lorr, M. (Eds.). (1994). *Differentiating normal and abnormal personality*. New York: Springer.

Szymanski, L. S., & Wilska, M. (1997). Mental retardation. In A. Tasman, J. Kay, & J. A. Lieberman (Eds.), *Psychiatry* (Vol. 1, pp. 605–635). Philadelphia: Saunders.

Trull, T. J. (1992). *DSM-III-R* personality disorders and the five-factor model of personality: An empirical comparison. *Journal of Abnormal Psychology, 101*, 553–560.

Trull, T. J., & Widiger, T. A. (1997). *Structured Interview for the Five-Factor Model of Personality*. Odessa, FL: Psychological Assessment Resources.

Trull, T. J., Widiger, T. A., & Burr, R. (2001). A structured interview for the assessment of the five-factor model of personality: II. Facet-level relations to the Axis II personality disorders. *Journal of Personality, 69*, 175–198.

Turner, R. M., & Dudek, P. (1997). Outcome evaluation of psychosocial treatment for personality disorders: Functions, obstacles, goals, and strategies. In H. H. Strupp, L. M., Horowitz, & M. J. Lambert (Eds.), *Measuring patient change in mood, anxiety, and personality disorders* (pp. 433–460). Washington, DC: American Psychological Association.

Wakefield, J. C. (1992). Disorder as harmful dysfunction: A conceptual critique of *DSM-III-R's* definition of mental disorder. *Psychological Review, 99*, 232–247.

Wakefield, J. C. (1999). Mental disorder as a black box essentialist concept. *Journal of Abnormal Psychology, 108*, 465–472.

Westen, D. (1997). Divergences between clinical and research methods for assessing personality disorders: Implications for research and the evolution of Axis II. *American Journal of Psychiatry, 154*, 895–903.

Westen, D., & Arkowitz-Westen, L. (1998). Limitations of Axis II in diagnosing personality pathology in clinical practice. *American Journal of Psychiatry, 155*, 1767–1771.

Widiger, T. A. (1993). The *DSM-III-R* categorical personality disorder diagnoses: A critique and an alternative. *Psychological Inquiry, 4*, 75–90.

Widiger, T. A. (1994). Conceptualizing a disorder of personality from the five-factor model. In P. T. Costa, Jr., & T. A. Widiger (Eds.), *Personality disorders and the five-factor model of personality* (pp. 311–317). Washington, DC: American Psychological Association.

Widiger, T. A. (1997). Personality disorders as maladaptive variants of common personality traits: Implications for treatment. *Journal of Contemporary Psychotherapy, 27*, 265–282.

Widiger, T. A., & Clark, L. A. (2000). Toward *DSM-V* and the classification of psychopathology. *Psychological Bulletin, 126*, 946–963.

Widiger, T. A., & Corbitt, E. (1994). Normal versus abnormal personality from the perspective of the *DSM*. In S. Strack & M. Lorr (Eds.), *Differentiating normal and abnormal personality* (pp. 158–175). New York: Springer.

Widiger, T. A., & Costa, P. T., Jr. (1994). Personality and personality disorders. *Journal of Abnormal Psychology, 103*, 78–91.

Widiger, T. A, & Frances, A. J. (1985). The *DSM-III* personality disorders: Perspectives from psychology. *Archives of General Psychiatry, 42*, 615–623.

Widiger, T. A., Frances, A. J., Spitzer, R., & Williams, J. (1988). The *DSM-III-R* personality disorders: An overview. *American Journal of Psychiatry, 145*, 786–795.

Widiger, T. A., & Lynam, D. R. (1998). Psychopathy from the perspective of the five-factor model of personality. In T. Millon, E. Simonsen, M. Birket-Smith, & R. D. Davis (Eds.), *Psychopathy: Antisocial, criminal, and violent behavior* (pp. 171–187). New York: Guilford.

Widiger, T. A., Mangine, S., Corbitt, E. M., Ellis, C. G., & Thomas, G. V. (1995). *Personality Disorder Interview—IV: A semistructured interview for the assessment of personality disorders*. Odessa, FL: Psychological Assessment Resources.

Widiger, T. A., & Sanderson, C. J. (1995). Towards a dimensional model of personality disorders in *DSM-IV* and *DSM-V*. In W. J. Livesley (Ed.), *The DSM-IV personality disorders* (pp. 433–458). New York: Guilford.

Widiger, T. A., & Sankis, L. (2000). Adult psychopathology: Issues and controversies. *Annual Review of Psychology, 51*, 377–409.

Widiger, T. A., & Saylor, K. I. (1998). Personality assessment. In A. S. Bellack & M. Hersen (Eds.), *Comprehensive clinical psychology* (pp. 145–167). New York: Pergamon Press.

Widiger, T. A., & Trull, T. J. (1998). Performance characteristics of the *DSM-III-R* personality disorder criteria sets. In T. A. Widiger, A. J. Frances, H. A. Pincus, R. Ross, M. B. First, W. Davis, & M. Kline (Eds.), DSM-IV *sourcebook* (Vol. 4, pp. 357–373). Washington, DC: American Psychiatric Press.

Wiggins, J. S. (Ed.). (1996). *The five-factor model of personality: Theoretical perspectives.* New York: Guilford.

Wiggins, J. S., & Pincus, H. A. (1989). Conceptions of personality disorder and dimensions of personality. *Psychological Assessment, 1,* 305–316.

Williams, J. B. W. (1998). The *DSM-IV* multiaxial system: Final overview. In T. A. Widiger, A. J. Frances, H. A. Pincus, R. Ross, M. B. First, W. Davis, & M. Kline (Eds.), DSM-IV *sourcebook* (Vol. 4, pp. 939–946). Washington, DC: American Psychiatric Press.

Zanarini, M. C., Frankenburg, F. R., Sickel, A. E., & Yong, L. (1996). *Diagnostic Interview for DSM-IV Personality Disorders (DIPD-IV).* Boston, MA: McLean Hospital.

Zimmerman, M. (1994). Diagnosing personality disorders: A review of issues and research methods. *Archives of General Psychiatry, 51,* 225–245.

Zimmerman, M., & Coryell, W. H. (1989). *DSM-III* personality disorder diagnoses in a nonpatient sample. *Archives of General Psychiatry, 46,* 682–689.

The *DSM-III-R* Personality Disorders and the Five-Factor Model

NEO-PI-R domains and facets	PAR	SZD	SZT	ATS	BDL	HST	NAR	AVD	DEP	OBC	PAG
Neuroticism											
Anxiety	h		h	h/L	H			H	H		
Angry hostility	H	L		H	H	H	H			h	H
Depression			h	h	H		h/L	h	H	h	
Self-consciousness		L	H	**L**	**H**	H	H	H	h	h	
Impulsiveness				H	H						
Vulnerability			h		H	h	H	H	H		
Extraversion											
Warmth	l	L	L	l			H	L/H	**h**	L	
Gregariousness	l	L	L		**h**	h		L			
Assertiveness					**h**		H	L	L	H	
Activity						h		L			
Excitement seeking		**L**		H		h		L			l
Positive emotions	l	L			**h**	H					l
Openness to Experience											
Fantasy			H			h	H				
Aesthetics	l										
Feelings	l	L	L			H				L	
Actions	**L**					h		L			
Ideas			H			l					
Values			h							L	
Agreeableness											
Trust	L		L			h					
Straightforwardness	L			L	**L**	l	l				L
Altruism				L		L	L		H	L	
Compliance	L	h		L	L				H	L	L
Modesty	l			**L**			L		H		
Tender-mindedness	l			L			L		**h**		
Conscientiousness											
Competence	h					l	**h**				L
Order										H	
Dutifulness				L						H	L
Achievement striving		l			L		**h**		L	H	
Self-discipline				L		L					L
Deliberation				L						H	

Note. H, L = high, low, respectively, based on the third edition, revised, of the *Diagnostic and Statistical Manual of Mental Disorders* (*DSM-III-R*; American Psychiatric Association, 1987) diagnostic criteria; h, l = high, low, respectively, based on associated features provided in *DSM-III-R*; **H/h**; **L/l** = high, low, respectively, based on the clinical literature. Personality disorders: PAR = paranoid; SZD = schizoid; SZT = schizotypal; ATS = antisocial; BDL = borderline; HST = histrionic; NAR = narcissistic; AVD = avoidant; DEP = dependent; OBC = obsessive–compulsive; PAG = passive–aggressive.

Personality Disorders Proposed for *DSM-IV*

NEO-PI-R domains and facets	NEG	SDF	DPS	SDS
Neuroticism				
Anxiety			H	
Angry hostility	H			h
Depression		H	H	l
Self-consciousness			H	
Impulsiveness				
Vulnerability		H		
Extraversion				
Warmth				
Gregariousness				
Assertiveness	H			H
Activity				
Excitement seeking		L		
Positive emotions				
Openness to Experience				
Fantasy				
Aesthetics				
Feelings				
Actions				
Ideas				
Values				
Agreeableness				
Trust				
Straightforwardness		L		
Altruism		H		**L**
Compliance	L	L		L
Modesty				
Tender-mindedness			L	L
Conscientiousness				
Competence	L			
Order				
Dutifulness		L		
Achievement striving				
Self-discipline		L		
Deliberation				

Note. H/h, L/l = high, low, respectively, based on the proposed fourth edition of the *Diagnostic and Statistical Manual of Mental Disorders* (*DSM-IV*) diagnostic criteria (Task Force on DSM-IV, 1991); **H, L** = high, low, based on the clinical literature. Personality disorders: NEG = negativistic; SDF = self-defeating; DPS = depressive; SDS = sadistic.

The *DSM-IV* Personality Disorders and the Five-Factor Model

NEO-PI-R domains and facets	PAR	SZD	SZT	ATS	BDL	HST	NAR	AVD	DEP	OBC
Neuroticism										
Anxiety			H		H			H	H	
Angry-hostility	H			H	H		H			
Depression					H	H		H		
Self-consciousness			H			H	H	H	H	
Impulsiveness					H					
Vulnerability					H			H	H	
Extraversion										
Warmth		L	L			H			H	
Gregariousness		L	L			H		L		
Assertiveness								L	L	H
Activity										
Excitement seeking				H		H		L		
Positive emotions		L	L			H				
Openness to Experience										
Fantasy			H			H	H			
Aesthetics										
Feelings		L				H				
Actions			H							
Ideas			H							
Values										L
Agreeableness										
Trust	L		L		L	H			H	
Straightforwardness	L			L						
Altruism					L		L		H	
Compliance	L			L	L				H	L
Modesty							L		H	
Tender mindedness					L		L			
Conscientiousness										
Competence					L					H
Order										H
Dutifulness					L					H
Achievement striving							H			H
Self-discipline					L					
Deliberation					L					

Note. NEO-PI-R = Revised NEO Personality Inventory. H, L = high, low, respectively, based on the fourth edition of the *Diagnostic and Statistical Manual of Mental Disorders* (*DSM-IV*; American Psychiatric Association, 1994) diagnostic criteria. Personality disorders: PAR = paranoid; SZD = schizoid; SZT = schizotypal; ATS = antisocial; BDL = borderline; HST = histrionic; NAR = narcissistic; AVD = avoidant; DEP = dependent; OBC = obsessive–compulsive.

Description of the Revised NEO Personality Inventory (NEO-PI-R) Facet Scales

NEUROTICISM FACETS

N1: Anxiety

Anxious individuals are apprehensive, fearful, prone to worry, nervous, tense, and jittery. The scale does not measure specific fears or phobias, but high scorers are more likely to have such fears and free-floating anxiety. Low scorers are calm and relaxed; they do not dwell on things that might go wrong.

N2: Angry Hostility

Angry hostility represents the tendency to experience anger and related states such as frustration and bitterness. This scale measures the individual's readiness to experience anger; whether the anger is expressed depends on the individual's level of Agreeableness. Note, however, that disagreeable people often score high on this scale. Low scorers are easygoing and slow to anger.

N3: Depression

This scale measures normal individual differences in the tendency to experience depressive affect. High scorers are prone to feelings of guilt, sadness, hopelessness, and loneliness. They are easily discouraged and often dejected. Low scorers rarely experience such emotions, but they are not necessarily cheerful and lighthearted—characteristics that are associated instead with Extraversion.

N4: Self-Consciousness

The emotions of shame and embarrassment form the core of this facet of Neuroticism. Self-conscious individuals are uncomfortable around others, sensitive to ridicule, and prone to feelings of inferiority. Self-consciousness is akin to shyness and social anxiety. Low scorers do not necessarily have poise or good social skills; they are simply less disturbed by awkward social situations.

From the *Revised NEO Personality Inventory (NEO-PI-R) and NEO Five-Factor Inventory (NEO-FFI) Professional Manual* (pp. 16–18), by P. T. Costa, Jr., and R. R. McCrae, 1992, Odessa, FL: Psychological Assessment Resources. Copyright 1992 by Psychological Assessment Resources. Adapted with permission.

N5: Impulsiveness

In the NEO-PI-R, impulsiveness refers to the inability to control cravings and urges. Desires (e.g., for food, cigarettes, possessions) are perceived as being so strong that the individual can not resist them, although he or she may later regret the behavior. Low scorers find it easier to resist such temptations, having a high tolerance for frustration. The term *impulsive* is used by many theorists to refer to many different and unrelated traits. NEO-PI-R impulsiveness should not be confused with spontaneity, risk taking, or rapid decision time.

N6: Vulnerability

The final facet of Neuroticism is vulnerability to stress. Individuals who score high on this scale feel unable to cope with stress, becoming dependent, hopeless, or panicked when facing emergency situations. Low scorers perceive themselves as capable of handling themselves in difficult situations.

EXTRAVERSION FACETS

E1: Warmth

Warmth is the facet of Extraversion that is most relevant to issues of interpersonal intimacy. Warm people are affectionate and friendly. They genuinely like people and easily form close attachments to others. Low scorers are neither hostile nor necessarily lacking in compassion, but they are more formal, reserved, and distant in manner than are high scorers. Warmth is the facet of Extraversion that is closest to Agreeableness in interpersonal space, but it is distinguished by a cordiality and heartiness that is not part of Agreeableness.

E2: Gregariousness

A second aspect of Extraversion is gregariousness—the preference for other people's company. Gregarious people enjoy the company of others, and the more the merrier. Low scorers on this scale tend to be loners who do not seek—or who even actively avoid—social stimulation.

E3: Assertiveness

High scorers on this scale are dominant, forceful, and socially ascendant. They speak without hesitation and often become group leaders. Low scorers prefer to keep in the background and to let others do the talking.

E4: Activity

A high activity score is seen in rapid tempo and vigorous movement, a sense of energy, and a need to keep busy. Active people lead fast-paced lives. Low scorers are more leisurely and relaxed in tempo, although they are not necessarily sluggish or lazy.

E5: Excitement Seeking

High scorers on this scale crave excitement and stimulation. They like bright colors and noisy environments. Excitement seeking is akin to some aspects of sensation seeking. Low scorers feel little need for thrills and prefer a life that high scorers might find boring.

E6: Positive Emotions

The last facet of Extraversion assesses the tendency to experience positive emotions such as joy, happiness, love, and excitement. High scorers on the positive emotions scale laugh easily and often. They are cheerful and optimistic. Low scorers are not necessarily unhappy; they are merely less exuberant and high spirited. Research shows that happiness and life satisfaction are related to both Neuroticism and Extraversion and that positive emotions is the facet of Extraversion most relevant to the prediction of happiness.

OPENNESS TO EXPERIENCE FACETS

O1: Fantasy

Individuals who are open to fantasy have a vivid imagination and an active fantasy life. They daydream not simply as an escape but as a way of creating for themselves an interesting inner world. They elaborate and develop their fantasies and believe that imagination contributes to a rich and creative life. Low scorers are more prosaic and prefer to keep their minds on the task at hand.

O2: Aesthetics

High scorers on this scale have a deep appreciation for art and beauty. They are moved by poetry, absorbed in music, and intrigued by art. They need not have artistic talent nor even necessarily what most people would consider good taste; but for many of them, their interest in the arts leads them to develop a wider knowledge and appreciation than that of the average individual. Low scorers are relatively insensitive to and uninterested in art and beauty.

O3: Feelings

Openness to feelings implies receptivity to one's own inner feelings and emotions and the evaluation of emotion as an important part of life. High scorers experience deeper and more differentiated emotional states and feel both happiness and unhappiness more intensely than do others. Low scorers have somewhat blunted affect and do not believe that feeling states are of much importance.

O4: Actions

Openness is seen behaviorally in the willingness to try different activities, go to new places, or eat unusual foods. High scorers on this scale prefer novelty and variety to familiarity and routine. Over time, they may engage in a series of different hobbies. Low scorers find change difficult and prefer to stick with the tried-and-true.

O5: Ideas

Intellectual curiosity is an aspect of Openness that has long been recognized. This trait is seen not only in an active pursuit of intellectual interests for their own sake but also in open mindedness and a willingness to consider new, perhaps unconventional ideas. High scorers enjoy both philosophical arguments and brain teasers. Openness to ideas does not necessarily imply high intelligence, although it can contribute to the development of intellectual potential. Low scorers on this scale have limited capacity and, if highly intelligent, narrowly focus their resources on limited topics.

O6: Values

Openness to values means the readiness to re-examine social, political, and religious values. Closed individuals tend to accept authority and honor tradition; as a consequence, this type is generally conservative, regardless of political party affiliation. Openness to values may be considered the opposite of dogmatism.

AGREEABLENESS FACETS

A1: Trust

High scorers on this scale have a disposition to believe that others are honest and well intentioned. Low scorers on this scale tend to be cynical and skeptical and to assume that others may be dishonest or dangerous.

A2: Straightforwardness

Straightforward individuals are frank, sincere, and ingenuous. Low scorers on this scale are more willing to manipulate others through flattery, craftiness, or deception. They view these tactics as necessary social skills and may regard more straightforward people as naive. When interpreting this scale (as well as other Agreeableness and Conscientiousness scales), one must recall that scores reflect standings relative to other individuals. A low scorer on this scale is more likely to stretch the truth or to be guarded in expressing his or her true feelings, but this should not be interpreted to mean that he or she is a dishonest or manipulative person. In particular, this scale should not be regarded as a lie scale, either for assessing the validity of the test itself or for making predictions about honesty in employment or other settings.

A3: Altruism

High scorers on this scale have an active concern for others' welfare, as shown in generosity, consideration of others, and a willingness to assist others in need of help. Low scorers on this scale are somewhat more self-centered and are reluctant to get involved in the problems of others.

A4: Compliance

This facet of Agreeableness concerns characteristic reactions to interpersonal conflict. The high scorer tends to defer to others, to inhibit aggression, and to forgive and forget. Compliant people are meek and mild. The low scorer is aggressive, prefers to compete rather than cooperate, and has no reluctance to express anger when necessary.

A5: Modesty

High scorers on this scale are humble and self-effacing, although they are not necessarily lacking in self-confidence or self-esteem. Low scorers believe they are superior people and may be considered conceited or arrogant by others. A pathological lack of modesty is part of the clinical conception of narcissism.

A6: Tender-Mindedness

This facet scale measures attitudes of sympathy and concern for others. High scorers are moved by others' needs and emphasize the human side of social policies. Low scorers are more hardheaded and less moved by appeals to pity. They consider themselves realists who make rational decisions based on cold logic.

CONSCIENTIOUSNESS FACETS

C1: Competence

Competence refers to the sense that one is capable, sensible, prudent, and effective. High scorers on this scale feel well prepared to deal with life. Low scorers have a lower opinion of their abilities and admit that they are often unprepared and inept. Of all the Conscientiousness facets, competence is most highly associated with self-esteem and internal locus of control.

C2: Order

High scorers on this scale are neat, tidy, and well organized. They keep things in their proper places. Low scorers are unable to get organized and describe themselves as unmethodical. Carried to an extreme, high order might contribute to a compulsive personality disorder.

C3: Dutifulness

In one sense, conscientious means "governed by conscience," and that aspect of Conscientiousness is assessed as dutifulness. High scorers on this scale adhere strictly to their ethical principles and scrupulously fulfill their moral obligations. Low scorers are more casual about such matters and may be somewhat undependable or unreliable.

C4: Achievement Striving

Individuals who score high on this facet have high aspiration levels and work hard to achieve their goals. They are diligent and purposeful and have a sense of direction in life. Very high scorers, however, may invest too much in their careers and become workaholics. Low scorers are lackadaisical and perhaps even lazy. They are not driven to succeed. They lack ambition and may seem aimless, but they are often perfectly content with their low levels of achievement.

C5: Self-Discipline

Self-discipline refers to the ability to begin tasks and carry them through to completion, despite boredom and other distractions. High scorers have the ability to motivate themselves to get the job done. Low scorers procrastinate in beginning chores and are easily discouraged and eager to quit. Low self-discipline is easily confused with impulsiveness—both are evident of poor self-control—but empirically they are distinct. People high in impulsiveness cannot resist doing what they do not want themselves to do; people low in self-discipline cannot force themselves to do what they want themselves to do. The former requires an emotional stability; the latter, a degree of motivation that they do not possess.

C6: Deliberation

The final facet of Conscientiousness is deliberation: the tendency to think carefully before acting. High scorers on this facet are cautious and deliberate. Low scorers are hasty and often speak or act without considering the consequences. At best, low scorers are spontaneous and able to make snap decisions when necessary.

Diagnostic Criteria of *DSM-IV-TR* Axis II Personality Disorders

GENERAL DIAGNOSTIC CRITERIA FOR A PERSONALITY DISORDER

A. An enduring pattern of inner experience and behavior that deviates markedly from the expectations of the individual's culture. This pattern is manifested in two (or more) of the following areas:

    (1) cognition (i.e., ways of perceiving and interpreting self, other people, and events)

    (2) affectivity (i.e., the range, intensity, lability, and appropriateness of emotional response)

    (3) interpersonal functioning

    (4) impulse control

B. The enduring pattern is inflexible and pervasive across a broad range of personal and social situations.

C. The enduring pattern leads to clinically significant distress or impairment in social, occupational, or other important areas of functioning.

D. The pattern is stable and of long duration and its onset can be traced back at least to adolescence or early adulthood.

E. The enduring pattern is not better accounted for as a manifestation or consequence of another mental disorder.

F. The enduring pattern is not due to the direct physiological effects of a substance (e.g., a drug of abuse, a medication) or a general medical condition (e.g., head trauma).

CLUSTER A PERSONALITY DISORDERS

301.0 Paranoid Personality Disorder

A. A pervasive distrust and suspiciousness of others such that their motives are interpreted as malevolent, beginning by early adulthood and present in a variety of contexts, as indicated by four (or more) of the following:

    (1) suspects, without sufficient basis, that others are exploiting, harming, or deceiving him or her

(2) is preoccupied with unjustified doubts about the loyalty or trustworthiness of friends or associates

(3) is reluctant to confide in others because of unwarranted fear that the information will be used maliciously against him or her

(4) reads hidden, demeaning, or threatening meanings into benign remarks or events

(5) persistently bears grudges, i.e., is unforgiving of insults, injuries, or slights

(6) perceives attacks on his or her character or reputation that are not apparent to others and is quick to react angrily or to counterattack

(7) has recurrent suspicions, without justification, regarding fidelity of spouse or sexual partner

B. Does not occur exclusively during the course of Schizophrenia, a Mood Disorder With Psychotic Features, or another Psychotic Disorder and is not due to the direct physiological effects of a general medical condition.

Note: If criteria are met prior to the onset of Schizophrenia, add "Premorbid," e.g., "Paranoid Personality Disorder (Premorbid)."

301.20 Schizoid Personality Disorder

A. A pervasive pattern of detachment from social relationships and a restricted range of expression of emotions in interpersonal settings, beginning by early adulthood and present in a variety of contexts, as indicated by four (or more) of the following:

(1) neither desires nor enjoys close relationships, including being part of a family

(2) almost always chooses solitary activities

(3) has little, if any, interest in having sexual experiences with another person

(4) takes pleasure in few, if any, activities

(5) lacks close friends or confidants other than first-degree relatives

(6) appears indifferent to the praise or criticism of others

(7) shows emotional coldness, detachment, or flattened affectivity

B. Does not occur exclusively during the course of Schizophrenia, a Mood Disorder With Psychotic Features, another Psychotic Disorder, or a Pervasive Developmental Disorder and is not due to the direct physiological effects of a general medical condition.

Note: If criteria are met prior to the onset of Schizophrenia, add "Premorbid," e.g., "Schizoid Personality Disorder (Premorbid)."

301.22 Schizotypal Personality Disorder

A. A pervasive pattern of social and interpersonal deficits marked by acute discomfort with, and reduced capacity for, close relationships as well as by cognitive or perceptual distortions and eccentricities of behavior, beginning by early adulthood and present in a variety of contexts, as indicated by five (or more) of the following:

(1) ideas of reference (excluding delusions of reference)

(2) odd beliefs or magical thinking that influences behavior and is inconsistent with subcultural norms (e.g., superstitiousness, belief in clairvoyance, telepathy, or "sixth sense"; in children and adolescents, bizarre fantasies or preoccupations)

(3) unusual perceptual experiences, including bodily illusions

(4) odd thinking and speech (e.g., vague, circumstantial, metaphorical, overelaborative, or stereotyped)

(5) suspiciousness or paranoid ideation

(6) inappropriate or constricted affect

(7) behavior or appearance that is odd, eccentric, or peculiar

(8) lack of close friends or confidants other than first-degree relatives

(9) excessive social anxiety that does not diminish with familiarity and tends to be associated with paranoid fears rather than negative judgments about self

B. Does not occur exclusively during the course of Schizophrenia, a Mood Disorder With Psychotic Features, another Psychotic Disorder, or a Pervasive Developmental Disorder.

Note: If criteria are met prior to the onset of Schizophrenia, add "Premorbid," e.g., "Schizotypal Personality Disorder (Premorbid)."

CLUSTER B

301.7 Antisocial Personality Disorder

A. There is a pervasive pattern of disregard for and violation of the rights of others occurring since age 15 years, as indicated by three (or more) of the following:

(1) failure to conform to social norms with respect to lawful behaviors as indicated by repeatedly performing acts that are grounds for arrest

(2) deceitfulness, as indicated by repeated lying, use of aliases, or conning others for personal profit or pleasure

(3) impulsivity or failure to plan ahead

(4) irritability and aggressiveness, as indicated by repeated physical fights or assaults

(5) reckless disregard for safety of self or others

(6) consistent irresponsibility, as indicated by repeated failure to sustain consistent work behavior or honor financial obligations

(7) lack of remorse, as indicated by being indifferent to or rationalizing having hurt, mistreated, or stolen from another

B. The individual is at least age 18 years.

C. There is evidence of Conduct Disorder with onset before age 15 years.

D. The occurrence of antisocial behavior is not exclusively during the course of Schizophrenia or a Manic Episode.

301.83 Borderline Personality Disorder

A pervasive pattern of instability of interpersonal relationships, self-image, and affect, and marked impulsivity, beginning by early adulthood and present in a variety of contexts, as indicated by five (or more) of the following:

(1) frantic efforts to avoid real or imagined abandonment. Note: Do not include suicidal or self-mutilating behavior covered in Criterion 5.

(2) a pattern of unstable and intense interpersonal relationships characterized by alternating between extremes of idealization and devaluation

(3) identity disturbance: markedly and persistently unstable self-image or sense of self

(4) impulsivity in at least two areas that are potentially self-damaging (e.g., spending, sex, substance abuse, reckless driving, binge eating). Note: Do not include suicidal or self-mutilating behavior covered in Criterion 5.

(5) recurrent suicidal behavior, gestures, or threats or self-mutilating behavior

(6) affective instability due to a marked reactivity of mood (e.g., intense episodic dysphoria, irritability, or anxiety usually lasting a few hours and only rarely more than a few days)

(7) chronic feelings of emptiness

(8) inappropriate, intense anger or difficulty controlling anger (e.g., frequent displays of temper, constant anger, recurrent physical fights)

(9) transient, stress-related paranoid ideation or severe dissociative symptoms

301.50 Histrionic Personality Disorder

A pervasive pattern of excessive emotionality and attention seeking, beginning by early adulthood and present in a variety of contexts, as indicated by five (or more) of the following:

(1) is uncomfortable in situations in which he or she is not the center of attention

(2) interaction with others is often characterized by inappropriate sexually seductive or provocative behavior

(3) displays rapidly shifting and shallow expression of emotions

(4) consistently uses physical appearance to draw attention to self

(5) has a style of speech that is excessively impressionistic and lacking in detail

(6) shows self-dramatization, theatricality, and exaggerated expression of emotion

(7) is suggestible, i.e., easily influenced by others or circumstances

(8) considers relationships to be more intimate than they actually are

301.81 Narcissistic Personality Disorder

A pervasive pattern of grandiosity (in fantasy or behavior), need for admiration, and lack of empathy, beginning by early adulthood and present in a variety of contexts, as indicated by five (or more) of the following:

(1) has a grandiose sense of self-importance (e.g., exaggerates achievements and talents, expects to be recognized as superior without commensurate achievements)

(2) is preoccupied with fantasies of unlimited success, power, brilliance, beauty, or ideal love

(3) believes that he or she is "special" and unique and can only be understood by, or should associate with, other special or high status people (or institutions)

(4) requires excessive admiration

(5) has a sense of entitlement, i.e., unreasonable expectations of especially favorable treatment or automatic compliance with his or her expectations

(6) is interpersonally exploitative, i.e., takes advantage of others to achieve his or her own ends

(7) lacks empathy: is unwilling to recognize or identify with the feelings and needs of others

(8) is often envious of others or believes that others are envious of him or her

(9) shows arrogant, haughty behaviors or attitudes

CLUSTER C

301.82 Avoidant Personality Disorder

A pervasive pattern of social inhibition, feelings of inadequacy, and hypersensitivity to negative evaluation, beginning by early adulthood and present in a variety of contexts, as indicated by four (or more) of the following:

(1) avoids occupational activities that involve significant interpersonal contact, because of fears of criticism, disapproval, or rejection

(2) is unwilling to get involved with people unless certain of being liked

(3) shows restraint within intimate relationships because of the fear of being shamed or ridiculed

(4) is preoccupied with being criticized or rejected in social situations

(5) is inhibited in new interpersonal situations because of feelings of inadequacy

(6) views self as socially inept, personally unappealing, or inferior to others

(7) is unusually reluctant to take personal risks or to engage in any new activities because they may prove embarrassing

301.6 Dependent Personality Disorder

A pervasive and excessive need to be taken care of that leads to submissive and clinging behavior and fears of separation, beginning by early adulthood and present in a variety of contexts, as indicated by five (or more) of the following:

(1) has difficulty making everyday decisions without an excessive amount of advice and reassurance from others

(2) needs others to assume responsibility for most major areas of his or her life

(3) has difficulty expressing disagreement with others because of fear of loss of support or approval. Note: Do not include realistic fears of retribution.

(4) has difficulty initiating projects or doing things on his or her own (because of a lack of self-confidence in judgment or abilities rather than a lack of motivation or energy)

(5) goes to excessive lengths to obtain nurturance and support from others, to the point of volunteering to do things that are unpleasant

(6) feels uncomfortable or helpless when alone because of exaggerated fears of being unable to care for himself or herself

(7) urgently seeks another relationship as a source of care and support when a close relationship ends

(8) is unrealistically preoccupied with fears of being left to take care of himself or herself

301.4 Obsessive–Compulsive Personality Disorder

A pervasive pattern of preoccupation with orderliness, perfectionism, and mental and interpersonal control, at the expense of flexibility, openness, and efficiency, beginning by early adulthood and present in a variety of contexts, as indicated by four (or more) of the following:

(1) is preoccupied with details, rules, lists, order, organization, or schedules to the extent that the major point of the activity is lost

(2) shows perfectionism that interferes with task completion (e.g., is unable to complete a project because his or her own overly strict standards are not met)

(3) is excessively devoted to work and productivity to the exclusion of leisure activities and friendships (not accounted for by obvious economic necessity)

(4) is overconscientious, scrupulous, and inflexible about matters of morality, ethics, or values (not accounted for by cultural or religious identification)

(5) is unable to discard worn-out or worthless objects even when they have no sentimental value

(6) is reluctant to delegate tasks or to work with others unless they submit to exactly his or her way of doing things

(7) adopts a miserly spending style toward both self and others; money is viewed as something to be hoarded for future catastrophes

(8) shows rigidity and stubbornness

301.9 Personality Disorder Not Otherwise Specified

This category is for disorders of personality functioning that do not meet criteria for any specific Personality Disorder. An example is the presence of features of more than one specific Personality Disorder that do not meet the full criteria for any one Personality Disorder ("mixed personality") but that together cause clinically significant distress or impairment in one or more important areas of functioning (e.g., social or occupational). This category can also be used when the clinician judges that a specific Personality Disorder that is not included in the Classification is appropriate. Examples include depressive personality disorder and passive–aggressive personality disorder.

Depressive Personality Disorder

A. A pervasive pattern of depressive cognitions and behaviors beginning by early adulthood and present in a variety of contexts, as indicated by five (or more) of the following:

 (1) usual mood is dominated by dejection, gloominess, cheerlessness, joylessness, unhappiness

 (2) self-concept centers around beliefs of inadequacy, worthlessness, and low self-esteem

 (3) is critical, blaming, and derogatory toward self

 (4) is brooding and given to worry

 (5) is negativisitic, critical, and judgmental toward others

 (6) is pessimistic

 (7) is prone to feeling guilty or remorseful

B. Does not occur exclusively during Major Depressive Episodes and is not better accounted for by Dysthymic Disorder.

Passive–Aggressive Personality Disorder (Negativistic Personality Disorder)

A. A pervasive pattern of negativistic attitudes and passive resistance to demands for adequate performance, beginning by early adulthood and present in a variety of contexts, as indicated by four (or more) of the following:

 (1) passively resists fulfilling routine social and occupational tasks

 (2) complains of being misunderstood and unappreciated by others

 (3) is sullen and argumentative

 (4) unreasonably criticizes and scorns authority

 (5) expresses envy and resentment toward those apparently more fortunate

 (6) voices exaggerated and persistent complaints of personal misfortune

 (7) alternates between hostile defenses and contrition

B. Does not occur exclusively during Major Depressive Episodes and is not better accounted for by Dysthymic Disorder.

Author Index

Numbers in italics refer to listings in reference sections.

Subject Index

Numbers in italics refer to listings in reference sections

485

About the Editors

PAUL T. COSTA, JR., PHD, is chief of the Laboratory of Personality and Cognition at the National Institute on Aging's Gerontology Research Center in Baltimore, Maryland. He received his PhD in human development and clinical psychology from the University of Chicago. He has academic appointments in the departments of psychiatry and behavioral sciences at the Johns Hopkins University School of Medicine and at the Duke University School of Medicine, and is a clinical professor of psychiatry at the Georgetown University School of Medicine. He has also held academic positions at Harvard University and the University of Massachusetts at Boston. With his colleague Robert R. McCrae, Dr. Costa is co-author of the *Revised NEO Personality Inventory* and has published more than 250 journal articles and book chapters. A licensed clinical psychologist in Massachusetts, Dr. Costa is on the attending staff of the Johns Hopkins Sexual Behaviors Consultation Unit and enjoys teaching personality assessment to third year psychiatry residents.

THOMAS A. WIDIGER, PHD, is a professor of psychology at the University of Kentucky in Lexington. He received his PhD in clinical psychology from Miami University in Oxford, Ohio, and completed his internship at the Cornell University Medical College in Westchester, New York. Dr. Widiger has published over 200 journal articles and book chapters on personality and personality disorder. He is currently associate editor of the *Journal of Abnormal Psychology* and the *Journal of Personality Disorders*, and serves as Consulting Editor for a number of additional journals. He has served as the Research Coordinator for the American Psychiatric Association's 4th edition of the *Diagnostic and Statistical Manual of Mental Disorders* (*DSM-IV*) and was a member of the *DSM-IV* Task Force, the *DSM-IV* Personality Disorders Work Group, and the *DSM-IV-TR* Personality Disorders Text Revision Work Group.